To Larry
+ Joann
with affection
Marc

# INSTITUTIONAL ANALYSIS AND ECONOMIC POLICY

# INSTITUTIONAL ANALYSIS AND ECONOMIC POLICY

edited by

**Marc R. Tool**
Professor Emeritus of Economics
California State University, Sacramento

and

**Paul Dale Bush**
Professor Emeritus of Economics
California State University, Fresno

**KLUWER ACADEMIC PUBLISHERS**
Boston/Dordrecht/London

**Distributors for North, Central and South America:**
Kluwer Academic Publishers
101 Philip Drive
Assinippi Park
Norwell, Massachusetts 02061 USA
Telephone (781) 871-6600
Fax (781) 681-9045
E-Mail: kluwer@wkap.com

**Distributors for all other countries:**
Kluwer Academic Publishers Group
Post Office Box 322
3300 AH Dordrecht, THE NETHERLANDS
Telephone 31 786 576 000
Fax 31 786 576 254
E-Mail: services@wkap.nl

Electronic Services < http://www.wkap.nl>

**Library of Congress Cataloging-in-Publication Data**

Institutional analysis and economic policy / edited by Marc R. Tool and Paul Dale Bush.
p. cm.
Includes bibliographical references and index.
ISBN 1-40207-308-9 (alk. paper)
1. Institutional economics. 2. Economic policy. I.Tool, Marc R. II. Bush, Paul Dale.

HB99.5 .1555 2002
330--dc21 2002038903



*Printed on acid-free paper.*

Printed in the United States of America.

For

Lillian and Barbara

# CONTENTS


| | | |
|---|---|---|
| *Lists of Figures, Tables, Graphs* | | *ix* |
| *List of Contributors* | | *xi* |
| *Preface* | | *xiii* |
| | I | |
| 1 | Foundational Concepts for Institutionalist Policy Making<br>*Paul D. Bush & Marc R. Tool* | 1 |
| | II | |
| 2 | An Institutionalist View of Fiscal Policy<br>*Philip A. Klein* | 47 |
| 3 | Monetary Policy: An Institutionalist Approach<br>*L. Randall Wray* | 85 |
| 4 | Progressive Tax Policies<br>*Peter S. Fisher* | 115 |
| | III | |
| 5 | Promoting Economic Equity: The Basic Income Approach<br>*Charles M. A. Clark* | 133 |
| 6 | Welfare Reform<br>*Janice Peterson* | 157 |
| 7 | Universal Health Care in the United States: Analysis and Proposals<br>*Michael Keaney* | 183 |
| 8 | Social Security: Truth or Convenient Fictions?<br>*L. Randall Wray* | 219 |
| | IV | |
| 9 | Competing Perspectives on Economic Power and Accountability<br>*Edythe S. Miller* | 251 |
| 10 | Market Failure in Public Utility Industries: An Institutionalist Critique of Deregulation<br>*Harry M. Trebing* | 287 |
| 11 | The Abuse of Economic and Financial Power in the New Economy: Historical Patterns in the Creation of Modern Remedies<br>*Michael F. Sheehan* | 315 |

V

12 Toward Developmental Curriculum Reform: Teach What? To Whom? Why? 349
*Baldwin Ranson*

13 Policies to Provide Non-invidious Employment 379
*Deborah M. Figart*

14 Policy Implications of the New Information Economy 411
*William H. Melody*

VI

15 An Institutionalist Perspective on Environmental Goal Setting 433
*Kurt Stephenson*

16 Policy Concerns Regarding Ecologically Sound Disposal of Industrial Waste Materials 461
*F. Gregory Hayden*

VII

17 Globalization: An Institutionalist Perspective 493
*Gladys Parker Foster*

18 Global Industrial Policies 523
*Wolfram Elsner*

19 Recent Tendencies in Development Economics: Bringing Institutions Back In 549
*James M. Cypher*

*About the Authors* 577

*Index* 583

# FIGURES


2–1 Phillips Curve, 1960-1969
2–2 Phillips Curve, 1960-1999
2–3 Fiscal Policy vs. Fiscal Impact
2–4 GNP, Unemployment, and Federal Receipts and Expenditures, Quarterly, 1957-1959
2–5 Gross Domestic Product, Unemployment and Federal Receipts and Expenditures, 1988-1992
2–6 Total Government, Federal Government, and State and Local Government Receipts as a Percent of GDP, 1960-2000
16–1 Institutionalist Integrated System
16–2 Coase Theorem Bribe
16–3 Some of the Inputs and Outputs of a Brown Coal Fired Power Plant
16–4 Relationship Between Capital and Waste


# TABLES


2–1 Productivity, Unit Labor Costs, and Inflation 1960-1999
4–1 Income Inequality Before and After Income Taxes, 1980-2000
5–1 Average Percent in Poverty Over Business Cycle Peaks, 1959-1999
5–2 Basic Income Payments, 1999
5–3 Costs of Basic Income Systems, 1999
5–4 Federal Government Revenues
5–5 Income Distribution Effects of Basic Income System
5–6 Average Household Income by Quintile, 1999, with and without Basic Income
19–1 Median Unweighted and Weighted Growth in GDP Per Capita


# GRAPHS


5–1 Economic Growth and Poverty Rates, 1959-2000
5–2 Actual and Predicted Poverty Rates, 1959-1999

# LIST OF CONTRIBUTORS

Bush, Paul D., *Professor Emeritus of Economics*, California State University, Fresno. 1266 West Escalon Avenue, Fresno CA 93711

Clark, Charles M.A., *Professor of Economics,* St.Johns University, Jamaica NY 11439

Cypher, James M., *Professor of Economics*, California State University, Fresno, Fresno CA 93740-8001

Elsner, Wolfram, *Professor of Economics*, University of Bremen, Wilhelm-Herbst-Strasse 1A, D-28350 Bremen, Germany

Figart, Deborah M., *Professor of Economics,* Richard Stockton College, Pomona NJ 08240-0195

Fisher, Peter S., *Professor Urban & Regional Planning*, University of Iowa, Iowa City IA 52242

Foster, Gladys, *Professor of Economics (Ret.)*, University of Colorado at Denver. 6468 South Hudson Street, Littleton CO 80121-3542

Hayden, F. Gregory, *Professor of Economics,* University of Nebraska, Lincoln NE 68588-0489

Klein, Phillip A., *Professor Emeritus of Economics,Pennsylvania State University, 608* Kern Bldg., University Park, PA 16802.

Keaney, Michael, *International Department, Mercuria Business School,* Martinlaaksontie 36, FI-01620, Vantaa, Finland

Melody, William H., *Professor,* Center for Tele-Information , Technical University of Denmark. 2800 DK, Lyngby, Denmark.

Miller, Edythe S., *Professor of Economics (Ret.)*, Metropolitan State College, Denver. 580 Front Range Road, Littleton CO 80120

Peterson, Janice, *Senior Analyst*, US General Accounting Office,330 N. Piedmont St. #2, Arlington VA 22203

Ranson, T. Baldwin, *Professor of Economic (Ret.)*, Western State College of Colorado, 700 Kimbark Street, Longmont CO 80501

Sheehan, Michael, *Fisher, Sheehan and Colton*, 33126 SW Callahan Road, Scappoose OR 97056

Stevenson, Kurt, *Professor of Economics*, Virginia Tech University, Blacksburg VA 24061

Tool, Marc R., *Professor Emeritus of Economics*, California State University, 5708 McAdoo Avenue, Sacramento CA 95819-2516

Trebing, Harry M., *Professor Emeritus of Economics*, Michigan State University, 4568 Manitou Drive, Okemos MI 48864

Wray, L. Randall, *Professor of Economics*, University of Missouri, Kansas City, Kansas City MO 64110

# PREFACE

The purpose of this volume is to demonstrate how contemporary institutional economic analysis can be applied to the resolution of economic problems. All of the essays in this book challenge the conventional wisdom in the problem areas addressed. They advocate policy positions that often run contrary to views widely held by academic economists and policy makers alike. The general literature of institutional economics is unorthodox, beginning with its methodological foundations and continuing through the kind of policy analysis found in these pages.

The orthodox tradition in economics is commonly characterized as "neoclassical economics." Neoclassical economics fosters the myth that only "the market" can efficiently allocate a society's economic resources and equitably distribute its income. It provides the intellectual defense for capitalist ideology in which "free markets" are championed over democratic policy formation, which it contends is neither efficient nor equitable. For both professional economists and policy makers of a conservative political persuasion, neoclassical economics writes the script for a morality play in which the market is the "good guy" and the government is the "bad guy." As such, it undermines the belief that free societies can enhance economic welfare through the use of democratic processes in the formulation of economic policies.

Institutional economists eschew the myth of "the market" and reject in large part the neoclassical edifice upon which it is based. They view the economy as a system of institutions, in which market relationships are only one of numerous institutional structures upon which society depends for the provision and enhancement of the means of life. Moreover, institutionalists reject the notion of the "universal market," i.e., the idea that all market structures are essentially alike in their basic operations. There is a universe of difference between the market realities facing the Main Street USA business enterprise and those facing multinational corporations (MNCs).

Similarly, institutionalists reject the monolithic view of capitalism, i.e., the notion that there is one set of institutional arrangements that can be found in all "capitalist" economies. Institutionalists take the position that markets are embedded in the other institutions of society in such a way as to give any particular market characteristics that are peculiar to its historical, cultural, and geographical setting. Institutionalists also point out that while capitalist ideology identifies certain institutional features as common to all capitalist economies, real-world capitalist economies have many different institutional manifestations; therefore, it is fundamentally erroneous to presume that "one model fits all." The economies of the United States, Germany, Japan, and

Denmark, for example, while loosely referred to as "capitalist" economies, are quite different in the institutional structures that form their economic systems.

But perhaps *the* diagnostic characteristic of institutional economics is its focus on the process of institutional change. Institutional economists advance the hypothesis that the institutions of today have evolved through the cultural history of the community. As such, they embody the accumulated skills, technology, and vested interests of the past. Accordingly, institutional economists are concerned with the question of whether existing institutional structures are capable of nurturing the community's capacity to provide and enhance the means of life.

Institutional economists, relying on broad-based findings of social science, find that often given institutional structures fail to render the instrumental efficiency upon which the community depends in provisioning itself. Vested interests are capable of thwarting this instrumental efficiency through the use of economic and political power to enhance the well being of the few at the expense of the many. It is the conviction of institutional economists that while it may not be possible for society completely to eradicate vested interests based on the invidious distinctions embodied in racial and ethnic bigotry, the ability to pay, or the encapsulation of technology in order to preserve the status quo, social progress lies in diminishing their influence on the life process of the community. Thus, from the perspective of institutional economics, policy problems exist when the institutional structure (or some aspect of it) fails to provide instrumentally efficient, non-invidious outcomes that enhance the life processes of the community taken impersonally. The solution to such institutional impairment is institutional change that will eliminate the impairment. This focus on institutional change in both analysis and in policy formation gives institutional economics its unambiguous "evolutionary" orientation.

It is the task of this volume, then, to demonstrate how institutional analysis lays the foundations for economic policies that can ameliorate such problems as macro-instability, an inequitable distribution of income, resource misallocation, invidious employment practices, inadequate health coverage, environmental degradation, the abuse of corporate power, and the domination of the global economy by multinational corporations. As will be seen, all such problems require institutional changes for their resolution.

This volume is addressed to colleagues seeking pluralistic approaches to problem analysis, to upper division and graduate students in economics seeking more policy-relevant approaches to inquiry, to policy makers in government who seek more pertinent policy options for problems confronted, and to public citizens who are weary of mistaken admonitions to "let the market decide," and wish to refocus their public concerns and political participation.

The essays of this volume are provocative, candid, and timely. The contributors do not seek to flatter the vested interests of any political, business, or academic entity. As indicated above, they stand in opposition to the mainstream economic literature on the issues they address. In other words, these essays are non-ideological, challenging as they do those ideological doctrines that have dominated academic and public debates on these issues. The authors are interested in offering new ways of perceiving problems and of formulating solutions. We believe they have succeeded in doing so, thereby contributing to the reader's capacity to participate in the continuing re-creation of the economic process.

The authors of the papers comprising this volume were invited to contribute because of the high quality of their scholarship in the topical areas to which their papers are addressed, and, more broadly, because they are major contributors to the American tradition of the original institutional economics (OIE). This tradition of inquiry began with Thorstein B. Veblen over a century ago. It has been enriched by contributions of John R. Commons, Wesley C. Mitchell, Walton Hamilton, John Maurice Clark, John Dewey, Clarence E. Ayres, J. Fagg Foster, John Kenneth Galbraith, Dudley Dillard, Kenneth Boulding, Hyman P. Minsky, and their contemporary intellectual progeny, among others. John Maynard Keynes, Gunnar Myrdal, K. William Kapp, and Karl Polanyi in Europe shared, during their lives, an intellectual kinship with this American institutionalist tradition. The modes of inquiry advanced in contemporary *neoclassical* institutional economics (NIE), as in the writings of Oliver E. Williamson, R.H. Coase, Douglass C. North, and others, are not represented in this collection.

Finally, it should be noted that the authors of this volume are not proposing expedient or short run "quick fixes" for the problems addressed. In every case, they seek long term modifications of problematic structures. In so doing, they demonstrate why a democratic society must *continually* develop its skills, commitments, and capacity to enhance instrumentally warranted institutional adjustments to resolve problems as they emerge in the on-going life processes of the community.

# 1

# FOUNDATIONAL CONCEPTS FOR INSTITUTIONALIST POLICY MAKING

Paul D. Bush
Marc R. Tool

*The history of institutional thought is a history of concern for policy.*
F. Gregory Hayden (1993)

## INTRODUCTION

Institutional economics is a policy-oriented science. For over a century, it has contributed to the resolution of economic problems at the federal, state, and local levels. Institutional economists have continuously sought to identify and resolve the economic and political problems that impair the efficiency and equity with which the economy engages in the production of goods and services and the distribution of income. The topics of the chapters of this book illustrate the broad range of interests institutionalists exhibit in policy issues and the approaches they take in dealing with them.

Institutional economists reject the presumption of neoclassical orthodox economics that the self-serving practices of economic agents, operating in unfettered markets, necessarily serve the public interest. Institutionalists are in complete agreement with John Maynard Keynes who, nearly eighty years ago, took vigorous exception to orthodox notion that enshrined self-interest is a public good. Keynes put it this way:

> It is *not* true that individuals possess a prescriptive "natural liberty" in their economic activities. There is *no* "compact" conferring perpetual rights on those who Have or on those who Acquire. The world is *not* so governed from above that private and social interests always coincide. It is *not* so managed here below that in practice they coincide. It is *not* a correct deduction from the principles of economics that enlightened self-interest generally *is* enlightened; more often individuals acting separately

> to promote their own ends are too ignorant or too weak to attain even these. Experience does *not* show that individuals, when they make up a social unit, are always less clear-sighted than when the act separately ([1926] 1972, 287-288, italics in original).

The *laissez-faire* conception of the relationship of government to the economy, to which Keynes objected, has waxed and waned in the popular consciousness over the years. Keynes himself, in his publication of *The General Theory* (1936), contributed substantially to its waning during the first three decades following the Second World War, in consequence of which governments of the world's democracies assumed responsibility for the level of economic activity and, marginally, the distribution of income.

But in the last three decades of the 20th century, the administrations of Ronald Reagan, George Bush, and even that of William Clinton, subscribed to the doctrine of the "market *uber alles*," the market over all. The fundamental tenet of "Reaganomics," it will be recalled, is that the "government is the problem." Presumably, the solution to any economic problem is to "get the government off the businessman's back." Such a sentiment was reflected in large part by President Clinton's proud assertion that the "era of Big Government is over." It now appears that George W. Bush may well outdo his predecessors in advancing this ideological program.

The promulgation of this ideological perspective by leading politicians of both of the major political parties has received substantial assistance from neoclassical economists. In the view of orthodox rational expectations theorists, for example, macroeconomic stabilization policies are utterly futile because "rational" market responses to monetary and fiscal policies will completely nullify the desired outcomes of the policies. Economic policy therefore is constrained by the "real" forces at work in free markets. Thus, the capacity of a democracy to formulate economic policies is bounded by the more potent, and more "legitimate," forces of market processes.

Institutionalists argue vigorously to the contrary. As Keynes observed: "the chief task of Economists . . . is to distinguish afresh the *Agenda* of Government from the *Non-Agenda*; and the companion task of Politics is to devise forms of Government within a Democracy which shall be capable of accomplishing the *Agenda* ([1926] 1972, 288, italics in original). The papers comprising this volume refashion the Agenda of government as Keynes recommended. They look upon the "market *uber alles*" perspective as being destructive of the processes of self-governance in a democratic society. The alternative view offered by the authors of this volume is that, given the nature of institutions and institutional change, democratic policy making provides genuine solutions for economic problems through institutional adjustments. Such adjustments bound and shape markets, not the reverse.

The following sections of this chapter consider the tenets of institutional economics and an exploration of the connections between the practice of democracy and institutional change. The chapter will conclude with an introduction to the contributions of the authors.

# THE NATURE AND DEVELOPMENT OF INSTITUTIONAL ECONOMICS

## The Founders of American Institutional Economics

Institutional economics is the only school of economic thought indigenous to the United States. Contemporary institutionalists trace its origins to the works of Thorstein B. Veblen (1857-1929) and John R. Commons (1862-1945). Each made a unique contribution to the development of institutional economics. Veblen's works were based on his profoundly critical examination of the philosophical weaknesses of the emerging school of neoclassical economics.[1] He sought to provide economics with an evolutionary orientation quite different from that offered by the non-historical, deductively formulated theories of orthodoxy, which have, in fact, come to dominate the mainstream economic literature. Although Veblen addressed a wide variety of contemporary economic issues, he focused his work on a critique of orthodox thought, while offering tantalizing glimpses of a conception of economic reality that a truly evolutionary economics might produce. He did not, however, concern himself to any great extent with economic policy formation. Commons, on the other hand, was a policy economist *par excellence.* He and his students quite literally created numerous fields of economic policy analysis, which are now accepted as standard areas of economic policy studies. Among the fields in which they did pioneering work are: economics and the law, labor economics, workman's compensation, social security, public utilities, industrial organization, and the social control of economic activity. Many facets of Franklin D. Roosevelt's "New Deal" legislation, were formulated and later administered by institutional economists trained by John R. Commons. From the works of Veblen and Commons, contemporary institutional economics derives both its methodological independence from economic orthodoxy and its vigorous pursuit of economic policy free from the ideological blinders that narrow the vision of the neoclassical school. Both of these intellectual influences are clearly evident in the papers that appear in this volume.

## The Definition of Institutional Economics

The term "institutional economics" was coined in 1918 by Walton H. Hamilton (1881-1958) in his paper entitled "The Institutional Approach to Economic Theory," delivered at the annual meetings of the American Economic Association. In that paper, Hamilton set fourth five fundamental characteristics of "institutional economics" (Hamilton 1919). They are:

1. Economic theory should unify economic science.
2. Economics theory should be relevant to the modern problem of control.
3. The proper subject-matter of economic theory is institutions.
4. Economic theory is concerned with matters of process.
5. Economic theory must be based upon an acceptable theory of human behavior.

This characterization of institutional economics holds up pretty well as we contemplate the developments of the institutionalist literature over the eighty-four years since Hamilton set it forth. Nevertheless, some addenda and qualifications should be added to it. We will turn to these presently. But before we do, let us briefly consider what Hamilton's five characterizations entail.

### Economic Theory Should Unify Economic Science

Hamilton's first characterization that "economic theory should unify economic science" as a methodological principle is non-controversial as between institutionalists and neoclassical economists. But agreement on this general point cannot hide the vast difference there is in the views of these two schools of thought regarding the meaning of "unity" and how it is to be achieved. Neoclassical economists take great pride in what they regard as the unifying principle of their theoretical orientation: the principle of constrained maximization. A mathematical demonstration that this principle underlies all neoclassical theories, ranging from the theory of consumer's choice to the theory of production, was given by Paul A. Samuelson in his influential book, *Foundations of Economic Analysis* ([1947] 1958).

The principle of constrained maximization states, in effect, that all rational economic behavior is a matter of the economic actor (consumer or producer) making choices in such a way as to maximize some goal (for the consumer, utility; for the producer, profits) subject to some kind of constraint (for the consumer, limited money income; for the producer, the costs of acquiring scarce resources). This is the logic that lies behind the notion of "economic choice." It is consistent with a definition of economics that neoclassicists had used long before Samuelson published his book. According to this definition, "[e]conomics is the science which studies human behavior as a relationship between ends and scarce means which have alternative uses (Robbins [1935] 1962, 16). Contemporary textbooks often define the "economic problem" as the "allocation of scarce resources among alternative uses." Many neoclassical economists take the extreme position that any problem that cannot be defined in these terms lies outside the boundaries of economics. This exclusionary doctrine means that heterodox schools of economics thought, particularly institutional thought, lie outside the boundaries of the discipline. For example, they refer to the works of Veblen as falling within the realm of "sociology," not economics.

It is precisely this kind of narrow, deductively formulated notion of theoretical "unity" that Hamilton and all subsequent institutional economists working in the intellectual tradition of Veblen and Commons reject. As it turns out, the neoclassical unifying principle and its associated narrow definition of economics, would make Hamilton's other four characterizations of institutional economics impossible to apply as guiding principles for economic analysis. When Hamilton speaks of the necessity of economic theory unifying economic science, he has in mind the ability to explain the nature of various aspects of economic behavior "by pointing out the parts they play in this larger whole" [i.e., the economic system]. In this connection, he makes the interesting methodological point that the theoretical statements of institutional economics are "always tentative, always enriched by inquiries in particular fields . . ." (Hamilton 1919, 312). It is a basic tenet of institutionalist methodology that all theoretical constructs are subject to reformulation based on the findings of empirical research. In contrast, there is nothing tentative about the unifying theoretical principles of neoclassical economics. They are indubitable logical truisms, timeless and beyond historical modification. And, as institutionalists and other critics of the neoclassical school point out, the theoretical dogmas of neoclassical thought appear to be impervious to modification by empirical realities. These profound differences in the institutionalist and neoclassical methodologies are given considerable attention by the authors of the essays in this collection.

## Economic Theory Should Be Relevant to the Modern Problem of Control

At the time Hamilton presented his paper to the American Economics Association, he and others of similar intellectual inclination felt compelled to challenge the orthodox preoccupation with the doctrinal fiction that the market system could perform all the basic economic functions of society, which provides a "formal defense" of *laissez-faire*. The language used at that time to articulate the need to move beyond a blind faith in the market system was the term "the problem of control." This is the meaning of Hamilton's second characteristic of institutional economics. In the terminology of the late 20th and early 21st century, he was advocating a "paradigm shift" in the science of economics. Hamilton elaborated on this point in the following way:

> A shift in problems and a general demand for control has made institutional economics relevant. This shift has been due partly to a discovery that institutions are social arrangements capable of change rather than obstinate natural phenomena, partly to a consciousness that activity, once apparently voluntary, is controlled by subtle conventions and habits of thought, and partly to the bad taste which *laissez faire* has left with us. But, however it has come about, there is a demand for an economics relevant to problems of control (313).

What must be emphasized at this point is that the "problem of control" is not simply a matter of governmental "interference" with market forces, although government regulation of economic activity is a necessary aspect of the contemplated inquiry. In a broader sense an awareness of this problem focuses our attention on the way in which institutions regulate human behavior in all aspects of the human enterprise, particularly those activities deemed to be relevant to the economic system of society. This notion comes through most clearly in John R. Commons's characterization of his approach to institutional economics. "I here derive a theory of the part played by collective action in control of individual action" (Commons [1934] 1961, 1). This view is sometimes referred to as "methodological collectivism" in contrast to the "methodological individualism" of the neoclassical school. It should be noted immediately that neither Veblen nor Commons (or, for that matter, any of their contemporary followers) subscribed to the view that individual behavior is completely determined by "collective action." As will be seen below, institutionalists envision a dynamic interplay between the individual and society at large. Individuals are viewed as both the product of, and the creators of, culture. This conception of the individual stands in stark contrast to that postulated by the neoclassical school, which takes no account of the cultural determination of individual behavior or the manner in which actions of individuals bring about changes in culture. We will return to these considerations later in our discussion of human nature and institutional change.

**The Proper Subject-Matter of Economic Theory is Institutions**

In discussing this characteristic of institutional economics, Hamilton identifies a critical feature of both its analytical method and its approach to policy formation. In contrast to neoclassical economics, which presumes that knowledge of the economy can be constructed from the analysis of individual choice-making behavior, institutionalists focus on the primacy of institutional arrangements in organizing and coordinating the behavior of individuals as they go about the daily effort to make a living, that is, to provision themselves and their families and to participate in the productive processes of the community. This, says Hamilton, "requires a knowledge of specific institutions" (313). The types of institutional arrangements that must be understood encompass a bewildering variety social structures; one cannot be content to study only the logical implications of an imagined market system and hope to gain a grasp of economic reality. Hamilton puts it this way:

> . . . the development of industrial society is contingent upon a knowledge of the bundle of conventions and arrangements which make it up. The basis of material wealth in the machine technique, the scheme of natural rights which still inheres in the legal system, the resolution of all industry into a multitude of specialized and interdependent tasks, the rise of complicated business mechanism which intervenes between wealth and welfare, the concentration of direction in the hand of an industrial hierarchy, the scheme of arrangements known as the wage-system, which is the means by which the laborer establishes a connection with industry—these and a hundred other things like them must be recognized by one who would direct, or, if he be an economic theorist, watch, industrial development (314).

As will be pointed out below, considerable progress has been made over the span of the 20$^{th}$ century by institutional economists to clarify just what kind of analytical methodology would permit the kind of systematic analysis Hamilton envisions here. It will also be demonstrated below that changes in institutions becomes the primary focus of institutionalist policy making.

### Economic Theory Is Concerned with Matters of Process

In discussing this characteristic of institutional economics, Hamilton lays hold of a diagnostic feature of institutional analysis: its preoccupation with the phenomenon of institutional change. Hamilton captures the importance of institutional change in the following passage:

> Competition, property, the price structure, the wage system, and like institutions refuse to retain a definite content. Nor only are things happening to them, but changes are going on within them. A law, a court decision, a declaration of war, a change in popular habits of thought, and the content of property rights is affected . . . . Both by a change in its relation to other things and by subtle changes going on within, each of these institutions is in process of development. And, if this is true of particular institutions, it is likewise true of the complex of institutions which together make up the economic order (315).

The explanation of the changes that take place within and among institutions is the central task of institutional economics. The institutionalist effort to provide a theoretical explanation for institutional change is what makes institutional economics an "evolutionary" science in the sense that Veblen used the term.

A terminological clarification is in order here. When institutionalists refer to their analysis as being "dynamic," they are referring to the fact that their theories attempt to explain institutional change and the role it plays in policy formation. Neoclassical economists also refer to certain aspects of their work as "dynamic" analysis. But what they have in mind when they use the term is the "dating" of the variables of their models, making them functions of time. Thus, they draw a distinction between "static" equilibria" and "dynamic" equilibria. But it should be noted that even when they speak of "dynamic" equilibria, they continue to assume that the institutional structure remains unchanged (institutions are part of the *ceteris paribus* conditions), or they assume that institutions will change as necessary to accommodate the new "dynamic" equilibria (this is known as the *pari passu* condition). In either case, institutions are not themselves subject to direct examination. They are always taken as parameters of the model.[2] Thus, from the point of view of institutional economics, neoclassical economics is "static" in the sense that it does not attempt to deal with institutional change.

## Economic Theory Must Be Based Upon an Acceptable Theory of Human Behavior

In this characterization of institutional economics, Hamilton sets forth the institutionalist's rejection of the neoclassical conception of *homo economicus.* In a famous passage Thorstein Veblen characterized the hedonistic conception of economic man as a "lightening calculator of pleasure and pains, who oscillates like a homogeneous globule of desire of happiness under the impulse of stimuli that shift him about the area, but leave him intact. He has neither antecedent nor consequent" (Veblen [1919] 1942b, 73). Hamilton observes that "[i]n no respect does neoclassical economics more nearly resemble the body of doctrine from which it sprang than in its theory of the individual who knows the alternatives with which he is confronted and seeks his own greatest material good measured in pecuniary terms" (316). Such a conception of human nature, he says, ". . . neglect[s] the influence exercised over conduct by the scheme of institutions under which one lives and must seek his good" (317). Contemporary institutionalists would add that this conception of human nature prevents the economist from building any credible theory of society and the institutional structures of which it is composed.

The institutionalist view of human nature finds its first expression in the works of Veblen. Rejecting the notion that man is a "lightening calculator of pleasures and pains," Veblen argues that ". . . it is the characteristic of man to do something, not simply to suffer the pleasures and pains through the impact of suitable forces. He is not simply a bundle of desires that are to be saturated by being placed in the path of the forces of the environment, but rather a coherent structure of propensities and habits which seeks realization and expression in an unfolding activity" (Veblen [1919] 1942b, 74). To a very large extent, according to Veblen, the habits of thought that guide individual behavior are institutionally determined. Accordingly, he writes, "The wants and desires, the end and aim, the ways and means, the amplitude and drift of the individual's conduct are functions of an institutional variable that is of highly complex and wholly unstable character" (242-43).

The importance that this alternative view of human nature plays in institutional economics cannot be overemphasized. In a recent article, Geoffrey Hodgson raises the question: "What is the essence of institutional economics?" After considering a number of characteristics of institutional economics, he argues that it is this conception of human nature that sets it apart from all other schools of economic thought. "[T]he single most important characteristic of institutionalism is the idea that the individual is socially and institutionally constituted. . . . all the old [i.e., "original"] institutional economists, from Veblen to Galbraith, embrace the notion that the individual is molded by cultural or institutional circumstances (Hodgson 2000, 327). While Hodgson's intellectual exercise in trying to locate the "essence" of institutional economics may not be viewed by many institutionalists as a productive undertaking, they would not dispute his argument that this view of human nature is one of its diagnostic characteristics.

As indicated earlier, the institutionalist view of the relation of the individual to his/her institutional setting is one of dynamic interaction. While the individual is a product of institutional circumstances, he/she is also potentially a creative force in shaping and molding institutions. Returning to Veblen's assessment of this relationship, he sets forth the following observation: "The growth and mutations of the institutional fabric are an outcome of the conduct of the individual members of the group, since it is out of the experience of the individuals, through the habituation of individuals, that institutions arise . . ." (Veblen [1919] 1942a, 243). The methodological individualism of neoclassical economics simply cannot capture the dynamic complexity of this relationship between individuals and institutions. Therein lays its failure to produce a credible theory either of society, or of the economic system that exists within its institutional structure.

## The Distinction between the Original Institutional Economics (OIE) and the New Institutional Economics (NIE)

In concluding this initial discussion of the defining attributes of institutional economics, it is necessary to clarify a bothersome bit of terminology. The institutional economics discussed above is today referred to as the "old" or "original" institutional economics.[3] The preferred usage in this volume is the "original" institutional economics (OIE). The need for this terminology arises from the fact that over the last forty years there has emerged in the orthodox literature a school of economic thought that attempts to take into account the role of institutions and institutional change in the economy while remaining true to most of the methodological presuppositions of neoclassical economics. It has come to be called the "new" institutional economics (NIE).

In spite of their fundamental neoclassical orientation, some new institutional economists pay homage to John R. Commons as providing the basic inspiration for their work. See, for example, Oliver E. Williamson (1975, 3). While there are points of convergence in the analytical interests of practitioners of the OIE and the NIE, their methodologies and their policy prescriptions are at fundamental odds.[4] Returning to Hodgson's discussion of the "essence" of the OIE, he succinctly identifies the fundamental difference between the OIE and the NIE by noting that while the OIE "embrace[s] the notion that the individual is molded by cultural or institutional circumstances," this notion is "found neither in mainstream economics, nor in the new institutionalism" (Hodgson 2000, 327). He goes on to say, "[t]he tradition there is to take the individual as given. His or her preference function, even if it includes cultural variables as arguments . . . , is immanently conceived. The emphasis there is on "rational choice" with given preferences in specified circumstances. Welfare judgments are based on the assumption that the choice made by the individual is the 'best' one in the circumstances" (327-28).

The essays throughout this volume are written in the tradition of the original institutional economics (OIE). Although occasional references are made to the new institutional economics (NIE), it will be noted that they reflect the critical view that practitioners of OIE hold with respect to the NIE.

## Neoinstitutional Economics and the Theory of Institutional Change

Institutional economics flourished in the period between World War I and World War II. It was a dominant force both in academe and in the realm of economic policy making. While *laissez-faire* ideology dominated public discourse on economic problems, day-to-day problem-solving at both the state and national levels was greatly influenced by practitioners of institutional economics. The influence of institutional economics on policy formation reached its zenith during the administration of President Franklin D. Roosevelt. His "New Deal" was fashioned to a great extent by institutionalists who were the students of Commons and Veblen. Landmark legislation in the fields of social security, unionism and collective bargaining, public power (the Tennessee Valley Authority), and agriculture, to name but a few, was designed primarily by institutional economists.

But by the end of World War II, institutional economics had fallen into decline. Neoclassical economics rose to a position of dominance in institutions of higher learning, and the influence of institutionalists in the formulation of national economic policies began to wane. If one were to consult standard textbooks on the history of economic thought, one would find a general consensus among the authors that institutional economics disappeared from the scene by the end of the 1930s. Eric Roll, put it this way: "The 'institutionalist' school . . . is now [1942] almost completely dead, and

. . . intermittent attempts to revive it have invariably failed to arouse much interest" (Roll 1942, 498). Paraphrasing Mark Twain, news of the demise of institutional economics was a bit premature.[5]

Paradoxically, it was during the mid-1940s that, rather than taking its last gasp, this supposedly moribund school of economic thought had new life breathed into it. The new stimulus to institutional thought was provided by the works of Clarence E. Ayres (1891-1972) of the University of Texas. Ayres's contribution lay in his integration of Veblen's analysis of institutional change with the value theory of the great American philosopher, John Dewey (1859-1952). Ayres's work inspired a careful re-examination of institutionalist methodology and launched a new approach to institutional analysis, which came to be called "neoinstitutional" economics (Tool 1953; and Bush 1995). In its more restrictive meaning, the term "neoinstitutional" economics refers to the line of thought that is traced from the confluence of the ideas of Veblen and Dewey in the works of Ayres, to J. Fagg Foster, Ayres's leading protégé, and other American institutionalists influenced by Ayres and Foster. The editors of this volume, both of whom are students of Foster, are identified as "neoinstitutionalists" in this intellectual tradition.[6] In its broader meaning, the term "neoinstitutional" economics is used to identify the institutional economics written in a manner consistent with the Veblen-Commons tradition since the Second World War. Using this criterion, Allan G. Gruchy identified John Kenneth Galbraith, Gerhard Colm, and Gunnar Myrdal, as "neo-institutional" [Gruchy's spelling] economists (Gruchy 1974).

## NEOINSTITUTIONALISM

### The Neoinstitutionalist Methodology

There are two key elements in the neoinstitutionalist methodology: 1) the "Veblenian dichotomy," and 2) Dewey's pragmatic instrumentalist theory of value. Each of these elements is imbedded in a broader range of considerations. In the case of Veblen's "dichotomy," the notion arises in his effort to identify the evolutionary processes at work in all societies. In the case of Dewey's value theory, both his philosophy of democracy and his philosophy of science provide broad intellectual frames of reference in which the theory is formulated. In the following paragraphs, these two key elements of the neoinstitutionalist methodology will be briefly explained with particular emphasis on the manner in which Ayres and Foster integrated them into a coherent theory of institutional change.

## The Veblenian Dichotomy: The Case of Consumption

Veblen challenged two of the fundamental propositions of neoclassical economics: 1) that consumption is undertaken to maximize the utility of the individual consumer; and 2) that profits are the reward for productivity. In attacking the first proposition he formulated his famous notion of "conspicuous" consumption. In attacking the second proposition, he formulated his famous distinction between the "industrial employments" and the "pecuniary employments," or, to put it in less elegant terms, the distinction between "making goods" and "making money." The following paragraphs will provide a brief review of the meaning and significance of these two aspects of Veblen's thought.

It will be recalled from earlier remarks that Veblen rejected the Hedonistic conception of man that provided the philosophical foundation for the neoclassical theory of human nature, which he characterized as a "lightning calculator of pleasures and pains." In contemporary parlance, the neoclassical conception of the rational consumer is that of a person attempting to maximize utility subject to an income constraint. In the Veblenian view, "utility" signifies "pleasure" and "income constraint" signifies "pain," reflecting the utilitarian origins of the neoclassical conception of "rationality."

The meaning of utility in this context is "use value." Goods and services have "use value" to the extent that their consumption sustains and enhances human life. Veblen had no quarrel with the notion of use value as such. What he rejected was the notion that consumption is motivated by the desire to acquire "use value" alone. He argued that a major element of consumption is the acquisition and display of status, which he called "conspicuous consumption." Furthermore, he said, consumer goods (and to a lesser extent capital goods) are designed and produced in such a way as to appeal to the consumer's desire for "conspicuous consumption." The use of the technology and resources to produce goods and services that satisfy the consumer's desire for "conspicuous consumption" is his definition of "waste." While there may be reasonable limits to the desire to acquire "use value," even for the very rich, there is no limit to the desire for the acquisition of status, either for the rich or the poor. This means that irrespective of the level the technology and resources available to the community, there is a collective propensity to waste economic resources.

Probing more deeply into the notion of "conspicuous consumption," we find that it is prompted by "invidious distinctions" which form the foundation of the system of status and power within the community. This is such a critical notion in Veblen's system of thought, it is useful to review his definition of the term. An invidious distinction, he says, is a "comparison of persons with a view to rating and grading them in respect of relative worth or value—in an aesthetic or moral sense—and so awarding and defining the relative degrees of complacency with which they may legitimately be contemplated by themselves and by others. An invidious comparison is a process of valuation of persons in respect to worth" (Veblen [1899] 1975, 34). Racism, sexism, and ethnic and religious bigotry provide the bases for some of the more notorious forms of invidious distinctions. In addition, invidious distinctions based on blood lineage have a long history in both the East and the West. But it is the invidious distinction based on the "ability to pay" that is Veblen's preoccupation. The ability to pay is the invidious criterion operative in communities (such as capitalist societies) that have adopted the "pecuniary standard of living." Conspicuous consumption, then, is a public demonstration of one's ability to pay; which is to say, it is a demonstration of one's social status.

It is within this line of reasoning that one form of the Veblenian dichotomy emerges. Consumption entails two different kinds of social implications: on the one hand, consumption is the noninvidious means to sustaining the life process, impersonally considered; on the other hand, consumption is the primary determinant of one's status, judged by the invidious standard of the ability to pay. Veblen speculated that the "waste" involved in conspicuous consumption is probably embodied in all consumer goods and services to one degree or another.[7] For example, a BMW is a marvelously engineered automobile that will perform the instrumental function of transporting its owner from point A to point B. As one of the most expensive cars in the world, it also demonstrates the owner's ability to pay. Accordingly, the dichotomy is a matter of drawing an analytical distinction between the "invidious" and "noninvidious" aspects of consumption.

The capacity of the community to provision the noninvidious consumption of its members is determined by its technological capacity to "turn material means to account" (to use one of Veblen's famous phrases); it is, in other words, based on the state of the arts and sciences embodied in the community's fund of knowledge. In contrast, the community's allocation of resources to invidious (conspicuous) consumption turns on considerations of status and power. Those who have the ability to pay are, by virtue of their superior status, empowered to exercise discretion over the behavior of others. This perception has significant methodological and policy implications; for it requires that economic analysis undertake a direct investigation of the acquisition and use of power in the study of economic relationships. This analytical perspective provides institutional analysis with its robust policy relevance. The fields of public utility regulation and antitrust economics are cases in point. In Chapter 10, Harry M. Trebing explains how concentrations of corporate power brought about the deregulation of public utilities, and in Chapter 11, Michael F. Sheehan sets forth the institutionalist rationale for the continuing need for public policies to combat the abuses of economic power by giant enterprise.

### The Veblenian Dichotomy: The Case of Business Enterprise

Veblen's distinction between the "non-invidious" and "invidious" reappears in his discussion of the organization of business enterprise. The business sector of the economic system is composed of two interrelated, but fundamentally different types, of "employments." He calls them the "industrial" and the "pecuniary" employments (Veblen [1899] 1975, 208). The industrial employments, according to Veblen, entail the tools-skills nexus that makes possible the provisioning of the community through the production of life-sustaining goods and services. Without the industrial employments, the community could not survive. Such employments are "non-invidious" for the reason that they sustain the life processes of the community, defined in impersonal terms. The pecuniary employments, on the other hand, are "institutions of acquisition" (ibid.); they involve the struggle for *control* over the industrial employments and the effort to enhance one's status through the acquisition of financial advantage over others. These employments, Veblen contends, are "self-regarding," thus, "invidious" (239). Veblen introduced the dichotomy between pecuniary and industrial employments in *The Theory of the Leisure Class (1899)* and elaborated on it in *The Theory of Business Enterprise (1904).* The dichotomy became the anchor of his theory of business enterprise, with which he explained the foundations of economic power of the business elite, whose personal well-being was lodged in the pecuniary employments.

Veblen believed that the invidious pecuniary employments tended to dominate the non-invidious industrial employments in modern business enterprise. From the point of view of those engaged in the pecuniary employments it is "vendibility," not "serviceability" that is the controlling consideration in bringing products to market. "Vendibility" is an invidious criterion that means saleable at the highest possible profit; where "profit" is the name of the flow of income received by the propertied and business elite. It is uniquely a pecuniary criterion. On the other hand, "serviceability," is a non-invidious criterion which is applied in the industrial employments to appraise the capacity of goods and services to meet the needs of the community to maintain its life processes. Accordingly, he writes: "The interest of the community at large demands industrial efficiency and serviceability of the product; while the business interest . . . demands vendibility of the product . . . ." (Veblen [1904] 1975, 7157-158). While it is possible that "vendibility" and "serviceability" might indeed coincide in the production of some commodities and services, Veblen believed that in the normal case they diverged. "[P]ecuniary efficiency" (i.e., 'vendibility'), he says, "is on the whole incompatible with industrial efficiency" (Veblen [1899] 1975, 241; see also, Veblen [1904] 1975, 51). Given this divergence, it lies within the vested interests of those engaged in the pecuniary employments to dominate the industrial employments in the production and distribution of goods and services.

For Veblen, the "Captain of Industry" (as he called the practitioners of the pecuniary employments) was not necessarily the champion of technological innovation and industrial growth (Veblen [1923] 1964, 112-113).[8] On the contrary, Veblen argued that the "Captain of Industry" was more likely to engage in a "conscientious withdrawal of efficiency"—that is, create artificial scarcities—if doing so would keep prices high and increase profits (Veblen [1921] 1965, 1). He referred to this practice as "sabotage." In a passage that is most appropriate to the current rash of corporate scandals, Veblen observes that ". . . the corporation is always a business concern, not an industrial appliance. *It is a means of making money, not of making goods.* The production of goods or services, wherever that sort of thing is included among the corporation's affairs, is incidental to the making of money and is carried only so far as will yield the largest net gain in terms of money, all according to the principle of 'what the traffic will bear' . . . ." (Veblen [1923] 1964, 85; italics not in the original).

This brings to mind the testimony that David Roderick, the CEO of United States Steel (USS), gave in the early 1980s to a congressional committee investigating the shutting down of steel plants throughout the northeastern part of the US. Members of Congress were concerned about the impact these plant closings were having on the local economies in the region. In response to questions that clearly implied that the USS had a responsibility to keep the steel plants open, Roderick stated emphatically that: "United States Steel is not in the business of producing steel, it is in the business of producing profits!" In 1986, United States Steel changed its symbols from "USS" to "USX." An "X" replaced the world "Steel." Veblen's distinction between making goods and making money was thus validated by the CEO of one of the country's largest corporations.

In spite of these considerations, Veblen observes that ". . . there is a naïve, unquestioning persuasion abroad among the body of the people to the effect that, in some occult way, the material interests of the populace coincide with the pecuniary interests of . . . business men . . ." (Veblen [1904] 1975, 286). In this lament, Veblen puts his finger on the enabling myth that continues to vex any effort to develop progressive economic policies as we enter the 21st century, to wit: the belief that the unfettered "market" harmonizes the interests of business with the interests of the community at large. In Chapter 9, Edythe S. Miller explains how neoclassical thought has strengthened this myth by rationalizing the concentration and centralization of power in the corporate sector of the economy.

## Veblen's Concept of "Cumulative Causation" and Its Implications for the Theory of Institutional Change

Veblen's conception of evolutionary processes is captured in his notion of "cumulative causation." "[A]n evolutionary economics," he says, "must be the theory of a process of cultural growth as determined by the economic interest, a theory of a cumulative sequence of economic institutions stated in terms of the process itself" (Veblen [1919] 1942, 77). He goes on to say: "It is necessarily the aim of such an economics to trace the cumulative working-out of the economic interest in the cultural sequence. It must be a theory of the economic life process of . . . the community" (78). This means that an evolutionary economics must be able to explain the process of cumulative causation that affects changes in the community's institutional structure over time. Neoclassical economics fails in this respect to qualify as an evolutionary economics because it does not even pose this matter as a subject for scientific inquiry. It confines itself only to problems of cause and effect that can be isolated and configured into the problem of the allocation of scarce means among competing ends within a given institutional structure.

Veblen defines institutions as follows: ". . . institutions are, in substance, prevalent habits of thought with respect to particular relations and particular functions of the individual and of the community . . . ." (Veblen [1899] 1975, 190). The process by which institutions change in response to evolutionary forces at work in the society is complex; it is both the fundamental cause of social problems and the character of their resolution. Veblen captures the problematic nature of institutional change in the following passage:

> Institutions are products of the past process, are adapted to past circumstances, and are therefore never in full accord with the requirements of the present. In the nature of the case, this process of selective adaptation can never catch up with the progressively changing situation in which the community finds itself at any given time; for the environment, the situation, the exigencies of life which enforce the adaptation and exercise the selection, change from day to day; and each successive situation of the community in its turn tends to obsolescence as

> soon as it has been established. When a step in the development has been taken, the step itself constitutes a change of the situation which requires a new adaptation; it becomes the point of departure for a new step in the adjustment, and so on interminably (ibid. 190-192).

Institutional change, he emphasizes, occurs ". . . in the last analysis, through a change in the habits of thought of the individuals which make up the community" (ibid, 190). This is a critical feature of his theory of institutional change, for, as will be seen in the following section, it is a key to an understanding of the role the value system of the society plays in the process.

Veblen employed the "invidious"-"non-invidious" dichotomy in his explanation of institutional change. The non-invidious cultural factors contain within them the dynamic technological/social forces that give rise to institutional change. The invidious cultural factors, on the other hand, retard those technological innovations and institutional changes that are perceived to threaten existing patterns of status and power. The non-invidious tools/skills nexus of the industrial employments infuses an inherently dynamic process into the affairs of the community. Problem solving in the non-invidious aspects of the culture involves the mastery of cause and effect, the application of an appropriate technology, or technological innovation, to create an appropriate technology, and the concomitant adjustment of habits of thought and behavior. In contrast, the invidious aspects of the culture require what he called the "ceremonial" observance of status and power relationships and their rationalization through ideological myth structures. Such rationalizations, Veblen says, rely on "sufficient reason" as opposed to the efficacy of causality in providing social warrant for the invidious distinctions that lie at the heart of the ceremonial practices of the community (Veblen [1914] 1964, 323). The non-invidious practices of the community auger for institutional change, whereas the invidious practices of the community tend to defend the status quo.

In concluding these remarks on Veblen's theory of evolutionary social change, it should be noted that he did not believe that evolutionary processes are teleological, that is, focused on some definitive ultimate end. While individual behavior is everywhere teleological, the social processes of evolutionary change are not. There is no guiding hand of nature that points the process in the "right" direction. Social evolution is not necessarily a force for "progress." This is due to a variety factors, the two most important of which are; 1) human beings may not possess appropriate technologies with which to solve their problems; and, 2) the ceremonial-invidious practices of the community may impede the use of appropriate technologies in the problem-solving process. Indeed, Veblen held a rather pessimistic view about the capacity of humankind to adapt adequately to evolutionary forces impinging on its circumstances. Accordingly, he says: ". . . history records more frequent and more spectacular instances of the triumph of imbecile institutions over life and culture than of peoples who have by force of instinctive insight saved themselves alive out of a desperately precarious institutional situation . . . ." (Veblen [1914] 1964, 25). Left to itself, the evolutionary process is one of "blind drift."

We turn now to the elaborations that contemporary neoinstitutionalists have made on Veblen's evolutionary theory of institutional change.

## The Contributions of Ayres, Dewey, Foster, and Their Students

### Clarence E. Ayres's Integration of Veblen and Dewey

As indicated above, Clarence E. Ayres invigorated the methodology of institutional economics by integrating Veblen's theory of institutional change with John Dewey's philosophy of social value. Ayres perceived that Veblen's distinction between the "invidious" and "non-invidious" implied a conception of valuation that bore a remarkable resemblance to John Dewey's theory of "instrumental" valuation. Ayers's perception was validated by Dewey who saw little difference between his theory of instrumental valuation and Veblen's conception of "non-invidious" problem-solving in the community.

In Veblen's discussion of the dynamics of institutional change, he talked about the impact of technology on the institutional structure. Technological processes, he argued, required a matter-of-fact preoccupation with cause and effect at the exclusion of any consideration of status or power relations. Problem solving in the technological continuum of human experience is inherently dynamic as the solution to one problem (or set of problems) opens up new areas of possibilities for consideration. This has a dislocating effect on the status quo of the existing institutional structure. Workers imbued with intellectual habits that involve reasoning in terms of cause and effect are less likely to be inclined to adhere to ceremonial practices that rationalize their inferior economic status. They become, as Veblen said, "insubordinate." However, the institutional structure of the community responds only slowly, and most often, quite negatively, to technological innovations that might disrupt existing patterns of status and power. While an elite of vested interests are usually in a position to exercise economic and political power to protect its privileged status, the common folk also tend to be conservative with respect to social change and emulate the prejudices of the power elite in such matters. Thus there is, in the Veblenian analysis, a tension between technology and institutions.

Ayres probed the Veblenian dichotomy to elaborate the underlying value structures Veblen appeared to be working with in this analysis. It is very clear in Veblen's work that the ceremonial practices of the community rest upon myths and beliefs that are absolutistic and, beyond a certain point in their rationalizations through Holy Writs, myths, and ideologies, unyielding to critical examination. For Veblen, they are a species of an "animistic" habit of thought. They are pre-scientific. Consequently, the standards of judgments, i.e., the values by which behavior is correlated, in the ceremonial practices of the community lie beyond reasoned analysis of cause and effect. Such standards of judgment meet the standard of "ceremonial adequacy"; that is, they conform to the rationale of the existing pattern of invidious distinctions operative within the community. Ayres recognized this kind of value system as being identical to those John Dewey argued passionately against in his *Quest for Certainty* ([1929] 1984).

Absolutistic moral beliefs and the "quest for cognitive certainty," Dewey argued, rest upon the "need for security in the results of action" (Dewey [1929] 1984, 32). But the quest for certainty is precisely what scientific inquiry does not permit. What we learn from scientific inquiry, and what Dewey sets forth as one of the basic tenets of his pragmatic instrumentalist philosophy, is that "there is no belief so settled as not to be exposed to further inquiry" (Dewey [1938] 1986, 16). Absolute truth, in other words, is not attainable, nor is there any need to try to attain it. In contrast, science provides us with *tentative* small "t" truths about the world that we can act upon with confidence (but not certitude). Similarly, pragmatic instrumentalism offers a conception of value and valuation that is compatible with, and indeed integral to, scientific inquiry in particular and problem solving in general.

As standards of judgment, values can be formulated within the existential context of the problems addressed. They need not be imported from without the existential context, as would be the case if one attempted to employ universal values of an absolute character, the authenticity of which is guaranteed by widely accepted dogma and taken for granted. Whether the issue is one of trying to determine how to proceed with inquiry in a scientific laboratory, or whether it is one of trying to decide how to formulate a policy for the distribution of the community's income, it is necessary to adopt and employ standards of judgment (i.e., values) with which to correlate the behavior of the participants in bringing the enterprise to a successful conclusion. Instrumental valuation involves a consideration of means and consequences. An instrumental value is validated by the consequences that flow from it use as a standard of judgment. It is not validated by an appeal to its "authentic" origins in religious, philosophical, or ideological dogma. An instrumental value is employed because it contributes in some positive way to the continuation of the life processes; in science, it helps to keep the paths of inquiry open; in problem-solving generally, personal or social, it contributes to the on-going discovery of new possibilities in the human enterprise. Unlike absolute moral dicta, instrumental values are subject to re-examination and revision as human experience dictates. Finally, it must be reiterated that instrumental values and valuations stand in direct opposition to invidious distinctions and considerations of status and power. Such matters play no role whatsoever in instrumental logic precisely because they are derived from a universe of considerations that instrumental logic excludes from the realm of legitimate inquiry.

These observations are relevant to the neoinstitutionalist view of scientific objectivity. Following Dewey, neoinstitutionalists reject the fact-value dualism that is the foundation of the neoclassical economist's conception of scientific objectivity. According to this positivist doctrine, "objectivity" can only be achieved if normative propositions are expunged from scientific inquiry. Pragmatic philosophy teaches that this dualism actually blocks the path of inquiry because it obscures the normative judgments scientists actually make in the conduct of inquiry. Pragmatic philosophers and neoinstitutionalists grant that certain kinds of normative judgments are, indeed, contaminants of inquiry; these are normative judgments based on absolute moral injunctions, which are themselves beyond critique and revision. They are imposed on inquiry from without. But not all values that operate as standards of judgment are derived from absolutistic foundations. Instrumental valuation employs values, i.e., norms, that are "determined in and by the process of inquiry" (Dewey [1938] 1986, 496). They are the species of normative propositions that science requires to carry on inquiry. As Jacob Bronowski puts it, "[t]he values of science . . . have grown out of the practice of science, because they are the inescapable conditions for its practice" (Bronowski 1965, 58). Thus, "objectivity" in science is not a matter of expunging all normative propositions from inquiry; it is rather a matter of employing normative propositions that are appropriate to the process of inquiry; namely, those that arise out of instrumental valuations.

Instrumental valuations, are part of the common experience of humankind. They are found in the tools/skills nexus of the technological processes of the community. The standards of judgment adopted in the technological continuum of human experience are evaluated on the grounds of their instrumental efficiency. Values that meet the criterion of instrumental efficiency are said to be "instrumentally warranted." In contrast, values that meet the standard of "ceremonial adequacy" are said to be "ceremonially warranted."

A simple example may clarify the use of this language. In the world of work, there are "bosses" and workers. The relationship of the "boss" to workers involves both ceremonially warranted and instrumentally warranted modes of valuations, relating to the different roles the "boss" plays in the workplace. One role a boss plays is ceremonially warranted by the invidious distinction involved in the "master-servant" relationship. The authority of the boss to give orders is based on the invidious distinction drawn between "superiors" and "inferiors." Whether or not the boss's orders are reasonable or arbitrary and capricious, the worker has no choice but to obey them. In this dimension of the boss-worker relationship, the boss's authority is unquestioned *because of* his or her "superior" status. The legitimacy of the boss's right to give orders is judged by the test of "ceremonial adequacy."

A boss can also serve as supervisor, as in the case of the journeyman-apprentice relationship. In supervising the work of the apprentice, it is the responsibility of the journeyman to teach the apprentice how to use the appropriate tools to get the job done safely and efficiently. Their relationship is governed by a division of labor that is anchored in the tools/skills nexus of the technological process of the work they are doing. The apprentice follows the journeyman's orders because doing so is essential to learning how to get the job done properly. The authority of the journeyman to gives orders to the apprentice is judged by the test of "instrumental efficiency."

It does not take much time on the job before a worker can tell when the boss is giving orders "just to show who the boss is," and when the boss is giving orders that are instrumental to "delivering the goods," getting the job done safely and efficiently. It is important to note at this point that Veblen's belief that the pecuniary (invidious, ceremonially warranted) employments dominate the industrial (non-invidious, technologically grounded) employments is relevant to an understanding of the boss-worker relationship. It is a generally accepted myth, even within our "modern" society, that the ceremonially warranted, invidiously endowed "superior" status of the boss provides the "legitimacy" of his authority to act as a supervisor. His superior status is embedded in the institution of private property. Either as the owner of the property, or as the representative of "absentee owners," his superior status is warranted by the rights and privileges enjoyed by those who preserve the "sanctity" of private property.

Even though members of the community can tell the difference between the two types of authority exercised by the boss, they generally defer to the legitimacy of the ceremonially warranted behavior. They understand quite well that the invidious notion of the boss's "superiority" does not, in fact, have anything to do with "delivering the goods." They know that it is the instrumentally warranted division of labor within the technological continuum of activities that actually contributes to "delivering the goods." Nevertheless, the community's widely shared myth structure ensures compliance with these ceremonial practices. Members of the community willingly subscribe to the notion that a clearly defined system of invidious status relationships contributes to an orderly and predictable state of affairs in which "everyone knows his or her place." As a matter of received doctrine, it is believed that the alternative would be chaos. Thus, the ceremonial practices dominate the instrumental practices of the community. In Chapter 13, Deborah Figart demonstrates that ceremonially warranted invidious distinctions extend far beyond the boss/worker relationship in the world of work.

In his book, *The Theory of Economic Progress (1944),* Clarence Ayres advanced the idea that genuine social progress occurs when a society is able to increase its reliance on instrumentally warranted patterns of behavior in its problem-solving processes. This, of course, would involve the displacement of ceremonially warranted patterns of behavior, and this would, of necessity, entail institutional change. Herein lies the interweaving of Dewey's philosophy of value with Veblen's theory of institutional change. In working with the Veblenian dichotomy, Ayres followed rather closely Veblen's theoretical structure, in which he posited a tension between "technology" and "institutions." Applying Dewey's value theory, Ayres counterpoised ceremonial valuation with instrumental valuation, the former apparently being confined to "institutions" and the later to "technology."

The "apparently" in the previous sentence is prompted by the question of whether Ayres adhered to a strict distinction between the domains of "technology" and "institutions" in his application of Dewey's value theory. The matter is the subject of debate among some of Ayres's followers. Without delving into that dispute, it must be conceded that Ayres's use of terminology entailed some ambiguities that impaired the clarity with which the process of institutional change could be discussed.

## J. Fagg Foster's Contribution

J. Fagg Foster clarified these issues by offering a precise definition of the concept of an "institution" and the relationship of the instrumental and ceremonial patterns behavior within the institutional domain. He defined an institution as a set of *socially prescribed patterns of correlated behavior which have both instrumental and ceremonial aspects.* The theoretical advantage of this definition is that it avoids the ambiguities that are associated with such notions as "technological *institutions*" and "ceremonial *institutions.*" What Foster's definition does is offer a uniform definition of institutions and clearly identifies the "technological" (instrumental) and the "ceremonial" as attributes assignable to specific patterns of correlated behavior within the institutional structure. Thus, in the example given above, both instrumental and ceremonial patterns of behavior were found in the employment relationship between the boss and the worker. The boss's superior status was ceremonially warranted, whereas his or her role as a supervisor was instrumentally warranted.

At this point in the discussion, it is possible to identify precisely the meaning of the terms "value" and "valuation" as they are used by neoinstitutionalists in the discussion of the institutions and institutional change. "Values" are the standards (or criteria) of judgment by which behavior is correlated in "behavioral patterns." Thus, an "instrumentally warranted" pattern of behavior employs an instrumental value as a standard of judgment. In the employment relation example above, the behavior of the supervisor in giving the apprentice an order, and the apprentice's behavior in complying with that order, are correlated by the technologically determined division-of-labor in doing the work, an instrumental standard of judgment (value). When the boss is "throwing his or her weight around" and issues an order to an "inferior," a ceremonial value (the invidious distinction of status) serves as the standard of judgment by which the behavior of the "superior" and the "inferior" are correlated. Using this enriched conception of an institution, Foster's students have gone on to develop Foster's theory of "institutional adjustment" into a robust theoretical framework within which to address both analytical and policy issues.

Foster's theory of institutional adjustment consists of three principles: 1) the principle of technological determination: 2) the principle of recognized interdependence; and 3) the principle of minimal dislocation (see Tool 2000, 87-104). Foster's formulation of the *principle of technological determination* focuses on the fact that the dynamic for social change exists in the technological process of the community, not in its ceremonial practices. It should be noted in passing, that Foster was not a "technological determinist" as the term is often used in the literature. One can acknowledge the causal characteristics of technology without being a "technological determinist," as the following recitation of his theory of institutional adjustment demonstrates.

The technological process provides knowledge by which the community can assess the capacity of the existing institutional structure to support the life processes of the community. For technological innovations to contribute to the well-being of the community, they must be absorbed into the community's problem solving processes. However, technological innovation involves not only a change in the use of tools (and associated skills), it also involves a change in the way in which behavior is correlated within the institutional structure. Technological innovation entails the expansion of the use of instrumentally warranted values in the correlation of behavior. More often than not, this will require the displacement of ceremonially warranted patterns of behavior in the affected institutional domain. This, of course, would mean that traditional patterns of status and power may be disrupted. To the extent that such disruption is anticipated, there is resistance to the adoption of the new technology.

A social problem can be defined as a situation in which the community perceives a difference between "what is" and "what ought to be." Putting it in institutional terms, a social problem exists when the existing institutional structure fails to permit the community to make the best use of its fund of knowledge in sustaining the life processes of the community. In effect, technological innovation makes it possible for the community to distinguish between "what is" and "what ought to be." It not only delineates the institutional impairment, it also offers the means by which the community can identify its options in dealing this the problematic situation. But whether the community will be able to undertake the institutional change(s) necessary to achieve "what ought to be" depends on additional considerations covered under Foster's two other principles of institutional adjustment.

The *principle of recognized interdependence* addresses the question of what the community must take into account in assessing its institutional options. It highlights the fact that the solution to a social problem involves a conscious choice to undertake an institutional change. While institutions are composed of habitual patterns of thought and behavior, which provide a certain amount of social continuity and predictability of human behavior, they do not arise "spontaneously" out of some sort of social vacuum. They are consciously chosen at some point in the community's history as solutions to social problems. Once adopted, the new patterns of correlated behavior become habituated and they are taken for granted. Over a certain period of time, members of the community tend to presume that the existing institutional structure is "natural" and "proper," for the memory of man does not run to the contrary. This makes institutional change difficult, but not impossible.

In choosing among the institutional options facing the community, those who must alter their behavior need to be aware of how the new behavior will fit into the interdependent fabric of patterns of behavior in the affected institution, and how the changes in that institution will affect other institutions of immediate concern in the circumstances. It is not, of course, possible for the community to be omniscient. Judgments about interdependencies can be erroneous, and the full range of required institutional adjustments throughout the community cannot be predicted with any certainty. Indeed, the sense of not having sufficient knowledge about such matters can instill a conservatism that ultimately defeats needed institutional adjustments. But this fact does not nullify the importance of the principle of recognized interdependence. In addition to the principle of technological determination, the principle of recognized interdependence identifies a necessary condition for institutional change; it does not predict its inevitability. In anticipation of the upcoming discussion of the relationship of democracy to institutional change, it should be noted that while this discussion of the principle of recognized interdependence has been confined to an *analysis* of institutional change, it also has profound implications for the formulation of economic *policy*.

Foster's *principle of minimal dislocation* identifies what may be thought of as the sufficient condition for institutional change. This principle is based on the fact that the institutional structure is continuous through time (historical continuity) and through social space (an institutional "fabric"). It is composed of a complex of interconnecting socially prescribed patterns of correlated behavior, some of which are ceremonially warranted and some of which are instrumentally warranted. Institutional change dislocates old patterns of behavior as new patterns of behavior are introduced. It is entirely possible that a technological innovation may dislocate other related instrumentally warranted patterns of behavior as well as ceremonial patterns of behavior. It is universally recognized that technological obsolescence is a necessary side effect of technological innovation. Nevertheless, there may be instrumentally warranted aspects of the old technology that society might not wish to do without. For these reasons, if a particular institutional change is to take hold, it must involve a minimal dislocation of the institutional structure of the community.

Once again, this is an analytical conclusion, based on inquiry into the institutional structure and institutional change. But it also has profound policy implications. For example, it is abundantly clear that the "market shock therapy" prescribed by neoclassical economists for the transitional economies of the former Soviet block countries has produced near disastrous consequences for the countries involved (Tool 1995, 197- 211). In foisting the market *uber alles* ideology on these countries, little or no consideration was given to either of Foster's principles of recognized interdependence or minimal dislocation, and the world is now paying the price for neglecting them. In Chapter 18, Gladys P. Foster explores the implications of the neglect of these principles of institutional change in the "globalization" of the world economy.

Before we leave this discussion of the theory of institutional change one additional idea must be mentioned. It is called "*ceremonial encapsulation*" (Bush 1987; 1999). This notion refines the theoretical scenario of how technological innovations find their way into the problem-solving processes of the community. It envisions two phases to the process of institutional adjustment. In the first phase, "ceremonial encapsulation" occurs when the community initially responds to the existence of a technological innovation. The community's initial response is to absorb the technological innovation with its associated changes in correlated patterns of behavior only to the extent that it can do so without disrupting the existing system of status and power. In other words, the technological innovation is encapsulated within ceremonially patterns of behavior in such a manner as not to change the existing value structure of the community. The traditional patterns of dominance of ceremonially warranted behavior over instrumentally warranted of behavior are not disturbed. The expansion of instrumentally warranted behavior is strictly circumscribed by newly fashioned ceremonial practices designed for that purpose.

But whatever the degree of ceremonial encapsulation—with the exception of the case of a complete suppression of the technological innovation—this first phase of institutional adjustment does involve the introduction of new instrumentally warranted patterns of behavior in the form of the technological innovation. These new patterns of behavior can have what Galbraith calls (in a different context) a "demonstration effect." The use of instrumental standards of judgment in the correlation of behavior is perceived as being applicable to a wider range of behaviors; that is, the possibility of displacing ceremonial patterns of behavior with instrumental patterns of behavior begins to suggest itself to members of the community who have direct knowledge of the situation. George D. Santopietro provides a perfect example of this phenomenon (Santopietro 1995). Discussing changes in patterns of behavior in the environmental practices of the community, he demonstrates how the instrumentally warranted activity of recycling waste at home may "also lead [a person] to promote recycling in the workplace (or vice versa)" (Santopietro 1995, 521). He notes that "the psychological literature refers to this as 'transsituational influence on behavior'." The substitution of instrumentally warranted behavior (recycling) for ceremonially warranted behavior (exercising one's right to engage in ceremonial waste) in one situation opens up the possibility of making a similar substitution in another institutional setting.

One of the implications of the notion of "ceremonial encapsulation" is that at any time in the life of the community it is likely to possess a fund of knowledge that has been ceremonially sequestered and thereby made unavailable to the community in its problem-solving processes. Thus, ceremonial encapsulation is a process that reduces the community's efficiency in coping with its problems. A poignant case in point is found in the social constraints placed on the dissemination of information about contraceptive technology and the outright prohibition on abortion counseling in some localities. Both ceremonial practices clearly lower the community's efficiency in preventing teenage pregnancies.

Perhaps one the most dramatic examples of ceremonial encapsulation in the US in the 20$^{th}$ century was the subordination of the authority of atomic scientists to design and direct research to the control of the Atomic Energy Commission (AEC). The AEC saw as one of its major functions the vetting of atomic scientists for "security clearance." This was essentially an elaboration of ceremonial practices designed to keep the pursuit of inquiry in the field (an instrumental practice) within the control of those who possessed a superior knowledge of the "patriotic needs" of the country (a ceremonial practice). When J. Robert Oppenheimer, director of the Los Alamos atomic weapons laboratory, began to express concerns about increasing the destructive power of atomic weapons, he was called before an inquisition of the AEC and was ultimately stripped of his security clearance. This was like telling Noah Webster he could no longer be trusted to read the dictionary he had written. The "security apparatus" of the US government from the outset of WW II to the present has been a primary force in the ceremonial encapsulation of science and technology in our culture. Secrecy is not only the enemy of science; it is also the enemy of democracy.

Veblen's analysis of the manner in which the pecuniary employments regulate the industrial employments through the imposition of the standard of "vendibility" is a blue print for the analysis of "ceremonial encapsulation" in the corporate world. For the better part of the 20$^{th}$ century, the tobacco industry provided a textbook example of the kind of predatory practices Veblen contended were the primary *modus operandi* of the pecuniary employments, namely, "force and fraud." Through a highly organized, industry-wide effort to discredit competent scientific research that demonstrates a causal connection between the use of tobacco and the onset of life-threatening diseases, the industry effectively deceived the public concerning the true risks of tobacco use. And, in a strategy designed to escape regulation by the Food and Drug Administration, the industry sequestered the scientific knowledge generated by its own scientists that nicotine in tobacco is addictive. The industry's efforts to misrepresent and actually suppress scientific knowledge is a classic case of ceremonial encapsulation of technology. The consequences of the tobacco industry's successful encapsulation of science and technology prevented the community from making the highest and best use of its knowledge fund (which included the knowledge sequestered by the industry) in dealing with major public health problems. Although he does not use the term, William H. Melody, in Chapter 14, examines the evidence of the ceremonial encapsulation of information technology by giant transnational corporations as they attempt to secure dominant positions in global markets.

Analytically, the substitution of instrumentally warranted patterns of behavior for ceremonially warranted patterns of behavior is called "progressive institutional change" (Bush 1984). It involves a change in the value structure of the institution which decreases to the degree of ceremonial dominance over instrumental patterns. This is the second phase of institutional adjustment. This idea also has significant implications for economic policy formation, which will be explored in the next section of this chapter.

In 1979 an important normative proposition was added to the neoinstitutional literature. It is called the "social value principle" (Tool 1979, 293). The principle identifies the path of social progress as that "which provides for *the continuity of human life and the noninvidious re-creation of community through the instrumental use of knowledge*" (ibid, italics in the original). Logically, this principle is equivalent to "progressive" institutional change under conditions of minimal dislocation (Bush 1989, 459). It is, in other words, a normative extrapolation of the neoinstitutionalist theory of institutional change. In policy analysis, it serves as a welfare criterion stated in terms of a process. It will provide the normative compass for the discussion of the relationship of democracy to institutional change in the following section.

## POLITICAL FOUNDATIONS OF ECONOMIC POLICY

It is a well know fact that most governments today attempt to identify themselves as "democracies." But, as Francis M. Meyers noted almost fifty years ago, there is a "warfare" of democratic ideals that significantly muddies the waters when the meaning of democracy is at issue (Meyers 1956). This "warfare" of democratic ideals is not only waged among nations through self-serving propaganda in the international theater of ideological combat, it also goes on among political factions within a given nation. Serious differences of opinions over the meaning of democracy are often at the heart of policy disputes among economists. For example, while there is a rather loose agreement between neoinstitutionalists and neoclassical economists, such as Milton Friedman, that "freedom" has something to do with enhancing the individual's range of choice—Friedman speaks of the "freedom to choose" and institutionalists speak of "increasing the area of individual discretion"—their conceptions of the institutional realities that make "freedom" possible are at fundamental odds with one another. In recognition of the fact that views on "democracy" can vary widely among reasonable and thoughtful students of the subject, it is necessary that this discussion move to a more detailed consideration of the conception of democracy that is incorporated in the neoinstitutionalist analysis of policy formation.

## Democratic Sovereignty, Freedom, and Public Policy

The political system of society is a system of institutions that establishes, among other things, the legitimate locus of authority, known as "sovereignty," within the community. The notion of sovereignty is significant for the present discussion because it identifies how the society allocates political power. Political power may be defined as the exercise of discretion over the behavior of others. Reference has already been made to the use of power in economic affairs. It has been argued that the invidious distinctions at work in societies allows for the exercise of discretion over the behavior of others by those who are favored by the invidious distinctions. As will become immediately apparent, invidious distinctions also play a key role in the discussion of sovereignty.

For the purpose of the present discussion, we may distinguish between two forms of sovereignty: authoritarian and democratic sovereignty. Under a system of authoritarian sovereignty, the legitimate locus of authority rests with a political elite. This is, of course, the form of sovereignty that most of the world's population has experienced throughout history, including the present. Such political elites are identified through dominant invidious distinctions within the community: blood lineage defines the royal family that occupies the monarchy; religious criteria identify the "select" who rule in a theocracy; and ideological purity defines the "party faithful" who were the political elite in both Nazi and Communist regimes of the 20$^{th}$ century. Such systems of sovereignty are "authoritarian" because they posit the right of an elite to rule from the top down. Those who are subject to the exercise of discretion by a ruling elite are permitted to respond to political edicts only through obedience. Under such a regime, the population is composed of "subjects," not "citizens."

Democratic sovereignty, on the other hand, is based on the principle enunciated by Thomas Jefferson: "[G]overnments . . . [derive] their just powers from the consent of the governed." Under a system of democratic sovereignty, therefore, the legitimate locus of authority lies with the people; that is, the "governed." This is unambiguously a non-invidious identification of those who may participate in the governance of the nation. It means that those who are subject to the consequences of public policy must have the opportunity effectively to participate its formation, and, if necessary, its revision. Under such a regime, the population is composed of "citizens," not "subjects."

In a system of democratic sovereignty, the question arises regarding the accessibility of the political process to the participation of individuals. Obviously, this question never arises under a regime of authoritarian sovereignty. In addition, the articulation of the "public interest" under majority rule is a critical aspect of democracy. The diagnostic consideration here is not majority rule as such, but *how* majorities are formed, and in their formation, *how* the rights of the minority are protected. Crucial to these considerations is the freedom of speech and the role it plays in the formation of majorities. The institutional arrangements through which the polity addresses these questions represent some of the heaviest burdens carried by the political process in a democracy.

Another critical aspect of the political process is the role it plays in determining the standards of judgment by which behavior is correlated throughout the institutional structure of society. In the previous discussion of neoinstitutional analysis, the argument was advanced that there are two modes of value formation in society, the ceremonial and the instrumental. The political process influences and is influenced by these two modes of valuation. At the formal level, the political process generates constitutions, laws, codes, and so forth, that may be based on either ceremonial or instrumental considerations (or, perhaps, both). Two examples should help clarify this point.

Antimiscegination laws, which forbid intermarriage among the "races," and which remained on the books in the US until almost a decade after the World War II, are based on the invidious distinctions inherent in racism. Such laws, in other words, clearly impose an invidious standard of judgment on the correlation of behavior in the marriage relation. With respect to the question of freedom, it is also clear that such laws erode the freedom of individuals to exercise discretion over even the most intimate aspects of their lives. What is at fault here is not that governments can pass laws that restrain individual behavior, but that, in this case, the restraint was ceremonially warranted.

It should be noted that the notion of freedom as "freedom from restraint" (advanced by Milton Friedman and the Libertarians) throws the baby out with the bath water. It presumes that *any* governmental restraint on some forms of individual behavior must, of necessity, reduce the freedom of the community at large. This conception of freedom not only establishes an ideological bias against government regulation, it prevents any consideration of instrumentally warranted forms of governmental regulation.

An example of instrumentally warranted government regulations are traffic laws. They are based on a rational consideration of cause and effect embodied in the technology of automotive transportation. Such laws establish standards for the correlation of behavior, the "rules of the road," that are non-invidious, and, if followed, expand the area of discretion (genuine freedom) for all who use the roads, whether pedestrians or drivers. Under traffic laws, anyone who uses the road, irrespective of invidious considerations of status and power, can do so without taking undue risks. Instrumental to achieving this outcome is the restraint on certain forms of individual behavior, e.g., speeding, running red lights, turning without signaling, and so forth. In this instance, government restraint on some forms of individual behavior actually expands the area of discretion (freedom) for the individual, i.e., one does not have to be a hero or a daredevil in order to use the public streets. It expands freedom precisely because it is instrumentally warranted.

## Freedom of Speech and Majority Rule

It would be impossible for the citizens of a democracy to exercise their sovereign right of self-governance if they did not possess the freedom of speech. Keeping in mind the pragmatic instrumentalist view that there is no such thing as absolute truth, it must be recognized that in the neoinstitutionalist view the warrant for the freedom of speech is not the idea that free speech leads to a discovery of capital "t" truth. They quite frankly reject the hoary admonition "Seek ye the Truth and the Truth will make you free," for it clearly embodies the idea that there is a "Truth" out there, waiting to be discovered. What nurtures freedom is the process of open-ended inquiry and discourse. The pragmatic instrumentalist conception of "truth" is the notion of "warranted assertions." As indicated earlier, warranted assertions are propositions about the natural or social domain that we can act upon with some degree of confidence. They are created out of an effort to comprehend causal relationships and to use that comprehension as a basis for action in human affairs. A proposition is accorded the status of small "t" truth only provisionally. Such propositions must be bounded by qualifications concerning the extent to which they permit an understanding of cumulative causation in the natural and social domains. In short, truth is "constructed" through the process of inquiry. And the process of inquiry, it should be noted, is a social process. "An inquirer in a given special field appeals to the experiences of the community of his fellow workers for confirmation and correction of his results" (Dewey [1938] 1986, 484). Accordingly, the crucial consideration here is not the "truths" produced by inquiry, for they are mere stepping stones to further discoveries and are themselves subject to revision and may even be discarded; the crucial consideration is the process of inquiry itself. Thus, if a pragmatic instrumentalist were to rephrase the admonition cited above, it would be "Seek ye the (small "t") truth, and the *quest* will make you free."

Coupled with this conception of "truth," is the notion that freedom of speech must be universal; that is to say, the right to exercise the freedom of speech must not involve any form of invidious exclusion of individuals or groups of individuals within the community. It is the pragmatic instrumentalist view that cultural diversity is a critical element in the preservation of freedom in a democracy. Louis Menand captures this idea precisely in the following passage:

> The more individual variations, the greater the chances that the group will survive. We do not . . . permit the free expression of ideas because some individual may have the right one. No individual alone can have the right one. We permit free expression because we need the resources of the whole group to get us the ideas we need. Thinking is a social activity. I tolerate your thought because it is part of my thought—even when my thought defines itself in opposition to yours (Menand 2001, 431).

Returning to the earlier definition of a social problem, in order to discover both "what is the case" and "what ought to be the case," the widest possible consideration of views must be undertaken as a communal effort. This is possible only if the freedom of speech is a non-invidious, universal endowment of the community.

Conservatives have always scoffed at the idea that a universal exercise of the right of free speech can somehow ensure the quality of government, given the fact that intelligence is not equally distributed throughout the population. Alexander Hamilton's view that a great nation must, of necessity, be governed by the "rich, wise, and well-born," continues to carry weight in some circles. There certainly is a rationale for this idea if access to education is allocated on the invidious basis of the "ability to pay." The intellectual training required for political leadership under such a regime is, indeed, confined to an economic elite. But a system of public education, properly funded and administered, is the democratic antidote to the necessity of rule by the "rich, wise, and well-born." This explains why John Dewey and institutionalists (OIE) have long given the highest priority to public education as a pillar of a democratic society. A well-endowed system of public education is vital to the enrichment of the dialogue that must be the foundation of meaningful policy formation in a free society. Baldwin Ranson, in Chapter 12, sets forth an institutionalist analysis of how education in a democracy can strengthen the community's capacity to deal with the challenges of technological innovation and institutional change.

The outcome of free and open debate never results in unanimous agreement. The will of the majority, no matter how openly arrived at in the public forum, is, by definition, not the will of the minority. Freedom of speech is, nevertheless, necessary to guarantee the legitimacy of majority rule and to provide the minority with the voice necessary to protect its rights. It is the vital ingredient in the process that forms a responsible majority. In the following passage, Livingston and Thompson succinctly clarify the complex relationship that exists between voting majorities and minorities in a democracy.

> The minority is obligated to obey the laws passed by a majority, but not to believe that the majority or its laws are correct. The final political loyalty of both majority and minority is to the *process* through which majority opinion is formed and continuously tested . . . The process of majority rule puts limits on the power of temporary majorities and guarantees rights for temporary minorities (Livingston and Thompson 1971, 90, italics in the original.)

This perception of majority rule is based upon the idea that democracy is an open-ended, problem-solving process. The history of democracy has shown time and again that today's minority is tomorrow's majority. This fact alone operates to temper the arrogance of power wielded by temporary majorities.

## Democracy and Institutional Change

"The neoinstitutionalist democratic perspective," Rick Tilman has written, "is thoroughly instrumentalist in origins and outlook" (Tilman 1987, 1382). He goes on to say,

> the neoinstitutionalist theory of democracy involves acceptance of the virtue of change in the interest of progress. Indeed, it is primarily a process and a method for improving unsatisfactory situations. At its most sensitive, it is a form of experimentalism through which alternative ways of thinking and acting are tested. In the eyes of the instrumentalist, democracy is not a formalistic ideology sanctioning certain institutions and election procedures; nor is it a rationale that legitimates a particular system of property relations. Rather, the essence of democracy consists

> of the view that there are few, if any, social structures that cannot be abandoned or altered, for all social institutions are subject both to the collective will and the test of usage (Tilman, 1987, 1382-83).

In this passage, Tilman sets the stage for a consideration of the relationship between the neoinstitutionalist theory of democracy and its theory of institutional change.

The matter simply put is that neoinstitutionalists believe that democracy is the optimal mode of governance for achieving "progressive" institutional change under the conditions of minimal dislocation. Foster's principles of recognized interdependence and minimal dislocation make it clear that if a community is going to exercise discretion over the institutional changes that will shape its future, it must have a political system that permits the widest possible consideration of the technological and institutional alternatives it faces at any given point in time. Furthermore, the community functioning as a polity must be able to select among its alternative institutional futures in such a way as to maintain the continuity of human life and to achieve the noninvidious re-creation of itself through the instrumental use of knowledge; that is, to act in terms of the social value principle. Democratic processes of self-governance meet these requirements.

Under a system of democracy, institutional changes may be tailored to revamp the correlated patterns of behavior in a particular area problem by problem. Under majority rule, limited adjustments in the institutional structure can be made minimally dislocative as long as they are acceptable to the majority of those who must bear the incidence of the change in structure, and as long as the rights of those in the minority to seek more favorable adjustments are protected. In a democratic system, institutional adjustments are on-going, involving successive approximations until the community's expectations and the institutional outcomes are congruent. But successive approximations must, at some point, reach closure, not because further inquiry and public debate cannot be allowed, but because subsequent adjustments must wait upon assessments of the institutional changes already achieved. They must be tested in use. The fashioning of new habits, new routines, and new expectations is unsettling. There is insecurity about the expected outcomes. Therefore, institutional change must not be allowed to become functionally disabling. Accommodation of new patterns of behavior within the community takes time. The open character of a democratic polity permits the kind of self-correcting adjustments the process of progressive institutional change requires.

The conception of democracy presented here advances the notion that democratically established and maintained governments have the capacity to contribute to problem-solving processes of the community. Contrary to the basic premise of Reaganomics, government is not the problem, it is a viable part of the solution. However, the political reality is that the "market *uber alles*" mentality prevails not only in corporate board rooms, in the halls of Congress, and in the White House, but also in the service clubs of Main Street, USA. This has had a debilitating effect on the use of democratic processes in dealing with many of the nation's leading economic problems. As John Kenneth Galbraith has observed, "[m]oney, voice and political activism are now extensively controlled by the affluent, the very affluent and the business interests" (1996, 140). A plethora of well-financed, right-wing "think tanks" provide a steady stream of ideological rationalizations for government by and for the rich and the powerful (Stefanic and Delgado 1996). They are quick to denounce proposals for an active role of government in problem-solving as "populist," suggesting that populism is some sort of a negative influence in a democracy. It is certainly true that populism has always been associated with a distrust of concentrations of economic and political power, particularly the concentrations of corporate power. It is also the case that instrumentally warranted government action in a democracy focuses on the community's interest independent of considerations of status and power. Advocacy of government policies which favor the interests of the community at the expense of the vested interests is glibly dismissed by right-wing pundits as the promotion of "class" warfare.

The market "uber alles" mentality is based on the belief that there is an institutional structure (i.e., "the market") that is the right and best way for society to perform its economic functions. Any such unqualified endorsement of a given institutional structure, and the value system it entails, is the business of ideology. It is not the business of either science or democracy. Institutional economics is non-ideological precisely because it challenges the notion that any institutional structure is sacrosanct. It advances the view that it is the process of institutional change, not the permanency of any institutional structure that offers hope for progress. The test of efficacy of the policy proposals of institutional economics is not to be found in the deference these proposals show to a set of ideological preconceptions; the test lies in the capacity of democratically formulated policies to solve problems through carefully designed institutional changes.

## AN INTRODUCTION TO THE CHAPTERS

The chapters comprising this volume are grouped into six topical segments: Macro-stabilization policies, equity and security policies, power accountability policies, individual empowerment policies, environmental policies, and global development policies. A characterization of the basic thesis of each chapter is offered in the following paragraphs.

I

In Chapter 2, on fiscal policy, *Philip A. Klein* provides an institutionalist view of macro-economic management. Klein contends that "fiscal policy is arguably the most explicit embodiment of the institutionalist conviction that there is a constructive role for governmental intervention in the quest for stable satisfactory growth rates in the modern market oriented economy." He vigorously refutes the orthodox notion that there is such a condition as a "natural rate of unemployment" which is the "price we have to pay to keep inflation down." Drawing on the Keynesian tradition, he insists that the economy is not self-regulating and "that the deliberate manipulation of governmental expenditures and tax revenues can play a role in producing both more rapid and more stable growth rates for the economy."

In Chapter 3, on monetary policy, *L. Randall Wray* examines the recent history of banking and offers an assessment of the importance of monetary policy. He traces the emergence of the "Currency School," the Federal Reserve system, the discovery of the "deposit multiplier," the impact of the Keynesian contribution, recourse to open market operations, and the recent Monetarist approach to monetary policy. He notes that post WWII Keynesians were skeptical "of the potency of monetary policy." "As we begin the 21st century," he says, "orthodox thinking about monetary policy is in nearly complete disarray." Wray concludes that "the main monetary policy recommendation . . . is that central banks should abandon any pretense that they can influence the quantity of reserves or the quantity of money privately created. They can only set the overnight interest rate—the fed funds rate in the US. That, of course, sets the base interest rate."

In Chapter 4, on tax policy, *Peter S. Fisher* observes that institutionalists have challenged "the orthodox view of market efficiency, market failure, the alleged trade-off between efficiency and equity, and . . . the agnosticism of neoclassical economists regarding income distribution." For institutionalists, these orthodox dicta are largely irrelevant. Fisher's fundamental critique of these positions opens the way for "an institutionalist approach to tax policy." In particular, Fisher supports progressive taxation on egalitarian grounds. He rejects the idea that "tax breaks to business and the wealthy are justified as stimulants to investment and job creation." He affirms that "tax incentives are very costly and largely ineffective." He also explains the ways in which tax policy plays a significant role in the concentration of poverty in central cities. He concludes that "tax incentives are very costly and largely [ineffective]."

II

In Chapter 5, on basic income policy, *Charles M. A. Clark* contends that nearly "every human society has had some mechanism to promote economic equity." However, while "wealth and incomes are collectively created . . . . the rules that determine the initial distribution of incomes do not typically provide for the whole community." He argues "that rules that generate economic outcomes are not natural laws. . . . Markets are social institutions and are socially determined." He maintains that "economic equity . . . must include fairness in outcomes based on the criterion that all have a right to a decent standard of living. . . . A policy that would promote both equity and economic efficiency is the provision of Basic Income to all citizens as a right of citizenship."

In Chapter 6, on welfare policy, *Janice Peterson* suggests that "distributional issues and the pursuit of economic security . . . are at the forefront of institutional analysis and policy." She contends that "in the US, the determination of whose interests count . . . has reflected gender (as well as race and class) distinctions." "Welfare policy in the United States," she says, "often reflect[s] and reinforce[es] invidious distinctions between those seen as 'deserving' and 'undeserving' of assistance." "From an institutionalist perspective," she observes, "it is clear that the purpose of welfare reform and welfare policy should be poverty reduction and promotion of the institutional change necessary for low-income families to participate fully in the economy and society." She is concerned that "the changes in welfare provisions presently before Congress will increase hardships on current and future welfare recipients."

In Chapter 7, on health care policies *Michael Keaney* contends that "few would deny that the health care system in the United States is in crisis." He argues that "to conduct inquiry into the problems of universal health care from an *institutionalist* standpoint necessitates a complete reappraisal of our habits of thought, clusters of mores, structures of authority and social continuities." He seeks to provide "an explanation of the current crisis . . . and a vision of what its solution would entail. It encompasses discussion of the historical development of the US health care system, its current dysfunction, and barriers to the formulation and implementation of solutions that meet the normative criteria inherent in the social value theory of neoinstitutional economics. . . . [S]uch barriers," he says, are "formidable" but "they are not . . . insurmountable."

In Chapter 8, on social security policy, *L. Randall Wray* says that "there is no question that Social Security is under attack by well-organized and well-funded opponents. . . . [T]he enemies have been there from the beginning, but they had had little success until recently. The truth is that Social Security does not, and indeed cannot, face any financial crisis." He examines the program and then looks "at various 'reform' proposals —concentrating on the Clinton administration's plan and contrasting that with the Bush Commission's 'reforms'." He then proposes a "progressive reform for Social Security." His primary message is that, ironically, "the 'fictions' that originally helped to protect Social Security now stand in the way of sensible discussion about the nature of the program."

III

In Chapter 9, on competing perspectives on economic power and accountability, *Edythe S. Miller* explains that the existing neoclassical dominion over inquiry and policy advisories "reflects an orthodox viewpoint that encompasses a specific vision of human nature, a particular economic methodology and an explicit outlook on the design and workings of the economy. Advocacy of this viewpoint is now widespread, nationally and globally." Miller "examines the foundations of this pattern of thought and some of its applications." She advances the neoinstitutional view that "application of accepted neoclassical beliefs has contributed to the concentration and centralization of economic power in giant multinational corporations and the concomitant decline of democratic processes in the determination of economic policy." She believes "that acceptance of the neoclassical economic philosophy has profound and negative implications for survival of political democracy."

In Chapter 10, on market failure in public utilities (an institutionalist critique of deregulation), *Harry M. Trebing* argues that "public utility services are an integral part of the infrastructure of modern society. Typically these services are provided in capital intensive networks that link centralized supply with a wide range of diverse consumer classes." They "must be supplied in an efficient manner that is responsive to consumer needs. . . . Actions that are conducive to resource misallocation, inefficiency, or the discriminatory exercise of power must be constrained." Trebing examines the "deregulation process, the shortcomings of remedial steps, the growing evidence of market failure and the exercise of power." Rejecting deregulation, he provides an agenda for reform based on the long history of institutionalism's commitment to the public regulation of public utilities.

In Chapter 11, on the abuse of economic and financial power in "The New Economy," *Michael F. Sheehan,* contends that: "Since well before the time of Hobbs, it has been accepted that one of the major functions of government is to protect the general society from abuses by predators whether they are common criminals or the more well-dressed users and abusers of monopoly power. . . . This paper provides an evolutionary perspective on the monopoly abuses found at each of the several important stages of our national history" and how they were dealt with. "Without regulation," he argues, "economic relations tend to be heavily coercive. . . . [T]he strong will rob the weak . . . the monopolist [will rob] the consumer and competitor. Leaving the market to the mercies of monopolists . . . and financial and accounting con men inevitably results in substantial losses to most economic participants."

IV

In Chapter 12, on developmental curriculum reform, *Baldwin Ranson* assesses systemic reform of public education over the last several decades and finds it unsuccessful. The character of educational policy obviously impacts directly on the economy in providing a labor force with skills, and in providing citizens generally with warranted knowledge to assess economic policies and performance. Educators are presently seeking to adjust curricula to global trends of an "explosion of scientific and technological knowledge" and the "global aspiration for democracy." Through recourse to institutional analysis, Ranson argues that curriculum reform must close existing gaps in school performance. "Both the quality and the quantity of preparation of youths to use sci/tech inquiry and to participate in democratic society are much below technically possible levels. Closing these two gaps is necessary to eliminate opposition between educational quality and quantity [and to]. . . transmit the best theory and practice of sci/tech inquiry to all youths."

In Chapter 13, on policies to provide non-invidious employment, *Deborah M. Figart* contends that "progressive labor market policy should have as its goal the elimination of merely ceremonial distinctions in favor of polices that . . . develop human potential, capabilities and well-being. Workers should be treated fairly." She argues that "recognition of the worth of their work should not be excluded . . . on the basis of class identity, race-ethnicity, gender, nationality or sexual preference." She reminds us that "[t]he work of society is more than paid work." "It also entails the ongoing work of families . . . the social reproduction of the future labor force. Life's work . . . creates value and should be rewarded accordingly." She supports "policies that would stock the labor market with so-called 'good' jobs."

In Chapter 14, on the new information economy, *William H. Melody* explores a profound structural change in economic systems. "Technologically advanced economies are in the process of moving beyond industrial capitalism to information based economies." "This transformation," he says, "is being driven by the development and pervasive application of information and communication technologies and services." Melody "examines some characteristics of 'information' in the new information economy and the important policy issues and implications they raise." He argues that "[I]n the information economy . . . people will be the central resource attracting investment because information is essentially produced, stored, and applied by humans." "This suggests, he says, "that the information economy can provide for a considerable higher level of human development than the industrial economy."

V

In Chapter 15, on environmental goal setting, *Kurt Stephenson* explains that "at the most basic level, environmental policy can be thought of as addressing two fundamental questions:" how to establish and to achieve environmental goals. "Environmental goal setting addresses questions of what ambient physical, chemical and biological conditions should exist in our nation's air and water resources." "Once . . . identified," he argues, "the policy means to achieve those conditions—such as emission technology and performance standards, emission taxes and subsidies, transferable emission allowances, educational programs, or moral 'suasion'—must then be established." "[The] original institutional economics (OIE)," he contends, "offers unique perspectives to the study of environmental economics and policy" including its relevance "for developing an applied, policy-oriented research program" that affirms the "efficacy of democratic processes in environmental policymaking."

In Chapter 16, on the ecologically sound land disposal of industrial waste materials, *F. Gregory Hayden* alerts us to a major environmental problem. He contends that: "Improper waste disposal, in addition to resulting in disease problems for humans and other species, results in a loss of living systems upon which people and industry depend. The disposal of hazardous, toxic, and radioactive waste has been and will continue to be a serious and growing problem." Natural systems for disposing of industrial waste are being overloaded and destroyed. "The main reason for the dismal waste disposal record," he contends," is the fact that most . . . decision making regarding industrial production, pollution emissions, and waste disposal has been dominated by powerful corporations." "Corporate dominion," he argues, "must be challenged by public authority."

## VI

In Chapter 17, on policies relating to globalization, *Gladys Parker Foster* considers "a process of institutional change in the modes of intercourse among nations . . . prompted by technologies that increase the volume of exchange of knowledge, culture and commerce." She argues that "it is not globalization *per se* but the application of neo-liberal philosophy that is responsible for the dismal economic scene" globally. This global reliance on neo-liberal policy," she observes, "permits multinational corporations to set their own self-serving policies of price fixing, encapsulated technology, resource use, social indifference and market control." Drawing on contemporary neoinstitutionalism, Foster argues in support of democratic policy making, constraints on predatory economic conduct, reasoned and instrumental institutional adjustments, noninvidious developmental assistance, and continuing corporate accountability. Globalization, she argues, can be humane.

In Chapter 18, on global industrial policies, *Wolfram Elsner* argues that "globalization is a politically organized phenomenon with one-sided, regulated 'deregulations'—concessions and exemptions for capital interests, following the "neo-liberal" market ideology." "Transnational corporations," he says, "have successfully dominated trade, production, technology and prices in international, regional, and local markets." "This means that national and local cultures, that have developed unique characteristics through countless regional interactions in response to regional conditions, are under increasing pressure to adapt to and emulate the behavior of the wealthy, powerful, and 'successful' centers of the global economy." "In consequence, the global system increasingly loses its cultural diversity . . . ." He proposes a system of global industrial policy in which "the *global protection of cultural diversity must be the highest value of a global institutional reform*."

In Chapter 19, on recent tendencies in development economics, *James M. Cypher* "critically analyzes some major recent analytical tendencies in development economics." He focuses "on key points of contention within the field of study," including "the role of institutions and institutional innovation [play] in the context of development." He observes that "the preeminent development institutions are uncertain as to how they should respond to the proposition which they now espouse: institutions matter." In response, Cypher offers a persuasive critique of the conservative neo-liberal "Washington Consensus" of the International Monetary Fund and the World Bank. He contends that they have failed to deal effectively with development problems of the 1980s and 1990s. He refashions a theory of economic development in which the democratic state has a continuing role in the creation and effective use of institutional innovations.

## NOTES

1 It was Veblen who coined the term "neoclassical" economics. See Veblen [1919] 1942a; and Fayazmanesh 1998.

2 It will be noted later that the neoclassically oriented "new institutional economics" (so-called) breaks with the orthodox literature to the extent that it does try to take account of the role played by institutions and changes in them as they affect economic relationships.

3 The original institutional economics (OIE) also encompasses what will be identified in the next section as "neoinstitutional" economics.

4 For a thoughtful discussion of the similarities and differences between OIE and NIE, see Stanfield 1999.

5 Curiously, the notion still persists among neoclassical economists that the original institutional economics is dead and buried. In fact institutionalists have secured a solid professional footing in the establishment of three professional associations (two in the US and one in Europe) that sponsor research in institutional/evolutionary economics. The Association for Evolutionary Economics (AFEE) was founded in 1966. Its *Journal of Economic Issues* is currently in its thirty-sixth year of publication. It holds its annual meetings in conjunction with the Allied Social Sciences Association. The Association for Institutional Thought (AFIT) was founded in 1979. It holds its meetings annually in conjunction with the Western Social

Science Association in various venues in the western US. In 1989 the European Association for Evolutionary Political Economy (EAEPE) held its inaugural meetings in Keswick, England. It holds its annual meetings in various European venues.

[6] Several of the authors of the essays in this volume are also students of J. Fagg Foster: Gladys Parker Foster, Edythe S. Miller, and Baldwin Ranson.

[7] One implication of this line of reasoning, which Veblen did not pursue, is that the price of a commodity or service, reflects not only the value of its life sustaining properties, but also the "waste" entailed in its invidious capacity to demonstrate the consumer's status. Such a notion plays havoc with the neoclassical belief that price in a purely competitive market in the long run is equal to the minimum average cost to society of producing the commodity or service. Presumably, when price equals minimum long run average costs, the waste of scarce resources has been minimized. But if the Veblenian analysis is correct, an element of "waste" remains even when price equals minimum long run average costs.

[8] According to Veblen, the "Captain of Industry" started out, in the 19th century as the leader of those engaged in the industrial employments. But, he says, ". . . when the Captain of Industry then made the passage from industrial adventurer to corporation financier it became the ordinary care of his office as Captain to keep a restraining hand on employment and output, and so administer a salutary running margin of sabotage on production, at the cost of the underlying population (Veblen [1923] 1964, 112-113). In footnote #6 on page 113, he could not resist a bit of humor. There, he observes that "[a]s someone with a taste for slang and aphorism has said it, 'In the beginning the Captain of Industry set out to do something, and in the end he sat down to do somebody.' "

# REFERENCES

Ayres, Clarence E. 1944. *The Theory of Economic Progress.* Chapel Hill: University of North Carolina Press.

Bronowski, Jacob. 1965. *Science and Human Values*, revised edition. New York: Harper & Row.

Bush, Paul D. 1987. The theory of institutional change. *Journal of Economic Issues* 21 (3): 1075-1116.

———. 1989. The concept of "progressive" institutional change and its implications for economic policy formation. *Journal of Economic Issues* 23(2): 455-64.

———. 1995. "Marc Tool's Contributions to Institutional Economics." In Charles M. A. Clark, ed. *Institutional Economics and the Theory of Social Value: Essays in Honor of Marc R. Tool.* Boston: Kluwer Academic Publishers.

———. 1999. "Ceremonial Encapsulation." In *The Encyclopedia of Political Economy, Volume 1,* Phillip A. O'Hara, ed. London: Routledge, 80-81.

Commons, John R. [1934] 1961. *Institutional Economics, Volume 1.* Madison: University of Wisconsin Press.

Dewey, John. [1929] 1984. *The Quest for Certainty.* In *John Dewey : The Later Works, 1925-1953, Volume 4,* Jo Ann Boydston, ed. Carbondale: Southern Illinois University Press.

———. [1938] 1986. *Logic: The Theory of Inquiry.* In *John Dewey : The Later Works, 1925-1953, Volume 12,* Jo Ann Boydston, ed. Carbondale: Southern Illinois University Press.

Fayazmanesh, Sasan. 1998. "On Veblen's Coining of the Term 'Neoclassical'." In Sasan Fayazmanesh and Marc R. Tool, eds. *Institutional Method and Value.* Cheltenham, UK: Edward Elgar.

Galbraith, John Kenneth. 1996. *The Good Society: The Humane Agenda.* Boston: Houghton Mifflin.

Gruchy, Allan G. 1974. *Contemporary Economic Thought: The Contribution of Neo-Institutional Economics.* Clifton, N.J.: Augustus M. Kelley.

Hamilton, Walton H. 1919. The institutional approach to economic theory. *American Economic Review, Supplement No. 1,* 9 (March): 309-318.

Hodgson, Geoffrey M. 2000. What is the essence of institutional econom-ics? *Journal of Economic Issues* 34 (2): 317-329.

Keynes, John M. [1926] 1972. "The End of Laissez-Faire". *Essays in Persuasion. The Collected Writings of John Maynard Keynes, Volume IX.* London: Macmillan, St. Martin's Press, 272-294.

———. 1936. *The General Theory of Employment, Interest, and Money.* New York: Harcourt, Brace and Company.

Livingston, John C. and Robert G. Thompson. 1971. *The Consent of the Governed,* 3rd edition. New York: Macmillan.

Menand, Louis. 2001. *The Metaphysical Club.* New York: Farrar, Straus and Giroux.

Robbins, Lionel. [1935] 1962. *An Essay on the Nature and Significance of Economic Science.* London: Macmillan.

Roll, Eric. 1942. *A History of Economic Thought.* New York: Prentice-Hall.

Samuelson, Paul A. [1947] 1958. *Foundations of Economic Analysis.* Cambridge: Harvard University Press.

Santopietro, George D. 1995. Raising environmental consciousness versus creating economic incentives as alternative policies for environmental protection. *Journal of Economic Issues* 29 (2): 517-24.

Stanfield, James R. 1999. The scope, method, and significance of original institutional economics. *Journal of Economic Issues* 33 (2): 231-55.

Stefanic, Jean and Richard Delgado. 1997. *No Mercy: Conservative Think Tanks.* Philadelphia: Temple University Press.

Tool, Marc R. 1953. The Philosophy of Neoinstitutionalism: Veblen, Dewey, Ayres. Ph.D. diss., University of Colorado, Boulder.

———. 1979. *The Discretionary Economy: A Normative Theory of Political Economy.* Santa Monica: Goodyear Company, Inc.

———. 1995. *Pricing, Valuation and Systems: Essays in Neoinstitutional Economics.* Aldershot: Edward Elgar.

———. 2000. *Value Theory and Economic Progress: The Institutional Economics of J. Fagg Foster.* Boston: Kluwer Academic Publishers.

Veblen, Thorstein B. [1899] 1975. *The Theory of the Leisure Class.*New York: Augustus M. Kelley.

———. [1904] 1975. *The Theory of Business Enterprise.* Clifton, N.J.: Augustus M. Kelley.

———. [1914] 1964. *The Instinct of Workmanship and the State of the Industrial Arts.* New York: Augustus M. Kelley.

———. [1919] 1942a. "The Preconceptions of Economic Science, III." In *The Place of Science in Modern Civilisation.* Thorstein B. Veblen. New York: The Viking Press, 148-179.

———. [1919] 1942b. "Why is Economics Not an Evolutionary Science?" In *The Place of Science in Modern Civilisation.* Thorstein B. Veblen. New York: The Viking Press.

———. [1921] 1965. *The Engineers and the Price System.* New York: Augustus M. Kelley.

———. [1923] (1964). *Absentee Ownership.* New York: Augustus Kelley.

Williamson, Oliver E. 1975. *Markets and Hierarchies.* London: Collier McMillan Publishers.

# 2

# AN INSTITUTIONALIST VIEW OF FISCAL POLICY

Philip A. Klein[1]

## OVERTHROWING THE SHACKLES OF THE IMMEDIATE PAST

Fiscal policy is arguably the most explicit embodiment of the institutionalist conviction that there is a constructive role for governmental intervention in the quest for stable satisfactory growth rates in the modern market oriented economy. As such it is, therefore, at the same time an equally explicit rejection of the conventional mainstream belief that the best course is almost invariably to leave the economy to the not invariably tender mercies of the market.

This view of macroeconomic policy is largely due to the impact of Keynes, although it must be added that institutionalists have not always been unanimous in their admiration for Keynes. A major appraisal of fiscal policy from an institutionalist perspective was the 1984 examination by Wallace Peterson, surely one of the outstanding institutionalists of his generation working on macroeconomic problems. He wrote, "For nearly two decades the United States and other major industrial democracies have struggled to reach full employment without inflation.  None have succeeded, a failure that has caused people and professional economists to question much contemporary economic theory as well as the policy measures based upon this theory" (Peterson 1984, p. 69). Peterson goes on to note that Keynesian principles had been relied upon by most industrialized countries for the period 1945-1970 with considerable success in creating sufficient stability and sufficiently strong growth so that the world had managed to avoid the kind of major depression which in the 1930s had caused many to question the future validity of market-oriented economies. The Keynesian assertion that the Great Depression was brought about in large part by inadequate aggregate demand and subsequently exacerbated by a variety of forces, was pretty widely accepted as well.

The 1970s changed all that. For the first time industrial economies suffered double digit inflation and pretty high unemployment at the same time. As Peterson puts it, the critical unanswered question at the end of the 1970s was "Is it possible for systems of market capitalism to enjoy simultaneously full employment and stable prices ?" (*Ibid.*, p. 69).

From an institutionalist perspective what has happened to fiscal policy in the past half century illustrates a number of the most critical insights of institutional economics. Peterson in his very first sentence speaks of full employment without inflation as the goal. Modern mainstream economists would no doubt chastise him for using a very old fashioned term–full employment, instead of the more modern and tranquilizing term,–keeping unemployment down to "the natural rate." They would perhaps be struck as well with the fact that employment gets mentioned first. Modern discussion of the objectives of macroeconomic policy invariably put the emphasis on controlling inflation, often to the exclusion of any mention of unemployment at all. As we shall see, unemployment is most typically considered in connection with discussions of the Phillips Curve, an infamous chapter in recent macroeconomic theory discussions. The Phillips Curve is utilized for a variety of purposes but most particularly to suggest that in the fight to control inflation, higher unemployment may be one of the unavoidable by products, however unfortunate this may be. This notion permeates many a discussion of macroeconomic policy nowadays. It is customarily presented as "the price we may have to pay to keep inflation rates down." Accordingly, examination of the Phillips Curve and the assertions that it has elicited is a major task in the pages to come. More generally, what has happened to fiscal policy, and in particular the manner in which it has for much of this period been rendered impotent as a tool of macroeconomic stabilization, can be best explained only by consideration of a number of well known institutionalist tenets.

Accordingly, we need to begin by consideration of how fiscal policy, a potentially potent weapon with which to pursue economic stability as well as economic growth, was rendered virtually useless for much of the period since the early 1970s.

# THE THEORY-POLICY LINK IN ECONOMIC ANALYSIS

## The Keynesian Insight

Any consideration of the role of fiscal policy must begin with the contributions of John Maynard Keynes. Modern economic theory began its existence with the emphasis on microeconomic theory. Classical economists believed there was little if any need for public policy because in a competitive world the operation of the economy could be "left to the market." It was Keynes' effort to understand the economic chaos brought on by the Great Depression of the 1930s that brought the attention of economists to macroeconomic theory. Keynes put macroeconomics on the map, so to speak. More than that, he concluded that left to its own devices the "Underemployment equilibrium" which, he argued, might well describe the state of the major industrial market economies, characterized as they were by widespread unemployment, low output, sluggish growth and widespread misery, might continue indefinitely unless and until steps were taken to reinvigorate them. As Keynes himself put it, ". . . it is an outstanding characteristic of the economic system in which we live that, whilst it is subject to severe fluctuations in respect to output and employment, it is not violently unstable. Indeed it seems capable of remaining in a chronic condition of sub-normal activity for a considerable period without any marked tendency either towards recovery or towards complete collapse" (Keynes 1936, p. 249). In consequence of this, leaving economic activity to market forces was not for Keynes a necessarily promising path to pursue in the urgent need to restore macroeconomic performance to a viable condition.

Fiscal policy was introduced as an option in these circumstances. Fiscal policy is here defined as the deliberate manipulation of federal expenditures and tax rates so as to inject stimulus into the economy in the form of governmental expenditures financed with deficits in times of cyclical contraction and withdraw overall governmental stimulus by taxing more than is expended in times of cyclical expansion so as to reduce inflationary pressure.

It should be pointed out that from this perspective Keynes was profoundly institutionalist in his approach. From the outset institutionalists have insisted that the focus should be on the economy as it actually is, with the express purpose of illuminating market failures so that public policy could be brought to bear on overcoming them. That is why institutionalists, reacting to the way in which mainstream economists dwell lovingly and at length on the welfare implications of the competitive model, brought forth a major dissent from mainstream theory. In precisely the same way Keynes, bolstered no doubt by all the evidence he saw all around him, dissented from the classical assumption that, thanks to Say's Law and the assumption that flexible wages would always produce full employment, the phenomena of modern business cycles could be reduced to mere short-run self-correcting disturbances. If indeed they were self-correcting, there was, happily, no need for public policy.

Instead of taking the classical approach and describing an ideal macro economy, Keynes faced the actual macro economy and described it, as we say, "warts and all." The actual economy, Keynes said, might indeed generate macroeconomic equilibria that were anything but satisfactory. The actual economy could achieve equilibrium with widespread unemployment (the aforementioned "underemployment equilibria") or equilibrium with unacceptable inflation rates. Hence, Keynes's theory emphatically opened the way to asserting the critical necessity for developing sound feasible macroeconomic policy. Keynes certainly had a role for monetary policy, but he did think that in the immediate aftermath of a major downturn it might be highly unlikely that monetary policy alone could rescue the economy from possible disaster. Hence there were times (e.g., most particularly after the 1929 downturn) when fiscal policy was the only possible discretionary policy.

If Keynes infuriated socialists by in effect trying to find a way to save capitalist economies from disintegrating, he also infuriated the mainstream neoclassical economists. He not only disputed their views that the macro economy, like the micro economy, was self regulating and could be "left to the market." He presented interventionist policy as a logical outcome of his theory. New classical economists e.g., Friedman and other monetarists, later the supply-siders (Wanniski, Laffer, et al.) and the rational expectations group (Lucas, Barro, Sargent, et al.) were from the outset, therefore, desperate to find a way to dispute Keynes' assertion that unsatisfactory performance might be a logical outcome from time to time of the operation of any major macro economy.

In short, Keynes examined the functioning of the real economy, and came to the conclusion that it was not at all times adequately self-regulating. Therefore, in its functioning it could not be guaranteed to avoid clashing with prevailing societal values concerning the minimal material standards on which all participants in the economy had a right to count.

An outcome of Keynes's macroeconomic analysis was to produce a theory from which emanated a legitimate and necessary role for the federal government. We shall see that in the U.S. this formed the basis for the Employment Act of 1946. It was this policy above all that the mainstream could not abide. Robert Lucas has gone so far as to describe the impact of the Employment Act of 1946 in these words: "There is nothing subtle . . . in the effects of the act . . . on the practice of monetary economics in the postwar period. Renamed *macroeconomics*, this subdiscipline *defined* itself to be that body of expertise the existence of which was presupposed in the Employment Act . . . "[2]

Needless to add, without Keynes and his *General Theory*, there would never have been an Employment Act. They (Lucas, et al.) searched, therefore, for ways to restore the world of macroeconomic theory to its pre-Keynesian condition. With the stagflation of the 1970s and the emergence of the rational expectations brand of new classical economics they found a way–or at least they thought they found a way–to accomplish that long sought objective.

The implications of all this for fiscal policy were explicitly spelled out. Said Lucas, "In 1966, it seemed to many that we had one theory which could quantitatively link fiscal policy to economic performance with sufficient accuracy that it could be responsibly applied to policymaking. In 1977, we know we have none" (Lucas 1983, p. 267). The disparagement of fiscal policy played an especially important role in this endeavor, because it was fiscal policy which actually depicted a way in which the federal government could intrude into the day to day operations of the otherwise market-driven macro economy. Getting rid of fiscal policy was an integral part of the task of selling a view of government as largely and profoundly pejorative. Fiscal policy debates became the center of the daily effort to get the government out of intervening in the economy and disparaging the role of government generally.

How far the mainstream has gone in the effort to restore economic theory to its pre-Keynesian perspective is suggested by the observation that an increasing number of Departments of Economics simply ignore macroeconomics as a legitimate branch of economic theory. The important matters can be considered in what is referred to as "The Micro foundations of Macroeconomics." New classical economists are convinced that the role of market allocation in the modern economy is well on the way to re-assuming the commanding position from which Keynes's insistence on "Under employment equilibrium" had grabbed it. As a viable and legitimate outcome for the operation of the market system, under employment equilibrium had seemingly fatally undermined the classical system.

Accordingly we pause to consider the mainstream depiction of government generally before turning to the way in which institutionalists depict fiscal policy.

## The Role of Government–Us or Them?

It is instructive to consider the approach to government customarily taken by political scientists. However wedded they may be to the idea of political democracy, devotion to "leaving it to the people" never seems to require the obsessive attention to shrinking the role of government which devotion to "leaving it to the market" requires of mainstream economists. Both disciplines recognize the necessary role government plays in providing for security against both external and internal threats. But that is about as far as agreement extends. Political scientists devote most of their attention to perceived flaws in the way self-governance works. They spend much time and attention on relations between representatives and their constituencies, how Veblen's "vested interests" exert their special kind of impact on the operations of legislative and executive bodies, and the role of government in ensuring that the wishes of the collectivity (which is all the voters) gets effectively translated into policy decisions.

This tacit acceptance of the positive and essential role of government contrasts sharply with the mainstream economists' view. At one extreme this includes the views of "public choice" economists like Buchanan. He argues that merely entering public service is likely to corrupt one so that carrying out honestly and responsibly the duties of public life, so that government can function, requires assuming more than can credibly be justified. Buchanan, for example, fairly early in his writing on public choice commented, "Honesty, as an attribute of exchange, is a quality that we acknowledge to be appropriately encouraged by internally applicable moral codes and by externally imposed legal sanctions. There is no comparable encouragement of a quality in political 'exchange' that corresponds to 'honesty' in market dealings" (Buchanan 1985, p. 89).

There is circularity in this position. To assume that the market operates efficiently and appropriately to achieve the results attributed in an earlier and simpler day by mainstream economists to the operation of the invisible hand is, of course, to assume also that there is no need for government. If there is no need for government and government officials are not likely to perform responsibly then "that government is best which governs least" is quite literally true. If there is no need for government, finally, it is because the system does operate reasonably well in its absence.

Other mainstream economists take a less extreme view, but they all regard government as at best something to be viewed with suspicion. Politicians love to harangue audiences with exhortations to the public not to "let them take it away from us." This leads to the view of fiscal activity, as mainly creating a large public debt. Debt, of course, is "bad" because it represents what "we" owe "them." But of course, as economists never tire of pointing out (to the likes of President Eisenhower who was, I think, the first to refer to "the great burden of debt we are placing on our grandchildren,") to the extent that the borrowing of the government represents Treasury bonds sold to the domestic public, the public debt is quite literally also the public asset. Undeniably a large amount of outstanding bonds creates some difficulties, but that "we" will have to find a way to pay "them" is a formulation which clearly overlooks the detail that the "them" getting paid off in exchange for maturing bonds will largely be the same grandchildren to whom the President was referring. While beginning public finance students will understand all this, it is rhetorically much more effective to worry about our grandchildren's debts and forget about their credits. Semantics is an underrated aspect of public discourse and referring to the "nest egg" going to our grandchildren as a result of how we finance public expenditure would be regarded by many as a serious lapse in not only fiscal responsibility but morality as well.

This is not an argument particularly favoring public expenditures. It may well be most appropriate to argue that funds can be spent wisely or foolishly in the private sector and wisely or foolishly in the public sector. If indeed that seems a correct observation, sound fiscal policy emanates partly from determining what expenditures are best made in the public sector and which in the private sector. That said, it is clear that there is considerable consensus at this point on the wisdom of a variety of public expenditures going considerably beyond expenditures on defense and shoring up domestic security. No one any longer questions the essential correctness of having a social security system, although suggestions to "privatize" parts of it appear in various quarters. On both sides of the Atlantic, and despite the efforts of administrations devoted to admiring "the miracle of the market" and to downplaying market faults, the percent of GDP devoted to the public sector has been remarkably stable for quite a few years. For example, when Reagan became president the percent of GDP devoted to Federal expenditures was 18.7% and when he left office the percentage was 18.2%. In George Bush's years in office the federal share fell from the 18.2% just noted to 17.7% (*Cf.*, *Economic Report of the President*, 2001, p. 274 and p. 371). We shall return to this state of affairs at the end of the paper. We are arguing only that the fury with which the role of the public sector is debated masks the considerable common acceptance of a public sector presence in a large variety of areas today. It is in what is said and written that the reluctance to grant a significant role for the public sector is most obvious and where the rhetorical venom is most vitriolic.

## THE LEGITIMACY OF THE NORMATIVE IN ECONOMIC POLICY CONSIDERATIONS

### Dynamic View of the Collective Ought in Action

Before we can consider fiscal policy in action in recent years, there is one last preliminary matter to introduce. A well known difference between institutional economics and conventional mainstream economic theory is the insistence of the latter that the discipline is a "positive" science and that normative considerations have no place in its deliberations. Institutionalists have long insisted, for example, that restricting the consideration of welfare matters to the confines of Pareto Optimality is inadequate. Their contention that a welfare norm which begins by assuming the distribution of income and wealth is given, is fatally flawed from the outset. To accept these as given, despite the fact that both are two of the more controversial manifestations of any economy is, in effect, to assert that the scientist is comfortable with whatever distributions may exist. Institutionalists insist that what one is comfortable accepting inexorably reflects a value position quite as clearly as to insist that these distributions "ought" to be changed in this or that manner. The institutionalist view has largely fallen on deaf years.

In view of this very normative view of "positive economic theory," it is interesting to consider what Keynes's perspective produced. In the United Kingdom it led to the Beveridge Plan–a program for reaching "full employment." (Beveridge was perfectly aware that full employment did not "mean literally no unemployment." He used a common sense definition–"full employment . . . means more vacant jobs than unemployed men"(Beveridge 1945, pp. 18-19)).

In the United States it lead to the first explicit statement by the U.S. Congress that the Federal Government had a responsibility to work actively toward explicit macroeconomic goals. "The Congress hereby declares that it is the continuing policy and responsibility of the Federal Government to use all practicable means . . . to promote maximum employment, production, and purchasing power" (U.S. Employment Act of 1946).

In the words of Edwin G. Nourse, first Chairman of the Council of Economic Advisors (which was set up under the Employment Act), "The distinctive character of the Employment Act was that it accepted responsibility on the part of the Federal Government to make systematic study of its several policies and programs to see that they move consistently toward maintaining the health of the economy and continuous high utilization of the nations's resources" (Nourse 1953, p. 67). This activist interventionism on the part of the Federal Government is a principal aspect of the Keynesian heritage. What happened to this simple notion of full employment at the hands of neo-classical economic theorists?

Just as the medical profession has not regarded it as a hopeless violation of the scientific method to base its work on an oath which embraces "good health" as a goal, the Employment Act of 1946 suggested a normative role for public economic policy by embracing a view of the "good economy." Following in Keynes's footsteps, the Act announced that "underemployment equilibrium" was a bad outcome for a modern market economy.

What have mainstream American economists made of the Employment Act in the intervening years? Although subjected to some clarification in the Humphrey Hawkins Act of 1978 (it set a 3% inflation rate and a 4% unemployment rate target) the Act has never been repealed, nor has there been an active effort to get it repealed. There was a contention that inflation needed more explicit attention than it got in the Act. But the assertion that "maximum purchasing power" requires "minimum price increases" thereby covering the dangers of inflation, has thus far been considered an adequate inclusion of inflationary dangers by most economists.

But a curious thing has happened, discussed below in connection with the Phillips Curve. Our positive mainstream economists have managed to contend with some success that there is no inconsistency in eschewing normative positions, on the one hand while, on the other, asserting that inflation is very bad for the economy and if necessary higher unemployment may be "the price we must pay" to avoid it. Accordingly they have in various ways and by various means tried to convince both economists and the public that the Employment Act at the very least reversed the macroeconomic priorities. In that Act maximum purchasing power (low inflation rates) was indeed the first mentioned goal. (Note that Nourse avoided the question by referring to "high utilization" of the Nations's resources). Today whatever intervention by the federal government in the operation of the economy could, in their view, be justified revolved around keeping inflation rates low–not reducing unemployment. Indeed there are economists who argue that an inflation rate of zero is the only appropriate objective.

No one would argue that the only unemployment we should tolerate would be frictional and/or some seasonal unemployment. Indeed one of the "accomplishments" of modern economics has been to complicate the notion of "full employment" to the point where arguably that objective cannot (or need not) be defined at all. As noted above, Beveridge, though he understood perfectly well about frictional, seasonal, and even some structural unemployment, had no difficulty in setting a full employment objective for the UK economy which was not difficult to understand. The promulgators of the Employment Act of 1946 were similarly not thrown off the track by the presumably insurmountable obstacles in setting this goal for the United States in a comprehensible way.

Some years ago I suggested that one could usefully refer to current views about such matters as macroeconomic goals as "the collective ought" (Klein 1984, pp. 45-68). The term underscores that any economy is at any given time based on *a value floor*–an implicit set of norms conforming to currently accepted standards for efficiency, equity, freedom, security, and humaneness. They clearly can differ from economy to economy, which is why institutionalists insist that any economy can be comprehended only when examined in the context of the culture within which it is found. Each economy has its own value floor.

Here is one place where institutionalism not only is compatible with Keynesianism but extends it in a meaningful way. In contemplating fiscal policy Keynes argues only that there are times when public expenditures can be salutary, even if financed from borrowing. Keynes is always careful not to characterize the nature of the expenditures involved. In a famous passage he asserts that increased expenditure from whatever source and for whatever reason can help: "In so far as millionaires find their satisfaction in building mighty mansions to contain their bodies when alive and pyramids to shelter them after death, or, repenting of their sins, erect cathedrals and endow monasteries or foreign missions, the day when abundance of capital will interfere with abundance of output may be postponed. 'To dig holes in the ground,' paid for out of savings, will increase, not only employment, but the real national dividend of useful goods and services. It is not reasonable, however, that a sensible community should be content to remain dependent on such fortuitous and often wasteful mitigations when once we understand the influences upon which effective demand depends" (Keynes 1936, p. 220). Keynes does not go far enough. It is in deciding what precisely constitutes "useful goods and services" that the community determines its own collective ought at any given time. In the months before the terrible tragedies of September 11, 2001 there was considerable evidence that in the United States the collective ought was coming to demand greater expenditures for a prescription drug program to assist low income families with that expenditure, greater public expenditure on improving public education, and a number of other items moving debate about public expenditures well beyond the agreed upon national defense.

Some years ago I commented, ". . . unlike mainstream economists, institutionalists are not ethically neutral–they do not assume that *what is* represents the ideal. They are not radical either, in that they do not have a predetermined notion of 'what ought to be" against which they measure 'what is.' Rather they have a view of efficiency that examines the political economy and asks how well does this economy play its part in shaping and channeling as well as transmitting the ongoing values of its participants?" (Klein 1994, p. 189).

If the events of September 11$^{th}$ opened up whole new areas of critical and arguably mandatary public expenditures as societal values adjusted to this brutal change in the country's position, it underscored the fact that Keynes unnecessarily stressed ridiculous expenditures even if only to make his point. Any democratic market oriented economy is always engaged in refashioning for a new era the previously agreed upon public expenditures to shore up currently perceived inadequacies in existing health and welfare standards which are inexorably reflected in the panoply of purposes to which public funds of the moment are devoted. In this sense the collective ought refers to the ever emerging normative position determined by existing community attitudes.

What we suggest here is that the value floor established at any given time is also consistent with the normative parameters which that society has established for the pursuit of scientific research. To this extent economic theory needs to be directed to the best possible economic policy with which to pursue fulfillment of the parameters at any given time. This is a meaningful way to contemplate the character of the normative framework of economic research. Hence, it can surely govern the improvement of macroeconomic policy with which to pursue the goals of the Employment Act of 1946.

## The Phillips Curve and "Positive" Macroeconomic Analysis

We have suggested that as between attitudes toward inflation rates and unemployment rates the "positive stance" of mainstream macroeconomics has drifted to the decidedly normative conclusion that fighting inflation is the more critical objective and unemployment may simply have to be tolerated. This conclusion has emerged in large part because of the long preoccupation of mainstream economists with the Phillips Curve.

Most of the Phillips Curve story is familiar territory and we need not pause long to recapitulate it. A brief retelling of the highlights will suffice for us to make the necessary points relevant here. Introduced by the English economist, A.W. Phillips, roughly half a century ago it originally dealt with the historical relationship between money wages and unemployment in the

UK over a period of close to one hundred years. Phillips concluded that there was an inverse relationship between the unemployment rate and the rate of change in the inflation rate (Phillips 1958, pp. 283-299). This was later broadened by others to incorporate the so-called natural rate of unemployment, inflationary expectations, short and long runs, and other refinements. The original Phillips Curve as envisaged by Phillips is often presented as shown in Figure 1 for the decade of the 1960s. A decade is scarcely as convincing a period historically as half a century but economists of all persuasions made the most of the 1960s. Non-interventionist economists accused those they regarded as interventionists of using this "precise relationship" as a license to "fine tune" the economy–since this Phillips Curve enabled one to quantify the "price" one must pay in inflation rate increases for unemployment rate decreases, or vice-versa. Macroeconomic policy was thought to include both monetary and fiscal policy. Noninterventionists drew a somewhat different conclusion: the Phillips Curve proved that it was impossible to get unemployment rates down without driving inflation rates up.

In the fullness of time the simple relationship of the 1960s became more complicated. Today the so-called Phillips Curve produces a picture like the one shown in Figure 2. What does this mean? Economists had a field day. First it was concluded that the simple curve was shifting to the right. (Initially this shift was because of changes in the expected inflation rate. Later it was explained as the result of shocks to aggregate supply (e.g., OPEC). Economists seemed to ignore the simple conclusion that a reliable functional relationship which "shifts" in almost every time period is not a very reliable functional relationship. (Imagine a demand curve which "shifted every market period"–would the presumed relationship embedded in the curve actually exist? If so, no curve would ever last beyond a single price-quantity combination!).

Milton Friedman and Edmund Phelps had concluded that the curve depicting the 1960s was a "short run curve" and that in the long run there in fact was not a trade–off between inflation rate changes and unemployment rates.[3] In the long run the Phillips curve became a vertical line at the "Natural Unemployment Rate." This rate, defined variously, in effect suggests that there is structural unemployment that is beyond amelioration and that when one adds it to frictional and seasonal unemployment it produces a marvelous new concept, The "Full Employment Unemployment Rate." It plays a pivotal role in the non-interventionist ("leave it to the market") argument. The bottom line was that quite a lot of unemployment could be included here. If getting rid of it would accelerate inflation, then getting rid of it was not wise policy. In effect, the more unemployed persons that could be categorized this way, the smaller was the group of unemployed persons that policy makers smaller was the group of unemployed persons that policy makers needed to worry about.

Actually, Friedman and Phelps carried their conclusion one step further. They argued that the short run Phillips Curves (like the one covering the1960s) indicated the relationship between the two variables which existed when the expected inflation rate was given. But efforts to reduce unemployment would drive the inflation rate up and the longer it stays up the more impossible it would be for that rate to remain the expected rate–so it would shift up and a new higher short run Phillips Curve relationship would develop–one with a higher expected inflation rate built in. The encompassing result was a conclusion that this "positive analysis," perhaps only by coincidence, conformed to the normative predilections (non-interventionism) of the proponents. That conclusion is that efforts to reduce unemployment would lead to accelerating inflation rates and so would only exacerbate an already bad situation. Thus was born the NAIRU–the non-accelerating inflation rate of unemployment. This is the natural rate of unemployment; it is the lowest rate of unemployment which will not trigger unacceptably high accelerating rates of inflation, and therefore, the rate below which it is futile to try to get the unemployment rate to fall.

One of the oddities of all this is that the only way to tell whether one has tried to push the unemployment rate below the natural rate–that is, the rate below which the subsequent inflation rate becomes unacceptably high–is to wait and see what happens. Any time, therefore, that one has an unacceptable inflation rate it must perforce have been because in an earlier period policy makers tried to get the unemployment "too low"–that is, below the natural rate. The natural rate in turn drifted up for a number of years and then was declared to have begun to fall. These changes were made in an effort to keep this lowest feasible unemployment rate in line with what actually happened to unemployment. The latter had an infelicitous tendency throughout the 1990s to fall.

Friedman and others concluded from all this that inflation rates could not be brought down without an accompanying recession. Empirical evidence suggested that a falling inflation rate could invariably be associated with recessions in a number of countries. Some years ago I examined the relationship between recessions and inflation rates for a number of market economies (Klein 1994, p. 273-280). It was perfectly true that of the 49 comparable recessions thirteen were not accompanied by declines in inflation. For the rest, sometimes the inflation rates began to fall before the recession's onset, sometimes after. Sometimes the inflation rates were again on the way up before the associated recession was over. We asked finally how long on the average did the inflation rate stay down when engineered by enduring a recession to get it down? The answer for the recessions covered was on average eleven months. In light of this, it is at least fair to ask whether that is a long enough period to justify the misery which goes with recession. Instead of attempting to derive policy from the by now admittedly short run conjectural Phillips Curve, would it not be better to search for some long run solutions which would not require accepting the dubious proposition that there is an enduring trade off between recession and lower inflation rates?

In the end the debate about the Phillips Curve was converted to presumed corroboration of the proposition that activist stabilization policy including fiscal policy was a futile endeavor at best and a convenient means of exacerbating the otherwise probably tolerable state of the macro economy at worst. This became known among mainstream economists as the "policy ineffectiveness theorem." An outgrowth of Robert Lucas's Rational Expectations Hypothesis it is defined by Samuelson and Nordhaus as "A theorem which asserts that, with rational expectations and flexible prices and wages anticipated government monetary and fiscal policy cannot affect real output or unemployment" (*Ibid.*, p. 435). Now we see why macroeconomics is no longer a "real field."

Along with the total misreading of what was involved in "Keynesian Fiscal Policy," to which we turn below, it prevented any useful efforts to improve fiscal policy because the enormous tide of public debt which developed in the 1980s made any use of activist fiscal policy impossible.

## AFFIRMING THE PARITY OF UNEMPLOYMENT AND INFLATION IN POLICY CONSIDERATION

The above discussion indicates that in recent years much of the debate about macroeconomic policy has suggested that the principal objective has to be keeping the inflation rate down, even if this has meant tolerating higher unemployment rates. In mainstream economics in general there has long been a tendency to underscore the importance of the role of the entrepreneur, mostly through a variety of measures designed to protect and/or raise profit rates and

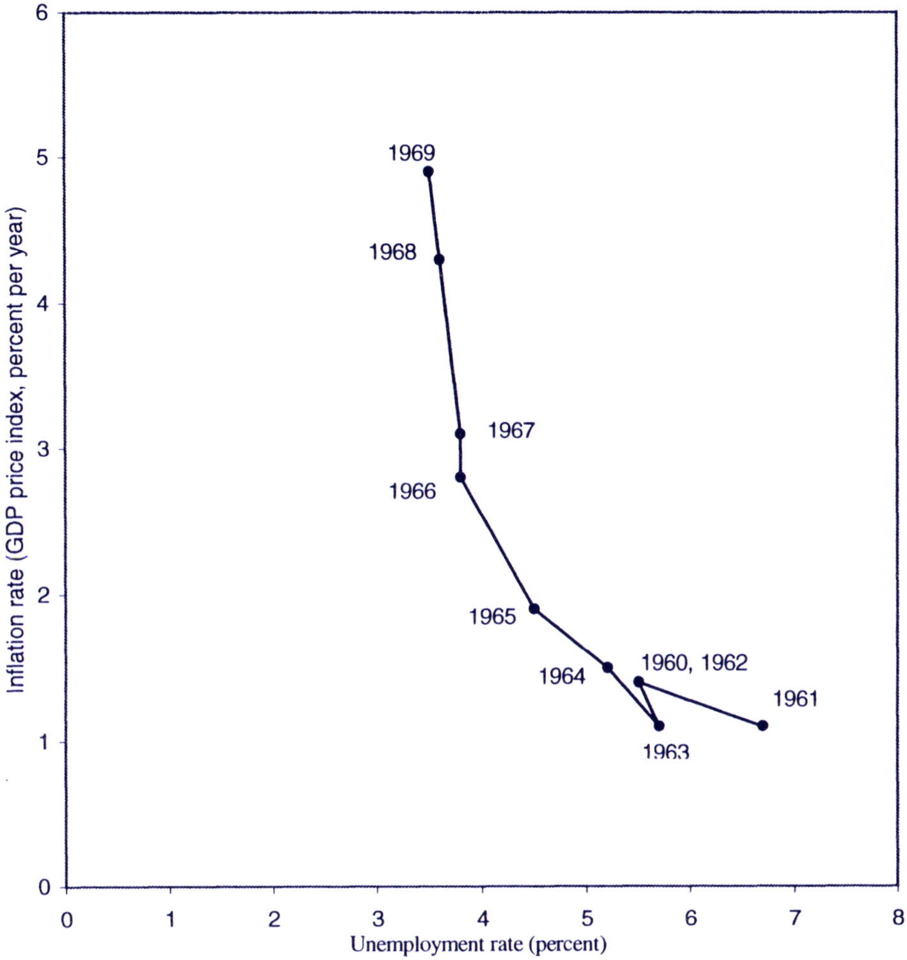


*Figure 1*
*Phillips Curve (1960-69)*

Note: 1960 and 1962 share identical percentages.
Source: Economic Report of the President 2001.

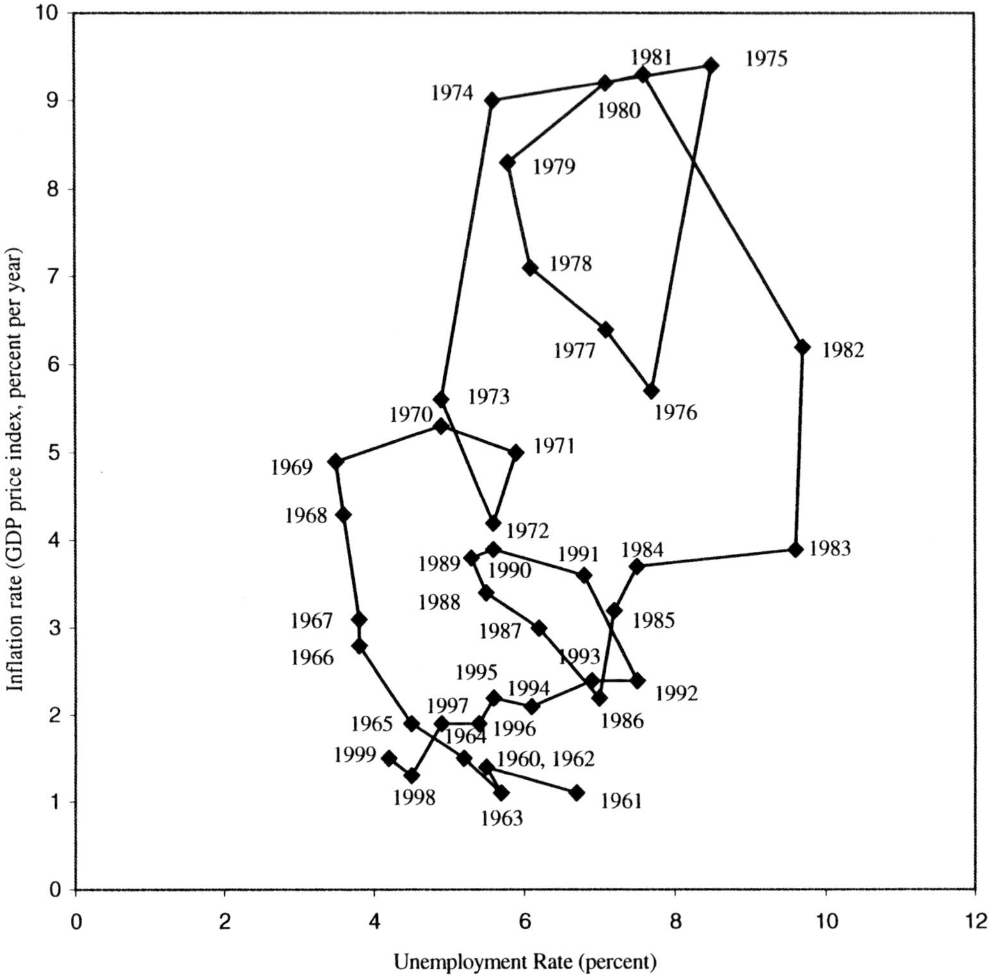


*Figure 2*
*Phillips Curve (1960-1999)*

Note: 1960 and 1962 share identical percentages.
Source: Economic Report of the President 2001.

all asserting the importance of strengthening the incentive to invest.

At the same time the role of labor has tended to be downplayed. If higher profits strengthen the incentive to invest, higher wages merely add to costs thereby fueling inflation. Oddly, profits never seem to have anything to do with inflation nor do wages add to the incentive or ability to consume thereby strengthening the economy.

Discussions of the profit rate, particularly the corporate profit rate, assume implicitly that high corporate profits presage future health for the economy. Elementary textbooks, on the other hand, have been reporting more or less faithfully the decline in Union membership for many years (from a high of 26.6% of the Labor Force in 1945 to a current low of 13.5%.[4] This elicits no perceptible reaction from economists. I have seen no discussion of declining union membership reflecting the view that a weak union movement holds any perils, (or any encouraging signs, either, for that matter). The wide-ranging discussions of an earlier era dealing with the virtues of a healthy atmosphere for collective bargaining are no longer encountered.

All this is relevant to our discussion of fiscal policy only because the quiet assumption of an earlier era was that the essential motivation for producing in an enterprise economy was the profit motive and the major technique for strengthening that motive was to develop public policy considered helpful in increasing the prospect for future sales. That belief could be real or illusory–either way it might encourage economic expansion.

Today the discussion, probably influenced by the debate about the Phillips Curve we have just summarized, is that the profit motive needs strengthening and that keeping (wage) costs down is a primary means for accomplishing this.

Without belaboring the point we note only that underlying this presumed discussion of positive economic theory are a number of highly normative assumptions and implications. Therefore, the debate about public policy is inescapably and profoundly normative.

## Some Critical Fiscal Distinctions

Before we can consider fiscal policy in connection with the performance of the economy in the past quarter century there are some terms frequently misused which we need to define carefully. It seems most useful to define fiscal policy as we did earlier–the deliberate manipulation of federal tax policies and federal expenditure policies in an effort to have a conscious impact on the performance of the aggregate economy. This parallels the use of "monetary policy" as a term meant to convey that conscious effort is being made to manipulate the growth of the money supply so as to have an impact on the rate of expenditures representing aggregate demand and hence the macroeconomy. Fiscal policy is customarily regarded as stimulating when expenditure growth relative to tax growth results in a net injection of expenditures into the economy and regressive when expenditures relative to taxes are successfully manipulated to generate a net withdrawal of expenditures from the economy.[5]

One critical aspect of fiscal policy is no longer very controversial; it does not require deliberate action in response to cyclical changes. This structural element is the automatic stabilizers. To the extent that the income tax is progressive, rising disposable income brings larger tax revenues because more taxpayers move into higher tax brackets. The reverse occurs in contraction. Since the number of tax brackets has been reduced in recent years, the system is less progressive. On the expenditure side, virtually all the welfare expenditures go up in recession and down in expansion automatically.

## New Focus on Fiscal Policy

It is now possible, therefore, to distinguish *fiscal policy*, which we have just seen focuses on the *intent* leading to the deliberate policy behind the extant taxes and expenditures, and *fiscal stance*, which merely *records* the net impact on the macro economy of whatever taxes and expenditures happen to be on the books. Fiscal stance has been defined as "The expansionary or contractionary implications for the economy of the government's budgetary policy . . . more precisely, it represents an attempt to summarize in a single measure, the combined effect on aggregate demand, and therefore potentially on real output and income, of all the various decisions taken by government in respect of public expenditure, taxation, and other sources of revenue which go to make up a national budget" (Ward 1987, p. 367).

This definition at the outset is confusing because the use of the word "policy" conveys intent about the results which may or may not be the case. The continued use of the definition is therefore more helpful in conveying the haphazard set of circumstances which influence tax and spending decisions.

The objection to the use of the word "policy" in the first sentence has to do with our assertion that this word should be limited to deliberate manipulations with a fiscal objective in mind. Fiscal stance refers to the total impact of fiscal activity on the macro economy whether intended to contribute to specific impact or not. The distinction is important because the use of the term "fiscal policy" was originally associated with Keynes's theory and viewpoint. It is worth remembering that what Keynes advocated was balancing the federal budget over the business cycle rather than over any arbitrary time period such as a year. He advocated creating a federal deficit only during recession in order to augment private aggregate demand with greater public demand in order to rid the economy of "underemployment equilibrium." But equally important was the notion that budgetary surpluses in good times would reduce the size of private aggregate demand by adding a negative government expenditure component in order to reduce "over employment (inflationary) equilibrium."

If Keynes stressed the latter less than the former it was only because in the context of the 1930s it was less important. In the United States, Keynes's views were given flesh by the Research and Policy Committee of the Committee for Economic Development which, in the words of Alvin Hansen, "placed at the center of their program . . . compensatory cycle policy. They did not favor a year-by-year balanced budget; instead they favored what they called a 'stabilizing budget policy.' This involved a scheme which provided automatically for a budgetary surplus in boom years and a budgetary deficit in depressed years" (Hansen 1964, pp. 546-547).

The result, therefore, of "Keynesian fiscal policy" in the long run, given the way in which the US and other market economies have functioned historically–that is, for economies where "good times" were far more prevalent than "bad times"–ought to have resulted over time in budgetary surpluses, and consequently, shrinking public debts. It is, therefore, a monumental misinterpretation of Keynes to argue, as has frequently been heard, that the "Keynesian fiscal policy" of the 1980s was responsible for the quadrupling of the US public debt in that decade. The debt quadrupled for a very simple (and profoundly *un-Keynesian*) reason–the Federal government spent more than it was willing to tax, with the result that it perforce borrowed to pay for the rest.

It is, therefore, fundamentally important to distinguish expenditures and taxes that are the result of macroeconomic goal–oriented activity from those which are not related to their impact on the economy at all. Instead they simply have whatever impact they have that originated in tax or expenditures decisions made for other reasons.

Even distinguishing fiscal policy from fiscal stance is not a sufficient instrument to use in evaluating federal expenditures and taxes for their fiscal policy impact. Unfortunately, one cannot tell what is in the minds of the Congress, for example, by simply looking at total government expenditures and total taxes and computing the difference.

The cyclical state of the economy impinges on these magnitudes. In recent years some of these problems have been approached by distinguishing the *structural budget* from the *actual budget* and the *cyclical budget*. The actual budget shows how much the recorded deficit or surplus for each year is.

The structural budget is based on what existing tax and revenue parameters would produce (deficit or surplus) were the economy operating at its potential output. The cyclical budget is the difference between the other two–it indicates the effect of the business cycle on the budget–that is by how much expenditures and tax revenues are affected by the impact of the business cycle during any given year. In the end we shall be forced to conclude that estimating the structural budget in practice is a highly complicated matter, and the actual estimates may, therefore, be of dubious accuracy. Nevertheless conceptually the distinctions still seem important.

In order to consider this problem it is necessary to distinguish carefully between the "automatic" or "built-in stabilizers" and discretional fiscal policy. In recent years the automatic stabilizers, as we saw earlier, have been fairly widely accepted and are certainly the least controversial part of fiscal policy. The term is used to refer to those measures passed by the Congress which result in automatic changes in the percent of income which is taxed as personal income rises or falls and similarly those measures which result in automatic changes in the levels of government expenditures as a percent of personal income, as the latter rises or falls.

Thus in Figure 3 the tax curve suggests that there are more or less constant changes in the tax revenues as income rises. They reflect not just the increase which would accompany a proportional tax, but an increase reflecting the degree of "progressivity" in the tax rate structure. Progressivity, of course, refers to the degree to which the *percentage* taxed or spent increases with rises in income. The steepness of the curve reflects that progressivity. It was, to be sure, far larger in an earlier era when the United States had as many as fifteen or more tax brackets, with a different percent tax rate pertaining to each. Now we have only a few tax brackets, and the difference between the marginal tax rates for the highest and lowest tax brackets has been drastically reduced. The difference in marginal tax rates for different income tax brackets illustrates what is meant by built-in stabilizers. They result in different tax rates automatically as income changes without any new legislation having to be adopted.

Similarly, we have a number of kinds of expenditures (unemployment compensation, welfare measures, etc.) which also increase or decrease automatically as personal income goes up and down with fluctuations in employment. Accordingly the slopes of the two curves in Figure 3 reflect the impact

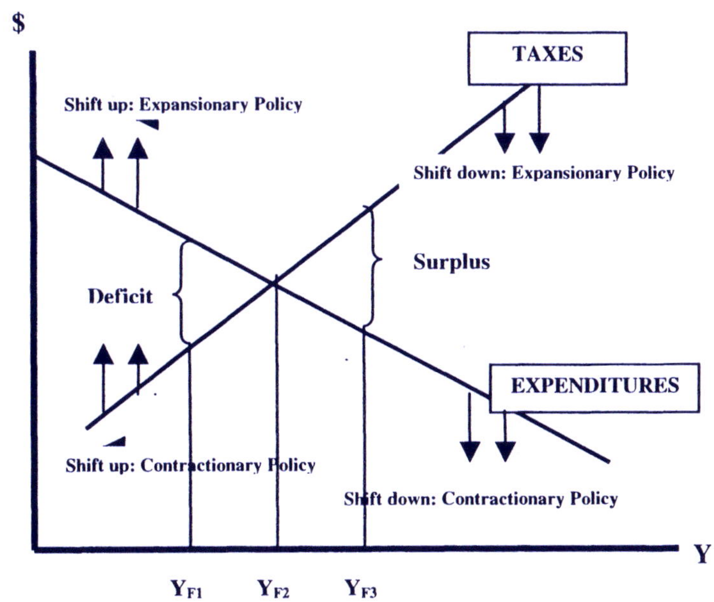


*Figure 3. Fiscal Policy vs. Fiscal Impact*

of the extant automatic stabilizers on the operation of the macro economy. Discretionary fiscal policy can be contrasted with the automatic stabilizers because the former requires new and explicit legislation by the Congress in order to be put into effect. It is often criticized as taking too long to be effective as a stabilizer–by the time the Congress recognizes that inflation or recession is imminent, holds hearings, formulates a piece of legislation, and passes it the stage of the business cycle is likely to have changed drastically. Over the years this objection has been confronted by efforts to speed up this process. The notion of a "public works shelf"–a set of proposed public projects planned and budgeted in advance, so as to be able to be activated in atimely fashion, has been a principal effort in this direction. It was advanced a number of years ago. In Figure 3 the possibilities from discretionary policy are illustrated by shifts up and down in the two functions, as shown.

What the figure shows, importantly, beyond the relationship of both taxes and expenditures to personal income changes is the impact of the business cycle on the results of given tax and expenditures polices. It has been argued that only if one asks what will the tax revenues be at full employment and what will the total government expenditures be at that point can you say whether on balance the extant fiscal stance associated with present fiscal policy is inflationary, contractionary, or neutral. Thus the figure shows the impact on the economy of the same tax measures and expenditure measures, buttheir fiscal impact depends on where one regards "full employment" to be. Even if full employment is as murky a concept as modern mainstream economists have managed to make it, it is still possible to argue that fiscal measures are inflationary onl when they produce deficits when the economy is beyond full employment.

Thus if YF1 represents full employment, the fiscal stance would be expansionary (creating a deficit) even if, thanks to the business cycle the economy is so far above YF1 that there is an actual surplus. On the other hand, any time there is a budgetary surplus (as for example when the full employment level is at YF3) the fiscal impact is contractionary. This remains true, even if, due to the cycle, the economy is so far below YF3 that there is an actual deficit. Only if by chance "full employment" were at YF2 would the structural budget be in balance and, therefore, have a neutral effect on the macroeconomy. We argue that there is merit conceptually, therefore, in the term "structural budget" even though the actual measurement of the magnitudes involved, not to mention their calculation, is highly problematical. It is the structural budget which shows the "implicit" surplus or deficit in the extant tax and expenditure system.

Examination of these problems takes us beyond the scope of this essay, but a cursory review of their nature is useful because it shows why even useful concepts can be extremely difficult to produce both realistically and accurately with the statistics we have available. Making the relationships which lie back of Figure 3 realistic requires correctly estimating the way in which the components which make up the automatic stabilizing system–the individual taxes and individual expenditures–change as personal income changes. For economists this means correctly estimating the income elasticities of all these components. These calculations are in the hands of the Congressional Budget Office. The chart is useful in suggesting the dynamics of how any actual budget surplus or deficit can only be translated into its fundamental impact on the economy if one abstracts from the cyclical impact on the discretionary variables in place at any given time. (*Cf.*, Footnote 6 below for a more detailed explanation of how these tax and expenditure yield curves are derived. Yield curves show annual return on fixed-interest assets against their years to maturity).

The difficulties begin with the notion of "Potential GDP" which was introduced in the Kennedy administration and was prepared by the Council of Economic Advisors each year until the Reagan administration stopped the practice. The calculation of the potential GDP involved beginning with some base line GDP, and adjusting it each year for the change in hours of labor worked, the change in productivity (based on changes in technology and resultant knowledge), and the change in the capital stock. In its heyday potential output, though always an estimate, was often referred to as though it were a "real statistic" as in "potential output has grown about 3% annually over the last half-century" (Samuelson and Nordhaus 1992, p. 399).

The "hypothetical full employment rate" is the second non-existent number. It is the estimate of what the unemployment rate would be were the economy operating at the potential GDP. Sometimes this is clarified by suggesting that above this GDP, inflation rates are "unacceptably high."

Beyond this, the government receipts and expenditures are hooked to various levels of income by complicated formulae. The most current and perhaps most reliable estimate is done by the Congressional Budget Office. Darrel Cohn and Glenn Follette, economists at the New York Federal Reserve Bank, have written a paper summarizing the underlying technique. They begin with the New York Federal Reserve technique for estimating the impact of the automatic stabilizers on the budgetary surplus or deficit as income changes.[6] That these calculations are highly tentative seems clear. In attempting to put numbers to a heuristic device such as Figure 3 it is important to remember that the provisions in the various statutes governing automatic stabilizers are subject to constant change and adjustment. Moreover it is equally important to remember that discretionary fiscal policy can be factored into the schematic device only approximately as is indicated in the figure.

In sum, the potential GDP, the precise unemployment rate that goes with any estimate of what we mean by a fully employed economy, and the precise income level which at any given time attaches to any estimate of the full employment income level are subject to myriad actual and statistical influences which make them slippery concepts at best. The justification for all this seems primarily to be in underscoring the important point that the actual budget deficit or surplus in any given year is no proper guide to whether fiscal policy (recall that this phrase means deliberately trying to influence the level of income), is expansionary or contractionary.

## Fiscal Policy Versus Fiscal Stance–A Tale of Two Recessions

We have been at pains to suggest that there is little or nothing about the behavior of federal expenditures and federal tax revenues as they have been carried out in the past quarter century which could by any stretch of the imagination be labeled "Keynesian." Keynes's basic notion was that they should be manipulated so as to create net injections into the economy (deficits) during recessions and net withdrawals (surplus) from the economy during expansions. This was the fundamental basis of "counter cyclical fiscal policy." We saw that balancing the budget over the cycle rather than over any arbitrary period could not possibly lead to mounting public debt unless the economy managed to suffer more or less chronic recession. For that possibility we briefly allude to the secular stagnation hypothesis.

We noted that critics of fiscal policy with some justification discussed the timing difficulties involved in introducing discretionary changes in tax and expenditure measures in a system where such changes had to be initiated in a relatively cumbersome and inflexible legislative system. Some suggestions have been made to attempt to deal with these problems, such as the creation of a public works "shelf" of potential program subjects underwritten by the federal government and ready to be introduced in fairly short order.

Nevertheless timing fiscal policy has always been recognized as a complex matter. Some years ago Wilfred Lewis did a study of fiscal policy in which he attempted to assess fiscal policy in action through a number of postwar recessions (Lewis, Jr. 1962). He discussed fiscal policy not only from the theoretical perspective but also with reference to the practical difficulties created by the problem of correctly timing fiscal flows and changes in them, coping with the differences in viewpoints of various congressmen involved in the process, as well as resolving differences between Congress and the Administration.

One of the last recessions he covered is that of 1957-58. The variables he considers are indicated in Figure 4. Lewis accepts the notion of a "hypothetical high employment" standard, so that recession reflects the actual GNP fall from the pre-recession peak level to the recession trough and then traces the gradual recovery to its pre-recession level in the subsequent expansion. The figure shows that unemployment behaved reasonably as expected, rising during the contraction, lagging a bit in response to the trough and rising for at least two more quarters. Thereafter it fluctuated a good deal for a number of quarters.

It is most especially the story of expenditures and tax revenues to which we must pay attention. It is what happens to federal receipts and expenditures over the cycle which determines the budgetary balance. Figure 4 shows that the surplus was shrinking before the peak as there was decreasing need for any federal intervention to cool off the economy in late expansion. Shortly after the business cycle peak the federal fiscal stance shifts from being contractionary to being expansionary. Hence, throughout most of the contraction shown, the deficit is growing although much more slowly after the previous peak level has been achieved. Without belaboring the complexities we may simply note that expenditures and receipts were generally moving counter cyclically. Part of this was, of course, due to the behavior of the automatic stabilizers. But the rest was due to discretionary action. By putting both together it was possible to say that the impact of federal expenditures and tax policies was to utilize the stabilizing potential inherent in deficits and surpluses. The figures suggest that the fiscal stance at that time was genuinely stabilizing. Only if one assumes that conditions such as those prevailing in much of 1958 were generally typical would the deficits over time be larger than the surpluses. The period in short illustrates the use of "Keynesian fiscal policy."

We have attempted to duplicate most of these variables for the most recent official completed recession, that of 1990-1991. The results are shown in Figure 5. The business cycle reached a peak in the second quarter of 1990 and a trough in the first quarter of 1991.[7] GDP rose slowly until the end of 1991 and then began expanding more rapidly and indeed it reached its recovery point early in 1992. In the study from which Figure 4 is derived the author, Wilfred Lewis wrote, "The phase designated as 'recovery' is intended to represent the period from the trough quarter in GNP to the time the economy returns to high employment. The percentage of the labor force employed is used as the primary means of indicating recovery, not because labor is the only underused resource during recession and recovery, but because this is probably the best single statistic available to indicate the extent to which production resources in general are being utilized" (Lewis 1981, pp. 3-4).

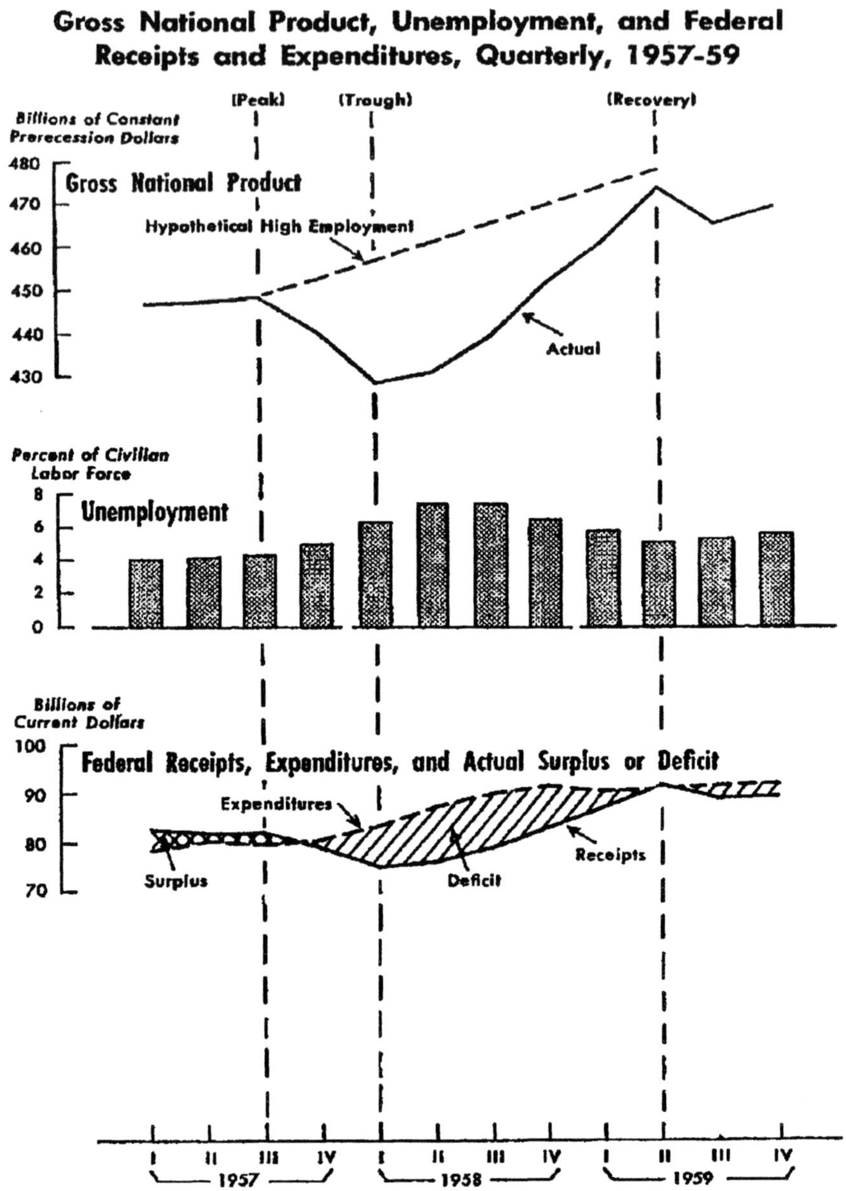


Figure 4

*Gross National Product, Unemployment, and Federal Receipts and Expenditures, Quarterly, 1957-59.*

Source: Adapted by author from *Federal Fiscal Policy in the Postwar Recessions; Studies of Government Finance*, Wilfred Lewis, Jr. (Ed.), Wash., DC: Brookings Institute 1962, p. 190.

Comparison of the data in Figure 4 and Figure 5 above shows that the unemployment rate behaved very differently in the later recession. The unemployment rate stayed elevated for a number of years. We have chosen, therefore, to measure recovery in terms of the time from the trough to the return of GDP to its peak level. Obviously what has changed has been labor productivity. Overtime a previous peak level would become increasingly less acceptable as technological progress increases productivity. (This is precisely what the hypothetical high employment GDP anticipates).

What happened to unemployment rates during this period? The second panel in the figures tells the story. Unemployment lagged the cycle as is often the case. It rose throughout the recession and for three quarters into recovery. Only when GDP had recovered to its previous peak level did it fall. Thereafter it fluctuated.

The behavior of federal expenditures and tax receipts during this period, unlike the other variables considered, show virtually no indication of any cyclical impact. The expenditures are larger than the tax receipts in every quarter in the period covered as indeed they were from every quarter for the twenty-five years preceding the mid-1990s when we finally managed to produce a federal surplus, initially small, for the first time in many years.

We wish to underscore the point that this period gives no sign of what we have defined as Keynesian fiscal policy–having expenditures and/or tax revenues deliberately vary so as to reflect the stage of the business cycle. Instead they reflect not stabilizing policy, but simple arithmetic–the government did not try to stabilize the economy but only to buy more than it was willing to pay for. Hence, like any other economic unit, borrowing was the only alternative. The fiscal stance reflects the net effect of all tax and expenditure decisions. To repeat, only if they are directed toward stabilizing the macro-economy can they be called "fiscal policy" and only in those circumstances could they fairly and accurately be called "Keynesian." The two episodes illustrate clearly the difference between "fiscal policy" and "fiscal stance."

## Reassessing the Usefulness of Fiscal Policy

An essential aspect of any institutionalist assessment of economic theory is its usefulness in making the economies of the real world function better (Veblen's phrase was "enhancing the life process" (Veblen [1899] 1994, p. 99)). That is the underlying reality which governs much of what we have discussed

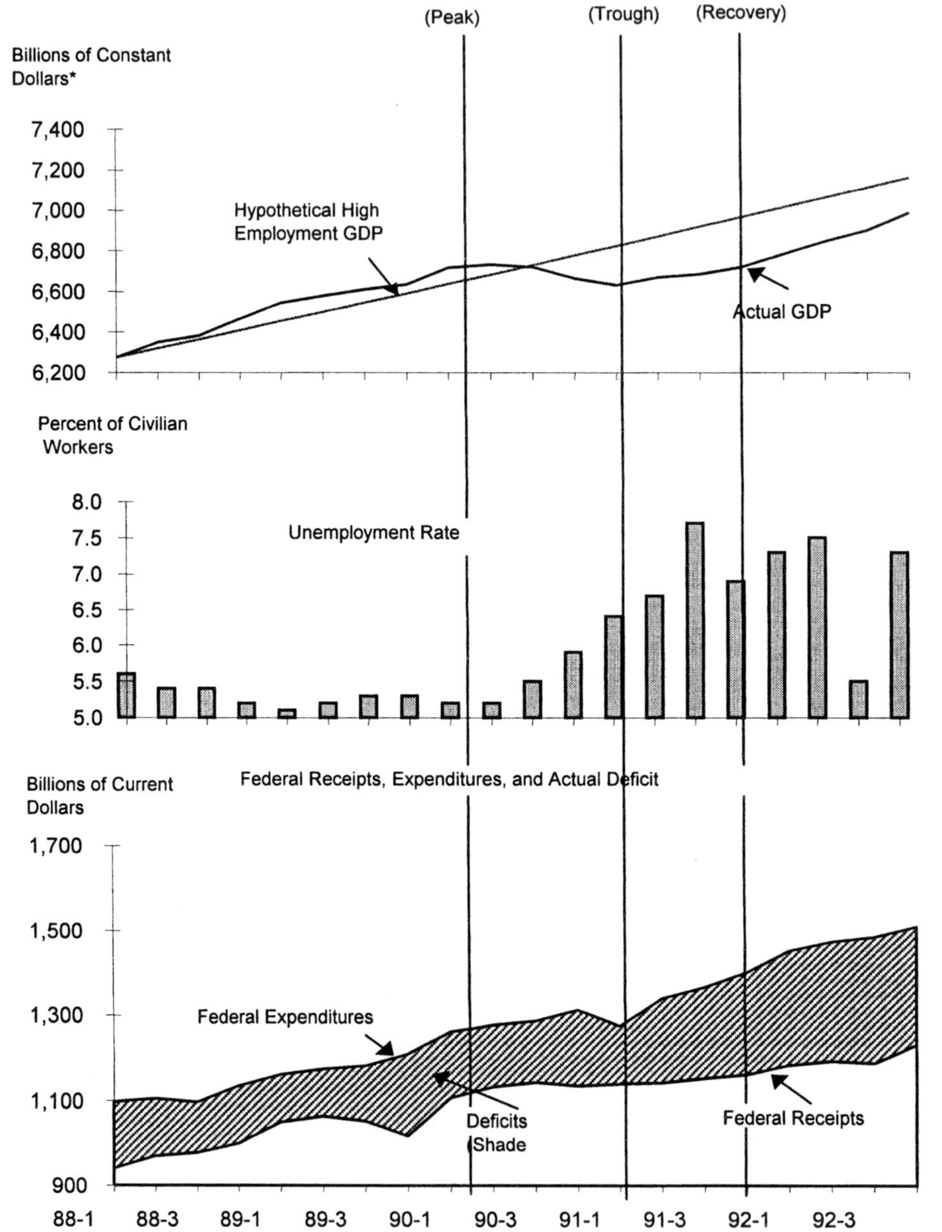


*Figure 5*

*Gross Domestic Product, Unemployment, and Federal Receipts and Expenditures, Quarterly, 1988-92*

Sources: GDP *Economic Report of the President* 1993 except 1988 and 1989—*Economic Report of the President*, 1992.

*Billions of chained (1996) dollars.

thus far. It is the central truth which makes normative analysis critical to institutionalist consideration of economic policy. In the case of fiscal policy we may say that it has a role to play in bringing "the collective ought" to bear on how the macro economy functions.

In the past the task assigned to fiscal policy has been described variously. As we have seen for Keynes the task was to balance the federal budget over the business cycle rather than over arbitrary time periods such as years. We may refer to this simply as "counter-cyclical fiscal policy." Paul Samuelson referred to it as "compensatory fiscal policy," to suggest it was designed simply to compensate for the fluctuations of the business cycle, (Samuelson 1970, p. 337). He also distinguished the secular stagnation case, originally developed by Alvin Hansen, in which mature capitalist economies have increasing difficulty achieving what at the time was referred to as "Full Employment." Were fiscal policy to be utilized in this case–it was sometimes referred to as "fully compensatory counter-cyclical fiscal policy"–the presumption was that the budget would more or less always have been in deficit. In this case the resulting public debt would indeed grow secularly. It most particularly would *not* be an example of Keynes' view of how fiscal policy ought to be used.

We argue, therefore, that institutionalists assess fiscal policy in pragmatic terms. In this connection it is instructive to summarize the view taken in the early 1980s by Wallace Peterson. He surveyed the functioning of the American macro economy in the period 1960-1982 and summarized the essential data as shown in Table 1 (Peterson 1984).

For Peterson, this table tells a powerful story: 1) productivity in the U.S. had deteriorated significantly; 2) money wages grew at a rapidly increasing pace in the period he covered despite three recessions in the 1970s; 3) the rise in wages coupled with the fall in productivity produced (inevitably) steadily rising unit labor costs; and 4), prices however measured grew roughly in proportion to unit labor costs. Peterson is at pains to underscore that one could not conclude from his data that workers' demands for higher wages were the cause of inflation. He notes that often money wages lag behind price changes, leaving workers trying to "catch up." Indeed, Peterson argues that concentrated power, ". . . lodged in the giant corporation enables it to shift readily onto prices the burden of increased wages" (*Ibid.*, p. 87). On the basis of these considerations, Peterson calls for a "workable incomes policy."[8]

It is striking what has happened in the 1990s. We have added the relevant data to Peterson's table. In comparison to Peterson's findings for the earlier era: first, productivity, though down in the first half of the 1990s, is up now close to the highest rate it has achieved since 1960-64.[9] Secondly, wages have grown at a lower rate since 1980 than they grew in any one of the periods Peterson studied after 1964. Thirdly, if rising wages and falling productivity produced rising unit labor costs in the earlier periods, in the 1990s we find the reverse. Unit labor costs in 1995-99 were lower than for any period since the first one (1960-64) Peterson examined.

Interestingly, the recent period in an important sense supports Peterson's view. In the 1980s he had argued that while the rate of increase in nominal wages was a major determinant of the inflation rate, the latter was also heavily influenced by the expected inflation rate. Thus, contrary to the Phillips Curve argument that suggests that a recession was the only way to bring down inflation, Peterson argues that if the *expected* inflation rate were lowered this could achieve the same result, (and far less painfully) and nothing was more likely to lower expected inflation than to lower inflation itself.

The 1990s was a remarkable decade characterized as it was by low inflation, low unemployment, no recession, healthy growth rates, sustained consumer confidence in the future of the market economy and a long rising stock market which did not weaken until the first years of the new century. As for fiscal policy, only as the annual budgetary deficits dwindled and ultimately were replaced by surpluses did the possibility of being able to use government expenditures and taxes to stabilize macroeconomic performance–that is, did the use of fiscal policy as an active adjunct to monetary policy and incomes policy–even become a viable possibility.

Accordingly, with the new millennium the possibility of reestablishing counter cyclical fiscal policy as a legitimate and effective aid in achieving the kind of macroeconomic performance which accords most with the collective ought was once more something which, for the first time in very many years, could even be realistically contemplated.

## A Realistic Look at the Public Sector

We have tried to show that a major reason that fiscal policy has become such a contentious issue is that it really serves as something of a stalking horse for a fundamental point of conflict between mainstream and institutionalist economists. Not only does the mainstream believe that the market really is mostly self-regulating, they go one step further and, in line with the "us" versus "them" approach to the public sector which conforms most to their overall perspective, they continue in their rhetoric if no place else, to fight for a

| Period | Productivity | Compensation Per Hour* | Unit Labor Costs | Inflation Rates | |
|---|---|---|---|---|---|
| | | | | GNP Deflator | CPI |
| 1960-64 | 2.9% | 3.9% | 1.0% | 1.2% | 1.2% |
| 1965-69 | 1.9 | 5.8 | 3.6 | 3.3 | 3.4 |
| 1970-74 | 1.4 | 7.5 | 6.0 | 5.3 | 6.1 |
| 1975-79 | 1.3 | 8.6 | 7.2 | 7.4 | 8.1 |
| 1980-82** | 0.7 | 9.1 | 8.8 | 8.6 | 10.0 |
| 1990-94 | 1.6 | 4.0 | 2.4 | 2.6 | 3.6 |
| 1995-99 | 2.3 | 3.7 | 1.4 | 1.5 | 2.4 |

*Table 1*

*Productivity, Unit Labor Costs, and Inflation: 1960-99*
*(in percent, annual average rates of change)*

Sources: 1960-82-Wallace C. Peterson, "Economic Stabilization and Inflation," *Journal of Economic Issues*, Vol. XVIII(1), March 1984, p. 79. Data from *Economic Report of the President*, 1983, p. 208.
*Wages and salaries plus all fringe benefits, including employer contributions.
**Three year Period.
1990-1999 added by the author to Peterson's table. Data from *Economic Report of the President*, 2001, all except CPI, p. 333. CPI p. 347.

smaller government, by which they mostly mean a smaller federal government. We present one final piece of evidence, therefore, as a sobering reminder of how accepted many aspects of federal involvement in the economy have become. Figure 6 shows federal, state and local, and total government revenues as a percent of GDP from 1960 to today.

Overall government receipts as a percent of GDP have grown slightly in the years shown (from about 25% to perhaps 31% of GDP). But close inspection shows that the increase has largely been in the shaded area–that is, in state and local receipts as a percent of GDP. The federal share has increased only slightly–from about 18% to 20%.

It is interesting to examine the changes by presidential administrations. Federal spending as a percent of GDP did not increase during Kennedy's brief presidency. The Johnson administration is regarded as a "big spending" period–the Great Society programs were all funded during this time. Yet, the federal budget as a percent of GDP grew only about 2%. During the Nixon administration there was some fluctuation, but the federal share of GDP was little changed. The Ford years are something of a surprise–his administration was, of course, the shortest in the period under review, yet somehow he became associated with a rare drop (about 1%) in federal receipts as a percent of GDP. The Carter presidency exhibits a mild increase in the percent share of the federal government. Reagan, on the other hand, whose administration produced the most vivid anti-big government rhetoric of any of the administrations under re view here, left office with the federal government's share of GDP only slightly below what it was when he took office. Bush in his four years managed a very slight decrease. Federal government receipts as a percent of GDP grew by a little over 2.5% during the first six years of the Clinton Administration. This was virtually the only period during which the state and local share did not increase more than the federal share.

What all this shows, of course, is how difficult it is to reduce the influence of the federal government in the current US macro economy. The labyrinthine processes by which federal expenditures are determined is a topic that is well beyond the scope of this essay. In the end, what we can conclude is that the role of the public sector in the present US economy, though hotly debated in the public discourse, is in many respects more widely accepted than the rhetoric would suggest. The debate is about marginal changes. This was underscored in the fall of 2001 in the aftermath of the tragedy of September 11th. The ease with which bipartisan support built for "stimulus expenditures" to ward off prolonged recession was symptomatic of the degree to which public spending had been accepted.

The degree of acceptance is one of the obstacles to real flexibility in utilizing the tax and expenditure levers to achieve greater growth with stability, which is the underlying objective of fiscal policy.

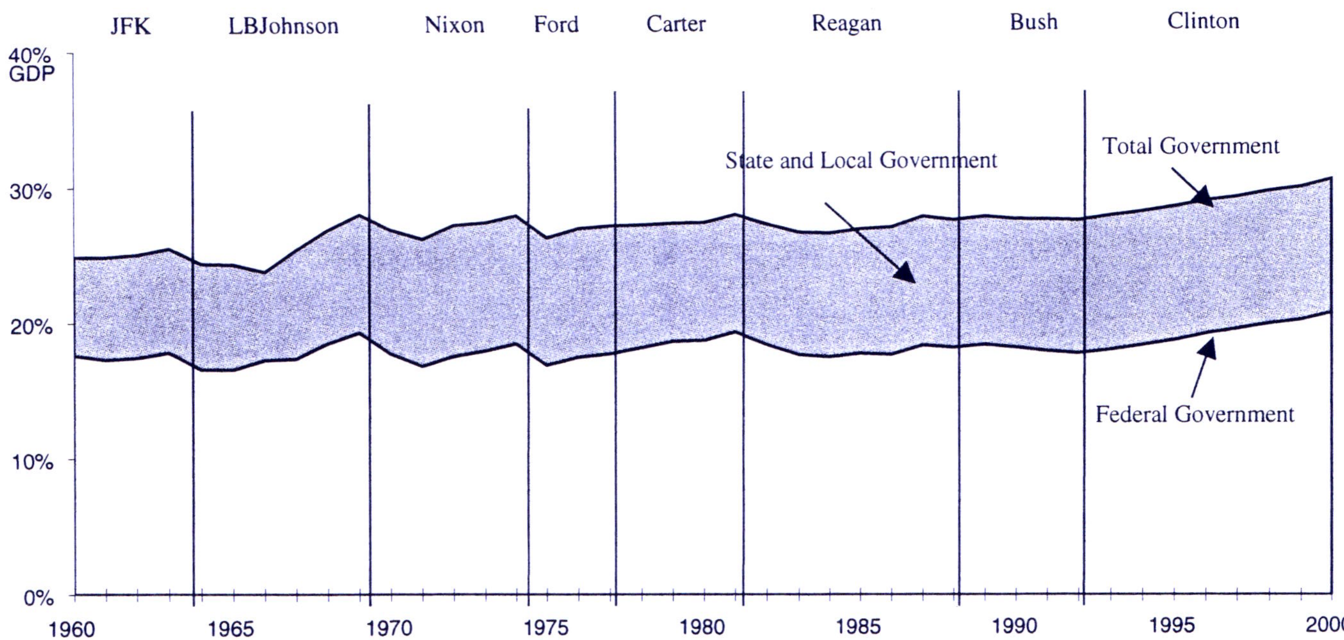


*Figure 6*
*Total Government, Federal Government, and State and Local Government Receipts as a Percent of GDP 1960-2000*

Source: Bureau of Economic Analysis, National Income and Products Accounts, 2001. GDP–Table 1-1, Total Government Receipts–Table 31, Federal Government Receipts–Table 32.

## CONCLUSION

If there is one tenet most institutionalists would readily agree to, it is that in the end the role of economics is to assist in the basic task of "enhancing human life," to use Veblen's widely quoted phrase.

Arguably the major divide between institutionalists and mainstream economists (who probably have nothing against enhancing human life) is that for the mainstream the market itself is the principal agent for whatever improvements get made in the performance of an economy. For institutionalists enhancing human life means going as far as seems prudent with the market but recognizing that there is a continuing and critical role for the public sector.

Fiscal policy, it turns out is a pivotal area in this dichotomy. Originating with Keynes, whose theory provides the bedrock foundation for the assertion that governmental power can be constructively used to improve the performance of the economy, it asserts that as part of constructive interventionism, the deliberate manipulation of government expenditures and tax revenues can play a role in producing both more rapid and more stable growth rates for the economy.

In asserting that economic theory needs to be assessed from the perspective of improving economic policy, fiscal policy is, therefore, one of the first areas to be encountered. For genuine believers in "leaving it to the market" there can be no fiscal policy because there can be no use of federal powers to affect the macro economy.

We have seen earlier that for economists like Robert Lucas the whole field of macroeconomics is tainted with the implicit assertion that federal intervention has a role to play. They would, therefore, go back to monetary policy which they can view as mostly a private bank activity. The Lucas view ironically suggests the significance of fiscal policy, as we have defined it in this paper. It is the outgrowth of macroeconomic theory (for which read Keynesian macroeconomic theory). It is Keynesian macroeconomic theory which makes interventionism both logical and instrumental in improving the economic life of the participants in such an economy. It is not the "trashing" of the market that is sometimes charged, but the recognition that the operation of almost any market will from time to time need help from purposive governmental activity in order to function properly. It is further the recognition that even in the best of times there are some activities that are best handled by governmental resource deployment. Keynesian fiscal policy makes clear how macroeconomic theory can be applied so as to improve the quality of life in modern market economies. If Keynesian theory led to the injudicious macroeconomic interventionism that Lucas has charged, what does this suggest for microeconomics? Micro theory has presumably been used to justify antitrust activity and other forms of public intervention in the workings of the market-oriented economy. If the economy is as self-regulating at both the micro- and the macro-level as Lucas and other new classical economists contend, the modern economy can presumably be likened to a perpetual motion machine. The theory of how perpetual motion machines continue moving successfully and without exogenous guidance has never been considered to be anything more than an interesting intellectual exercise–rather like theories about winning at chess.

We have been at pains to suggest that all recent Administrations have–whether they liked it or not–ended up accepting a remarkably large proportion of the evolving public economy. Whether or not this continues it is highly unlikely that many aspects of the modern welfare state will be challenged except in marginal ways.

Discretionary fiscal policy may be an inheritance from Keynes, but it is also a logical and significant outgrowth of the whole institutionalist perspective which has always argued in non-doctrinaire fashion that a successfully functioning modern economy must be a combination of a well organized and efficient private sector and a well organized and efficient public sector. They both have their place and they each need to recognize the importance of the role for the other sector.

# NOTES

[1] Gladys Foster, James K. Galbraith, and L. Randall Wray provided valuable advice. I am grateful to the Economic Cycle Research Institute in New York City for producing the charts for me. In particular Dimitra Visvicki and Jean Maltz have my gratitude. At Penn State my secretary, Nancy Cole, worked diligently to improve the manuscript. The remaining errors are, of course, mine.

[2] Robert E. Lucas 1981, "Rules, Discretion, and the Role of the Economic Advisor," in Lucas, Robert E. (ed.), *Studies in Business Cycle Theory*, Cambridge, MIT Press, 1981 Paperback Edition, 1963, 250. Italics in original.

[3] Growing out of work by Milton Friedman and Edmund Phelps; the "Natural Rate of Unemployment" is attributed to them both, Friedman 1968, 1-17 and Phelps, 1970.

4 The earlier figure is from Bureau of Labor Statistics, *Directory of National Unions and Employee Associations.* The later figure is from Bureau of Labor Statistics, Current Population Survey reported in *Employment and Earnings. Cf.*, especially the issue of February, 1994. An additional 14.9% of the labor force was "represented by unions" but these figures have been available since 1983 and are not customarily included in reporting the size of union strength.

5 More precisely the most expansionary fiscal impact results when expenditures increase while tax rates decrease, and the most contractionary impact results when taxes increase while expenditures decrease. In between it is possible to have increases in both, in which case the impact depends on which increases the most and how much the difference is between the two rates. Or finally it is possible to decrease both in which case the fiscal impact depends on the relationship between the two rates of decrease.

6 For the complete discussion of the New York Federal Reserve attempt to flesh out the Congressional Budget Office approach, see Cohen and Follette 2000, 35-73. The question asked is what would the automatic fiscal stabilizers in their current form yield in revenues and expenditures at various possible income levels at any given time? This technique as noted in the text involves estimating the income elasticities attached to the current personal tax system and including such factors as the statutory tax rate, variables reflecting the distribution of wage earners and their tax liabilities, and the impact of various indirect business taxes to get the variation of tax receipts by yearly income. On the expenditures side calculations are made for the various transfers and grants involved in the welfare system in place at any given time. These include the Food Stamp program, the earned income Credit, welfare (Aid to Dependent Children, Temporary Assistance for Needy Families, Disability Insurance, etc.).

7 This record belies the common view that recessions last at least two quarters. The National Bureau of Economic Research dating committee take a far more complicated view of the task of dating recessions. (As this essay was completed, the dating committee declared a business cycle peak had occurred in March 2001. This illustrates the point being made. Not until the fall of 2001 did a quarter of GDP exhibit an absolute decline).

8 Principally Peterson called for a policy directed at large corporations with great economic power which would curtail their ability to pursue administered pricing policies which exacerbated inflationary pressures.

9 So important did Peterson regard the decline in productivity that he wrote a book on the implications of it, *Silent Depression*, published in 1994. In that book Peterson commented, "The most important *single* fact about the American economy is the productivy slowdown since 1973. If one had to point to a single cause for the silent depression this would be it–the slowdown in productivity growth" (Peterson 1994, pp. 171-172). We add only that much of the analysis of that book is germane to the economy of the initial years of the next millennium, Peterson's comment notwithstanding, although the "longest peacetime expansion" was just beginning when Peterson published his book. On the other hand, there has been a continued deterioration in the inequality of income distribution, the rising cost of many essentials (health care, education, etc.) and many other factors that Peterson argues have contributed to the silent depression.

# REFERENCES

Beveridge, William H., 1945. *Full Employment in a Free Society.* New York: W.W. Norton and Company, Inc.

Buchanan, James M., 1985. *Liberty, Market, and State: Political Economy in the 1980s.* New York: New York University Press.

Cohen, Darell and Glenn Follette, 2000. "The Automatic Fiscal Stabilizers: Quietly Doing Their Thing." In *Economic Policy Review*, FRBNY.

*Economic Report of the President*, 2001. US Government Printing Office.

Friedman, Milton, 1968. The Role of Monetary Policy. *American Economic Review* 58:1-17.

Hansen, Alvin H., 1964. *Business Cycles and National Income.* New York: W.W. Norton & Company, Inc.

Keynes, John Maynard, 1936. *The General Theory of Employment, Interest, and Money.* New York: Harcourt Brace and Company.

Klein, P.A., 1984. Institutionalist Reflections on the Role of the Public Sector. *Journal of Economic Issues* 18(1):45-68. Reprinted in *Beyond Dissent, Essays in Institutional Economics,* Philip A. Klein, (ed.), Armonk, New York: M.E. Sharpe, 1994.

Klein, Philip A., 1994. "What's Natural About Unemployment?" In *Beyond Dissent, Essays in Institutional Economics,* Philip A. Klein, ed., Armonk, New York: M.E. Sharpe. Reprinted in *Analyzing Modern Business Cycles*, Philip A. Klein, ed., Armonk, NY: M.E. Sharpe, 1990.

Lewis, Jr., Wilfred, 1962. *Federal Fiscal Policy in the Postwar Recessions.* Washington, DC: The Brookings Institution.

Lucas, Robert E., 1981. *Studies in Business Cycle Theory.* Cambridge: MIT Press, Paperback Edition, 1983.

Lucas, Robert E., 1981. A Review: Paul McCracken et al, "Towards Full Employment and Price Stability," A Report to the OECD by a group of Independent Experts. In Robert E. Lucas, ed., *Studies in Business Cycle Theory.* Cambridge: MIT Press, 1963:262-270.

Lucas, Robert E., 1981. "Rules, Discretion, and the Role of the Economic Advisor." In Robert E. Lucas, (ed.), *Studies in Business Cycle Theory*, Cambridge, MIT Press: Paperback Edition, 1963.

Nourse, Edwin G., 1953. *Economics in the Public Service.* New York: Harcourt Brace and Company.

Peterson, Wallace C., 1984. Economic Stabilization and Inflation. *Journal of Economic Issues* 18:69-100.

Peterson, Wallace C., (1994). *Silent Depression*, New York: W.W. Norton & Company.

Phelps, Edmund S., 1970. "The New Microeconomics in Employment and Inflation Theory." In *Microeconomic Foundations of Employment and Inflation Theory*, Edmund S. Phelps et al., eds., New York: Norton.

Phillips, A.W., 1958. The Relation Between Unemployment and the Rate of Change of Money Wages in the United Kingdom, 1861–1957, *Econometrica,* new series, Nov. 1958; 25:283-99.

Samuelson, Paul A. and William Nordhaus, 1995. *Economics, 16th Edition.* New York: McGraw-Hill, Inc.

Samuelson, Paul and William D. Nordhaus, 1992. *Economics, 14th Edition*. New York: McGraw Hill Book Company.
Samuelson, Paul, 1970. *Economics, 8th Edition*. New York: McGraw-Hill Book Company.
US Employment Act of 1946, Public Law 304, 79th Congress. United State Government Printing Office.
Veblen, Thorstein, [1899] 1994. *The Theory of the Leisure Class*, New York: Penquin Books.
Ward, Terry, 1987. "Fiscal Policy." In *The New Palgrave Dictionary of Economics* 2, John Eatwell, Murray Milgate, and Peter Newman, eds. London: The Macmillan Press, Ltd.

# 3

# MONETARY POLICY: AN INSTITUTIONALIST APPROACH

L. Randall Wray

## A BRIEF HISTORICAL OVERVIEW

While this chapter will not present a detailed history of monetary policy, it is useful to first take a quick look at the evolution of thinking about the nature of monetary policy. We will first examine the famous Currency School-Banking School debates of the early 19th century, then turn to the insightful analysis of Walter Bagehot. We next turn to the creation of the Federal Reserve System (Fed) and early 20th century thinking about the role of the central bank. The discovery of the "deposit multiplier" in the 1920s as well as the developing understanding of open market operations had a very large influence on the post-WWII theory of central bank control of the money supply. While post-war "Keynesian" economists were skeptical of the potency of monetary policy, the Monetarist approach gradually gained adherents and came completely to dominate thinking about monetary policy by the last quarter of the 20th century. However, Monetarism experienced a quite remarkable turn-around of fortunes at the end of the century. As we begin the 21st century, orthodox thinking about monetary policy is in nearly complete disarray. However, there are themes that run through the 20th century and even the 19th century that offer some guidance in reformulating and creating a truly institutionalist approach to monetary policy.

### Pre-War Monetary Policy

There are many similarities between the Currency School-Banking School debate of the 19th century and the 1960s-1970s debate between Monetarists and "Keynesians." (When I use the term "Keynesian" in quotes, I mean the bastardized version of Keynes popularized by Samuelson and his followers, and best exposited in the ISLM model. This is to be contrasted with Keynes's own thoughts and those of his followers, the Post Keynesians.) The debate centered around the relation between money and spending, on the ability of the central bank (the Bank of England) to control the quantity of money, and on the relation between the quantity of money and the external balance (Wray 1990). The Currency School tended to follow the "Classical" view that an increase of the money supply would be fully reflected in a rise of prices—in other words, they accepted what has come to be known as the proposition that money is neutral. Further, because the resulting inflation would make domestic output noncompetitive, this would tend to cause a trade deficit. On a gold standard, this would then cause a gold outflow, which would cause the money supply to decrease (as there would be less gold to back it) and force prices to fall. Hence, the "specie-flow" mechanism would tend to restore balance by automatically reducing the supply of money.

If, however, some portion of the money supply was not backed directly by gold, the specie-flow mechanism could not work because an outflow of gold would not necessarily reduce the money supply. For example, if private bank notes circulated as part of the money supply, and if these were not strictly convertible to gold (or to government currency that was itself strictly convertible to gold), an increased supply of private bank notes could cause inflation and result in a persistent trade deficit. For this reason the Currency School wanted to tightly constrain the issue of private bank notes by requiring that private banks hold specie or Bank of England notes in an amount equivalent to their private bank note issues. The Bank of England would be able to control private money creation simply by controlling its own emission of notes—which would serve as the required reserves of the private banks. In short, like modern Monetarists, adherents to the Currency School approach believed that "required reserves" would give to the central bank control over that portion of the money supply that is privately created, and that this would in turn allow the central bank to limit inflationary pressures that would cause trade deficits.

The Banking School, on the other hand, denied that "excessive" creation of private bank notes is the cause of inflation. They argued that bank notes are issued only on demand, and only because someone wants to hold or spend them. Any excessive notes would be returned to banks for redemption or to repay loans—what has been called the "law of reflux." Indeed, the Banking School denied that private banks have any discretionary influence over the quantity of bank notes outstanding—private money creation is "endogenously" determined by the customers of banks. Further, central banks could not affect the quantity of private notes issued, but rather would affect only the terms on which they were offered in loans. In other words, central bank policy operated not on the quantity of money but rather on the interest rate—restrictive policy would increase interest rates.

Note, however, that the Banking School argued that the law of reflux would not apply to a government-issued "fiat" money that was not convertible. As it was not redeemable for gold, a government fiat money could be issued in excess without refluxing back to government. Hence, a government fiat money could indeed be excessive and could thereby contribute to inflation—and could cause a trade deficit. However, as privately issued money would reflux to the issuers, so long as it was redeemable, it could not directly affect inflation or the trade balance.

Like some modern day "Keynesians," the Banking School saw monetary policy as operating indirectly, only through its affects on interest rates. Thomas Tooke, the foremost Banking School theorist argued that "(I)t is only through the rate of interest and the state of credit, that the Bank of England can exercise a direct influence on the foreign exchange" (Tooke 1959, 124). According to Tooke, proper monetary policy would not worry about the quantity of money but instead would attempt to stabilize interest rates: "[T]he greater or less liability to variation in the rate of interest constitutes, in the next degree only to the preservation of the convertibility of the paper and the solvency of banks, the most important consideration in the regulation of our banking system" (ibid).

Unfortunately, as is often the case, the persuasiveness of the position of the Banking School was lost on policy makers. Parliament adopted the Currency School principles in its Act of 1844, which tried to limit private bank note issue by placing a ceiling on their issue and by constraining Bank of England note issuance. Tooke's analysis some years later was harsh: "As the result of a careful examination of the principle on which the Act of 1844 was founded, and of the experience of its working since the time when it came into operation, I have no hesitation in giving it as my opinion that it is a *total, unmitigated, uncompensated*, and, in its consequences, *a lamentable failure*" (Tooke 1848, vol IV, 402). "The variations, in the rate of interest, during the year 1847, have exceeded in frequency and extent any of which there is to be found an example in the commercial history of this country" (Tooke 1848, vol IV, 400). As we'll see later, one could say much the same of the Federal Reserve's application of Monetarist principles in the early 1980s.

Over time, England developed what we might call a "mono-reserve" system in which private banks promised to redeem their own liabilities (initially taking the form of bank notes, but eventually mostly taking the form of deposits) for Bank of England notes. Private banks thus held some Bank of England notes in vaults, but most of their reserves took the form of deposits in key London banks, which in turn held deposits on the Bank of England. In a sense, the whole banking system "pyramided" reserves on the Bank of England, which gave it tremendous power in determining interest rates. It could cause "tight money" by calling in advances made to London banks or brokers, or it could raise the interest rate required in its discount of bills, or it could simply refuse to discount bills altogether. When faced with tight money, London banks would call in overdrafts and force correspondent country banks to sell consols or stock. This tended to cause bond prices to fall and interest rates to rise. (Sayers 1957, 125-7; Wray 1990, 51) In this way, the Bank of England could affect market interest rates.

When England ran a trade deficit, the Bank of England would face an external drain of specie. It would then institute a tight money regime to attract bullion inflows seeking higher interest rates. However, an external drain would often generate an internal drain: bank customers might notice a drain on bank reserves, become worried over the stability of banks, and hence try to obtain loans and discount bills before credit was cut off. Worse, they would try to withdraw deposits or redeem notes. This would lead to a further (internal) drain of reserves of the Bank of England, which would tighten money even further to stem the drain. A panic would result whenever the Bank of England acted like it might not provide the reserves needed by the private banks. Indeed, the Bank of England would frequently sell securities to replenish its own reserves—simply adding pressure on private banks.

By the last quarter of the 19$^{th}$ century, Bagehot forcefully argued that this was precisely the wrong policy (Bagehot 1927). He believed that one of the most important functions of a central bank is to act as a lender of last resort. He recognized that in any mono-reserve system, the monopoly supplier of that reserve must supply reserves *without limit* whenever the banking system faces a panic. The way to stop a run on reserves is to demonstrate to the public that private bank liabilities can be, and will be, redeemed on demand for the ultimate reserve. This would restore confidence and stop bank runs. Note that Bagehot's recommendation is consistent with the Banking School's preference for policy to aim at interest rate stabilization, while the Bank of England's actual policy only caused interest rates to rise even further during a panic.

Bagehot's influential book was published in 1873, and his recommendations were gradually incorporated within the dominant view of economic theorists. By the end of the 19$^{th}$ century, the Bank of England endorsed Bagehot's theory in its policy. When the Federal Reserve System was established in 1913, one of the principal justifications for its creation was the recognition that the panic of 1907 might have been prevented or at least attenuated if a national lender of last resort had been in existence. In a mono-reserve system based on liabilities of the central bank, reserves can always be expanded without limit as the central bank lends reserves (at the discount window, by discounting eligible "bills"), or provides them through open market purchases of assets. Hence, the Federal Reserve Act of 1913 charged the Fed with furnishing "an elastic currency" and "the means of rediscounting commercial paper" (Meulendyke 1989, 18). For many years thereafter, the guiding principle of the Fed was the "Real Bills Doctrine" under which the Fed was to rediscount eligible paper (thus make loans of reserves to member banks) on demand to meet the needs of trade. (Meulendyke 1989).

The original Act did not provide for open market operations. Since WWII in the US, we have become accustomed to central bank open market operations—purchases and sales of government debt—and to the impact these have on banking system reserves. However, before WWII, the outstanding stock of government debt was generally not large (except following wars), and banks typically got their reserves at the discount window by submitting eligible paper for discount. WWI had also increased the supply of government debt, and just like private banks, the Fed had purchased some of this debt as an interest-earning asset. It was not until the 1920s that the effect of open market operations by the central bank was generally understood. It was also at this time that the "deposit multiplier" was discovered: an open market purchase would create reserves that were believed to permit a multiple expansion of deposits (Meulendyke 1989). While some commentators at the time noticed that an open market operation that increased/decreased bank reserves would simply lead to offsetting activity at the discount window (as discounts fell/rose), this recognition was gradually lost as Currency School-type thinking was revived after WWII in a particularly virulent, Monetarist, form.

Monetary policy during the Great Depression has received a bad rap. Some have faulted the Fed for "allowing" half of all banks to fail. If the Fed was created in 1913 to save banks facing a run, why did it stand by as bank after bank had to close its doors? A simple, but not complete, answer is that the Fed saw as its mandate the charge to lend reserves to otherwise solvent banks. In other words, the Fed was supposed to provide liquidity by discounting "good" bills, but was not supposed to save banks whose bills (and other assets) were questionable. The banks that were failing were not merely illiquid, they were also insolvent because their assets had collapsed in value. The far less valid, but nearly universal, complaint about the Fed, however, is the absurd Monetarist claim that the Fed reduced the money supply, and, hence, caused the bank failures. This view has been popularized by Friedman and Schwartz (1963), who claim that tight monetary policy by the Fed turned a downturn into a long depression. As evidence, they point out that the money supply and bank reserves declined during the depression; since they believe that the Fed determines the quantity of money through the deposit multiplier and its control over bank reserves, the Fed deserves the blame.

Actually, the Fed intervened immediately and forcefully in 1929, buying $125 million of Treasury securities the day of the stock market crash, five times the maximum weekly amount it was authorized to purchase, and doubling Fed holdings in one day. (Muelendyke 1989; Wray 1998a, 99) However, as the asset price deflation spread, and as the depression forced down production and prices of goods and services, defaults on loans snowballed throughout the economy. In this environment, banks were forced to default on their own commitments (the demand and savings deposits of their customers) and/or reduce their loan portfolios (due to lack of good borrowers). Hence, the money supply fell because of the depression and it is rather silly to claim that the depression could have been avoided if only the money supply had continued to grow rapidly.

There is only one sense in which Friedman and Schwartz are correct in claiming that tight money policy contributed to the depression. Until the US went off the gold standard, the Fed did indeed worry about loss of its gold reserves if there were a run on US dollar-denominated assets. Hence, the Fed's interest rate policy was constrained because the US interest rates could not drop significantly below those of other countries—ignoring expectations of exchange rate movements—without draining gold. Thus, if a lower interest rate might have had a marginal, positive, influence on borrowing and spending, then one could argue that monetary policy should have been "looser." However, this was not possible so long as the dollar was redeemable for gold.

## Post-War Policy

During WWII, federal government deficits reached to nearly a quarter of GDP, leading to large issues of treasury debt. The Fed agreed in 1942 to peg the three-month Treasury bill rate at 3/8 of one percent to keep government interest costs low; longer-term bonds were informally pegged at somewhat higher rates. In effect, the T-bill rate operated as a floor for interest rates, and by keeping it low this tended to keep interest rates on private debt low (at a markup over the rate paid by government, with the differential determined largely by default risk and capital risk). After the war, the Fed was concerned with the potential for inflation and wanted to abandon the peg so that it would be free to raise rates to fight inflation. In 1947 the Treasury agreed to loosen the reigns on the Fed, which raised interest rates. The Fed continued to lobby for greater freedom to pursue activist monetary policy, resulting in the 1951 Accord in which the Fed abandoned its commitment to maintain low interest costs for the government. Henceforth, the Fed would manipulate the interest rate to implement countercyclical monetary policy.

After the War, banks were flush with government debt. Gradually, the Fed's emphasis moved from the discount window to open market operations. During the 1950s, the fed funds market was created and evolved to become the primary private "market" for excess reserves. Before the development of the fed funds market, a bank needing reserves would sell government bonds; banks with excess reserves would buy government bonds to obtain earning assets. The fed funds market allowed surplus banks to lend reserves directly to deficit banks, often requiring that borrowing banks put up government bonds as collateral. The fed funds rate gradually became the key short-term, base, interest rate.

After the 1951 Accord, the Fed—for political reasons—did not announce interest rate targets. Its newly won independence required that it proclaim that it was not pegging rates. However, it is clear that the Fed was targeting Treasury bill rates until the mid 1960s, when it switched to a fed funds target because the fed funds market had by then become the primary means for reserve adjustment by individual banks. Any aggregate deficit of reserves would immediately place pressure on the fed funds rate, inducing Fed provision of reserves to keep the rate from rising above target. Not only did the fed funds rate serve as an almost immediate indicator of reserve positions, but a fed funds target did not have the political baggage that accompanied a bills rate target (which determined the government's cost of issuing debt). Of course, the two rates would be inextricably linked, but it was politically easier for the Fed to increase the fed funds rate than it would be to explicitly raise government interest costs. Over the post war period, the Fed also began to rely on repurchase agreements and reverse repos rather than on outright open market purchases and sales in order more finely to tune market conditions.

The discovery of the reserve effects of open market operations and the discovery of the deposit multiplier, together with the growing post-depression consensus that government "ought" to try to use monetary and fiscal policy in a countercyclical manner, led to the belief that the Fed should try to increase the growth of the money supply in a downturn and reduce its growth in a boom. To be sure, economists were not unanimous in their belief that this would do much good. The typical "Keynesian" believed that while monetary policy might be fairly effective in a boom (tight money policy could slow money growth and hence slow growth of spending), it probably would have little effect in a recession. It was said that one "cannot push on a string"—the Fed would not be able to encourage loan-making activity and thereby increase the money supply if no one wanted to spend. Hence, most economists believed that in a recession, fiscal policy would be more effective than monetary policy in stimulating demand.

The notion that a central bank can influence reserve and monetary aggregates had been around for quite some time, as indicated above, however, the Fed did not adopt formal monetary targets until 1970, with the express purpose of bringing down inflation by reducing money growth. Still, during most of the 1970s, the Fed explicitly adopted the fed funds rate as the operating target used to hit intermediate (monetary aggregates) targets. If the rate of growth of the money supply were above the Fed's target, it would raise the fed funds rate target. Unfortunately, the 1970s saw "stagflation" so the Fed was continually in inflation-fighting mode.

In October 1979, the new Chairman, Paul Volcker, announced a major change of policy. The Fed would henceforth use the growth rate of M1 as its intermediate target, with reserves as the operating target, while it would allow the fed funds rate to rise as high as necessary to allow achievement of this goal (Fazzari and Minsky 1984). The Fed would calculate the total reserves consistent with its money target, then subtract existing borrowed reserves to obtain a non-borrowed reserve operating target. However, in practice, when the Fed did not provide sufficient reserves in open market operations (as it hit its non-borrowed reserve target), banks would simply turn to the discount window, causing borrowed reserves to rise (and, in turn, causing the Fed to miss its total reserve target). Because required reserves are always calculated with a lag (Moore 1984, Wray 1998a), the Fed could not refuse to provide required reserves at the discount window, thus, it found it could not control total reserves. Further, the rate of growth of M1 exploded beyond targets in spite of consistently high interest rates that resulted from the Fed's tight policy (the fed funds rate reached above 19% during April 1980 and hit 20% in January 1981). So the Fed found it could hit neither its reserve nor its M1 targets. The attempt to target nonborrowed reserves ended in 1982 while the attempt to hit M1 targets was abandoned in 1986 (Meulendyke 1989; Fazzari and Minsky 1984). Still, the Fed continued to announce and tried without success to hit M2 targets during the rest of the 1980s. The attempt to target growth of monetary aggregates finally came to an official end in 1993 after more than a decade of miserable failure.

The fate of Monetarist doctrine in academic circles nearly mirrors its fate in policy-making. Over the course of the 1960s and 1970s, Monetarism gradually rose in favor, from virtual obscurity to accepted doctrine. As "Keynesianism" lost its following in the 1970s—largely due to stagflation—use of fiscal policy to tame the business cycle lost credence. Hence, in the 1980s, Monetarism, rejection of fiscal policy, and exclusive use of monetary policy in a countercyclical manner became increasingly accepted among academicians. By the mid 1980s, it would not have been far wrong to claim that academic macroeconomists were all Monetarists. At the end of the decade, however, Monetarist doctrine was in question because the Monetarist experiment at controlling the money supply had been such a disaster in the US (and also in the UK) (B. Friedman 1988). That is a remarkably quick turn-around for accepted doctrine.

Both theorists and policy makers quickly abandoned the belief that the Fed could control the money supply and that the money supply determines the rate of spending and thus of inflation. Paradoxically, a "cult of Greenspan" (the Board of Governors chairman who had replaced Volcker in 1987) developed in the US and abroad. While no one could put into words exactly how he single-handedly whipped inflation and created a "Goldilocks" economy (neither too hot to cause inflation nor too cold to cause unemployment) in the last half of the 1990s, virtually all analysts came to believe that the Fed somehow is responsible for not only keeping inflation in check, but also for keeping real GDP growth at potential. The Greenspan-led Fed became so bold as to announce immediately after each Federal Open Market Committee (FOMC) meeting exactly what the fed funds rate target would be—something the Fed had never before done. The financial press deconstructed every word uttered by Chairman Greenspan in the 1990s, trying to anticipate the Fed's next action. Whether he hinted that inflation was around some corner or other, or that the stock market suffered from "irrational exuberance", or that the "New Economy" offered rapid productivity growth as far as the eye could see, every Greenspan speech moved financial markets. The Greenspan Fed changed interest rate targets frequently—first up to fight invisible but incipient inflation, then down to forestall a slump. Every quarter-point change of the fed funds rate target was supposed to have a monumentally important impact on production, prices, and employment. Every improvement of the unemployment rate and every downward click of inflation was proof positive of Greenspan's guiding hand. While Al Gore was said to have claimed to have invented the internet, everyone knew that Al Greenspan had suckled and nurtured NASDAQ and the New Economy. His efforts did not go unrewarded: he was reverently treated in Bob Woodward's *Maestro* (the title says it all); and he won the highly valued "Enron Prize," funded by a high-tech energy speculation firm that went bust during the Fall of 2001 in the most spectacular and expensive bankruptcy in US history—at just about the precise moment that Greenspan had lost his luster.

While Greenspan's fall from grace has not, as yet, been quite so impressive as that of NASDAQ and Enron, and while it has lagged the demise of Monetarist doctrine, it may well be as complete by the time this volume hits the streets. As of late winter 2002, the stock market has fallen significantly and is poised for collapse; the Goldilocks New Economy is long dead—dead and gone; every component of Greenspan's highly touted IT sector is reeling; unemployment is rising faster than at any time since the Great Depression; household net wealth has fallen—for the first time ever in US history; and the private sector is suffering under record debt levels as bank customers default, as bank profits fall, and as we move down the path to massive and widespread bank insolvency. The Fed has lowered interest rates a dozen times, or so—to no avail. No doubt Greenspan feels like the guest who has overstayed his welcome and regrets the fact that he did not retire with his saintly wings intact in 2000 and thereby avoid the fall from Maestro to dot-com sucker in a matter of months. His speeches are now but an irrelevant embarrassment, having no measurable impact on financial markets. The most articulate and inflation hawkish of the Fed's governors, Larry Meyer, has refused to serve another term—preferring the relatively certain and carefree life of a private economic forecaster over serving as a member of a thoroughly discredited Fed Board of Governors.

## IS THERE AN ALTERNATIVE APPROACH TO MONEY?

Where to begin? Institutionalists reject the entire orthodox corpus, including the view of money advanced, the pseudo history adopted, the theory of the role that money plays in the economy, and orthodox policy analysis and prescription. In the orthodox story, money comes out of markets, created by barterers to reduce transactions costs. Above all a handy medium of exchange, money plays no *essential* role in orthodox theory—our economy would function in substantially the same manner even if we were to ban money from the system and return to barter. Indeed, modern technology should allow barter-based markets to function without entailing many transactions costs of the sort that money's creation was supposed to have eliminated. At most, orthodox economists debate about the conditions under which money might have some short-run non-neutrality; in the long run, according to orthodoxy, money's neutrality is assured. Finally, as discussed above, most mainstream theoretical approaches presume that money is under control of the "monetary authorities"—in theory, if not in practice. Only Austrians and Real Business Cycle Theory (RBC) aficionados deviate from this "exogenous" money approach, although Austrians do so in order to imagine a utopia of "free" banks without an evil government or central bank, while RBC theorists do so in order to make money "super-duper" neutral. Neither fringe approach warrants further inquiry.

In contrast, most heterodox economists, including institutionalists, adopt an "endogenous" money approach similar to the views of the Banking School examined above. Privately issued money (mostly bank deposits today) is issued only on demand, that is, only because someone has deposited cash or is willing to take out a loan. The latter activity has been concisely described by Post Keynesians as "loans make deposits" because when a bank accepts a borrower's IOU it simultaneously creates a bank deposit. The idea that privately created money could be "excessive" is ludicrous, for as the Banking School explained, any excess would "reflux" to banks. Those with "extra" bank deposits would retire loans, withdraw cash, or buy something (the latter of which just shifts the deposits about; the first two activities reduce bank deposits in the aggregate). It is literally impossible for banks to force excess money onto the economy because there must be willing borrowers in order for banks to create deposits.

The second important point made by Post Keynesians is that "deposits make reserves," reversing the interpretation of the deposit multiplier. They emphasize that reserves cannot be a discretionary variable from the point of view of the central bank. There are a number of reasons for this. Many, including Basil Moore (1988), have argued that because required reserves (in those nations that have them) are always calculated with some lag, based upon deposits that are "history" (issued by banks at some point in the past), banks cannot adjust deposits to cope with a position of insufficient reserves to meet requirements. This means that only reserves can be adjusted—so that a bank caught short will turn to the fed funds market. However, if the system as a whole is short, at least one bank will not be able to meet requirements. In practice, central banks always and automatically lend reserves to such banks, booking a shortfall as an overdraft or loan of reserves. If they did not, they would force the bank to fail to meet legal mandates. Further, if the central bank did not provide desired reserves, banks with insufficient reserve levels would bid the fed funds rate above target. (Note that the reverse is also true: if the system as a whole has excessive reserves, the fed funds rate is bid below target—at the limit it will fall nearly to zero.) Hence, an orderly fed funds market requires that the central bank provide/drain reserves to eliminate deficiencies or surpluses.

In addition, timely and orderly check clearing among banks requires that the Fed automatically provide reserves as required. Banks use reserves for net clearing of checks (recall the discussion of a mono-reserve system). If the Fed refused to routinely make up for aggregate reserve shortfalls, the payments system could not operate smoothly. Indeed, if the Fed stopped lending reserves as needed, checks would bounce. If a bank was suspected of nearing a position of a shortage of reserves, other banks would refuse to accept its checks. It is because the Fed always credits reserves to the account of a receiving bank without first ensuring that the bank upon which a check is drawn has sufficient reserves that bank checks always clear at par. Indeed, this was a primary purpose of the creation of the Federal Reserve System, before which bank notes commonly circulated below par. Finally, payments to the Treasury by bank customers (tax payments, mostly) are also made using bank reserves. Imagine the problems that would be created if a taxpayer's check to the IRS bounced because her bank did not have sufficient reserves! Again, in practice the Fed always provides reserves to banks as needed to meet reserve requirements, to clear checks among banks, and to make payments by check to the Treasury.

If the central bank cannot control reserves in a discretionary manner, and if the deposit multiplier is reversed, and if the supply of privately created money is essentially determined by the demand for loans, then what *can* the central bank control? Leaving aside regulatory and supervisory issues for the moment, the central bank only has one policy tool: the overnight interbank lending rate, or fed funds rate (called the bank rate in the UK). This rate can be hit with a great degree of accuracy, indeed, as mentioned above, the Greenspan Fed began to simply announce what the target would be, and the fed funds rate would nearly instantly move toward the target. All the Fed must do to keep the actual rate at the target is to ensure that banks have the quantity of reserves they require or desire; if the rate rises above/falls below the target, the Fed adds/drains reserves until the rate aligns with the target. While some at the Fed would like for us to believe it is all very complicated and hence that it requires teams of highly trained economists to provide detailed analyses and forecasts of future demand for reserves, that is mostly obfuscation to protect budgets, jobs, and the Fed's reputation.

Turning to the "nature" and "origins" of money, institutionalists reject the orthodox notion that money is essentially a commodity that functions primarily as a medium of exchange, invented to reduce transactions costs. Institutionalists and other heterodox economists insist that money is "social" in its nature. As Ingham puts it "money *necessarily* consists in *social relations* between economic agents and between them and a monetary 'authority. . . ." (Ingham 2000, 19) Or, as Neale argues: "all monies are *parts of larger systems* of economic and social relationships" (Neale 1976, 4). Further, Neale warns that "Despite the fact that many a text on money says that money originated in the inconveniences of barter, that money was invented as a medium of exchange. . .neither historical evidence nor argument by analogy from contemporary non-literate societies lends support to this speculative history" (Neale 1976, 8-9) .

Admittedly, any story of the origins of money is necessarily speculative for two reasons. First, we must decide what "social relation" from the past qualifies as something we are willing to label "money." Neale argues that it is best to think of "monies" rather than "money" because those social relations vary widely by society. He emphasizes that in most pre-capitalist societies the range of social relations associated with use of a "special purpose money" was much narrower than those we now associate with "general purpose money." For example, we would now likely include medium of exchange, unit of account, means of debt settlement, and store of value as functions that are served today by general purpose money. However, in previous societies (and in non-literate societies today) there have been "special purpose monies" that served only one or two of these functions but not the others. The second problem is that it is possible and even likely that the origins of money lie in a very distant past for which we have no easily interpretable records; indeed, many believe that money predates writing. (It has long been believed that writing was invented to keep track of nominal debts, although the history of writing is probably as complex as the history of money. See Schmandt-Besserat 1989.) Hence we will probably never have a completely satisfying story of the origins of money.

Still, it is tempting to speculate on money's origins. There are three plausible alternatives to the orthodox story. Heinsohn and Steiger (1983) argue that money developed not out of a barter economy but when private property and loans developed. Following Keynes, they emphasize that early monetary units were based on a specific number of grains of wheat or barley. (Keynes 1982, 233-36) Later, metals (such as iron, copper, silver, or gold) were used as money, with the value denominated in those grain units of measurement. According to their argument, the first money was created when private property (so many units of grain) was loaned with the expectation of payment of a greater sum of grain in the future. Eventually, grains of wheat or barley would be used as a universal equivalent to measure value of all types of alienable private property to reduce transactions costs, acting as a unit of account in all creditor-debtor relations. Gradually, representative money, in the form of metal but still denominated in these grain weight units, could be loaned, used as a medium of exchange, and used to settle debts. Hence, Heinsohn and Steiger focus on money as a unit of account developed in these early loan agreements, and the "thing" used as money is important primarily because it represents the loan agreement that is denominated in the unit of account.

A second approach has been advanced by Hudson (2001), who has developed an alternative thesis for the origins of the money of account in Babylonia. He argues that money originated within the temple and palace communities for internal accounting purposes. Like Heinsohn and Steiger, his story also emphasizes the importance of loans, however, he argues that early loans were made by the temple and palace communities to the "external" sector. Thus, rather than focusing on private property and loans between individuals that gradually become standardized in a grain unit of account, Hudson believes the unit of account was created within the early bureaucracies. Clearly, his argument focuses more on the social nature of the origins of money and hence is probably more appealing to institutionalists.

A third approach has been developed by the great numismatist, Grierson, and elaborated in Goodhart (1989, 1998) and Wray (1998). According to this view, money evolved out of the pre-civilized practice of *wergeld*; or to put it more simply, money originated not from a pre-money market system but rather from the penal system (Grierson 1977, 1979; Goodhart 1998). An elaborate system of fines for transgressions was developed in tribal society. Over time, authorities transformed this system of fines paid to victims for *crimes* to a system that generated a variety of payments *to* the state (Innes 1932). Until recently, *fines* made up a large part of the revenues of all states (Maddox 1769). Gradually, fees and taxes as well as rents and interest were added to the list of payments that had to be made to authority. To be clear, this authority should be seen as a gradually evolving institution—from early temples, to palace communities, to feudal kings, and finally to democratically elected representative governments—with varying degrees of sovereign power. All that was required was some sort of authority able to levy obligations on a population—anything from fines or tithes to fees and taxes. While *wergeld* payments did not require a unit of account (the fines were assessed in the form of particular items or services to be delivered to victims), payments to the authority were gradually standardized, measured in a money of account.

This approach has been called the "Chartalist" or "taxes-drive-money" approach. It is also closely related to Knapp's "state money" approach. Briefly, this view emphasizes the important role played by "government" in the origins and evolution of money. More specifically, it is believed that the state (or any other authority able to impose an obligation—whether that authority is autocratic, democratic, or divine) imposes an obligation in the form of a generalized, social unit of account—a money—used for measuring the obligation. The next important step consists of movement from a specific obligation—say, an hour of labor or a spring lamb that must be delivered—to a generalized, money obligation. This does not require the pre-existence of markets, and, indeed, almost certainly predates them. Once the authorities can levy such an obligation, they can then name exactly what can be delivered to fulfill this obligation. They do this by denominating those things that can be delivered, in other words, by pricing them. To do this, they must first "define" or "name" the unit of account. This resolves the conundrum faced by methodological individualists and emphasizes the social nature of money and markets.

Note that the state can choose anything it likes to function as the "money thing" denominated in the money of account, and, as Knapp emphasized, can change "the thing" any time it likes: "Validity by proclamation is not bound to any material" and the material can be changed to any other so long as the state announces a conversion rate (say, so many grains of gold for so many ounces of silver) (Knapp 1924, 30). What Knapp called the State money stage begins when the state chooses the unit of account and names the thing that it accepts in payment of obligations to itself—at the nominal value it assigns to the thing. The final step occurs when the state actually issues the money-thing it accepts. In (almost) all modern developed nations, the state accepts the currency issued by the treasury (in the US, coins), plus notes issued by the central bank (Federal Reserve notes—green paper—in the US), plus bank reserves (again, liabilities of the central bank)—that is, the monetary base or high powered money (HPM). The material from which the money thing issued by the state is produced is not important (whether it is a gold coin, a base metal coin, paper notes, or even numbers on a computer tape at the central bank). No matter what it is made of, the state must announce the nominal value of the money thing it has issued (that is to say, the value at which the money-thing is accepted in meeting obligations to the state).

Many orthodox economists are "metallists" (as Goodhart, 1998, calls them), who argue that until this century, the value of money was determined by the gold used in producing coins or by the gold that backed up paper notes. However, in spite of the amount of ink spilled about the gold standard, it was actually in place for only a relatively brief instant. Typically, the money-thing issued by the authorities was not gold-money nor was there any promise to convert the money-thing to gold (or any other valuable commodity). Indeed, throughout most of Europe's history, the money-thing issued by the state was the hazelwood tally stick. Other money-things included clay tablets, leather and base metal coins, and paper certificates. Why would the population accept otherwise "worthless" sticks, clay, base metal, leather, or paper? Because the state agreed to accept the same "worthless" items in payment of obligations to the state. Contrary to orthodox thinking, then, the value of the money-thing issued by the state was not determined by its intrinsic value, but rather by the nominal value set by the state at its own pay offices (at which it accepted payment of fees, fines, and taxes).

In the orthodox story, barter is replaced by use of a medium of exchange; due to its inherent characteristics, barterers soon settle on gold (or another precious metal) as the most efficient medium of exchange. In order to reduce transactions costs involved in assessing purity and weight, this metal is stamped and coined. However, it has long been established that the first coins were issued in Lydia and East Greece, probably no earlier than the third or fourth quarter of the seventh century BC, and long after other forms of complex financial instruments, local markets, and long distance trade had been established. If precious metal coins were indeed invented to reduce transactions costs, one wonders why it took so long to discover them. Further, while coins might have been important to the Greek world and perhaps to the Roman world, they played a relatively unimportant role throughout most of European history. Numismatists, such as Kraay (1964) have challenged the economistic thinking of orthodoxy by arguing that coins were invented to standardize payments made by and to the state.

In a detailed study of the origins of coinage in Greece during the seventh century BC, Kurke (1999) links the creation of coins to "a seventh/sixth century crisis of justice and unfair distribution of property," that was eventually decided in favor of a democratically-leaning city state against a hostile elite (Kurke 1999 p. 13). In her view, "the minting of coin would represent the state's assertion of its ultimate authority to constitute and regulate value in all the spheres in which general-purpose money operated simultaneously—economic, social, political, and religious. Thus, state-issued coinage as a universal equivalent, like the civic *agora* in which it circulated, symbolized the merger in a single token or site of many different domains of value, all under the final authority of the city" (Kurke 1999, 13). By tying the invention of coinage to the special circumstances of Greece during that period, Kurke's analysis makes it clear why coins were so unimportant to other societies, before and since. Further, as Kurke makes clear, since coins are nothing more than tokens of the city's authority, they could have been produced from any material. The choice of gold should be viewed as something of a coincidence, resulting from the particular hierarchy of metals in elite gift exchange extant in Greece at that time. In other words, and in contrast to the orthodox story, there is nothing inherent in gold (or silver, or copper) that guarantees its adoption as the money thing. A state is theoretically free to name anything it wants, although the historical circumstances might dictate that one thing is preferred over others.

Once the state has created the unit of account and named that which can be delivered to fulfill obligations to the state, it has generated the necessary pre-conditions for development of markets. All the evidence suggests that in the earliest stages the authorities provided a full price list, setting prices for each of the most important products and services. Once prices in money were established, it was a short leap to creation of markets. This stands orthodoxy on its head, by reversing the order: first money and prices, then markets and money-things (rather than barter-based markets and relative prices, and then numeraire money and nominal prices). The next step was the recognition by government that it did not have to rely on the mix of goods and services provided by taxpayers, but could issue the money-thing to purchase the mix it desired, then receive the same money thing in the tax payments by subjects/citizens. This would further the development of markets because those with tax liabilities but without the goods and services government wished to buy would have to produce for market to obtain the means of paying obligations to the state. As Heinsohn and Steiger (1983) say, the market is the place to which one turns for earning the means of debt settlement, including the means of tax settlement. This is quite different from the orthodox view that markets develop so that individuals may maximize utility by trading consumables.

The final theoretical topic to be tackled concerns money's supposed neutrality. The discussion thus far should make it clear that money cannot be neutral, as it is not simply a medium of exchange invented to lubricate market exchange. If, as I have hypothesized, money originated as a means to move resources to the public or state sector, then it clearly had a "real" impact. If, as Heinsohn and Steiger speculate, money was invented in private loan contracts, it played a crucial role in an important social relationship—that between debtor and creditor. Further, if one views the market as a place for earning the means of settling debts (both private debts and tax debts), rather than as a place to which one turns to increase utility through mutually beneficial trades, then one sees the market as a fundamentally monetized institution. Regardless of the origins of money and markets, institutionalists have always distinguished between the technical aspects of production and the pecuniary considerations involved in producing for markets. In the modern capitalist economy, the primary purpose of production is not to exchange for other consumables, but to "make money"—that is, to sell at a profit. The most famous characterization of capitalist production is Marx's M-C-M', according to which the capitalist begins with money (M) to produce commodities (C) to sell for more money (M'). Keynes advanced what he called the "monetary theory of production", emphasizing the same point; Dillard (1980) explicitly adopted Keynes's terminology, as have many institutionalists. (See also Wray 1993.) If modern production begins and ends with money, money cannot be neutral. Indeed, rather than arguing that money is a veil that hides "real" activity (as Friedman does), one might more accurately argue that money is the "real" variable that motivates production while the "real" output that results is just a veil that obscures the true purpose of individual decision making of capitalist production.

## AN ALTERNATIVE VIEW OF FISCAL AND MONETARY POLICY

In the orthodox approach, the government must tax, borrow, or "print money" in order to spend. If the government borrows, that is likely to place upward pressure on interest rates, "crowding out" investment. If it prints money, that is likely to generate inflation. While most economists do not insist that government continuously balance its budget, limiting its spending to its tax revenue, they do believe that a perpetual deficit is to be avoided. Not only would it cause interest rates or inflation to rise (depending on whether the deficit were financed by borrowing or money creation), it could also eventually cause government insolvency and default on its obligations. During the last two decades of the twentieth century, "fiscal discipline" was increasingly imposed in most developed nations and in many developing nations (especially those that had fallen under the control of the IMF and World Bank). Indeed, several developed nations (including Japan, the US, Canada, the UK, and Australia) actually ran significant surpluses in some years during the final decade of the century. This was almost universally cheered by economists, as an antidote to the budget deficits that had been common in the post war years.

Institutionalists have always rejected such notions. They have always taken the pragmatic approach perhaps best espoused in Lerner's functional finance approach: "The central idea is that government fiscal policy, its spending and taxing, its borrowing and repayment of loans, its issue of new money, and its withdrawal of money, shall all be undertaken with an eye only to the results of these actions on the economy and not to any established traditional doctrine about what is sound or unsound" (Lerner 1943, 39). Further, institutionalists have recognized that the notion that government borrowing "crowds out" private borrowing is really based on either the loanable funds argument or on the supposition that the supply of money is fixed. Foster (1981) was among the first to recognize how revolutionary was Keynes's argument that investment *creates* an equivalent amount of saving; similarly, a government deficit must also create an equivalent amount of saving. Hence, a government deficit cannot absorb saving that would otherwise have gone to finance investment. Further, given the endogenous money arguments provided above, it is clear that government borrowing could not reduce the amount of "money" available for firms to borrow from banks.

Banks create money when they make loans, and no amount of government deficit spending would reduce bank ability to create deposits for firms to use to finance investment.

These are powerful arguments, even if they appear rather simple. However, they can be strengthened by adding the Chartalist or taxes-drive-money approach. When a modern government spends, it issues a check drawn on the treasury; its liabilities increase by the amount of the expenditure and its assets increase (in the case of a purchase of a good produced by the private sector) or some other liabilities are reduced (in the case of a social transfer). The recipient of the check will almost certainly cash it at a bank, in which case either the recipient will withdraw currency, or (more likely) the recipient's bank account will be credited. In the former case, the bank's reserves are first increased and then are reduced by the same amount. In the latter case, bank reserves are credited by the Fed in the amount of the increase of the deposit account. The bank reserves carried on the books as the bank's asset and as the Fed's liability are nothing less than a claim on government-issued money, or, a leveraging of High Powered Money (HPM). In other words, Treasury spending by check really is the equivalent of "printing money" in the sense that it increases the supply of HPM. Unless bank required reserves happened to increase by an equivalent amount, the banking system will typically find itself with excess reserves after the treasury has spent, creating HPM.

The important thing to notice is that the Treasury can spend before and without regard to either previous receipt of taxes or prior bond sales. In the US, taxes are received throughout the year (although not uniformly as tax payments are concentrated around April 15 and other quarterly due dates). These are mostly paid into special tax accounts held at private commercial banks (Bell 2000). It is true that the Treasury transfers funds from these private bank accounts to its account at the Fed when it wishes to spend, but this is really a reserve maintenance operation designed to minimize effects on reserves that result when the Treasury issues checks. When the Treasury spends, bank reserves increase by approximately the same amount (less only cash withdrawals) so that the simultaneous transfer from tax accounts is used to neutralize impacts on bank reserves. These additions to/subtractions from reserves are carefully monitored and regulated by coordination between the Fed and the Treasury, but this should not confuse analysts about the processes at work. The Treasury spends by having the Fed emit HPM; that HPM is simply a liability that can be increased at will. The Treasury does not need to transfer deposits from private banks to the Fed in order to spend; it needs to do so simultaneously with spending only to minimize reserve effects.

On the other hand, tax payments by households lead to a reserve drain as the Treasury submits the checks to the Fed for clearing, at which point the Fed debits the bank's reserves. Things would be much simpler and more transparent if tax receipts and Treasury spending were perfectly synchronized. In that case, the Treasury's spending would increase reserves, and the tax payments would reduce them. If the government ran a balanced budget there would be no net impact on reserves. In this case there would be no need for the complex coordination between the Fed and Treasury using tax and loan accounts because there would be no reserve effects so long as the budget were balanced.

However, let us suppose that the timing were synchronized but that spending exceeded tax revenues so that a budget deficit resulted. This means that after all is said and done, there has been a net injection of reserves. It is possible that the extra reserves created happen to coincide with growing bank demand for reserves—in which case the Treasury and Fed need do nothing more. More probably, the net injection of reserves resulting from budget deficits would lead to excess reserves for the banking system as a whole. The receiving banks would offer them in the fed funds market, but would find no takers. This would cause the fed funds rate to begin to fall below the Fed's target, inducing the Fed to drain reserves either through an open market sale or by reducing its discounts. When the Treasury runs a sustained deficit, quarter after quarter and year after year, the Fed would find it was continually intervening to sell bonds; obviously, it would eventually run out of bonds to sell. This is why, over the longer run, responsibility for bond sales designed to drain excess reserves from the system must fall to the Treasury—which faces no limit to its own sales of bonds as it can create new bonds as needed.

While it may sound strange, we conclude that Treasury bond sales are not a borrowing operation at all, but are in fact nothing but a reserve draining operation. This becomes apparent when one recognizes that the Treasury cannot really sell bonds unless banks already have excess reserves, or unless the Fed stands by ready to provide reserves the banks will need to buy the bonds. If the Treasury typically tried to first "borrow" by selling bonds *before* it spent, it would be trying to drain reserves it will create only *once* it spends. As it drained required or desired reserves, it would cause the fed funds rate to rise above the Fed's target—inducing an open market purchase and injection of reserves by the Fed.

Another way of putting it is that the government spends by issuing IOUs, and the private sector uses those IOUs to pay taxes and buy government bonds. Obviously, if government spending were the only source of these IOUs, the private sector could not pay taxes or buy bonds *before* the government provided them through its spending. In the real world, government spending is the main, but not the only source, of the IOUs needed by the private sector to pay taxes and buy government bonds. In addition, the central bank provides its IOUs through discounts or open market operations, and these IOUs are perfect substitutes for Treasury IOUs. Unfortunately, most economists have become confused about all this because they do not understand the nature of the coordination between the Fed and the Treasury. Indeed, most economists do not understand that monetary policy has nothing to do with the quantity of money, but is concerned only with the overnight interest rate. The central bank's provision of, or removal of, reserves is nondiscretionary and is always merely in response to actions of the Treasury or the private sector. On the other hand, fiscal operations always impact reserves, and government deficits always lead to a net injection of reserves. Boulding came close to capturing this when he said:

> It's just as true as it is funny,
> That Deficits increase our money;
> In understanding this there lies
> The power of States to Stabilize.
> (Boulding 1958, 183)

The purpose of government bond sales is not to borrow reserves—a liability of the government—but is instead designed to offer an interest-earning alternative to undesired non-interest-earning bank reserves that would otherwise drive the fed funds rate toward zero. Note that if the Fed paid interest on excess reserves, the Treasury would never need to sell bonds because the overnight interest rate could never fall below the rate paid by the Fed on excess reserves. Note also that in spite of the widespread, orthodox, belief that government deficit spending places upward pressure on interest rates, it would actually cause the overnight rate to fall to zero if the Treasury and Fed did not coordinate efforts to drain the created excess reserves from the system. (For proof of this, note that for many years after the mid 1990s, the overnight interest rate in Japan was kept at zero, in spite of government deficits that reached 8% of GDP, merely by keeping some excess reserves in the banking system.) On the other hand, budget surpluses drain reserves from the system, causing a shortage that would drive up the fed funds rate if the Fed and Treasury did not coordinate actions to buy and/or retire government debt. Needless to say, orthodoxy has got the interest rate effects of government budgets exactly backwards.

One could think of government bonds as nothing more than HPM that pays interest—indeed, as described above, the government would never need to sell bonds if the Fed paid interest on excess bank reserves, or if the Fed's interest rate target were zero. Bond sales are not really a borrowing operation but are instead an interest rate maintenance operation. Obviously, however, banks are not the only entities in the private sector that would like to earn interest by holding government IOUs. Indeed, households and firms generally like to accumulate a portion of their net wealth in the form of interest-earning government debt. In a growing economy, the outstanding stock of government IOUs (both interest-earning and non-interest earning) will need to grow to keep pace with the demands of the private sector. This means that a government deficit should be the "normal," expected, situation. In contrast, sustained budget surpluses can be achieved only by draining the government IOUs held as net wealth. This is why government budget surpluses usually cannot be sustained for long—they reduce the private sector's disposable income (because taxes exceed government spending) and destroy private net wealth (by draining government IOUs), and hence set off tremendous deflationary impacts on the economy.

## MONETARY POLICY RECOMMENDATIONS

The main monetary policy recommendation that follows from this analysis is that central banks should abandon any pretense that they can influence the quantity of reserves or the quantity of money privately created. They should admit that they only set the overnight interest rate—the fed funds rate in the US. This of course sets the base interest rate; short-term interest rates on government debt are determined rather directly by the fed funds rate because the banking system uses government securities as a substitute for the fed funds market to adjust reserves at the individual bank level. Longer-term government debt is priced more complexly because it must include potential capital gains and losses that result from future changes to the fed funds rate target. When a central bank frequently changes its targets wildly—as the Fed has increasingly done since the mid 1960s—a great deal of uncertainty about future policy must be built into the pricing of longer term assets. Indeed, this is the primary reason that markets deconstructed every word uttered by Chairman Greenspan during the 1990s, trying to anticipate policy moves that would impact asset prices.

It is very difficult to see why a great deal of uncertainty about Fed interest targets is desirable. Wild swings of asset prices tend to reinforce uncertainty and encourage speculative behavior. As Keynes argued, "Speculators may do no harm as bubbles on a steady stream of enterprise. But the position is serious when enterprise becomes the bubble on a whirlpool of speculation. When the capital development of a country becomes a by-product of the activities of a casino, the job is likely to be ill-done." (Keynes 1964, p. 159) An "active" Fed that continually tries to surprise markets with interest rate adjustments promotes the casinos over enterprise. As Tooke argued in the quote above, "[T]he greater or less liability to variation in the rate of interest constitutes, in the next degree only to the preservation of the convertibility of the paper and the solvency of banks, the most important consideration in the regulation of our banking system" (Tooke 1959, 124). As the Fed's propensity to destabilize the interest rate has increased since the mid 1960s, speculative behavior has increased and economic performance has suffered. Obviously, other factors have also contributed to this and we cannot say with certainty that greater instability of interest rates has been the decisive factor.

The orthodox response is that the Fed must move interest rates countercyclically in order to help to fine-tune the economy—to fight inflation in booms and lower unemployment in recessions—hence, even if this contributes to greater instability of asset prices, the Fed cannot abandon its responsibility. There are, however, strong reasons to doubt that Fed policy has much impact on either unemployment or inflation. As discussed above, low interest rate policy in a slump does not seem to have much effect on spending—for fairly obvious reasons, consumers are reluctant to borrow when they fear losing their jobs, and firms are unlikely to invest as sales are falling.

Furthermore, the interest rate is really a redistributive variable, as for every interest payment there is an interest receipt. When the Fed lowers interest rates this does indeed benefit new borrowers and anyone with existing debt that can be reset at a lower rate. However, all those who rely on interest payments for income (particularly pensioners and financial institutions) suffer as rates fall. Interest income has increased greatly in the postwar period as the population has aged, and as workers have built up pension funds and other savings for their retirement years. The conventional argument is that interest payments represent a transfer from mostly low and middle income earners to the rich, hence, lower interest rates redistribute income from those with a low marginal propensity to consume toward those with a high propensity to consume. There is surprisingly little work on this, however. With the aging of western societies, the redistribution that results today from rising interest rates is probably mostly from firms and younger workers (especially from new homeowners with mortgages) toward elderly persons. It is not clear that this necessarily reduces the overall propensity to consume. More importantly, in a modern economy with a large outstanding stock of government debt, the redistribution is largely from government to households and firms. Indeed, if the stock of government debt were large relative to national income and to private debt, it is possible that lower interest rates actually depress spending because of the effect on private sector incomes as government interest payments fall. It is conceivable that Japan reached such a situation in the late 1990s, when short term interest rates effectively reached zero.

Can central banks stabilize the overnight interest rate? Yes, so long as they do not try to peg currency exchange rates. Recall from the discussion above that during the Great Depression the Fed worried that if it kept interest rates too low, the US would lose reserves of gold. Exchange rates are fixed on a gold standard and hence only adjustments of the interest rate could stem a "run" on dollar-denominated assets. In the modern world, countries do not operate on a gold standard, and most countries have adopted floating exchange rates. Hence, if the US were to keep interest rates lower than those abroad, it is possible that from time to time there might be downward pressure on the dollar. So long as the US allows the dollar to fall, it can maintain low interest rates without losing international reserves. Note that low interest rates do not necessarily cause currency depreciation—Japan's currency has remained exceedingly strong (many would say it was overvalued) even with overnight rates at zero. Exchange rates, like long term interest rates, are complexly determined and the overnight interest rate is only one factor that goes into their determination. However, in any event, so long as exchange rates are indeed flexible, a nation's overnight interest rate is "exogenous" and can be set anywhere the central bank wants to put it.

What else *should* a central bank do? We have dealt with the issues that are most closely related to orthodox views on monetary policy reserves, money aggregates, inflation, and interest rates. In addition, we have addressed Bagehot's recommendation that the central bank must operate as a lender of last resort—still among the most important functions of the central bank.

There is also a wide array of other important central bank functions:

*Setting required reserve ratios*: While orthodox economists believe that required reserve ratios give the central bank leverage over private money creation, we have seen this is false. Others believe that maintenance of reserves makes banks safer because they hold a liquid asset. However, if a central bank stands ready to discount eligible assets, a bank does not need to hold reserves for liquid purposes. Indeed, it could be argued that required reserves in excess of the level of reserves that would be held voluntarily for clearing purposes acts like a tax on banks (forcing them to hold assets that do not earn a return). If this lowers bank profitability it could actually reduce bank safety and soundness. The UK does not have legal reserve ratios; Canada has recently moved to a system in which the required reserve ratio is zero. On balance, there is probably little argument in favor of retaining legal requirements, and in practice, legal ratios in the US are now so low that they probably are not very binding especially given all the innovations banks use to reduce requirements (such as sweep accounts).

Finally, as discussed above, government spending creates bank reserves, and reserve requirements force banks to hold non-earning reserves rather than earning government bonds. Hence, one might conclude that reserve requirements lower government "borrowing" costs (a point frequently made by populist groups such as COMER in Canada). However, the government can have any "borrowing" cost it wants, including zero, merely by setting the fed funds rate target at that level. It seems a bit strange to argue that banks, alone, should earn zero if the government has decided that everyone else can earn a positive return by holding government liabilities. Alternatively, as discussed above, the Fed could pay interest on reserves—in which case the difference between bank reserves and treasury bills disappears. Equivalently, the Fed could allow banks to count interest-earning government liabilities as reserves to meet requirements.

*Credit Controls*: Many support use of the Fed to try to channel credit to some areas, and to discourage it from others. Some have argued for asset-based reserve requirements to discourage banks from holding some kinds of assets. For example, if the Fed wanted to encourage home mortgage loans but discourage commercial real estate loans, it could require reserves against the latter, but exclude home mortgages from reserve requirements. The same sort of result can be obtained by risk-weighting assets and requiring greater net equity ratios against riskier assets (as is done with the Basle Accord), or simply by imposing a tax on bank purchases of riskier assets. All such requirements work by reducing the relative return on unfavored assets. Others have emphasized that central banks can impose margin requirements on borrowers, requiring them to put up liquid assets as collateral—raising the cost of borrowing. In the US, the Fed has the authority to change margin requirements on stock purchases, so that buyers are constrained in the percent of borrowed funds they may use to purchase stocks. During the NASDAQ boom after the mid 1990s, the Fed refused to raise margin requirements, although some believe this would have constrained the boom.

*Encourage provision of financial services:* Relatedly, many American analysts want to use the Fed and other monetary authorities (including other regulatory agencies such as the FDIC, the Comptroller of the Currency, and state banking regulators) to encourage an increased supply of credit to areas thought to be underserved. Most importantly, some studies have shown that financial institutions have traditionally discriminated against certain groups (racial minorities, women) and have "red-lined" some neighborhoods (drawn a "red line" around neighborhoods to which they would not provide many services, including loans). Note that redlining is not exactly the same as discrimination—while red-lined areas typically were neighborhoods with a high proportion of minority residents, even white males living in them would be denied banking services simply because they lived in red-lined areas. The Community Reinvestment Act in the US forced banks to report on the services provided in their own self-defined business area, and many analysts believe this has played an important role in reducing discrimination and red-lining activity. In addition, it has often been believed that more credit needed to be supplied to finance certain activities deemed to have significant social worth. This led to creation of Government Sponsored Enterprises (essentially institutional arrangements that put government guarantees behind loans initiated by private lenders) that have targeted lending to favored groups such as homeowners (Fannie Mae), students (Sallie Mae), farmers (Freddie Mac), and veterans. (Stanton 1991)

*Supervision and regulation:* Many economists have argued that bank regulation and supervision is a necessary corollary to central bank lender of last resort activity as well as to implicit and explicit government guarantees (such as those offered through FDIC and the Government Sponsored Enterprises). If government intervenes to prevent or contain failures, then adverse incentives are created. While all modern, developed, economies regulate and supervise financial institutions, the US is fairly unusual in the degree to which responsibilities are shared by the Fed, the FDIC (and in the past, the now-defunct FSLIC), the FHLBB, the Comptroller, and state regulators. There have been sensible proposals to streamline and consolidate these activities in the US, but they have never made much headway. Part of the problem is that financial institutions have been very important campaign contributors, and seats on House and Senate committees that have anything to do with financial institutions are highly prized as campaign cash cows. Since the early 1970s, most changes to supervision and regulation have been free-market-oriented, designed to unleash "entrepreneurial initiative." The most notorious example is the series of legislative maneuvers that succeeded in "freeing" US savings and loans associations to "market forces," playing a significant role in creating the thrift crisis of the 1980s that required a massive government bail-out (Wray 1998b).

More recently, the Glass-Steagall Act (that had separated commercial banking from investment banking since the Great Depression) was eroded, first for the biggest financial institutions, allowing commercial banks to become involved in equities markets. As this chapter is being written, the deregulation chickens are coming home to roost as the Enron fiasco spreads to Enron's partner banks, including J.P. Morgan and Citi-Group. It is also becoming apparent that the mostly self-regulated accounting firms played an important role in hiding Enron's financial mis-dealings, just as they had done in the Saving and Loan fiasco a dozen years earlier. Unregulated markets seem to do well when they are doing well, and remarkably poorly when the offal hits the fan. It is too soon to forecast how this will all play out, but a very serious and prolonged recession is likely to contribute to such a financial mess that there will be a sea-change of policy, away from laissez-faire and back toward New Deal-era sorts of reforms.

## REFERENCES

Bagehot, Walter. 1927. *Lombard Street: A Description of the Money Market.* London: John Murray,

Balbach, Anatol B. 1981. How controllable is money growth? *Federal Reserve Bank of St. Louis Review* 63 (April): 5.

Bell, Stephanie. 2000. Do taxes and bonds finance government spending? *Journal of Economic Issues* 34 (Sepember): 603-620.

Boulding, Kenneth. 1950. *A Reconstruction of Economics.* New York: John Wiley & Sons.

———. 1958. *Principles of Economic Policy.* Englewood Cliffs, NJ: Prentice-Hall.

Brunner, Karl. 1968. The role of money and monetary policy. *Federal Reserve Bank of St. Louis Review* 50 ( July): 9.

Cook, R.M. 1958. Speculation on the origins of coinage. *Historia* 7: 257-62.

Davidson, Paul. 1978. *Money and the Real Worl.,* London: Macmillan.

Davies, G. 1994. *A History of Money from Ancient Times to the Present Day.* Cardiff: University of Wales Press.

Dillard, Dudley. 1980. A monetary theory of production: Keynes and the Institutionalists. *Journal of Economic Issues* 24 ( June): 255-273.

Fazzari, Steve and Hyman Minsky, 1984. Domestic monetary policy: if not Monetarism, what? *Journal of Economic Issues* 18 (March): 101-116.

Friedman, Benjamin. 1988. Lessons on monetary policy from the 1980s. *Journal of Economic Perspectives* 2( summer): 51-72.

Friedman, Milton. 1969. *The Optimal Quantity of Money and Other Essays.* Aldine, Chicago.

———. and Anna J. Schwartz. 1963. *A Monetary History of the United States, 1867-1960.* Princeton: Princeton University Press.

Foster, J. Fagg. 1981. The reality of the present and the challenge of the future. *Journal of Economic Issues* 15 (December): 963-968.

Goodhart, Charles A.E. 1989. *Money, Information and Uncertainty.* Cambridge, Mass: MIT Press.

———.1998. Two concepts of money; implications for the analysis of optimal currency areas. *European Journal of Political Economy* 14:407-432.

Grierson, Philp. 1979. *Dark Age Numismatics.* London: Variorum Reprints.

———. 1977. *The Origins of Money.* London: Athlone Press.

Heinsohn, Gunnar and Otto Steiger 1983). *Private Property, Debts and Interest or: The Origin of Money and the Rise and Fall of Monetary Economies.* Naples, Italy: University of Bremen.

———. 1989. "The Veil of Barter: The Solution to the 'Task of Obtaining Representations of an Economy in Which Money is Essential,'" in J. A. Kregel. ed. *Inflation and Income Distribution in Capitalist Crises: Essays in Memory of Sydney Weintraub.* Washington Square, New York: New York University Press.
———. 2000. "The Property Theory of Interest." In *What Is Money.* John Smithin. ed. London & New York: Routledge
Hudson, Michael. 2001. "Public-Sector vs. Individualistic (and Debt vs. Barter) Theories of the Origins of Money.".Manuscript.
Ingham, Geoffrey. 2000. "'Babylonian Madness': On the Historical and Sociological Origins of Money." In *What is Money,* John Smithin, ed. London and New York: Routledge.
Innes, A. M. 1913. What is Money? *Banking Law Journal* May :377-408.
———. 1932. *Martyrdom in Our Times: Two Essays on Prisons and Punishment.* London: Williams & Norgate, Ltd.
Kaldor, N. 1985. *The Scourge of Monetarism.* London: Oxford University Press.
Keynes, John Maynard. 1964. *The General Theory.* New York, Harcourt-Brace-Jovanovich.
———. 1973. *The Collected Writings of John Maynard Keynes, Volume XIV, The General Theory and After: Part II Defence and Development.* Donald Moggridge, ed.London and Basingstoke: Macmillan, Cambridge University Press.
———. 1982. *The Collected Writings of John Maynard Keynes, Volume XVII.* Donald Moggridge, ed. London and Basingstoke: Macmillan, Cambridge Uni. Press.
———. 1983. *The Collected Writings of John Maynard Keynes, Volume XI, Economic Articles and Correspondence, Academic.* Donald Moggridge, ed. London and Basingstoke: Macmillan, Cambridge University Press.
———. 1972. *The Collected Writings of John Maynard Keynes, Vol. IX, Essays in Persuasion.* Donald Moggridge, ed. London and Basingstoke: Macmillan.
Knapp, Georg Friedrich. 1973 [1924]. *The State Theory of Money.* Clifton: Augustus M. Kelley.
Kraay, C.M. 1964. Hoards, small change and the origin of coinage. *Journal of Hellenic Studies* 84: 76-91.
Kurke, Leslie. 1999. *Coins, Bodies, Games, and Gold.* Princeton, New Jersey: Princeton University Press.
Lerner, Abba P. 1943. Functional finance and the federal debt. *Social Research* 10: 38-51.
———. 1947. Money as a creature of the state. *American Economic Review* 37 May: 312-317.
Maddox, Thomas, Esq. [1769] 1969. *The History and Antiquities of the Exchequer of the Kings of England, in Two Periods,* Vols I & II, Second Edition, NY: Greenwood Press.
Marx, Karl. 1909. *Capital, Volume III.* Chicago: Charles H. Kerr and Company.
Meulendyke, Anne-Marie, 1989. *US Monetary Policy and Financial Markets,* New York: Federal Reserve Bank of New York.
Minsky, H.P. 1986. *Stabilizing an Unstable Economy.* New Haven: Yale University Press.
Moore, Basil. 1988. *Horizontalists and Verticalists: The Macroeconomics of Credit Money,* Cambridge, Cambridge University Press.
———. 1984. Contemporaneous reserve accounting: Can reserves be quantity-constrained? *Journal of Post Keynesian Economics* 7(1): 103-113.
Mosler, Warren. 1995. *Soft Currency Economics,* 3rd edition (Private publication).
Neale, Walter C. 1976. *Monies in Societies.* San Francisco: Chandler & Sharpe.
Papadimitriou, Dimitri, and L. Randall Wray. 1996. Monetary Policy Uncovered: Flying Blind: The Federal Reserve's Experiment with Unobservables. *Public Policy Brief, No. 15.* Annandale-on-Hudson: Jerome Levy Economics Institute, Bard College.
———. 2001. "Minsky's Analysis of Financial Capitalism." In *Financial Keynesianism and Market Instability.* Riccardo Bellofiore and Piero Ferri. eds. Cheltenham, UK: Edward Elgar.

Papadimitriou, Dimitri, Ronnie Phillips, and L. Randall Wray. 1993. A Path to Community Development: the Community Reinvestment Act, Lending Discrimination, and the Role of Community Development Banks. *Public Policy Brief, No. 6.* Annandale-on-Hudson: Jerome Levy Economics Institute, Bard College.

Rousseas, Stephen. 1986. *Post Keynesian Monetary Economics.* Armonk, New York: M.E. Sharpe.

Sayers, R.S. 1957. *Lloyds Bank in the History of English Banking.* Oxford: Clarendon Press.

Schmandt-Besserat, Denise. 1989. "Two Precursors of Writing: Plain and Complex Tokens." In *The Origins of Writing*, Wayne M. Senner, ed. Lincoln and London: University of Nebraska Press.

Stanton, Thomas H. 1991. *A State of Risk: Will Government-Sponsored Enterprises be the Next Financial Crisis?* New York: Harper Business.

Tooke, Thomas. 1959. *An Inquiry into the Currency Principle: the Connection of the Currency with Prices and the Expediency of a Separation of Issue from Banking.* London: The London School of Economics and Political Science.

———. and Newmarch. 1848. *History of Prices and the State of the Circulation from 1792 to 1856.. Volumes III and IV.* New York: Adelphi Press.

Veblen, T. 1919a. *On the Nature and Uses of Sabotage.* New York: Oriole Chapbooks.

———. 1919b. *The Industrial System and the Captains of Industry.* New York: Oriole Chapbooks.

Wray, L. Randall. 1998a. *Understanding Modern Money: The Key to Full Employment and Price Stability.* Edward Elgar: Cheltenham.

———. 1990. *Money and Credit in Capitalist Economies: The Endogenous Money Approach.* Aldershot: Edward Elgar.

———. 1993. The monetary macroeconomics of Dudley Dillard. *Journal of Economic Issues* 27 (2): 547-560.

———. 1998b. "The Political Economy of the Current US Financial Crisis." In *The Political Economy of Economic Policies.* Philip Arestis and Malcolm Sawyer, eds. Houndsmills, Basingstoke, Hampshire, and London: Macmillan Press.

# 4

# PROGRESSIVE TAX POLICIES

Peter S. Fisher

## INTRODUCTION

Institutional economists have not had a great deal to say about tax policy, at least directly. Nonetheless, they have had a great deal to say about the orthodox view of market efficiency and market failure, about the alleged trade-off between efficiency and equity, and about the agnosticism of neoclassical economists on issues of income distribution. In this chapter, we show how these ideas form the basis for an institutionalist approach to tax policy. We then apply this approach to three of the most important issues of taxation in current policy debates: the assault on progressivity in taxation and the taxation of wealth, the use of tax law and tax incentives to influence individual and corporate decisions, and the relation between local government taxation and the increasing polarization of metropolitan areas along lines of race and class.

## AN INSTITUTIONALIST APPROACH TO TAX POLICY

The neoclassical approach to the analysis of government is founded on two claims: (1) that market failure theory allows economists to make normative prescriptions about the efficiency of government actions, but (2) that the impossibility of making interpersonal comparisons of utility prevents economists from saying anything about issues of income distribution. Institutionalists reject both claims.

Market failure theory is founded on the premise that market outcomes are efficient unless proven otherwise. It begins, in other words, with a powerful bias in favor of private, market solutions to social problems and against government action, referred to invariably as "intervention," a loaded term implying that government is the alien force and markets the natural and more fundamental process. Institutionalists, on the other hand, recognize that markets themselves are an institution created by collective action. Markets can function only to the extent that government defines and enforces property rights and contracts. Government is prior to markets.

Warren Samuels (1989, 430-432) has put the issue well:

> The critical question always concerns what interests are to be protected by government, whether designated "property" (or "rights") or otherwise. . . . Government is, perforce, an object of control in a perpetual contest to have interests protected by government, whether as legal rights, as property. . .as immunities from the rights of others, or as beneficiaries of government programs. . . .What is normally considered "intervention" is not the intrusion of government in an area in which government hitherto has been absent but the change of the interests to which government gives its support or which government is used to support.

Institutionalists take a pragmatic approach: society should choose, collectively, whichever tool is more effective for the problem at hand. Establishing rules for privately owned businesses to produce and exchange goods and services, including rules creating a new kind of institution, the corporation, is just one way to ensure that society is provided with the means to live and prosper. Other ways include government provision, cooperative societies, private contracting and franchising, regulation of private monopolies, and subsidies to non-profit organizations. Institutionalists, like most citizens, are inclined to choose among these alternatives in a pragmatic fashion. Proof of market failure is not a necessary condition for government action to be valid. Neoclassical economists, on the other hand, provide the dogma to justify solutions that entail the least amount of collective control and leave the largest scope of action for private firms to enlarge their profits.

The orthodox presumption in favor of markets—that they operate efficiently and measure social value, unless proven otherwise—leads to a presumption in favor of taxes that are neutral, or that entail the least interference with market outcomes. Institutionalists, lacking reverence for the market and with a more empirical bent than neoclassical theorists, are inclined to find market failure a pervasive condition. Tax neutrality in such circumstances merely preserves the inefficiency of market outcomes. And since institutionalists accord no special status to market outcomes, in terms of who is rewarded in the marketplace, they are unlikely to believe that tax policies that redistribute income "interfere" with efficient markets. This leaves them free to judge tax policies on grounds of social efficiency in a much broader sense, and on grounds of fairness, which brings us to the second point.

As Harold Groves (1964, 242) has pointed out, neoclassical economists have concluded that "economists as economists can say nothing about policy proposals which would improve the lot of some people but worsen that of other people. Since this would be true of nearly all policy changes and policy is of the essence in economic inquiry, it follows that economics is largely much ado about nothing." Institutionalists, instead, point out the conservative, status-quo bias inherent in such ostensible agnosticism, and tend to pursue in their own professional careers a much more activist role in issues of public policy, including advocacy of policies to better the lot of those least well off.

Tax policies, and public policies generally, to an institutionalist, should be judged in terms of how they affect the "life process"—the health and well-being of the citizenry, which in turn is a fundamental prerequisite to economic progress (see, for example, Peach, 1987; Tool, 1979). They reject the notion that taxes should merely promote efficiency in private markets, which can then be relied on to maximize the value of goods and services produced. It is obvious that markets have failed massively to create a society in which goods and services are produced and distributed in a way that maximizes the well-being of present and future generations. Problems of poverty and its often-attendant ills—malnutrition, family break-up, substance abuse, poor education, and a lifetime of poor job prospects—plague American towns and cities. To ignore this 900-pound gorilla while fretting that all attempts to create greater equity create an unfortunate trade-off in loss of "efficiency," is, to an institutionalist, not just spurious agnosticism but shameful irresponsibility.

Neoclassical economists also accord little attention to the issue of power. While they discuss market power, it is important only to the extent that it affects prices. Broader issues of economic power are simply defined out of the discipline. Institutionalists, on the other hand, are concerned with the effects of economic power internally within organizations, about the effects of power on communities, and about the effects of economic power on political institutions and processes. Taxation as an instrument for the redistribution of economic power then has a rightful place on the agenda for public debate.

## THE ASSAULT ON PROGRESSIVE TAXATION

The case for progressive taxation of incomes and for taxation of wealth can be made on a variety of grounds. First, there is a simple appeal to egalitarian principles, based perhaps on the assumption that differences in income and wealth have as much to do with luck and circumstance as they do with ability and effort. Second is the notion that taxes should be, as John R. Commons put it, "proportioned *directly* according to a person's ability to pay" (1934, 819).

While the ability-to-pay principle might be interpreted as a rationale for a proportional tax—a constant percentage of income—it can also be argued that ability to pay is best measured by one's *discretionary* income, income above that needed to purchase the basic necessities of life. "There is a social interest in allowing individuals to retain enough means after taxation to maintain themselves in health, vigor, and informed citizenship. . . .Taxation according to ability to pay simply means that a nation, viewed as a family, satisfies it most urgent wants before it indulges in superfluities" (Groves, 1964, 25). This is no doubt the logic behind standard features of state and federal income taxes such as the large "zero-bracket amount"—the amount of income that goes untaxed—as well as the standard deduction and personal exemptions. Even a flat rate tax becomes progressive overall if it includes a large credit or exempts a substantial initial share of income.

Imagine, for example, a simple tax on income. For each family, income up to the poverty threshold for a family of that size is exempt entirely from tax. Such an exemption is a comprehensive substitute for standard deductions and personal exemptions or child credits and ensures that no one is taxed into poverty. (It could, of course, be set at some percentage of the poverty threshold, such as 125%.) For a family of four in 2002, $18,104 would be exempt. All income above that level would be taxed at 27% (the federal marginal tax rate that would apply to income above about $46,000 in 2002).

Consider the effective tax rate on families of four at different income levels. As income rises from $25,000 to $75,000, the effective rate rises from 7.4% to 20.5%. The tax is quite progressive. But at higher income levels, the average rate increases only modestly—it doesn't reach 25% until income reaches $250,000—and gradually approaches 27% at very high incomes. While such a tax has merit, its progressivity levels off and it fails to tax very heavily those at the top of the income distribution.

A flat rate tax fails, in other words, to impose much tax on those sources of income most likely to be derived from inherited wealth, from speculation or great good fortune, from economic rents deriving merely from ownership of scarce resources, and from monopoly profits deriving from concentrations of economic power. The case for a more progressive rate structure, where additional higher rate brackets come into play at higher income levels, can thus be made on the Veblenian grounds that the incomes of the rich are derived largely from unproductive activity rather than from earnings. An additional rationale is that they reduce the ability of the wealthy to translate economic resources into political influence, thereby distorting democratic processes. In 1999, the richest 20% of households derived 30.5% of their income from capital: rent, interest, dividends, and realized capital gains; for the richest 1% of households, capital income accounted for 58% of total income (Mishel, Bernstein and Schmitt, 2001, p 85). Furthermore, 58% of all capital income went to the top 20% of households and 18% went to the richest 1%.

Perhaps the most fundamental argument for more progressive taxation is simply that taxing the rich more heavily permits lighter taxation of the poor. Alleviating poverty, in turn, promotes greater health and productivity, and fuller participation in politics and society, of all citizens.

Since the first days of the Reagan administration, and even earlier through the rise of conservative think tanks and their success in getting their messages in the media, there has been a concerted attack on progressive taxation and on the belief systems supporting it. We are told that the plight of the poor is largely due to their own failures and to failures of government policy. We are told that we live in a meritocracy, where high incomes are merely a reward for high productivity and entrepreneurialism. We are told that the rich must be taxed lightly because the rich are the ones who invest and create jobs. Social Darwinism has made a comeback in the form of a pro-market, anti-government ideology that leaves the losers to fend for themselves and leaves the richest with their spoils of victory intact. And we are told that to point out these things is to fan the flames of class warfare.

The result has been a decline in the progressivity of the overall tax system in the United States. Corporate income taxes have declined in importance at all levels of government, from 16% to 11% of total federal-state-local tax revenue between 1970 and 1999.[1] Cuts in the federal income tax have been skewed in favor the highest income taxpayers. Devolution of responsibilities from the federal to state and local governments in the 1970s and particularly the 1980s meant increasing reliance on state and local revenue sources; the state & local share of tax revenues rose from 37% in 1970 to almost 45% by 1990.[2] State income taxes are generally much less progressive than the federal, and sales and property taxes, both regressive, remain the dominant taxes, accounting for about two-thirds of state-local tax revenue in the 1980s and 1990s. User charges (also regressive) have assumed increasing importance in financing state and local government as well. Most importantly for the issue of progressivity, there has been a very successful assault on inheritance and estate taxes at the federal and state levels since the mid-1990s, even though these taxes hit just a small percentage of the wealthiest estates.

These shifts towards more regressive forms of taxation conceal another trend: income taxes themselves, the mainstays of progressive taxation, have been changed significantly in the 1980s and the 1990s. These changes have further eroded the progressivity of the tax system. The best summary measure of progressivity or regressivity is the degree to which the tax system renders the distribution of income more or less unequal. A proportional tax has no effect on inequality, while a progressive tax makes the after-tax distribution of income less unequal than the before-tax distribution. A commonly used summary measure of the degree of income inequality is the Gini coefficient, which takes on a value between 0 and 1, with higher values indicating a greater degree of inequality.

As can be seen in Table 1, the distribution of income became substantially more unequal in the last two decades of the 20th century. But the trend was more pronounced for after-tax income, because the tax system did less to redistribute income in 2000 than it did in 1990 or 1980. (Federal and state income taxes, social security payroll taxes, and the earned income tax credit (EITC) are included in this analysis.) In 1980, taxes produced a nearly 7% reduction in inequality as measured by the change in the Gini; by 2000, the effect of taxes was only a 4% reduction in inequality.

*Table 1.* Income Inequality Before and After Income Taxes, 1980-2000

| | Gini Coefficient | | | Percent change |
|---|---|---|---|---|
| | 1980 | 1990 | 2000 | 1980-2000 |
| Income Measure | | | | |
| Market income before taxes[1] | 0.462 | 0.487 | 0.506 | 9.5% |
| Income after income taxes and EITC | 0.430 | 0.461 | 0.486 | 13.0% |
| Percent reduction in inequality due to taxes | 6.9% | 5.3% | 4.0% | |

[1] Money income less government transfers, plus capital gains and health insurance supplements to wages and salaries.

Source: U.S. Census Bureau, Historical Income Tables - Experimental Measures, Table RDI-5. Index of Income Concentration (Gini Index), by Definition of Income, 1979 to 2000. http://www.census.gov/hhes/income/histinc/rdi05.html

These shifts in tax policy have been possible in part because corporate interests and the wealthy have been able to exert direct influence on the political process to advance their interests, and in part, because they have been able to exert influence on the media and shift the ideological center to the right. The forces that in the past have produced progressive policy changes—prolonged recession (the 1930s) or widespread civil unrest (the 1960s), both of which threaten to undermine the legitimacy of concentrated income and wealth—have been replaced by a new world order characterized by greater economic competition internationally and at the same time a greater independence of corporate power from national sovereignty.

## TAXES AS ECONOMIC INCENTIVES

The last two decades of the twentieth century saw a remarkably widespread acceptance of the idea that economic activity can be promoted effectively using tax incentives. While demand-side tax cuts have fallen out of favor, increasingly tax breaks to business and to the wealthy are justified as a means of stimulating investment and creating jobs. Accelerated depreciation, investment tax credits, and targeted jobs credits began at the federal level, but they quickly became the mainstay of economic development policy at the state level in the 1980s and 1990s (Eisinger, 1988; Fisher, 1985). Localities, meanwhile, began to rely increasingly on property tax abatements to spur investment in their communities. State enterprise zone programs sprang up in the early 1980s and their use continued to expand, within states and by adoption in more states, through the 1990s. While tax incentives received their initial impetus from the recession of the early 1980s and from a perception that capital had become increasingly mobile and location decisions increasingly competitive, incentives have increased in importance through good times and bad, including the long expansion of the 1990s (Fisher and Peters, 1998).

Both support and criticism of tax incentives can be found in the writings of institutionalists. John R. Commons referred to the "police power of taxation," a phrase based on the US constitution's welfare clause (that government has a responsibility to promote the general health, safety and welfare), commonly relied upon as the rationale for government regulation of private activity and hence for the "police powers" of state and local government. Taxes, Commons argued, are invariably regulative as well as revenue-raising devices. "If we look at a tax from the police-power standpoint of what may be expected as the economic results of the tax, then we shall inquire: What will be the best inducements to individuals to increase the commonwealth by increasing their own wealth?" (Commons, 1934, 819).

This statement by Commons should not by any means be taken as an endorsement of trickle-down economics. Commons recognized that the police power could be used to promote narrow class interests. His argument is that we should recognize the regulatory role of taxes and should judge the regulatory effects on the basis of how they contribute to the commonwealth, rather than to private wealth; that is, are the effects a public benefit or not? Some contemporary institutionalists, on the other hand, have argued for eliminating all "tax preferences" under the income tax, in effect stripping it of its regulatory role (e.g., Galbraith, 1973; Peterson, 1982).

The issue is probably best sorted out by relying, in classic institutionalist fashion, on empiricism and pragmatism. There is in fact a vast empirical literature on the effectiveness of tax policy in stimulating investment. The general conclusion is that, at the state level, tax incentives have a measurable but quite small effect on economic activity (Bartik, 1992; Wasylenko, 1997). The consensus among these writers is that, when considering interstate differences in taxes, the elasticity of economic activity (investment or jobs) with respect to taxes is only in the range of -.2 to -.4. That is, a 10% tax cut would produce a 2% to 4% increase in business activity. But there remains skepticism among some that this conclusion is that firmly established (Peters and Fisher, 2002).

The problem for those who would promote taxes as an economic development incentive is that state and local taxes are simply not a large enough share of business costs to alter location and investment decisions in the majority of cases. Labor, energy and transportation costs will dominate such decisions, along with projections of the market for the firms' products. Furthermore, the lack of effectiveness also makes tax incentives a very expensive strategy as well. The elasticities cited earlier imply that only about 10% of new investment can be attributed to state-local tax incentives, given the 25%-30% tax cut represented by the typical incentive package. That means that the direct revenue gains from the 10% of investment attributable to the incentives is more than offset by the losses entailed in granting the incentives to the other 90%, which would have happened even in the absence of incentives (Peters and Fisher 2002).

Opponents of economic development incentives at the state and local level often argued that they amounted to a zero-sum game. That is, to the extent that they do have some effect, they merely alter the location of economic activity but do not increase overall investment or employment. Others have pointed out that it may in fact be a negative-sum game: tax incentives may induce firms to choose locations that otherwise would not have been the least-cost and most efficient locations, reducing the overall efficiency of the economy.

One can concede that this might be the case (a negative or zero-sum game) even without agreeing with those orthodox economists who base their criticisms of incentives on a belief that taxes should be "neutral" (e.g., Burstein and Rolnick, 1995). Incentives are indeed non-neutral—they bias decisions in favor of certain locations, certain industries, and certain kinds of productive factors (typically capital rather than labor)—but the notion that the state-local tax system would be approximately neutral in the absence of incentives is largely a pipe dream. States and localities exhibit enormous variation in their effective tax rates on business income overall, by economic sector, and by capital- versus labor-intensive investments, even without incentives (see Fisher and Peters, 1998). The institutionalist critique, then, is not that incentives represent a departure from an ideal, competitive equilibrium in which taxes represent efficient prices for public services, but that they represent costly tools that do not, for the most part, enhance the commonwealth. They do not create public benefits, but instead merely enhance after-tax profits.

Before dismissing all economic development tax incentives out of hand, it is important to consider a special class of incentives that would seem on the surface to be more justifiable. These are geographically targeted incentives that attempt deliberately to alter location by directing activity to pockets of unemployment and poverty through an enterprise zone strategy. The argument is that relocation in such instances is a positive sum game because the personal and societal benefits of expanding employment in depressed, poverty ridden neighborhoods are so great that they exceed the loss of benefits to better-off communities that would otherwise have been the chosen sites for new investment.

Unfortunately, research on enterprise zones has shown that they, also, are very costly and largely ineffective tools for bringing additional employment to distressed areas (Peters and Fisher, 2002). The cost per job could easily exceed $80,000. Furthermore, bringing jobs to poor neighborhoods does not do as much to increase employment of the residents of those neighborhoods as one would hope. Labor markets are metropolitan, not local, so that most of the new jobs go to persons from outside the neighborhood; furthermore, the other barriers to employment of the poor remain: poor education, lack of labor market attachment, racial discrimination

One suspects that the popularity of tax incentives rests on two factors. First, tax cuts are always an easier strategy politically than expenditure programs. Many states, and the federal government, now publish tax expenditure reports that show the annual cost of tax incentives, in the hopes of putting these programs on the same footing as direct expenditures. But regardless of the fact that incentives represent an expenditure of public funds aimed at a very narrow set of beneficiaries, they can still be characterized by politicians as tax cuts rather than expenditure increases. Once embedded in the tax code, they are immune from the annual appropriation process and become entitlements, and therefore very difficult to repeal.

The second factor explaining the widespread use of tax incentives is that the distributive effects are skewed towards corporations and the rich and that these groups exert undue influence on the legislative process. Tax incentives become another device for relieving taxes on those groups and further reducing the progressivity of the tax system. The effective state-local corporate income tax rate declined by about 40% from the late1980s through the late 1990s (Maguire, 2000). This trend is attributable in substantial degree to the increasing prevalence and generosity of tax incentives. A study of taxes in 20 of the most heavily manufacturing states found that, in just the eight years from 1990 to 1998, tax incentives for manufacturing industries grew on average from about 10% of gross taxes to 29%, and the effective corporate income tax rate on new investment fell from 4.4% to 3.1% (Fisher, 2002).

By cutting corporate income taxes, other state taxes must be raised or services cut. In the 1990s, states showed a pronounced preference for raising regressive sales taxes in the early part of the decade when the recession cut into revenues and tax increases were needed. In the latter 1990s, when the economy was booming and tax cuts were in order, most states lowered progressive income taxes, individual or corporate, instead of rolling back the sales tax increases (Johnson and Tenny, 2002).

Thus for pragmatic reasons, it would be easy to stake out an institutionalist position against tax incentives generally, or at least incentives with an ostensible economic development rationale. The use of such incentives cannot be shown to have beneficial effects on the economy; there is a political bias in favor of their overuse; they are subject to little scrutiny; and their proliferation has altered the tax system in the direction of greater regressivity.

## LOCAL TAXATTION AND METROPOLITAN FRAGMENTATION

The final issue in tax policy that we address from an institutionalist perspective is the system of local taxation that prevails in US metropolitan areas and the effects of that system on income distribution and the spatial segregation of the population by economic class and race. Does fragmented government contribute to the problems of poverty and inequality?

The social consequences of poverty are well documented (Duncan and Brooks-Gunn, 1997). It is also well established that the effects of poverty are aggravated when poverty is concentrated geographically (Brooks-Gunn et al, 1997). The social pathologies of crime and substance abuse are fostered by concentrations of poor families in inner-city neighborhoods. The absence of adults with stable and permanent connection to the labor force in such communities produces extraordinarily high rates of joblessness among youth, who lack role models with good jobs and who have little contact with individuals who are networked into the job market, and who are in a position to inform them of jobs and help them obtain those jobs. Schools in poor areas are likely to be poorly funded, to have a high turnover of teachers, to perpetuate low expectations of achievement, and to have low high school graduation rates, condemning youth to a life of poor jobs, at best.

Concentrated poverty thus exacts an enormous cost on society in terms of the loss of human potential, the loss of economic productivity, and the high social overhead costs associated with providing services and income support to populations unable to fend for themselves. While the causes of poverty in general are many and complex, taxes clearly play a role in the concentration of poverty in central cities. Metropolitan areas in the US are fragmented into local governments, each with its own regulatory powers and taxing authority. The average metropolitan area in 1992 contained 90 local governments (US Bureau of the Census, 1994). Suburban jurisdictions use their regulatory powers—zoning, subdivision regulations, and rental housing regulations—to minimize the tax burden on their own residents. They do this by making it difficult or impossible to build affordable housing, particularly rental housing. Requirements for large lots, attached garages, minimum floor area, and the like, and lack of areas zoned for higher density housing, can effectively exclude low and moderate income families (Orfield, 1997). The suburbs thus exclude those who are likely to consume more than the average share of services while contributing less than the average share of taxes.

The incentives to engage in such "fiscal zoning" will be there as long as local governments play a major role in service provision, particularly education, and as long as they rely heavily on local property taxes to finance those services. These policies prevent many lower income families from following the exodus of jobs to the suburbs. Increasingly, the middle class has been moving out of the central city neighborhoods, including middle class blacks, leaving behind areas of more concentrated poverty.

Local government has thus become a device for the middle and upper income classes to preserve and protect their economic status by creating enclaves of wealth, with moderate taxes and quality public services. The poor, meanwhile, become increasingly isolated in the central cities and older declining suburbs. Not only does this isolation exacerbate and perpetuate the problem of poverty, it depersonalizes poverty for the non-poor and allows the middle class to go about their comfortable lives without confronting neighbors who suffer the devastations of poverty. It relieves them of responsibility for the problems of "the city" and fosters the perpetuation of mythology about the character of the poor, about crime, drugs and dysfunctional families. Solutions to the problem of poverty become more difficult to achieve.

Would greater access to the suburbs improve the well-being of poor families? There is, in fact, evidence that this is the case, from studies of the "Gatreaux Progam" in Chicago. This program provided assistance in the relocation of poor families from distressed neighborhoods in Chicago to suburban areas. The results showed that poor, black families that relocated to middle-income, largely white suburbs fared better on a number of measures than similar families who remained in poor, predominantly black Chicago neighborhoods. The adults were more likely to find stable employment, the children were more likely to achieve success in school.

The simple dichotomy between poor central city and rich suburb is, however, an outdated caricature. The reality is that the problems of the central cities have spread to older, inner-ring suburbs. Many such suburbs are now in worse condition than the central cities, since these older suburbs often have similar concentrations of poor families but lack the downtown commercial tax base of the central city (Orfield, 1997).

Research in recent years has attempted to document the extent to which the fortunes of city and suburb are tied together. Some have found that metropolitan areas with less inequality and less segregation have more healthy economies (e.g., Ledebur and Barnes, 1992.) Others have found the linkages more complex; in some cases rapid growth appears to cause large income disparities, while in other cases causality is reversed, inequality dragging down the attempts to achieve faster metropolitan growth (Phillips and Lucy, 1996). David Rusk (1993) found that where central cities were able to grow in spatial extent (through annexation), per capita income in the central city was nearly the same as in that city's suburbs. On the other hand, cities unable to expand had per capita incomes just 68% of the average in places outside the central city.

The problems of political fragmentation and economic/racial segregation can be attacked at the metropolitan-regional level. Regional solutions can be fairly limited, at least to begin with. Metropolitan areas already have regional agencies for transportation planning (MPOs, or Metropolitan Planning Organizations.) Some have created their own regional agencies for performing a limited range of other activities; regional special districts are frequently established to achieve economies of scale in the provision of water or sewer service. Similarly, where school districts are independent of municipalities, district boundaries may extend well beyond the central city, reducing or eliminating, at least potentially, the disparity in resources between city and suburban schools.

In some smaller metropolitan areas, county government can effectively function as a regional government for a central city and its suburbs. With countywide taxes financing countywide services, the fiscal problems of fragmentation are ameliorated and the financial incentives for suburbs to engage in exclusionary practices are reduced. For the most part, however, county government functions have remained fairly limited, typically encompassing health and social services. Still, to the extent that these services are demanded disproportionately by the poor, such countywide provision helps alleviate the burden on places with large concentrations of poor families. At present, there are only a handful of places that have gone beyond this sort of "limited-function regionalism" by actually merging municipal and county governments: Miami-Dade County Florida, Nashville-Davidson County Tennessee, Indianapolis-Marion County Indiana, and Lexington-Fayette County Kentucky.

Less ambitious, but no more politically viable, are strategies that aim at redistributing revenue within a metropolitan area. The regional tax-base sharing system put in place by the Minnesota legislature in the early 1970s for the seven-county Twin Cities Metropolitan area has its flaws, but it does reduce incentives for fiscal gamesmanship by requiring any city to share 40% of all new commercial and industrial property tax base with the entire region (Orfield, 1997). The revenue from the shared tax base is then distributed among cities inversely in proportion to their commercial/industrial tax base per capita. While this clearly redistributes revenue, it does so in a somewhat inconsistent fashion. The city of Minneapolis is a net contributor of tax base because of the commercial property value downtown, despite having a disproportionate share of the region's poor. Wealthy bedroom suburbs with no poor families can be net gainers because they have little or no commercial valuation, though they have high overall tax base per capita. This plan has not resulted in a noticeably more egalitarian distribution of the population within the Twin Cities MSA, nor has it been imitated elsewhere.

More promising, in theory, are state revenue sharing programs that redistribute state taxes in inverse proportion to a locality's wealth, as measured by the income of its residents or by tax base per capita (Fisher, 1981). Such programs are common in the financing of schools, but are rare for general-purpose local governments. County-wide sales taxes that are then shared with local governments or school districts on a per capita or per pupil basis also amount to redistributive revenue sharing. It is probably easier for a state government to enforce such redistribution, either through state aids or by means of sharing requirements attached to county option tax enabling legislation, because the redistribution is obscured to an extent. For example, raising the state income tax to finance per capita grants to localities can be characterized merely as the sharing of revenues; the fact that it redistributes from income-rich places to income-poor places is obscured.

While it may be easier to enact redistributive measures when the redistribution is less direct and visible, this is not necessarily a virtue. Even if fiscal resources are more evenly distributed, and even if the incentives for fiscal zoning are reduced, the motivation for exclusion remains. In part this is because exclusionary practices may be less about money and more about perceptions that lower income families bring crime and violence and drugs with them, and more about just plain racism. Poverty rates among blacks and Hispanics remain far above poverty rates for non-Hispanic whites, so that exclusion by income can be a thinly-veiled effort to exclude by race. It may well be that what we need, more than a redistribution of funds (though that is clearly needed), is better recognition of our interdependencies and an enhanced sense of social responsibility. Regional cooperation may be more important than merely regional revenue sharing.

There has been a revival of interest in regional governance recently, in academic circles but also in more popular writings (Pastor et al, 2000; Calthorpe and Fulton, 2001). These writers have more or less ambitious visions for the role of regional government. They all begin, however, with the same premise: that municipal boundaries are artificial, obscuring the interdependencies that exist across the region and obscuring the basic economic and social reality, which is a "regional city."

One can think of new regional revenue systems that make this interdependence explicit. We should avoid calling these systems "sharing" or "redistribution," since such terms imply that we are taking something that belongs to one group and giving it to another. Instead, they should be presented simply as regional revenues. The state government can apply a carrot and stick approach, restricting purely local revenue sources while allowing new taxes that can only be applied on a regional basis and used to finance regional governmental functions. In order to take advantage of such revenue sources, local governments would be forced to talk with one another, and to form new regional forms of service provision and governance, including, importantly, the regulation of land development.

Clearly the existing institutions of local government and finance have failed us and we should not expect then to provide the basis for a more humane society in which all can participate equally. They are institutions for the preservation of inequality, institutions of isolation and exclusion. We need instead institutions that reflect the fundamental truth that "we're all in this together." Development of such institutions is a daunting but essential task.

## CONCLUSIONS

An institutionalist approach to tax policy begins with a recognition that the neoclassical focus on efficiency, market failure and tax neutrality provides little basis for addressing the most important tax issues facing the US today.
Arguments about the non-neutrality of tax incentives miss the point and fail to gain any traction in public debates. The more pragmatic and empirical approach of institutionalists leads to the conclusion that incentives are simply very costly and largely ineffective, and that they worsen income inequality. Their non-neutrality is not the problem; they are simply poor tools for the

attainment of economic growth or even for attainment of a more equitable distribution of growth.

Much of the economics profession also embraces agnosticism about the appropriateness of progressive taxation; mainstream economists have little to say about the increasing inequality of incomes and the lessening effects of tax policy in reducing that inequality. For institutionalists, inequality and poverty are critically important issues on the public policy agenda and responsible policy analysts should use their professional expertise to address them. There is plenty to be said; simply documenting the extent and consequences of inequality and the role of tax policy in perpetuating or aggravating poverty is a task that economists are well equipped for. The barrier is a professional culture in mainstream economics that disciplines those who get their hands dirty in such debates and rewards instead the building of mathematical models, technically impressive but utterly irrelevant. Institutionalists should, and usually do, embrace and perpetuate a more socially responsible professional culture that is at the same time grounded in a sound and empirical methodology.

# NOTES

[1] Figures cited in this paragraph relating to shares of tax revenue are from the following sources: American Council on Intergovernmental Relations, 1997, Table 28; US.Bureau of the Census 2002; and USOffice of Management and Budget, 2002.

[2] The state-local share declined to 41% by 1999, due largely to the rapid increase in Federal individual income tax receipts. This trend was fueled largely by the run-up in the stock market in the latter 1990s and the enormous capital gains that resulted; since capital gains accrue overwhelmingly to those at the top of the income distribution, most are taxed at the highest marginal rate. This trend came to an end with the bear market of 2001 and 2002, which may well have produced a drop in the income tax as a share of total taxes, back to a more normal level. State-local tax revenue for these years is not yet available to confirm this hypothesis.

# REFERENCES

American Council on Intergovernmental Relations (ACIR). 1997. *Significant Features of Fiscal Federalis,,Volume 2, Revenues and Expenditures.1995*. Washington, DC: ACIR.

Bartik, Timothy J. 1991. *Who Benefits from State and Local Economic Development Policies?* Kalamazoo, Michigan: W.E. Upjohn Institute for Employment Research.

Brooks-Gunn, Jeanne, Greg Duncan, and J. Lawrence Aber, eds. 1997. *Neighborhood Poverty, Vol. I: Context and Consequences for Children.* New York: Russell Sage Foundation.
Burstein, Melvin L., and Arthur J. Rolnick. 1995. Congress should end the economic war between the states. *The Region (Federal Reserve Bank of Minneapolis)* 9 (March): 3-19.
Calthorpe, Peter, and William Fulton. 2001. *The Regional City.* Wash. DC: Island Press.
Commons, John R. 1934. *Institutional Economics: Its Place in Political Economy.* New York: The Macmillan Company.
Duncan, Greg J., and Jeanne Brooks-Gunn, eds. 1997. *Consequences of Growing Up Poor.* New York: Russell Sage Foundation.
Eisinger, Peter. 1988. *The Rise of the Entrepreneurial State.* Madison: University of Wisconsin Press.
Fisher, Peter. 2002. Tax incentives and the disappearing state corporate income tax. *State Tax Notes* 23: 767-774.
———. 1985. Corporate tax incentives: The American version of industrial policy. *Journal of Economic Issues* 19: 1-19.
———. 1981. State equalizing aids and metropolitan tax base sharing. A comparative analysis. *Public Finance Quarterly* .9: 449-470.
———and Alan Peters. 1998. *Industrial Incentives: Competition among American States and Cities.* Kalamazoo, Michigan: W.E. Upjohn Institute for Employment Research.
Galbraith, John Kenneth. 1973. *Economics and the Public Purpose.* Boston: Houghton Mifflin.
Groves, Harold. 1964. *Financing Government.* . Sixth edition. New York: Holt, Rinehart and Winston.
Johnson, Nicholas, and Daniel Tenny. 2002. *The Rising Regressivity of State Taxes* Washington, DC: Center on Budget and Policy Priorities. Available at www.cbpp.org.
Ledebur, Larry C., and William R. Barnes. 1992. *Metropolitan Disparities and Economic Growth.* Washington, DC: National League of Cities.
Maguire, Steve. 2000. *Average Effective Corporate Tax Rates.* Congressional Research Service Report, February 28. Washington, DC.
Mishel, Lawrence, Jared Bernstein , and John Schmitt. 2001. *The State of Working America, 2000/2001.* Washington, DC: The Economic Policy Institute.
Orfield, Myron. 1997. *Metropolitics.* Washington, DC: Brookings Institution.
Pastor, Manuel, Jr., Peter Dreier, J. Eugene Grigsby III, and Marta Lopez-Garza. 2000. *Regions that Work: How Cities and Suburbs Can Grow Together.* Minneapolis: University of Minnesota Press.
Peach, James T. 1987. Distribution and economic progress. *Journal of Economic Issues* 21: 1495-1529.
Peters, Alan, and Peter Fisher. 2002. *State Enterprise Zone Programs: Do They Work?* Kalamazoo, Michigan: W.E. Upjohn Institute for Employment Research.
Peterson, Wallace. 1982. *Our Overloaded Economy.* Armonk, New York: M. E. Sharpe.
Phillips, David L. , and William H. Lucy. 1996. *Central City Disparities, Growth and Metropolitan Prosperity: 59 Metropolitan Areas in the South,1970-1990.* Report to the Center for Urban Development, Virginia Commonwealth University for the Partnership for Urban Virginia.
Rusk, David. 1993. *Cities Without Suburbs.* Baltimore: Johns Hopkins University Press.
Samuels, Warren. 1989. Some fundamentals of the economic role of government. *Journal of Economic Issues* 23: 427-433.
Tool, Marc R. 1979. *The Discretionary Economy.* Santa Monica: Goodyear Publishin Company.
US Bureau of the Census. 2002. United States State and Local Finances by Level of Government, 1998-99. Available on the census website at http://www.census.gov/govs/estimate/9900us.html

US Bureau of the Census. 1994. *Census of Governments 1992, vol. 1, no. 1, GovernmentOrganization.* Washington, DC: US Government Printing Office.

US Office of Management and Budget. 2002. Budget of the United States Government, Historical Tables: Table 2.1—Receipts by Source: 1934-2007, and Table 2.5—

Composition of "Other Receipts": 1940-2007. Both tables available on the web at http://www.whitehouse.gov/omb/budget/fy2003/hist.html

Wasylenko, Michael. 1997. Taxation and economic development: The state of the economic literature. *New England Economic Review* (March/April): 37-52.

# 5

# PROMOTING ECONOMIC EQUITY: THE BASIC INCOME APPROACH

Charles M. A. Clark

## WHAT IS ECONOMIC EQUITY AND WHY IS IT IMPORTANT?

It is no accident or coincidence that just about every human society has had some mechanism to promote economic equity. From the Old Testament's redistribution of wealth through the Jubilee to the modern welfare state, a common feature of human society has been the redistribution of wealth and incomes to account for those who have not been adequately provided for by the given "rules of the game" that determine income allocation. This constant feature of social living shows that there is a need to account for factors besides existing property rights in determining the ability of individual community members to subsist and thrive. The reason that such redistribution schemes are a fundamental feature of human societies is that wealth and incomes are collectively created, but often the rules that determine the initial distribution of incomes, usually based on power and property rights, do not typically provide for the whole community. Many people in the community are not currently economically productive but still need to be provided for to ensure the economic sustainability of the community (children and the elderly). Furthermore, many factors besides what is necessary to promote future production influence what the initial distribution of income will be (such as a lucky hunter), thus it may be harmful to the health of the community to allow such inequalities to persist.

Anthropologists have long known of these features of human society, yet they are often ignored when analyzing modern capitalist economies. The need for redistribution is just as necessary today as it was for our ancestors. Our economy produces a distribution of income that has levels of inequality well beyond any instrumental need to send out the market signals of differential incomes in order to coordinate economic activities. Power and property rights, totally disconnected to issues of effort and productivity, greatly influence the distribution of incomes in modern capitalist economies (Clark 1996). This "market driven" level of inequality causes serious problems for the long run health of the community. First, it creates a situation of insufficient aggregate demand, that is the economy is not able to purchase the amount of goods it has the potential to produce simply because those with needs do not have the adequate resources to satisfy them. Second, many are unable, given the "rules of the game" for distribution to secure sufficient incomes to support themselves and their families. Without some mechanism to redistribute incomes these people will eventually perish or become hostile to the existing political order. Lastly, gross inequalities, especially when they cannot be justified based on economic necessity, weaken the social bond (some might say the social capital) of the society, and thus lead to great strains and costs of the society as a whole, diverting resources towards protecting existing property relations and away from meeting human needs. Thus the economic pie as a whole shrinks. Hence, the importance of economic equity.

The most common definition of equity is fairness. However, left like this, the definition is vague; for what constitutes "fairness"? If it merely means that one gets one's due out of market transactions, then an overly narrow (purely procedural) definition of equity is being used, which can lead to very inequitable outcomes in practice. The older and more exact meaning of equity, derived from the field of Jurisprudence, defines equity as referring to provisions to supplement or correct the outcomes of the law. That is, it is long recognized that the outcomes of a strict adherence to the law or rules often produce results that are contrary to either the spirit of the laws or society's intent, thus causing a need for adjustments in the outcome. This adjustment is equity in the classical sense of the word. In terms of the economy, this means that following the laws and rules that guide the economy will often produce outcomes that might be in accordance with the restrictions of justice in that everyone has followed the letter of the law, yet which are socially or morally unacceptable. To give an example: market wages might not be at levels that can support a family at a decent level, and in many cases can be below the subsistence level. Thus it has been common for societies to intervene in such market outcomes to ensure that certain social minimums are met. Strict adherence to the logic of economic theory suggests that all market outcomes, as long as they are the result of free actions, are necessarily fair (equitable) and that it would be unfair (a violation of justice) to interfere with such outcomes. Yet this conception of equity not only ignores the second and older definition of equity, it is a mere tautology, for it assumes that all market outcomes are equitable, and the proof of this is that they are market outcomes. Market outcomes need to be evaluated using criteria other than the market, and all market economies have eventually adopted this approach, for markets often produce unacceptable outcomes.

An examination of how particular societies solve the central economic problem of how to provide for their material reproduction shows that equity considerations (questions of fairness not only in procedures, but also in terms of outcomes meeting socially desirable standards) are important at every level of economic activity. We can see this by breaking down the economic problem into its three basic component parts, the three economic questions all societies must answer: What to produce? How to carry out production? To whom to distribute the benefits of economic production? All three of these questions have both necessary and discretionary aspects—necessary in that the forces of nature place restrictions on how we address each question and discretionary in that these natural forces do not wholly determine our answers. In fact, as a society develops and becomes more affluent the discretionary aspect grows and the restrictions of nature shrink. We see this clearly in our first question: What to produce? Nature tells us that we must produce sufficient food, clothing and shelter to meet the community's basic physiological needs, and that these are appropriate for the community's natural environment (climate, available resources etc.), yet in an affluent society such as the United States the limits imposed on us by nature are rather small. Thus the role of discretion looms much larger and we must ask ethical questions when deciding what to produce. When the outcomes of the economy violate our sense of decency and fairness we must intervene and adjust these outcomes. In our economy what gets produced is determined mostly by those with the most money (with a large role for advertisers). Thus, the wants of affluent suburbanites for SUVs and very large houses take precedence over the needs of those on low incomes for adequate transportation and shelter (which often go unmet).

Equity issues are central also to the second question—how to carry out production—for this question is not solely about what technology to use, but what is more important, about the social division of labor, i.e., who gets what jobs. As income, status and how much one gets to participate in society are often determined by one's job, this is not a trivial matter. Our necessary component to this question is that we must come up with a system of allocating jobs and tasks in a manner that those who get particular jobs have the ability to do them adequately. However, here, as elsewhere, discretion plays the bigger role, for most jobs provide the majority of the skills and training necessary to do them in the form of on-the-job training. As almost all hiring decisions are discretionary, the potential for exclusion of groups without connections to the "good jobs" (friends or family) is great and thus society must intervene to allow access to good jobs for all willing and able to work.

How a society distributes the benefits of its economic production is the classic equity issue, and we can see that it is clearly related to the first two questions. The distribution of wealth and incomes greatly shapes the demand for goods and services (as well as political decisions), and thus what society will produce, as well as the ability to achieve the right credentials and connections to get the most desirable jobs. Our major constraint on how we distribute incomes and wealth is that it has to be done in a manner that contributes to future production. Too much inequality hampers the ability of society to materially reproduce itself, both on the production side (under fed and ill housed workers will be much less productive than their potential) and on the demand side (the primary cause of the Great Depression was inadequate aggregate demand caused mostly by the high levels of income inequality generated by the economy of the roaring 20's), while perfect equality (everybody gets the same income regardless of job or effort) might produce disincentives to work hard, acquire skills, undertaking difficult jobs and innovate. In the mythology of our economy, incomes are determined by how much one contributes to the marketplace, thus such outcomes are "fair and just" (from each according to their abilities, to each according to their deeds). Yet the reality is that power determines incomes more than anything else, and this power is distributed not according to the necessary requirements of an efficient economy, but according to past income and wealth and how the "rules of the game" are set. Incomes are determined by bargaining, and how well you can bargain is determined by your initial position and the context of the bargaining process (laws, regulations and customs).[1] If you belong to a strong union, or if your industry has considerable market power (few competitors) or if you have the political clout to get the government to set the rules in your favor, and most important, if you can exclude others from competing against you, and encourage them to compete against each other, you will have significant power and can greatly determine your income. The less economic power you have the lower your income will be. Throughout the history of capitalism, the incomes of the most powerless have frequently fallen to below subsistence levels and these groups have been able to share in the economic progress generated by capitalism only through intervening in market outcomes, either through the government (minimum wages, social protection expenditures) or through collective action (unions and collective bargaining). The rules of the market are created by those with power and thus have never benefited the poor and marginalized, and have only benefited the middle class to the extent that they have been able to influence these rules through collective action.

The rules that generate economic outcomes are not natural laws. The market outcomes are not natural phenomena like the weather, something we can complain about but cannot change. Markets are social institutions and the rules are socially determined. Most often the rules are created to benefit those with the power to adjust or set the rules, but they can be adjusted to promote greater equality and inclusion. And if changing the rules is too difficult or costly, then equity dictates that we intervene after the fact to produce outcomes that will ensure that *all* benefit and *all* can contribute.

## SOCIAL JUSTICE REQUIRES EQUITY AND EFFICIENCY

In most discussions of the economy, questions of economic equity are peripheral to what economists and policy makers are really interested in—economic growth. In fact, when equity does enter the discussion it is seen as in opposition to economic efficiency. This is the famous, or infamous, depending on ones' perspective, "Big Trade-off" between equity/equality and efficiency. This idea of a necessary trade-off between equity/equality and economic efficiency is so fundamental to how economists think about these issues that they often merely dismiss any call for greater equity without giving it any serious thought or analysis. Yet, the requirements of social justice call for both equity and efficiency and suggest that they support, rather than oppose, each other.

The idea of a trade-off between equality and efficiency became solidified in economic theory with the famous book by Arthur Okun, *Equality and Efficiency: The Big Trade-Off* (1975). Okun argued that market economies, in order to operate efficiently, must necessarily generate a certain level of income inequality. The reason is simple enough. Markets must pay higher incomes to get people to take more difficult or stressful jobs, or to acquire the necessary education and skills which some jobs require, and for entrepreneurs to undertake higher levels of risk with their investments. In order to generate greater levels of equality, Okun contended, this market mechanism would have to be hampered with, thus weakening the role of price signals and thus lowering the efficiency of markets. Okun stated that public policies that promote equality are like transferring water from one well to another. Inevitably some will spill in the process. This spillage from these leaky buckets (equality promoting policies) is lost economic efficiency, which means that the economy will produce less Gross National Product than it could have. It is ironic that this analysis has since been used to argue against re-distributive economic policies, for the main point of Okun's book was that the United States could well afford considerable spillage in order to achieve the more important goal of greater equality.

The central weakness in Okun's analysis is its contention that market outcomes are necessarily efficient. If one defines efficiency as market outcomes, then it is natural to measure efficiency with Gross National Product (GNP), which measures the total of all market exchanges for final goods and services. It is well known that this is a poor measure of economic and social well-being for it includes many economic transactions that do not promote the well-being of the community (such as crime; illness; pollution) while excluding activities that do promote well-being (household production, caring for children and elderly; volunteer work). In fact, much of the economic growth in the US economy in the past thirty years has been social decay by another name. To give an example: the rise in divorce rates and family break-ups causes a considerable increase in market transactions (two homes, multiple appliances, paid child-care, divorce lawyers, fast food; psychological counseling etc.). Arthur C. Pigou, a famous English economist of the early 20$^{th}$ century, once quipped that when a man married his housekeeper, the country's national income declined (because now the activities of the housekeeper will not be provided as a market exchange). We have been promoting economic growth by doing the opposite. This is one reason why so many feel they are not experiencing the beneficial effects of the "good" economy. Market outcomes might be the most profitable for those with economic power, but they are rarely the best possible outcome for the entire population, especially the poor and marginalized. As we saw above, the market only considers the demand of those with money. The voices and needs of those without money are not considered. Thus our current economy at its peak in 2000, considered the envy of the world, still produced an outcome with 32 million people living in "official" poverty, with millions more living in actual poverty. Any outcome that excludes 32 million people cannot be considered efficient by any definition based on human needs and decency. Not only are these 32 million individuals being excluded from the benefits of what the economy actually produced, their potential contribution to the economy and society is lost, thus society as a whole is poorer than it needs to be. Society is operating at its most efficient level when all are contributing to their fullest potential, with non-market contributions being given their due importance.

Economists often equate equity with equality, thus creating a straw man. You would have a hard time finding anyone who advocates perfect equality in incomes (everyone receives the same income). In fact such equality would be a violation of most conceptions of social justice, in that all people do not have equal needs. An adequate income for all is the equity criterion asserted by the UN Declaration on Universal Human Rights as a human right. Yet rights need to be balanced with responsibilities, thus there is a necessary second component to social justice. The right of all to a decent standard of living is coupled with the responsibility of all to contribute to the well-being of the community (though this does not have to be in the form of paid employment. The parent who cares for their children and raises them to respect others and to be good citizens is certainly contributing the economic and social well-being of society). However, many are prevented from fulfilling this responsibility by social structures that erect barriers to their social participation. One such barrier is the extreme poverty that too many Americans experience. An adequate income is a minimum criterion to social participation and to contributing to the well-being of the community. This is the minimum criterion of social justice, the adequate provision to all so that they can lead a decent life and contribute to their fullest potential toward the well-being of the community. *Equity promotes real efficiency.* It is not a trade-off, but two sides of the same coin.

This is not merely a theoretical case we are making here. The experience of the past 50 years confirms that when we promote greater equality and equity, we are at the same time promoting a more efficient economy. One example of this is the provision of universal access to education regardless of ability to pay. Education helps to break down barriers to the poor and marginalized, generating greater equality and dramatically improving the productivity of workers and the economy. Expenditures on education do more to promote economic growth than spending on anything else. We should remember that the period from WWII to 1973, often called the "golden age of capitalism" experienced both falling levels of income inequality, a breaking down of barriers to the poor and the fastest growing economy ever experienced in the USA. This widening of social participation was a key ingredient to this economic progress. The Reagan experiment can be best seen as an attempt to promote economic growth by increasing income inequality (a rather perverted use of the equality/efficiency trade-off), yet its success was due to good old fashion Keynesian deficit spending. The 1990s boom was built on speculation and historic levels of consumer debt. None of these paths to economic growth are sustainable. Only a growth strategy built on promoting equity and real efficiency is sustainable (economically, politically, socially and environmentally) in the long run.

## A RISING TIDE WILL NOT LIFT ALL BOATS[2]

When President Kennedy made his famous "a rising tide lifts all boats" statement he was expressing the idea that the best policy for reducing poverty is to promote economic growth. This same belief was behind Ronald

Reagan's experiment with "trickle-down economics." The political benefits of using economic growth to fight poverty are fairly obvious, for they allow the problem of poverty to be tackled without requiring any sacrifice from the more affluent. Both major presidential candidates in the recent election also highlighted this faith in economic growth eliminating poverty. Both Bush and Gore stated the need to keep the economy growing in their position papers on poverty policy, with Gore taking the position that "fiscal discipline" would provide for a healthy economy.

The welfare reform policies of the 1990's are different from the "Great Society" programs of the 1960's essentially in their belief that economic growth is enough, that government support programs are a hindrance to getting out of poverty. All that is necessary for government to do is provide the right incentives for getting out of poverty. Only if one believes that the economy will provide sufficient jobs and incomes to bring everyone willing to work out of poverty, does it make sense to pursue social policies designed to increase the poor's willingness to work and expect that to be enough to eliminate poverty. Much of the success or failure of these experiments will depend on whether economic growth will be enough to significantly reduce poverty in America.

## Relationship between Economic Growth and Poverty

The theoretical linkage between economic growth and the number of people below the poverty rate is fairly straight forward. More economic growth leads to potentially more income for all. If any of this increase in income "trickles down" to the poor we will get a rise in their standard of living and a reduction in the poverty rate, *ceteris paribus*. If one looks at the long term relationship between economic growth and the poverty rate (or numbers in poverty), it is clear that there has been a close and inverse relationship between the rate of economic growth and the poverty rate, with increases in GNP coinciding with declines in the poverty rate, and when economic growth slows down, or when the economy experiences negative growth in GNP (recession), the poverty rate rises. We can see this in two ways. In Graph 1 below we see the relationship between economic growth and poverty, as measured by the official poverty rate.

**Graph 1**
**Economic Growth and Poverty Rates, 1959-2000**

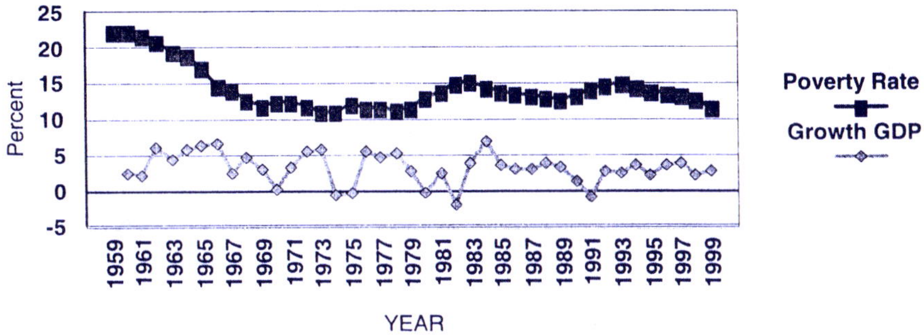


Source: U.S. Census and BLS

In this Graph we see that the poverty rate fell consistently from 1959 to 1973 when it hit its all time low of 11.1 percent, and since then it has fluctuated around 13 percent (plus or minus 2 percentage points).

The secular trend upward of the poverty rate can be seen in Table 1 below, which gives the average poverty rate for each of the business cycles from 1959 to 1999. Here we see that the poverty rate reached its lowest average level in the 1973-79 cycle and has been rising with each successive business cycle.

**Table 1**
**Average Percent in Poverty over Business Cycle Peaks, 1959-99**

| Years | Poverty Rates % |
|---|---|
| 1959-67 | 19.1 |
| 1967-73 | 12.5 |
| 1973-79 | 11.6 |
| 1979-89 | 13.6 |
| 1989-99 | 13.7 |

Source: U. S. Bureau of the Census, P60-201.

Economic growth's ability to reduce poverty has been greatly weakened since the early 1980's (see Blank 1993 and Mishel, Bernstein and Schmitt, 1999. pp. 292-4). Using a model based on the work of Rebecca Blank, we have estimated the effects that various macro economic variables have had on poverty rates in the United States from 1959 to 1980 and carried forward these variables up to 1999 to see how these variables influenced the poverty rates in the 1980s and 1990s.

**Graph 2**
**Actual and Predicted Poverty Rates, 1959-1999**

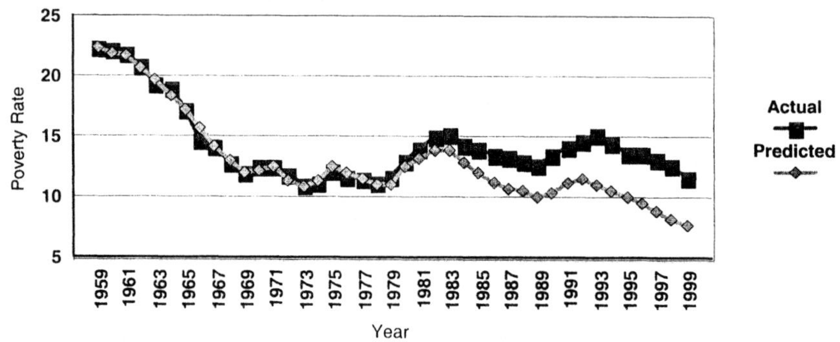


Source: Authors Calculation

In Graph 2 above we see both the actual and predicted poverty rates. We see that the factors that reduced poverty (all economic growth related) before 1980 failed to have the same impact after 1980. Had the relationships of the 1960s and 1970s held, we would have expected a significant drop in poverty rates to historic lows, reaching 7.8% in 1999. What has changed from the 1960's to the 1990's? The rise in income inequality is the main cause of the inability of economic growth to significantly reduce poverty. Just about all of the income gains of the past 20 years have been concentrated in the hands of the richest 20 percent of the population, thus leaving little to trickle down to the poor. The reason that the rich have been the main beneficiaries of this economic growth (unlike in the 1950 and 1960s) is because of the change in the balance of power (economic and political) brought about partly by the rise of the "New Economy." As we will see the changes brought about by the "New Economy" have greatly weakened the ability to spread the benefits of economic growth more equitably.

## CHALLENGES OF THE "NEW ECONOMY"

So far we have argued that economic equity is not merely following the letter of the law, but has to include fairness in outcomes based on the criteria that all have a right to a decent standard of living and a right to participate to their fullest capabilities in promoting the well-being of the community. These dual criteria of social justice mean that we must promote both efficiency and equity. Efficiency without equity (ensuring all share in the benefits of economic progress), that is economic growth alone, will not reduce poverty. Here we will look at the complex problem of how to promote equity and a prosperous economy in the context of "globalization" and the "New Economy."

Few would doubt that the economies of the world are going through a period of rapid change and transformation. Whether this is a "New Economy" or merely an acceleration of the evolutionary trends of the past two hundred years is a question for academics to debate. What is beyond debate is that many of our old assumptions and beliefs about the economy and the institutions and structures that determine economic outcomes no longer hold. In many ways we are at a turning point in economic history not unlike the one Karl Polanyi wrote about in his classic *The Great Transformation* (1944). Three points that Polanyi emphasized are worth keeping in mind when considering the current transformation. First, technological change requires institutional change, that is, society must change the "rules and habits" by which the economy and society are organized. Second, institutional changes generated by the economy will shift the costs of the new production methods to those with the least power and influence, the poor and workers. Third, and finally, these changes will generate a social backlash by those adversely affected by the new economic order. Polanyi used the development of the Industrial Revolution to illustrate these points, but we can take our present economies in transition to make the same points.

## Why 20th Century Economic Institutions Do Not Fit the 21st Century Economy

One of the reasons that the post WWII period was the "golden age" of capitalism is that its social and political institutions underwent a dramatic change to complement the advances in economics and technology. The creation of the Welfare State played a key role in this economic progress because it helped to spread the benefits of economic progress to all, or at least to most. These efforts at inclusion were necessary not only for the generation of economic progress, but also because they allowed for stronger democratic institutions and a stronger civil society. The model used for structuring the economy so that all or most of the citizens shared in the benefits of economic progress has been called (at least in the English speaking countries) the Keynes-Beveridge model.

**Assumptions of Model:**

*Full employment as the norm.* The experience of the wartime economies showed that Keynes's policy suggestions worked and that full employment could be achieved. If there were bouts of unemployment, they would be temporary and short-lived. Keynesian fiscal and monetary policy would keep the economy at or near full employment.

*Productivity gains were passed on to workers.* Various institutions were set up to ensure that the gains of economic progress would be widely shared. Most of these involved intervention in various labour markets: with labour unions; work place regulations; minimum wages; subsidized benefits such as health care and retirement pensions and a progressive tax system that checked the growth of income inequality.

*One worker per household.* Under the Keynes-Beveridge model, each household should be able to have a standard of living within the accepted norms of a decent quality of life provided one of the household's adults participated full time in the labour force. Wage increases that reflected productivity gains allowed for rising standards of living, while also supporting non-market contributions to the economic and social life of the community and household.

**Macro and Micro Policies**

*Necessary Macroeconomic Policies Included*: Fiscal policies (the ability to raise and lower taxes and spending levels, including deficit spending, in order to regulate aggregate demand); monetary policy (ability to raise or lower interest rates to counter inflation and influence aggregate demand) and trade policy (use of trade barriers to protect home production and the use of trade surpluses to generate aggregate demand and use imports to fight inflation, and after 1971, the ability to manipulate one's currency to influence trade and inflation).

*Necessary Microeconomic Policies included*: price regulation; investment subsidies; minimum wages and other wage regulations; labour regulations (on all aspects of work and remuneration); intervention in capital, land and resource factor markets, and the use of taxes and subsidies to promote greater levels of income equality, and income supports for those who, for what ever reason, could not compete successfully in the market economy. (In many countries there were strict demarcations between those who had legitimate reasons for their lack of success in the market economy, such as age, illness, unemployment, and those who did not. This is the Elizabethan demarcation between the deserving and non-deserving poor).

It is only with these assumptions and complementary macro and micro economic policies that the Welfare State was able to insure that all or most of society was able to share in the economic progress of the post WWII era. Starting at the beginning of the 1970s however, these conditions started to falter, and the Welfare State economies started to come under increasing strain. The first and second oil shocks dramatically reduced the aggregate demand for the goods and services that these economies produced. The extra revenues that went to pay for the increasingly higher energy cost meant reductions in money being spent on domestically produced goods and services, which translates into higher unemployment rates. Furthermore, the higher energy costs lead to inflation. Thus you had the infamous *stagflation*, rising prices *and* unemployment levels. The rising unemployment levels prevented the use of Keynesian fiscal policies to fight inflation (tax increases), as aggregate demand was already insufficient. Thus a monetary policy of high interest rates was used to fight inflation. This had an even greater dampening effect on aggregate demand, and by the end of the 1970s and early 1980 s many countries had double-digit levels of unemployment.

The flexibility and mobility that are the chief characteristics of the "New Economy" run counter to the structure of the Welfare State, which achieved its goal of income security by creating inflexibilities. The goal of economic security is a worthy one; in fact no society can call itself decent and civilized that doesn't provide a decent minimum level of economic security. If the advanced capitalist economies are to remain functioning democracies and are to pursue long-term prosperity and maintain their strong civil societies, then their main challenge will be to ensure that all share in the benefits of the "New Economy." To understand how this can be achieved, we must first look at what are the driving forces of the "New Economy": technological change; trade liberalization; increased capital mobility (capital/financial flows); and labor market flexibility.

**Technological Impact**

Not a day seems to go by without a new technological marvel being heralded in the press. No doubt the pace of technological change has been accelerating, much like it did for the first "great transformation." At such a quick pace, it is no wonder that most analysts have not looked at the potential long term economic implications of these advances. The changes in the technology of production have the potential to generate technological unemployment at an unprecedented scale (Rifkin 1995). Unless demand grows just as fast, this increasing productivity will lead to millions of workers without jobs in the paid labor force. The major source of unmet needs that can meet this demand for goods and services are the poor, both in the rich countries and in the Third World, but although they have unmet needs, they lack the money to meet these needs. New methods of distributing income will be needed so that these needs get met.

## Trade Liberalisation

Trade liberalisation is a fact of the "New Economy." The only question is whether it will be limited to regional trade agreements or to a global system (as proposed with the WTO). One of the ways that countries have spread the benefits of economic progress down to workers and the poor has been by protecting these workers from foreign competition. Unions do this nationally, but in an international economy, this is achieved through trade policy. There are two basic forms of trade policy: tariffs and trade barriers; and currency policy. Tariffs and trade barriers provide protection for workers and businesses in that they reduce competition from low-cost foreign producers. Currency policy allows the government or central bank to reduce the cost of production domestically by lowering the exchange rate of the currency (this also makes foreign goods more expensive), promoting exports and reducing imports. These two important tools for raising the standards of living of domestic workers and ensuring that the benefits of economic progress are more widely shared have been partially or completely eliminated. A new set of institutions is needed to ensure that the benefits of the "New Economy" will be widely shared.

## Capital Mobility

One of the most dramatic aspects of the "New Economy" is the increase in capital mobility, the ability of money to enter and exit economies, leading to rising investment levels, and often to speculation and economic crisis (Asian-crisis, Mexican Crisis, Latin American Crisis etc.). One of the effects of capital mobility is the fall in the share of income going to workers and the rise in the share going to capital. Another effect is the change in the rules of the economy. Due to the increased mobility of capital, real interest rates have increased, the result of higher levels of risk and uncertainty in the post Breton Woods world. This too contributes to more income inequality. More than any other development of the "New Economy," the increased capital mobility has weakened the relative position of workers, thus promoting greater income inequality. Short of massive international capital controls, some other means needs to be devised for more equitably distributing the benefits of economic progress.

### Labor Market Flexibility

As with the other factors mentioned above, a key method of spreading the benefits of economic progress down the economic ladder has been through the regulation of labor markets, either by the government or by unions. Many of these regulations only are successful to the extent that they create rigidities. These rigidities allow wages to rise, with the cost being shifted to another sector (either a fall in profits or in higher prices). Declining unionization rates and falling government support for worker protections have lead to greater labor market flexibility, but at the cost of reducing the ability to distribute the benefits of economic progress more widely, thus furthering the case for the need for new institutions to achieve equity.

## NEW OPPORTUNITIES: THE BASIC INCOME SOLUTION

Guy Standing (1999) has noted:

> Every era of capitalist triumphalism creates the basis for renewed social struggle to ameliorate inequalities, a struggle to limit the new mechanisms of inequality. Every technological revolution has been accompanied by ruling elites calling for more flexibility (or whatever the word at the time) from workers and for more "discipline" over them. In such times, momentarily, the forward march of social progress seems to be halted, even reversed. Then, once a vision of an alternative, viable system of distributive justice has crystallised, the state has moved in that direction, to re-embed the economy in society. Then—perhaps—in directions that were not previously foreseen—the forward march resumes ( Lerner, Clark, and Needham 1999, 106).

The inability of the old institutions to deal with the problem of promoting economic equity in the context of the "New Economy" requires us to come up with some new ideas. The failure of "Welfare Reform" to help the poor and marginalized shows that going backwards will not work either. What is needed is a new way of looking at the role of work in our economy and society. Following John Paul II (1991), we must take a broader view of work, one that includes all forms of social participation and contributions. As fewer full-time paid employment opportunities will be available, we cannot rely on such employment as the only rewarded way in which someone can contribute to the economic and social well-being of the community. Furthermore, we must recognize that paid employment and the market will not provide a decent minimum income for all. We must devise systems of support that provide a decent level of income and which do not create barriers to further development. We must help the poor, not regulate them.

One policy that is being debated in many European economies that would promote both greater equity and economic efficiency is the provision of a Basic Income to all citizens as a right of citizenship.[3] Such an income would be tax-free and would not go down when one's income increases, thus avoiding poverty and unemployment traps (creating inefficiencies). It also supports all the necessary and valuable activities in the social economy, activities upon which the social health of our society depends but which currently go unrecognized and unsupported.

In the previous section we have noted that the "New Economy" requires flexibilities that weaken the ability of the Welfare State to promote economic equity. The Welfare State approach of regulating the poor creates many barriers to escaping poverty (poverty traps) and other disincentives, as well as taxing the fiscal and economic health of the overall economy. The "workfare" approach of reducing benefits and tightening eligibility has at best lead to higher levels of hidden poverty and shifted the responsibility of providing necessary assistance for the poor to private charities and churches which do not have the resources to adequately deal with this problem. The only option being proposed to these admittedly inadequate systems is the Basic Income proposal, which provides, through its universality and security, an effective social safety net and also promotes an efficient and flexible economy. Thus the choice seems to be between income security or economic flexibility or (with a Basic Income System) both income security and economic flexibility. The first two options do not offer attractive alternatives, for they frequently, in essence, pit the social classes against each other, with income security benefiting those at the lower end of the economic ladder, while a reduced welfare state (workfare) benefits those who are already well off (in terms of reduced tax rates). With its ability to offer both income security and labor market flexibility, Basic Income gets beyond this trade-off by providing a means through which all Americans will be able to benefit from the economic progress being created by this new economy.

Basic Income is a generic term that fits many different types of proposals (or at least is applied to many proposals). The main differences are twofold: 1) different levels of benefits, from a full Basic Income, with benefit levels set at the official poverty level, to a partial Basic Income set at a lower level; and 2) how the Basic Income system will be funded. Most Basic Income proposals include a flat income tax as their sole, or primary, source of funding. Such a funding mechanism is not an essential aspect of Basic Income. Alaska has a Basic Income system with their Permanent Fund, which is supported by revenues generated by their oil and gas reserves. A flat income tax is often used because it is the easiest source of tax revenues for the person developing a Basic Income proposal to estimate and model. As these proposals have been, for the most part, developed by individuals and groups with very limited resources, this is their only option. Were a system to be developed by either a government agency or a well-endowed research institute alternative modes of taxation could easily be developed, and the tax on income could be dramatically reduced.

For the purpose of furthering the discussion on Basic Income I am presenting a rudimentary Basic Income system for the United States as if it were instituted in 1999. The system is designed to replace the entire social welfare and income assistance system in the United States with the exception of Social Security (a good case can be made for including Social Security in the system, but that is not done here.) In this section we will present this proposal, along with some analysis of its effects on income distribution. We present this Basic Income System for America not as an actual proposal, but as a hypothetical proposal that allows the issues raised by a Basic Income proposal to be discussed. Much further work, requiring resources beyond those at our disposable, would be required to develop a complete American Basic Income proposal.

## Hypothetical American Basic Income System

The following Basic Income proposal is based on 1999 figures, with the population levels, income distribution and payment rates as they were in 1999. The proposed Basic Income system is a full Basic Income system, meaning that the levels of payment are set so that everyone is brought above the poverty line (for 1999). The Basic Income system would have annual payment levels at:

**Table 2**
**Basic Income Payments, 1999**

| Age | Payment |
|---|---|
| Under 18 | $3,500 |
| Adult | $8,667 |
| Over 65 | $7,990 |

This will have the following costs:

**Table 3**
**Costs of Basic Income System, 1999**

| Age | Payment | Population (Millions) | Costs ($ Millions) |
|---|---|---|---|
| Under 18 | $3,500 | 70.2 | 245,697 |
| Adult | $8,667 | 167.95 | 1,455,640 |
| Over 65 | $7,990 | 34.54 | 275,975 |
| **Total** | | | 1,977,311 |

The total costs of our Basic Income proposal would be just under 2 trillion dollars. Add to this the cost of the other functions of the Federal Government, which in 1999 totaled $1,465,333 ($1,703,040 million minus $237,707 million, income security funds to be cut under a basic income proposal). Thus the total costs of the Federal Government would be $3,442,644 million.

Funding for the Basic Income system, as well as for the Federal Government in general, would be through a flat tax on all incomes at a rate of 35.8%. Federal government expenditures on income security would be cut, with the exceptions of pensions and social security. The flat income tax would replace the current income tax system. All other taxes collected by the Federal Government would remain. There would be no income tax deductions. State and local tax and benefits systems in our example are left untouched, although obviously they would change dramatically (i.e., be reduced or eliminated, leading to reductions in local and state taxes). All funding for health, veteran's programs, education, and housing remain.

**Table 4**
**Federal Government Revenues**
(Millions)

| | |
|---|---|
| Flat Tax | $2,576,970 |
| Corporate Taxes | $184,680 |
| Social Insurance | $611,833 |
| Excise Taxes | $70,414 |
| Total | $3,443,897 |

Thus, under this proposal the total expenditures of the Federal Government would be $3,442.6 billion, while the total revenue would be $3,443.9 billion, leaving a small surplus of $1.3 billion.

## Distributional Impact

Using the 1999 consumer expenditure survey data, I have simulated how such a policy would effect the distribution of income in the United States. Table 5 presents the results of this simulation.

**Table 5**
**Income Distribution Effects of Basic Income System**

| Income Quintile | Without BI (1999) | With Basic Income (1999) |
|---|---|---|
| Bottom | 3.5 | 8.22 |
| 2nd | 8.65 | 12.22 |
| 3rd | 14.86 | 16.96 |
| 4th | 23.93 | 23.39 |
| Top | 49.06 | 39.2 |

Source: Author's calculations. Totals may not equal 100% due to rounding.

In Table 6 we see the average household income for each household quintile, and their gain or loss due to the Basic Income system.

**Table 6**
**Average Household Income by Quintile, 1999**
**Without and With BI**

| Income Quintile | Without BI | With BI | Difference |
|---|---|---|---|
| Bottom | $7,101 | $16,714 | $9,613 |
| 2nd | $17,576 | $24,826 | $7,250 |
| 3rd | $30,186 | $34,448 | $4,262 |
| 4th | $48,607 | $47,515 | $-1,092 |
| Top | $99,656 | $79,622 | $-20,034 |

Source: Author's calculations.

Introducing a Basic Income system in the United States like the one proposed would have the dual effect of lifting everyone above the "official" poverty level, and dramatically reducing the level of income inequality. We will now turn to the arguments for and against such a policy.

## ARGUMENTS FOR AND AGAINST BASIC INCOME

One of the most interesting aspects of the Basic Income discussion is the wide ideological range of its supporters (and its critics).[4] The idea of something like a Basic Income system was first fully developed by Thomas Paine in the late 18th Century. Recent supporters include liberal economists John Kenneth Galbraith and James Tobin and conservative economists James Meade and Herbert Simon. Both Richard Nixon and George McGovern discussed proposals that were, in some regards, similar to a Basic Income. Such a diverse list of supporters causes some confusion in that many of the arguments for a Basic Income contradict other supporting arguments (usually based on what the person feels is wrong with the existing system).

### Views of Conservatives

The conservative case for a basic income centers on two economic prepositions: 1) unemployment is caused by imperfections in the labor market; and 2) standard policies (Keynesian) designed to reduce poverty and promote full employment instead cause inflation. The best example of the first proposition is James Meade's work (especially Meade 1989). His argument is as follows. Under the current system, wages are downwardly rigid during recessions. This downward rigidity prevents the labor market from reaching the market-clearing price, thus causing mass unemployment. The sources of this rigidity are the rational choices of those who retain their jobs during the economic downturn and the lack of any mechanism for those without jobs to influence the labor market. By partially separating income from work, the incentive of workers to fight against wage reductions is considerably reduced, thus making labor markets more flexible. This allows wages, and hence labor costs, to adjust more readily to changing economic conditions. It is thus argued that this increased efficiency in the labor market, particularly the responsiveness of wages to conditions of excess labor supply, would lead to full employment and greater economic growth.

The second reason conservatives support Basic Income policies stems from Milton Friedman's advocacy of a negative income tax. Friedman proposed a negative income tax as an alternative to Keynesian Demand management policies, which he felt were inflationary, and created large government bureaucracies. Negative income taxes (and a Basic Income) would give the money directly to the poor without causing inflation or big government.[5]

Some conservatives argue against Basic Income proposals on two grounds. First, it is argued that such policies require high tax rates to fund them and conservatives are almost always against high taxes. Second, they feel that giving a non-means tested payment will damage the incentive to work. These incentives are also lessened by the high tax rates just mentioned. Thus they feel that these types of policies will lessen the labor supply and reduce economic growth and efficiency.

Both the conservative case for and against Basic Income policies came up short when evaluated from the perspective of what we know about labor markets and incentives. The case for requires unemployment to be caused solely by market imperfections, yet the primary cause of unemployment is inadequate aggregate demand. Improving wage flexibilities will do little to improve this inherent problem of advanced capitalist economies; in fact it might make it worse (unless there is a basic income system in place, then it will not necessarily make things worse). The case against basic income rests on the notion that high taxes or benefits will reduce the labor supply, but the preponderance of the evidence shows that such factors are not important for the labor supply of adult males and single females. It is only married women whose labor supply is greatly influenced by tax and benefit levels. Thus the impact on economic growth and efficiency will not be great.

### Views of Liberals

The liberal case for a Basic Income policy stems from the fact that it allows those in poverty more opportunities to raise themselves out of poverty, in large part because of the elimination of the poverty and employment traps. Furthermore, liberals see the universality of Basic Income systems as a means of preventing individuals from falling through the social safety net, as well as taking away the stigma of being poor and on public assistance. Some liberal economists feel that a Basic Income system will strengthen the position of workers in their bargaining with employers. They also note that a Basic Income, paid to each individual, greatly empowers women and promotes communitarian values, citizenship and equality.

The liberal argument against Basic Income policies is a reaction to the labor market flexibility argument put forward by conservatives. Some liberal economists have argued that a Basic Income system will lead to wage substitution and weaken society's commitment to promoting full employment in the traditional Keynesian sense. Yet for this to happen you would have to repeal the minimum wage laws and eliminate unions and labor legislation.

The great Institutionalist economist, C.E. Ayres wrote that the institution of a universal guaranteed income "would . . .restore the reality of free private enterprise" (Ayres 1966, 161). His argument is based partly on the positive aggregate demand effects such a system would have and partly on the great liberating effect economic security has on individuals. All societies attempt to provide some form of economic security. This is due to the simple fact that as individuals we are poor and that we only achieve affluence through the cooperation of others, i.e. life in society. On the level of societies, this economic security allows for experimentation and knowledge creation. Communities that are living hand to mouth do not have the time or the resources to break from their poverty through technological or institutional change. The risk of failure is too great (starvation) for them to undertake such a gamble. The same is true for poor individuals in an affluent society. Economic security provides the support for experimentation and risk taking, what would be called in business circles as entrepreneurship, allowing the poor to find their way out of poverty.

## CONCLUSION

The dual problems of persistent poverty and rising income inequalities are a real threat to the health and well being of the United States. Under the hey day of the Welfare State the government was able to affect the "rules of the game" for distributing income by creating inflexibilities that shifted power down the economic ladder and thus allowing them to demand a larger share of the economic pie. Globalization and the "New Economy" are increasingly making it difficult or impossible for governments to achieve these same results without significant costs to the competitiveness of the economy. New policies are needed to promote economic equity in a way that does not create these inflexibilities. A Basic Income system allows for the promotion of greater economic equity (in our proposal it reduces the official poverty rate in the United States to zero) while also getting the government out of the business of regulating the poor and creating stigmas and barriers to getting out of poverty. Furthermore, a Basic Income system helps to support those in atypical forms of employment, as well as those who contribute to society in the social economy and not through paid employment. Lastly, a Basic Income system is a recognition of the fact that wealth and income are socially created, with our technological and intellectual heritage being the most important factor of production. All of us are inheritors of these gifts from our forbearers, yet currently most of the benefits of this inheritance do not reach all of our citizens. A Basic Income system ensures that all share in the benefits of economic progress, while maintaining the flexibilities that ensure future economic progress.

## NOTES

[1] See Clark (1996) for an Institutionalist approach to explaining income inequality.

[2] This section is based on Clark (1999, 43-53).

[3] For an excellent overview of recent Basic Income proposals see Widerquirst (2001a and 2001b). Also see http://www.usbig.net/ for more information on Basic Income.

[4] This section is based on Clark and Kavanagh (1996).

[5] There are many significant differences between Friedman's negative income tax and the Basic Income outline here. The two most glaring of these are 1) the level of payment (at the official poverty line) is much higher than Friedman argued for, and 2) all Basic Income payments in this proposal are tax free and thus free of poverty traps. Friedman's proposal had a high withdrawal rate, thus high poverty traps.

## REFERENCES

Ayres, Clarence E., 1966. "Guaranteed Income: An Institutionalist View." In *The GuaranteedIncome: Next Step in Economic Evolution?* R. Theobald, ed. Garden City, New York: Doubleday & Company.

Blank, Rebecca M. 1993. "Why were Poverty Rates so High in the 1980s?" In *Poverty and Prosperity in the USA in the Late Twentieth Century*, Dimitri B. Papadimitriou and Edward N. Wolff, eds. New York: St. Martin's Press.

Clark, Charles M. A. 1996. "Inequality in the 1980's: An Institutionalist Perspective." In *Inequality: Radical Perspective on Institutionalist Race, Gender, Class and Nation.* William Dugger, ed. Westport, CT.: Greenwood Press.

———. 1999. "Does a Rising Tide Lift All Boats? How Poverty has Become Immune to Economic Growth." *Vincentian Chair of Social Justice* Vol. 5.

———. 2002. *Basic Income Guarantee: Promoting Equity and Efficiency in the Irish Economy*. Dublin: Liffey Press.

———, and Catherine.Kavanagh. 1996. Basic income, inequality, and unemployment: rethinking the linkages between work and welfare. *Journl of Economic Issues 30:399-406*

John Paul II. 1991. *Laborum Exercens*. Vatican.

Lerner, Sally, Charles M. A., Clark and Robert Needham. 1999. *Basic Income: Economic Security for All Canadians*. Toronto: Between the Lines.

Meade, James E. 1989. *Agathotopia: The Economics of Partnership*. Aberdeen: Aberdeen University Press.

Mishel, Lawrence, Jared Bernstein, and John Schmitt. 1999. *The State of Working America,1998-99*. Ithaca: Cornell University Press.

Okun, Arthur. 1975. *Equality and Efficiency: The Big Trade-Off*. Washington: Brookings.

Polanyi, Karl. 1944. *The Great Transformation*. Boston: Beacon Press.

Rifkin, Jeremy. 1995. *The End of Work*. New York: G.P. Putnam Sons.

Standing, Guy. 1999. *Global Labour Flexibility*. London: Macmillan Press Ltd.

Widerquist, Karl. 2001. Perspectives on the guaranteed income, Part I. *Journal of Economic Issues* 35:749-757.

———. 2001 Perspectives on the guaranteed income, Part II. *Journal of Economic Issues* 35:1019-1030.

# 6

# WELFARE REFORM

Janice Peterson

## INTRODUCTION

In the *Preface* of this volume, the editors state that the common purpose of the volume's various chapters is to "demonstrate how contemporary institutional economic analysis can be applied to the resolution of economic problems." Institutional economics is characterized as "unorthodox," challenging the myth that "only 'the market' can efficiently allocate a society's economic resources and equitably distribute its income." The unorthodox methodological foundations of institutional economic analysis lead to policy analysis that challenges the "conventional wisdom" in the problem areas it addresses.

There is probably no area in which institutional economics differs more from the mainstream than in its treatment of the problem areas of income inequality and poverty. Rejecting the presumed trade-off between efficiency and equity that dominates mainstream approaches to these problems, institutionalists are primarily concerned with the question of "whether existing institutional structures are capable of nurturing the community's capacity to provide and enhance the means of life." This places distributional issues and the pursuit of economic security for all members of society at the forefront of institutional analysis and policy.

This chapter examines institutional economic policy analysis in the context of contemporary US welfare policy debates. The first section provides an overview of the framework that institutional economic policy analysis brings to the study of welfare reform. The second section examines recent welfare reform legislation, its impacts, and the contemporary debate regarding its future. The chapter concludes with some thoughts on the relevance of institutional economics to this on-going process of institutional change.

# INSTITUTIONAL ECONOMIC POLICY ANALYSIS

Institutionalist approaches to economic policy have their roots in the fundamental principles of institutional political economy. In particular, institutionalist conceptions of the economy and the economic role of the government lead to very different analyses of distributional issues and policies than those prevalent in mainstream economics, and provide the basis for institutionalist analyses of the US welfare state.

## Social Provisioning and Instrumental Efficiency

Institutionalists define "economics" as the study of social provisioning and see the economy as an evolving set of institutions engaged in the process of providing for the material needs of its members. The central focus of economic analysis is not on the choices of autonomous individuals interacting in competitive markets in response to scarcity, but on the actions of socialized and acculturated human-beings engaging in the provisioning process in many settings (which can include markets, as well as families, communities, and government activities).

In this context, the "efficiency" or "inefficiency" of a particular economic outcome is seen quite differently than it is in mainstream economic analysis. Institutionalists define inefficiency in terms of the waste resulting from resource allocation based on pecuniary values and invidious distinctions, including "preventable unemployment, employment of individuals at less than potential, and denial of participation because of invidious attitudes towards members of specific groups" (Miller 1996, 88). The goal of economic activity is not traditional allocative efficiency, but "instrumental efficiency"—that which promotes the "continuity of human life and the non-invidious re-creation of community" (Tool 1979, 293). Inequality and poverty represent fundamental failures of the economy to achieve instrumental efficiency: "Deprivation of income means deprivation of genuine economic choices. Since effective choice is essential for effective economic participation, the non-availability of adequate flows of money income to significant portions of the community drastically impairs their instrumental efficiency" (Tool 1979, 303-304).

Despite the seriousness of the problems presented by inequality and poverty for both the individual and society, these problems are often "evaded by characterizing those in poverty with invidiously rooted attributes" (Tool 2000, 195), or are justified with "enabling myths" about the behavior of the poor or the sources of inequality (Dugger 1989, 6). Consequently, the first step in addressing these problems is the recognition that distributional arrangements are strongly influenced by "the norms of the prevailing institutional arrangements" and that they are largely "discretionary"—that is, "determined by the conscious decisions of persons with the power and position to do so" (Peach 1988, 78). The role of economic policy in this context is to promote institutional change that leads to more instrumentally warranted patterns of behavior and outcomes.

Institutionalists call for a much more activist role for government policy in promoting such institutional change than is typically found in mainstream economic and policy analyses (Petr 1984). In addition, institutionalist thought holds that the government is inherently, even unavoidably, "involved" in the economy at all times. Institutionalists argue that the government, through its definition and enforcement of the working rules, defines the economy and legitimizes the power relationships, institutions, and beliefs that shape economic outcomes (Samuels 1989). Thus, the conceptual separation of "the economy" from "the state" found in mainstream definitions of the "private" and "public" sectors provides an incomplete and distorted picture of both the operation of the market economy and the broader social provisioning process. Further, the traditional emphasis on "private" market activity devalues the necessary provisioning activities that the government performs.

The government is seen to be intimately involved in the process of social provisioning and to have a necessary role to play in the provision of economic security. In this process, however, the government is never neutral—it shapes the economy by giving support to the interests of some participants and not to others. The relevant policy question is never "how much government intervention is desirable?" but "whose interests are being served?" (Samuels 1989). Thus, the economic role of the government is a complex and often contradictory one. The government both defines and is defined by the status quo distribution of power (Samuels 1989), and thus, may provide a vehicle for the amelioration of social and economic problems at the same time that it supports that status quo and resists change (Stanfield 1991).

## The US Welfare State: Provisioning and Inequality

Both the necessity of government action and the contradictory nature of such action are important themes in institutionalist analyses of the "welfare state" —defined as "the use of the power of the central government to protect people from the income loss inherent in industrial society" (Peterson 1985,

602). Institutional economic analysis views the welfare state as a response to the insecurities of industrial market capitalism. These insecurities manifest themselves in the disruption of the income flows necessary to settle the reciprocal relationships of a market society, and the welfare state has evolved to "circumvent stoppages of the usual pecuniary flow." This has typically involved the addition of a new income stream—"independent income"—that is independent of market exchange and imputed productivity, and traditionally, involves no explicit quid pro quo (Hamilton 1984).

The stream of independent income takes different forms in different industrial societies, but it is generally associated with some system of income transfers. Although mainstream economic analysis tends to focus on the allocative efficiency of income transfer programs, institutionalists emphasize that the public acceptability of such programs often has little to do with their efficiency defined in market terms. It is consistency with "social values, norms and beliefs" that is the crucial factor, with programs that appear to be provided "as a matter of right for some good or service" finding the most acceptance. That is, programs that are structured in such as way as to resemble reciprocal exchange have typically been seen by the public to have more legitimacy, and have received more public support, than those that are viewed as a unidirectional flow (Waller 1987).

This point has very important implications for the study of US welfare policy. For many decades, discussions of "welfare reform" have focused on policies designed primarily for poor single-mother families. The public acceptability of such programs has been affected by deeply held, and sometimes conflicting, "social values, norms, and beliefs" about the appropriate roles of women (particularly those who are mothers). In addition, determining the meaning of reciprocity has been complicated by the fact that women's relationships to the traditionally accepted pecuniary income flows of the market economy have often differed from those established by men, and that their contributions outside of the market economy have often been devalued economically.

This reflects what feminist economists have identified as another important "public-private" distinction in mainstream economic thought—the conceptual separation of the "public sphere" of the economy from the "private sphere" of the home and family. The market economy has been defined as the only legitimate sphere of economic activity, and thus, the social provisioning activities that take place within the home have been defined as private, and therefore, non-economic (Waller and Jennings 1990). Women have traditionally been associated with the private sphere, thus defining their relationship with the market economy as contingent and their work in the home as non-economic. Consequently, the ways in which the government has attempted to "circumvent stoppages of the usual pecuniary flow" and to reduce economic insecurity have differed for men and for women. Programs for men have been viewed as responses to disruptions in the economy and have sought to assist them as workers, while programs for women have been viewed as responses to disruptions in the family and have been designed to assist them as mothers (Silverberg 1985; Nelson 1990).

Thus, the government's response to economic insecurity has not been the same for all groups of US society. Throughout the history of the US welfare state, the determination of whose interests count, and how they will be served, has reflected gender (as well as race and class) distinctions. The government, through the programs of the welfare state, has promoted economic security for many, while at the same time it has instituted and reinforced various forms of inequality (Peterson 1996). This is reflected in the "dual" or "two-tiered" structure of the US welfare state, which makes a sharp distinction between "social insurance" and "public assistance" programs. This distinction has been particularly important in defining what is meant by "welfare" and the issues that have come to dominate "welfare reform" discussions.

## The Dual Welfare State

Social insurance and public assistance programs provide benefits of different degrees of adequacy and coverage to different groups in society. Social insurance programs are designed primarily to protect workers and their families from loss of income due to retirement, illness, disability, or unemployment. They are tied to previous employment and earnings, and their benefits are typically viewed as "earned" income. Public assistance programs are designed to provide financial support to certain categories of the poor. Benefits are means-tested and typically lower than those provided through social insurance programs (Peterson and Petersen 1994; Peterson 1997). These two different flows of "independent income" are structured and administered very differently, and consequently, convey very different meanings about the "worthiness" of their recipients. Social insurance transfers, which have the appearance of being tied in some way to reciprocal exchange, have had a great deal more public support than public assistance, or "welfare," transfers.

The hierarchical "two-tiered" structure of the dual welfare state limits the welfare state's potential for progressive redistribution by essentially "helping most the people who need it the least." Those individuals most likely to have access to the "top-tier" social insurance programs are also the ones most likely to receive private pensions, sick leave, and health insurance. In addition, public spending on the poor through public assistance has consistently been much smaller in magnitude than social insurance spending. Thus, any redistributive gains that may have been provided to the poor through public assistance do not compare with the superior benefits to the middle- and upper-classes through social insurance (Gordon 1994, 6, 300).

This structure also fosters the enabling myths that further legitimize various forms of inequality (Peterson 1997). Although the terms "income support" and "welfare state" are used to include both public assistance and social insurance programs, Americans "make a sharp conceptual and evaluative distinction" between them (Skocpol 1988, 296)—public assistance is considered to be "welfare," while social insurance is not. The contemporary pejorative meaning of "welfare" derives from this distinction, which "labels only some programs 'welfare' and understands others to be in a different category" (Gordon 1994, 1).

The gendered nature of this structure can be seen in the development of the two Progressive era programs—Mother's Pensions and Workmen's Compensation (both enacted in 1911)—which provided early models for the distinction between public assistance and social insurance. While both programs attempted to address the increased economic insecurity of the time, they represented very different approaches to public provisioning—one primarily focused on women (Mother's Pensions) and the other primarily focused on men (Workmen's Compensation) (Silverberg 1985; Nelson 1990).

Mother's Pensions were designed to aid poor children in families that had lost the support of a male bread-winner (Abramoviz 1988, 190-194), while Workmen's Compensation was designed to protect workers and their families from income loss due to disability or death in industrial accidents (Silverberg 1985; Polakow 1993). These two programs differed tremendously in their administrative designs and procedures. In particular, the eligibility and decision rules in Mother's Pensions were not as standardized and automatic as those used in Workmen's Compensation, and the behavior of Mother's Pensions recipients was considered in their continued eligibility while the behavior of Workmen's Compensation recipients was not (Nelson 1990, 141-142; Polakow 1993, 55; Gordon 1994, 46).

While Mother's Pensions set an important precedent through the provision of public "outdoor" (non-institutionalized) aid to the poor (Katz 1986, 128-129), the characteristics of this program also set the pattern for future "welfare" programs. Even among the supporters of Mother's

Pensions, there was concern about the "pauperizing tendencies" of public assistance. This concern was addressed by providing benefits to "deserving mothers" only and by keeping such benefits extremely low (Gordon 1994, 49-52). Administrators of the program distinguished between "deserving" and "undeserving" mothers on the basis of their adherence to (class- and race-defined) gender norms and notions of proper "moral behavior." "Unsuitable home" requirements were used to exclude many of the women who needed aid the most. As a result, the vast majority of Mother's Pensions recipients were white and widowed (Nelson 1990, 141-142; Polakow 1993, 55; Gordon 1994, 46, 50-52).

The introduction of Mother's Pensions and Workmen's Compensation established important patterns that would be replicated in the federal legislation that followed in the Social Security Act of 1935. The Social Security Act, in response to the economic insecurity of the Great Depression, firmly established the role of the federal government to provide economic security and broke the traditional reliance on private charity and local aid. At the same time, the Social Security Act instituted the dualistic structure of the US welfare state, carefully distinguishing between social insurance programs—Old Age Insurance and Unemployment Insurance—and public assistance programs—Aid to Dependent Children (the federal version of Mother's Pensions), Old Age Assistance, and Aid to the Blind.

The social insurance programs as constructed were the core of the Social Security Act, stressing the systemic insecurity of industrial market capitalism and the need for the public to assist the victims of such insecurities in a dignified manner (Gordon 1994, 149). [See also Randall Wray's Chapter on Social Security in this volume.] The social insurance programs also incorporated assumptions of traditional gender roles and the family wage, and assumed that women would benefit from social insurance as the economic dependents of wage earning males (Gordon 1994, 179). In addition, the occupations covered, as well as the type of employment history and wage levels required for eligibility, excluded many women wage earners, as well as workers from racial/ethnic minority groups, from these programs (Quadagno 1994, 157; Abramovitz 1988, 250).

Recourse to traditional gender ideology also helped shape the development of the largest public assistance program, Aid to Dependent Children (ADC). Like Mother's Pensions, the ADC program reflected the concern that single mothers, if forced to support themselves through wage labor, could not adequately nurture and supervise their children. And, like the supporters of Mother's Pensions before them, proponents of ADC stressed that it was a program for "deserving mothers" only. State and local control of the program gave ADC officials a great deal of discretion in determining who fit these criteria. Initially, the majority of ADC recipients were white widows (Abramovitz 1988, 315).

The 1939 amendments to the Social Security Act established Survivor's Insurance (SI), a social insurance program providing benefits for the widows and children of men covered by the Old Age Insurance program. This extended the stratification of the welfare state by creating a dual income support system for single mother families and their children (Peterson and Petersen 1994). As the white widows of industrial workers shifted from ADC to SI, the ADC population became increasingly stigmatized (Quadagno 1994, 119-120). During the 1960s, after becoming Aid to Families With Dependent Children (AFDC) with the addition of grants for mothers, a number of barriers to eligibility (i.e., residency requirements) and "moral supervision" (i.e., "suitable home" tests) were eased. With the resulting expansion of the program, and the continuing shift of the composition of the recipient population toward mothers considered "undeserving," the program became increasingly controversial and received less public support (Mink 1995, 175).

Beginning in the 1970s, welfare reform discussions became increasingly focused on moving welfare recipients into paid work (Albelda 1999), with the increasing labor force participation of middle- and upper-income mothers with young children often invoked as the rationale for this policy focus (Cohen and Bianchi 1999). This argument, however, has been fraught with contradiction, with many of the most passionate supporters of the notion that "welfare mothers" should work outside the home also being the most vocal proponents of policies that facilitate the ability of middle- and upper-income mothers to choose to stay home with their young children (Mink 1998). This argument has also ignored some important aspects of mothers' labor force participation. While the labor force participation of married mothers has increased dramatically, and married mothers often make critically important contributions to family incomes, the vast majority of married mothers in the United States are not the sole breadwinners for their families (Cohen and Bianchi 1999).

Thus, with its "blend of mothers' provisions and worker exclusions affecting women" (Mink 1995, 172), the income support system established by the Social Security Act initially aided women as mothers not as workers, despite the economic realities that denied exclusive domesticity to many women. This has meant not only that women's relationship to the welfare state has differed from men's, but that this relationship has varied among women themselves according to social and economic rank and marital status (Mink 1995, 172). Changes in the structure of the economy and in the socio-economic roles of women in the decades following the Social Security Act have made this distinction even more destructive. The welfare state has consistently failed to address the needs of women wage earners, creating a situation where many working mothers have faced “two bad choices—employment or ‘welfare,’ both on inferior terms” (Gordon 1994, 301). It is within this context that the most recent welfare reform legislation needs to be understood.

# US WELFARE REFORM

Today, the term “welfare reform” generally refers to the 1996 Personal Responsibility and Work Opportunity Reconciliation Act (PRWORA), which replaced AFDC with the Temporary Assistance to Needy Families (TANF) block grant. This legislation changed the structure of income support for poor families in the United States in a number of very significant ways, including the elimination of the individual entitlement to cash public assistance, the institution of a “work-based safety-net" for poor families with children, and the inclusion of "family formation" issues among the welfare system's primary goals.[1]

The TANF program must receive Congressional reauthorization by September 30, 2002, and it is expected that Congress will consider changes to the TANF program as part of the reauthorization process. Although this chapter will be completed prior to the final TANF reauthorization debate and the passage of any TANF reauthorization legislation, the issues brought to this debate by activists and researchers provide valuable insights into the nature of contemporary welfare policy in the US and are likely to remain important as welfare policy enters its next phase after TANF reauthorization. This section begins with an overview of some of the key elements and major impacts of the TANF program (as established by the welfare reform legislation of 1996); this is followed by a discussion of some TANF reauthorization issues and advocacy goals.[2]

## Key Elements of TANF

The changes in welfare policy associated with the establishment of the TANF program are extensive, including revisions in federal law, state law, and state and local implementation practices. Typically, provisions in federal law, and the policy decisions made by states within this framework, have received the most attention in TANF reauthorization discussions. The provisions in federal law most often identified as the key elements of TANF include the elimination of the entitlement to cash assistance and the introduction of block grant funding, mandatory work requirements, sanctions, and a five year time limit on cash assistance (Haskins, Sawhill and Weaver 2001a, 8). In addition, TANF includes a number of specific "family formation" provisions.

**Elimination of Cash Welfare Entitlement**

In many ways, the most radical change associated with the 1996 legislation is the elimination of the individual entitlement to cash public assistance. Under the AFDC program, states were required to aid all families eligible under state income standards; this is no longer the case. It is now left up to the states to determine when and under what conditions they will provide cash public assistance to poor families. While the federal law prohibits states from using TANF funds to assist certain categories of individuals or families, there is no requirement that a state provide assistance to any individual or family (Committee on Ways and Means 2000, 353; Greenberg et al. 2000, 6; Pavetti 2000, 44; Haskins, Sawhill and Weaver 2001a, 8).

**Block Grant Funding**

Under the AFDC program, the federal government paid at least half of all benefit costs on an open-ended basis, with federal welfare spending increasing as AFDC caseloads rose. The TANF program, however, is funded as a block grant, providing a fixed sum ($16.5 billion per year) to states through fiscal year 2002 (Haskins, Sawhill and Weaver 2001a, 8; Haskins, Sawhill and Weaver 2001b, 2). Each state receives a lump sum of federal funds, representing roughly what the state received in AFDC and AFDC-related funds in (or near) 1994. Each state also has a maintenance-of-effort requirement, which obligates it to continue spending 75 to 80 percent of the amount it spent on AFDC and AFDC-related expenditures in 1994 (Committee on Ways and Means 2000, 353; Greenberg and Laracy 2000, 9). Although states have a great deal of discretion in spending these funds, they must meet certain federal requirements, including work requirements, sanctions, and a cumulative five year time limit on federally funded cash assistance.

**Work Requirements**

The 1996 law requires that an increasing share of the total TANF caseload be engaged in specific work activities that are listed in the law. States must require all recipients to participate in these work activities after they have received no more than two years of assistance, although states may choose to exempt those with a child under 12 months. (Committee on Ways and Means 2000, 353; Haskins, Sawhill and Weaver 2001a, 8). In the federal law, education and training activities count toward the work participation requirements to a very limited extent (Greenberg and Laracy 2000, 9; Greenberg et al. 2000, 7). In addition, most states have adopted a "work first" approach to moving welfare recipients into the labor market, which emphasizes the rapid placement of recipients into jobs for which they are currently qualified (Pavetti 2000, 46).

### Sanctions

Under the TANF program, states must reduce the cash TANF benefit of adults who fail to meet the work requirement designed by the state. Thirty-seven states have chosen to implement "full family sanctions," meaning they can end the entire cash TANF benefit of families that fail to meet work requirements (Pavetti 2000, 46; Haskins, Sawhill and Weaver 2001b, 4). In addition, the federal government will reduce the block grant of states that fail to have the specified percentage of their caseload engaged in work activities (Pavetti 2000, 44; Haskins, Sawhill and Weaver 2001a, 8).

### Five Year Time Limit

States may not use federal TANF funds to provide assistance to a family that includes an adult who has received federally funded TANF assistance for a total of five years over his/her lifetime. States may allow exceptions for up to 20 percent of families currently receiving assistance. States also have the option of adopting a shorter time limit, or using their own funds to continue cash assistance beyond the five year limit (Committee on Ways and Means 2000, 353; Greenberg et al 2000, 6-7; Haskins, Sawhill and Weaver 2001a, 9).

### Family Formation

The stated purposes of TANF refer to the "family formation" goals of promoting marriage and two-parent families and reducing non-marital childbirths. TANF has a number of family formation provisions, including: changed rules concerning assistance to two-parent families (giving states more flexibility to serve more two-parent families); the establishment of the "illigitimacy bonus" (rewarding states with highest reduction in their non-marital birth ratio who have also reduced their abortion rate); the denial of assistance to some minor parents (who are unmarried, not in school, and not living with relatives or other adults); and, the establishment of federal funding for "abstinence only" sex education. States have the option of adopting policies that deny assistance to the children born to unmarried teen mothers and to additional children born to families receiving welfare (the "family cap") (Committee on Ways and Means 2000, 1408; Greenberg et al. 2000, 13-14).

## Impacts of TANF

The literature examining the impacts of TANF is quite extensive and covers a wide range of outcomes, including those involving welfare caseloads, employment, earnings, income, poverty, and family formation. The research findings that have received the most attention from those who argue that welfare reform is a success report on welfare caseloads and employment; the findings on earnings, income, and poverty are much more mixed. Family formation outcomes, while very important in recent welfare reform rhetoric, have received far less attention in the evaluation literature.

### Welfare Caseloads and Employment

The most widely cited impact of welfare reform is the decline in the number of families receiving cash public assistance. The national welfare caseload reached its peak in 1994, with over 5.0 million families receiving cash public assistance. By the time of TANF's passage in August of 1996, caseloads had declined to 4.4 million families; after the passage of TANF the rate of decline in the caseload escalated, falling by more than 50 percent to 2.1 million families in June 2001 (Committee on Ways and Means 2000, 352; Greenberg and Laracy 2000, 10; Falk et al. 2002, 2).

Another widely cited impact of welfare reform is the increase in the employment rates of various groups of single mothers. National labor force data indicate that, after a decade of little change, the number of single mothers participating in paid work rose by 25 percent between 1993 and 1999, including a 50 percent increase in the number of never-married mothers who were employed (Haskins, Sawhill and Weaver 2001a, 4). By 1999, 71 percent of single mothers were employed, an employment rate exceeding that for married mothers (Committee on Ways and Means 2000, 1408). Among TANF recipients work has also increased, from roughly 8 percent of adults in fiscal year 1994 to 28 percent in fiscal year 1999 (Falk et al. 2002, 2). In addition, both state and national studies consistently show that roughly 60 percent of those who have left the TANF program are employed shortly after leaving the program (Bernstein and Greenberg 2001, 13; Haskins, Sawhill and Weaver 2001a, 4).[3]

## Earnings, Income, and Poverty

The findings on earnings, income, and poverty are less positive than those on welfare caseloads and employment. Research on "welfare leavers," for example, consistently finds that those leaving welfare for employment are typically entering jobs paying below-poverty-level wages (an average of roughly \$6.00-\$8.00 per hour) and are not receiving employer-provided benefits such as health insurance or paid sick or vacation leave. In addition, many of these families fail to receive key public income supports—including childcare assistance, Medicaid coverage, and Food Stamps—even though their incomes are low enough to make them eligible to receive these benefits (Committee on Ways and Means 2000, 1409; Greenberg and Laracy 2000, 11; Greenberg et al. 2000, 8; Pavetti 2000, 48-49; Bernstein and Greenberg 2001, 13; Savner, Strawn and Greenberg 2002, 4, 6).

The growth in the total incomes of these families has also been disappointing, particularly in light of the significant increases in employment. Even though the increase in employment (even at low wages) has increased the aggregate earnings of poor single mothers as a group, for many families average income has increased very little, if at all, because the increase in earnings has been offset by the loss of welfare benefits. Among the poorest single mother families, average incomes have actually fallen despite increased earnings (Primus and Daugirdas 1999, 6; Committee on Ways and Means 2000, 1413; Pavetti 2000, 48; Haskins, Sawhill and Weaver 2001a, 5; Neuberger, Parrott and Primus 2002, 3).

Despite early predictions that welfare reform would increase poverty, official poverty statistics show that as the caseload has declined each year, so have both the overall poverty rate and the rate of child poverty (Haskins, Sawhill and Weaver 2001a, 4). In 2000, the child poverty rate was 15.7 percent, down from 22 percent in 1993 (Falk et al. 2002, 2). Declines in caseloads have greatly exceeded declines in poverty, however, thus substantially reducing the portion of poor families who receive public assistance (Primus and Daugirdas 1999, 5-6; Committee on Ways and

Means 2000, 1412; Greenberg 2000a, 1). In addition, "deep poverty" (defined as family income below 50 percent of the poverty level) has increased among some single mother families, indicating that some of the poorest single mothers and children have become poorer (Porter and Dupree 2001, 17; Pavetti 2000, 48-49; Haskins, Sawhill and Weaver 2001a, 4).

### Family Formation

To date, less attention has been paid to the impacts of the family formation initiatives than to the welfare-to-work provisions of TANF. Although recent data show that in the 1990s teen pregnancy rates fell, non-marital birth rates stabilized, and the percentage of children living with two parents increased, many analysts conclude that it is unlikely that welfare policy changes were the driving force behind these changes (Fremstad and Primus 2002). Program evaluations that have addressed family formation issues suggest welfare policy changes have had a limited impact. For example, the majority of evaluations of welfare-to-work programs that examined marriage and birth rates for single parents report no impacts, and studies of state AFDC waiver initiatives that included "family cap" policies have found inconclusive results (Committee on Ways and Means 2000, 1444-1445).

## TANF Reauthorization Issues and Goals

The research findings on the structure and impacts of TANF raise a number of issues for consideration and debate in the context of TANF reauthorization. Perhaps the most fundamental issue to be addressed is the primary purpose of TANF (and of welfare reform more generally). A number of other issues are also likely to be raised, including the funding of TANF, the structure and implementation of time limits and sanctions, the effectiveness of current "welfare-to-work" strategies, and the impact of an economic recession.

### Primary Purpose of TANF: Reducing Poverty vs. Increasing Marriage

The Personal Responsibility and Work Opportunity Reconciliation Act (PRWORA) states that the purposes of the TANF program are to assist needy families, to fight "welfare dependency" by promoting work and marriage, to reduce non-marital births, and to encourage the formation and maintenance of two-parent families (Committee on Ways and Means 2000, 354; Haskins, Sawhill and Weaver 2001b, 2). As the TANF program has been implemented, reducing "welfare dependency" has received the greatest emphasis, and success in meeting this goal has been measured largely in terms of declining caseloads and increasing employment among poor single mothers. There are many who continue to see this as the primary goal of welfare reform and argue that reducing caseloads and increasing employment among poor single mothers should remain the primary policy focus. But, as welfare reform enters the next phase, many researchers and advocates from across the political spectrum are critical of this focus, with those on the left arguing that welfare reform should focus on reducing poverty and those on the right arguing that welfare reform should focus on increasing marriage and reducing "illegitimacy."

Many progressive researchers and welfare advocates argue that welfare reform has not focused enough on improving the economic well-being of poor families with children. They emphasize that although caseloads have fallen and employment has increased, "welfare reform has not fundamentally improved the living standards of many of the families it has affected" (Bernstein and Greenberg 2001, 11). From this perspective, changing the law's central focus from caseload reduction to poverty reduction should be the top priority for TANF reauthorization. This position grounds a policy agenda for TANF reauthorization that calls for increasing TANF funding and for reforms in key elements of TANF, such as work requirements, time limits, and sanctions (Edelman 2000; Bernstein and Greenberg 2001; Savner, Strawn, and Greenberg 2002, 7-14 ).

Many conservative researchers and activists, on the other hand, argue that the family formation purposes of TANF are its most fundamental goals and should be at the forefront of reauthorization reforms (Murray 2001; Rector 2001b). The inclusion of these provisions in the 1996 legislation was inspired, to a great extent, by the work of Charles Murray, who asserts that "illegitimacy is the single worst social problem of our time—more important than crime, drugs, poverty, illiteracy, welfare or homelessness because it drives everything else" (quoted in Greenberg et al. 2000, 13). This position grounds a policy agenda for TANF reauthorization that seeks to further limit the access of poor single mothers to public assistance and to aggressively promote marriage to those who receive it (Murray 2001; Rector 2001b; Fremstad and Primus 2002).

Progressive researchers and activists from a variety of perspectives question the use of government programs to promote marriage, emphasizing the fact that while polls show "most Americans continue to prize and value marriage as an important life goal," there is "a great deal of uncertainly about the appropriate role of the government with respect to marriage" (Greenberg et al. 2000, 16). In addition, it is stressed that if the emphasis of such programs is on "quantity" rather than "quality," marriage promotion activities could end up encouraging unstable or high conflict marriages (Fremstad and Primus 2002).

Feminist researchers and activists have expressed the strongest opposition to marriage promotion policies. Stephanie Coontz and Nancy Folbre, for example, argue that "lack of marriage is sometimes a symptom rather than a root cause of poverty, and that encouraging people to marry without giving them long term support systems may do more harm than good." They argue that while it is appropriate for public policy to eliminate disincentives or penalties for marriage, it does not follow that marriage promotion should be the centerpiece of antipoverty policy. They argue that the current pro-marriage policy agenda is misguided because it does not recognize that poverty may be the cause of non-marriage and that "the quality and stability of marriages matter" tremendously. It also fails to recognize that two-parent families also experience "the economic stresses that put children at risk," and that single parenthood "does not lead to poverty if women have access to jobs, education, and child care" (Coontz and Folbre 2002).

**Funding of TANF**

It is expected that the funding level of the TANF block grant will also be an issue of debate in reauthorization discussions. Funding levels for TANF were based on the size of the caseload in 1994, and, given the dramatic decline in the caseload since that time, it is argued by some that federal TANF funding is now too high and should be cut back (Haskins, Sawhill and Weaver 2001b, 2; Rector 2001b, 8). Welfare advocates and many researchers, however, argue that the remaining caseload has many unmet needs and that welfare-to-work strategies may become increasingly expensive and require more funds to adequately serve this population. In addition, it is argued that as welfare reform enters the next phase, more attention should be given to assisting low-income working families more generally through the provision of work supports. A reduction in funding is also seen to reduce the ability of states to cope with a recession. Thus, an important goal for many advocates is increasing (or at least maintaining in real terms) federal levels of TANF spending and state maintenance-of-effort dollars (Greenberg and Laracy 2000, 14; Greenberg et al. 2000, 10; Falk et al. 2002, 3; Neuberger, Parrott and Primus 2002).[4]

## Time Limits

Time limits—seen by many as the "hallmark of welfare reform"—remain one of its most controversial features and are also likely to be addressed in some way in Congressional TANF reauthorization discussions. While supporters of time limits argue that they play "an enormous symbolic role" (Rector 2001a, 267), many welfare researchers and advocates argue that in the context of mandatory and strictly enforced work requirements there is no rationale for placing arbitrary time limits on welfare receipt. In addition, there is particular concern that those families who remain on welfare, and who are likely to be affected by time limits, have significant barriers to employment and will face serious hardships when assistance ends, especially in the context of a recession. Many advocates argue that, at the very least, the federal time limit structure should be revised to provide more flexibility in assisting working families – by, for example, "stopping the clock" when a parent is employed, caring for young children, or going to school—and increasing exemptions for those who cannot find and maintain employment due to barriers such as caring for a chronically ill or disabled child or having experienced domestic violence (Edelman 2000; Greenberg 2000b; Greenberg et al. 2000, 11; Haskins, Sawhill and Weaver 20001b, 4; Falk et al. 2002, 3).

## Sanctions

Sanctions also continue to be a controversial element of the TANF program that many feel should be addressed in TANF reauthorization discussions. Supporters of strict sanctions argue that they "send an important message that the state is serious about changing behavior" (Rector 2001a, 266) and are necessary for the implementation of mandatory work requirements. Research on sanctions shows they are, in fact, widely and routinely used: in some states, as many as a third of the cases are under sanction or have received a sanction (Haskins, Sawhill and Weaver 2001b, 4). Critics of current sanction policies report research findings that show many of the families who have lost assistance through sanctions are among those with the least education and most severe barriers to employment, and often do not understand why they are being sanctioned (Bernstein and Greenberg 2001, 13; Pavetti and Bloom 2000, 258-260; Haskins, Sawhill and Weaver 2001b, 4; Goldberg 2002). Welfare advocates call for increased state and local accountability in terms of sanctioning policies, the institution of federal protections against arbitrary sanctions, and increased outreach and services to promote compliance and resolve obstacles prior to sanctioning (Edelman 2000; Greenberg 2000b; Greenberg et al. 2000, 11-12).

**Effectiveness of Current Welfare-to-Work Strategies**

The desirability of the "work first" approach to moving welfare recipients into employment—that is, giving highest priority to finding a job and limiting the extent to which education and training can count as work activities—is another likely issue for debate during TANF reauthorization. Research findings that "welfare leavers" generally have low earnings, face high levels of job instability, and have little upward mobility have raised serious concerns about this approach. Many researchers and advocates argue for a redefinition of "work activities," placing more emphasis on education and training, and the expansion of education and training opportunities for low-wage workers (Edelman 2000; Greenberg 2000b; Falk et al. 2002, 3). Further, it is argued that nontraditional job training opportunities should be expanded and made available for welfare recipients to enhance their ability to move into jobs paying living wages (Negrey et al. 2001)

Another important question is how well existing welfare-to-work strategies serve families where the adults face high and/or multiple barriers to employment, such as lack of work experience, poor education, poor physical or mental health, a chronically ill or disabled child, substance abuse, or domestic violence. Research on the current welfare caseload suggests that those who have not already left welfare for work are likely to have serious and multiple barriers to employment (Blank 2000, 18; Greenberg and Laracy 2000, 11-12). Research has also shown that recipients with barriers to employment have lower earnings on average, are less likely to find jobs, and are more likely to lose assistance because of a sanction than recipients without barriers (Goldberg 2002). Those families who have left welfare without work (about 40 percent of welfare leavers) also appear to be among those with the most severe barriers to employment (Greenberg 2000a, 2; Greenberg et al. 2000, 8). Many researchers and advocates argue that addressing the needs of these parents and families—the so-called "hard to serve" or "hard to employ"—is one of the primary challenges of the next phase of welfare reform (Edelman 2000; Greenberg 2000a; Greenberg 2000b).

**Impact of an Economic Recession**

Welfare reform has been aptly characterized as a "fair weather ship." The strong economy of the mid-to-late 1990s contributed significantly to what are widely seen to be the positive outcomes (i.e., falling welfare caseloads and increased employment rates among single mothers) associated with welfare reform (Bernstein 2001, 3; Bernstein and Greenberg 2001, 12). Mary Jo Bane has argued that "the country was enormously lucky that welfare reform was implemented in the midst of the best economic expansion this country has had in decades" (quoted in Toner 2002).

While it is not fully known at this time what the full impact of welfare reform will be in the context of an economic recession, the changes in welfare program design have "almost surely made less-skilled women (particularly single mothers) more vulnerable to the economy" (Blank 2000, 19). More single parents are working than ever before, and many are employed in cyclically sensitive sectors (Bernstein 2001, 3). The current economic downturn has already resulted in job losses among low-skilled workers, and previous research suggests that the employment options of former welfare recipients will be limited in a recession (Holtzer 2000, 2). In addition, welfare caseloads are rising: in September 2001, TANF enrollment in 21 states and Guam exceeded year-earlier levels, although the national total remained 4 percent below that of the previous year (Burke 2002b, 1). Recent TANF caseload data show that between September 2001 and December 2001, caseloads increased in 40 states (Richer, Sankarapandian and Greenberg 2002).

Little has been done to make the structure or funding of the TANF program responsive to an economic downturn. Key features of TANF, such as time limits, are insensitive to the business cycle. Currently, there are no provisions to provide further federal cash assistance through TANF to former recipients who have met their lifetime time limits, even during a recession (Bernstein 2001, 3; Peterson 2000, 523). This inflexibility in time limits is a particular concern given that many former TANF recipients who lose their jobs are not eligible to receive Unemployment Insurance (UI) benefits (Peterson 2000).

In addition, the shift from providing cash public assistance as an entitlement to providing it through a block grant means that federal welfare spending is no longer counter cyclical. This places much more of the financial burden for responding to increased economic need on states, many of which operate under a balanced budget requirement in their constitution and may be limited in their ability to respond (Bernstein 2001, 3; Blank

2001, 4). The 1996 legislation did provide TANF with three provisions designed to financially assist states in a recession (i.e., the ability to carry over block grant funds, a loan fund, and a contingency fund), but these provisions are generally seen to be inadequate and in need of "serious reworking to be entirely effective in a recession" (Blank 2001, 1).[5]

Concerns about the impacts of TANF in a recession and the ability of states to respond to increasing economic need raise additional issues for TANF reauthorization. Some analysts focus on strengthening the anti-recession provisions currently within TANF, while others argue that a counter cyclical component should be built more directly into the TANF block grant, by, for example, tying additional federal funds to changes in unemployment rates or other indicators of economic need (Holtzer 2000, 6; Blank 2001, 6). In addition, there are calls for further increasing the flexibility of time limits, such as allowing states to issue more exemptions from time limits during a recession and to extend eligibility for recipients who are participating in welfare-to-work activities but are not able to acquire the employment and/or earnings they need to leave the program (Blank 2001, 6). Increasing the flexibility of work requirements, by, for example, allowing more education and training activities to count as work participation, is also seen to be particularly important in a recession (Holtzer 2000, 5).

## CONCLUSION

Institutionalist approaches to economic policy recognize that "the structure and performance of the political economy is at all times largely a consequence of choices made by individuals in positions of discretion in government, industry, and elsewhere. The existing economy is a myriad of prior choices; through the making of new choices, its structure is modified. "Problems are resolved only through institutional change" (Tool 1984). Welfare policy in the United States reflects many decades of choices and institutional change, choices that have sought to address economic insecurity while often reflecting and reinforcing invidious distinctions between those seen as "deserving" and "undeserving" of assistance.

The debate surrounding the reauthorization of the TANF program once again brings to light the choices society can make in addressing the needs of low-income families. Researchers and advocates who view the primary purpose of welfare reform as poverty reduction tend to support increases in TANF spending, more flexible time limits (or their elimination), more protections against arbitrary sanctions, more flexible and realistic work requirements, and more emphasis on education and training for TANF recipients. Those who view the primary purpose of welfare reform as caseload reduction and/or the promotion of a particular family structure typically support a different set of choices, limiting TANF spending, making the program more restrictive, and shifting resources to programs that support "family formation" goals (such as promoting marriage).

Going into the final debate on TANF reauthorization, different combinations of these policy choices have been presented for consideration. Several bills have been sponsored by members of Congress that make poverty reduction a primary goal of TANF, offer bonuses for poverty reduction, and include many of the reforms to the program promoted by progressive researchers and welfare advocates (Burke 2002a; Burke 2002b).[6] The National Governors Association has also called for an increase in the TANF block grant and the ability of states to expand the definition of work activity to include more job training, education and drug abuse treatment and to relax time limits (Goldstein 2002b; Pear 2002). The Bush administration, however, proposes to revise TANF by increasing work requirements and providing states new subsidies to encourage marriage (Goldstein 2002c; Milbank and Goldstein 2002; Toner 2002; Toner and Pear 2002). In addition, the Bush proposal keeps the block grant at the same level of funding, with no adjustment for inflation (Goldstein 2002a; Parrott 2002).

The choices made with respect to the primary purpose of welfare reform and the components of the new safety net will have important implications for the future of TANF and US income support policy more generally. From an institutionalist perspective, it is clear that the purpose of welfare reform and welfare policy should be poverty reduction and promotion of the institutional change necessary for low-income families to participate fully in the economy and society. It is possible for welfare reform legislation to make poverty reduction a primary goal, to eliminate unrealistic, counter-productive and harsh elements of TANF, and to improve the economic prospects of working poor and low-income families. It is a question of the political will to promote instrumentally warranted institutional change. While it is true that the issues associated with the provision of economic security for low-income families go far beyond those addressed in TANF reauthorization, as Peter Edelman has argued, "the welfare system is in many ways the 'canary in the coal mine' that signals the quality of our national commitment to low-income families" (Edelman 2002), and the outcome of TANF reauthorization will provide an important context for income support policy in this new century.

# NOTES

[1] Despite the emphasis on family structure throughout the history of the AFDC program, prior to the implementation of TANF "no federal program expressly sought to influence marital status" (Greenberg et al. 2000, 13).

[2] This discussion focuses closely on what are often seen to be the core elements of TANF. The 1996 law includes a number of additional important provisions not discussed here, including those relating to the treatment of non-citizens, child support enforcement, and child care. For an overview of these elements of welfare reform, and the reauthorization discussions surrounding them, see Greenberg et al. 2000.

[3] How much of the decline in caseloads and the increase in employment is due to welfare reform, and how much is due to the strong economy is widely debated. Existing studies do not provide a definitive answer (Haskins, Sawhill and Weaver 2001a), but many indicate that the economy played a substantial role in both the decline in caseloads and increase in employment (Bernstein 2001; Bernstein and Greenberg 2001).

[4] Because the TANF block grant has been funded at a fixed level that is not adjusted for inflation, its real value fell by more than 11 percent between September 1997 and September 2002 (Neuberger, Parrott, and Primus 2002).

[5] The most potentially important anti-recessionary feature of TANF is a $1.96 billion "contingency fund," authorized (through September 2001) to provide additional money to states in times of increased economic need. Critics argue, however, that the criteria established for obtaining these funds were outdated and difficult for states to meet, and that funding levels were inadequate to assist a large number of states facing financial difficulties (Blank 2001; Neuberger, Parrott and Primus 2002).

[6] Early TANF reauthorization legislation introduced by members of Congress include: S. 940/H.R. 1990 (Leave No Child Behind Act) developed by the Children's Defense Fund and sponsored by Senator Dodd and Representative George Miller in almost identical form; H.R. 3113 (TANF Reauthorization Act) sponsored by Representative Mink, and H.R. 3626 (Next Step in Reforming Welfare Act) sponsored by Representative Cardin (see Burke 2002a and Burke 2002b for an overview).

# REFERENCES

Abramovitz, Mimi. 1988. *Regulating the Lives of Women: Social Welfare Policy from Colonial Times to Present.* Boston: South End Press.

Albelda, Randy. 1999."Welfare Reform." In *The Elgar Companion to Feminist Economics.* Janice Peterson and Margaret Lewis, eds. Cheltenham UK: Edward Elgar, 750-757.

Bernstein, Jared. 2001. "The Fair Weather Ship in a Storm: How Will Welfare Reform Do in a Recession?" A paper prepared for a National Urban League Briefing. Washington, DC: Economic Policy Institute (February 16).

_______. and Mark Greenberg. 2001. Reforming welfare reform. *The American Prospect* January 1-15: 10-16.

Blank, Rebecca. 2000. "Declining Caseloads/Increased Work: What Can We Conclude About the Effects of Welfare Reform?" A paper presented at the conference Welfare Reform Four Years Later: Progress and Prospects, Federal Reserve Bank of New York (New York, November).

_______. 2001. "Welfare and the Economy," Welfare Reform & Beyond Policy Briefno. 7. Washington, DC: The Brookings Institution (September).

Burke, Vee. 2002a. "Recent Welfare Developments." *CRS Welfare Reform Briefing Book.* Washington, DC: Congressional Research Service, The Library of Congress. (revised February 19).

_______. 2002b. "Welfare Reform: An Issue Overview." *CRS Issue Brief for Congress.* Washington, DC: Congressional Research Service, The Library of Congress. (revised February 19).

Cohen, Philip and Suzanne Bianchi. 1999. Marriage, children, and women's employment: What do we know? *Monthly Labor Review* (December): 22-31.

Committee on Ways and Means, US House of Representatives. 2000. *2000 Green Book*, Washington, DC: US Government Printing Office.

Coontz, Stephanie and Nancy Folbre. 2002. "Marriage, Poverty, and Public Policy." Council on Contemporary Families Discussion Paper, prepared for the Fifth Annual Council on Contemporary Families Conference (New York, April).

Dugger, William. 1989. *Radical Institutionalism: Contemporary Voices.* Westport, CT: Greenwood Press.

Edelman, Peter. 2000. Controversy: Knowing what we do know, how should Congress change welfare reform? *The American Prospect Online* 11, 15 (June 19-July 3). (www.prospect.org).

_______. 2002. Reforming welfare–take two. *The Nation* (February 4). (www.thenation.com).

Falk, Gene, Vee Burke, Melinda Gish, Carmen Solomom-Fears, Joe Richardson and Emilie Stoltzfus. 2002. "Welfare Reauthorization: Brief Summary of Issues for the 107th Congress." *CRS Report for Congress.* Washington, DC: Congressional Research Service, The Library of Congress. (revised January 22).

Fremstad, Shawn and Wendell Primus. 2002. *Strengthening Families: Ideas for TANF Reauthorization.* Washington, DC: Center on Budget and Policy Priorities.

Goldberg, Heidi. 2002. *Improving TANF Program Outcomes for Families with Barriers to Employment.* Washington, DC: Center on Budget and Policy Priorities.

Goldstein, Amy. 2002a. "Welfare: New Plans, Old Budget," *Washington Post*, February 7.

_______. 2002b. "Governors Detail Welfare Goals," *Washington Post*, February 22.

_______. 2002c. "Welfare Reform Plan Unveiled.," *Washington Post*, February 27.

Gordon, Linda. 1994. *Pitied But Not Entitled: Single Mothers and the History of Welfare.* New York: The Free Press.

Greenberg, Mark. 2000a. "Looking Ahead to Reauthorization of TANF: Some Preliminary Thoughts." A presentation to the Bi-Partisan Welfare Reform Seminar for Senior Congressional and Administration Staff. Washington, DC: Center for Law and Social Policy.

_______. 2000b. "Controversy: Knowing What We Do Know, How Should Congress Change Welfare Reform?" *The American Prospect Online* 11, 15 (June 19-July 3). (www.prospect.org).

_______. and Michael Laracy. 2000. "Welfare Reform: Next Steps Offer New Opportunities." Neighborhood Funders Group, Policy Paper no.4. Washington, DC: Center for Law and Social Policy.

_______. Jodie Levin-Epstein, Rutledge Hutson, Theodora Ooms, Rachel Schumacher, Vicki

Turetsky and David Engstrom. 2000. *Welfare Reauthorization: An Early Guide to the Issues*. Washington, DC: Center for Law and Social Policy. (July).
Hamilton, David. 1984. The myth is not the reality: income maintenance and welfare. *Journal of Economic Issues* 18 (March): 143-158.
Haskins, Ron, Isabel Sawhill and Kent Weaver. 2001a. "Welfare Reform: An Overview of Effects to Date," Welfare Reform & Beyond. Policy Brief no.1. Washington, DC: The Brookings Institution. (January).
________. 2001b. "Welfare Reform Reauthorization: An Overview of Problems and Issues," Welfare Reform & Beyond. Policy Brief no.2. Washington, DC: The Brookings Institution. (January).
Holtzer, Harry. 2000. "Unemployment Insurance and Welfare Recipients: What Happens When the Recession Comes?" Assessing the New Federalism Project, Series A, no. A-46. Washington, DC: The Urban Institute. (December).
Katz, Michael. 1986. *In the Shadow of the Poor House: A Social Hiistory of Welfare in America*. New York: Basic Books.
Milbank, Dana and Amy Goldstein. 2002. "Bush Welfare Plan Would Increase Work Requirements." *Washington Post*, February 26.
Miller, Edythe S. 1996. "Seen Through the Glass Darkly: Competing Views of Equality and Inequality in Economic Thought." In *Inequality: Radical Institutionalist Views on Race, Gender, Class, and Nation*. William M. Dugger, ed. Westport, CT: Greenwood, 87-99.
Mink, Gwendolyn. 1995. *The Wages of Motherhood*. Ithaca, NY: Cornell University Press.
________. 1998. *Welfare's End*. Ithaca, NY: Cornell University Press.
Murray, Charles. 2001. "Family Formation." In *The New World of Welfare*. Rebecca Blank and Ron Haskins, eds. Washington, DC: The Brookings Institution, 137-160.
Negrey, Cynthia, Stacie Golin, Sunhwa Lee, Holly Mead and Barbara Gault. 2001. *Working First But Working Poor: The Need for Education and Training Following Welfare Reform*. Washington, DC: Institute for Women's Policy Research.
Nelson, Barbara. 1990. "The Origins of the Two-Channel Welfare State: Workmen's Compensation and Mothers' Aid." In *Women, the State and Welfare*. Linda Gordon, ed. Madison, WI: University of Wisconsin Press.
Neuberger, Zoe, Sharon Parrott and Wendell Primus. 2002. *Funding Issues in TANF Reauthorization*. Washington, DC: Center on Budget and Policy Priorities (revised February 5).
Parrott, Sharon. 2002. *The TANF Related Provisions in the President's Budget*. Washington, DC: Center on Budget and Policy Priorities (February 7).
Pavetti, LaDonna. 2000. Welfare policy in transition: redefining the social contract for poor citizen families with children, *Focus* 21 (Fall): 44-50.
________. and Dan Bloom. 2001. "Sanctions and Time Limits." In *The New World of Welfare*. Rebecca Blank and Ron Haskins, eds. Washington, DC: The Brookings Institution, 245-264.
Peach, James. 1988. "Distribution and Economic Progress." In *Evolutionary Economics Vol II: Institutional Theory and Policy*. Marc Tool, ed. Armonk: NY: M.E. Sharpe, 77-111.
Pear, Robert. 2002. "Governors Want Congress to Ease Welfare Work Rules." *New York Times*, February 24.
Peterson, Janice and Carol Petersen. 1994. Single mother families and the dual welfare state. *Review of Social Economy* 52 (Fall): 312-338.
Peterson, Janice. 1996. "Social Provisioning and Inequality: Women and the Dual Welfare State." In *Inequality: Radical Institutionalist Views on Race, Gender, Class, and Nation*. William Dugger, ed. Westport, CT: Greenwood, 141-152.

_______. 1997. Ending welfare as we know it: The symbolic importance of welfare policy in America. *Journal of Economic Issues* 31 (June): 425-431.

_______. 2000. Welfare reform and inequality: The TANF and UI programs. *Journal of Economic Issues* 34 (June): 517-526.

Peterson, Wallace. 1985. The US welfare state and the conservative counter revolution. *Journal of Economic Issues* 19 (September): 601-641.

Petr, Jerry. 1984. Fundamentals of an institutionalist perspective on economic policy. *Journal of Economic Issues* 18 (March): 1-17.

Polakow, Valerie. 1993. *Lives on the Edge: Single Mothers and their Children in the Other America.* Chicago: University of Chicago Press.

Porter, Kathryn and Allen Dupree. 2001. *Poverty Trends for Families Headed by Working Single Mothers, 1993-1999.* Washington, DC: Center on Budget and Policy Priorities.

Primus, Wendell and Kristina Daugirdas. 1999. "Several Suggestions for Improving the Work-Based Safety Net and Reducing Child Poverty." Joint Center on Poverty Research Working Paper. Chicago: Joint Center on Poverty Research. (September).

Quadagno, Jill. 1994. *The Color of Welfare: How Racism Undermined the War on Poverty.* New York: Oxford University Press.

Rector, Robert. 2001a. "Comment." In *The New World of Welfare.* Rebecca Blank and Ron Haskins, eds. Washington, DC: The Brookings Institution, 264-267.

_______. 2001b. Testimony Before the Subcommittee on Human Resources of the House Committee on Ways and Means, Hearing on Welfare Reform. Washington, DC. (March 15).

Richer, Elise, Vani Sankarapandian and Mark Greenberg. 2002. "Impact of Recession and September 11 Seen on Welfare Caseloads," Washington, DC: Center for Law and Social Policy.

Samuels, Warren. 1989. Some fundamentals on the economic role of government. *Journal of Economic Issues* 23 (June): 427-33.

Savner, Steve, Julie Strawn and Mark Greenberg. 2002. *TANF Reauthorization: Opportunities to Reduce Poverty by Improving Employment Outcomes.* Washington, DC: Center for Law and Social Policy. (January).

Silverberg, Helene. 1985. Private mothers and public policy: women, welfare and the state. *The Cornell Review of Social Relations* 18 (Spring): 1-12.

Skocpol, Theda. 1988. "The Limits of the New Deal System and the Roots of Contemporary Welfare Dilemma." In *The Politics of Social Policy in the United States.* Margaret Weir, Ann Shola Orloff and Theda Skocpol, eds. Princeton: Princeton University Press, 292-311.

Stanfield, J. Ronald. 1991. The dichotomized state. *Journal of Economic Issues* 25 (September): 765-780.

Toner, Robin. 2002. "Helping the Poor in the Post-Welfare Era," *New York Times*, (March 3.)

_______. and Robert Pear. 2002. "Bush Plan on Welfare Law Increases Work Requirement," *New York Times*, February 26.

Tool, Marc. 1979. *The Discretionary Economy: A Normative Theory of Political Economy.* Santa Monica, CA: Goodyear.

_______. 1984. Economic policy for the 1980s and beyond: an institutionalist agenda. (Editor's Introduction). *Journal of Economic Issues* 18 (March).

_______. 2000. *Value Theory and Economic Progress: The Institutional Economics of J. Fagg Foster.* Boston: Kluwer Academic Publishers.

Waller, William. 1987. Transfer program structure and effectiveness. *Journal of Economic Issues* 21(June): 775-783.

________. and Ann Jennings. 1990. On the possibility of feminist economics: the convergence of institutional and feminist methodology. *Journal of Economic Issues* 24 (June): 613-622.

# 7

# UNIVERSAL HEALTH CARE IN THE UNITED STATES: ANALYSIS AND PROPOSALS

Michael Keaney

*Over the past decade or more, health conditions have worsened for Americans of every age: infants, adolescents, adults and the elderly. Reduced services, less public funding or increased costs have triggered all manner of negative consequences running from higher infant mortality rates, to the recurrence of nineteenth-century diseases, to more modern kinds of health epidemics. On most comparative indexes, the United States ranks last in health care but first in health costs among the world's industrialised countries* ( Petras and Morley 1995, 75).

*From the point of view of both fairness and effectiveness, healthcare, US style, has to be seen as a disaster* (Whitney 2001, 43).

*By almost every measure, the US health care system is failing* (Blank 1997, ix).

## INTRODUCTION

Few would deny that the health care system in the United States is in crisis. Regardless of political viewpoint, it is a rare person indeed who can express satisfaction with the status quo. This, despite the fact that the US spends more on health care than any other country. Whether as a proportion of GNP (13.5% in 1997) or per capita ($4,000), there is little denying the significance of health care expenditure to the US economy. Yet while the populations and governments of other countries struggle with the problems of rising costs and tightening budgets, you might wonder why it is that, in the midst of relative and absolute plenty, the US system should be so crisis-ridden.

This chapter seeks to provide both an explanation of the current crisis, and a vision of what its solution would entail. It encompasses discussion of the historical development of the US health care system, its current dysfunction, and barriers to the formulation and implementation of solutions that meet the normative criteria inherent in the social value theory of critical institutionalism. While acknowledgement is made of such barriers, however, formidable as they may appear, they are not treated as insurmountable. On the contrary, the "inquiry task is to make arguments and proposals that will stimulate public discussion and social action" (Tool 1996, 121). In this case, the very concepts of health and care require reconstruction. This necessitates a fundamental reappraisal of our institutions, originally defined in 1909 as the "settled habits of thought common to the generality of men" by Thorstein Veblen (1990, 239), and more recently conceived as "a cluster of mores that configures power or authority over things and people that are relevant to the material and social continuity of human life" (Stanfield 1996, 132). Thus, to conduct inquiry into the problems of universal health care from an *institutionalist* standpoint necessitates a complete reappraisal of our habits of thought, clusters of mores, structures of authority and social continuities. In the words of Karl Marx, what is required is no less than a ruthless criticism of all that exists.

## METHODOLOGICAL PREAMBLE

It will be recognized that American or critical institutionalism, as a branch of economic inquiry, does not command the vast resources available to the practitioners and users of neoclassical economics. As a result it suffers from something akin to a low recognition factor. One consequence of this is that others, similarly dissatisfied with the dominant form of economic theory and analysis, are developing alternative concepts and methods that, at the very least, bear close resemblance to those of critical institutionalism. Similarly, within the domains of other social science disciplines, work is being conducted that shares a strong affinity with the legacy of Thorstein Veblen and his intellectual successors.

The collapse of the Soviet Union for many discredited the Marxist theoretical enterprise. In point of fact future intellectual historians may point to the latter's liberation as a result of the tumultuous events of 1989-91. For Marx never offered a blueprint of socialist nirvana; his primary strength was as an analyst of the emergent economic system he christened capitalism. And of all the political economists whose work Veblen criticized as he formulated his own unique position, Marx alone was recognized for having bequeathed a theoretical corpus that "as a whole has an air of originality and initiative such as is rarely met with among sciences that deal with any phase of human culture," characterized as it was "by a certain boldness of conception and a great logical consistency" (Veblen 1990, 409). Praise, indeed, from the hypercritical Veblen. But Veblen recognised that the Marxist duality of class, based on ownership of the means of production, was too simplistic *on its own* to analyze the complexities of a reality in which human beings could not be reduced to rational utility-maximizers, whether as capitalists or proletarians. While Marx, the theoretician, was careful to avoid this assumption, Marx the politician-polemicist was concerned to offer a message of hope to those whom he saw as both in need of, and the vehicle of, human emancipation. Veblen's more pessimistic view of the human prospect allowed him to develop concepts and apply these with analytical precision without the "distraction" (as he mostly saw it) of political organizing.

In a subject as complex as health care, a simple, orthodox Marxist two-class model will yield some insights regarding the structural environment in which human action takes place. Indeed, as the influence of neoclassical economic "reasoning" becomes more prevalent, a Marxist critique offers a powerful rebuttal to the remorselessly privatizing "logic" of orthodox theory and practice. In addition, a Marxist critique will make reliable predictions as regards the evolution of the health care system as market-based reforms seek to emulate the neoclassical models that work so well on paper, but which ignore the crucial element of power. Therefore Marxist analysis of the status quo makes a vital contribution to our understanding of the present predicament. But alone, it is not enough.

Critical institutionalism, in keeping with the philosophical tradition of John Dewey, accepts the open-endedness of inquiry in recognition of a world that is in constant flux. Our institutions provide structure, a modicum of reliability and even reassurance. A wholly volatile world would be an intolerable place for a species that habitually, *instinctively*, seeks to impose order upon its environment. Problems of obsolescence arise, however, when these structures inhibit the full development of human personality and community, in order to serve narrow, vested interests. The purpose of inquiry is to expose such institutions to critical scrutiny, in line with the generic ends of life, defined as "idle curiosity" (critical inquiry in the service of human betterment), the "parental bent" (altruism), and the "instinct of workmanship" (self-actualization and the enrichment of community through the development and application of skilled labor)—"the arts," in Dewey's terminology (see Tilman 1996, 125).

Marx, Veblen and Dewey have each contributed to the development of a form of critical inquiry that is *dialectical* in its method. In other words, they recognized the tensions arising from the duality of continuity and change. Marx wished to recast social life in its entirety, believing it to be possible; Veblen, much as he wished to achieve such a goal was too pessimistic to believe in it, given his reading of history and anthropology; Dewey offered, via his articulation of the means-ends continuum, a vehicle by which the ruthless criticism of all that exists could be reconciled with the inevitability of continuity and our constantly changing appreciation of the universally applicable guide to valuation whose principal features Dewey himself regarded as fundamental to his conception of the democratic community: "a life of free and enriching communion" (Dewey 1954, 184).

Utopian? No. Part of that ruthless criticism of all that exists includes subjecting our aspirations, our beliefs, our values to that same piercing scrutiny. We must scrutinize that which we regard as desirable, together with our assumptions of what is possible. The latter are often the subject of manipulation via the propagation of *enabling myths* that legitimate the continuation and development of invidious distinctions serving vested interests. These interests are complex, and especially so in as ambiguous a topic for investigation as health care. But if there were ever an area of inquiry that demonstrated the absolute necessity of challenging the "there is no alternative" mantra that has characterized government policies since the beginning of the Great Capitalist Restoration (Stanfield and Stanfield 1996), then health care is surely it.

## THE LAY OF THE LAND

The crisis afflicting health care provision in all advanced countries derives from the escalation of costs. State-administered health care systems are subject to the pressures of fiscal crisis (O'Connor, 2001). Growing tax resistance among electorates, together with corporate lobbying driven by a logic of "privatize the profits, socialize the costs," led to the neoliberal ascendancy spearheaded by Milton Friedman and Friedrich A. Hayek. Even now, this quarter-century old structural adjustment program frames the debate concerning the appropriate economic role of the state, and was at least partly responsible for the failure of the much-vaunted Clinton health care plan in 1993. The system that plan intended to replace, the "market-based" system of private insurance with bolt-on federal and state assistance for the disadvantaged, is similarly driven in its development by a focus on cost containment. No wonder, then, that the field of health economics has mushroomed during the last thirty years. For the same conditions that create the fiscal crisis of the capitalist state in fact apply to the provision of all public goods. As Robert Blank says of US health care, "Every group wants reform but only if someone else ends up paying for it" (Blank 1997, x). It is a manifestation of the "privatize the profits, socialize the costs" rationale that is fundamental to capitalism and the cause of what orthodox economists euphemistically call "externalities" (see O'Connor 2001, 9).

Criticisms of orthodox health economics are legion.[1] Like all neoclassical approaches, orthodox health economics involves assuming the status quo as given, and proceeds to define the problem as one of allocating scarce resources in the most "efficient" manner. This is accomplished by a reductionism whereby actors are assumed to be individuals, each with their own utility functions and all rational maximizers. The consequences of this methodological approach are, at best, a very selective insight into specific problems of resource allocation; more usually, a serious distortion of the problem situation, which is refashioned to meet the demands imposed upon it by an otherwise inappropriate tool of analysis; and, at worst, a deliberate abuse of the mantle of science in the ideological service of vested interests.

Sometimes orthodox microeconomics can shed light upon problem situations (see Hildred and Watkins 1996). If we take the example of disease prevention, then, as this applies to the health of individuals, it is relatively simple to assess the costs and benefits of a program designed to reduce or even eradicate a particular ailment, as with cancer screening. However, if a cancer prevention program were to take account of social phenomena that may contribute to a cancer's prevalence, then the retention of neoclassical analysis would distort both the design and appraisal of such a program. As Shiell and Hawe (1996, 242) explain, health promotion campaigns that "focus on the structural or socio-economic causes of ill-health" via "the empowerment of communities such that they are enabled to take control over their own collective health" will yield benefits that orthodox analyses "systematically underestimate." This is because "notions of outcome based on the absence of disease are too narrow to capture the full effects of community development programmes." John Dewey's contributions to the critical institutionalist theoretical corpus highlight the shortcomings of a crude, rationalistic methodological individualism. The problems of community development were central to Dewey's political philosophy, and will be the subject of further discussion below.

The third type of intervention involving neoclassical economic analysis concerns the deliberate obfuscation and distortion of facts, all in the name of science, but all in the service of vested interests. This sort of activity is hardly new: in the propaganda struggle of private business interests against public ownership of utilities during the 1920s, vested interests went to great lengths to promote and further entrench themselves:

> Although [Samuel] Insull had originated and expanded the organized propaganda movement throughout his own empire, it had in a short time encompassed nearly all electric utilities in the country. . . . Anyone who

> worked on a newspaper or magazine, served in a legislature, or worked in a library; who planned programs for civic and service clubs; the teachers and preachers, editors of house organs, publishers—all were courted, persuaded, and often paid to exalt the private utilities as the epitome of public service, honor, and human concern. The effort was so extensive and relentless that rarely was there any rebuttal, analysis, or objection . . . .
>
> The managing director of the National Electric Light Association, M. H. Aylesworth, issued an exuberant advisory directive to member utilities in a 1923 speech that became part of Federal Trade Commission investigation records. What it lacked in subtlety, it possessed in explicit counsel on how to buy an educator.
>
> I would advise any manager who lives in a community where there is a college to get the professor of economics—the engineering professor will be interested anyway—interested in our problems. Have him lecture on your subject to his classes. Once in a while it will pay you to take such men and give them a retainer of one or two hundred dollars per year for the privilege of letting you study and consult with them. For how in heaven's name can we do anything in the schools of this country with the young people growing up, if we have not first sold the idea of education to the college professor? (see Rodgers 1972, 70 – 72).

Today the health care industry is investing many thousands of dollars in the promotion of corporate health and welfare, and often at the expense of those most in need. The methods employed have developed a certain degree of sophistication. Arm's length think tanks, rather than hired individual consultants, provide a sheen of scientific legitimacy, sufficiently funded as they are to employ teams of researchers, all of whom possess doctorates and other credentials earned from reputable institutions. As with utilities in the 1920s, the focus of attack is on state regulation and administration. Foremost among such "think tanks" is the Independent Institute, whose resident and associate scholars loudly proclaim their independence from vested interests as they ply their trade.

The first question to ask, when presented with such a claim, is: "independent of what?" Cursory investigation reveals that, for the Independent Institute, independence is defined solely on the basis of its relationship to government via state and especially federal institutions. Taking its cue from the theory of regulatory capture formulated by George Stigler (1971) and subsequently modified by Sam Peltzman (1976), the Independent Institute adheres to classical liberalism's inherent mistrust of the state in all matters economic, which finds expression in the burgeoning literature on public choice, law and economics, and the so-called "new" institutionalism.[2] Its academic advisors read like a who's who of the above approaches to economic analysis: James M. Buchanan, George Gilder, Deirdre N. McCloskey, William A. Niskanen, Arthur Seldon, William F. Shughart II and Robert D. Tollison, to name only a few. The Institute is weighing into the current debate surrounding US health care provision in a variety of ways, including the publication of a strongly promoted collection of essays "showing" how superior are market-based systems (see Feldman 2000).

The Independent Institute's research director, Alexander T. Tabarrok, may not enjoy the academic fame of some of his advisor colleagues, but he is no less busy in the service of "independent" thought. Pharmaceutical giant Pfizer has, for an extended period, been advertising in broadsheet newspapers and news magazines (including the *Financial Times* and *The Economist*) via its sponsorship of the "Pfizer Forum," where guest "experts" are invited to ruminate on a health care topic in approximately 700 words. Among these is Tabarrok, whose contribution argues against the imposition of drug price controls by governments. Quoting a study published by the American Enterprise Institute (another ideologically-charged "think tank"), Tabarrok finds fault with the *methodology* of government studies that "incorrectly" survey only a few selected drugs, and do not account for the quantity of drug prescriptions. In this way government efforts to control prices are ineffectual: "Suppose, for example, that seven drugs are more expensive in the US than in Canada and three are cheaper. If the three which are cheaper are prescribed more often than the seven which are more expensive, in which country are drugs truly less expensive?" (Tabarrok 2000). Even more damningly, according to Tabarrok, government studies have compared wholesale with retail prices, therefore reaching erroneous conclusions. The answer is for the United States to "continue to insist upon the protection of intellectual property rights in other countries, and should equally call on our trading partners, such as Japan and France, to let the market set pharmaceutical prices, not government bureaucrats."

At the time of writing Pfizer is leading an assault by large pharmaceutical companies against European-style health care policies that involve government-mandated purchasing of drugs and other supplies. Attempting to enlist competitor companies like Eli Lilly and GlaxoSmithKline, Pfizer is threatening to withhold new treatments from France unless the French government permits higher drug prices. Similar action is being promised for Canada and Austria pending meetings with politicians (Michaels et al. 2001). Such policies have repercussions elsewhere, as in Japan, where the government estimates prices on the basis of a weighted average of costs in other markets. Of course the idea that "the market" should set prices, rather than "government bureaucrats," ignores the oligopolistic structure of the pharmaceutical industry, coupled with the statutory monopoly that constitutes the "protection of intellectual property rights." These very same rights are being abrogated throughout the poorer countries as pharmaceutical companies and their agents engage in "biopiracy," "discovering" new medicines and patenting these, thereby enclosing what has been the common property of indigenous peoples for centuries.

While "price-fixing" arrangements exist in several individual states in the US (for example Maine, an object of Tabarrok's and thereby Pfizer's wrath), the last major effort aimed at reforming the US health care system and thereby universalize coverage—the Clinton health care plan of 1993—ended in ignominious failure. At least in part this was due to a high-powered lobbying and public relations campaign by corporations like Pfizer, whose strategy is symbiotically linked with the current trajectory of US health care development.[3] Indeed, that trajectory is driven largely by the convergent interests of pharmaceutical companies, insurers and the medical profession, among others that drive the progressive technocratization and privatization of health care. Thus the "independence" touted by hired guns like Tabarrok must be weighed against the corporate interest to which they are, at best, so blind. But so too must the assumptions underlying the status quo be subjected to ruthless criticism, if only because, with such universality of agreement concerning the US health care system's endemic crisis, there is no logical alternative.

## PATHOLOGIES OF THE SYSTEM

As it is currently constituted, the US health care system is an interlocking set of different interests that converge upon those of the wider community. In so doing they serve to elevate the individual at the expense of the social. While the US system is "market-based," its privatization is as much cultural as it is legal. Health care is a package of products that is tailored to individuals. In this it is no different from any other commodity traded under capitalist conditions. Patients are treated as consumers who purchase a bundle of entitlements according to the package they have chosen. Of course health care is quite unlike other more mundane commodities for various reasons, elaborated below. Nevertheless, in a "market-based" system such as exists in the US (and in the so-called "quasi-market" reforms enacted in other countries including Britain), this idea of consumer sovereignty, drawn directly from mainstream textbook microeconomics, informs the treatment of health care by policymakers and most mainstream commentators, and is, to varying degrees, the dominant ideology in the public consideration and presentation of health care issues. This ideology was a significant contributor to the failure of the Clinton plan.

According to Lewis Hill and Robert McComb, Clinton's plan to universalize coverage on the basis of a German-style play-or-pay system (where employers either provide insurance for their employees or pay taxes to fund state-provided coverage) failed largely because it was perceived to be too radical, too bureaucratic, and too complicated. Relegated to a "superficial" status is the apparently "little or no consultation with the leaders of business, labour, and the healthcare professions from the private sector" (Hill and McComb 1996, 24). Yet how could it be possible that a plan, enjoying opinion poll support of 71% at its outset in February 1993, would see that support shrink to 59% the following September and bottom at 33% the following year? Assuredly, a well-funded and carefully planned public relations campaign by and on behalf of pharmaceutical companies and health insurers had its effect. Roger Feldman of the "Independent" Institute is certain that the plan failed, not because of television commercials depicting a representative family experiencing doubts over their future coverage ("Harry and Louise"), but because "the American people were not willing to entrust the government with running the health care system" (Feldman 2000, 2). Evidence of this could be found simply by turning to the popular press, which "intuitively understood" this. If this were true, then the *audited* expenditure, in excess of $120 million, of health care interests opposed to the Clinton plan, must rank as one of the most cost-ineffective interventions ever recorded in health care history (see Dowd 1997, 100-104).

For whatever reasons, Hill, McComb, and Feldman ignore the lengths to which corporate interests can and do go to achieve their goals. Television commercials would be a fraction, albeit significant, of a public relations campaign encompassing *all* news media. Tapping into the individualistic ideological underpinnings of the "American dream" would not be difficult in normal times, but the period in question was also marked by an overwhelming popular frustration with federal government that was quite remarkable for its intensity and its timing, considering that it had arisen *during* the Reagan-Bush presidencies that had, supposedly, rolled back the frontiers of the federal state. Activating a succession of academics-for-hire and other spokespersons and commentators would hardly have been beyond the resources of those interests concerned to prevent the Clinton health care plan from succeeding. Any future effort at reform would do well to acknowledge this fact.[4] And, of course, there are those who genuinely do believe in the market ideal with all the fervency of a religious believer or committed ideologue, and who take it upon themselves to stamp out "error" at home and propagate their message (and impose their model) of "free" markets abroad.

This dominant ideology of consumerist individualism serves corporate interests very well, and mitigates against whatever social currents leading toward greater collective awareness and solidarity. Blank (1997, xvi) notes that the concept of health care as a collective activity is common to all European nations (including even Britain) despite variations in system design. In the US, however, "individualism and the belief in the private sector negates a similar view," resulting in a much more narrowly defined notion of public good. In health care, as in most other matters, the crucial concept underlying this is "choice," which has been portrayed as under threat every time the issue of health care reform has reared its head. According to the conventional wisdom, the threat of the removal of choice was too much for the American people, who opted instead for the retention of the system that is its very embodiment. Therefore, it is worth examining both the nature and extent of choice commonly exercised by the users of the US health care system.

## The Mythology of Choice

Given that, in 1997, "at least 35 million citizens have been left outside the insurance system and have no assurances of access to health care resources" (Blank 1997, ix) it might be worth pondering over what sort of "choice" is being proffered by the guardians of individual liberty and entrepreneurialism. Clearly, when such a large segment of the US population "have been left outside" the system, as opposed to having opted out of it, it is worth considering what is the practical meaning of the enshrinement of individual choice as the paragon of social virtue, especially when the US outstrips all other countries in per capita health care expenditure.

That health care expenditure is heavily skewed toward heavy users of the system is partly a result of the heavy reliance on "technological" solutions to health care problems that are themselves subject to invention by cultural forces that reinforce the recourse to those same "solutions." These interrelated cultural and technological factors are discussed below. Similarly related, but more fundamental, is the notion of choice and the concept of the consumer as it is applied to health care (among other goods).

Consumerism is an ideology that has come to pervade, to varying degrees, the societies of advanced countries, west and east, and is held up as an aspirational model for citizens of less developed countries, "emerging markets" and "economies in transition." The latter, especially, have been bombarded with propaganda equating "freedom" with consumerism. In all of this the model is based upon the US experience, as the "land of opportunity" became the "land of plenty" in the post-1945 period. Such visible material affluence was, and is, vigorously promoted in commercial advertisements and has come to define for many the image of what it is to be "American." US institutions, whether state, private or social, are as involved in the propagation of this model, leading some to wonder whether or not "globalization" is simply another word for "Americanization."[5] This is "because the United States is the only country in the world today offering a model of a global society" (Berndtson 2000, 167). Yet while citizens of other countries have recourse to nationalist defenses against such cultural imperialism, in the United States the "free market" model and its associated consumerism is often portrayed as patriotic.[6]

In keeping with the remorseless logic of capitalist development and the associated application of neoclassical economic "reasoning,"[7] the consumerist model has become entrenched in both popular and "informed" treatments of health care. Health care is a set of packages manufactured by health care producers and "sold" to consumers based upon the rubrics of choice as exercised in a market setting. Scarce resources are allocated supposedly on the basis of "willingness to pay."[8] Of course in reality life is not so simple, and, given the unpredictable nature of a person's or public's health, institutions have been designed that mitigate that unpredictability. Insurance schemes exist whereby individuals, whether personally or via their employers, can subscribe to a prescribed level of care in accordance with the price of that scheme. In addition, the elderly can, via the federally-administered Medicare program, have government assistance with hospital costs and some other specified treatments.

Aside from the obvious difficulties inherent in the exercise of "choice" by patients whose knowledge of medicine and care is most likely insignificant in comparison with that of their professional care-givers (see Keaney 1999), it will be clear that the "choice" facing supposed consumers is most often made at one further remove, circumscribed as it is by the limitations of insurance cover and personal affluence, in addition to expertise. Yet the history of US health care reform throughout the 20$^{th}$ century has been one in which government efforts to extend coverage have been met with opposition predicated on the supposedly inalienable right of individual choice. Presently, this is the banner with which the pharmaceuticals industry is attempting to stave off tighter price regulation, by highlighting the cost to future generations of discoveries foregone owing to the reduction of profits to be reinvested should price controls be implemented. The Bush administration's proposals for prescription drug discount cards for Medicare have been tailored to avoid conflict with the pharmaceuticals industry, which administers the distribution of prescription drugs via pharmacy benefit managers—intermediaries between companies and patients (McGregor and Michaels 2001). The insurance industry mobilized against the Clinton plan ostensibly to protect individual choice. When Lyndon Johnson's administration was attempting to extend health care coverage via the creation of the Medicare and Medicaid programs, it was the American Medical Association that fought a rearguard action against reform, again in the name of individual choice. On this occasion it was the patient's right to choose a physician that was supposedly under threat.[9] And, of course, Harry Truman's efforts to universalize coverage almost twenty years earlier failed miserably because of the entrenched opposition of vested interests.

Thus has the ideology of individual choice conspired to restrict access to those least endowed with it. Choice has been a persistent, consistent enabling myth that has allowed vested interests to thwart or distort egalitarian reforms. One of these vested interests has been the medical profession itself. The mythology of choice has combined with the "medicalization" of health care, in a process of cumulative causation, to contribute significantly to the present crisis. This medicalization of care represents another barrier obstructing progress toward a more equitable health care system.

## Unhealthy Alienation

Ever since Adam Ferguson (1966) wrote of the socially divisive effects of the division of labor, social philosophers from Adam Smith through Karl Marx to Thorstein Veblen and John Dewey have pondered the mixed blessing that is ever-greater specialization. It was Smith, most famously, who highlighted the greater technical efficiency and thereby productivity arising from specialization, but was equally mindful of the dulling effect such specialization would have on the workers in his notional pin factory. Veblen's critique of mainstream economic theory rested, in part, on his identification of *empirical* technical efficiency as exhibited by skilled industrial workers, as against the notional allocative efficiencies of the business system, as he termed it. Thus Veblen often appears overly sanguine regarding the division of labor, as compared to, say, Marx, whose conceptualization of class, resting upon ownership of the means of production, involved the alienation of the worker from the fruits of his or her labor. Dewey, too, was concerned that the tyranny of economics should not be given such free rein that notions of citizenship, community, even humanity itself, would be diminished as a result.[10]

All of these commentators have shed light on important aspects of increasing specialization. As these relate to health care, we will focus initially on the gains. Undoubtedly, as the world of learning has divided and sub-divided into myriad branches of science, our collective knowledge of and mastery over our environment has been enhanced beyond measure. Medicine and health care have benefited from an impressive array of discoveries: new cures, palliatives, treatments, procedures, and preventative measures. All these have resulted in the eradication or substantial reduction of major diseases (smallpox, polio, typhoid, cholera), whilst prolonging life for the average citizen of the developed world. But even these achievements rest upon the existence of a supportive institutional infrastructure, not least public hygiene (refuse collection, sewerage facilities and clean water) and education. This has been illustrated most graphically in the decline of the former Soviet Union, and most graphically in Russia, where, according to the World Health Organization, between 1987 and 1994 the risk of premature death among males increased by as much as 70%, recovering only slowly since, owing to the collapse of state-administered infrastructure and the Western-assisted plunder of state assets that was privatization. The World Bank, in its World Development Report of 1997, admitted as much when it identified that a crucial problem facing all developing countries was a "crisis of state effectiveness" (see Panitch 1998).

A central contradiction of the market fundamentalism informing much academic and policy discourse is that the methodological prerogatives of neoclassical economics force economists to reduce complex wholes to more "manageable" units, which can then be arranged according to the "logic" of the theory. Not only is this a reversal of standard scientific practice (empirical reality is, by definition, deficient to the extent that it does not adhere to the theoretical model!), but the consequent "externalities" are conveniently excised from the analysis, thereby rendering the analysis of practical use only to neoclassical economists, at best, and, more often, to vested interests well served by such "trained ignorance." In health care, this reinforces the "medicalization" process mentioned earlier by undervaluing public health and disease prevention initiatives (Shiell and Hawe 1996) whilst emphasizing the importance of technologies developed in response to individual patients' care needs. And where these "needs" are themselves manufactured by the medical profession, the "value" derived from their fulfillment is "cost-effective" to the extent that patients' subjective utility is maximized (Hildred and Beauvais 1995). This amounts to a tautology behind which lies a serious conflict of interest: patients are told they have a problem by the medical-industrial complex, and its solution depends upon the administration of a specially developed "cure" or palliative by a medical practitioner, often in collaboration with the company responsible for the new technology, and whose own verdict of the outcome will, depending upon the intervention, significantly shape the patient's own "utility." In such fashion are many medical technologies introduced, thereby driving costs *upward*, rather than generating savings, as is supposed to be the outcome of market-based systems. As Blank (1996, 322) remarks, "there is little doubt that the market system has the potential to exaggerate the diffusion of medical technologies that are expected to be profitable."

Meanwhile, having separated "health care" from other relevant social factors through its equation with medical intervention, arguably the most important contributors to the health of individuals and communities are ignored. As Blank (1997, 56) reminds us, "Health status is more closely correlated with many nonmedical factors including adequate water and sanitation, good nutrition, decent housing and socioeconomic factors." In institutionalist parlance, health status is closely, positively correlated with the level of real income.

The most radical critic of the medicalization of health care has been Ivan Illich. Like others, he highlights the truly significant collective gains achieved through the improved provision of social infrastructure and cleaner environment, as compared to the contributions of specific medical treatments, which are "never significantly related to a decline in the compound disease burden or to a rise in life expectancy" (Illich 1976, 29). But Illich's most damning criticism concerns what he calls the iatrogenesis resultant from the increasing hegemony of the medical model of health care. Aside from clinical manifestations of iatrogenesis (pain, sickness or death resulting from medical care), there are, perhaps, even greater social and cultural aspects to consider. According to Illich, the hospitalization of ill-health has resulted in the alienation of patients from their own homes and families—provision of care and support outside the hospital system is somehow deviant. Cultural iatrogenesis occurs when medicine and the medical profession provide explanations and prescriptions that supplant individuals' own sense of their situation, or even their own ability to deal with the inevitable: "Western man has lost the right to preside at his act of dying" (Illich 1976, 210).

While Illich's rhetoric is provocative, there is sufficient truth in what he says to instil unease. The subtitle of his book, *The Expropriation of Health*, captures the essence of his and others' criticisms. The medical model of health care, combined with consumerism, results in the unhealthy alienation of individuals from their own bodies, as the care for these is entrusted to others as a matter of "choice." While we might not wish to legislate for lifestyles, given the abuses to which that course of action has been put in the past (racism, homophobia, patriarchy), there is a growing discontent among insurance subscribers that their ever-increasing contributions are going to pay for the irresponsibility of others. Blank warns that this privatized form of fiscal crisis is going to, if it has not already begun to, force the pace of public discussions about health care rationing.

The medical-industrial complex driving the development of new health care technologies bears much responsibility for this. Capitalism's insatiable appetite for accumulation demands feeding, and where companies cannot achieve growth in existing markets, new ones must be made, either through the development of export markets, or the creation of new products for which there is sufficient demand. Exporting is subject to ongoing controversy over intellectual property rights, which pharmaceutical companies have sought to protect in spite of the appalling toll of suffering and death that citizens of impoverished countries must endure because of the costs involved. New products, on the other hand, comprise two types: genuine improvements in intervention via the invention of new technologies for existing maladies, and, more sinisterly, technologies invented to "solve" equally invented problems.

To take genuine improvements first: since most major improvements in health have been achieved through better social infrastructure (real income), most new discoveries will be subject to a process of diminishing returns. Increasing specialization dictates that the numbers served by new technologies will decrease. This is not to denigrate such innovation, but it does constitute a use of resources that, under other circumstances (for example, democratic control), could as easily be employed elsewhere. This is more complex in the field of mental health care, where seemingly new diagnostic innovations are, by their nature, subject to extreme controversy. The medicalization of mental and emotional processes designated as "syndromes" increases individual dependency upon medical expertise, whether technological (prescription drugs) or personal (therapy). At the same time, the objectification of psychological "conditions" alienates the individual from his or her mind, as professional intervention is deemed the most appropriate recourse at times of stress (Vandenburgh 2001, 67, provides a list of references that discuss the social construction of psychiatric disorders).

This can also have reactionary social consequences, as Dana L. Cloud highlights. Therapeutic discourse has become increasingly prominent in the public domain since the end of the Vietnam war. According to Cloud, while there is much of value in this attention to the psychological damage wrought by all kinds of events (war, alcoholism, domestic abuse, persecution, and so on), there is also a material purpose served by the privatization of human suffering:

> Racism, sexism, and capitalism pose significant obstacles to individual mobility and well-being; their roles in structuring social reality, however, are obscured in therapeutic discourses that locate the ill not with the society but with the individual or private family. . . .The rhetorical function of therapeutic discourses in such contexts is to encourage audiences to focus on themselves and the elaboration of their private lives rather than to address and attempt to reform systems of social power in which they are embedded (Cloud 1998, xiii, xiv).

Of course, as the number of diagnosed "conditions" and associated medical technologies proliferates, the upward pressures on costs threaten to spiral further out of control. Fiscal crisis is biting the private sector also. Earlier efforts to mitigate this through "managed care" have exhausted the savings to be made, and costs are now rising once again, bringing closer the day of reckoning that the revised Clinton health care legislation sought to postpone.

## Mismanaged Care

By now it will be apparent that the hegemonic medical model of health care is riven with contradiction: the vested interests served by the enabling myths of individual choice have accumulated social costs including vast inequalities in access to health care despite the world's most abundant health care system; over-reliance on medical technologies leading to the alienation of individuals from their own bodies, minds and social surroundings; focus on narrow specialisation at the expense of basic social infrastructure; and deepening fiscal crisis resulting from the medical-industrial complex's efforts both to meet and manipulate the public's desire for ever more professional care, itself founded upon an individualistic ideology that deems "choice" an inalienable right.

While the US federal government can be relieved it does not face the dilemmas of other governments, which have to wrestle with the funding problems posed by the financing of state health care systems similarly subject to fiscal crisis, the day of reckoning is coming ever closer. Ever since the health care costs explosion began in the 1960s, successive administrations have attempted to grapple with the contradictory goals of widening coverage (an electoral advantage) whilst containing costs (popular in theory, less so in practice). We have already seen some of the compromises into which Presidents have found themselves pushed, whether through lack of political nous, courage, or sufficient support. While this has suited certain vested interests, including both the insurance industry and the medical establishment, it has merely deferred the moment when the issue of health care rationing requires to be addressed explicitly.

Since the 1970s, there has been a growth in managed care schemes. Originally this was driven by the Nixon administration's alarm at the rising costs of Medicare (Rubin and White-Means 2001, 241). This growth has accelerated in the last decade due to rising inflation in the health care industry —as high as 20% per annum. As a result, whereas in 1987 95% of those receiving health coverage from their employers received almost full repayment for medical services that they themselves had selected, by the end of the 1990s that figure has been halved and is still decreasing, as employers select the health maintenance organizations (HMOs) on behalf of their employees (Tauber 1999, xiii).

HMOs are the most common type of managed care organizations, which serve as contractual intermediaries between patient (or employer scheme or government program) enrollees and care providers. HMOs receive a fixed payment in advance for all medical care received by a group. In this way they bear financial risk, and can experience severe financial difficulty, even to the point of bankruptcy. Patients enrolled in HMO-administered programs receive care only from specified hospitals and physicians, pharmacies and therapists, and must adhere to the administrative requirements of their program (follow prescribed procedures, seek approval, fill forms, and so on). The HMO must contract with a sufficient number of physicians and hospitals (serving as a provider network), and often employs a gatekeeper physician to administer primary care and control costs (in the manner of British general practitioners following the 1991 "internal market" reforms).

The configuration of management controls exercized by HMOs and other types of managed care organization (for instance, preferred provider organizations—PPOs—that combine the managerial controls of HMOs with the flexibility of unmanaged fee for service provision) is too large to be examined in detail here.[11] It is sufficient to note that greater numbers of those with health care insurance are finding themselves switched to schemes that involve greater managerial discretion over which hospitals, physicians, and treatments are covered. This is especially true of the aftermath of the Clinton health care plan, whose failure accelerated the rise of managed care, which, in the words of Hill and McComb (1996, 25), "is a rational market response to escalating costs."[12]

This industry restructuring, involving price competition among providers in response to HMOs, themselves under pressure from newly-formed associations of employers seeking to boost monopsonistic bargaining power, resulted in a temporary reduction in health care insurance costs. While Hill and McComb regarded this development positively, others were not as convinced. Blank (1996, 1997) has consistently warned against the wilful ignorance of rising costs on the part of the public and government, pointing to the material, systemic bases of fiscal crisis. And now that the "shake-out" resulting from that restructuring has worked its way through to completion, costs are set to resume their upward trajectory. It is not difficult to guess who will bear the brunt.

While insurers lobby the US Food and Drug Administration to recommend switching certain high cost medicines from prescription to over-the-counter status (see Pilling 2001), counter-lobbying by the pharmaceutical industry will limit the gains to be expected from that approach.[13] Payment of providers by insurers is already slow and cumbersome, and has contributed significantly to the demise of non-profit community hospitals (*The Economist*, 2001). This leaves one, altogether more promising route for insurers. Having already risen by 11% in 2001, insurance premiums are set to increase by at least a further 13% in 2002.[14] According to *Business Week*, "there's little doubt big annual price hikes are again becoming the norm." Only this time, the costs are being passed on by employers to their employees. This is because the much-touted restructuring of the Clinton years, yielding so much by way of effiency savings, also resulted in further concentration in the insurance industry, and price competition has all but evaporated. Employers, therefore, are now faced with the problems of fiscal crisis as never before, and, naturally, it is their employees that are seeing their health care benefits shrink. Rising in popularity among employers is the usage of "defined-contribution plans," in which employers' health insurance premiums are capped and responsibility for cost-containment is shifted further onto the employee. Some employers even go so far to reckon that they can handle billing for services rendered rather than pay inflated premiums. (see Weber et al. 2001).

## Prognosis: Negative

The pathologies of the US health care system, explored in this section, have exposed a crisis-ridden entity that remains in thrall to the very forces driving it toward collapse. Without radical change, the most likely outcome will be the continuing polarization of health care usage between those who can afford to use ever more expensive medical technologies prescribed as the definitive interventions, while the rest enjoy either a much-diminished insurance coverage, or no coverage at all. What is required is no less than a root-and-branch refashioning of health care, US-style.

While this chapter has already employed certain analytical tools of institutionalist origin, the next section will explore, in greater detail, how a projected health care reform program could be modelled according to a critical institutionalist perspective.

## AN INSTITUTIONALIST PRESCRIPTION

While this chapter has been sharply critical of the status quo, and, especially, the hegemony of a particular version of medical intervention as a health care model, it has been necessary to focus on where we are now, and how we came to be here. This has permitted reasoned speculation about the likely trajectory of future events, suggesting that, without a major upheaval, the US health care system will continue to fail more and more of its citizens. This penultimate section focuses on some of the arguably necessary changes involved in its envisioning of a more equitable health care system.

Just as the separation of economics from politics and the other social sciences is an abritrary and artificial demarcation, so, too, is the notion that health lies solely in the domain of the medical profession. Even to widen that attribution to include other caring professions is only a mildly ameliorative conceptual shift, however desirable a broader perspective than the predominant medical-curative model of care. No less than a comprehensive reconsideration of what we mean by health is required in order to gain some purchase over the otherwise intractable issues pertaining to universal health care.

Institutionalism, as a tradition of political economy, is well placed to serve here. The steady development of its theory of social value has clarified the end-in-view of institutionalist inquiry: "We now affirm that that direction is forward which provides for *the continuity of human life and the noninvidious re-creation of community through the instrumental use of knowledge*" (Tool 2001, 293, italics in original). Marc Tool's social value principle encapsulates decades of critical institutionalist inquiry whilst developing it further. The concern with technical efficiency that marked the work of Veblen and especially Clarence Ayres is, as William M. Dugger (1995) has highlighted, re-channelled into a concern with democratic participation and ownership—a most appropriate redress in health care matters, as we shall see further.

In his revealing dissection of US health care, Robert Blank argues repeatedly that the ultimate test of any system of care is whether or not it meets its "primary goal . . . to maximize the collective health of society, not individual medical benefit" (Blank 1997, xviii). The social value principle's identification of the "non-invidious re-creation of community," and critical institutionalism's longstanding concern with what Veblen called the "generic ends of life,"[15] is thoroughly consistent with this criterion.

It has already been remarked that the greatest advances in societal health have been achieved through the development of social institutions—the public infrastructure that ensures the provision of education, clean water, refuse collection, unpolluted environment, and so on. Where these factors are lacking, there is a marked increase in ill-health. Another chief social determinant of health status is financial income. Blank (1997, p. 60) cites a study by R. G. Wilkinson (1992) in which it is calculated that "approximately two-thirds of the variation in mortality rates in developed nations is related to the distribution of income in the population." Other studies have made more explicit linkages between morbidity and mortality rates and particular manifestations of inequality based on race (for instance, King and Williams 1995; Hayward et al. 2000; Shi 2001). Clearly, socioeconomic provisioning is a fundamental determinant of a community's health status. In selecting those aspects of the present system most necessitating reform, I propose that we focus on the following key factors: real income, community development and public health, the patient-provider relationship, and the medical profession itself. Attention to these is vital to a more effective US health care system, and all, to some extent, relate to the role of the state.

## Real Income

Critical institutionalists have been at the forefront in the development of a concept of real income that encompasses more than the financial, important though that is. According to Tool (2001, 72), real income can be defined simply as "goods and services." The capitalist form of economic organization discriminates in favor of private property, and value, in accordance with neoclassical theory, is judged in accordance with the price individual consumers are prepared to pay in economic transactions involving the exchange of private property rights. In this way, goods and services are typically conceptualized as tradeable because excludible. "Problems" arise because, of course, not all goods are like that. They are problematized because they do not fit into the conceptual framework employed by mainstream economists, and so vast new tracts of inquiry open up in response: solving the problems posed by "externalities," agency theory, and public choice approaches, to name only a few. However, when we approach social problems from an ontologically different perspective, the difficulties imposed by an inappropriate conceptual framework disappear. The test of the new perspective is whether it reduces the needless methodological obstructions that impede the full development of human personality and community. Critical institutionalism's recasting of real income as the "requisites to civilized existence" (Tool 2001, 73) is a step in this direction—indeed, a recovery of much that has been lost by mainstream economics in its exogenization of factors deemed "non-economic."

Beyond this initial foray, we must infer the composition of real income from the specifications of its converse: social costs. Here, critical institutionalists have long been developing analyses of the deficiencies of our economic system and mainstream theories, whether as a result of "private affluence amid public squalor" (Galbraith 1998), the deleterious effects of our economic system upon the environment (Kapp 1971), or, simply, the ceremonialization of social institutions in the service of vested interests (Veblen 1992). Thus Tool (1995, 121) defines social costs as "demonstrable disruption or impairment of the knowledge-driven flow of real income and output" in relation to the social value principle highlighted above. Manifestations of social costs that relate to health care include "conspicuous waste, environmental destruction, blighted lives, needless deaths, deprived learning, invidious discrimination . . . ." (ibid.).

The US health care system, as it is currently configured, practices invidious discrimination against the poor (often those most in need of care), resulting in blighted lives and needless deaths. The paltry provisioning of public health promotion programs adds to this, constituting deprived learning. But instead of treating health care as a good to be purchased by an individual consumer, it ought, instead, to be included in any consideration of real income, as that relates both to individuals and communities. And this should be linked with the idea of a basic income, since health is a function of socioeconomic status.[16] In other words, a basic income should be a basic *real* income.

## Community Development and Public Health

"Too much medicine is not good for health. Not only does it divert resources from useful endeavors, but it also produces ill health and disrupts traditional social and cultural institutions and values that are central to good health in the broader sense" (Blank 1997, 50).

As detailed above, the "privatization" of health care—its conceptualization in the public mind as a consumption good—has been detrimental to public health promotion programs that, arguably, would do more good for the re-creation of community, than the present development of technologies by the medical-industrial complex, aimed at treating ever more particular conditions afflicting mainly fewer and fewer individuals. Meanwhile greater emphasis upon a more participative approach to health care (in accordance with Blank's call for the assertion of positive rights that encompass personal responsibility as well as entitlements) is essential to the democratization of the system. What is required is a reconceptualization of health care as a community asset, collectively owned *and developed* by the members of the community together, and not simply the province of specialists and professionals who, unchecked, can pursue agendas that are not in accordance with the wider interest. The recasting of the patient-provider relationship, discussed below, acts as a further constructive response to the present problem situation. But what is required is what philosopher Larry Hickman (1990) has called "responsible technology": responsive, *regenerative* inquiry that draws upon the collective knowledge and experience of the community to meet the evolving problem situations requiring solution, or at least, amelioration. In other words, the health care system itself, and its constituent parts, must, both as a result of democratic participation and in order to strengthen it, "focus on constructive institutional adjustments," in accordance with the general principles of instrumental inquiry and democratic governance elaborated by Tool (1998).

In order to achieve this, it will be necessary for the federal government to grasp the nettle so bitterly contested for decades, and support, financially and administratively, a universal health care system. To those who would charge that this is an unseemly "socialization" of health care, the answer is that, even excluding Medicare, health care in the US is already socialized, albeit within the private sector. The problems of fiscal crisis have been shifted onto insurers which, in turn, have shifted it onto managed care organizations, which, in turn, have tried to pass them on to providers and patients (the latter with greater success, unsurprisingly). To those who would charge that this would represent a further bureaucratization of the health care system, the answer is that, thanks to the accumulation of accomodations made with vested interests, government regulation of health care (itself unavoidable) is a messy patchwork that confuses where it should clarify, wastes where it should generate efficiency. Care providers must negotiate a regulatory jungle comprising conditions set by local, state and federal governments. Meanwhile, what of the bureaucracies employed within the insurance industry? A unified system of administration would yield some, not insubstantial savings (though these should not be overestimated[17]), but, perhaps more importantly, it would also be a pre-requisite for equitable provision of health care resources, whether according to geography, technology, or socioeconomic status. It need not entail an intrusive command-and-control system overly cumbersome in its regulation—arguably that is what exists just now in the US: "Merely qualifying for reimbursement requires mastery of a staggering number of contractual arrangements. Hospitals in densely populated areas may accept as many as 200 different health-care plans" (*The Economist* 2001). Meanwhile other developed countries have universal systems guaranteed by the state that are far more efficient administratively than the US health care system.

As for health promotion programs, these can be more than financed by the money currently spent by providers and insurers alike on marketing their services, as well as the public relations exercises mentioned earlier. Universal care does not need to be marketed, but useful information geared toward the promotion of healthier lifestyles and more efficient resource use most certainly does. This would be a fulfillment of Dewey's envisioning of "the perfecting of the means and ways of communication of meanings so that genuinely shared interest in the consequences of interdependent activities may inform desire and effort and thereby direct action" (Dewey 1954, 155).

The democratic community will also have to come to terms with the limitations of finite resources (an issue studiously avoided in the imagery of advertising), and will need to consider how to prioritize its expenditures accordingly. This will encompass social attitudes toward death itself.[18] The experience of the state of Oregon, where citizens have been able to "vote" for their preferred health care expenditures as part of the state administration's effort to universalize care, while imperfect, offers a beginning for a consideration that is long overdue. In this connection, state and local governments could retain sufficient autonomy to be able to work within general guidelines established by federal authorities, in accordance with an established basic income as part of the more general application of the social value principle to policymaking. Such mechanisms are in place now, as already noted—what is required is greater uniformity of standards, thereby enhancing transparency and guaranteeing each US citizen a basic level of real income, but enabling local communities to work out how best to achieve that level in accordance with local preferences. Where local resources would not be sufficient to meet the basic real income level, federal government can arrange fiscal transfers to redress the balance.

Such an extension of state or government power does not, of itself, guarantee the wise use of warranted knowledge in accordance with the social value principle. As Galbraith warned:

> public ownership is not a promising solution for privately exercised power if the state itself is the instrument of such power. . . .All organization excludes interference from outside or above; its goals are those which serve the interest of its members. This is the behavior of an organization before it is taken over by the state; it will be its behavior after it has been taken over. This will be especially certain if its operations are technical in character and its power is derived from more or less exclusively possessed information (Galbraith 1973, 219).

At all levels, government will require to be more fully democratic than at present. Democratizing the state—"to put democratic content into the democratic forms (or procedures) of the bourgeois liberal state"—is a prerequisite of the good society (O'Connor 1998, 310; see also Keaney 2001b). As Galbraith affirmed only recently, "The decisive step toward a good society is to make democracy genuine, inclusive" (Galbraith 1996, 139). Part of the democratization of the state and its bureaucracy would involve instilling an ethos of craftsmanship commonly attibuted to "the professions" within the state administration itself, rendering it a truly *public* administration. This concern, as Tilman and Brown (1995) have demonstrated, has strong antecedents in the work of Veblen and C. Wright Mills. It runs strongly counter to recent developments in the West, where the idea of public service has been consistently degraded in favor of notions of private entrepreneurship and business prerogatives. Yet, arguably, it has never been more necessary than now, at a time when the public's faith in the ability of "its" institutions to perform is unprecedentedly low.

Thus, once again, health care reform entails more than mere tinkering with existing structures. It requires the levels of participation in decision-making envisaged by Dewey (1954) in order that the social costs endemic to the present system are eradicated.

## Reconstructing the Patient-Provider Relationship

Throughout the foregoing discussion, criticisms have been levelled at the medical technocracy that serves as the hegemonic model of health care. While interest groups like the American Medical Association are culpable in this and related developments, there are physicians who are troubled, if not profoundly dissatisfied, with the present arrangement and its widely predicted failure. While not going so far, at least rhetorically, as Ivan Illich, Alfred I. Tauber has crafted a thoughtful meditation on the dilemmas facing the medical profession, in many ways echoing what Douglas Dowd foresaw in the aftermath of the failed Clinton health care plan. Dowd predicted the growing "proletarianization" of doctors as their profession loses the trappings of earlier times, "now that doctors find themselves simultaneously losing income *and* professional dignity (diktats from insurance companies replacing their medical judgments. . . ." (Dowd 1997, 103). While some provider organizations are restructuring incentives to encourage doctors to "drum up business" (discussed below), Tauber is more concerned about the effects of "a medical system that has become increasingly hostile to my standards of care for my patients" (Tauber 1999, xv).

For all the above criticisms levelled at the medical-industrial complex, the doctor-patient relationship remains, rightly, the central component of any health care system. When the system itself disfigures or distorts that relationship (thereby creating a social cost), it is the system that requires reconfiguration. As has already been argued, such a reconfiguration is long overdue and absolutely necessary. "I am a physician, not a health care manager, nor a politician. My interests concern serving the patient. Medicine is a calling based on a special social relationship" says Tauber (1999, xiv). This special social relationship has been recognized in Western culture since at least the time of Hippocrates, and analogues are evident in other non-Western cultures. This is not to ceremonialize a once useful technology: rather, it is to recognize the continuing importance of a crucial aspect of health care. Even with greater individual and community responsibility for the promotion and maintenance of good health, occasions will arise where skilled practitioners are required to make considered interventions informed by professional expertise. Part of a physician's intrinsic reward, like that of other professionals (in the various branches of education, for example), is the *art* of care: the application of combinations of scientific knowledge and career experience in specific, unique circumstances. Tauber admits that this professional freedom is theatened by the encroachment of what, in institutionalist terms, is essentially the pecuniary interest.

The worrying aspect of this is that Dowd's vision of proletarianized doctors joining the ranks of disenfranchized patients in demanding a more equitable health care system ignores some notable precedents. Writing originally in the 1960s, John Kenneth Galbraith imagined that, thanks to the increasing specialization and bureaucratization of industrial society, greater reliance on the "educational and scientific estate" would result in the colonization of its liberal ethos to other sectors of the political economy more usually governed by the pecuniary interest. Writing his introduction to the fourth edition of *The New Industrial State* twenty years later, Galbraith remarked that these liberal values had been thwarted by President Reagan's purpose "to assert the virtues of a narrower pecuniary preoccupation in public life and society" (Galbraith 1985, xxxv). Managed care, and the goals of for-profit care providers more generally, represent the assertion of pecuniary preoccupations over and above those of health care practitioners, some of whom, at least, can be relied upon to accommodate that interest.

Much commentary exists on the impact of cost containment measures upon the quality of health care. For some, managed care means damaged ethics (Coney 1997). Physicians are forced to act as gate-keepers on behalf of performance-assessed administrators (whose performance criteria are profit or savings-related). In the United Kingdom there is evidence that some doctors practise "cream-skimming": turning away higher risk patients because they are too costly (Boseley 1999). Meanwhile, those physicians not rewarded according to how *little* they treat their patients (an antidote to overzealous prescribing, perhaps, but ethically troublesome as we have seen) can be subject to converse, but equally perverse, incentives. In a detailed study, sociologist Henry Vandenburgh charts a form of what he calls "organizational deviance" as routinely practised in private psychiatric hospitals in Texas. There, "federal guidelines that have otherwise outlawed kickbacks in return for patients" are being circumvented via the provision of part-time medical directorships, which hospitals award to those physicians who refer the most patients (see Vandenburgh 2001). This enables hospitals to award higher payments. The organizational deviance is the routine infringement of community norms: the secrecy attached to this sort of practice is, according to Vandenburgh, sufficient evidence of its abnormality. No one would feel comfortable in openly admitting of such practice, and for good reason.

If we are to eradicate these social costs, the institutional reforms discussed above will go a long way to removing the perverse incentives that support such invidious distinctions. But an alternative view of the central patient-doctor relationship is still necessary to complete what is, of necessity, a preliminary sketch of a reformed health care system. Once again, the model offered by critical institutionalism is thoroughly consistent with the social value principle.

The historical emphasis on patient autonomy and individual choice has proven misleading, when compared against empirical reality. Real patient empowerment within a reformed system of health care would involve a similarly empowered care practitioner, able to exercise clinical judgment in a process of inquiry that is a *partnership* between patient and professional, and, by extension, the wider community that the professional serves. This is vital to restoring the trust that various commentators note has been lost as a result of various social and economic changes during the last 50 years (Tauber 1999; see also McMaster 2001 on the British health care system). Certainly, for-profit providers recognize the importance of this relationship—so much so that it is usually central to their marketing campaigns:

> Perhaps the best snapshot of today's medicine is the TV commercial or newspaper advertisement depicting a smiling nurse or doctor looking with apparent compassion at either a child or an elderly patient. Why? First, the doctor-patient relationship is primary. Just as beer commercials feature beer bottles, and car commercials feature cars, health care advertisements show the profession's essential relationship. Medicine is caring. But there is a second, perhaps more subtle reason the media attempts to capture an ostensibly normal scene of compassion. I suspect that they recognize that the five-minute clinic visit, the cog-in-the-wheel

> attitude so rampant in today's health care facility, is the source of great anxiety (Tauber 1999, xii).

Doctors, patients, and other care practitioners ought to be regarded as *partners* in a process of inquiry geared toward the solution of an identified set of problems relating to the health of the patient concerned. This ethos of partnership should extend throughout provider organizations, effectively reconstructing care processes as multidisciplinary ventures. This involves recognizing the vital input of nursing, pharmacy, and professions allied to medicine, as in the development of integrated care pathways in the British National Health Service (Campbell et al. 1998; Keaney 2001, 159). Patients should not feel required to supplement minimalist hospital provision by hiring their own nurses (Trafford 2001).[19] Nor should they automatically consider malpractice suits when outcomes are less than ideal—such expectations only lead to defensive medicine, hardly conducive to the craftsmanship essential to its practice. In addition, as with the increasing burden of expectation placed upon medical technologies (sold as infallible) to provide "perfect" births, heavy recourse to litigation can result in a shortage of medical expertise, as it has done in obstetrics (MacLennan 1993).

But the proper restoration of the patient-doctor relationship to its central status depends not only upon the design of provider institutions. Just as public expectations need to readjust to more realistic levels, so, too, must those involved in the medical-industrial complex machinery re-orient their interests away from activities supposedly more glorious and rewarding than patient care.

## A Prescription for the Medical Profession

A persistent complaint of many within and around higher education is the low status accorded to its supposedly central activity: teaching. Instead, recognition and reward accrues to those who "research"—an activity usually measured by the volume of publishing, whether books or articles in peer-reviewed academic journals. With the growth of higher education and the consequent increase in the number of personnel, there has been a proliferation of publications purporting to push back the frontiers of ever more specialized areas of knowledge. As "star" researchers gain professional kudos and attract grants financing ever more research activity, lower-paid teaching assistants take their place and conduct those activities most people would assume to be the fundamental *raison d'être* of an institution of higher learning.

Similarly, most people would expect those entering the medical profession to look forward to a career of saving and enhancing lives, of relieving suffering and providing comfort to the afflicted. It would come as something of an unpleasant surprise to read Tauber's account of his own medical education:

> I am a scientist. I trained as a biochemist and I spent the better part of my formative years as a physician in the laboratory. Success as a basic researcher assured my rapid climb up the professorial ladder. I learned the key lessons for academic advancement from a mentor at Harvard, himself a highly productive researcher, who in my opinion contributed more to the welfare of the public than one hundred—or for that matter, one thousand—ordinary clinicians, if any such comparison could be made. But that career model, whether translated into the prosaic concerns of doctors making money or academics wishing to rise in the medical school hierarchy, must strike most patients as callous, even severely selfish. Different models of excellence clearly have their place, but in the setting of the clinic, the patient is concerned with his or her own care, not the self-aggrandizement of the doctor. Yet the rewards in our medical schools do not traditionally go to the teacher or the committed clinician, but rather to the competitive clinician-scientist, dedicated to (depending on your point of view) the expansion of knowledge, or more cynically, the accrual of grants, prestige, and overhead dollars for the university. In either case, under the rubric of science, the medical establishment has almost universally (until quite recently) rewarded the successful researcher at the expense of the clinician (Tauber 1999, 21-22).

The medical establishment has also, as we have seen, resisted every effort by the federal government to broaden the coverage of health care in the US. The irony of this is that, owing to the medical establishment's own response to the opportunities provided by Medicare, the costs of that program mushroomed. It has only been when its autonomy has been threatened that the medical establishment has reminded the public of the importance of its professional skill and the freedom required to achieve clinical excellence. This is true, but, in the circumstances, disingenuous, because the medical establishment has consistently resisted enactment of measures that would achieve better clinical outcomes for the population as a whole, depicting itself as striking a blow for individual choice (usually its own).

According to Tauber, increasing public dissatisfaction is altering the behavior of the medical profession. Predictably, it is being driven by a developing discourse of patient rights. Under pressure from politicians, administrators and the insurance industry, it makes political sense for the medical profession to get on board this bandwagon, all other things being equal. The trouble is that, regardless of the impossibility of all other things remaining equal, the focus on individual rights has been a key constituent factor of the complex forces that have brought the health care system to its current crisis-ridden state.

Tauber's own scholarship provides a clue to the nature of the necessary reform of the medical profession. He revisits a debate whose outcome decisively shaped the development of medicine as an institution in the US—one that bears a striking resemblance to the cleavages within economics and the other social science disciplines. William Osler (1849-1919) and Francis Peabody (1881-1927), both leading academic and practising physicians, advocated a model of medical practice that held the patient-doctor relationship to be sacrosanct, built upon trust and the personal commitment of the clinician to the patient's welfare. The Osler-Peabody model could be described as humanistic. In opposition was a model of health care that was founded upon the fashionable precepts of positivism, emphasizing the laboratory model of science and its related detachment. This found clear articulation in the publication of the Flexner Report in 1910, having been commissioned by the "orthodox" medical establishment as a blueprint for the development of medical education. As Tauber (1999, 11-12) relates, in accordance with the report, "the new physician was to be taught that clinical medicine was but a branch of pathophysiology. The vector of interest was firmly drawn *from* the laboratory *to* the bedside. . . .The paragon became the sophisticated researcher; and the clinician immersed in anecdote and intuition, though still valuable where science had yet to advance, became a relic of a displaced medical folk art." Osler and Peabody lost the argument, and the subsequent hegemony of the "scientific" model, in large part financed by the federal government through the National Institutes of Health, is a major component of the medical-industrial complex that has so alienated patients and communities from what was once a central feature of community life: the family doctor.[20]

A reformed medical profession must recover its humanistic ethos, and offer incentives that reward patient care *at least* as much as it does scientific research. This would involve refashioning medical education, and would even entail re-instituting a professional discipline founded upon its own principles, and not necessarily those of other disciplines. The present efforts of some medical schools to teach the humanities as an integral part of the curriculum are a promising development in the right direction.

## CONCLUSION

This chapter has detailed an array of serious faults undermining the ability of the US health care system, as presently constituted, to provide adequate care for the whole of its population. Rather than tinkering with that status quo, however, I have suggested that health care needs to be reconceptualized before we can even begin to refashion our institutions in accordance with the social value principle of critical institutionalism. This has involved examining issues normally outside the area of inquiry pertaining to health care—merely a reflection of how inadequate reductionist orthodoxy is when addressing such complex issues. A reformed health care system will be intimately tied to reforms of the political system (the state, government, the public), and the economy (basic income, welfare provision). An obvious factor, neglected in the foregoing discussion, is our collective and individual relationship to the environment. There will be other errors of omission, whether of similar magnitude or of greater specificity to health care, that I have inadvertently committed. Nevertheless, it should be clear that, thanks to the analytical precision afforded by the precepts of critical institutionalism, the status quo is grossly inadequate and quite untenable. Nothing less than a root-and-branch reconstruction of the institutional complex that constitutes the US health care system is required. If we are to improve the welfare of citizens and achieve the end that is the full development of human personality and community, expressed by Thomas Jefferson as "life, liberty and the pursuit of happiness," then the reconstruction of the US health care system according to the principles outlined above will, I believe, help to achieve that most desirable and admirable goal.

## NOTES

1. For a small selection, see Hildred and Beauvais (1995), Keaney (1997), Loughlin (1996), and McMaster (2001).

2. A recent example of this sort of argument is that of Irving Louis Horowitz (1999). He has publicly endorsed the work of the Institute, specifically lavishing praise on its contribution to the health care debate (Feldman 2000) as "top-flight." See http://www.independent.org/. For an extended critique of Horowitz and the classical liberal state/society dualism, see Keaney 2001a.

3. Eyeing the world from an investor's point of view, on December 28, 2001, the Lex Column of the *Financial Times* provided a concise summary of big pharmaceutical companies' recent history and future prospects: "Ageing populations and rising living standards bringing pressure for better healthcare, allied with technological innovation, have underpinned near double-digit compound annual growth in pharmaceuticals revenues through two decades. Most big pharmaceuticals companies boast operating margins above 20 per cent. Opportunities provided

by the genomics revolution to "customise" treatment and disease prevention to individuals support a robust long-term prognosis." In other words, for as long as current trends continue, these vested interests look set to accumulate ever greater profits. No wonder, then, that they should be less than enthused by the issue of universal health care. The US market currently accounts for at least 60 per cent of pharmaceutical profits (Pilling 2001).

4. This is certainly the case with regard to the promotion of new treatments. Citing the work of Jeanne Kassler (1994), Blank (1997, 38) notes that "a large proportion of health stories, pehaps as high as 90 per cent . . . are initiated by public relations firms funded by the medical establishment. Press releases and video news releases launching new procedures are often presented as objective news stories without investigative analysis. Local evening news shows with limited budgets are particularly likely to run these promotional stories without challenge because they lack staff capable of putting the release in proper perspective. However even the networks and major daily newspapers have become dependent on this new form of advertising."

5. This is the argument of George Ritzer (1999, 44), who sees the "bombardment" of consumers worldwide with US products and advertisements as "better described by the term *Americanization* than *globalization*; the latter would indicate more or a multidirectional relationship among many nations."

6. In the aftermath of the September 11, 2001 attacks on the United States, the Bush administration and allied agencies exhorted the already heavily indebted US consumer, hung over from the excesses of the Clinton years, to spend whatever money they could in order to support the economy. This may count as the first formal privatization of fiscal policy on record.

7. This long and mutually rewarding association is the subject of Dowd (2000).

8. For an explanation and defense of "willingness to pay," see Donaldson et al. (1997). A succinct critique of this and neoclassical health economics generally is provided by David Seedhouse (1997).

9. The irony of this is that the ideology of individual choice prevented the federal government from instituting cost control mechanisms in the Medicare apparatus —mechanisms that would have mitigated the fiscal crisis that, almost immediately, afflicted the Great Society reforms. "Events later proved, as the historian Allen Matusow has argued, that Medicare was a 'ruinous accommodation between reformers and vested interests.' But in the context of 1965 there was no politically feasible alternative. Any effort to alter the delivery system for health care in the United States, or change the way in which health care was financed, faced certain defeat. Twenty years later Wilbur Cohen recalled that 'it wasn't possible in 1965 to put cost controls in it. It would have never passed Congress. That would have been federal control, which was the whole political issue at the time. . .'"(Andrew 1998, 105).

10. Writing in 1946, Dewey argued: "The position that economics is the sole conditioning factor of political organization, together with the position that all phases and aspects of social life, science, art, education and all the agencies of public communication included, are determined by the type of economy that prevails is identical with that type of life to which the name 'totalitarian' justly applies" (Dewey 1954, 227). While written in the context of a consideration of Soviet communism, this applies no less to the "market fundamentalism" of our own times. Agreeing with Rousseau that the interdependence resultant from economic development "makes it possible and worth while for the stronger and abler to exploit others for

their own ends, to keep others in a state of subjection where they can be utilized as animated tools" (155), Dewey rejected Rousseau's half-joking suggestion of a return to "independence based on isolation." Rather, "the only possible solution" was, and remains, "the perfecting of the means and ways of communication of meanings so that genuinely shared interest in the consequences of interdependent activities may inform desire and effort and thereby direct action." As we shall see, this is an urgent requirement of any fundamental reform of health care.

11, A useful, clear introduction is provided by Thomas E. Getzen (1997, chapter 10).

12. Hill and McComb are, on balance, sanguine about the consequences of the Clinton administration's failure. The "rational market response" they identify brought about "overdue reforms" in which excess capacity among care providers enabled a restructuring of supplier relationships. In this way employers banded together thereby boosting monopsonistic power and exercising bargaining leverage over HMOs. In turn, HMOs rearranged their provider networks by forcing the providers into price competition and achieving lower costs as a result. This has proven to be a temporary palliative, however, as costs have begun their inexorable rise once more.

13. Not suprisingly, the FDA is a target of the Independent Institute, which decries its restrictions on medicine advertising as the propagation of potentially fatal ignorance (Rubin 2000). Yet it is the *success* of pharmaceutical companies' marketing efforts that contributes to the fiscal crisis of US health care: "According to the National Institute for Health Care Management Foundation, a research group, spending on prescription drugs shot up 19 per cent to $131bn last year, bringing the increase in the past two years to 40 per cent. Much of that, it found, was due to soaring demand for a small number of brand-name drugs heavily advertised on television" (Pilling 2001).

14. "The cost of popular point-of-service managed-care plans, which give employees a broad choice of doctors, jumped 14.1% between July, 2000, and July, 2001, reports Segal Co., a New York-based benefits consultant. Claims for health-maintenance organizations jumped 11.2%, while more traditional fee-for-service claims rose 11.9% . . . . Drug spending alone, driven by the development of new medicines and evermore aggressive marketing, may rise 16% next year" (Weber et al. 2001).

15. Namely, the full development of human personality and community. These are symbiotically linked: the removal of one would, at the very least, be detrimental to the other. Hence Dewey's warnings against "absolutistic" or totalitarian systems of thought and policy. Today's totalitarianism is the market fundamentalism that would reduce all human relationships to exchange transactions.

16. Galbraith (1973, 262) describes the provision of a guaranteed income as a "most urgent" reform. While he has moderated his view somewhat, owing to what he perceives as the changed circumstances governing the politically possible, others are developing a rich literature on the subject (see Clark, this volume). And, just as health care should be incorporated into any consideration of basic income, so, too, should be what is currently defined as "welfare" (see Peterson, this volume).

17. Blank (1997, 86) cites a study demonstrating that administrative costs in the US health insurance system were 11 times higher than those of the Canadian single payer system in 1988. This is controversial, however, as others argue that costs are "dramatically understated"

because of "hidden" items that do not conform to the US model. In any case, Blank, while applauding the idea of reducing administrative costs, cautions against any over-optimistic notions of vast sums able to be redirected to health care for as long as the current medical model of care persists.

18. It is a remarkable feature of such an ostensibly religious society as the US that so much money and effort is spent in the postponement of what, according to Christian belief, is a "homecoming."

19. "Anecdotal evidence suggests that more and more patients are hiring private nurses or nursing assistants when they go to hospital. Private agencies that supply nurses' aides report a dramatic rise in requests from patients in hospital in the past few years. Sitters or certified nursing assistants do not give medications or insert IVs. They provide the personal touch. A sitter will help a patient to the bathroom, a deliver a meal. If a patient is frightened, a sitter holds his hand. At night, a sitter watches that a patient doesn't fall out of bed or become wedged between the bed railings and the mattress, where the patient might suffocate. The growing use of sitters reflects the turmoil in health care during the 1990s. Hospitals are being squeezed to provide more intensive care at less cost. Lower reimbursement rates from managed-care plans and government programs have pressured hospitals to cut expenses and trim staff. Patients tend to be sicker and older. That leaves fewer nurses to deal with more needy patients and more complex therapies" (Trafford 2001).

20. A fuller account is provided by Tauber (1992).

# REFERENCES


Andrew, John A. III. 1998. *Lyndon Johnson and the Great Society*. Chicago: Ivan R. Dee.

Berndtson, Erkki. 2000. "Globalization as Americanization." In *Power in Contemporary Politics: Theories, Practices, Globalizations*. Henri Goverde, Philip G. Cerny, Mark Haugaard and Howard Lentner, eds. 155-169. London: Sage Publications.

Blank, Robert H. 1996. The medical marketplace and the diffusion of technologies. *Health Care Analysis* 4(4): 321-324.

_______. 1997. *The Price of Life: The Future of American Health Care*. New York: Columbia University Press.

Boseley, Sarah. 1999. "Patients 'struck off' by GPs for being uneconomic." *The Guardian*, September 13.

Campbell, Harry, Rona Hotchkiss, Nicola Bradshaw, and Mary Porteous. 1998. Integrate care pathways. *British Medical Journal* 310: 1315-1318.

Cloud, Dana L. 1998. *Control and Consolidation in American Culture and Politics: Rhetoric of Therapy*. Thousand Oaks, CA: Sage Publications.

Coney, Sandra. 1997. To the uninformed: managed care means damaged ethics. *Health Care Analysis* 5(3): 252-258.

Dewey, John. (1927) 1954. *The Public and its Problems*. Athens, OH: Swallow Press.

Donaldson, Cam, Shelley Farrar, Tracy Mapp, Andrew Walker and Susan Macphee. 1997. Assessing community values in health care: is the 'willingness to pay' method feasible? *Health Care Analysis* 5(1): 7-29.

Dowd, Douglas. 1997. *Against the Conventional Wisdom: A Primer for Current Economic Controversies and Proposals*. Boulder, CO: Westview Press.

_______. 2000. *Capitalism and its Economics: A Critical History*. London: Pluto Press.
Dugger, William M. 1995. "Beyond Technology to Democracy: The Tool Legacy in Instrumentalism." In *Institutional Economics and the Theory of Social Value: Essays in Honor of Marc R. Tool*. Charles M. A. Clark, ed., 195-207. Boston: Kluwer Academic Publishers.
*Economist, The*. 2001. "Reconstructive surgery. " January 27.
Feldman, Roger D. 2000. "Introduction." In *American Health Care: Government, Market Processes, and the Public Interest*. Roger D. Feldman, ed. 1-12. New Brunswick, NJ: Transaction Publishers.
Ferguson, Adam. (1767) 1966. *An Essay on the History of Civil Society 1767*. Edinburgh: Edinburgh University Press.
Galbraith, John Kenneth. 1973. *Economics and the Public Purpose*. Boston: Houghton Mifflin.
_______. 1985. *The New Industrial State*, 4th edition. Boston: Houghton Mifflin.
_______. 1996. *The Good Society: The Humane Agenda*. Boston: Houghton Mifflin.
_______. 1998. *The Affluent Society*, 40th anniversary edition. Boston: Houghton Mifflin.
Getzen, Thomas E. 1997. *Health Economics: Fundamentals and Flow of Funds*. New York: John Wiley and Sons.
Hayward, Mark D., Eileen M. Crimmins, Toni P. Miles and Yu Yang. 2000. The significance of socioeconomic status in explaining the racial gap in chronic health conditions. *American Sociological Review* 65: 910-930.
Hickman, Larry A. 1990. *John Dewey's Pragmatic Technology*. Bloomington and Indianapolis, IN: Indiana University Press.
Hildred, William, and Fred Beauvais. 1995. An instrumentalist critique of cost-utility analysis. *Journal of Economic Issues* 29(4): 1083-1096.
Hildred, William, and Larry Watkins. 1996. The nearly good, the bad, and the ugly in cost-effectiveness analysis of health care. *Journal of Economic Issues* 30(3): 755-775.
Hill, Lewis E., and Robert F. McComb. 1996. A post-mortem on the Clinton healthcare proposal: Lessons from history and hopes for the future. *International Journal of Social Economics* 23(8 ): 21-28.
Horowitz, Irving Louis. 1999. *Behemoth: Main Currents in the History and Theory of Political Sociology*. New Brunswick, NJ: Transaction Publishers.
Illich, Ivan. 1976. *Limits to Medicine: Medical Nemesis: The Expropriation of Health*. Harmondsworth: Penguin.
Kapp, K. William. 1971. *The Social Costs of Private Enterprise*. New York: Schocken Books.
Kassler, Jeanne. 1994. *Bitter Medicine: Greed and Chaos in American Health Care*. New York: Birch Lane Press.
Keaney, Michael. 1997. Can economics be bad for your health? *Health Care Analysis* 5(4): 299-305.
_______. 1999. Are patients really consumers? *International Journal of Social Economics* 26(5/6): 695-706.
_______. 2001a. State versus society: the political sociology of Irving Louis Horowitz. *Critical Sociology* 27(3).
_______. 2001b. "The Role of the State in the Good Society." In *Economist with a Public Purpose: Essays in Honour of John Kenneth Galbraith*, Michael Keaney, ed., 67-94. London: Routledge.
King, Gary, and David R. Williams. 1995. "Race and Health: A Multidimensional Approach to African-American Health." In *Society and Health*, Benjamin C. Amick III, Sol Levine, Alvin R. Tarlov and Diana Chapman Walsh, eds., 93-130. New York: Oxford University Press.
Loughlin, Michael. 1996. Rationing, barbarity and the economist's perspective. *Health Care Analysis* 4(2): 146-156.

MacLennan, A. H. 1993. Who will deliver the next generation? *Medical Journal of Australia* 159(4): 261-263.

McGregor, Deborah, and Adrian Michaels. 2001. "Bush backs discount cards for Medicare." *Financial Times*, July 13.

McMaster, Robert. 2001. "The National Health Service, the 'Internal Market', and Trust." In *The Social Economics of Health Care*, John B. Davis, ed., 113-140. London: Routledge.

Michaels, Adrian, Geoff Dyer and Raphael Minder. 2001. "Pfizer threatens to withhold new treatments from France." *Financial Times*, December 10.

O'Connor, James. (1973) 2001. *The Fiscal Crisis of the State*. New Brunswick, NJ: Transaction Publishers.

_______. 1998. *Natural Causes: Essays in Ecological Marxism*. New York: Guilford Press.

Panitch, Leo. 1998. 'The State in a Changing World': social-democratizing global capitalism? *Monthly Review* 50(5): 11-22.

Peltzman, Sam. 1976. Toward a more general theory of regulation. *Journal of Law and Economics* 19(2): 211-248.

Petras, James, and Morris Morley. 1995. *Empire or Republic? American Global Power and Domestic Decay*. New York and London: Routledge.

Pilling, David. 2001. "A bitter pill." *Financial Times*, May 21.

Ritzer, George. 1999. *Enchanting a Disenchanted World: Revolutionizing the Means of Consumption*. Thousand Oaks, CA: Pine Forge Press.

Rodgers, William. 1972. *Brown-Out: The Power Crisis in America*. New York: Stein and Day.

Rubin, Paul H. 2000. "Ignorance is death: the FDA's advertising restrictions." In *American Health Care: Government, Market Processes, and the Public Interest*, Roger D. Feldman, ed. New Brunswick, NJ: Transaction Publishers.

Rubin, Rose M., and Shelley White-Means. 2001. "Medicare HMOs: The Promise and the Reality." In *The Social Economics of Health Care*, John B. Davis, ed., 240-254. London: Routledge.

Seedhouse, David. 1997. Tautology and value: the flawed foundations of health economics. *Health Care Analysis* 5(1): 1-5.

Shi, Leiyu. 2001. The convergence of vulnerable characteristics and health insurance in the US. *Social Science and Medicine* 53(4): 519-529.

Shiell, A., and P. Hawe. 1996. Health promotion, community development and the tyranny of individualism. *Health Economics* 5(3): 241-247.

Stanfield, James Ronald. 1996. *John Kenneth Galbraith*. New York: St. Martin's Press.

———.and Jacqueline Bloom Stanfield. 1996. "Reconstructing the Welfare State in the Aftermath of the Great Capitalist Restoration." In *Inequality: Radical Institutionalist View on Race, Gender, Class and Nation*, William M. Dugger, ed., 127-139. Westport, CT: Greenwood Press.

Stigler, George J. 1971. The theory of economic regulation. *Bell Journal of Economics* 2(1): 3-21.

Tabarrok, Alex. 2000. Drug price controls: a 'cure' worse than the disease. *Pfizer Forum*, http://www.pfizerforum.com/english/tabarrok.shtml, accessed December 18, 2001.

Tauber, Alfred I. 1992. The two faces of medical education: Flexner and Osler revisited. *Journal of the Royal Society of Medicine* 85: 598-602.

_______. 1999. *Confessions of a Medicine Man: An Essay in Popular Philosophy*. Cambridge, MA: MIT Press.

Tilman, Rick. 1996. *The Intellectual Legacy of Thorstein Veblen: Unresolved Issues*. Westport, CT: Greenwood Press.

———. and John H. Brown. 1995. Thorstein Veblen, C. Wright Mills and the possibilities of a public administration. *International Journal of Social Economics* 22(1): 3-15.

Tool, Marc R. 1995. *Pricing, Valuation and Systems: Essays in Neoinstitutional Economics.* Brookfield, VT: Edward Elgar.

_______. 1996. "Choose Equality." In *Inequality: Radical Institutionalist Views on Race, Gender, Class and Nation.* William M. Dugger, ed. 103-126. Westport, CT: Greenwood Press.

_______. 1998. "Instrumental Inquiry and Democratic Governance." In *Institutionalist Theory and Applications: Essays in Honour of Paul Dale Bush, Volume 2,* Sasan Fayazmanesh and Marc R. Tool, eds. 1-29. Northampton, MA: Edward Elgar.

_______. (1979) 2001. *The Discretionary Economy: A Normative Theory of Political Economy.* New Brunswick, NJ: Transaction Publishers.

Trafford, Abigail. 2001. "Don't trust the hospital, bring your own nurse." *The Guardian Weekly,* January 18-24.

Vandenburgh, Henry. 2001. Physician stipends as organizational deviance in for-profit psychiatric hospitals. *Critical Sociology* 27(1): 56-76.

Veblen, Thorstein. (1919) 1990. *The Place of Science in Modern Civilization,* New Brunswick, NJ: Transaction Publishers.

_______. (1899) 1992. *The Theory of the Leisure Class.* New Brunswick, NJ: Transaction Publishers.

Weber, Joseph, with Michael Arndt, Laura Cohn and others. 2001. This is gonna hurt. *Business Week International,* September 17.

Whitney, W. T., Jr. 2001. Market failures in US medicine. *Monthly Review* 52(9): 41-45.

Wilkinson, R. G. 1992. National mortality rates: the impact of inequality? *American Journal of Public Health* 82: 1082-1084.

8

# SOCIAL SECURITY: TRUTH OR CONVENIENT FICTIONS?

L. Randall Wray

## INTRODUCTION

There is no question that Social Security is under attack by well-organized and well-funded opponents. As my colleague, Max Skidmore, has documented, the enemies have been there from the beginning, but they had had little success until recently (Skidmore 1999). Originally, the program was attacked on the basis that it was dirty pinko socialism. The framers of the Social Security Act had taken such claims into account when they formulated the program to look something like a pension plan, with "contributions" and "benefits". Americans came to believe that they deserved benefits because they had "paid into" the program. Hence, rather than being seen as welfare and socialistic, the program came to be seen as little different from a private retirement plan. For several decades, this effectively quashed criticism.

However, beginning in the 1980s the critics seized on an apparent weakness. Slower economic growth after 1970, lower birth rates, and longer life spans all supposedly threatened the long run financial viability of Social Security. The enemies renewed a two-pronged attack. First, they began a campaign to convince younger people that because of shaky finances, they would never collect benefits equal to what they would pay into the program. This was a particularly easy sell for higher income "yuppies" because the redistributive aspects of the program provide fairly low "money's worth" returns for the "pension" provided by Social Security to higher income individuals. Second, the Greenspan Commission was formed to "resolve" the long run financial "problems", mostly through very large payroll tax increases. This helped to reinforce the claim that Social Security is a "bad deal" for younger workers—who saw take-home pay fall during a period in which labor was already under attack by the Reagan administration.

After the Greenspan Commission had "solved" the financial problems, the Social Security Administration adopted increasingly pessimistic assumptions for its long run forecasts—as documented by Skidmore (1999;

2001) and by actuary Langer (2000a, 2000b). Not surprisingly, a "looming financial crisis" reappeared, and hysteria about reforming Social Security was revived. Taxes would have to be raised, benefits would have to be cut, and, more importantly, the return on Trust Fund assets would have to be increased. As the stock market performed well from the early 1980s, and then picked up the pace in the 1990s, eventually resulting in what Chairman Greenspan labeled the "irrationally exuberant" dot-com frenzy, the enemies saw a chance to eliminate the program through privatization. This, of course, had always been the goal, but now it was possible to play the role of "savior" of the system, while killing it. The "friends" of Social Security, mostly Democrats and Big Labor, saw a chance to exploit popular fears. They would play along with the enemies, pretending there really is a financial problem, so that they could save Social Security and thereby win votes. All the polls showed that voters trust Democrats more on Social Security, hence, given a choice between Republican schemes to "save" the program through privatization or Democratic plans to "save" it by placing the Trust Funds "off limits", the voters would choose the Democrats.

The Democrats were given a huge boost in the late 1990s when the federal budget appeared poised to run surpluses as far as the eye could see. Hence, President Clinton proposed to take a portion of the surplus and add it to the Trust Fund. Essentially this would allow double-counting of the surplus run by Social Security, since most of the budget surplus accrued because payroll taxes far exceeded program benefit payments (Wray 1999). Al "lockbox" Gore used this as his sole campaign issue—proposing to lock-up surpluses in a very large box hidden away from greedy Republicans who would otherwise fritter-away revenues through tax cuts for the rich. A wide variety of economists embarrassed themselves by claiming that this was "good economics" (Wray 1999). I was told by economic advisors to both top Democrats and Big Unions that they realized it was all nonsense but they believed it was politically pragmatic to endorse such silliness. But, of course, we now know with perfect hindsight that it all backfired. Gore looked like an idiot in debates with a candidate who made Dan Quail look like a poster child for Mensa by comparison. President Bush appointed a new Commission to reform Social Security, appointing only those on record as supporting privatization.

And yet, even after all this, the "friends" of Social Security still insist that the terms of the debate should be limited to the best way to enhance the Trust Fund to provide for future retiring baby boomers. Hence, they want to put only *part* of the Trust Fund into the stock market. They are willing to go along with giving "individual ownership" over some portion of payroll taxes paid—with an option to increase one's contribution, and perhaps to individually manage some portion of one's "funds". They are also willing to accept a mandated rising retirement age, curtailment of benefits for future retirees, and payroll tax increases. They allow the enemies to continue to push the notion that Social Security is nothing but an involuntary pension scheme. They insist that the original provisions that were designed to counter charges of "socialism" cannot be changed. And even after the dot-com bust they cannot make any significant headway against the arguments of the privatizers. These "friends" are the best enemies Social Security could have.

As a supporter of Social Security and as an educator, I believe that the best way to save the program is to tell the truth about its finances. The truth is that Social Security does not, and indeed cannot, face any financial crisis. Further, the Trust Fund does not in any way, shape, or form protect Social Security. Many "supporters" who understand the economics of this still want to accumulate a Trust Fund on the argument that it provides "political protection" against privatization and program cuts. But that is obviously false—it is precisely because there is a Trust Fund that the privatizers are making headway. If there were no Trust Fund, there would be nothing to privatize. I will first examine the program, then will look at various "reform" proposals—concentrating on the Clinton administration's plan and contrasting that with the Bush Commission's "reforms", and then will propose a progressive reform for Social Security. My primary message will be that the "fictions" that originally helped to protect Social Security now stand in the way of sensible discussion about the nature of the program.

## THE SOCIAL SECURITY ACT AND ITS TRANSFORMATION TO AN ADVANCE-FUNDING MODEL

The American preference for self-reliance delayed creation of a system of social insurance until the Great Depression of the 1930s, while Germany had adopted an extensive social insurance system as early as 1883. Our reluctance was finally overcome by general recognition that individual thriftiness and willingness to work hard might not be sufficient to keep poverty at bay—especially poverty among the elderly, the vast majority of whom were not able to accumulate sufficient financial wealth to see them through their final years. The provisions of the Social Security Act (signed into law by President Roosevelt on 14 August 1935) were carefully tailored to avoid any hint of *welfare* or *socialism*, by modeling the program along the lines of a private insurance scheme. In the case of the old-age insurance portion of Social Security (OASI), the counterpart to insurance premiums was mandatory taxes, assessed equally on employee and employer. Employees who earned an established minimum income per year, and who worked a minimum number of years would be eligible for annual benefits. A degree of *individual equity* would be maintained, with those who paid-in more receiving greater benefits upon retirement. OASI would not be means-tested, reflecting American preferences against *welfare*. These provisions helped to make the Social Security Act the most successful and enduring of the New Deal programs, indeed, many analysts claim that Social Security is the most popular federal government program ever adopted. (See Skidmore 1999 for an excellent overview of the program.)

It is interesting to note that institutionalists played a major role in formulating the Social Security Act of 1935—mostly students of John R. Commons, who is generally acknowledged as a leading pioneer in the development of social legislation in the United States. Arthur J. Altmeyer, who served as Chief Executive of the program from 1937-1953, emphasized this as follows:

> John R. Commons did not actually participate in the drafting of the Social Security Act or in the research leading to the recommendations upon which the act is based, yet his teachings and general philosophy of social legislation had a profound influence upon those who were charged with the responsibility for developing a social security program for the nation. The President of the United States, members of his Cabinet, and the technical staff upon which they relied were all familiar with the contributions that Professor Commons had made in the field of social legislation, particularly labor legislation. Indeed, a number of Commons' former students served as senior advisers to the President and his Cabinet Committee on Economic Security, which made the recommendations upon which the Social Security Act is based. They were selected for the very reason that they were known to have worked with Professor Commons in the drafting and administration of social insurance laws which were precursors of the social insurance provisions of the Social Security Act (Altmeyer 1963, 123).

Altmeyer went on to observe: "It is not too much to say that the philosophy underlying the Social Security Act is the same philosophy which Professor Commons expounded to his students throughout the years" (1963, 124).

While the framers were wary of charges of socialism, in truth, however, Social Security never closely approximated a private insurance plan, and changes to the Social Security Act over the years have moved it ever further from that model. (Altmeyer insisted that "Social Security will always be a goal, never a finished thing because human aspirations are infinitely expandable . . . just as human nature is infinitely perfectible" (President's Commission, 2001, 7). The 1935 Act contained several other programs in addition to old-age security: unemployment benefits, pensions for elderly poor, means-tested assistance to poor children, grants to states to provide services for the blind or disabled, funds for vocational rehabilitation, and funding for public health services. Amendments to the Act added benefits for wives and for widows and children of deceased workers, advantages for low-income and short-term workers, benefit coverage for the self-employed, benefits for the disabled, and medical benefits (under Medicare, added in 1965). Thus, while Americans still tend to think of Social Security as a system of "retirement insurance", in fact over 26% of the beneficiaries of OASI (which excludes medical and disability benefits covered in the broader OASDHI) in 2001 were spouses or survivors of covered workers. Further, Social Security benefits are inflation-indexed, an advantage that is not usually available (at any price) in private pension plans. All of this is usually forgotten in the debates about reform, particularly by reformers who compare individual returns to retirees, only, with those that would be generated by a private pension fund. In the discussion that follows, we will focus on the aspects of Social Security that relate most closely to issues surrounding aging and retirement, however, it must always be kept in mind that Social Security is a much bigger program with broader coverage, and any reforms must take account of the large percent of beneficiaries without *normal* work histories who would be left behind by the privatization schemes.

US workers began to pay payroll taxes for Social Security in 1937 and the first benefits were paid in 1940. (Among the first beneficiaries was Ida May Fuller of Ludlow, Vermont, who paid a total of $24.75 in Social Security taxes, lived to age 100, and collected $22,889 in benefits!) Over the years, tax rates were increased, percent of the workforce covered grew, and benefits were expanded. A substantial change was made in 1972, when automatic cost-of-living adjustments to benefits were added. The next few years experienced high inflation and slower real economic growth–together these raised program benefit payments and lowered growth of tax receipts, generating the first *crisis* for Social Security when it was feared that receipts might fall below expenditures. This led to the first significant cut-backs in the program's history, with inflation-adjustments temporarily delayed, tax rates increased, and some benefit cuts for civil servants. By the early 1980s, it was believed that these changes had not been sufficient, so a commission was appointed (with future Fed Chairman Alan Greenspan at its head) to study the long-term financial situation of Social Security.

One significant issue that had arisen was the *aging* of the US population—a typical demographic change experienced in all the developed nations due to falling death and fertility rates (number of children born per woman). This was compounded by the *baby boom bulge* created in the early post-war period when fertility rates rose and remained high until the *baby boom boost* of the 1970s. Combined with rising longevity, this ensures that the baby boomers will create a relatively large number of elderly Social Security beneficiaries between 2015 and 2035. By the same token, unless fertility rates (or net immigration) rise spectacularly in the early years of the twenty-first century, there will be fewer workers paying payroll taxes relative to the benefits paid to baby-boomers. While the problems created by the Baby boom bulge receive most of the press, falling fertility rates and rising life expectancy are common experiences in all the major developed nations, leading to various social challenges that result from an aging population. Indeed, on current projections, Social Security will experience its greatest financial (and real) problems *after* all the baby-boomers will have died.

The *Greenspan Commission* published findings that resulted in the most significant changes made to Social Security since addition of Medicare in 1965. These included higher tax rates, imposition of taxes on Social Security benefits, and phased increases to the normal retirement age. Most importantly, the 1983 revisions changed Social Security from *pay-as-you-go* to *advance funding*. In a pay-as-you-go (or, *paygo*) system, current-year revenues are balanced against current-year expenditures. In other words, if payroll tax receipts in the year 2000 just covered benefits that year, we might say that the program was financially sound. Similarly, we could project spending and receipts for each of the next 75 years; if receipts were equal to, or greater than, spending in every one of those years, we could conclude that the program was in sound financial shape. If we found that receipts were lower than expected spending in one or more years, we could adjust tax rates (or benefit payments) for those particular years. (Note that a temporary shortfall in one year could be offset by a surplus in another so that tax rates and benefits would not have to be adjusted so often. Indeed, an OASI Trust Fund was created on January 1, 1940 as a separate account in the US Treasury, with surpluses in one year used to "purchase" special Treasury debt that could be "sold" in other years to "cover" temporary shortages) (Skidmore 1999, Social Security Administration, 2002).

The Greenspan Commission claimed the aging of America creates a special financing problem that could be resolved through financial fixes. During the late 20$^{th}$ and early 21$^{st}$ centuries, OASDI was projected to run large annual surpluses, but sometime during the second decade of the 21$^{st}$ century, the program would begin to run annual deficits. Indeed, it was feared that the deficits would eventually become so large that it might be politically infeasible to raise taxes or cut benefits by the amount required to return the program to balance in each year. For this reason, it was decided that the paygo system should be abandoned in favor of advance funding. In an advance funded system, near-term annual surpluses would be accumulated in a Trust Fund, which would purchase special US Treasury securities to earn interest. When program spending fell below tax revenues, interest earnings could be used to supplement revenues. At some point in the future, taxes plus interest earnings would fall below annual benefit payments, however, the Trust Fund could begin to "sell" its portfolio of treasury securities to make up the difference. (Actually, these are special securities that cannot be sold. Thus, they are merely turned back to the Treasury, which is supposed to credit Social Security with "cash".) In this way, surpluses over the first three or four decades could be used to offset annual deficits during the final decades, ensuring long-term financial solvency.

## Long-term Prospects

The changes made in 1983, including the move to an advance funded system, were believed at the time to have resolved the long run challenges created for Social Security by the aging of its population. Over subsequent years, the Board of Trustees developed a rigorous method of financial accounting for the program that reported detailed projections for the next 10 years (its "short-range" forecast) and a projection for the next 75 years (its "long-range" forecast) to capture the effects of demographic shifts, as well as alternative assumptions regarding economic factors such as economic growth. By the end of the 1990s, they had settled on use of three alternative scenarios for the long-term forecasts: "high cost" (pessimistic), "intermediate cost", and "low cost" (optimistic). The long-term financial status of the program is summarized in a calculation of the "actuarial balance" for the 75-year period. This is the difference between the "summarized income ratio" (the ratio of the present value of payroll taxes to the present value of taxable payroll) and the "summarized cost rate" (the ratio of the present value of expenditures to the present value of the taxable payroll) over the valuation period. This is essentially similar to any comparison that must discount future revenues and costs to determine long-term net revenues. When the summarized income rate equals or exceeds the summarized cost rate, the program is said to be in actuarial balance. If the difference is negative, the program is in actuarial imbalance with an *actuarial gap*, measured as a percent of taxable payroll. For example, if discounted revenues fell short of discounted benefit payments by an amount equal to 1% of taxable payroll, this is said to represent an actuarial gap of 1%. An immediate increase of payroll taxes by a total of 1% (half on employers and half on employees) would close the gap.

The "long run actuarial balance" calculated after the Greenspan Commission changes was reported as positive in 1983. With each subsequent year, however, the reported actuarial balance became increasingly negative—reaching –0.44 in 1986, –0.91 in 1990, –1.46 in 1992 and rising above –2% of taxable payroll by 1994, requiring more than a one-percentage-point tax rate increase on each of employer and employee to close the actuarial gap (Social Security Administration, 2002). This was mostly due to adoption of increasingly pessimistic economic assumptions by the Board of Trustees (Skidmore 1999, 2001; Langer 2000a, 2000b). As an alternative to tax increases, the gap could be closed either through benefit cuts or by increasing the rate of return earned on Trust Fund assets. In fact, many proposals for reforming Social Security include provisions that would simultaneously pursue all three alternatives: tax increases, benefit cuts, and higher earnings. In addition, some proposals would move Social Security operations closer to a private insurance fund model, or, indeed, replace Social Security with a privately-operated (and even purely voluntary) retirement system. Before turning to such proposals, let us examine the actuarial gap as well as the underlying causes of the gap.

According to the Social Security Administration's 2002 projections, on intermediate-cost assumptions, the program achieved actuarial balance only for the first 25 years; over the fifty year period, the actuarial gap was –0.95, while it reached –1.87 for the entire 75 long-range forecast. Note, however, that on low-cost assumptions, the program maintained actuarial balance for the whole period, while on high-cost assumptions the program had an actuarial gap even for the first 25 year period. This shows how critical are the assumptions used in the forecasts. Note also that any *crises* are relatively far into the future; indeed, even on high-cost assumptions, the actuarial imbalance is quite small for the first quarter of the 21st century. The 2002 projections showed a significant improvement over the projections that had been made in 1999, with the 75-year gap falling from –2.07 to –1.87 on intermediate assumptions—mostly reflecting improved assumptions regarding economic performance. This, in turn, reflected the "Goldilocks" expansion of the last half of the 1990s. It was somewhat ironic that Social Security's "day of reckoning" (the date at which it would "go broke") was postponed by a year or two with each new Trustee's report in the late 1990s.

According to the 2002 projections, the OASDI Social Security Trust Funds would rise from $1.4 trillion in 2002 to $3.4 trillion in 2010 and peak at well over $7 trillion after 2025 before declining to zero by 2041 (note that the 2002 report postponed this latter date by 6 years compared with the 1999 projections). Using low cost assumptions, the Trust Fund would continue to grow over the entire 75 year period, reaching more than $87 trillion by 2080. On the other hand, the Trust Fund would reach only $4.5 trillion in 2020 according to high-cost assumptions, and would then be depleted quickly, falling to zero by 2029. In other words, if Social Security is analyzed as if it were a private pension plan, it will apparently experience a crisis in 2029 or 2041 using high cost or intermediate cost assumptions, although on low cost assumptions it would not experience crisis. Most analysts focus on the intermediate-cost projections, according to which Social Security revenues would be sufficient to cover only 73% of expected expenditures in 2041 and only two-thirds of expected expenditures in 2076.

Let us quickly summarize the main demographic and economic assumptions that underlie the projections: fertility rates, immigration, labor force participation rates, longevity, growth of real wages, and taxable base. Together, fertility rates, immigration rates, longevity, and labor force participation rates determine the size of the pools of workers and retirees. It is frequently noted that the number of Social Security beneficiaries *supported* by workers will rise sharply in coming years. This is important, because Social Security revenues come from payroll taxes on workers (and their employers), while beneficiaries are largely (but not solely) retirees. For example, the number of OASDI beneficiaries per 100 covered workers was 31 in 1975, but this will rise steadily between 2010 and 2075 when it reaches 55 on intermediate-cost projections. To put it another way, while the US had just over 3.3 workers per beneficiary in 2000, it may have only 1.8 by 2075. Thus, the *financial burden* required of future workers to provide for OASDI beneficiaries could increase by almost a factor of two. On the other hand, workers in 2075 are projected to support fewer young people due to low fertility rates. If we add the under age 20 population to the age 65 and over population to obtain a *dependent* population (most of whom would not be expected to be working), we find that the *dependency ratio* (the ratio of dependents to workers) actually peaked at 0.95 in 1965, fell to 0.71 by 1995, and will rise only slightly to 0.83 by 2075. In other words, the parents of the baby-boomers supported more dependents in the mid 1960s than any generation is likely to support in the future. This is the *real burden* faced by future workers, and is almost always forgotten in debates about the "burden" on future generations.

As the number of beneficiaries rises relative to the number of workers paying Social Security taxes, this negatively impacts the actuarial balance. As mentioned, this results in part from falling fertility rates, which reduces the size of the younger population from which workers can be drawn. Fertility rates (children born per woman) stood at just over 2 at the end of the 1990s and was projected to fall to 1.95 under the intermediate assumptions. If the fertility rate were to rise back to 3.7 (where it stood in 1957), as much as 90 percent of the actuarial gap would be eliminated. On the other hand, falling fertility rates can be offset by rising net immigration (since immigrants can add to the worker pool, paying payroll taxes) and by rising labor force participation rates (the number working or seeking work per 100 population). In the late 1990s, net (legal and illegal) immigration reached about 960,000 per year. In their intermediate projections, however, the Trustees assumed that annual net immigration would fall to 900,000 and remain there throughout the 75 year period. Additional net immigrants above that level would reduce the actuarial gap. The Trustees also project that labor force participation rates for men will fall (from 75.5% in 1997 to 74% by 2075). In recent years, labor force participation rates for women have been rising sharply (reaching 60% in 1997). The Trustees project that this will nearly level-off (reaching only 60.6% by 2075). If male labor force participation rates did not fall (for example, if men increasingly chose to work beyond age 65), and if female rates rose, some of the actuarial gap would be eliminated. Finally, the Trustees project that death rates will fall, which adds to the actuarial gap because increased longevity increases program costs more than it increases revenue.

These are the main demographic assumptions that underlie the projected actuarial balance of the program. While most of the debate over the program's solvency focuses on these unfavorable demographic trends, they were well-known by the Greenspan Commission and the 1983 adjustments should have taken care of them. In fact, the reason for the *looming Social Security crisis* lays not in the demographics, but rather in the increasingly pessimistic economic assumptions adopted by the Trustees in their reports in the 1980s and 1990s, although to some extent, the Goldilocks boom attenuated some of the pessimism by the end of the 1990s. The main economic assumptions that lead to the financing gap are low growth of real wages and a falling taxable base. In 1999, the Trustees projected that real wages would grow at only 0.9% per year; this was raised to 1.1 percent in the 2002 report. Real wage growth, in turn, is related by assumption to productivity gains. The Trustees assume that productivity will grow at just 1.6% annually over the long-range period–well below long-term US averages. Real wages will grow more slowly than productivity because the Trustees assume that hours worked will fall, and that a larger portion of worker compensation will take the form of benefits (largely not subject to payroll taxes). If real wages were to grow at 2 percent per year, as much as half of the actuarial gap would be eliminated. The Trustees also project that the unemployment rate will settle on 5.5% through the 75 year period; lower unemployment rates increase revenues more than they raise benefit payments and hence would help close the actuarial gap.

Finally, the Trustees have projected that the taxable base will fall from 41 percent of GDP in 2002 to only 35 percent in 2080. This is for two reasons. First, Social Security uses a payroll tax, taxing wages and certain kinds of self-employment income. Other types of income, for example interest income, are exempt. If these rise as a share of national income, the percent of income subject to the Social Security tax will fall. Second, payroll taxes are levied only on a portion of one's wage income–determined by the contribution and benefit base. In 2001, OASDI taxes were applied only to the first $80,400 of employment income (the contribution and benefit base for that year; this base is increased each year with rising nominal average wages). The Trustees have assumed that the taxable base will fall both because a smaller portion of income will be received in the form of wages and because a higher percent of wages will accrue to those with earnings above the contribution and benefit base. Therefore, by 2080 little over a third of national income will be taxed by OASDI.

We might question the usefulness of calculating an actuarial balance over a 75 year period. Projection of demographic trends, and, more importantly, economic variables over such long periods is inherently difficult, and relatively small changes to assumptions can change the projections significantly. Some analysts have argued that projections are based on rather pessimistic economic assumptions. For example, according to intermediate cost projections, real GDP is projected to grow at 2.7% and productivity will grow at only 1.6% per year. In fact, labor productivity has grown at a rate of approximately 2% per year since 1870, and at 2.7% per year between WWII and 1973, while real GDP grew at an annual rate of 3.7% from 1870 to 1973. If productivity and GDP grew at rates equal to US long-term trends, Social Security's financial problems would be eliminated. On the other hand, US economic performance after 1973 has generally been worse than long-term averages, and some claim it is more prudent to project weak performance into the future than to presume that high growth might return. On the other hand, it has been noted that these pessimistic assumptions were incongruously adopted in the Trustee forecasts during the "Goldilocks" 1990s expansion, when US economic performance did return toward historical averages. (Ironically, precisely as the Goldilocks expansion has collapsed, the Trustees have revised assumptions, increasing productivity and GDP growth projections and postponing the "day of reckoning" by several years.) Furthermore, some have argued that the assumptions adopted may not be internally consistent. For example, if labor force growth rates and immigration are as low as the Trustees have assumed, one might expect that real wage growth should be higher than the assumed 1.1 percent as excess demand for labor pushes up its relative return, and labor productivity growth should also be higher as firms substitute capital for scarce labor.

More fundamentally, it is not clear that a national, public, retirement system ought to operate as if it were a private pension fund, building reserves today that earn interest and can be depleted in future years. In, say, 2041 when the Trust Fund needs to "sell" securities to the Treasury, the Treasury will have to raise taxes, cut other spending, or run deficits (likely leading to security sales in the new issue market) to "cover" retirement of debt held by Social Security. As we'll examine in more detail below, this is exactly what the government would have to do even if Social Security had no Trust Fund at all! Suppose Social Security were operated as a paygo system, with each year's receipts equal to each year's spending. When revenues begin to fall below benefit expenditures, the government would have to increase taxes, reduce other spending, or run deficits to "cover" the difference—exactly the same actions it would take with an advance funded system. Hence, when Social Security begins to run deficits, existence of a Trust Fund cannot really provide "finance" to the government to "cover" its spending. Further, unlike a private firm, the US government's revenues are not "market-determined" and do not limit its spending. Hence, while government cannot really build up a trust fund, it also does not need to do so.

What really matters is whether the economy will be able to produce a sufficient quantity of real goods and services to provide for both workers and dependents in, say, the year 2041. If it cannot, then regardless of Social Security's finances, the real living standards of Americans in 2041 will have to be lower than they are today. Those who take this approach argue that any reforms to Social Security made today should focus on increasing the economy's capacity to produce real goods and services, rather than on ensuring positive actuarial balances. For example, policies that might encourage public and private infrastructure investment will ease the future burden of providing for growing numbers of retirees. In a sense, this would be a *real* reform rather than a financial reform, although it is possible that financial reforms might encourage greater investment. For example, and as we will now discuss, some advocates of privatization argue this will encourage more investment by entrepreneurs. Note, however, that even with the Trustee's rather pessimistic economic and demographic assumptions, real living standards are projected to rise substantially for both workers and retirees throughout the 75 year long-range period. Accordingly, Social Security does not face a real crisis.

## REFORM PROPOSALS

Let us turn to some of the most important reform proposals. Perhaps the most extreme would be to abolish Social Security altogether, leaving it up to individuals to decide how to provide for their retirement. (However, it should be recalled that Social Security is not simply an old age security program; privatization could leave widows, dependents, and disabled persons without a safety net.) Some reformers recognize that individuals generally underestimate the future costs of retirement, thus, some sort of mandatory minimum contribution levels should be maintained even if the program were privatized. Another variation would maintain basic coverage in a mandatory, government-run program, but would allow individual control over supplemental investments in privately-run pension funds. “Liberals” have tended to oppose privatization and have instead focused on ramping up the Trust Funds, perhaps by diverting some of the government’s budget surpluses to the program, or by increasing returns by allowing the Trustees to invest a specified portion of the Trust Funds in private equities.

### “Liberal” Reforms

In his 1999 State of the Union Address, President Clinton offered his “liberal” proposal for "saving" Social Security by "committing" 60 percent of projected government budget surpluses (or, $2.7 Trillion) for the next 15 years to that purpose. This is a variation on the last theme listed above: trying to increase the size of the Trust Funds in the near-term in order to provide more “financial where-with-all” to cover deficits in the program later. The president's plan relied critically on several assumptions. Most obviously, it relied on running budget surpluses far into the future. The president's unbounded optimism allowed him to claim, "We are on a course for budget surpluses for the next 25 years." Unfortunately, our nation has *never* run budget surpluses for such a period: every time we had significant surpluses, the economy quickly collapsed into a depression that created budget deficits. It is interesting to note that only two years later—by 2001—the federal budget surpluses had collapsed with the economy, generating budget deficits “as far as the eye can see.” Close examination of the president's projections revealed that the federal government was expected to run a significant "on-budget" deficit through 2003, with "off-budget" revenues accounting for most of the projected surpluses. These off-budget revenues mostly came from Social Security surpluses—in other words, surpluses in Social Security more than offset deficits in the rest of the budget. According to projections of the Social Security Trustees made at the time, payroll tax revenues would have exceeded OASDI expenditures by $119 billion in 2003, with the surplus rising to $159 billion in 2008. Looking at the two projections together shows that the president's projected surplus of $150 billion in 2003 would have been achieved mainly thanks to the $119 billion surplus run by Social Security. In other words, 60 percent of federal budget surpluses—created for the most part by Social Security—would have been added to the surpluses already run by Social Security in order to "save" Social Security! Those surpluses proved to be a mirage, but, in any case, Al "lockbox" Gore lost the election because the population could not understand (and should not have understood!) the crazy accounting proposed by the Democrats.

However, the real question remains: Will setting aside any surpluses really have helped ease the budgetary burden of the baby boomers' retirement? To answer this question, one must understand that when OASDI runs a surplus, the Treasury creates an interest-earning IOU, a nontradable bond, that is held by the Social Security Trust Fund. This IOU is essentially a debt the government owes itself. Because the overall federal budget (including off-budget revenues) was at the time projected to run surpluses over the foreseeable future, the Treasury would have actually retired some outstanding bonds held by the public each year, with the amount retired being somewhat less than the projected surpluses. Curiously, the gross federal debt would actually have risen by nearly $600 billion by 2003 *in spite of projected surpluses* because the Treasury would have created debt to be held by OASDI. Thus, while it is true that the public would have held fewer bonds, the government would have become increasingly indebted—*to itself*.

Even if the federal government could have maintained a balanced budget forever, the Treasury would have gone into debt by another $2.5 trillion by 2020 as it issued bonds to be held by the Trust Fund. Remember, this is debt that would have been created so that the government could owe itself. President Clinton's plan would have increased the government's indebtedness (to itself) by another $2.7 trillion because the Treasury would have issued debt equal to 60 percent of the government's surpluses to be added to the Trust Fund's accumulation of bonds. The greater the budget surpluses, the more indebted the Treasury became! To complicate the already Byzantine nature of these finances, the Treasury pays compound interest on all this debt by issuing more IOUs to the Trust Fund—the higher the interest rate, the more the government owes itself and, hence, the sounder Social Security becomes. If you can follow the accounting logic of all this, the Clinton administration (and Enron!) may have had a position for you (See Summers and Yellin 1999 for a defense of the Clinton plan.)

Would this debt—whether it had been "set aside" or not—have helped to provide for retiring baby boomers? If you were to write yourself IOUs to provide for your retirement and put them in a safety deposit box, would you rest comfortably, assured that you would be able to purchase all the necessities of life in 2027 (the projected year during which the Trust Fund will have to begin to "sell" its assets to cover current account deficits)? Of course not. But isn't that what President Clinton's plan amounted to? No—actually his plan was even worse. What if a pension fund approached you with a retirement plan according to which you were to pay a safety deposit box fee equal to 2 percent of your annual income so that you could safeguard your own IOUs to be taken out of the box in 2027 and sold in order to raise the cash required to support you in your old age? You would rightly argue that if sales of your own IOUs could really support you in your old age, you would prefer to write them in 2027 rather than paying the 2 percent annual fee; that would at least allow you to consume, or to save, the 2 percent in the meantime.

President Clinton's plan consisted of taxing current workers about 2 percent more of their payrolls than is needed to cover all OASDI expenditures, writing IOUs that would be stored at the Treasury, and then taking out the IOUs in 2027 and turning them back over to the Treasury, which would then increase taxes or deficit spend—exactly what would have had to be done regardless of the existence of the Trust Fund. Unless retirees can eat Treasury bonds, the president's plan would have done nothing to provide for them.

Milton Friedman made a similar argument. He pointed out that paying taxes today to build up a trust fund cannot help provide for future retirees. Indeed, a trust fund is little more than an accounting gimmick.

> Taxes paid by today's workers are used to pay today's retirees. If money is left over, it finances other Government spending—though, to maintain the insurance fiction, paper entries are created in a "trust fund" that is simultaneously an asset and a liability of the Government. When the benefits that are due exceed the proceeds from payroll taxes, as they will in the not very distant future, the difference will have to be financed by raising taxes, borrowing, creating money or reducing other Government spending. And that is true no matter how large the "trust

fund" (Milton Friedman, "Social Security Chimeras," *New York Times,* January 11, 1999, A17).

It makes no sense to tax current workers more than is needed to equate to current expenditures simply to allow the government to increase its debt to itself to maintain the subterfuge that this somehow will allow it to avoid doing what it must do in 2027. Current workers could enjoy a tax cut now, and this would have no impact whatsoever on what must be done in 2027 to provide for retirees.

The current notion behind the operation of OASDI as an advanced-funded system is to accumulate financial assets now, in the belief that these can be depleted in later years when Social Security program expenditures exceed the revenues that will be generated from a shrinking taxable base. In other words, the "saving" represented by the annual surpluses will be accumulated over the next two decades and more in order to provide for future "consumption" by retiring baby boomers. Clearly, the retirees will not be able to "consume" the Trust Fund (which will consist solely of nonmarketable bonds backed by the full faith and credit of the US government). They will need a "real" basket of consumer goods when they retire. The question is this: Can the current generation, as a whole, save in real terms for its future retirement?

If the current generation were to abstain from consumption, dig holes, and bury goods and services to be excavated and consumed some-20-odd years hence, we could clearly provide for future consumption by saving (in real terms) today. Presumably, the pharaohs had something like this in mind when they buried goods, as well as those who would provide services, with them in the pyramids. However, today, outside of the stockpiles of a handful of "survivalists," this sort of real saving is not significant. That is, most of the consumption that occurs in, say, 2027 will have to be provided for by production in that year, with the notable exception of owner-occupied housing. In other words, the Social Security Trust Fund (and all other public and private pension funds) is "saving" only in financial terms, in the hope that retirees will be able to purchase real goods and services at the time they retire for consumption at that date.

Is it possible for society to do anything today to increase the quantity of goods and services that can and will be produced in 2027 for consumption not only by retirees but also by all non-retirees (working or not working)? If not, the financial savings represented by the Social Security Trust Fund (and all the other public and private pension savings) can affect only the *distribution* of goods and services produced in 2027. The current debate, then, seems to center around a fear that if we do not "reform" Social Security, the retiring baby boomers will not get a sufficient share of society's output in 2027 or some later year.

If this is really what the debate is all about, Clinton's proposal (which represents the "liberal" end of the spectrum of reformists) does no good. His reform aimed to increase the size of the Trust Fund and its rate of growth over the future (by "investing" a portion of it in the stock market to obtain higher returns than those expected from its government bonds), thereby postponing the "day of reckoning" by 55 years, according to calculations made by his administration. However, unless accumulation of the Trust Fund actually enhanced society's ability to produce goods and services in the year 2027, the amount to be distributed would be exactly the same whether the Trust Fund had been larger or smaller. The only economic justification for an accumulation of assets is the belief that it will increase the distribution going to retirees. However, there is no way to guarantee that the accumulation of assets in the Trust Fund would actually bring about this result, and it is not clear that a larger fund would result in a more desirable distribution.

Is there a better and more direct way to ensure that the distribution will be shifted toward retiring baby boomers? Yes—through the tax system. In the year 2027, if it is decided that the elderly should get a larger share of the distribution, then payroll taxes would be increased (reducing disposable income of workers and thus their consumption), while also allowing benefit payments to the elderly to rise.

It would be far more straightforward simply to increase the tax on workers in the year 2027 and increase the benefits paid to retirees at that time than to try to accumulate financial reserves over the next 20-odd years in the hope that the OASDI Trustees could affect distribution by turning bonds back to the Treasury, which would then sell bonds in the year 2027 in an amount equal to the cash it would turn over to OASDI. This could work smoothly only if those who obtained income from working in the year 2027 decided to reduce consumption in the year 2027 in order to buy bonds offered by the Treasury. It is possible, perhaps likely, that the asset sales would merely depress asset prices and that the competition for consumption by workers and retirees would drive up prices of goods and services. While it is conceivable that the net result would be a greater distribution going to the elderly, that is not a foregone conclusion. Why not simply use the tax system in the year 2027 or 2041 or 2075 to guarantee the desired result?

In conclusion, "liberals" want to increase the size of the Trust Fund, or to increase return on Trust Fund assets. However, as was noted above, when the Trust Fund sells securities back to the Treasury, the Treasury will have to cut other spending, raise taxes, or run deficits (and likely sell securities to the general public) to equal the payments made to the Trust Fund. Furthermore, like most financial fixes, these reforms will not necessarily increase future productive capacity. Nor is it necessary for the federal government to actually run surpluses for it to simply credit the Trust Fund with more securities. The Treasury can add securities worth any amount to the Trust Fund at any time (in principle, it can add an amount equal to the entire Social Security shortfall today, thereby "resolving" any financial difficulties). Alternatively, the Treasury could simply agree to pay a higher interest rate on Trust Fund assets—paying whatever interest rate that would eliminate the actuarial gap. While somewhat ludicrous, these alternatives emphasize that accumulating a Trust Fund of Treasury securities really cannot resolve future annual deficits in the Social Security program. They also show that there cannot be a "financial problem" at all, as government can always pay all mandated benefits simply by issuing checks.

The burden of providing real goods and services to retirees in 2020, 2030, or 2075 will be borne by workers in those years regardless of the tax imposed today. And if the amount to be produced cannot be increased by actions taken today, then the burden that will be borne cannot be reduced by anything we do today. Nothing Clinton and other "liberals" have proposed will reduce the burden placed on workers in the year 2020. They merely asked workers today to make a sacrifice by paying unnecessarily high taxes without in any way shifting the burden from future workers. This is pain without gain and is bad public policy.

## Conservative "Reforms"

Some conservative reformers advocate privatization simply as a matter of principle—for example, Milton Friedman has long argued that there is no justification for mandatory participation in a public system. (Feldstein 1999) Others emphasize that as currently designed, Social Security has a strong redistributional element—both within and across generations (Peterson 1996). They typically use a *money's worth* estimate to calculate a return to one's contributions based on expected benefits. Those with high earnings and thus high contributions receive low returns when they eventually collect benefits, while those with low earnings receive higher returns. Many beneficiaries never actually contribute, thus, contributions of others are said to be *redistributed* to them. Returns also vary greatly by generation; early participants in Social Security received very good returns on their contributions, but returns for later generations are much lower. (Old Ida May Fuller is often trotted out to exaggerate this difference—as mentioned, she got a "return" of nearly $23,000 on an "investment" of only $24.75). In 1940 there were 42 workers per Social Security beneficiary, versus just over three today. This is used by the enemies of Social Security to emphasize how impossible the finances are today. However, the number of workers per beneficiary fell very rapidly in the early years of the program—from 42 in 1940 to 16.5 in 1950, and to 5.1 by 1960—and all that without any crisis! By contrast, the decline from 3.4 today to 2.4 in 2080 looks positively miniscule—a point never emphasized by Social Security's "friends" or "enemies". Thus, some reformers emphasize that reform should be geared toward ensuring better money's worth outcomes for contributors, both within generations and across generations. It should be noted, however, that while some attention was paid to such equity concerns in the original Social Security Act, money's worth was not a high priority in the beginning and most amendments since have moved the program ever further from this sort of equity.

Still, most reformers in recent years have pushed privatization to resolve the long-range financial imbalance of Social Security, with money's worth calculations playing a smaller role. It is argued that under current arrangements, the Trustees can hold only government bonds with relatively low interest rates. Allowing investments in the stock market and other private assets could increase returns on the Trust Fund. Such arguments were given a tremendous boost by the spectacular performance of US stock markets from the mid 1980s through 2000. Many proponents argued that equity markets should earn real returns of about seven and a half percent per year—as they have averaged since the 1920s—probably more than double the real return on government debt. Over the long-range 75 year period, these higher returns are said to resolve Social Security's financial problems.

However, there are several objections. First, there will be a costly transition period as the system becomes privatized, during which current workers must "finance" the cost of the existing Social Security system (paying taxes to "finance" the benefits going to current retirees), plus the costs of building up their own "retirement funds." Thus, a fairly large, immediate, tax increase will be required, and must remain in place for several decades until all those covered under the old system have died.

Second, it is probably inconsistent to argue that real GDP growth will average 2.7% per year, little over two-thirds its long-term average, without affecting growth of equity prices. Critics have shown that this implies either that the share of distribution of national income going to profits must grow to implausibly high levels. Indeed, Dean Baker has calculated that wages must be *negative* by 2070, or that price-earnings ratios, already at all-time highs in 2000, must rise to truly astronomical levels, on Baker's calculation, to 485-to-1 by 2070 (Baker 1997, 1998; also Mueller 1998). On the other hand, privatizers believe that the influx of money into stocks would generate more investment and thus higher economic growth.

Third, privatization might place unacceptable levels of risk on workers. Even if the stock market were to grow at an average rate of over 7.5% per year, there could be relatively long periods of below-normal growth. In the past, equity prices have been fairly flat for decades at a time. Unlucky workers whose retirement happened to come after a long period with little growth of stock prices could face deprivation during retirement. Furthermore, if workers are given individual control over their retirement accounts, they might do poorly even if the markets as a whole are doing well.

Fourth, numerous small retirement accounts can be very costly to administer and supervise. Current costs of administering Social Security are exceedingly small—well under one percent of revenues. Privatizers often point to the Chilean example as evidence that a private system can produce high returns for contributors, however, overhead costs in Chile are above ten percent. While private fund managers were initially supportive of the move to privatize, they have become less enthusiastic as they have come to realize the logistics of managing many small accounts for lower income workers. (Darby and Celarier 1999)

Fifth, the interest "earned" on government securities held by the Trust Fund is at an administered rate. It can be set anywhere government wants. Hence, it can be set at the 7.5% rate that equities are supposed to earn—or at 15% and thereby trounce stock returns (Eisner 1998). Finally, critics note that privatization schemes do not, and probably cannot, offer the same kinds of coverage currently offered by Social Security. For example, private pension plans do not offer inflation indexing, as Social Security does (Baker 1998). As discussed, Social Security also offers coverage for many individuals without significant work histories. If the program is privatized, a new social safety net would have to be created to cover individuals who would not be able to purchase private insurance.

Furthermore, as emphasized above, what really matters is the economy's capacity to produce real goods and services in the future. Hence, if the amount that can be produced will not be sufficient to provide the level of consumption desired by all generations in the future, it will be necessary to either boost production or to ration consumption. Extending the normal retirement age (which is essentially a benefit cut) will keep workers in the labor force longer, and will reduce the number of years they must be supported during retirement. Increasing taxes on future workers will leave them with less income and lower purchasing power, ensuring more of the nation's output can go to retirees. Cutting future OASDI benefits will do the opposite—allocating more output toward workers and others with incomes that are not dependent on

Social Security. Fortunately, given increases to worker productivity that reasonably can be expected to occur, plus increases to production facilities that are likely to take place as a result of public and private investment, it appears quite likely that future workers and future retirees will enjoy higher living standards than do their counterparts today–in spite of the aging of America.

## President Bush's Commission to "Modernize" Social Security

On July 24, 2001, President Bush's Commission on Social Security Reform approved its draft interim report (2001a) proclaiming that the Social Security system was "conceived and designed for a different era and a different economy" and that it now is "broken" and requires a "fundamental restructuring." The report was immediately attacked by a wide variety of critics, who recoiled at its tone and apparent biases. (Goldstein 2001; Aaron, Blinder, Munnell, and Orszag 2001) Representative Robert Matsui (D-Calif.) characterized the report as "an attempt to frighten the American public." House Democratic Leader Richard Gephardt (D-Mo) echoed this sentiment when he argued that the commission was "trying to undermine public confidence" in Social Security. While the Commission's Co-Chairs conceded that "broken" was a poor choice of words, they insisted that the program is "unsustainable" and that the interim report accurately reports the facts surrounding the looming crisis. In December 2001, the Commission released its final report (2001b), which summarized the main conclusions of the interim report—trying to smooth-over some of the more outlandish statements—but mostly focusing on three different privatization schemes favored by the Commission.

Paul Krugman, a *New York Times* columnist, dismissed the interim report as "sheer, mean-spirited nonsense" (Krugman 2001). While I believe he was correct, he did not clearly identify the nature of the "mean-spiritedness" pervading the report. The Commission repeatedly claimed that while Social Security may have served us well in the past, it is now nothing but an old workhorse that must be put out to pasture, to be replaced by a young Wall Street-bred filly. But the Commission's real mean-spiritedness was directed against future Congresses. The reports repeatedly argued that the main defect of the current program is that it relies on the continued goodwill of Congress. When (if?) Social Security revenues fall short of promised benefit payments, those evil politicians of the future may be unwilling to continue to put the "full faith and credit" of the federal government behind those promises. Thus, the program must be "overhauled," in the view of the Commission. The

Commission was rather short on specifics in the interim report, but it noted that "in any retirement system a lack of legal ownership is a source of insecurity." Hence, "overhaul" was a euphemism for taking Social Security out of the hands of future Congresses through the creation of individual retirement accounts "owned" by beneficiaries and managed by those same Wall Street wizards who did such a wonderful job losing all the funds that flowed into dot-coms. The Co-Chairs hastened to add in their post-meeting press conference that this measure would not amount to privatization.

However, the Final Report belied that claim by pushing three different partial privatization scams. The main justification was, as mentioned, the Commission's "concern" that "because Social Security provides no property rights to its contributors—the Supreme Court has twice so ruled—a worker could easily work forty years then die and own not a penny of the contributions he has made for retirement benefits he will never collect" (p. 7). This statement is quite interesting for the manner in which it twists the Supreme Court's ruling into a justification for dismantling a social safety net. The Court was quite right to reject the claim that "contributors" have "property rights" in Social Security. From the beginning, Social Security was set up to pay benefits to those who met program requirements. A dead worker, by definition, could not meet requirements. (In Chicago, it is said, voters have "property rights" that allow them to continue to cast ballots long into the sweet hereafter, a model the President's Commission appears to want to adopt for Social Security!) Her survivors, however, could well qualify for benefits as laid out in program rules. While it is true that the rules for benefits include provisions linking payments to qualifying income earned (and the rules provide benefits that are more generous for retired workers than for survivors), total benefits received over one's lifetime have never been directly linked to payroll taxes paid (recall Ida May Fuller!). The Commissioners expressed faux concern for "minorities with shorter life spans than the white majority," who often die before they can collect benefits. If only they had "ownership rights" to their taxes, they could leave an inheritance to their survivors! Better yet, let them play the stock market so they can leave an "estate" to their heirs!

As President Bush had directed the Commission: "The idea works very simply. A young worker can take some portion of his or her payroll tax and put it in a fund that invests in stocks and bonds;" and the Co-Chairs added "the magic of compound interest now commences to work its wonders" (8). Three partial privatization plans were introduced in the Final Report. The first allows workers to voluntarily "invest" two percent of their taxable wages in a personal account, and a portion of their benefit payments will then depend on the performance of this account. The second model allows workers to put four percent of taxable wages into a personal account and attempts to resolve Social Security financial problems through large transfers from federal government general revenue. The third model asks workers to make voluntary contributions above payroll taxes, then has the federal government provide matching contributions to personal accounts. Again, large transfers are required from federal government general revenue. Hidden in the Report is the recognition that none of these privatization schemes will pay a level of benefits much beyond what the current system promises to workers (Model 1 actually proposes benefit cuts for workers; Model 2 proposes benefit cuts for high-wage workers; Model 3 gives small benefit increases to low and high wage workers), even though it is assumed the personal accounts are largely invested in stocks that are supposed to generate real returns of 6.5%, and even though some of the revenue shortfall (generated by diverting payroll taxes to personal accounts) is made up by annual contributions of general fund revenue of $40 billion.

The Co-Chairs illustrated the case of an individual in Model 3 who works from age 21 to 65, and who pays an additional 1% above the payroll tax (matched by the government), does well in the stock market, and amasses a huge portfolio worth $101,000 in constant 2001 dollars at retirement. There isn't much discussion of downside risks (what happens if the stock market tanks) nor of protection against inflation (automatically provided in the current system but abandoned in the privatization scheme). And, again, the Commission mostly ignores the fact that Social Security is much more than a pension plan. For an "estate" of $101,000, workers would accept more risk, higher tax rates, and large "transfers" from general fund revenues? Wonder of wonders, "reform" and "strengthening" and "modernization" of Social Security leaves the average beneficiary worse off than under the current system! The exercises in the Final Report simply bring home the message that average individuals cannot accumulate sufficient financial wealth to see them through retirement—something the framers of Social Security understood all too well. That $101,000 "estate" would provide only four years of retirement at the benefit level already written into current law for a high wage worker retiring in 2052; or five years for a medium wage worker. So much for the wonders of compounded interest!

This brings us again to the central issue, which is the real burden of providing for future retirees. Today, as the Commissioners correctly surmised, for each retiree there are three workers producing Winnebagos, supervising shuffleboard games aboard Caribbean cruises, and fertilizing golf course greens. In the future there will be two workers per retiree; hence, the "real burden" on each will rise, regardless of the method adopted for financing Social Security. Indeed, the real burden will rise even if Social Security in its current form is “retired”, as the Commissioners advocated. Even if privatization could provide each retiree with more financial wherewithal to buy Winnebagos, take cruises, or play golf, tomorrow’s workers will still face a higher real burden of supporting more retirees. That burden can only be alleviated by increasing the number of workers (via more immigrants or more children per family, for example), reducing the number of retired people (via a higher retirement age or more smoking-related deaths, for instance), or increasing worker productivity.

It is almost impossible to conceive of a future so horrible that two workers in 2050 would not be able to do the work of three workers today. I expect that productivity growth over the next 50 years will create a whole new set of problems, precisely because it will be difficult to find enough useful work for all those highly productive workers of the future. But let us envision the worst-case scenario, favored by the Commission, in which it becomes necessary to take positive, discretionary actions to raise worker productivity. Will the Commission's favored reform, privatization, succeed? The commission ruefully notes that to provide for retiring baby boomers, the nation must save and invest more, in order to increase the productivity of tomorrow's workers. The Commissioners choose to believe that "ownership" of the payroll taxes paid would allow individuals to "save," thus providing funds directly to capital markets that would convert them into productivity-enhancing investments.

That all sounds very nice. Let us imagine for a moment that Wall Street has learned from the errors of its recent past, so that individual savings pumped into stocks won't disappear into dot-com lands of the future. Will a privatized "retirement" system encourage more individual investment in real brick-and-mortar-and-machines capital? It is not sufficient to encourage individual "saving," for saving can take any form, from stuffed mattresses to sovereign debt to Rembrandts. Economists distinguish between "liquid" (cash, bonds) and "illiquid" (factories) as well as between low-risk (bank CDs) and high-risk (telecom stocks) investments. It is a fundamental principle of portfolio management that one does not begin with high-risk and illiquid investments; only when a portfolio provides sufficient liquidity and low-risk returns to meet basic needs should chances begin to be taken. As actuary David Langer (2000a,b) observes, professional actuaries recognize that private pension funds presume that Social Security provides a safety net for almost all retirees. Without such a safety net, prudent fund managers would have to adopt far safer positions. If the nation were to return to the pre-New Deal days in which most individuals had to rely on their own financial acumen for retirement (and on their children when that proved insufficient, as it did for most of the elderly), it is doubtful whether the supply of individual savings (including those professionally managed) flowing to Wall Street would actually increase. Far from promoting individual security-as the report claims it would-privatization would create insecurity because it would make individuals vulnerable to the fate of fickle financial markets. That is not likely to promote more investment in productivity-enhancing capital.

The Commissioners are correct when they argue that too many Americans have little or no savings and that too many will accumulate insufficient financial wealth to see them through their retirement years. However, the Social Security program is not the cause of this state of affairs, nor can partial privatization of the program do anything but worsen it. The real source of the problem is the growing inequality of income and the deterioration of opportunities for advancement for too many Americans.

## CONCLUSIONS: TOWARD PROGRESSIVE REFORM

From the perspective of the Social Security Trust Fund, its holdings of non-marketable Treasury debt can be counted as an asset. However, from the perspective of Uncle Sam, the Trust Fund does not in any way ease future financial "problems". The assets held by the Trust Fund are similar to the IOUs a wife might hold against her husband. She will not be able to buy any groceries with them, although so long as she trusts her husband she can count them as real claims on which he will some day make good. Similarly, when the time comes, Uncle Sam can make good on Trust Fund claims by emitting checks, which might entail budget deficits.

While I understand the argument that supporters of Social Security ought to pretend as if the Trust Fund really does ease future financial burdens of supporting retiring baby boomers, I believe that in the long run, honesty is the best policy. Once Americans know the true facts about Social Security, they will stop worrying about Trust Funds, lock-boxes, and looming "financial crises." What matters is Congressional Good Will, and so long as the full faith and credit of the US government stands behind Social Security, all promised future benefits will be paid.

For the past 60-plus years, US voters have held their politicians to a litmus test according to which the basic features of the Social Security program would remain off-limits. While there have always been critics of the program, including Ronald Reagan (beginning with his notorious "Operation Coffee Cup" speeches), the naysayers have never stood a chance. Most changes made in the past actually expanded the program, creating more benefits, and casting a wider net, while gradually raising payroll tax rates. The only truly significant modification came in 1983, with the Greenspan

Commission's change from a "pay-as-you-go" arrangement to an "advance-funded" system that would accumulate hundreds of billions, even trillions, of surpluses. This modification required payroll tax increases that would generate the surpluses necessary to buy non-marketable Treasury debt, purportedly putting Social Security on sure footing because the debt could be turned back to the Treasury as needed when the baby boomers retired, eliminating any future need to rely on the political goodwill of politicians. In the United States, it is believed that many things get better with time, with the notable exceptions of Social Security's finances and the intentions of Congress.

Ironically, Bush's Commission is now using this surplus to push forward its privatization agenda. It claims that because the surplus was accumulated in the form of Treasury IOUs, future retirees are still subject to the whims of future Congresses because when the time comes to retire those IOUs, politicians might refuse to raise other taxes, cut other types of spending, or borrow in order to come up with the necessary funds to pay to Social Security. Instead, we need to provide "legal ownership" of those surpluses directly to prospective beneficiaries. That way, Congress will not be able to refuse payment. (Déjà vu all over again!) The argument that politicians will find Social Security recipients of the future any easier to ignore than those of the past strains credulity—especially since the percentage of the population that will collect Social Security has grown steadily and will continue to grow significantly in coming years. I expect that future voters will continue to hold politicians' feet to the fire of Social Security and assert their resolve to keep the program intact. The true reason for the "urgent" need to privatize is that the enemies of the program fear that as baby boomers reach retirement age, it will be politically impossible to dismantle the program, hence, the Bush Commission's "last ditch effort" to gut the program today.

Still, let us give the Commissioners their due: at some point in the future, cash revenues might fall short of spending—the Greenspan commission's reason for advocating a transition to an advance funding scheme. However, as the Bush Commission's Interim Report emphasizes, the sale of Social Security Trust Fund assets may improve Social Security's budget situation, but not the overall federal budget position. From the perspective of Uncle Sam, the Trust Fund is nothing but an accounting construction, and when Social Security tries to "cash in" its assets, the Treasury will have to raise other taxes, cut other spending, or simply let its budget expand (reducing its overall surplus, if one exists at the time, or expanding its overall deficit). The Commissioners presume and hope that Uncle Sam will do nothing of the kind; rather, Congress will choose instead to slash Social Security benefits. For the reasons discussed above, this seems highly improbable.

Is there another solution? The size of the eventual financial shortfall amounts to about 2.5 percent of GDP in 2075. Therefore, to completely resolve the looming financial "crisis," without worsening the overall federal budget balance, will eventually require some combination of spending cuts and tax increases amounting to 2.5 percent of GDP. The Bush Commission's Interim Report adopted extreme scare tactics in its discussion of possible scenarios: raising taxes imposed on a couple by $2,295 per year by 2050 or, more ominously, eliminating the Departments of Education, Interior, Justice, Veterans Affairs, and Commerce, along with the EPA, NASA, HUD, and the NSF. As Krugman correctly pointed out, President Bush's tax cut will eventually reduce federal revenue by about 1.7 percent of GDP. (Krugman 2001) Did any of his supporters note that this would require elimination of most of the above-named departments and agencies?

Social Security is unusual because it was based from the beginning on the fiction that its revenues are the source of the funds used to pay benefits. In reality, this has never been the case. Social Security checks come from the Treasury, just like any other form of government spending. Technically, the Treasury can continue to pay Social Security benefits even if payroll tax receipts fall to zero. When the percentage of the population receiving Social Security benefits was small relative to that of the working population paying payroll taxes, it was politically useful to maintain the fiction of separate accounts. However, as we've seen, while there were five workers for every retiree in 1960, that ratio is now three to one, and it will fall eventually to about two to one. At the same time, the percentage of national income that is subject to payroll taxes has fallen and will continue to fall-from above 40 percent today to 35 percent by 2075.

Hence, to move 2.5 percent more of GDP to Social Security revenues would require a large increase in the payroll tax rate that is imposed on the current tax base—indeed, the Commission's report claims that payroll tax rates would have to rise by 37 percent by 2050 to eliminate the projected shortfall. However, a small tax increase imposed on a much broader base could easily increase revenue by 2.5 percent of GDP. At the limit, if the tax base included all national income, a Social Security tax rate of only 6.7 percent would equal all benefits to be paid in 2075! Contrast that with the current payroll tax rate of 12.4 percent of covered earnings (6.2 percent levied on both workers and their employers). In other words, rather than seeing tax rates rise over the coming decades, we could actually have much lower tax rates if the tax base were expanded. In 1960 it may well have made sense to pretend to finance Social Security on the basis of a payroll tax, given that there were plenty of workers to tax and few beneficiaries to support. However, as that ratio has continued to fall, it has made increasingly less sense to maintain such pretensions. As our population matures and the financial and real burdens of providing for a large number of longer-lived individuals rises, those burdens should be more equally shared-by high-income earners and even by those who receive non-wage income. Thus, let us pretend that a much lower tax rate on a much broader tax base "pays for" Social Security. Financial crisis resolved!

Most importantly, it is time for progressives to revisit the design of the program. While it made political sense in the 1930s to avoid any charges of socialism, the attempt to make Social Security operate as if it were like a private pension plan is now an albatross. The public should be told the truth. Social Security is an intergenerational assurance program. Those of working age must produce all the goods and services for themselves and also for the young, the aged, and disabled persons. We then need to formulate a distributive scheme to ensure that some portion of output gets transferred from the working to the nonworking. Capitalist systems rely on the market and financial system to achieve such a transfer. It is easy enough to provide the financial where-with-all so that the nonworking have access to society's output. The government merely needs to cut checks. Social policy must decide how much purchasing power to put into the hands of Social Security beneficiaries; it may well decide that different amounts should be provided to survivors and disabled persons than the amounts that are provided to those who had qualified work for some specified amount of time. Social policy might also want to link benefits to one's income earned over a life-time of work. There are also strong, progressive, reasons *not* to do this. The issues need to be brought out into the open and debated without the complications arising from lies and myths about how the program is funded.

The other side of the coin is the tax system. The ultimate purpose of taxes is to create a demand for the government's currency. (See Wray, this volume, Chapter 3.) There is also a subsidiary goal of using taxes to discourage certain behaviors (hence, the need for sin taxes). Taxes on activities tend to discourage those activities. It makes little sense to use a payroll tax, since that discourages firms from employing workers, and reduces the incentive to work for pay. Further, it makes little sense to try to match payroll tax revenues to Social Security benefits—just as it would make little sense to impose a particular tax to "pay for" national defense. As noted above, a tax on all income is preferable to a payroll tax. It is still far from the ideal tax, because it discourages an activity (earning income) that we mostly do not believe should be discouraged. An ideal tax would be one that could not be avoided or evaded, but would not discourage activity society desires. Further, strong arguments can be made for a progressive tax system, based on ability to pay. A progressive income tax, with the same rate imposed on income from any source, is probably acceptable, both economically and politically. We might still, however, come up with a better tax—say, a progressive tax on one's dwelling (with strong progressivity ensured by taxing square—or cubic—footage at an increasing rate). Avoidance would mean homelessness; evasion would be fairly difficult; and the "sin" of excessive living space would be discouraged. Maybe Henry George was on the right track, after all.

What is most important is to delink in the public mind taxes paid-in and benefits paid-out. The Trust Fund should be eliminated. Money's worth calculations should cease. Congressional goodwill should be emphasized, cultivated, and maintained at the ballot box. Social responsibility for survivors, dependents, those with disabilities, and those who are retired should be renewed. That is the proper and progressive way to reform Social Security. Convenient fictions cannot help and are, indeed, dangerous.

When we broach the topic of Social Security in my university class on economic policy, I ask students which of them doubts that the program will exist for them when they retire. Most raise their hands. Before they study the issues involved, most support elimination of the program, or at least some sort of privatization. After they have delved into the topic, they come to understand that if the program is analyzed strictly as a pension fund, it is a bad deal for most of them. But they also understand that Social Security is not simply or even primarily a retirement plan. Many experts have argued that it is actually an insurance system, providing a wide range of benefits that private insurance systems cannot offer, at least at a reasonable cost. I prefer to think of it as a social assurance program because "insurance" tends to bring to mind actuarial tables and reserve funds. The federal government does not, need not, and indeed cannot accumulate reserve funds—a point I have argued for years, and one the Bush Commission (as well as Milton Friedman!) has come to recognize. However, Social Security benefits can and will be paid, without regard to the program's revenues, so long as congressional will is maintained.

I have found that even though Social Security is a hard sell to my students as a retirement program, it is an immediate and easy sell as an assurance program. I simply pose the following question: Are you willing to pay about 6.7 percent of your income to Social Security in order to gain assurance that your parents, grandparents, and great-grandparents (not to mention your widowed Aunt Sally with her children) will not have to live in your home with you? One-hundred percent of my students have thus far agreed that on these terms the program is a good deal. Even leaving aside all the other "assurance" benefits for survivors and disabled people, this implicit, intergenerational promise—that Social Security will provide a minimum income sufficient to bring the vast majority of elderly persons above the poverty line, while allowing them to live with dignity and more or less independently—enjoys broad popular support.

## REFERENCES

Aaron, Henry J., Alan S. Blinder, Alicia H. Munnell, and Peter R. Orszag. 2001. "Response to the Co-Chairs of the Commission." July 23. Washington, DC, and New York: Center on Budget and Policy Priorities and The Century Foundation. www.socsec.org/new/Special Sections/bushcommission.html

Advisory Council on Social Security. 1997a. *Report of the 1994-1996 Advisory Council. Vol. I: Findings and Recommendations*. Washington, DC: Government Printing Office.

———. 1997b. *Report of the 1994-1996 Advisory Council. Vol. II:Report of the Technical Panel on Trends and Issues in Retirement Savings, Technical Panel on Assumptions and Methods and Presentations to the Council.* Washington, DC: Government Printing Office.

Altmeyer, Arthur J. 1963. "The Development and Status of Social Security in America." In *Labor, Management, and Social Policy: Essays in the John R. Commons Tradition.* Gerald G. Somers, ed. Madison University of Wisconsin Press.

Arnold, R. Douglas, Michael J. Graetz, and Alice H. Munnell, eds, 1998. *Framing the Social Security Debate: Values, Politics, and Economics.* Washington: National Academy of Social Insurance.

Baker, Dean. 1998. "Saving Social Security in Three Steps." Briefing Paper. Washington, DC: Economic Policy Institute.

———. 1997. "Saving Social Security with Stocks: the Promises Don't Add Up." The Century Foundation, www.tcf.org/publications/social_security/saving_ss/introduction.html

Ball, Robert M. with Thomas N. Bethell. 1998. *Straight Talk about Social Security: An Analysis of the Issues in the Current Debate*. New York: The Century Foundation Press.

Darby, Rose and Michelle Celarier, 1999. "Where's the Payoff?" *Investment Dealer's Digest* August 1999. 2-8.

Eisner, Robert. 1998. *Social Security: More, Not Less*, New York: Century Foundation Press.

Fagnoni, Cynthia. 1999. "Social Security and Minorities: Current Benefits and Implications of Reform." United States General Accounting Office, Testimony before the Subcommittee on Social Security, Committee on Ways and Means, House of Representatives, GAO/T-HEHS-99-60, February 10.

Feldstein, Martin S., ed. 1999. *Privatizing Social Security.* Chicago : University of Chicago Press.

Friedman, Milton, 1999. "Social Security Chimeras." *New York Times*, January 11. A-17. Goldstein, Amy. 2001. "Social Security Findings Criticized." *Washington Post*, July 25. A01.

Krugman, Paul. 2001. "2016 and All That." *New York Times,* July 22. Langer, David. 2000a. "Cooking Social Security's Deficit." *The Christian Science Monitor*, January 4.

———. 2000b. "Social Security vs. Stock." Op-ed. *Christian Science Monitor*, June 19: 19. Mueller, John. 1998. "The Stock Market Won't Beat Social Security." *Challenge* vol 41. no. 2, March/April . 95-117.

Papadimitriou, Dimitri B., and L. Randall Wray. 1999a. *Does Social Security Need Saving?* Public Policy Brief No. 55.Annandale-on-Hudson, NY: The Jerome Levy Economics Institute.

———. 1999b. *How Can We Provide for the Baby Boomers in Their Old Age?* Policy Note 1999/5. Annandale-on-Hudson, NY: The Levy Economics Institute.

Peterson, Peter G. 1996. *Will America Grow Up Before It Grows Old?* New York: Random House.

President's Commission to Strengthen Social Security. 2001a. "Draft Report of the President's Commission to Strengthen Social Security." Staff draft. Revised July 18 and 23. www.socsec.org/new/Special_Section/bushcommission.htm(July18)www.csss.gov/repor/ 7-23-Draft-Report,.pdf (July 23).

President's Commission to Strengthen Social Security. 2001b. "Strengthening Social Security and Creating Personal Wealth for All Americans: Report of the President's Commission." December 2001. http://www.csss.gov/reports/Final-report.pdf.

Skidmore, Max J. 1999. *Social Security and its Enemies: the Case for America's Most Efficient Insurance Program*, Westview Press: Boulder, Co.

———. "What Happened to the Social Security Surplus? An examination of the Trustee's Projections." Paper presented at a conference, "The Social Security 'Crisis': Critical Analysis and Solutions," University of Missouri. Kansas City. November 12, 2001.

Social Security Administration. 1999. *Annual Report of the Board of Trustees of the Federal Old Age and Survivors Insurance and Disability Insurance Trust Funds*. Washington, DC: Government Printing Office.

Social Security Administration. 2002. *Annual Report of the Board of Trustees of the Federal Old Age and Survivors Insurance and Disability Insurance Trust Funds*. Washington, DC: Government Printing Office.

Summers, Lawrence, and Janet Yellen. 1999. "Saving the Surplus will Protect Retirees. "*Wall Street Journal*, February 18.

Williamson, John. 1997. "Should Women Support the Privatization of Social Security?" *Challenge* Vol 40. no. 4. July/August, 97-108.

Wray, L. Randall. 1999. *The Emperor Has No Clothes: President Clinton's Proposed Social Security Reform.* Policy Note 1999/2. Annandale-on-Hudson, NY: The Levy Economics Institute.

———. 2001. "Killing Social Security Softly with Faux Kindness: The Draft Report by the President's Commission on Social Security Reform." Policy Note 2001/6. Annandale-on-Hudson, NY:The Levy Economics Institute.

# 9

# COMPETING PERSPECTIVES ON ECONOMIC POWER AND ACCOUNTABILITY

Edythe S. Miller

## INTRODUCTION

The economic beliefs that have become increasingly dominant in economic policy formation for the past quarter century are derived primarily from neoclassical economic orthodoxy. This orthodox viewpoint has its basis in an economic ideology that encompasses a specific vision of human nature, a particular economic methodology, and an explicit outlook about the design and workings of the economy. Based upon these neoclassical presuppositions, this ideological perspective demands the application of specific policies. General acceptance of this set of ideas has tended to wax and wane to some extent over the years, but in recent years it has enjoyed widespread approval. Advocacy of this viewpoint has spread from economic scholars to opinion makers, to politicians and to the public at large. The policies required by this set of ideas have been applied in the United States, and worldwide, for the past generation. This chapter will examine the foundations of this pattern of thought and some of its applications. It will contrast with this viewpoint the philosophy, and related policies, of the institutionalist school, a major alternative to neoclassicism. It then will examine how the application of accepted neoclassical beliefs has contributed to the concentration and centralization of economic power in giant multinational corporations and the concomitant decline of democratic processes in the determination of economic policy.

It is a thesis of this paper that acceptance of the neoclassical economic philosophy has profound implications for the maintenance and survival of political democracy. Among the qualities required for viable democracy are that public policy be popularly determined, that those who determine policy feel the incidence of that policy, and that a climate exists in which free inquiry and experimentation are encouraged and dissent respected. A system that breeds highly concentrated market power and severe distributional inequality violates the first two of these principles. A system that requires allegiance to one set of ideas, and requires that all economic policies be strictly in conformance with those ideas, tolerates neither dissent nor experimentation. It will be argued that the economic experience of recent years confirms this interpretation.

## THE HOLD OF ECONOMIC IDEOLOGY

Recent US economic performance and economic policy has been shaped by mainstream, neoclassical economic thought, the accepted economic orthodoxy in this country and much of the world. It is not a newly minted line of thought; it comes to us almost intact from our intellectual forebears. It is the school of economics that historically has been the received wisdom, but perhaps never held so firmly and by so many as it is at present. Accepted alternatives are difficult to find, whether one searches the academic establishment, the economics texts, political expression, popular media, or common opinion. The major political parties rival each other in expressions of fealty to this body of thought. It is identified as "the American way," yet comes to us initially from abroad and, in modern times, has been exported extensively. This set of ideas is the basis of formal academic economics worldwide, and broadly sets the agenda for economic belief, inquiry, and policy. That the ideas are so widely approved may reflect the disappearance of political alternatives that aver loyalty to other economic schools of thought, although it predates this development. It may be a reflection of a present tendency, a carryover from the past, to identify capitalism with freedom, and freedom with free markets, a matter to which we shall return. But whatever the reason, the present strength and durability of the model is indisputable. Even alternative thought now is forced into this mold (for example, the new Keynesian school, the new institutional economics); giving us such oxymorons as neoclassical Keynesianism and neoclassical institutionalism. And never before has academic dissent seemed so weak or so unwelcome. It is a contention of this paper that the predominance and pervasiveness of this line of thought go a long way toward explaining the state of our modern economy and of our political system.

### The Basic Model

The neoclassical model incorporates a view of human nature, an economic methodology, and a perception of the workings of the economy based upon specific laws of economic motion. It is grounded in a belief in the existence of universal principles that determine end results. At the heart of the model is the concept of methodological individualism. The focus is upon the lone individual, with "given" tastes and preferences, making decisions about purchases and sales, consumption and saving, labor and leisure. The aggregate of these decisions is held to determine national outcomes. All individual decisions are apprehended as based upon self-interested, rational (in a cost-benefit sense), hedonistic, maximizing criteria. Price is conceived as the variable that equates supply and demand in the goods market and in the labor market. If demand exceeds supply, an increase in price will result in market clearing. If supply exceeds demand, a fall in price has the same effect. The individual is viewed as passive, non-purposive, responding robot-like to the sole stimulus of price. Over a century ago, in his famous critique of economic orthodoxy, Thorstein Veblen characterized the neoclassical economic individual (the "rational economic man") as: ". . .a lightning calculator of pleasures and pains, who oscillates like a homogeneous globule of desire of happiness under the impulse of stimuli that shift him about the area, but leave him intact. He has neither antecedent nor consequent. He is an isolated, definitive human datum, in stable equilibrium except for the buffets of the impinging forces that displace him in one direction or another. Self-imposed in elemental space, he spins symmetrically about his own spiritual axis until the parallelogram of forces bears down on him, whereupon he follows the line of the resultant. When the force of the impact is spent, he comes to rest, a self-contained globule of desire as before" (1961a, 73-4).

The model adopts, by definition, a condition of full employment. Markets (goods and labor) "clear" through the expedient of flexible prices. If they do not clear, the fault lies with inflexible prices or other "disturbances." A market clearing position is an equilibrium position. An equilibrium condition is a state of rest. Departures from this state occur only in the event of a disturbance; the removal of the disturbance results in a return to equilibrium. It is the simplest of models. All aggregates are strictly summations of individual schedules. It is a closed system. It abstracts from any factors that would open it to influence from outside the model. It leaves out of account as given or exogenous all circumstances that would add complexity or subtlety: technology, income distribution, consumer taste and preference, custom, habit, individual and collective history, communal influence of any kind. It is timeless, a-historical, and a-social.

## Neoclassical Methodology

The neoclassical methodology embraces an a priori, hypothico-deductive ideal. Over the years, the model has become ever more formalized and mathemetized. But irrespective of the specifics of any of its models, deductive logic is employed to discover antecedent economic law, which is to be carried through to its ultimate conclusion. Logical consistency is favored, and reality ignored. Veblen describes neoclassical economic thought as grounded in natural law that embraces a normal order of things derived from an accepted ideal of conduct. The normal order is comprised of private property, the rights of ownership, and freedom of contract. Individual private exchange and contract is the natural course of business enterprise; government intervention is "unnatural," artificial and coercive, serving to throw sand in the gears of optimality and interfere with individual freedom. Laws of the normal or natural specify the ends to which the system tends, which are accepted as good, right and proper. The body of natural laws and rights thus are posited as embodying truth and merit, serving as an apologia for the status quo (Veblen 1961c, 150). Natural law controls the movement toward approved ends by "exercis[ing] some sort of coercive surveillance over the sequence of events" (1961a, 61, 65). A Shakespearean-type "tide in the affairs of men" prevails. The model clearly is deterministic. Ends are pre-determined. They also are worthy. Though proclaimed as *wertfrei* and therefore objective, the model equates the status quo with what should be, making the ultimate value judgment. The system is positivist and absolutist. It banishes uncertainty; both ends and means of individual action are fully specified.

The neoclassical school accepts the definition of economics set forth by Lionel Robbins in 1932 (Robbins 1984, 16): it is seen as the study of the allocation of scarce resources to given ends. The ends given are those denoted above, and are incontestable. That means and ends are viewed as separate and distinct is one of many examples of the acceptance by the neoclassical school of Cartesian dualisms. Means and ends, theory and practice, thought and action, learning and doing—all are viewed as unrelated and independent. Ends are not viewed as colored by the means used to attain them; theory is separate and uninformed by its application in practice; thought and action are isolated; learning is not influenced by doing. Economics is viewed strictly in an allocative sense. Delimiting the economic problem to resource allocation within the productive process establishes efficiency, narrowly defined in its allocative sense, as the paramount economic pursuit. Any broader elements of efficiency are disregarded. Equity issues have no place in the mix. Full employment and the full use of resources explicitly are accepted as premises of the system. Anything less, by definition, must be voluntary or frictional, or subsist because of unwelcome system "disturbances"—an obtrusive government, wage stickiness, the endurance of custom. Resources are viewed as invariably scarce; the model is one of limited resources. Given that resources are limited and that full employment prevails, opportunity cost is the operative concept. The school can be built only if resources are withdrawn from private construction; public spending is a "drag" on economic activity, it "crowds out" private expenditure. This despite the fact that the world often has experienced enduring gluts of resources—unused capacity, goods that could not find buyers, widespread unemployment. It is perhaps the ultimate irony that the definition itself first was promulgated in the depths of the depression of the 30s.

In Robbins's view of the economic world, the concept and influence of the social or communal is ignored. The whole is no more than the sum of its individual parts. The model incorporates a one-way flow from individuals to community. Thus, individuals with innate tastes and preferences determine the manner and shape of production. Their consumption, driven by innate preferences revealed through their purchases, is a vote for the production of particular goods and services. The productive process conforms accordingly. Consumer sovereignty prevails. And this, in keeping with the moral stance of the model, is as it should be. Judgments about the state of our consumer society are not justified. If a higher proportion of resources is devoted to the production of extravagances and luxury goods, or products of war, than to schools and hospitals and parks, so be it. The importance of the social, communal, habitual, customary, emulative in shaping individual tastes is not recognized. The role of business itself in developing and shaping the market for its product is ignored. Business only responds to the demands it encounters – it provides individuals with that which they desire. What could be more agreeable?

## Power and Freedom

In this model there is no role for accumulations of power. Freedom is defined strictly in individualistic terms. Individuals have decisive control; the consumer is sovereign. Power imbalances between employer and employee, producer and consumer simply are not recognized. If the goods and services produced are not those desired by consumers, the consumer will withdraw his/her vote, and cast it in other directions. If the terms of the labor bargain are not to the laborer's liking, he/she has the ability to withhold his/her productive effort, and redirect it. In this model, alternative purchases and employment always are viable options. And the worker has ultimate authority to decide between work and "leisure," as if the alternative to work for all workers is a Caribbean cruise. Alfred Marshall's representative firm remains the applicable and relevant business model in the economics texts. It has only been quite recently that this theoretical framework has even acknowledged the existence of business conglomeration (Miller 1993). And when business aggregation eventually is recognized, it is viewed as unrelated to the question of power. Firms are formed, it is claimed, so as to minimize transaction costs. The choice between firm and market (spot transactions) is strictly a cost-benefit matter. In any event, in this view of things firm formation and consolidation of power in no way constrains freedom. In this model, freedom is defined strictly as absence of coercion or restraint applied by political collectivities, rather than as in any sense also related to achievement of an enhanced ability to perform. Government is viewed as the ultimate force or constraint, with trade unions running a close second. Their roles, and those of all collectivities with the exception of the business firm, are to be kept to a minimum. In this way, freedom is identified with free markets, and capitalism itself with freedom.

The neoclassical economic theory has had a remarkable run. Despite some trimming around the edges in later formulations, and increasing model complexity, sophistication, and mathematization, the basic model remains unchanged to this day. It continues to hold the allegiance of economists, and to be accepted as the touchstone for professional recognition as an economist. The few changes that have been made in the model are for the most part non-substantive—a matter of extending or deepening the basic model. For example, in the "new institutional economics" bounded rationality is substituted for rationality, opportunism for self-interest, and transaction costs are added to production costs. The theory of contestable markets substitutes contestability for competition. These changes maintain the market ordered and inspired structures and behaviors and the competitive creed that are at the heart of the basic model. That is, the central model remains intact, and is the one applied for policy purposes. The questions to be explored then are—to what extent is the acceptance and application of this framework responsible for current economic conditions, are those conditions acceptable, and is there another way, a preferable way, that will result in a different set of outcomes? We will take last things first. Before going on to examine some practical current economic problems and the response to them of policy makers applying accepted dogma, we will explore an alternative paradigm.

## AN ALTERNATIVE PERSPECTIVE

The alternative perspective is that of institutional economics, in many respects almost a mirror image of neoclassical economics. Institutional economics is evolutionary, indeterminate, realistic, non-predictive, and perceives uncertainty as an inevitable aspect of the human condition. It does not conflate "what is" and "what should be." It is resolutely and implacably normative. Because "what is" is often viewed as subject to improvement, the interest of institutional economists consistently is directed toward reform, whether reform directly of the economy or indirectly of the economy through reform of economics itself. Individual institutional economists do not necessarily focus attention equally upon these types of reform. Some, such as John R. Commons, are primarily interested in political and economic reform. Commons advances proposals, for example, for public utility regulation, unemployment compensation, and other such programs—looking to the protection and security of the more vulnerable members of society in order to improve that society. Veblen, in contrast, principally is interested in the reform of economics itself, and directs primary attention to the unrealistic assumptions and premises of traditional theory. Although not equally engaged by these different aspects of reform, each necessarily explores both aspects, as need most institutional economists, in view of the mutuality of theory and practice. In addition, institutional economics is realist, that is, grounded in matter-of-fact knowledge (Bush 1993, 72-3). Its realistic focus commands recognition of the existence of such phenomena as power as well as the existence of such problems as unemployment and poverty. It also ensures that the examination of such issues looks to underlying, rather than simply to superficial causes; for otherwise, proposals for reform could not be expected to solve problems or effect desirable change.

Recognition of the desirability of reform and of the paralysis of prevailing wisdom in the face of existing economic problems makes institutional economics hospitable to other schools of economics and other disciplines with such alternative social and economic perspectives. For example, the thinking of the philosophers of the American pragmatic school of philosophy is a bulwark of much institutionalist thought. Philosophers such as Charles S. Peirce and John Dewey see a society guided, not by an invisible hand, but by a very visible one. That is, they envision a system in which policies designed and implemented by humans determine results, rather than results being preordained and predetermined.

In addition, there is early recognition by institutionalists of the importance and far-reaching consequences of the insights of John Maynard Keynes and his followers. Institutionalists share the Keynesian recognition of the significant role played by uncertainty in human decision making and the sequence of economic events. Moreover, institutionalists, like Keynesians, see the individual and social waste wrought by widespread unemployment, and view it as a devastating and unnecessary cost to society. Institutionalists recognize the underlying wisdom of Keynes's perception that it is better to employ individuals to dig holes and fill them up again, or Joan Robinson's ironic observation that it is preferable to engage people to paint the Black Forest white than to permit the impoverishment of lives through unemployment. Better, of course, for persons to be productively employed to fulfill social needs, but if objection to this is met, nonproductive employment is preferable to no employment at all.

J.M. Clark suggests that labor should be considered a fixed cost for society, even if a variable one for business. Just as the firm need maintain a fixed capital stock in the face of declining demand, so must society maintain its labor supply, or bear the cost of its erosion (Clark 1981, 15-16, 384-5). Institutionalists view human abilities unutilized as a primary form of waste, and the highest form of inefficiency. An efficient economy is one that "works" fully and smoothly for its members. This assessment has both a macro and a micro aspect. At the macro level, it means the provision of a universally accessible economic and social infrastructure to bind together the individual parts. At the micro level, it means providing the means universally to fulfill individual potential for self-realization through full participation in the society.

## An Institutionalist Perspective on Power

Institutionalists, in contrast to neoclassicals, recognize the existence and significance of imbalances of power in all economies. Where neoclassical economists see individuals and firms strictly as reactive agents responding to forces beyond their control, and therefore as powerless, institutionalists recognize that power is very much a part of any economy. Reform of the economy, or any social reform, will involve changing the reward and power structure of the society, and the dissemination or redistribution of power. In any change there will be winners and losers.

To understand the institutionalist interpretation of the concept of power, it perhaps is best to start with the distinction institutionalists draw between technology and institutions, or between the instrumental and the ceremonial. This distinction is so identified with Veblen that it often is denominated the "Veblenian dichotomy." But this important distinction appears in one form or another in much, if not most, institutionalist work, and is not confined to the work of Veblen. Almost all of Veblen's followers and many of his institutionalist contemporaries employ the concept. One finds it for example in Commons's differentiation between the going concern and the going plant. The distinction is one between business and industry, between making money and making goods.

Veblen points out that the purpose of business is to make money, of industry to produce goods. The businessman does not have the social good in mind. To the contrary, it is self-aggrandizement that occupies his thoughts and drives his efforts. Veblen sees both technology and institutions as habits of thought and action. Technology is reality based, grounded in the matter-of-fact and occurring in real time. It involves instrumental thought and action, reasoning from cause to effect. Technology is driven and made possible by the accumulated knowledge and the cultural heritage of the community; a common stock, jointly created and held. Technological advance is driven by such factors as workmanship, curiosity, and concern for humanity, both present and future (styled "the parental bent" by Veblen). The institutional or ceremonial aspect of life is moored in rank, authority, dominance—it is emulative, exploitative, self-serving and self-aggrandizing. It is important to recognize that instrumental and ceremonial behavior patterns exist simultaneously and interactively within organizations and operate similarly for individuals. The going concern is part of the going plant—there is no division between them. The individual acts at one and the same time on serviceable or productive and status or dominance driven grounds. The family, the plant and the school, for example, are amalgams of nurture or industry or learning and simultaneously of hierarchy and distinction.

The individualist and marginal productivity basis for production and distribution found in the neoclassical model is challenged by the view of technology as a common stock. Apprehending production as the result of group knowledge and group effort, and distribution as based upon bargaining power, rank, and authority, the core of the ceremonial aspects of life, challenges the very basis of neoclassical economics. Neoclassical theory, by grounding distribution theory in the individual contribution to the total product, justifies any prevailing distribution of income and wealth. The differentiation between industry and business, between making goods and making money, focuses attention upon a particular set of problems in the economic world. The role of industry is to produce goods, of business to make a profit. The institutionalist view of business enterprise directly confronts the neoclassical view that market forces invariably are sufficiently strong to prevent centralization of private power, and development of firm dominance. An important stratagem used by business to fulfill its moneymaking purposes, according to Veblen, is that of sabotage, which he defines as the "conscientious withdrawal of efficiency." Sabotage includes the ability to withhold from production so as to increase price. Veblen describes it as: "such habitual recourse to delay and obstruction of industry and such restriction of output as will maintain prices at a reasonably profitable level . . ." (1965, 7).

It is important to put this into context. Businesses can effectuate sabotage because they are not strictly creatures of the uncontrolled market. They are able to withhold from production because they are possessed of market power. But this is to society's disadvantage. It results in a smaller product, a shrinking pie. It removes the potential for improvement in the conditions of life for the many, in pursuit of the pecuniary advantage of the few. It is made possible because certain of the economic actors possess a high degree of market power. Dewey points out that: "...in the conduct of industry and exchange generally the technological factor is obscured, deflected and defeated by `business'" (1991, 182). Institutionalists maintain that the neoclassical faith in the ability of the free market to achieve the best of all possible worlds is misconceived. Because it is not free, but is instead controlled, the "free market" does not achieve efficiency even in the narrow neoclassical allocative view of the term, much less as perceived by institutionalists. Institutionalists define efficiency as the maximization of social output in pursuit of social good, and in terms of waste avoidance and the fulfillment of human potential. The institutionalist definition of efficiency has a sizeable equity component.

## Humans as Social Beings

Institutional economics recognizes the interrelationship of the social and the individual. Veblen points out that "man has never lived an isolated, self-sufficient life as an individual, either actually or potentially" (1961, 324), and adds that our life history is the history of human communities. He sees production and consumption as communal endeavors. Commons's very definition of an institution as "collective action in restraint, liberation, and expansion of individual action" (1961, 73) underscores the communal nature of human existence and the role played by the social and the collective both in penalizing and supporting individual action. Dewey points out that: "Habit is the mainspring of human action, and habits are formed for the most part under the influence of the customs of a group" (1991, 159). Humans are born into a social environment with a particular set of mores and customs. They are creatures of habit, convention, custom and humanly created law. But they also are animated by curiosity, workmanship, concern for fellow human beings, both present and future. As such, they effect change upon their societies, even as communal forces shape them. Persons primarily act out of habit and custom. Community standards both sanction and reward individual effort. Individuals act in conformance with social mores or suffer the consequences, even as at the margin they collectively forge novel approaches to the solution of problems.

Societies have always been characterized by the existence of particular power structures. Identification of privileged and authoritative groups varies by era. Historically, power has vested in different elites—the church, royalty, business, and finance. But the reality of the existence of power does not vary. The locus of power—like all ceremonial aspects of society—is replacemental. Technology, in contrast, the accumulated knowledge of the community, is developmental.[1] It involves reasoning from cause to effect, from means to end, with ends upon achievement becoming means to further ends. Institutionalism accepts no final or ultimate ends; all ends are viewed as provisional. Moreover, means and ends are not dichotomized, but partake of each other. Ends are influenced by the means utilized to achieve them.

Technology is by nature experimental. It functions through application of trial and error that includes both deduction and induction and adds to that a process, to use Peirce's term, of "abduction" (1958, 367-9; Miller 1998, 139).[2] The emphasis is upon hypothesis formation and testing. This process does not result in absolute truth, but rather in acquiring knowledge that is tentative and corrigible. This is knowledge, to use Dewey's phrase, that is "warrantably assertable;" that is, knowledge that we are justified in believing. The search is not so much for truth as for understanding. The knowledge in question is contextual, true for a particular time and place, and not necessarily for all time nor for all situations. It thus is not morally absolute; but nor is it morally relative, based as it is in reality.

The focus therefore of the study of economics is on consecutive change, on evolution—the process of change in society and change in the human agent as part of that society, a process that takes place continuously and unendingly. Institutionalism views equilibrium as both unrealistic and inapplicable to real world problems. There is no "resting place" in the real world; the real world has no final terms or ultimate ends. It is absurd to expect that a society when moved from "equilibrium" by some "disturbance" will return to that "equilibrium" when the "disturbance" is removed. The process of change is indeterminate and uncertain. Indeed, it is uncertainty that drives much human action. And since indeterminacy is a prevalent condition, the future cannot be predicted. Changing environments will effect changes in individuals who, in turn, will reformulate their environments. The future is unknown and unknowable. Actions and policies need be evaluated in terms of their consequences (Dewey 1991, 202-3), subject to change if these are unfavorable. Since consequences cannot be fully known in advance, experimentation and flexibility is required. In all of this, it is not perfection that is sought, not maximization, nor optimality, to use the neoclassical terms, but serviceability—to use Veblen's designation, or reasonableness—to use the terminology employed by C.E. Ayres.

There may be no greater distinction between the neoclassical and the institutionalist rendition of economics than their respective views on the existence and use of power in the economy. John Kenneth Galbraith points out that neoclassical economics removes power from the subject matter of economics (1973, 2). It portrays the firm strictly as a price-taker that produces in accord with consumer direction. The firm is viewed as subservient to the market. Employers and employees are viewed as equally capable of controlling personal outcomes, the employee every bit as able to withdraw his/her labor, as is the employer of withholding the job. The consumer is portrayed as directing production, rather than as manipulated in his/her purchases. Galbraith claims that in eliding power, neoclassical economics "destroys its relation with the real world" (1973, 2).

Institutionalists paint a different picture. They see an economy awash in power. Firms are more often price makers than price takers. Employees, with "shallow pockets" and minimal staying power, are at a bargaining disadvantage. Consumers often are driven by motives of emulation and status, and are manipulated by producers in consumption decisions. Veblen's *Theory of the Leisure Class* documents the emulative and status driven motives behind consumer life styles. Galbraith's *Affluent Society* recounts the public squalor that persists, despite vast public need, amidst private affluence and profligacy. In a process designated by Galbraith as a "revised sequence" (1967, 221-8), consumers are shown as subject to a barrage of signals and blandishments from business that shape their tastes, and influence buying habits and purchases. Consumers do not direct the market, they are directed. Firms control the market, rather than being under its control.

## Policy Implications

Policy prescription varies with perspective. Neoclassicals extol market solutions, and insist that the market should be left free to work its magic. Intervention, interference, "disturbance" of market solutions will thwart the superior outcomes of markets. Institutionalists, in contrast, in the face of what they perceive as persistent imbalances of power, argue for intervention. The only realistic and sufficiently strong counterbalance—in Galbraith's words, "countervailing power"—to dominant corporate power is alternative forms of collective power—government action or worker association. And yet, labor unions in recent years have lost both favor and membership. The climate of opinion in regard to labor organization became increasingly negative over the post-World War II period, with legislation, management practice, and public opinion turning increasingly hostile. In response, labor organizations steadily lost ground in the US over this period, with membership declining from a peak of about 35 percent in the early 1950s to a low of 11 percent in 1995 (Kuttner 1997, 98-100). At the same time, and not coincidentally, but rather stemming from the same cause, government action also increasingly is disfavored; in the name of a free market, deregulation, privatization and liberalization have proliferated. Government fiscal rectitude is celebrated, and government activity and the provision of public services is discouraged.

Viewed through an institutionalist prism, it seems evident that the least favored, most vulnerable groups increasingly are losing out. It is not true that the rich and the poor suffer equally when public services are neglected. The rich have the financial ability to opt out of unsatisfactory conditions. Acceptance of a neoclassical dogma that touts the free market as the panacea for all economic problems fosters the emergence of two societies, separate and unequal. There is little question that this has consequences for economic democracy.

The sections that follow pursue this theme in regard to several subject areas. The subject areas were chosen arbitrarily, others would have served as well. It will be evident that in each case, the definition of both problem and solution is strongly influenced by economic perspective. The question that engages us throughout, the underlying if unstated theme of each of these sections, is that of the appropriate role of the state in a capitalist economy. Should these matters be left entirely to the market, be handled entirely by the state, or is there some combination of market and state that should be utilized for these purposes? Neoclassicists see almost no role for the state, and even the minimal role that they traditionally have assigned it has been diminished with time. Institutionalists, in contrast, argue that while the state undoubtedly has a role in almost every type of economic activity, that that role must be worked out on a case by case basis, depending upon the problem. That is, they urge that these problems be approached experimentally, and that the solutions be evaluated on the basis of their consequences.

## THE NEW ECONOMY: DEREGULATION, ECONOMIC CONCENTRATION, AND ANTITRUST

In the neoclassical economic model, there is no more cherished policy principle than that of limitation of the size and scope of government. This canon takes pride of place over all others. Intervention by government in business is considered not only unnecessary, but also iniquitous; it breeds inefficiency, retards innovation, and prevents market forces from moving the economy in desirable directions. The existence of market imperfections is recognized, but over the years has become increasingly minimized as a problem. Natural monopoly is claimed to be less extensive than heretofore believed. Market flaws are held to be less formidable than previously thought. Attempts to cure market failure through government intervention must lead to end results worse than those wrought by imperfect markets, because of the potential for government failure; that is, the cure is held to be worse than the disease. Government failure has become the new catch phrase in the modern orthodox economic litany. Government failure is viewed as more common, more pervasive, and more detrimental than market failure. Determination by markets, even imperfect markets, has come to be widely viewed as preferable to control by government. It is maintained that market forces are sufficient to control deficiencies even in imperfect markets. This line of thought has been growing in acceptance for about the last half century. Increasingly, it is identified as the "new" and the only "true" economics. A policy of deregulation is an important building block in this line of thought.

### The Assault on Regulation

The regulation of industries serving in imperfect markets was viewed as an important governmental function from at least the time of the Great Depression until the 1960s. Beginning in about the late 1960s and strongly gaining ground into the 1970s and thereafter, policies of deregulation have been vigorously pursued and have found increasing favor in the US and worldwide. In the US, federal transportation was fully deregulated. In the natural gas industry, policies of partial and then full deregulation of pricing, entry liberalization, and open access for transmission pipelines were adopted. There was increased reliance upon market oriented tools such as negotiation and private contract in the natural gas industry and auctions in telephony. In compliance with these principles, the Federal Energy Regulatory Commission (FERC) separated the commodity and transport functions of natural gas, allowing end users to negotiate directly with suppliers. The Federal

Communications Commission (FCC) put the nation's airwave spectrum up for bid.

**Electricity**

In electricity, the 1992 Energy Policy Act (EPA) created a new class of producer to include both utility affiliated and non-affiliated wholesale producers, designated "exempt wholesale generators" (EWGs), so named because they were to be exempt from state regulation. FERC issued a series of orders aimed at the implementation of the EPA by requiring the unbundling of generation and transmission. Unbundling was calculated to create competition among generators and open access to the transmission grid. States also were heeding the call to deregulate. Characteristically, the state of California was a first mover on this, and California electric deregulation has become the most celebrated of the state electric deregulation experiments. California's recent experience with soaring prices, lack of reliability and rolling blackouts under deregulation has by now become well known. However, even before the worst of the troubles in California in 2000-01 there were auguries of things to come. Heat spells in the summers of 1998 and 1999 had similarly perverse, if less dramatic, results. At the time of the California electric deregulation climax about two dozen states were moving toward retail competition. The California debacle seems at least temporarily to have slowed the previously rapid march of the states toward electricity deregulation (Pearlstein 2001, 6).

Deregulation of these industries had been touted as a move that would result in lower prices, improved service, greater efficiencies, and increased innovation. Deregulation was equated with competition. It has become evident that deregulation and competition are not identical, nor even equivalent. In some cases, deregulation was followed by an initial burst of lower prices for consumers. But even then, the final result typically is a situation in which there are winners and losers. The winners generally include the new entrants and high users of the commodity or service. In virtually all of the fixed and transportation utilities, under deregulation large customers are courted with new services and discounted prices. Among the losers are the core customers who endure higher real prices and poor service.

In California and elsewhere, unregulated generators in electricity learned how to game the system (Pearlstein 2001, 6).[3] Recent evidence indicates that electricity traders such as Enron also were gaming the system, using ploys such as "round-tripping," that is, two players purchasing and selling the same amount of electricity from each other, and the creation of artificial congestion on transmission lines to increase revenues and manipulate markets (Pulliam and Blumenstein 2002, A1). Deregulated traders and marketers of gas and electricity were becoming increasingly concentrated, with marketers frequently the deregulated affiliates of natural gas pipelines and electric utilities (Trebing 2001, 397). Institutional economists long have pointed to the business practice of distinguishing physical assets and capitalized value of business, inflating the latter by the inclusion of such factors as "good will" and anticipated earnings, and thereby distorting the actual facts of the case, to say nothing of the signals to potential investors. Time and again history has proven institutionalists correct in this matter. The present is no exception. The important role played in partially deregulated electric and telecommunications industries by bloated balance sheets and aggressive accounting treatments of transactions such as asset swaps once again proves their point.

The California electricity deregulation experiment culminated in bankruptcy or near bankruptcy for the largest utilities in the state, and the eventual capping of wholesale rates. Enron also filed for bankruptcy, but not before it wreaked massive damage on consumers, employees and investors. Some of the other states experimenting with electricity deregulation experienced closing of plants and loss of jobs as a result of electricity price escalation. The resulting political upheaval led to the capping of rates in many of these states as well (Pearlstein 2001, 6). Free market advocates maintain that the problem does not lie with deregulation itself. Instead they claim that the problem lies with the design of the deregulatory scheme. In California, for example, wholesale prices were allowed to rise, while retail prices were capped. They maintain that if retail prices had been allowed to float, utilities would have been kept whole. It is probable, however, that had such a plan been adopted, the resulting political outcry would have been sufficiently intense, and the attack on deregulation sufficiently strong that the status quo could not have been maintained.[4] The lesson, if we choose to heed it, is the recurring one that the production and distribution of electricity and, indeed, of utility service in general, is a complex matter, and must be handled differently than are such matters in markets for fish or rutabaga.

### Telecommunications

In telecommunications, the 1984 AT&T divestiture left the seven divested regional Bell holding companies (RBHCs, also the Bells) in control of the local loop; that is, local service remained a monopoly. The goal of the 1996 Telecommunications Act was to rectify this situation and produce competition in local markets. This was to be achieved through the offer of the not inconsiderable carrot of entry into long distance markets by RBHCs in their home territories, but only after a demonstration that the RBHCs had opened their networks to competition. It was anticipated that this would provide the necessary incentive to ensure competition in local markets. However, amidst charges and counter-charges, by competitors that the Bells were engaging in stalling and delay, and that their asking prices for the lease of Bell lines was too high,[5] and by the Bells of cherry picking on the part of competitors, competition remains elusive. And cable did not effect the expected significant inroads into local service.

The result is that local service even today remains substantially a monopoly.[6] At the same time, service problems are mounting (for example, Blumenstein and Mehta 2000, A1; Jacobs 2000, R34). Telephone utilities have unique operating characteristics, including production in segmented markets characterized by different demand elasticities. These attributes serve to encourage price manipulation between customer groups and neglect of the investment base.

## Consolidation and Concentration

During this period of deregulation, and fed by similar convictions about the efficacy of market forces and the inadvisability of government intervention, a merger and acquisition (M&A) movement was gaining momentum. In transportation, a series of mergers resulted in the survival of only two Western and two Eastern rail systems. A similar merger pattern emerged in the energy industries, including mergers of potentially rivalrous electric and gas companies. The trend in mergers in past years has been sharply upward. For example, the dollar value of pending and completed mergers in the energy industries increased from $8.9 billion in 1994 to $312.5 billion in 2000 (Trebing 2001, 397). FERC has been generous in its treatment of mergers. Of the 29 applications reviewed between 1996 and 2000, conditions were imposed on operational control of the transmission network in only three cases, and limited divestiture of generation was required in only one case (Trebing 2001, 399).

The merger activity in telecommunications dwarfed that in most other areas for most of the decade of the 1990s. Telecommunications ranked in first or second place among all industry sectors in the US in its volume of announced merger and acquisition activities in eight of the eleven years between 1990 and 2000 (Blumenstein 2000, R4). A recent chair of the Federal Trade Commission (FTC) points out that the number of merger applications filed under the Standard Industrial Code classification for communication increased by almost 50 percent between 1995 and 1999. During these years, the total dollar value of applications increased eightfold, to more than $266 billion (Pitofsky 1999, 2).

In the process, the configuration of the telecommunications industry changed. The RBHCs, spun off as seven companies in the AT&T divestiture, are now down to four. Envisioned as potential geographic rivals, they are merging instead. Bell Atlantic combines with Nynex and acquires the non-Bell company GTE (and the new name, Verizon). SBC (formerly Southwest Bell) combines with PacTel and then with Ameritech. The long-distance and fiber optic company, Qwest, acquires US West. Only Bell South is neither acquirer nor acquiree. The result is a striking consolidation of power in local telephone markets. The four RBHCs control more than ninety percent of the nation's local phone lines. The power of control over bottleneck monopoly focal points is demonstrated by the fact that average phone bills for local service have climbed 17 percent since passage of the 1996 Telecommunications Reform Act (Young, et. al. 2002, A1). Competitive local exchange companies (CLECs) had been expected to provide strong competition to the Bells when the Telecommunications Reform Act was passed. Instead, today they seem fast becoming an endangered species. At the end of 2000 there were 330 CLECs, in 2001 this number had dwindled to 150 (Dreazen et. al. 2002, A1), and the outlook for those remaining is not favorable. Moreover, local phone companies are increasing their presence in long-distance markets (Young, et. al. 2002, A1), and this trend also is expected to continue.

At the same time, AT&T acquires TCI and MediaOne at a high cost and the incurrence of massive debt, and becomes, to all intents and purposes, a cable company. Then, continued loss of customers, earnings setbacks and plunging stock prices lead AT&T to a series of reorganizations. A recent reorganization breaking up the company into multiple parts just about ensures that AT&T will not be able to fulfill its dream of becoming the cable rival to and substitute provider for local telephony, and a one-stop provider of multiple services (Miller 2001, 389). Moreover, after several disastrous years of high debt and plunging stock prices, AT&T Broadband, AT&T's cable TV unit, was put into play for acquisition (Deogun and Solomon 2001, A1). Its purchase by Comcast appeared to end AT&T's "huge and costly foray" into the cable-TV business, putting it back to where it started—"a long-distance phone company with a declining business" (Young 2001b, B1). If the combination of AT&T and Comcast is approved as expected, it also will result in three companies controlling 65 percent of the cable business. In the years after 1996 when cable television was deregulated and consolidated into a few companies, cable television rates increased 36 percent (Dreazen et. al. 2002, A1). In each of these areas, there are fewer and fewer players, in possession of greater market power. These monopoly and oligopoly markets are characterized by price increases and severe service problems. Telecommunications is clearly a sector in turmoil. Moreover, none of the profound changes in the sector has met much, if any, regulatory resistance, or even received widespread public attention.

The centralization movement extends beyond telephony into related fields, spreading to the broadcast industries. Prior to 1995, networks were barred from engaging in both production and syndication; that is, they could not own the shows they aired. With the change in those rules, and subsequent mergers of networks and studios, networks may now supply themselves with programs. The rule change permitted the combinations of Disney and ABC, and Viacom and CBS.[7] Thus, Disney is able to supply ABC with programming, and Viacom to supply CBS. The restructuring of the broadcast industry permits the reconfigured companies to favor their own shows in terms of selection, placement, and cancellation, irrespective of the merits of the programs. This suggests that profitability will be allowed to drown out standards of newsworthiness, journalism, entertainment and culture; that is, that business is triumphing over industry. All of these developments, along with such additional events as the AOL-Time Warner merger, raise serious questions about how the combination of content and conduit will affect consumers. There is also the question of how it will affect the public interest requirement that the sources of consumer information be diverse and reflect many shades of opinion. A narrowing of sources and types of information delivered would make a mockery of the freedom of choice in the name of which this movement has been occurring.

There are impending signs that further erosion of current rules aimed at maintaining media diversity is imminent. The FCC now is considering changes to the rules that prevent a TV broadcaster from owning stations that reach more than 35 percent of the total US population. The changes also would end restrictions on the proportion of self produced content a cable company may offer on its system, and would eliminate the rule that prevents companies from controlling newspapers and TV stations in its market (Dreazin 2001a, B11). FCC limitations against broadcast networks' ownership of local television stations and the prohibition against cable providers owning in-market television stations are under attack in federal district court (Seiberg 2001, A19). There is little question that overturning rules such as these could set the stage for a new round of mergers and acquisitions in the broadcast industry. The relaxation of rules is an additional indication that the locus of control of information content and flow is narrowing and increasingly coming under the dominance of centralized power. Under such a new configuration it is difficult to envision how diversity will be ensured; that is, how, as information channels narrow down to a few powerful entities, availability to the public of diverse, unconventional and unorthodox varieties of speech and communication could not decrease.

## The Merger Movement

The utility industries are not unique in regard to merger activity during this period of time. The same phenomenon is evident in the wider economy. For example, in its report to Congress in April 2000 the FTC noted that the number of merger applications it had received had more than tripled over the course of the decade, from 1529 in fiscal year 1991, to 4642 in fiscal year 1999. It added that it expected the number to increase to even higher levels in the year 2000. The dollar value of mergers had shown a similar growth, increasing eleven-fold over the decade (Pitofsky 2000, 2). The FTC also reports upon the restraint that it exercises in its handling of merger applications. In its 1998 report it explains that the number of "problematic mergers" are small in relation to the total. Over the decade, an average of only 32 transactions per year were either challenged or abandoned. In 1997, 70 percent of all applications were quickly approved. The FTC had questions sufficiently significant to warrant substantive review in only 14 percent of the total, with unresolved questions warranting further review for only 4.5 percent of the total (Pitofsky 1998, 4). It is clear that government oversight over industry consolidation is being held to a minimum.

The merger phenomenon was both national and worldwide. Internationally, in 1996 the dollar value of M&A activity summed to $1 trillion, with an upward trend continuing thereafter. In 1996 alone, six of the transactions exceeded $10 billion, with more than 100 equal to or greater than $1 billion. The dollar volume of US 1996 M&As was nearly twice the dollar volume, and the number of transactions twice the number of transactions, as in the peak merger year of the 1980s (Lipin 1997, A1). In the 1990s, year by year, the dollar values of mergers beggar those of preceding years. Mergers valued in the tens of billions were becoming increasingly common. The AT&T-TCI and the WorldCom-MCI transactions were in the $30 billion range; the Bell Atlantic-GTE and the SBC-Ameritech transactions in the $50 billion range (Cauley 1998, A3; Mehta 1998, A3). The year 1999 saw $670.5 billion in mergers in telecommunications alone, more than twice the 1998 value of $296.7 billion (Blumenstein 2000, R4). The 1990s merger trend also differed from that in the 1980s in that the mergers of the earlier decade were to a large extent characterized by antagonism, as evidenced in hostile takeovers, corporate raiding and leveraged buyouts. In the 1980s, many companies also were taken over for their break-up value (Pitofsky 1999, 2). In contrast, the merger activity of the 1990s has been likened to the takeovers that created big oil, big steel and conglomerate auto companies in the beginning of the twentieth century (Wayne 1998, 2G), that helped to transform the American economy of that age. The merger activity occurring today promises to have at least an equal effect.

A number of possible explanations of the strength of the merger movement in the decade of the 1990s have been advanced, of varying reasonableness. Among these is the dramatic run-up in stock prices, making stock purchases or stock and debt purchases of companies, and sometimes of much larger by much smaller companies, a seemingly "cheap and easy" route to acquisition. This however seems more a facilitating factor than a causal explanation. Another reason advanced, somewhat curiously in the context of normal economic discourse and definitions, is the growing importance of the global economy. Companies, or so the argument goes, see the need to increase size so as to "compete" in an international economy in which they face large companies. This seems a novel definition of "competition," but there is little doubt that the leaders of many companies see a certain logic to the claim. In any event, it appears more justification than explanation. An additional attempt at explanation of even less credibility is that the merger movement was caused by deregulation, that it was the "shock of deregulation" that led to the merger movement (Andrade, et.al. 2001, 104). This is a type of *post hoc, ergo propter hoc* logic that carries little conviction. Instead, it is more reasonable to trace each of these movements, that is, deregulation and the merger movement, to a single cause—the anti-government bias that has undergirded every aspect of our public life in recent years. The explanation of the strength of both the deregulation and the merger movements that in this author's view deserves the greatest weight is that of the new permissiveness of regulators and courts to the specter of concentration in this new economy. The willingness of regulators, legislators and courts in recent decades to overturn protective rules, and to accept unprecedented conglomeration, is palpable.

## Governmental Response

There is little doubt that there have been cycles in official attitudes about economic concentration in the US over time. This is evidenced both in court findings and enforcement agency actions. From the end of World War I to the late 1930s, mergers and consolidation were viewed quite permissively. Thereafter, in the wake of the depression of the 1930s, and continuing through the 1960s, there was antipathy toward economic concentration. But in the early 1970s, after a sustained attack by Chicago School economists and lawyers against "antitrust activism," there was another attitudinal shift (Kovacik and Shapiro 2000, 46-54). Courts and enforcement agencies increasingly began to rely upon the interpretation of market power found in the theory of contestable markets; that is, the ability of markets to behave competitively irrespective of market concentration. Contestability denies the importance of economic concentration as long as the potential for competition exists. The potential for competition is seen to exist if there are no legal barriers to entry and exit, irrespective of the technical and operational characteristics of specific industries. The simple removal of entry and exit barriers, therefore, is claimed to secure the benefits, even if not the fact, of competition. Courts and enforcement agencies changed their antitrust criteria to reflect a skepticism about a market concentration/market power relationship (Baker 1999, 181-3).

Until then, Section 7 of the Clayton Act commonly was used to block any merger that "substantially decreases competition or tends to create a monopoly." This was the "incipiency standard," the intention of which was to block market power in its incipiency. In practice, the incipiency standard was interpreted broadly. Starting in about the mid-1970s, the interpretation was narrowed (Salop 1987, 3). The new Department of Justice (DOJ) and FTC horizontal merger guidelines issued in the early 1980s added such variables as efficiency benefits and the likelihood of market entry to economic concentration and market share considerations as among those to be considered in antitrust proceedings. Potential cost savings of a merger were to be allowed to compensate for increases in market power (Salop 1987. 6).

A subsequent revision a few years later permitted even mergers that could be expected to increase price so long as significant cost savings could be demonstrated. The demonstration could take the form of a showing of increased economies of scale or technological advance (Salop 1987, 8). Antitrust activity took as a goal the achievement of "Chicago-style" efficiency —the fulfillment of static allocational efficiency with its focus upon wealth maximization and increased consumer surplus (Curran 2001, 3). It also was accepted that the "new competition" (potential entry) could hinder the exercise of market power, a notion clearly derived from contestable market theory (Baker 1999, 183). So supplicant-friendly had these agencies become that the specification in the new guidelines of the means by which companies could demonstrate that a merger will result in cost savings was characterized by a *Wall Street Journal* reporter as "a roadmap for making their case before the government" (Wilke 1997, A3).

Correspondingly, in successive reports to the Congress by the FTC, its members make repeated reference to the need to consider factors other than the affect upon competitiveness in merger proceedings. The Chair points out that commission analysis in merger proceedings, previously a matter of strict reliance on market share/market structure data, now must take account of many additional factors. Specifically, he notes that it is important for the Commission to recognize and give appropriate weight to "the potential efficiency effects of mergers." He adds that it is not necessary to reach the question of merger efficiencies unless the merger appears to pose a serious threat to competition, but when it does, it is necessary to take account of valid claims of merger related efficiencies (Pitofsky 1998, 5, 10). A commissioner testifies: "The potential for anticompetitive effects does not end the inquiry in a typical merger investigation. Where the potential for anticompetitive effects is a close question, the potential efficiencies generated by the merger must be considered. Cognizable efficiencies include economies of scale, integration of production facilities, plant specialization, and lower transportation costs. . . . In a close case, an agency may refrain from challenging a merger if it appears that the merger would generate efficiencies" (Thompson 1999, 8).

There seems little question that changing beliefs of decision-makers resulting in changes in rules and regulations is an important contributory cause, and perhaps the single most important cause, of the relaxation of antitrust activity by government enforcement agencies and the changed direction of the courts. This bears on issues both of regulation and antitrust. Chicago School economists had been pressing their case for decreased government involvement in business at least since the end of World War II. The poor economic performance of the US economy during the 1970s became Exhibit 1 in their brief; the result, it was claimed, of an excess of government involvement in the economy. The poor performance also gained Chicago theorists a willing, even enthusiastic, audience and lent credence to their anti-government calls for decreased taxes, decreased expenditures, deregulation, and tolerance of, even enthusiasm for, concentration. The new economics cautioned against interference with business integration. The "New Institutional Economics," one of the offshoots of Chicago economics and a leading branch of the new economics, claimed that business decisions about economic integration are made on the basis of minimization of transaction costs; that is, on efficiency grounds. Interference constituted an obstruction of efficiency. An increasing number of theoretical models of "government failure" were published in the economics literature. The stars were in alignment for a crackdown on government activism.

It is interesting to note that much of the deference given efficiency rests on a balancing of actualities against potentialities. When it comes to deregulation and centralization the increase in market power is real. However, any claimed increase in efficiency, or entry, or technological advance, or innovation is not. Instead, it is potential and quite possibly illusory. It may or may not come to pass. It also should be reiterated that efficiency as defined by neoclassical economics is static in nature—the allocation of scarce resources to their highest (that is, most remunerative) uses, the minimization of costs so as to maximize receipts. The doctrine of cost minimization also ignores the fact that costs and receipts are but two sides of the same coin. A cost to business is an income to its constituent groups—or, to use the current expression, its stakeholders. The reduction of the wage bill of the corporate sector is not an unmixed blessing for the economy as a whole. Nor does the static concept of efficiency speak to the broader conception of efficiency used in institutional economics; for example, the efficiency that results from the smooth and cohesive interaction of the economy, and the broad availability to consumers of essential network services.

There is little question that performance in imperfect markets is in general suboptimal, even by neoclassical standards. That is, by definition output in these markets is smaller and price is higher than in competitive markets. However, utility industries demonstrate additional distinctive characteristics that should command attention. They manifest such attributes as the existence of network and coordination economies, high up-front investment requirements, large sunk costs, a large proportion of joint in total costs, market segmentation with market-specific demand elasticities, and a large element of necessity in demand. Markets such as these are particularly subject to manipulation through such stratagems as price discrimination, cross-subsidization, and disinvestment in core, noncompetitive markets. And because they produce a necessary commodity, with no readily available substitutes, consumer exposure to exploitation is high. These operations require tough oversight and a skeptical attitude on the part of overseers, unlikely to be achieved in a milieu in which priority is given to the desirability of pro-market, anti-regulation attitudes and credentials in the very selection of regulators. In recent electricity and telecommunications cases, even such minimal oversight as would have been expected to be provided by outside accountants and investment and banking analysts seems to have foundered in the mire of strong conflicts of interest and insider dealings. The tendency has been to accept at face value the warrants of those who should be, because of the importance to consumers and the economy of the services supplied, subject to persistent challenge and high standards of proof.

This is not to suggest that regulation itself should not be subject to change in the face of technological change and resulting changes in industrial performance. These industries entail both monopoly elements, such as transmission lines and the local loop, and competitive ones, such as telephone equipment. But in addition, there are many gray areas. Although there are gains to be achieved by opening competitive elements to market control, strict oversight is required in monopoly markets and to ensure that monopoly power in these markets is not used to secure differential advantage in ancillary markets. This in itself will require experimentation. To make the blanket judgment, as often has occurred in recent years, that all markets are competitive, or potentially so, is foolhardy, and will continue to yield perverse results.

Official attitudes are based on interrelated climates of opinion and enacted law. There is little doubt that in recent years the favored proposals of the business interests that swell political campaign coffers (for example, Hamburger et. al. 2001, A1) have received both a sympathetic hearing and favored treatment in the corridors of power. In all of this, the big players are clearly calling the shots. Moreover, as oversight capabilities of campaign finance enforcement officials are reduced, also partly in response to the embrace of small government, the influence of those with deepest pockets increases. At bottom, preexisting economic dominance is reinforced, with economic position determined, not by natural market forces, but by relative power, wealth and bargaining strength. In a world characterized by pervasive market power, this can only be countered by matching power. As previously noted, only such strong collectivities as government or labor organizations have the potential to counter the monopoly strength of the organized corporate sector, but the strength and influence of both government and labor have declined. At the same time, the power and sway of business, buttressed by the neoclassical economic doctrine and the shield given by "friends in high places," has increased. That the responsibility for decision-making in our society has been ceded in so large part to powerful and unaccountable business interests bodes poorly for economic democracy.

## GLOBALIZATION

Globalization refers to linkages among and economic integration of nations with respect to production, trade and aid. That such linkages exist is not a new development; international connections historically have been present. The nature of the linkages, however, depends upon the standards and rules that govern them, and these evolve and change over the years. In recent years the US, in keeping with its "super-power" status and its superior bargaining strength, has been the predominant influence in rule setting for the World Trade Organization and multilateral organizations such as the World Bank and the International Monetary Fund. The US position in regard to the rules for such relations has been the same over the last few decades irrespective of the party in power and is sufficiently coherent to have been labeled the "Washington Consensus."

The principles of the Washington consensus are those that also have influenced US national policy. That is, they flow from ideals of economic orthodoxy and are directed toward goals of minimizing the role of government and maximizing market control, in this case in respect to international trading partners or aid recipients. The principles include such axioms of orthodoxy as: the exercise of fiscal discipline in public expenditure, decreased marginal tax rates, decreased government subsidies, liberalization of trade and of direct investment, elimination of capital and currency controls, a movement from fixed to market determined exchange rates, privatization and deregulation. (Mandle 2001, 31-2). The principles also favor granting a high level of freedom of action to multilateral corporations and financial institutions. The influence of neoclassical economics in shaping these principles, with their emphasis upon limiting government, reliance on markets, and independence of action for the private sector, is evident. Foreign aid agencies routinely insist that developing nations live out the fantasies of the developed world by conditioning aid on acceptance of these "consensus" rules and standards.

## Trade and Capital Mobility

The case for free trade is based upon the Ricardian free market model of comparative advantage. The logic of comparative advantage runs along lines of capitalizing upon differences, that is, of realizing the benefits of specialization. Trade is seen to occur because of exogenous differences in tastes, technologies or factor endowments. The theory holds that a production shift toward increased utilization of the factor of production in abundant supply in a country will allocate resources most productively to the benefit of all. It relies upon relative as opposed to absolute advantage, and is based upon the marginal productivity model. It goes without saying that in less developed countries unskilled labor is the abundant and capital the scarce factor. In this view, the result of liberalized trade, with production based upon comparative advantage, will be more productive resource allocation, more rapid technology transfer, wage increases for the abundant factor, economic growth, and convergence among industrialized and non-industrialized countries.

As with mainstream theory in general, free trade theory presents a supply side model. Macroeconomic measures to maintain economic health through full employment and growth are downplayed. Economic well-being is assumed to be the by-product of the free play of market forces. The model also is static. One purpose of economic development should be to *change* the comparative advantage of less developed countries. Permanently assigning these nations to positions of primary product providers will dampen most hope of true development, which markedly differs from mere growth. It is also possible that following a course set in accord with assumed market forces might actually discourage growth.

The relaxation of controls on international capital mobility is strongly advocated by the International Monetary Fund and the US Treasury and was adopted by many developing countries. External political pressure was not the only reason for the adoption of such measures. Developing countries also liberalized capital accounts to finance their increasing deficits and imports (Berg and Taylor 2000, 9-11). The experience of the developing world with liberalized capital movements has not been a uniformly happy one. So long as free trade includes the free movement of capital it often will be inherently unstable. Sudden speculative inflows and equally sudden and speculative outflows of capital have often led to recession and currency collapse (Rogoff 1999, 22-3).[8] Many of the numerous financial crises in the developing countries of the world have resulted from and been intensified by speculative activity (Palley 2001, 72).

## Economic Consequences

In many developing countries there is a repeated pattern of crisis, imposition of austerity measures by lending agencies, increased unemployment, decreased real wages, and decreased incomes. For example, a study of globalization and liberalization in nine developing and transitional countries found mixed results, but the data demonstrated in general that sustained growth was not the experience of these countries. Employment growth was found to be "slow to dismal," and an increase in inequality over previously high levels was the rule. Most of the countries studied experienced deterioration in both economic growth and social equity as an accompaniment of liberalization. Countervailing social policies that governments in principle could have put into effect were not adopted, possibly because the governments lacked the capacity to do so (Berg and Taylor 2000, 53-4). But in any event, the imposition of countervailing social policies also is discouraged by the dominant orthodoxy and rules of the game that call, if anything, for a reduced government presence.

Globalization and increased integration have had a number of additional side effects. In developing nations, the ability of multinational firms to move operations weakens the ability of host nations to ensure that the power of the firm over employees is not abused and that firms contribute their fair share to national welfare. However, technological progress in such areas as communications, information and transportation has increased firm choice of location. Developing nations are aware, because they are aware that the low cost of operations was the initial attraction, that attempts to protect employees, increase taxes or impose environmental standards could lead to decreased investment or relocation. In these nations, the potential mobility of the firms also gives them increased leverage in matters of national policy making (Mandle 2001, 26). The low wages normally paid impose poor living standards on workers with no favorable options, and their very lack of options often is proffered as sufficient justification for the low wage policy. Workers, it is maintained, have improved standards of living even at such low wage rates and poor conditions of work, than they would if these firms, and the employment opportunities they represent, were not present.

At the same time, in developed nations the increased firm mobility granted by globalization gives firms greater bargaining power over their domestic labor force, weakens domestic institutions and norms, such as trade unions and environmental standards, and erodes the financial foundations of social support systems (Rodrick 1998, 83-5). Employers in developed nations use measures such as threats of offshore transfers of operations, with their accompanying actual and threatened layoffs and outsourcing, as assists in a "race to the bottom" that involves downwardly spiraling wage structures, conditions of work, industrial standards and worker unionization and protection in general.

Developing countries obviously cannot choose whether or not to abide by the standards insisted upon by international lending agencies. The wish of the international agencies becomes command for the supplicants. They adopt the standards or the aid is not forthcoming. However, the standards themselves with their "tighten your belt" and austerity implications may well have harmful effects on the economies of these nations.

Globalization has led so far to an increase in the economic power of business in developed nations. The centralization and consolidation of business observed in the US in recent years occurred also on a global scale. There were sharp increases in multinational mergers, acquisitions and joint ventures. Yet, multinational corporations face even fewer constraints than do those that operate within national borders, even in the current era of relaxed national regulation. First of all, the more far-flung an operation the less amenable it is to oversight and control. Moreover, the defenses against abuse of business power that were attained at the US national level were achieved only after many hard fought battles over many years and do not exist at the global level. There is no Federal Communications Commission, no Federal

Trade Commission, no Securities and Exchange Commission, no Fair Labor Standards Board, and no antitrust laws in the global economy because there is no global government. Even in the attenuated and circumscribed state in which these protections now operate in the US, they afford a measure of protection absent in the international economy.

This is not to suggest that we should or could return to a golden era of pre-globalization. It is to suggest that economic growth and full employment in the nations involved must be a consideration for any global trade and financial system to yield reasonable results. Such a system need not be protectionist, but human rights need be given consideration at least equal to property or intellectual rights. More than at any time in the 50 odd years that have elapsed, when it comes to globalization and economic integration, the world needs the arrival of a new Keynes to formulate and articulate a reasonable system, complete with updated bancor, that encompasses such principles.

It is clear that when it comes to considerations of democracy and autonomy for the population at large, and accountability for powerful business interests, these are even less in evidence in developing nations than at the US domestic national level. This obviously is not a new development. However, it is troubling that the situation is not improving despite the avowed intentions of the nations of the developed world over many years. Intentions, however, need be translated into appropriate policy. The application of neoclassical principles of small government, market determination, free trade, and maximum freedom of action for large multinational corporations is unlikely to yield either economic democracy or improved conditions of economic life for the populations of developing countries. Moreover, the situation in the world economy is unquestionably one of a starkly unequal distribution of income and power. In such circumstances, it is the powerful players who make the rules. The great majority of the populace in the developing nations of the world will have neither acknowledged voice or opportunity otherwise to participate fully and meaningfully in their societies, among the more important conditions for democratic governance, until such time as redistribution of income and power occurs.

## CONCLUSION

It is common to hear talk of "command and control" economies, in pejorative reference to the former Soviet Union, or other Communist nations. However, the economic system that has taken shape in the US in the last quarter century is one of command and control of the direction of the economy and of the economic, cultural and social patterns of life and livelihood by a business elite and its political handmaidens. The policies that have been put in place during this period have followed closely the orthodox neoclassical agenda and its philosophy of individualism, market control and limitations on government activity. That ideas have consequences is demonstrated, if demonstration indeed is required, by the results of the implementation of these policies. At the national level, policies of deregulation and privatization have resulted in increases in corporate concentration and market power, adversely affecting the lives and livelihoods of the more vulnerable members of the society. At the international level, the result has been severe economic volatility and general deterioration from a status that was unpropitious from the outset.

John Dewey emphasized that evaluation of actions or policies must turn on their consequences. The standard of evaluation should be whether the policy solves the problem to which it is addressed and improves conditions of life and experience. The standard of evaluation employed by mainstream economists and the policy makers who follow their guidance is not whether policies solve problems or improve conditions, but how closely they adhere to model ideals. The success of a policy of deregulation is measured by whether legal entry and exit barriers have been eliminated; evaluation of a policy of free trade runs along the lines of whether trade barriers have been relaxed. In this view of things, adherence to the ideal of the model is an end in itself, irrespective of its consequences for the level and quality of life.

Dewey notes that freedom of inquiry, the dispersal of its conclusions and the ability to experiment are essential conditions of democracy (1991, 166-7, 65). He observes that policies for social action must be in the nature of experiments and thus should "be treated as working hypotheses, not as programs to be rigidly adhered to and executed." He adds that such policies should be applied only "subject to constant and well-equipped observation of the consequences they entail when acted upon, and subject to ready and flexible revision in the light of observed consequences" (1991, 202-3). Marc Tool similarly notes the importance to viable democracy of "a problem solving approach of successive approximations" (1998, 24). Conformity to an ideal pattern is the very antithesis of such an approach.

As noted above, John Kenneth Galbraith argues that in consistently removing the issue of power from its subject matter, orthodox economics "destroys its relation with the real world" (Galbraith 1973, 2). In the real world, the enlargement of market power has meant that the economic system increasingly is dominated by powerful corporations able to influence, and often to determine, the level and allocation of prices and costs, the amount and type of output, even consumer preferences and behavior. As institutionalists from Veblen to Galbraith and beyond have demonstrated, it is not consumers whose preferences hold sway in the market (consumer sovereignty), but producers who manipulate consumer tastes and preferences to determine the "what, how and to whom" of production. They also, by their ability to determine the "how much" of production (that is, their ability to withhold from production— Veblen's "sabotage") are able to determine the terms of trade. It is unarguable that powerful business interests who have the ear of public officials and policy makers also have increasingly dominated the political system, and therefore are able to affect, if not to control, the rules of the game.

These matters speak to the issue of democratic governance. The existence of market power bears on issues of accountability and responsiveness (Tool 1998, 14, 21). The imbalance in power removes for decision-makers—in this case, the business interests—the requirement either for accountability for their actions or for responsiveness to real world problems. As revelations of recent months have demonstrated, powerful players often are not required, or do not see themselves as required, to play by societal rules—rules about conflicts of interest and inside dealings are not considered applicable to those at the center of power. Moreover, powerful policy makers are able to exempt themselves from the incidence of their policies, an essential aspect of the correction of mistakes. If public services are inadequate, the rich provide for themselves privately. When public schools deteriorate, they send their children to private academies. If public transport worsens, they have easy recourse to private transportation. If public disorder becomes too great, they barricade themselves behind high, barbed-wire walls and barred windows. When public policing is inadequate to the task, they contract privately for protection. The poor have no such ability; they have no recourse but to experience the consequences of these conditions. Moreover, as the rich and eventually the middle class withdraw from the ambit of these services, the services tend to deteriorate even further.

If decision-makers do not experience the consequences of their actions, they do not recognize the existence of a problem, much less discern the need for a remedy. An increase in poverty or inequality seems unlikely to affect their lives except as improvement, as it serves to increase their personal wealth. Moreover, any such increase is justified according to the incorrect and misleading dicta of orthodox economics with its intimations of the need for the savings of the rich to ensure capital formation to maintain a prosperous economy. An increase in market power thus is explained as both merited and socially beneficial, contributing both to the economic product and the cherished efficiency norms of orthodoxy.

Extremes of power and wealth do not establish the basis for a viable national or international society. Rather, they explain much of the economic instability that we have witnessed during the last quarter century or so. They cannot fail to breed ill will and violence. They do not bode well for national or international political stability. A residence with barbed-wire walls and barred windows makes for an uncomfortable dwelling place, even for those lodged more or less safely behind them. Extremes of power and wealth have consequences as well for the moral tone of society. The powerful are able to set the rules and standards for those below them on the social and economic ladder who, in turn, perceive that they are controlled by circumstances they had no hand in shaping. Moreover, a society based only on rational (in an orthodox economic sense) self-interest in which individual effort is focussed only upon acquisition of increasing quantities of wealth, material goods and discretionary power over others is not only elitist and anti-democratic, and a breeding ground for discontent and disorder; it also will have lost all sense of community.

# NOTES

[1] The ceremonial/technological distinction made by institutionalists is a differentiation of distinct thought and behavior patterns. Thus, when referring to technology, institutionalists have reference to a means of reasoning from cause to effect, rather than to a collection of artifacts. In this context, technology is not a matter of nuts and bolts, but of ways of thought and behavior. Similarly, the ceremonial or institutional has reference to habits of thought and action based upon authority.

[2] Strictly speaking, Peirce identifies abduction, or hypothesis formation that seeks explanation for a phenomenon that is not understood, as the first stage of inquiry. Deduction and induction are identified as the second and third stages of inquiry. He maintains, however, that neither deduction nor induction contributes to new knowledge. "Deduction explicates; Induction evaluates; that is all." It is abduction that results in scientific breakthroughs (1908,70-71).

[3] As part of the California deregulation program, utilities were encouraged to sell most of their generating plants to unregulated merchant generators such as Duke Energy (Pearlstein 2001, 7).

[4] For example, average wholesale power prices were $12 per megawatt hour in mid-1998. In June 2000, they reached $120 per megawatt hour, and during a cold spell in November 2000, they climbed to $200 per megawatt hour (Smith 2000a, A1). In December 2000, the average price increased to nearly $300 per megawatt hour, and reached heights of $1400 per megawatt hour (Smith 2000b, A2).

[5] The Federal Communications Commission (FCC) has fined both SBC and Verizon for inferior service provided to rivals seeking interconnection to their networks. SBC has also been censured by the FCC for providing the agency with false information in connection with its

applications to provide long-distance service in some of its states (Young 2001a, B5; Dreazen 2001c, B6).

[6] Nevertheless, two of the RBHCs, SBC and Verizon, have been authorized to provide long distance service in several of the states in their home territories. To date, Qwest and Bell South have not yet been approved to supply this service in any of the states that comprise their home territories. Applications currently are in the works by the RBHCs to provide long distance service for additional states (Dreazin 2001b, A3).

[7] The Fox network is owned by News Corporation, and NBC by General Electric.

[8] The financial instability has been sufficient to evoke calls for reform. One measure proposed that has received attention is an international currency transaction tax (the so-called Tobin tax, named after James Tobin who originally proposed it) to be applied to all transactions involving exchange of financial assets denominated in another currency. The tax is proposed in the interest of decreasing financial instability by increasing the cost of and therefore decreasing the amount of speculation in international markets (Palley 2001, 70-71). Although it is possible that a Tobin tax could have the desired effect it is, of course, a piecemeal approach to the problem. Its effectiveness would be increased if it were part of a more general program of reform.

## REFERENCES


Andrade, Gregor, Mark Mitchell and Erik Stafford. 2001. New evidence and perspectives on mergers. *Journal of Economic Perspectives* 15: 103-120.

Baker, Jonathan B. 1999. Policy watch: Developments in antitrust economics. *Journal of Economic Perspectives 13:181-194*

Berg, Janine and Lance Taylor. 2000. External liberalization, economic performance, and social policy. Working paper Number 12, Series I. Center for Economic Policy Analysis (CEPA), New York: New School University, available at www.newschool.edu/cepa.

Blumenstein, Rebecca. 2000. Who's on first? *The Wall Street Journal*, September 18. R4.

———. and Stephanie N. Mehta. 2000. As the telecoms merge and cut costs, service is often a casuality. *The Wall Street Journal*, January 19. A1.

Bush, Paul D. 1993. "The Methodology of Institutional Economics" In *InstitutionalEconomics: Theory, Method, Policy,* Marc R. Tool, ed. New York and Dordrecht: Kluwer Academic Publishers. 59-107.

Cauley, Leslie. 1998. AT&T to acquire TCI for 37.3 billion. *The Wall Street Journal* June 25. A3.

Clark, J. Maurice. (1923)1981. *Studies in the Economics of Overhead Costs.* Chicago. University of Chicago Press.

Commons, John R. (1934) 1961. *Institutional Economics.* Madison: University of Wisconsin Press.

Curran, William J., Jr. 2001. Markets, morals, or wealth? Delusions of a standardized antitrust value. *Review of Industrial Organization.* 19: 3-18.

Deogun, Nikhil and Deborah Solomon. 2001. Cold call: Comcast bid gives AT&T breakup plan an unexpected push. *The Wall Street Journal,* July 10. A1.

Dewey, John. (1927) 1991. *The Public and its Problems.* Athens, Ohio: Swallow Press, Ohio University Press.

Dreazin, Yochi J. 2001a. FCC plans to ease ownership rules for TV networks. *The Wall Street Journal,* April 9. B11.

———. 2001b. FCC clears the way for Verizon to offer long-distance service in Massachussetts. *The Wall Street Journal,* April 17. A3.

———. 2001c. FCC chides SBC for giving agency false information . *The Wall Street Journal,* October 17. B6

———. Greg Ip and Nicholas Kulish. 2002.Why the sudden rise in the urge to merge and form oligopolies? *The Wall Street Journal,* February 25. A1.

Galbraith, John Kenneth. 1967. *The New Industrial State.* New York: The New American Library.

———. 1973. Power and the useful economist. *American Economic Review* 63: 1-11.

———. 1996. *The Good Society: The Humane Agenda.* Boston: Houghton Mifflin.

Hamburger, Tom, Laurie McGinley and David S. Cloud. 2001. Influence market: Industries that backed Bush are now seeking return on investment. *The Wall Street Journal,* March 6. A1.

Jacobs, Karen. 2000. Not at your service. *The Wall Street Journal,* September 18. R34.

Kovacic, William E. and Carl Shapiro. 2000. Antitrust policy: A century of economic and legal thinking. *Journal of Economic Perspectives* 14:46-52.

Kuttner, Robert. 1997. *Everything For Sale.* New York: Alfred A. Knopf.

Lipin, Steven. 1997. Concentration: merger wave gathers force. *The Wall Street Journal,* February 26. A1.

Mandle, Jay. 2001. Reforming globalization.*Challenge 44:24-38.*

Mehta, Stephanie. 1998. Bell Atlantic, GTE confirm merger plan. *The Wall Street Journal,* July 29. A3.

Miller, Edythe S. 1993. The economic imagination and public policy: Orthodoxy discovers the corporation. *Journal of Economic Issues* 27: 1041-1058.

———. 1998. "Institutional Economics and Eternal Verities: A Contribution to the Discussion." In *Institutional Method and Value,* Sasan Fayazmanesh and Marc Tool, eds., Cheltenham, UK and Northampton Massachussetts, USA: Edward Elgar. 130-144.

———. 2001. The impact of technological change on market power and market structure. *Journal of Economic Issues* 35: 385-394.

Palley, Thomas. 2001. Destabilizing speculation and the case for an international currency transactions tax. *Challenge* 44: 70-89.

Pearlstein, Steven. 2001. The disaster of deregulation. *Washington Post National Weekly Edition,* September 10-16. 6-7.

Peirce, Charles S. (1908) 1958. "A Neglected Argument for the Reality of God." In *Values in a Universe of Change,* Philip P. Weiner, ed. Garden City, New York: Doubleday Anchor Books.

Pitofsky, Robert 1998. Statement of the Federal Trade Commission concerning mergers and corporate consolidation in the new economy, June 16. Available at www.ftc.gov/os/1998/9806/merger98.tes.htm.

———. 1999. Prepared statement of the Federal Trade Commission before the Committee on Commerce, Science, and Transportation, United States Senate, November 8. Available at www.ftc.gov/os/1999/9911/telcomergerspitofsky.htm

———. 2000. Statement of the Federal Trade Commission before the Committee on the judiciary, United States House of Representatives, April 12. Available at www.ftc.gov/os/2000/04/antitrusttimony.htm

Pulliam, Susan and Rebecca Blumenstein. 2002. SEC broadens investigation into revenue-boosting tricks. *The Wall Street Journal,* May 16. A1.

Robbins, Lionel. (1932) 1984.*An Essay on the Nature and Significance of Economic Science.* New York: New York University Press.

Rodrick, Dani. 1998. Has globalization gone too far? *Challenge* 41: 81-94.

Rogoff, Kenneth. 1999. International institutions for reducing financial instability. *Journal of Economic Perspectives* 13: 21-42.

Salop, Steven C. 1987. Symposium on mergers and antitrust. *Journal of Economic Perspectives* 1:3-12.

Seiberg, Janet. 2001 Media links foreseen.*The National Law Journal* September 24. A19.

Smith, Rebecca. 2000a. California law shows how not to structure deregulation. *The Wall Street Journal,* November 27. A1.

——— .2000b. Regulators move to keep California utilities solvent. *The Wall Street Journal, December 22. A2.*

Thompson, Mozelle W. 1999. Prepared statement of the Federal Trade Commission before the Committee of the Judiciary, United States House of Representatives, July 28. Available at www.ftc.gov/os/1999/9907/electricityHR.htm.

Tool, Marc R. 1998. "Instrumental Inquiry and Democratic Governance." In *Institutionalist Theory and Applications,* Sasan Fayazmanesh and Marc R. Tool, eds. Cheltanham, UK and Northampton, Massachussets, USA: Edward Elgar. 1-29.

Trebing, Harry M. 2001. New dimensions of market failure in electricity and natural gas supply. *Journal of Economic Issues* 35:395-404.

Veblen, Thorstein. (1898) 1961a. "Why Is Economics Not an Evolutionary Science?" In *The Place of Science in Modern Civilization and Other Essays. New York: Russell & Russell.*

———. (1900) 1961b. "The Preconceptions of Economic Science III." In *The Place of Science in Modern Civilization and Other Essays.* New York: Russell & Russell.

———. (1908) 1961c. "On the Nature of Capital." In *The Place of Science in Modern Civilization and Other Essays.* New York: Russell & Russell.

———. (1921) 1965. *The Engineers and the Price System.* New York: Augustus M. Kelley.

Wayne, Leslie. 1998. Merger mania reshaping America. Reprinted from *The NewYork Times* in *The Rocky Mountain News,* January, 25. 2G.

Wilke, John R. 1997. New antitrust rules may ease path to mergers. *The Wall Street Journal,* April 9. A3.

Young, Shawn. 2001a. SBC has paid big penalties for service to rivals. *The Wall Street Journal,* August 8. *B5.*

———. 2001b. AT&T's long, troubled trip back to its past. *The Wall Street Journal*, December 21. B1.

Young, Shawn, Yochi J. Dreazin and Rebecca Blumenstein. 2002. How effort to open local phone markets helped the baby bells. *The Wall Street Journal,* February 11. A1.

# 10

# MARKET FAILURE IN PUBLIC UTILITY INDUSTRIES: AN INSTITUTIONALIST CRITIQUE OF DEREGULATION

Harry M. Trebing

## INTRODUCTION

There is a general consensus that public utility services are an integral part of the infrastructure of modern society. Typically, these services are provided by capital intensive networks that link centralized supply with a wide range of diverse customer classes—ranging from residential to large industrial customers in both urban and rural settings. These networks constitute the platforms that support all sectors of the economy and contribute to the productivity gains and income growth of those using the networks. In addition, when successful these network platforms facilitate the expansion of markets, thereby further increasing productivity, wealth, and the attainment of social goals.

Because of their crucial role, it is a fundamental requisite that these services must be supplied in an efficient manner that is responsive to consumer needs. Actions that are conducive to resource misallocation, inefficiency, or the discriminatory exercise of power must be constrained because of their adverse ramifications. Satisfying these conditions is a prerequisite for both advanced and developing nations if they are to participate in the information revolution and in the globalized economy. However, the proper form of governance for achieving these goals has become an intensely contested issue. The aggressive champions of free markets have argued that deregulation and competitive market forces will do a far better job of achieving efficiency gains, lowering prices, and assuring a better deployment of resources than any system of economic regulation or public ownership. Defenders of regulation have essentially fought a rear guard action, pointing to potential abuses but nevertheless losing ground as various levels of government have moved toward dismantling traditional regulatory practices.

In the year 2000, all participants in this debate received a major shock as a series of heretofore unanticipated corporate failures, collapsing stock prices, and disclosures of manipulative executive strategies created a new distrust of both business enterprise and the credibility of long-standing financial and accounting safeguards. Enron, the world's largest deregulated energy trader, collapsed in 2001 creating the second largest bankruptcy in US history. At the same time, there was growing evidence that Enron and the other major energy traders had manipulated and rigged wholesale prices, thereby driving these prices to unprecedented high levels during periods of peak demand. Across the board, those electric and gas utilities with deregulated marketing and trading affiliates suffered major declines in share prices. In telecommunications, the new long distance carriers—World Com, Global Crossing, and Williams—that had been heralded as the harbingers of growth in the new information age, appeared to be near collapse. World Com exacerbated its plight by fraudulently understating expenses to show profits instead of losses for five consecutive quarters ending in early 2002. This constituted one of the nation's largest accounting frauds. Overexpansion, flagrant merger and acquisition programs, heavy debt burdens, and a recession combined to drive both World Com and Global Crossing into bankruptcy in 2002. World Com had the distinction of surpassing Enron to create the largest bankruptcy in US history. Nor were the regional Bell holding companies immune. Qwest was particularly hard hit when its stock fell by more than 90 %, and the Board of Directors apparently demanded the resignation of its chief executive officer because of his highly questionable strategies. The once impregnable AT&T and major telecom equipment manufacturers also suffered heavily from these changes. The *Wall Street Journal* reported that the cumulative fall in share values for the entire telecom sector approximated $2 trillion with more than 500,000 telecom workers losing their jobs.[1]

For these energy and telecommunications firms, failure and bankruptcy resulted in massive employee layoffs and hardships, but apparently had little immediate impact on those executives who took advantage of earlier bonuses, stock options, and insider trading to garner great personal wealth. For the public, however, the safeguards were gone. Arthur Andersen had served as both consultant and auditor for Enron, World Com, Global Crossing, and Qwest, among others. On June 15, 2002, Arthur Andersen was found guilty of duplicity in camouflaging from public scrutiny the extent of these failures (C. Bryan-Low 2002, c-13).

Public policy is at an impasse. Congress is pursuing investigations but there is no consensus regarding the remedial steps that should be taken. Only the proponents of free markets still adhere to the vision of complete economic deregulation and privatization of publicly owned utilities. But there is growing disenchantment with such ideological solutions and at the same time there is equal distrust of traditional regulation. For many, "the regulatory guard dogs have become lap dogs" (Moyers 2002).

This paper will seek to examine the broad patterns of change in the telecommunications and electricity industries to better place these events in perspective. The deregulation process, the shortcomings of remedial steps, and the growing evidence of market failure and the exercise of power will be considered. Finally, an agenda for reform based on the long history of institutionalism's commitment to the public control of enterprise will be set forth.

## ORIGINS OF DEREGULATION

In the past telecommunications and electricity were supplied primarily by regulated private firms in the US and Canada, and by public enterprises in much of the rest of the world. Regulation took the form of extensive control over the rate of return on assets, the approval of new and existing investment, the approval of the firm's capital structure, control over the quality of service, approval of prices for retail sales, and control over the entry or exit of firms in the market. This regulatory process has been carried out by independent commissions deriving much of their data from uniform systems of account.

From 1945 to 1969, this system of regulation appeared to work reasonably well. Total factor productivity in electricity, natural gas, and telecommunications increased at an average annual rate that exceeded that of US manufacturing. After 1970, conditions deteriorated rapidly. Industry performance was adversely affected by the energy crisis, general inflation, cost overruns for nuclear power plants, rapid changes in telecommunications technology that created new pressures for entry, and chronic periods of under and over supply of natural gas that led to rationing followed by price discrimination. These changes culminated in retail price increases that created widespread dissatisfaction. Regulation was blamed for most of the evils that had taken place. At the same time, three powerful proponents of deregulation emerged. These included (1) large industrial buyers of energy and tele-communications who aggressively sought major price concessions; (2) new entrants who perceived significant opportunities for profits; and (3) a new generation of utility management that saw the utility as a cash cow that could support new ventures in lucrative deregulated markets.

The case for deregulation relied heavily on the implicit gains associated with free markets. It was argued that deregulation would create new profit incentives for efficiency as well as new forms of supply that would be superior to anything that had prevailed in the past. New entry would rapidly erode the market power of the incumbent firm and serve to limit profits to reasonable levels. As a result, market forces would put the most efficient infrastructure in place. Government intervention would consist primarily of steps to assure open access to networks. This would benefit all customers by giving access to more markets and increasing the total traffic on all networks.

Once deregulation had been achieved, proponents of free markets argued that these gains would be swiftly realized. New entry would be successful and rapid. Market dominance would disappear and new services and offerings would enhance consumer choice. Much of this enthusiasm for deregulation was also used to justify the privatization of publicly owned utility systems in other nations. The World Bank and International Monetary Fund aggressively promoted privatization supplemented by "light" transitional regulation.

There is no doubt that traditional regulation performed poorly in many cases, but this does not justify accepting deregulation on the basis of the hypothetical superiority of a purely competitive model. Rather, deregulation must be evaluated by an analysis of actual performance over the past 20 years or so to determine both its successes and its failures. This examination will also provide a far better insight into the determinants of market failure and the potential options for reform. Also, if an evaluation of deregulation were confined to positing the theoretical advantages of free markets over flawed regulation there would be a strong incentive to treat any examples of market failure as transitional aberrations that can be corrected simply by inventing new market-oriented solutions.

Telecommunications and electricity will be examined in terms of each industry's response to deregulation, followed by an analysis of the consequences of these actions.

## TELECOMMUNICATIONS' RESPONSE TO DEREGULATION

Telecommunications markets were liberalized in 1968-69 when new microwave technology created the possibility of alternative sources of supply and the Federal Communications Commission (FCC) permitted foreign attachments, primarily terminal equipment, to be added on the

AT&T network. AT&T's draconian response to the threat of new microwave entry led to a Department of Justice action that culminated in the 1984 divestiture of AT&T long distance and equipment manufacturing from the seven regional Bell operating companies that provided local service. The latter became the seven regional Bell holding companies (RBHCs). Between 1984 and the passage of the Telecommunications Act of 1996, virtually all legal barriers to entry were removed at the interstate level for long distance carriers. The regional Bell holding companies, in turn, would be permitted to enter in the long distance market only if they could demonstrate that they had opened their local exchange markets to competition. At the same time, privatization in the UK and New Zealand created comparable conditions for liberalized entry, while France Telecom (FT) and Deutsche Telekom (DT) were mandated to provide open entry beginning in 1998. The first condition for the free market had been satisfied—at least from a legal standpoint. During this period, merger and acquisition standards were greatly relaxed.

Proponents of deregulation were delighted to note that there was a wave of new entrants in both the local exchange and long distance markets. At the local level, more than 30 competitive access providers had appeared by 1993 and the long distance interexchange carriers (IXCs), competitive local exchange carriers (CLECs), and the cable industry threatened to provide local telephone service. In the provision of broadband telecommunications, a new rivalry appeared to be emerging between cable companies and the incumbent local exchange carriers (ILECs) offering digital subscriber line (DSL) service. In the long distance market three major firms prevailed. AT&T was the largest, World Com was the second based on an aggressive program of mergers and acquisitions,[2] and Sprint was third.

At the local exchange level, horizontal mergers reduced the original seven regional Bell holding companies to four systems and one of these, Bell Atlantic, acquired independent General Telephone and Electronics (GTE). Both the four RBHCs and the three largest IXCs engaged in significant overseas expansion.[3] AT&T created World Partners, AT&T and British Telecom formed Concert, and Sprint, DT, and FT created Global One. Concert and Global One were joint ventures to establish broadband international networks. During this same period there was a massive expansion of fiber capacity, growing numbers of mergers and joint ventures, and the rapid growth of wireless affiliates. This rapid expansion was enthusiastically supported by the financial markets in the belief that telecommunications was on the cutting edge of the information age and a major player in the new economy. Massive amounts of debt capital were readily financed facilitating mergers and acquisitions, and stock prices for both carriers and equipment suppliers hit astronomical highs. The old standard under regulation that the market price should equal the net book value per share (based on original cost) was gleefully swept aside.

The telecommunications bubble burst in 2000. In part, this was due to the recession but more fundamentally it was attributable to the failure of anticipated earnings to materialize for IXCs, CLECs, and equipment suppliers. A major causal factor was the failure of the IXCs and CLECs to reach the final customer without being dependent on high access fees or other entry barriers set by the RBHCs. At the same time, only a small fraction of the fiber optic capacity (perhaps 5%)[4] was being effectively utilized and the broadband market was not developing as rapidly as anticipated.

## ASSESSING THE TELECOMMUNICATIONS AFTERMATH

There are seven significant consequences of telecom deregulation. First, market entry at the local exchange level has been essentially unsuccessful in eroding the market power and dominance of the four regional Bell holding companies. These RBHCs typically retain 95-96% of the local exchange market and all systems including wireless are dependent upon the local network at some point. The threat from the CLECs never materialized. In fact, between April 2000 and April 2001, the stock prices of 28 CLECs and broadband carriers fell by 94%. The IXCs, including AT&T Wireless, did not fare much better, as their stock prices fell by 70%. The RBHCs, on the other hand, experienced only a 39% decline in stock prices over this period,[5] although Qwest's price continued to fall substantially due to its entry into precarious new ventures. Indeed, AT&T and World Com suffered badly. The heavy debt burden and failure to vertically integrate successfully have caused AT&T to undergo a voluntary divestiture with the spin-off of wireless and the eventual sale of its cable properties to Comcast,[6] leaving affiliates only a shell of the former giant. World Com was floundering badly before June 25, 2002, when the firm's internal audit revealed that $3.8 billion in expenses (primarily related to access fee payments to ILECs to reach final customers) had been capitalized instead of being treated as an expense, with the result that 2001 and the first quarter of 2002 showed a profit instead of a loss. The *Wall Street Journal* noted on June 26, 2002, that this "could be one of the largest accounting frauds ever."[7] The major wireless carriers also experienced depressed stock values.

Second, international collaborative efforts and joint ventures appear to have fallen into disfavor. Global One and Concert were abandoned as too costly or unneeded. Whenever possible, horizontal and vertical growth by the incumbent seems to be the preferred course.

Third, there has been a new shift in market dominance from the IXCs to the RBHCs. In the future, it is reasonable to anticipate that the RBHCs will engage in aggressive vertical integration as they seek to establish positions of dominance in both the traditional long distance markets and in the broadband market through the promotion of DSL. At best, the constraint of rivalry between the cable carriers and the RBHCs will take the form of duopoly in a given geographic market.

Fourth, competitive entry did not bring about new systems of supply using new technology. Teligent, which would have used fixed radio relay to bypass the local system, has gone bankrupt with the CLEC collapse. Global Crossing, which held the promise of new transoceanic use of submarine fiber networks, went bankrupt and, in many ways, replicated the Enron experience. The entry of Microsoft into cable through an investment of $10 billion in the major cable systems did not produce the hoped-for breakthrough in new technology that would have upgraded cable into a highly competitive supplier of all forms of media, Internet, voice, and data services (Buckman 2002, A-1).

Fifth, the number of complaints regarding poor quality of service increased significantly with deregulation. There is evidence that investment related to service quality has declined under the pressure to achieve profit goals.[8] Under traditional return on investment regulation no such incentive existed.

Sixth, so-called "light regulation" proved largely ineffectual. The FCC applied price cap regulation to the RBHCs, but this did little or nothing to control oligopolistic pricing strategies. Similarly, the FCC attempt to use resale of services by entrants or the sale of unbundled network elements to promote entry at the local exchange level has met with little success. New entrants simply could not get a sufficient market share to become economically viable.[9] Furthermore, the prospects for bilateral negotiation of access fees between major carriers to encourage interconnection and entry continue to be less than promising.[10]

Seventh, financial markets did not operate in a fashion that assured efficient resource allocation. Rapid overexpansion was followed by a harsh contraction that only worsened the plight of the telecom players. The equipment suppliers also facilitated overexpansion by granting credit to the CLECs and others to build capacity when the prospects of success were very poor. As a result, the equipment suppliers found that accounts receivable and inventories grew faster than sales revenues.

Apparently conditions of market failure in telecommunications have forced free market advocates to realign their arguments in order to support continued adherence to deregulation. First, market concentration and market power at the local exchange level are relegated to the status of a niche problem rather than an area of principal concern. It is argued that new technology and changing market boundaries require that a new frame of reference be established in which the relevant market involves both landline and wireless services as well as a greatly broadened market that includes local, long distance, and international communications. These factors are used in combination to minimize the relative significance of high concentration at the local exchange level and negate the "essential facility" or monopoly focal point argument as it is applied to the local exchange.

Second, proponents of deregulation criticize any effort at regulatory intervention to force open access to broadband capacity, whether provided by cable or ILEC, to allow competitors to reach retail customers. They argue that mandating open access will diminish the prospect of achieving high profits and therefore diminish the incentive to make new investments in broadband networks. For deregulation advocates, the preferred choice is to let the ILECs and cable systems go at each other in a head-to-head confrontation.

Third, deregulation proponents continue to call for across-the-board removal of price controls as soon as possible so that investment decisions will be driven by market considerations.

Fourth, the concept of serial monopoly is gaining respectability in telecom circles. It argues that current monopoly is transitory and that it will be eradicated by technological advance to create a new generation of monopoly that will also be eradicated over time. High profits and potential entry become the keys to success while direct regulation becomes the corrupting factor in this process of change.[11]

These arguments are little more than an apologetic that tends to ignore the structural changes and behavioral strategies taking place in telecommunications. A failure to intervene for fear of affecting profit expectations will simply reinforce already high levels of concentration and establish an even stronger basis for manipulative price and investment strategies designed to achieve dominance. At the present time, the only effective control of market power in telecommunications is the widespread prevalence of redundant capacity, particularly in fiber optics. But the classical solution to oversupply is merger and collaborative behavior on the part of major players – both of which are clearly anticompetitive.

## THE MOVE TOWARD ELECTRICITY DEREGULATION

The initial step toward deregulation came in 1978 with passage of the Public Utility Regulatory Policy Act, which opened the door to non-utility generation and pluralism in electricity supply. For the first time, new non-utility sources of generation could come on line. Pressures for further liberalization led to the Energy Policy Act of 1992, which was designed to promote the deregulation of electricity at the wholesale level. The Federal Energy Regulatory Commission (FERC) began implementation of the Act in Orders 888 and 889 (1996), which required the functional unbundling of generation from transmission to facilitate new entry into the generation field. This was a pioneering effort to weaken the vertical integration that had been a characteristic of the electric utility industry since its inception. FERC then issued merger guidelines in Order 596 (1996) to establish broad standards for comparing pre- and post-merger concentration. This decision included reli-ance on the Herfindahl-Hirschman Index[12] to set a numerical standard for permissible levels of market concentration. The transmission grid was generally believed to be a monopoly focal point, so FERC issued Order 2000 (1999), to prescribe guidelines that would promote independent action on the part of transmission operators to prevent overt discrimination against non-utility generation. It must be emphasized that functional separation was not the same as full structural separation of the grid and the imposition of common carrier status on the transmission network. Essentially, FERC took a step-by-step approach to implement the wholesale deregulation of electricity. It eschewed a comprehensive restructuring plan as was done by the Securities and Exchange Commission (SEC) in the 1930s.

State deregulation of electricity focused on the retail market; that is, sales to final customers rather than sales between generating and transmission-distribution entities. In 1996 California and Pennsylvania took the most dramatic steps toward retail deregulation. California created a power exchange to facilitate transactions between buyers and sellers and an independent system operator to manage transmission scheduling and pricing. Pennsylvania introduced a shopping credit, or benchmark reference price, that would facilitate consumer choice between rival suppliers. Both states promoted utility divestment of generation. By 1999, one-half of the states had introduced some form of electricity deregulation.

## ELECTRICITY'S RESPONSE TO DEREGULATION

The electricity response involved the creation of spot and futures markets for trading megawatt hours (MWH), which led to the creation of new traders, brokers, marketers, and resellers. The volume of trading grew at an exponential rate. The market trading of electricity as a commodity created much greater price volatility and a higher premium for risk. Estimates indicate that a given MWH could trade ten times before it reached the final customer. Such trading produced the highest degree of price volatility of any commodity traded on futures exchanges, far exceeding that of natural gas and oil. At the same time there was new entry into wholesale deregulated generation, and new entry into retail markets.

Deregulation also involved implementation of two additional corporate strategies. First, there was a substantial increase in horizontal mergers and cross-industry mergers. The goal appears to have been the establishment of a strong market base with the vigorous purchase and sale of generating and distribution properties. Electric utilities also created deregulated marketing and generating affiliates, acquired natural gas facilities, and formulated new holding company systems to take advantage of a potentially lower cost of capital through financial synergism. US utilities moved overseas aggressively, particularly into the United Kingdom, with a reciprocal expansion of privatized UK systems into the US.

Second, new pricing concepts were introduced. Incumbent utilities sought to shift the cost of deregulation to retail customers, particularly basic service customers. This cost involved so-called stranded plant and purchased power contracts that were perceived to be uneconomic in a deregulated market setting. The incumbent utility would seek to have these stranded costs shifted to retail customers through a surcharge on all sales or a surcharge imposed on all power transmitted over the transmission grid. The negative impact on potential competitors was clearly obvious since they would have to pay a surcharge to cover the incumbent utility's stranded costs.

Deregulation also introduced the concept of a market clearing price that would determine which generation units would be run. If a generator would submit a bid price that was less than the market clearing price, then that unit would run. If the bid price were greater than the market clearing price, that unit would not run.

Another aspect of pricing involved an attempt to protect retail customers during the transition period by establishing maximum retail prices called "standard offers." A low standard offer would constitute a form of limit entry pricing that would foreclose entry and assure the retention of customers. If a residential or small business customer were to reject the standard offer and purchase power from a new entrant, then it would be vulnerable to being dropped by that supplier during a peak period. In that case, the customer would have to return to the utility as the default supplier, but this service would probably require a higher price since the utility would have to contract for additional power during the period of constrained supply. Large industrial buyers of electricity could use their oligopsony power to negotiate price concessions. There is evidence that some utilities offered special contracts which tied the large customer to the utility for 6-10 years in return for a promise to match a lower price offered to other large buyers or a lower price offered by a new entrant.

## ASSESSING THE AFTERMATH OF ELECTRICITY DEREGULATION

It has become increasingly evident that electricity deregulation has at least six significant adverse consequences. First, growing concentration has permitted discretionary pricing behavior on the part of suppliers – particularly during peak periods or during periods of constrained supply.[13] The simplest form of pricing behavior has involved withholding generation by oligopolistic suppliers to raise price. For example, the number of power plants out of service in California in August 2000 was five times greater than the number that were out in August 1999. During the same general period (6/29/99-6/29/00), on-peak wholesale prices increased 9.7 times while usage remained relatively constant. A more sophisticated variant of this pricing behavior involved using high-cost generation to determine the marginal supply price for electricity and then earning economic rent on the more efficient intramarginal power plants. The last MWH offered for sale sets the marginal supply price for all sales and each supplier will participate in the economic rents on the basis of the spread between that price and the cost of efficient intramarginal capacity. Bidding the high cost units to establish a high marginal supply price became an obvious oligopolistic strategy. There is evidence of this practice in the United Kingdom over the period 1991-2000. (See UK Office of Gas and Electricity Markets 2000.)

The most intriguing form of deregulated price abuse appears to have taken place among deregulated traders in the new wholesale power markets. The collapse of Enron and internal Enron correspondence have produced fascinating insights into these practices.[14] Ricochet trades involved buying power in California at capped prices, moving it out of state and then reselling it back to California at higher uncapped prices. The so-called Death Star strategy involved scheduling fictitious deliveries over badly congested transmission lines in order to receive congestion relief payments from the California grid operator for diverting this traffic to alternative routes or simply canceling a fictitious delivery. Round-trip trades involved swaps between two or more traders to sell the same energy back and forth at the same price. The goal was to inflate revenues from trading without incurring any risk, thereby misleading investors about the size and liquidity of the market. It would also have the incidental effect of conditioning buyers to anticipate higher prices. The governor of California has claimed that these rigging practices extorted about $30 billion from the state.[15]

There is growing evidence that these trading practices have been carried on by traders other than Enron. Mirant, Reliant Resources, Dynegy, Duke Energy, CMS Energy, Williams, and Xcel Energy are prominent examples. Some of these were trading entities created by parent utilities. There is also clear evidence of manipulative trading behavior throughout the western states, as well as Texas, Michigan, and Pennsylvania. In Pennsylvania, the state commission's investigation of PPLCorp's trading practices focused on trading capacity credits. Capacity credits are typically purchased by distribution companies to secure generation capacity to meet future demand. But PPL had bought up the capacity credits so that a 4% demand increase left these distribution companies with no choice but to go to PPL and pay the higher prices. The mid-Atlantic wholesale market price increased from $5 MWH to $177 MWH during the first quarter of 2001.

Second, with deregulation there is no incentive to maintain traditional reserve margins. The standard for such margins has been 15%. In 1996 the reserve margin for the US was 18.9% and 15.9% for the Mid-Continent Power Pool (MAPP). For 2005 the US margin is forecast to be 13.4% and only 3.3% for MAPP.[16] This situation is worsened because with deregulation there will be a growing dependence on generating capacity from undisclosed sources. As a consequence there will be less coordination between generation and transmission planning which, in turn, can adversely affect reliability.

Third, the transition process created a variety of conditions under which gains could be transferred to the firm while costs were shifted to basic service customers. As previously noted, many commissions permitted the incumbent firm to recover stranded costs by assessments against retail customers. At the same time, when the utility sold its generation plant to new entrants, the sale price of these units significantly exceeded the book value by an average of 93.4% over the period 1996-1999. As David Penn notes, these premiums over book value in California were transferred to the parent holding company and kept separate from the utility affiliate which was pleading for a rate increase to cover transitional costs (Penn 2001, 10). This process of cost shifting will be aggravated whenever large buyers of power are able to negotiate concessions, thereby leaving residual customers to finance stranded costs.

Fourth, deregulation has not given residential and small business customers an opportunity to choose. Meaningful options are lacking if choice is measured by the number of customers who have moved to alternative suppliers. By late 2000, the number of residential customers actually shifting from the utility ranged from 1.7 % in California to 9.3 % in Pennsylvania. In many states the situation is worsened because the alternative supplier is simply the marketing affiliate of another utility. The number of independent suppliers has rapidly disappeared. All of these factors combined to severely restrict consumer choice.

Fifth, the questions pertaining to market concentration have yet to be addressed. FERC policy appears to lack focus in establishing merger guidelines. Over the period 1996-2000, the total value of the 29 mergers that took place was $358.6 billion. In only three cases did FERC impose conditions on the operational control of the utility's transmission network, and in only one case did FERC impose a limit on divestiture (at the request of a state commission).[17] Even though these mergers substantially increased concentration and undoubtedly produced a high Herfindahl-Hirschman Index, not a single application was denied because of the HHI test. FERC also continues to struggle with the problem of how to handle the transmission grids. Transmission access clearly holds the potential for restricting trading and new entrants into generation. There is an obvious conflict when the same holding company owns a share in a regional transmission organization while at the same time owning a distribution network as well as deregulated trading and generation affiliates.

Sixth, electricity deregulation has not created any major breakthrough in new technology. Combined cycle gas turbines were created by equipment manufacturers during the monopoly period. Since that time there have been no significant changes, nor have there been significant advances in environmental protection. In fact, green power, based on the deployment of renewable sources (wind, biomass, solar, etc.), will not be favored by deregulated generators or traders unless mandated to do so by law. This explains why 14 states have required utilities and other suppliers to provide varying quotas of green power for consumers in the future. There is little doubt that a deregulated market will contain a bias against high-cost renewables. Furthermore, it should be noted that the municipally owned power system in Jacksonville, Florida, has been in the forefront of developing green power from renewable sources (Fialka 2002, A-20). This initiative did not come from private, profit-maximizing entities. In passing it should be noted that one of the side effects of deregulation has been the elimination of state commission initiatives that dealt with demand side management and integrated resource planning. Both of these concepts were designed to promote an optimal mix of efficient energy supply, conservation, and generation from renewable sources.

## THE ULTIMATE CONSEQUENCE OF DEREGULATION: FLAGRANT ABUSE OF POWER

The following three case studies provide excellent examples of how management can strive in a deregulated environment to achieve market dominance and wealth. Enron, Global Crossing, and Qwest moved in a short period of time to attract virtually unlimited funding that could be employed in aggressive programs of acquisition and merger, entry into new markets, and the enrichment of top management. This process was accompanied by fraudulent representation of revenues and profits, insider trading, concealment of debt, corrupted or ineffectual auditing (as noted earlier, all three had Arthur Andersen as auditor), and political action to circumvent or manage government intervention.

Enron moved from a traditional natural gas utility in 1985 to become the seventh largest firm (based on revenues) in the US in 2000. It established a preeminent position in natural gas, electricity, broadband, water, and environmental rights trading. Enron was the major player in regional trading hubs, where it promoted price volatility and then introduced risk-hedging instruments to counter the resultant volatility. It also expanded overseas, acquired domestic utility properties, and sought to "brand" energy sales by creating New Power Holdings as a marketing affiliate. New Power would make sales directly to residential customers.

To keep this complex of operations moving forward, Enron had to overstate revenues and profits and understate costs and debt liabilities. This was accomplished through off balance sheet transactions, in-house transactions, and the shifting of debt to bogus affiliates. At the same time, Enron aggressively promoted deregulation of electricity and gas at state and federal levels, secured congressional exemption of its derivitive trading practices from oversight by the Commodity Future Trading Commission, and possibly made off-the-record representations to Vice President Cheney's Presidential Task Force on Energy Policy (Davis 2001, A-10). All of these practices would have been forbidden or disallowed under traditional regulation because a commission had authority to prescribe accounting standards, review new security issues and mergers, and disallow political contributions.

On December 2, 2001, the aggregate impact of Enron's activities led to its collapse and bankruptcy. The results of this collapse, which in large part can be attributed to the abuse of power, were far reaching. First, when share prices dropped from $90 to $0.23 per share, there were severe repercussions throughout the entire financial community as retirement and pension funds, mutual funds, and individual shareholders suffered significant losses. Second, residential and small business consumers were directly affected when Enron was able to sustain high prices through trading strategies in the wholesale power markets. These inflated prices translated into high retail prices. These consumers were also adversely affected when New Power Holdings abandoned service and forced customers to return to default suppliers. Third, Enron's collapse increased the risk of commodity trading and the final prices to all consumers. In fact, Enron's manipulation of spot markets had a highly detrimental effect on futures markets. Fourth, Enron's collapse has created a shift toward dealing with those traders who are affiliated with a parent company that has a substantial, tangible asset base. This will strengthen the role of major holding companies that have both marketing affiliates and major investments at all stages of public utility production and distribution. This will further enhance the attractiveness of market concentration. Fifth, the credibility of independent auditing was shattered, again increasing the risk premium associated with the trading process. The winners in the Enron collapse were clearly the executives who benefitted from exorbitant salaries, bonuses, stock options, and insider trading. As the *Wall Street Journal* noted on June 17, 2002, "Enron paid top managers $681 million even as stock slid . . . (in 2001) . . . up to Dec. 2, 2001 when it filed for bankruptcy-court protection" (Kranhold and Pacelle 2002, B-1).

Global Crossing was formed in 1996 to create a global, fiber optic, broadband network covering 27 nations. Global's first transatlantic undersea fiber cable was enthusiastically received. Financial markets responded by making massive amounts of debt and equity capital readily available. Global

Crossing's stock hit an all-time high in 1999, when the total market value of that stock was higher than that of General Motors. However, Global Crossing soon confronted the oligopolistic strategies of the incumbent carriers, notably AT&T and MCI, who countered with aggressive pricing and marketing practices. It was difficult to match the rivals' price reductions because of Global's heavy debt financing, which put a floor under its price structure. Global's share of the transatlantic market fell from 50% to 15%, and large customers began to drop out. Interestingly, large customers appear to place a premium on highly reliable telecommunications service as well as on price. Global Crossing sought to handle the problem by falsifying revenues and profits, pursuing more acquisitions, and applying heavy political pressure whenever possible to strengthen its position. In reality, most of Global Crossing's assets were essentially worthless goodwill that arose from the overpayment for acquisitions. As part of its acquisition program Global Crossing did try to stabilize its revenue base by acquiring the Rochester Telephone System. These efforts were in vain, and on January 28, 2002, it filed for bankruptcy. The same general pattern of winners and losers emerged, as in the case of Enron. Once again exorbitant executive compensation was much in evidence.

Qwest was formed in 1996 to aggressively create fiber optic networks. Qwest challenged Global Crossing in the search for attractive acquisitions, and it succeeded in acquiring US West (one of the four large RBHCs stemming from AT&T divestiture). This acquisition was described as "a trout swallowing a whale." Again, the goal apparently was to use the RBHC as a source of stable income and cash to finance Qwest's new adventures. However, Qwest never made a profit. As the *Wall Street Journal* noted, "If Qwest did not have US West, they'd be in bankruptcy" (Solomon 2002a, A-1). Like Global Crossing, much of Qwest's asset base was goodwill, which had to be written off. Qwest tried to rescue itself by further acquisitions and by making secret deals with competitors who would agree not to oppose its efforts to expand into the long distance market (Solomon 2002b, A-1). More important, however, Qwest made a desperate effort to improve its profit position by making massive layoffs of US West employees, but these reductions would translate into a denigration of basic service. Qwest's precarious position caused its stock to fall by 90% over the 12-month period ending in mid-2002. This was exceptionally poor performance for an RBHC, and it posed an additional burden on basic telephone customers by raising the company's overall cost of capital when it was necessary to invest in improved service. In effect, the costs of acquisition and rapid expansion were being shifted, insofar as possible, to basic service customers, while executives again received high levels of compensation.

These three case studies reveal the broad, negative ramifications of the exercise of power. It is totally incorrect to argue that the ultimate failure of two of the three firms demonstrates an efficient market and justifies deregulation. Instead, the development of infrastructure was jeopardized and resources were badly misallocated. Furthermore, the distributional consequences were worsened by falsification and manipulation so that the collapse in stock values, poor service, discriminatory prices, and increased costs fell disproportionately on the general public while the responsible executives captured considerable wealth. The SEC is currently conducting investigations, but if Congressional hearings and the press are indicative of the remedial measures that may be adopted, these will consist only of narrow accounting reforms and improved auditing.[18] What is absent is a recognition of the full range of steps that must be taken to curb the future exercise of power.

## AN INSTITUTIONALIST APPROACH TO REFORM

The confrontation between those promoting deregulation and those advocating some form of reregulation ultimately becomes a debate over the appropriate role for the involvement of the state in economic activity. This debate is, of course, not new. In the late 19$^{th}$ century, the basic positions were clearly set forth by Herbert Spencer and Henry Carter Adams.

Spencer argued that society will achieve the best possible results if everyone is given unregulated economic freedom to pursue individual action. This view was widely accepted in both Great Britain and the US by many persons, including John Stuart Mill. Although Mill added a note of caution that laissez faire was not a "doctrine of science," he still believed that laissez faire should be the general practice, and that "any departure from it, unless required by some great good, is a certain evil."[19] This tradition was carried forward by Arthur T. Hadley, for whom direct economic regulation was anathema and any intervention should consist merely of publishing information about public utilities and railroads so that rational individuals could make informed decisions (Hadley 1892, 142-145). Variants of this philosophy are clearly embodied in the policy prescriptions advocating deregulation as proposed by the Chicago School, public choice advocates, and much of mainstream neoclassical economics.

In contrast to Spencer, Mill, Hadley, et al., Henry Carter Adams focused directly on the need to create a purposeful role for the state in economic activity. He rejected both English laissez faire and the German concept of the organic state as guidelines, commenting that "The fundamental error of

English political philosophy lies in regarding the state as a necessary evil: the fundamental error of German political philosophy lies in its conception of the state as an organism complete in itself. Neither the one nor the other of these views is correct" (Adams [1887] 1954, 82). Instead, Adams strove to develop a "wholly different system of thought" for the roles of both government regulation and competitive action because he felt that each was essential to the development of a highly organized society. Furthermore, the goal should be to maintain a harmonious relationship or balance between state intervention and competitive action. The benefits of competition "can never be realized through the uncontrolled play of private interests" (85). Unconstrained competition will force moral values to the lowest level (or what today would be characterized as a race to the bottom); but it will also deny the public the benefits inherent in cases where monopoly organization yields the greatest efficiency, and it will also promote weak and inefficient government (89). With respect to realizing the gains of monopoly organization, Adams notes that a "well organized society will include no extra-legal monopolies of any sort" (104). Rather, society must be secured against the "oppression of exclusive privileges administered for personal profit" (104). With this protection it can enjoy "such advantages as flow from concentrated organization" (104). He classifies industries on the basis of constant, diminishing, and increasing returns, with direct state control focusing primarily on the latter.

Adams refined and applied his views on the role of the state throughout his academic career and long government service. As the first statistician in the newly created Interstate Commerce Commission, serving from 1887 to 1911, he was particularly effective in applying statistics and accounting tools in the public control of enterprise. Adams deserves great credit for developing the uniform system of accounts during this period. His accounting model would permit the classification and valuation of assets (primarily railroad property), the determination of operating revenues, the calculation and review of operating expenses, and the estimation of net operating income. This income could then be expressed as the percentage return on net assets to judge the reasonableness of the rate of return. This conceptual framework could also be used to disallow expenses and charges not properly assigned to the ultimate consumer. Over time, this accounting system created a valuable data base for the application of rate base/rate of return regulation. Private accounting was totally inadequate for this task and highly vulnerable to fraudulent manipulation. In passing, one can only speculate that if these accounting strictures had been applied to the new activities created under deregulation, much of the current scandal would have been prevented.

A number of regulatory economists built on the Adams approach. These included B.H. Meyer (1903), John R. Commons (1924), Martin G. Glaeser (1939, 1957), E.W. Clemens (1950), and James C. Bonbright (1961).[20] Collectively these institutionalists refined the public utility concept and the basic tenets of economic regulation. Regrettably, none of their work received recognition in the subsequent move toward deregulation and acceptance of pure market solutions.

Adams' search for a harmonious balance between competition and regulated enterprise is particularly important at the present time, but it is becoming increasingly difficult to define and differentiate between these sectors in the wake of deregulation. Deregulation has promoted massive concentration but it will be a major challenge to determine whether this concentration reflects inherent economies (Adams' increasing returns criterion) or a drive to achieve market dominance. At the same time, deregulation has produced a host of new entities that directly or indirectly affect price, quality, and availability of service. But again, it is difficult to determine what type of demarcation, if any, should be made between regulation and competition insofar as traders, resellers, brokers, merchant generators, and broadband suppliers are concerned. A question can also be raised whether non-price constraints on quality of service should be introduced for each of these activities. Nevertheless, all of these decisions will have to be faced in any program of regulatory reform.

## A PROPOSED INSTITUTIONALIST AGENDA FOR REFORM

The following proposal for reform begins with a definition of the network, then proceeds to argue for the full structural separation of that network. New responsibilities are imposed on the network to better monitor market behavior. Service obligations are also imposed on deregulated marketers, traders, and resellers. Finally, regulation should assume a greater responsibility for industry-specific planning to evaluate public benefits and costs and industry performance.

In defining the economic content and boundaries of the network it is not sufficient simply to define the network as a power grid, a pipeline system, a distribution plant, or a local telephone facility. These definitions are too static and far too limiting. Rather, a network should be envisioned as a commons, composed of a collection of services and activities that are provided under conditions where pervasive network and coordination economies combine to lower costs and improve functionality.[21] This definition of a commons stands in sharp contrast to the classic commons, which was typified by the term "tragedy of the commons" because that involved a communal resource vulnerable to over use, private exploitation, and eventual exhaustion. In the definition proposed here, full use of the commons will actually improve the overall performance of the resource. It is equally imperative that everyone have full, non-discriminatory access to the network since many of the attendant services provided are affected with the public interest.

A primary test for the existence of these economies, as embodied in a commons, is the ability of usage to reduce the real average and incremental costs for each service below those costs that would prevail if each service were provided on a stand-alone basis. Professor Glaeser's alternative justifiable expenditures theory can be readily adapted to determine whether these cost conditions exist (Glaeser 1939). The theory could be applied as follows: First, the direct (avoidable) cost of each service would be subtracted from the total system cost. This would yield the common/joint costs. These common/joint costs would be assigned to each service on the basis of the relative benefit which that service receives from being included as part of the network. The relative benefit is measured by the difference between each service's direct and stand-alone cost. Each service would then be assigned its direct plus its allocated common/joint cost. If this combined cost is less than its stand-alone cost, then pervasive network and coordination economies exist and that service or activity should be a legitimate part of the network. Where no such economies exist, then the stand-alone cost will be equal to or less than the combined cost of providing the service over the network, and there would be no cost-based rationale for incorporating the service as an integral part of a commons-network complex.

There is another advantage in applying the Glaeser model for it prescribes the revenue contribution of each service or activity. This is far preferable to relying on demand-based price discrimination to determine each service's contribution.

The next step is to establish structural independence for the consolidated network function. The network must be structurally separate and fully independent from those using the system in all matters pertaining to management, planning, pricing, and finance. The concept of structural separation is not new. It is embodied in the Commodities Clause of the Hepburn Act of 1906.[22] The network would continue to stay under regulation. Its prices would be cost based rather than market based, and it would typically have common carrier status.

The creation of an independent network complex would provide an excellent opportunity to monitor the strategies and behavior of all deregulated entities using the network. With reporting requirements established by the appropriate regulatory agency, the network could gather information on the gaming of supply, the adequacy of service by class of customer, average and marginal cost-price spreads by class of customer, foreclosure tactics, and the exercise of oligopsony power. This oversight would give the regulator a first-hand picture of the actual operation of highly concentrated industries. It would also constitute a major step toward correcting the asymmetric imbalance of available information that puts regulators at a chronic disadvantage. Each network would give comprehensive information by industry to the pertinent state and federal regulators. In defense of this approach it should be noted that the California grid manager was among the first to report the price rigging strategies of the traders in electricity in 2000-2001, while FERC was completing two investigations which led that agency to conclude that there was little evidence of abusive pricing practices. FERC has now introduced a third investigation based on more informative reporting from those directly involved (Benson and Lee 2002, A-3).

Regulated networks will, of course, be utilized by a wide variety of deregulated buyers and sellers. These include media and information providers, Internet systems, data processors, energy traders, marketers and merchant generators, natural gas producers, and others. These networks will also be used by both investor owned and publicly owned distribution systems. On the demand side, there will still be readily differentiated customer classes.

Some regulators and free market advocates will be resistant to imposing strong service obligations on supposedly deregulated suppliers for fear of restricting competitive entry. However, where reliability and continuity of service are crucial, the regulator must go beyond requiring a simple termination notice or some proof of financial integrity. There are far too many examples where non-regulated electricity marketers have abandoned service during peak periods, thereby forcing customers back on the default supplier at higher rates. Similarly, deregulated telecom entrants and resellers have frequently abandoned or denigrated service. All deregulated suppliers should be compelled to post a bond sufficient to cover any penalty or inconvenience incurred by customers because of abandonment of service, and to submit a prescribed accounting statement (covering a balance sheet and income statement) for the affiliate. By the same token, any deterioration in service should result in holding the supplier liable for a significant penalty payment to consumers continuing until the problem is corrected. Where no improvement occurs, then there should be provision for abandonment of the contract to supply service. A marketer that cannot satisfy these conditions is simply shifting risk and cost to the retail customer.

In those cases where consumer choice is minimal or non-existent, or where buyer aggregation is ineffectual, the network must accept responsibility for providing retail service. When low-income customers are denied service, then the network should provide subsidized service with these costs treated as a social overhead cost to be borne by all network users.

Finally, the regulatory reform process requires the strengthening of industry specific planning. Such planning would consider public benefits and costs, societal values, and overall industry performance. Public benefits and costs would include both market externalities and net societal gains associated with direct regulatory intervention in particular problems. An evaluation of industry performance would focus on network reliability, reserve margins, promotion of innovation—particularly in broadband telecommunications—and the development of renewable energy resources. It would also include an attempt to refine merger and acquisition guidelines.

Much of the industry-specific planning is necessitated because structural separation of the network *per se* does not automatically assure first-rate performance. There may be cases where vertical integration rather than structural separation will achieve a better capacity utilization, better forecasting, and better long-term capital investment. Similarly, there are cases where structural separation has led to a breakdown in performance and cost shifting to the public sector. British Railtrack is an outstanding example. When British Rail was privatized, Railtrack was given responsibility for operating the actual railroad network. Responsibility for operating the passenger and freight trains was given to 25 newly formed train operating companies. There were endless disputes between Railtrack and the train operators—with each blaming the other for deteriorating service and worsening safety. Railtrack finally declared bankruptcy on October 10, 2001, and the government was forced to assume responsibility for new rail infrastructure investment. This British model of structural separation demonstrates the continuing need for regulatory oversight and planning.

The establishment of effective merger and acquisition (M&A) guidelines is another area that must be an integral part of the planning process. With deregulation there has been a rash of electricity, natural gas, and telecommunications M&As, both domestic and international. These assets are being bought and sold with very little regulatory oversight. The problem of formulating M&A guidelines is complicated by the fact that the enhancement of overall efficiency of the network must be considered, together with the fact that M&As enhance concentration and market power. In cases where full structural separation of the network is achieved, this problem will be much easier to resolve. But where the network still remains an integral part of holding company systems, despite token efforts to disassociate network access or pricing from the whole assemblage of holding company activities, the task is much more difficult. Under these circumstances, the following questions must be satisfactorily answered: (1) Will the M&A enhance the overall net efficiency of the network system? (2) Will these efficiency gains be distributed in an equitable fashion? (3) Could these gains have been achieved through means other than M&As? Attention must also be given to the fact that growing concentration translates into dominance or tight oligopoly. W.G. Shepherd has been highly critical of the 1992 Department of Justice/Federal Trade Commission guidelines designed to maintain competition (Shepherd, Shepherd, and Shepherd 2000). He believes that they place far too much emphasis on potential entry and potential competition while dismissing a thorough study of the actual competitive conditions within an industry. Professor Shepherd would impose a 25-30 per cent limit on any market share emerging from an M&A transaction.

There are also measurement problems if the Herfendahl-Hirschman Index is used to evaluate concentration and market power. HHI does not typically reflect transmission access, physical constraints, the distribution of ownership of supply, cross-industry convergence, or concentration during periods of peak demand. It is also difficult to apply HHI where the service is provided by a deregulated marketer who utilizes the underlying network. An HHI of ownership of the underlying network would not pick up the tactics of a deregulated marketer who contracts for inputs, leases transport and distribution capacity, and purchases other network services to provide rebundled service. In effect, the marketer becomes a network manager with a strong incentive to block the entry of rivals, constrain supply, and raise price. Assuming that these marketers purchase inputs from diverse sources to serve a wide range of retail markets, it is extremely difficult to track market concentration for these vertically integrated contracting entities.

The actual practice of regulatory planning is a largely unexplored area. In the past commissions have focused on either case-by-case adjudication or rulemaking on specific problems that, in turn, strongly reflect a procedural process that may not include all affected parties or public concerns. Whatever planning has taken place has typically come from Congress or the Executive Branch with relatively limited input from state and federal regulators. One exception was the Wisconsin Advanced Plan (1975-1999). The Advanced Plan was introduced to integrate electric utility forecasting with the construction of transmission and generation capacity. Over this period there were eight planning cycles typically involving an estimation of need and an assessment of supply options. Interestingly, the latter included, in addition to traditional generation, expedited siting, competitive bidding, demand-side management or conservation, and renewable sources of power. In retrospect, this planning process appears to have worked well for Wisconsin until the passage of the Energy Policy Act of 1992. EPACT created uncertainty for the utilities and a growing reluctance to invest in new capacity. Faced with the threat of potential power shortages, the legislature chose to deregulate and rely on market forces. Clearly, the Wisconsin experience indicates that legislative action must build upon commission experience and that commissions must have the authority to implement the plan. It also suggests that regulatory planning should be held accountable by requiring annual reports to legislatures and Congress. This would assure that Congressional intent is based to a large degree on actual experience in the field rather than on lobbying pressures. Hopefully, these suggestions will assure that infrastructure industries will continue to contribute to growth and prosperity in the future.

## NOTES

1 The telecom bust ". . . has wiped out about $2 trillion in stock market wealth, losses which are dampening household spending. Billions more stand to be lost on defaulted telecom debt . . ." R. Blumenstein and Scott Thurm (2001, A1 and A6; see also J. Sandberg, D. Solomon, and R. Blumenstein 2002, A-1).

2 World Com's meteoric rise was the result of an aggressive acquisition program that included Wiltel, UUNet, MFS, Brooks Fiber, and MCI, among the 60 acquisitions. This program established World Com as a member of the long-distance oligopoly.

3 The RBHCs had a strong incentive to invest in overseas properties because they were foreclosed from entering the interLATA long distance market until they satisfied specific conditions designed to expedite open entry in local exchange markets.

4 The *New York Times* reported that over 100 million miles of optical fiber had been laid around the world from 1999 to 2001. "Only 5 percent of fiber in the ground is on." Accordingly, investment in fiber optic networks has declined sharply. In Europe, DT, BT, and others invested $125 billion to acquire licenses to provide advanced wireless services. In view of slow demand growth and potential excess wireless capacity, they are seeking to renegotiate license payments and share some wireless network costs (Romero 2001, A-1).

[5] Alabama Public Service Commission Docket No. 17821, *Generic Proceeding to Establish Price for Interconnection Services and Unbundled Network Elements, 2001.* These data were supplied to the author by Dr. Robert Loube, consultant, Washington, D.C.

[6] In December 2001, AT&T appeared to be ending its foray into cable TV with an agreement to sell this operation to Comcast for $44 billion. It had originally purchased these cable operations (primarily TCI) for $100 billion. AT&T Chairman C. Michael Armstrong would become chairman of the new AT&T Comcast. AT&T Wireless has been spun off as a separate company. This will leave only AT&T's consumer long distance business and a unit that serves business customers (Young 2001, B-1).

[7] *Wall Street Journal*, June 26, 2002, A-1. World Com's stock price fell from a high of $64.50 in 1999 to $0.83 on June 27, 2002.

[8] Robert Nelson has set forth a detailed examination of deteriorating quality of service after passage of the 1996 Telecom Act, with particular emphasis on Michigan's experience. Comparative RBHC data are also included. Measures include capital expenditures per switched line, percentage of dissatisfied customers, and local service repair repeats. Nelson recommends penalties for poor performance ( Nelson 2001).

[9] David Gabel notes that ". . . entrants incur prohibitive fixed costs that make it uneconomical for them to compete with ILECs. With a 10% market share, new entrants face unit costs nine times those of ILECs, while with a 20% market share new entrants face monthly costs 4 times those of the incumbents." He concludes that the 1996 Telecom Act has failed to promote competition in local telecom services and that public policy should continue to rely on traditional regulation of ILECs for the foreseeable future (Gabel 2002, 5).

[10] Bilateral bargaining suffers from a number of problems. Interconnection with a competitive incumbent gives the incumbent control over a portion of the entrant's cost of service thereby placing the entrant at a disadvantage. Also, any loss of market share will jeopardize the incumbent's profits and make entry foreclosure a preferred strategy. Since each party's net gains will be severely impacted, a joint profit maximizing price for access and interconnection will be difficult to both determine and implement.

[11] For a defense of continued reliance on market forces and a discussion of serial monopoly, see Faulhaber (2002, especially 17-22). The relationship of serial monopoly to Schumpeterian change is clearly evident.

[12] The Herfindahl-Hirschman Index (HHI) is a measure of market concentration. It is calculated by obtaining the market share of each firm, squaring that market share, and adding together all of the squared market shares. The HHI indicates substantial market power when the value is above the range of 1800-2000. The Index will be affected by the number of firms and the absolute share of each firm. Fewer firms and higher shares will increase the Index. The HHI does not directly consider demand elasticity and conditions of entry.

[13] Although there is evidence of retail price increases by selected regions and markets with deregulation, a definitive study of the impact on the average retail price of electricity cannot be made at this time because many of the transitional programs carry interim price caps. Experience in wholesale, deregulated markets provides better evidence of deregulated price behavior.

[14] For a general description of trading tactics, see Kahn (2002a). For FERC's disclosure order on energy trades, see R. Oppel 2002. For the spread of these trading practices to other states, see Kahn (2002b). For unsuccessful attempt to apply these trading practices to broadband telecom capacity, see Barboza (2002).

[15] See Kahn (2002a&b). These trading practices were also accompanied by rolling blackouts and stage 3 emergencies. Mention should also be made of the alleged strategy of Perot Systems Corp. Perot helped build the computer backbone of the state's trading market, but critics charge that Perot then distributed a guide to traders so they could find loopholes in the system to drive up prices. See Benson and Thurm (2002, A-3).

[16] Worsening reserve margins and deteriorating reliability are outlined by geographic regions in North American Electric Reliability Council (1998).

[17] Compiled from data supplied by Diane Moody, director of Statistical Analysis, American Public Power Association, Washington, D.C.

[18] For representative samples, see *Wall Street Journal* articles: Pulliam and Blumenstein (2002, A-1); Hamburger, Hill, and Schroeder (2002, A-8); Kranhold, Wartzman, and Wilke (2002, A-1).

[19] See: J.S. Mill, *Principles of Political Economy,* Book V ch. XI, Sec. 7. Herbert Spencer is discussed in Dorfman (see References: Adams, Henry Carter).

[20] For an extended discussion of the work of these economists, see Trebing (1994, 200-210). A common characteristic of this group was a belief in the continuing need to review public policy and regulatory institutions. That same spirit is embodied in contemporary institutionalists. As Edythe S. Miller has observed, "Regulation is no more constant than market power or technology; it must be changed to accommodate new realities" (Miller 2001, 390-391).

[21] Network economies typically arise from economies of scale and scope, joint production economies, access to pooled reserves, and access to routing alternatives. As a result, as network size increases the incremental cost of adding a service decreases and each service offered on a joint basis is cheaper than if it were offered on a stand-alone basis. Expansion of the network will also permit the interchange of product and service over a greater distance. In addition, technology can contribute to network economies by lowering costs. For example, Dense Wave Division Multiplexing greatly enhances the capacity of fiber optics. As one writer notes: "As technology evolves, you can add 4 times the capacity at one-quarter of the price" (Sender 2002, C-5).

Coordination economies arise from successfully matching diverse usage and demand patterns with a capital intensive supply network. It involves attaining high load factors, high diversity factors, and high capacity factors (or equivalent measures). Once realized, these operating economies will permit peak demand to be met with minimum investment, overall reliability to be improved, and network functionality to be enhanced.

These economies require a minimum firm size and a minimum market share. There may also be net externality benefits associated with network and coordination economies.

[22] The Reading Railroad wanted to exploit ownership of both anthracite coal properties and its rail system to exert market power over Eastern coal sales. The Commodities Clause required divestiture of the coal properties.

## REFERENCES

Adams, Henry Carter. 1887. "Relation of the state to industrial action," *Publications of the American Economic Association*, Vol. I, No. 6 (Jan.): 465-549. Reprinted and edited with introductory essay by Joseph Dorfman. New York: Columbia University Press, 1954. Alabama Public Service Commission. *2001. Generic Proceeding to Establish Price for Interconnection Services and Unbundled Network Element.* Docket No. 17821.

Barboza, D. 2002. "Energy trades echoed in broadband market." *New York Times*, May 17.

Benson, M. and Lee, B. 2002. "FERC widens its investigation into California's energy Market." *Wall Street Journal*, May 8.

Benson, M. and Thurm, S. 2002. "Perot Systems faces heat in California." *Wall Street Journal*, June 6.

Blumenstein, R. and Thurm , Scott. 2001. "Telecom sector's bust reverberates loudly across the economy." *Wall Street Journal*, July 25.

Bonbright, J.C. 1961. *Principles of Public Utility Rates.* New York: Columbia University Press.

Bryan-Low, C. 2002. "Foreman was last to be persuaded." *Wall Street Journal*, June 17.

Buckman, R. 2002. "Microsoft miscues turned TV foray into costly lesson." *Wall Street Journal*, June 14.

Clemens, E. W. 1950. *Economics and Public Utilities.* New York: Appleton-Century-Crofts.

Commons, John R. 1924. *Legal Foundations of Capitalism.* New York: Macmillan

Davis, B. 2001. "Chairman's deep political connections run silent." *Wall Street Journal*, November 29.

Faulhaber, Gerald R. 2002. "Access ≠ $Access_1$ + $Access_2$." Quello Center, *Third Annual Conference*, Washington, DC, March 26.

Fialka, J.J. 2002. "Florida utility finds it's not easy even trying to be green." *Wall Street Journal*, April 4.

Gabel, D. 2002. "Why is There So Little Competition in the Provision of Local Telecommunications Services?" Quello Center, *Third Annual Conference*, Washington, DC, March 26.

Glaeser, Martin G. 1957. *Public Utilities in American Capitalism.* NewYork: Macmillan.

———. 1939. "Those TVA Joint Costs." *Public Utilities Fortnightly* 24: Aug 31, 259; Nov.9,606; Dec.7, 733.

Hadley, A.T. 1892. *Railroad Transportation: Its History and Its Laws.* New York and London: B.P. Putnam's Sons.

Hamburger, T., G. Hill, and M. Schroeder. 2002. "World Com scandal spurs congress." June 27.

Kahn, J. 2002a. "Enron's many strands: the energy market; Californians call Enron documents the smoking gun." *New York Times*, May 8.

_______. 2002b. "Will it be California Redux?" *Wall Street Journal*, May 12.

Kranhold, K., Wartzman, R., and Wilke, J.R. 2002. "As Enron inquiry intensifies, mid level players face spotlight", April 30.

———. 2002b. "Will it be California redux?" *Wall Street Journal*, May 12.

Kranhold, K. and Pacelle, M. 2002. "Enron paid top managers $681 million, even as stock slid." *Wall Street JournaL,* June 17.

Meyer, B.H. 1903. *Railway Legislation in the United States.* New York: Macmillan.

Mill, John S. [ 1848 ] 1961. *Principles of Political Economy.* Book V, Ch.XI, Sec. 7. Ashley Edition. New York: Kelly.

Miller, E.S. 2001. "The impact of technological change on market power and market failure in Telecommunications." *Journal of Economic Issues* 2: 385-391.

Moyers, Bill. 2002. "Now with Bill Moyers." National Public Television broadcast. June 14.

Nelson, R.B. 2001. "Quality of Service and Open Access – A Complex Interrelationship,"Institute of Public Utilities, *33rd Annual Regulatory Policy Conference*, October 28-31, Williamsburg, Virginia.

North American Electric Reliability Council. 1998. *Reliability Assessment 1998-2007: The Reliability of Bulk Electric Systems in North America*, September.

Oppel, R. 2002. "Energy companies told to disclose offsetting trades." *New York Times*, May 22.

Penn, David W. 2001. "Convergence, Competition, and the Role of Publicly Owned Utilities," Fifth International Conference on Technology Policy and Innovation: "Critical Infrastructures." The Hague, The Netherlands. June 27.

Pulliam, S. and Blumenstein, R. 2002. "SEC Broadens Investigation into Revenue-BoostingTricks." *Wall Street Journal*, May 16.

Romero, S. 2001. "Shining future of fiber optics loses glimmer." *New York Times*, June 18.

Samuels, W.J. and E.S. Miller, eds. 2002. *The Institutionalist Approach to Public Utilities.* East Lansing: Michigan State University Press.

Sandberg, J., Solomon, D., and Blumenstein, R. 2002. "Inside World Com's unearthing of a vast accounting scandal." *Wall Street Journal*, June 27.

Sender, H. 2002. "Is Level 3 looking to acquire Global Crossing?" *Wall Street Journal*, April 9.

Shepherd, G.B., H.S. Shepherd, and W.G. Shepherd, 2000. "Sharper focus: market shares in merger guidelines." *Antitrust Bulletin* 45 (Winter): 835-885.

Solomon, D. 2002a. "Bad connection." *Wall Street Journal*, April 2.

———. 2002b. "States probe Qwest's secret deals to expand long-distance service." *Wall Street Journal,*April 19.

Trebing, H.M. 1994. "Public Utility Regulation, Institutionalist Contribution to." In *Elgar Companion to Institutional and Evolutionary Economics*, edited by G.M. Hodgson, W.J.Samuels, and M.R. Tool. Elgar: Aldershot England.

UK Office of Gas and Electricity Markets. 2000. *Introduction of the Market Abuse Condition into the Licenses of Certain Generator.* June.

Young, S. 2001. "AT&T's long, troubled trip back to its past." *Wall Street Journal,*December 21.

# 11

# THE ABUSE OF ECONOMIC AND FINANCIAL POWER IN THE NEW ECONOMY: HISTORICAL PATTERNS IN THE CREATION OF MODERN REMEDIES

Michael F. Sheehan[1]

*O' it is excellent*
*To have a giant's strength,*
*But it is tyrannus*
*To use it like a giant.*
*(Measure for Measure)*

## INTRODUCTION

Since well before the time of Hobbes, it has been accepted that one of the major functions of government is to protect the general society from abuses by predators, whether they be common criminals or the more well dressed users and abusers of monopoly power. The typical response of the predators to the imposition of government controls on their activities is to claim that the government is infringing on their fundamental free enterprise right to prey on their neighbors. With the great changes in the American economy arising in the period from the end of the Civil War to the present, the issue has become more pressing. The increase in the size of industrial, commercial, banking, and utility markets has led to the organization of combinations for the very purpose of extracting monopoly rents from competitors, property owners and consumers. The management of these enterprises justify their behavior on the grounds of natural law, Social Darwinism, laissez faire, and Neoclassical and Chicago School economics.

The targets and victims of this abuse have not been content to go quietly and have actively responded, from the time of the Granger Movement onward, with efforts to control these abuses through state and federal legislation. To understand the dynamics of antitrust activity in the New

Economy, it is necessary to comprehend the evolution of monopoly power and abuse in the US, the evolution of the responses to these problems, and the efficacy of the latter in controlling the former in the context of specific historical patterns. It would be a mistake to attempt to understand the historical development leading up to our present circumstances in comparative static terms, and indeed a comparative static approach, where 150 years of facts are heaped up on the floor and analyzed as if they had happened simultaneously, opens the history of the evolution of antitrust to the charge of being contradictory and disorganized.

This paper provides an evolutionary perspective on the monopoly abuses found at each of the several important stages of our national history and how previous generations of Americans have dealt with these abuses and the abusers. With the arrival of the 1990s and the challenges of this generation's particular "New Economy," there is a need to review both the status of new and continuing monopoly abuses and the toolbox of remedies crafted by past generations to assist in arriving at a reasoned judgment as to the character of the problem now and how best to deal with it.

## THE PROBLEM STATED

In 1925, in his *Social Control of Business*, John Maurice Clark wrote:

> The costs of industry have two different aspects or dimensions: the financial expense borne by the business enterprise, and the sum total of the burdens ultimately falling on everyone in the community as a result of the operations which this enterprise carries on. The latter consist ultimately of sacrifices incurred by human beings or damages suffered by them.
>
> [T]he efficacy of private enterprise as a system for producing a maximum of valuable things at a minimum true cost to the community depends in no small degree on how well the financial expenses [of the business] serve their purpose as representatives of the true costs. . . . And this depends in turn, more than anything else, on the quality and completeness of the system of law under which industrial processes are carried on. . . .Thus, in one way or another, the law plays a vital part in determining whether private enterprise is to be predatory and socially wasteful to an inordinate degree, or whether it is to be in the main serviceable and socially efficient (Clark 1939, 108-9).

Veblen, Commons and many others have demonstrated that while the economy is primarily composed of productive forces characterized by the spirit of workmanship, common sense and technological advance, these are always opposed by parasitic forces that diminish the productivity of the economy and the public's welfare through fraud, financial manipulation, abuse of monopoly power, adulteration of products, environmental contamination and a long list of other malefactions. (See, for example, Veblen [1904] 1932, 1918, [1921] 1963; Commons [1923] 1968). It is only necessary to review the daily newspapers in any American city to be regaled with the toll of fraud, theft, and mismanagement: e.g. Enron and the manipulation of west coast energy markets (with public losses in the billions), Enron's manipulation of stockholders and employee retirement funds, Capital Consultants' current saga of fraud involving employee pension plans (the largest in history), and Merrill-Lynch's payment of $100 million in damages for consciously misleading small investors, to name only four.

Juxtaposed to this perspective on the economy is the Panglossian view that there is a natural law that individuals acting in their own selfish interest, if left almost completely undisturbed by the state in their economic relations, will produce the best of all possible worlds. In this connection, much is often made of Adam Smith's comment that the businessman is, "[l]ed by an invisible hand to promote an end which was no part of his intention. Nor is it *always* the worse for society that it was no part of it. By pursuing his own interest he *frequently* promotes that of society more effectually than when he really intends to promote it" (Smith [1776]1937, 423. Italics added). Or as Alexander Gray puts it: "Such is the invisible hand whose intervention miraculously harmonizes the pursuit of gain with the promotion of the public good—the quasi-religious sanction of laissez faire" (Gray 1931, 146).[2]

Like the businessman, the churchman accepted inequalities among men as inevitable and desirable and maintained that those who had risen to the top were men of ability whereas those who had failed had only themselves to blame. 'God,' said Henry Ward Beecher, 'has intended the great to be great, and the little to be little.' He thought it a 'general truth' that 'no man in this land suffers from poverty unless it be more than his fault—unless it be his sin.' (Fine 1956, 118-9). Consistent with this is the classical/neoclassical position that the law should not concern itself with the distribution of wealth in the economy. For the elite nineteenth-century American lawyer, classical political economy was the best possible determinant of the rule of law. The best legal rule enlarged total social wealth, and the science of political economy provided the necessary instructions for making society wealthier. Explicit state involvement in the transfer of wealth was inherently suspect—because it made one person or interest group richer only by making another poorer. (Hovenkamp 1991, 4).

This world view was reinforced by the adoption of the trappings of Newtonian physics, emphasizing the belief that the economic world was essentially static, with the economy driven by its very nature toward a stable equilibrium affected only by local transitory variations. An example of this type of thinking can again be drawn from Adam Smith: "The natural price, therefore, is, as it were, the central price, to which the prices of all commodities are continually gravitating. Different accidents may sometimes keep them suspended a good deal above it, and sometimes force them down even somewhat below it. But whatever the obstacles which hinder them from settling in this center of repose and continuance, they are constantly tending toward it." (Smith [1776]1937, 58).[3]

H. H. Liebhafsky in a fine and colorfully written article describes the evolution of the classical and neoclassical thought on this point: "Eighteenth-century mystical (supernatural) natural law theories such as those of Blackstone and Justice Story, which stemmed from Aquinas[4], today have been replaced by the mythical (supernatural) secular law theories of Friedrich Hayek and Ludwig von Mises. The latter's telling sentence, 'the reality of the laws of praxology [the science of human choice] is revealed to man by the same signs that reveal the reality of natural law' . . ." (Liebhafsky 1976, 240). There was of course a strong political and ideological component to this. The reality of the particular "New Economy" of the early industrial revolution in England and America was at odds with an assertion that all was well economically. There was vast poverty and exploitation cheek by jowl with stupendous riches and conspicuous consumption. The management of resources and especially human resources was especially deficient. The defense of this status quo and its vested interests called for a sophisticated economic justification. Newtonian economics together with natural law, laissez faire ideology and Aristotelian class theory became a bulwark against those who asserted the need for reform.

To summarize, the four main pillars of the classical-neoclassical model are that the economy and its outcomes are benevolent or at least as good as possible under the circumstances[5], the economy is essentially static, distribution of output is irrelevant, and finally that the natural law of the economic system propels it to a stable equilibrium, with only relatively small variations—as Newton tells us, *natura non facit saltum*—nature makes no leaps.

## THE INSTITUTIONALIST RESPONSE

Yet during the 19th century four major forces were coalescing to challenge the classical/neoclassical point of view and the economic and social structure it supported. The first was the work of Darwin between roughly 1840 (*Voyage of the Beagle*) and 1871 (*Descent of Man*). The second was the rise of the great monopolies—especially the railroads—in America after the Civil War. The third was the rise of a new political economics proposing and justifying better ways of managing the economy to increase production and minimize abuses. And the fourth was the expansion of the vote, especially after 1920 with the extension of the vote to women, which provided a voice to many of the victims of economic abuse.

Darwin demonstrated to social scientists that societies are not static and that there is no heavenly "form" of a perfect economy that naturally guarantees a permanent, unchanging, and benevolent viability. Evolution and adaptation to ever changing conditions are the keys to viability. Change, and not stasis, is normal, and adaptation is normal. Moreover, economic activity is often based on coercion: the liberty of the fox is the death of the hen; men enslave men if there is nothing to stop them. Darwinism represented a revolution in habits of thought. The whole way of thought characterized by the natural order preconceptions was gone, as evolution, conceived as an endless process of cumulative change, replaced the old static view of things. (Hamilton 1970, 25).

Adopting Darwin's insights, it was apparent that the economic system, as well, was characterized by ongoing change, sometimes relatively slow, and sometimes dramatic. Hunters and gatherers evolved into town dwellers, allowing specialization and the division of labor and leading eventually to the invention of the machine, the railroad, the automobile, the airplane, and the computer. It also brought times of booms and busts, plagues and the end of the buffalo, rural electrification and the environmental revolution, the rise of the labor movement and the women's movement, and the right to vote for the working classes of both sexes. Societies and economies move through time facing an endless progression of shocks and changes.

Institutional or Evolutionary economics (i.e., the Original Institutional Economics [OIE]) arose in this environment out of the need to provide society a frame of reference which would permit the conscious adaptation of the economy towards goals articulated by the polity. In terms of fundamentals, Institutionalists opposed the classical/neoclassical interests on five points.

First, society and the economic system are subject to continual change and evolution, and societies that fail to adapt, fail.

Second, the economy is neither static, nor "benevolent," nor does it tend naturally toward a stable equilibrium.

Third, evolutionary economists emphasized that economic relations were liable to be based on coercion and abuse if not checked by the legal system. John Gambs holds that the chief difference is the emphasis the institutionalist places on coercion. The classical economist, assuming that the economic universe was a harmonious one free from restraint and coercion, emphasized freedom of enterprise and individual self-help without interference. Gambs contends that the institutionalist views the economic universe as a coercive one in which coercion is brought to bear on those least able to protect themselves. (Hamilton 1970, 9).

Fourth, as should be obvious to every unbiased observer, it matters *who* gets the output of the economy. If producers are deprived of the fruits of their labor by the predatory practices of monopolists, then they will have less incentive to continue in production and will have to raise their prices to cover the cost of the additional risk. Price gouging by monopolists against consumers is just as much theft as if they were confronted by a man in the street with a gun. One of the fundamental purposes of society is to enforce minimum standards of behavior and prevent private oppression.

And fifth, the economy exists within the framework of the legal system and working rules, and can be improved in the public interest through conscious policymaking.

As Marc Tool summarized it:

> Economic and social change is in large part discretionary. Men and women, in the main, make their own history. Change is not predetermined by some technological force or phenomenon. Neither is change a consequence of fate or a mere dance of atoms. All structure is a product of human creation; all structural change is a consequence of human choice. The economic order is amenable to reasoned control; there need be no deference to impersonal market forces . . . . (Tool 1979, 164).

This change in approach provided the philosophical justification and the analytical foundation for reform efforts from the last quarter of the nineteenth century up until the present to control abuses in the American economy and subject economic operations to minimum standards of behavior and performance. Once again, as J.M. Clark put it: "Thus, in one way or another, the law plays a vital part in determining whether private enterprise is to be predatory and socially wasteful to an inordinate degree, or whether it is to be in the main serviceable and socially efficient. (Clark 1939, 108-9).

## THE GREAT REFORM CENTURY: 1865–1965

The economy is a vast, complicated, ever changing set of relationships among people and institutions, characterized and motivated by coercion and cooperation, need and greed, altruism and crime. As the economy changes, new opportunities arise, new abuses occur, and old institutions—perhaps adequate under earlier conditions—become inadequate and need to be replaced or revitalized to control socially destructive behavior and take full advantage of new opportunities. This evolution occurs in all areas of the economy.

At the beginning of this period, for example, the failure of cities to plan for sewage disposal and clean water produced a raft of deadly diseases and large loss of life, which we now know are and were avoidable. (Halliday 1999). It took a great deal of struggle against the vested interests to bring the major bacteria-based diseases (cholera, typhoid, etc.) under control.[6] Yet as late as the 1970s regulatory legislation, in the form of the Clean Water Act amendments to the Federal Water Pollution Control Act of 1948 and the Safe Drinking Water Act of 1974, was still being passed to deal with the chemical blight the profit maximizing private sector was so blithely and ubiquitously bestowing upon an unsuspecting public.

In the early 1900s, 62 percent of boys aged 9 to 14 were in the paid workforce, and children as young as six worked in the factories and coal mines, often under appalling conditions, often up to 80 hours per week, almost always at the expense of getting a basic education, and almost always at the expense of their health.[7] The battle to control the industrial exploitation of children seesawed back and forth as the states passed reform legislation, and the Supreme Court struck it down. The matter was only definitively resolved with respect to industrial (but not agricultural) labor in 1938 with the passage of the Fair Labor Standards Act and the US Supreme Court's decision upholding it in *US v. Darby*, 312 US 100 (1941).

Reform also confronted the ongoing industrial slaughter of the workforce. In 1914 industrial accidents killed 35,000 workers and injured another 700,000. It was standard for there to be no compensation to the workers or their families. Workers injured on the job and unable to work were usually fired. (Sheehan et al. 2000, 9).[8] Attempts to get judicial redress were generally unsuccessful, the courts having adopted various doctrines—e.g. the doctrine that if you were killed on the job, your claim died with you—to protect the industrial interests. (Friedman 1973, 415). And, of course, as long as the costs to the workers and their families of unsafe workplaces were not brought home to industry, industry had no incentive to eliminate the conditions giving rise to the carnage.

The problem was first addressed at the state level. Wisconsin was the first in 1911 to implement a workers' compensation act. It was drafted by one of the greatest of the Institutionalist economists, John R. Commons, and his students in 1911 (Friedman 1973, 587; Brodie 1963, 165). Commons also pushed hard for one of the first unemployment insurance acts in the nation (eventually adopted), and one of the first state health insurance acts, successfully resisted by the vested interests in the form of the medical establishment and employers (Dorfman 1959, 379-81). It was as late as 1970 that the federal government finally addressed the problem of accidents and disease in the workplace with the passage of the Occupational Health and Safety Act (OSHA).

Similarly, failure to have the proper mechanisms in place for the macroeconomic control of the economy led to the great, but avoidable, depressions of the 1870s, 1890s and 1930s in the United States. Reform legislation to control abuses in financial markets included the Securities Act of 1933 and the Securities Exchange Act of 1934. The Federal Reserve System was created by the Federal Reserve Act of 1913 and took its current form with the Banking Act of 1935 (Lovett 1984, 42-54).

Without the great progressive reforms of city government in the first part of the $20^{th}$ century our cities would still be cesspools of vice, corruption, mismanagement and incompetence.[9] Similarly, without the anti-monopoly reforms adopted from the end of the civil war to the present, Americans as consumers, producers, property owners, and people would still be at the mercy of those whose control of concentrations of economic power enable them to abuse and warp the lives of average people.[10] All of this clearly demonstrates two things: first, the economy, if left unchecked, does *not* produce anything remotely approximating the best of all possible worlds, and second, democratic action through public policy can result in substantial improvements in societal outcomes compared to laissez faire outcomes.

Having set the stage and provided the context, it is now time to turn to a brief review of the historical development of the monopoly problem and the efforts of reform to confront it.

## MONOPOLY POWER IN AMERICA

The rise of the monopolies in America, most notably in the period from the Civil War to 1900, burdened workers, farmers, consumers, and competitors with a pointedly abusive set of economic relations. Empowered by political reforms that expanded the franchise, abused communities learned to use political power to put in place state legislation to control the major economic abuses facing them as producers and consumers.

Notable in this period was the fight against the railroads and related monopolies by the Granger Movement which, within 20 years of the founding of its first grange in Minnesota in 1867, had 20,000 local granges around the country and close to a million members (Geisst 2000, 23). The Granges were effective in getting a number of state legislatures to pass regulatory legislation targeted at controlling railroad abuses.[11] The power of the monopolies and the lack of effective legal remedies led to a variety of abuses. These included price discrimination, price gouging, tying requirements (grain elevators), bad service, high accident rates, predatory abuse of competitors and the destruction of small or local business, stock flotation scams and other schemes against small or minority shareholders, and a generally high-handed approach to dealing with the public.

Price discrimination took a number of forms. Many of the railroads charged non-preferred customers or classes of customers sharply higher rates than preferred customers. Most notorious in this respect were the secret rebate agreements made by Rockefeller's Standard Oil trust with the railroads carrying his product. Under these agreements the railroads charged his competitors higher rates and then made a rebate to him of some of the difference, thereby providing him a tremendous anti-competitive advantage.[12] The railroads also engaged in price discrimination to give a competitive advantage to affiliated entities, for example grain elevators. This allowed those entities to undercut and eliminate their competition. To the extent that the affiliates were successful in this way they could be relied on to book all their business with the affiliated railroad at monopoly rates.

Price discrimination was also applied by product type. If the railroad determined that the product in question produced a higher mark-up for the manufacturer or shipper, then the rate would be increased, even if the *cost* of carriage were the same or less. This same mechanism is, of course, employed today by the airlines, which go out of their way to discriminate between those who have to fly and those who don't, using a variety of gimmicks including the requirement to book far in advance and stay over a Saturday.

Long haul/short haul price discrimination was a particular problem for farmers. As Hovenkamp has observed, "more often than not the rate differentials were far out of proportion to actual direct costs. They were outrageously different. . . ." But the biggest protest against short–haul/long–haul discrimination arose from the fact that short hauls frequently cost *absolutely* more than long hauls, even though the short haul was contained completely within the long haul route" (Hovenkamp 1991, 153). These discriminatory pricing abuses were often in addition to the exploitation of local monopoly power–especially in the rural areas–through price gouging: the practice of charging rates substantially higher, relative to the cost of providing the service, in areas where there was no competitive provider.

Predatory pricing was also a problem. Cornelius Vanderbilt, for example, would lower rates low enough and long enough to attract his competitor's customers and force the competitor out of business, and then raise rates back to previous levels or higher once the customers no longer had a competitive alternative (Geisst 2000, 22). Other predatory practices were widespread:

> The Bureau's [of Corporations] 1913 report on the farm implement trust concluded similarly that International Harvester, which manufactured

> several lines of agricultural machinery, had a policy of entering exclusive dealing arrangements with every available dealer in a community. Each dealer was given the right to sell a particular Harvester line, but forbidden from selling the machinery of competitors. The result, concluded the report, was that Harvester's competitors were denied access to adequate retail outlets for their competing products (Hovenkamp1991, 336).

This monopoly power got more intense after the great railroad consolidation movement, beginning in 1890, which resulted in the merger of most of the nation's hundreds of small railroads into six great systems (Hovenkamp, 147). Small railroads were faced with the choice of either joining one of the great systems or being driven into bankruptcy by one of the merged powerhouses. By 1895 twenty five percent of the railroads were in receivership. (Hovenkamp, 148). This theme of monopoly consolidation would continue with the further merger of the Union and Southern Pacific, and Burlington Northern and Santa Fe railroads in the late 1990s, and with ongoing mergers of the great cable television and telephone companies in the same period, all to the disadvantage of competitors and consumers alike.

The early fight to control the monopoly abuses of network industries, most particularly the railroads and somewhat later the utilities, is instructive. Early on, the Granger movement attempted to ameliorate these problems through state legislation that established state railroad commissions to set maximum rates. Some of these commissions were successful, and some were disasters in terms of performance (Friedman 1973, 390). The response of the railroads was to the federal courts, where they initially lost in the resounding US Supreme Court decision in *Munn v. Illinois* (1877), which upheld state rate regulation of railroads and related facilities (in this case a grain elevator) as "businesses affected with the public interest" (Friedman 1973, 393). This victory was short lived. In *Wabash Railway v. Illinois* (1886), the Court decided that states were not entitled to regulate rates of rail traffic which did not begin and end in the state. If regulation of traffic in interstate commerce was to be done, it would have to be done at the federal level. This decision added popular impetus to the creation in 1887 of the federal Interstate Commerce Commission (ICC) to regulate the railroads.[13] The ICC, however, was hamstrung when, in *ICC v. Cincinnati (etc) RR*, 167 US 479 (1897), the Supreme Court held that the Commission did not have the authority to determine rates or to prevent long–haul/short–haul rate discrimination, if such discrimination was "necessary to meet competition" (Friedman, 394).[14]

This sequence of events has become something of a standard. Local abuses by entities with market power are subjected to state level control through the passage of reform legislation. The entity then uses its influence to shift the locus of the issue first to the federal courts and then through federal legislation to federal regulators. Since access to faraway federal regulators is proportionally more difficult and expensive for small fry, there is a reduced chance of either regulatory litigation or political interference if the regulatory or legislative locus can be made more distant.

## THE ANTITRUST ACTS OF 1890 AND 1914

By 1890 there were two opposing movements coming to a collision. The 1880s was the decade in which the trusts burst on the scene, and by 1890 the popular furor was intense. The most famous of these combinations was Rockefeller's Standard Oil Trust created in 1882, with other industries right behind: cotton oil (1884), linseed oil (1885); sugar, whiskey, envelopes, cordage, oil-cloth, paving pitch, school slate, meat, and gas all in 1887 (Friedman 1973, 405-6). At the same time, the ICC and the state commissions turned in less than satisfactory performances controlling the railroad combines and the problem of price discrimination (Friedman 1973, 405-6).

Faced with these outcomes, the opposition to the monopolies turned to Congress for the passage of federal anti-monopoly legislation. Congress somewhat unenthusiastically complied with the passage of the Sherman Antitrust Act in 1890. The Act had three major provisions:

> Section 1: Every contract, combination in the form of trust or otherwise, or conspiracy, in restraint of trade or commerce among the several States or with foreign nations, is hereby declared to be illegal.
>
> Section 2: Every person who shall monopolize, or attempt to monopolize, or combine or conspire with any other person or persons, to monopolize any part of the trade or commerce among the several States, or with foreign nations, shall be deemed guilty of a misdemeanor. . . .(Arnold 1940, 299-300).

And Section 7, which—given the poor record of federal enforcement of the Act— was vital, in that it not only created a private right of action for injured parties, but also provided a heavyweight deterrent in the form of triple damages and the award of attorneys fees (Arnold 1940, 135-6). The Act, however, only dealt with horizontal combinations and not with "vertical" mergers and related abuses. The purpose of the Act, as described by Thurmond Arnold (the head of the Justice Department's Antitrust Division), writing in 1940 with the backdrop of the Japanese Zaibatsu and the great German cartels, was to "prevent one thing, and one thing only—the private seizure of power over interstate commerce" which "recognize[s] no public responsibility" (Arnold 1940, 107 and 110).

The Act took the stage at a difficult time. The greatest depression the country had known hit in the 1890s, with a low point at the time of the Panic of 1893; in addition, there was the great shakeout of the railroad industry where roughly 25 percent of the railroads went into the hands of receivers, along with the great railroad consolidation of the same period with several hundred railroads, as noted above, being merged into six great combinations.

Yet once again, efforts by the government to address these monopoly abuses, this time with the Sherman Act in hand, were defeated by the Supreme Court. Using the Sherman Act, the government had brought an action against the American Sugar Refining Company–a virtually complete monopoly—when it attempted to acquire its only major remaining competitor. In ruling for the monopoly interests in *US v. E.C. Knight Co.* (1895), the Supreme Court held that the Sherman Act's ban only applied to "commerce" and that sugar refining (and manufacturing generally) wasn't "commerce" (Friedman 1973, 407). This was a particularly felicitous escape for the monopolies. At the time of the decision in *Knight* a second more intense phase of the trust movement had begun with 3,268 mergers being allowed in the years 1895 to 1905 (Hovenkamp 242 and 410, n.6).

When Teddy Roosevelt entered the presidency in 1901, enforcement got somewhat more active. Notably, the government's record at the Supreme Court improved. In the *Northern Securities Case*, 193 US 197 (1905), the court held that the acquisition by a holding company of a majority interest in two competing railroads was illegal and the holding company was ordered dissolved. Also in 1905, the Court found in *Swift & Co v. US* that Swift had combined with other large packers to depress the price of cattle at stockyards to the loss of farmers, and to fix the prices of meat in sales to wholesalers. The government, however, never put more than minimal resources into the enforcement of the Sherman Act. At the time of the Teddy Roosevelt administration (1901-9), when trust-busting was supposed to be at its peak, there were only five lawyers and four stenographers in the entire Antitrust Division of the Department of Justice, and the enforcement effort was spotty and episodic (Arnold1940, 170).

Yet during the subsequent Taft administration, the government did bring to a successful conclusion the most famous of all antitrust prosecutions. The US Supreme Court's 1911 decision against Rockefeller's Standard Oil trust was the culmination of a ferocious fight spanning at least 21 years, and is a perfect example of the time, expense, and difficulty of exercising control over the abusive behavior of a nationwide and fabulously wealthy monopoly.[15] The case was initiated in 1890 by the Ohio attorney general in state court challenging the trust in a *quo warranto* action to rescind the corporate charter of Standard Oil of Ohio, the entity holding the other companies in trust.[16] In

1892 the Ohio Supreme Court ordered the dissolution of the trust and prohibited the owners of the companies involved from reconstituting the trust.

Unfazed by this decision, Rockefeller adapted his approach by abandoning Ohio and the "trust" mechanism for holding the shares of the 65 companies involved, and created instead a "holding company" under New Jersey law to do the very same thing with the very same companies. This worked for four more years until 1906, when Teddy Roosevelt's Antitrust Division filed an action against the holding company under both Sections 1 and 2 of the Sherman Act.

Another six years would pass before the US Supreme Court would rule against Standard Oil in 1911 and order the holding company dissolved, just 32 years after it began its career of monopoly abuse. The decision, however, was consistent with the Supreme Court's long established (and continuing) love-hate relationship with abusive corporations. Though the Court ordered the divestiture of the companies, it also substantially restricted the scope of Section 1 of the Act by holding that the Act did not really outlaw, "[e]very . . . combination . . . in restraint of trade" but instead only "unreasonable" combinations in restraint of trade. Naturally, it would be for the courts to decide what was reasonable and unreasonable thereafter; and what better to help them than classical and neoclassical economics, the sorcery of monopoly exploitation, with its elaborate justification for almost any abuse.

During this period there were three other attempts by Congress to deal with the loopholes opened in the Sherman Act by the Court and to deal with strategic adaptations by monopoly interests to get around the legislation. In 1914, during the Wilson administration, the Clayton Act was proposed to outlaw: price discrimination, where preferred customers were favored to the competitive disadvantage of others; exclusive dealing and tying contracts (Section 3), where those purchasing products from one entity had to agree not to purchase or offer the products of competitors; acquisitions of competing companies or their assets to the disadvantage of consumers (Section 7); and interlocking directorates, whereby monopoly coordination might be achieved among "competitors" through the mechanism of appointing the same individuals to all the boards of directors (Section 8).[17]

The difficulty was that while the House wanted to detail the abuses to be outlawed, the Senate wanted to leave that to the newly created FTC. In the end Congress kept the detail but added the phrase, "where the effect may be to substantially lessen competition or tend to create a monopoly," which once again complicated the burden of proof and opened a door for the entry of the neoclassical defenders of monopoly power. Enforcement of the Clayton Act was directed to the Federal Trade Commission (FTC), also established in 1914 by the passage of the Federal Trade Commission Act.

## THE NEW DEAL

By the beginning of the New Deal it was clear that the Neoclassical competitive model was defective as an explanation of, and justification for, events in the economy. It maintained its place in academe only because of the commitment of the majority of economics and business professors to the American business creed. It was, as Veblen described it, the alliance of the captains of erudition with the captains of industry (Veblen 1918).

The model assumes an economy populated by innumerable small firms, all offering the same standard product, all are price takers, all face a perfectly elastic demand; there is easy entry and exit from the market, and there are constant returns to scale in production. As many industries became highly concentrated, however, it became apparent to those without ideological blinders that these preconditions were no longer (if ever) met, and many important markets were not "competitive." This was upsetting to the vested interests. The Neoclassical justification for the free enterprise, unregulated, system—that produces the best of all possible economic worlds—collapses when markets can no longer be characterized as "competitive." Insights in this area gave rise in the 1920s to what Blaug (1968, 398) calls the "heated debate over 'empty economic boxes.'"

Another difficulty with the model had to do with the theoretical ramifications of increasing concentration. Given the focus in this period on the heavy industries of railroads, petroleum refining, steel, utilities, etc., it was becoming apparent that while increasing concentration could be at least nominally ascribed to economies of scale and cost saving improvements in technology, once there got to be a single firm or cartel protected by barriers to entry, even true believers were having a hard time arguing that the theoretical mechanisms of the competitive market would produce the desired outcomes. Monopolies and cartels would not set prices at marginal costs, nor could they be expected to vigorously pursue productive technological innovations in order to lower prices. These insights were captured by the profound and well known, but largely untaught and unread, works of Edward Chamberlin (1933) and Joan Robinson (1933) on what came to be known as monopolistic competition.

The perfect competition model as the ideological apology for the operation of the economy-in-fact further crumbled with the publication in 1933 of Berle and Means's *The Modern Corporation and Private Property.* Berle was a Harvard law graduate and had worked in Brandeis' law firm after graduation, and Means was a young Columbia University economist at the time. The book had a profound impact, as it pointed out variances between the model and reality and the consequences of the divergence. Adam Smith's small enterprise run by mom and pop with little fixed capital, had transmogrified itself by 1933 into vast corporations with large fixed costs, with managers and financiers in nearly absolute control, and with the great majority of shareholders almost completely passive in the governance of the corporation. The interests of shareholders (especially minority and small shareholders) were often at odds with the interests of the managers, especially when the corporation was dominated by, and yoked to the interests of, higher level financiers, such as the House of Morgan, which viewed its control over the individual corporation as simply a tool for maximizing its own profits. The logic of the competitive model was broken when the model's assumptions about the maximization of enterprise profits under the atomistic conditions could no longer be maintained.

Furthermore, Berle and Means demonstrated that to maximize the scope of their power, managers of the large corporation have tended to expand the corporation vertically. This has several ramifications, but perhaps most importantly vertical integration gives the corporation a means to impair the operations of its competitors. Companies A and B use steel in manufacturing. Steel production is dominated by Company C. Company A then gains control of Company C, which gives it the opportunity to interfere to its competitive advantage with the relationship between the steel producer and Company B.

The move to expand the scope and control of management by bringing in-house more and more economic transactions previously mediated through the market, also resulted in the corporation losing its sense of what inputs really cost. The corporation had gotten so complex and multifarious that the separation of costs and profits for each product became, if not impossible, at least purely arbitrary. "Competition between a small number of units each involving an organization so complex that costs have become indeterminate does not satisfy the condition assumed by earlier economists, nor does it appear likely to be as effective a regulator of industry and of profits as they had assumed" (Berle and Means 1933, 351). This point was illustrated in the Microsoft trial by the testimony of Richard Schmalensee, Microsoft's main economics witness. "Persistent high profitability, a characteristic of Microsoft through most of the 1990s, was recognized by Microsoft's economic expert at trial, Professor Richard Schmalensee, as a 'good indicator of long run power.' When confronted in cross examination concerning Microsoft's profits on operating system sales, Schmalensee had to confess he did not know what they might be because Microsoft's accounting systems did not provide that information" (Flynn 2001, 681, n.75).

Interestingly, many of the defenders of vertical integration have argued that the market is a high cost and inefficient means for the corporation to acquire the necessaries of business and that integrated enterprises with planning and control by trained managers are better. See for example Chandler (1977, Chapters 9 and 13).[18]

These theoretical points had practical ramifications. The line of reform thinking epitomized by the work of Berle and Means had a substantial impact on New Deal thinking. In the short term it resulted in the passage of the 1933 Securities Act and the 1934 Securities and Exchange Act, whose purpose was to address abuses in the relationship between ownership and control. For example, they outlawed financial predation against small and minority investors, including the numerous devices for unloading worthless securities upon unsuspecting purchasers (Hawley 1966, 306). This was done through requiring substantial disclosure of financial information when the corporation attempts to sell shares or issue bonds, when insiders engage in insider trading, and in a variety of other circumstances, along with substantial penalties for violations. The 1934 Act complemented the 1933 Act by creating the Securities and Exchange Commission to oversee and ensure compliance by financial institutions and financial markets.

A second area of activity, once it was accepted that concentrated industrial power could not be assumed to be beneficent, was the passage of trust busting legislation against both the "money trust" and the "utility trust." This included the passage of the Glass-Steagall Act of 1934, which outlawed the combination of commercial and investment banking in the same enterprise and other abuses, and the Public Utility Holding Company Act in 1935, whose "death sentence" provision required the divestiture of the great electric industry trusts (Hawley 1966, 308-9).

Another major attribute of non-competitive markets, non-cost based price discrimination, was addressed with the passage of the Robinson-Patman Act (RPA) in 1936, adopted as an amendment to Section 2 of the Clayton Act. The RPA was named after Wright Patman, a Texas congressman and ally of Lyndon Johnson. The Act was a response to one of those purposefully crafted defects in Section 2 of the Clayton Act that permitted price discrimination as long as it was done "in good faith to meet competition," the result being that from 1914 to 1936 the FTC had never been able to win a price discrimination case. The Act passed both houses of Congress almost unanimously (Geisst, 152-3). It outlaws the practice of charging a high price to some customers and a low price to other customers where, "the effect of such discrimination may be substantially to lessen competition or tend to create a monopoly . . . or to injure, destroy, or prevent competition," except where the difference in price is related directly to differences in cost (Sullivan 1977, 809-10).

The Act has since been roundly condemned by Chicago School commentators as special interest legislation meant to protect inefficient local merchants from big box chain stores. Yet here is another case where neoclassical critics–the *ne plus ultra* of theoreticians—ignore their own theories whenever it suits them. As every neoclassical economist knows, price discrimination is impossible in a competitive market. If an entity can successfully discriminate, then it is exercising market power, and the gains involved are monopoly rents. Patman himself is on point: "[P]rice discriminations that are practiced frequently or regularly, and at will, with devastating effects, can only be employed by a seller who has market power approaching monopoly control over prices in the markets in which he operates (Geisst 2000, 154).

New Deal reform thinking was productive in providing alternative avenues for solving economic problems where concentrated markets were either unwilling or too predatory to be relied upon. For example, New Deal reformers also supported the economic respectability of public and cooperative enterprise as a replacement or surrogate for abusive corporations. Major examples of initiatives in this area include the Tennessee Valley Authority and others like it, the Rural Electrification Administration (McCraw, 1971) (Lilienthal, 1944), (Glaeser, 1957), and a variety of state and local enterprises (Hellman, 1972).

Finally, the New Deal created or strengthened a variety of regulatory agencies and commissions to implement minimum standards for particularly troublesome industries, including the Federal Power Commission, the Securities and Exchange Commission, the Federal Communications Commission, and a strengthened Federal Reserve Board (1935 Banking Act).

Let it be said once again by way of summary, that none of the abuses leading to these reforms could have occurred, and none of the Progressive, Institutionalist, and New Deal reforms would have been necessary, had the main thrust of neoclassical economics been true.

## THE NEW ECONOMY

### Reagan and the New Ideology

The ascent to the presidency of Ronald Reagan and his supporters in 1981 can be seen as the beginning of both a new ideology and a New Economy. It came in the wake of Lyndon Johnson's Vietnam War and Nixon's Watergate Scandal, both of which interposed a new distrust of government and upset the general level of satisfaction with the New Deal and its programs. It also came at a time when the power of New Deal thinking was gradually waning with the retirement of the leading lights of the New Deal from government service and the rise of a younger generation that had not been touched by the corporate abuses of the late 1920s and early thirties.

The 1970s were a period of serious trouble for the economy, with double digit inflation and very high levels of unemployment, especially in industrial areas in the east. Against this backdrop, the Reagan administration was elected in 1981 on,

> a promise, most of all, to return to a robust economy founded in a regime of corporate control, subject only to the discipline of "the free market." Public policy would no longer interfere with the efficient management of private property. At the same time, social roles and moral questions were brought out of the closet, out of the private sphere. Now they were seen as the social infrastructure, the foundation necessary for the resurgence of a "strong America." This "return" to "traditional values," with its imagery of "the free market" and its commitment to an economy subject only to "corporate control" was accompanied by a complex ideological inversion of public and private spheres–that is, a flip-flop in attitude about the proper subjects for public policy (Peritz 1996, 266).

This move meant that conservatives, and especially religious conservatives, would be enlisted on the side of freeing corporate power from antitrust and regulatory controls, while liberals and progressives would be occupied primarily in dealing with fights over the social agenda of the social conservatives on issues of race, abortion, gay rights, prayer in the schools, etc. It was and is a brilliant strategy.

"'Traditional values' meant that the government should not seek to distribute power by, for example, enforcing anti-race or anti-sex discrimination policies. Rather, they should 'allow' the play of 'the free market'–whether in employment, gender, or race relations. This domestic 'freedom of contract' regime [was] portrayed as necessary to unleash the economic power of American business. . . . [C]orporations were again being represented as economically rational, potentially efficient captives of regulation, yearning to be free" (Peritz, 266).

## The Reagan Economy and the Collapse of Enforcement

In the interim period between 1950 and 1981 there were several major antitrust cases brought by the government. Two of these involved computers and communications, the two core industries of the New Economy. These were the government's cases against IBM, filed by Ramsey Clark, Attorney General under Lyndon Johnson in 1969, and the case against AT&T, filed by Ford's AG, William Saxbe, at the end of 1974. Both companies had adopted policies that made it very difficult for competitors to sell products that required integration with the dominant technology that they controlled. Seeing the writing on the wall, IBM had been smart enough during the period of the litigation to begin to loosen up its tying arrangements and to allow entry for third party providers into the market for what had previously been all proprietary software. One of the companies that benefitted from this loosening up was none other than Microsoft (Geisst 2000, 275). In the end, the Reagan administration simply dropped the case.

AT&T, on the other hand, had resisted opening its system to interconnection, first in the Carterfone case and later in its running fight with MCI (Geisst, 265-270). The company also had a high level of vertical integration back into manufacturing, based on its huge Western Electric manufacturing subsidiary, and forward into its twenty-two local telephone operating subsidiaries. Almost all telephone equipment procurement was done in–house, with prices set administratively. Moreover, AT&T was seen to be double dipping against the interests of the public. Not only did it receive an excessive return on its investment in Western Electric when that company overcharged for new equipment, but when the cost of that equipment was rolled into the regulated rates of the captive local telephone companies, and the regulated profit rate applied to it, dollar profits from the operating companies were higher than they would have been if the equipment had been sold and purchased at a more reasonable price (Geisst, 266-270).[19]

Both cases were inherited by the Reagan administration when it assumed office in 1981. Reagan had appointed William Baxter to be head of the Antitrust Division. Somewhat surprisingly, he took a hard line against AT&T and insisted on a major reform of the company's structure. By 1982 the company agreed to a divestiture where its twenty-two local operating companies were sheered off into seven "Baby Bell" regional holding companies. In order to prevent a backdoor recombination, AT&T was prohibited from acquiring shares in these companies. The companies themselves were thereafter free to acquire their equipment on the open market. With the benefit of hindsight, it is startling that such a substantial case should be brought to such a dramatic conclusion by the Reagan administration. The AT&T case outclassed the Standard Oil case of 1911 both in size and remedy. Both the problem and the remedy were classic, even energetic, New Deal–style antitrust.[20]

Yet if anyone was foolish enough to believe that the AT&T case signaled the beginning of a campaign of aggressive antitrust enforcement by the Reagan administration, they were soon jarred out of their reverie. The administration in the form of Malcolm Baldrige, Reagan's Commerce Secretary, and Attorney General Edwin Meese didn't mince words, and went early and clearly on record in favor of the repeal of the Sherman, Clayton and Robinson-Patman Acts (Geisst, 283). Attorney General Meese claimed to have discovered "that big is not necessarily bad and that small and many [firms] are not of themselves necessarily good." Similarly, Commerce Secretary Baldrige characterizes antitrust as "based on economic theories with no relation to the present and future." He proposed that Congress repeal entirely the anti-merger provisions of the Clayton Act because, he believed, such a step "will increase the efficiency of US firms and strengthen their competitiveness in world markets." The President's Commission on Industrial Competitiveness, too, warned that "US antitrust law must recognize the potential efficiency of mergers and other business combinations" (Adams and Brock 1986, 379).

Part of the administration's new approach to antitrust enforcement was designed by William Baxter, as head of the Antitrust Division and erstwhile Stanford law professor. Baxter was one of those lawyers who had taken up Chicago-style economics and became an enthusiast. He made it plain he would not prosecute antitrust violations unless it could be proven that the violations were not "economically efficient" (Geisst,186-7). This economics litmus test would become one of the main pillars of the Reagan administration's approach to antitrust. Baxter did not stay long in the administration. His replacement as head of the Division was Douglas Ginsburg, a favorite of both Reagan and Meese. Ginsburg had studied law and economics at the University of Chicago under Richard A. Posner and George J. Stigler and was also an enthusiastic believer in Chicago-style economics, including the view "that economic analysis rendered many of the antitrust laws obsolete" (Geisst, 302). To further ensure that there would be no surprises from the Antitrust Division, Reagan cut its budget by more than half and heavily salted the Economics Section with Chicago School economists.

Having gotten the Department of Justice in line, Reagan proceeded to the next stage of his program for permanently crippling antitrust enforcement—the reorientation of the federal judiciary. By the end of his second term, he had appointed about half of the federal judges in the nation, and by the end of the subsequent Bush administration, they had together appointed about two thirds (Geisst, 304). Moreover, Reagan made a strong attempt to get Chicago-style opponents of the antitrust laws onto the Supreme Court. His first success in this area was the appointment of Antonin Scalia in 1986. His second try was in 1987 with the nomination of Robert Bork, a very conservative federal judge and one of the leading and most aggressive critics of the antitrust laws. Bork's nomination ran into difficulty, and was eventually defeated, due in part to his views on antitrust, but primarily because of his notably illiberal views on privacy and abortion (Friedman 2002, 525). Believing that the Senate would not reject two nominations in a row, Reagan then nominated the very conservative Douglas Ginsburg. But again, opposing forces were too strong, and Ginsburg's right wing credentials lost him the liberals, and the fact that he had once smoked pot lost him enough conservatives to defeat him as well (Geisst, 302-3). The seat was eventually filled in 1988 with the more moderate Anthony Kennedy.

Reagan administration policies, high unemployment rates, very high inflation rates, and changes in the computer and communications industries were coming into confluence to produce an unstable situation. At the same time Reagan began his broadside attack on regulatory institutions and the statutory limitations on corporate abuses; the gorillas confined in those cages were clamoring to be set loose on the economy, and set loose they were.

Throughout the late 1970s and into the Reagan era the merger trend had accelerated. This was abetted by low stock market prices (i.e., shares necessary to initiate a hostile takeover could be bought relatively cheaply), and Reagan administration moves against banking regulation that allowed thrifts to invest in junk bonds. Combine this with the chaining up of the Sherman and Clayton Act watchdogs, and the stunning abuses of the Reagan administration's junk bond–merger movement were loosed upon the nation. Hostile takeovers were the order of the day, and manipulators like Ivan Boesky, Michael Milken, and T. Boone Pickens became household names. New techniques and abuses were invented: golden parachutes and greenmail, poison pills and shark repellents. As Adams and Brock wrote at the time:

> The current merger mania is clearly out of control. Billion-dollar mega-corporations are roaming the Darwinian jungle, making helter-skelter acquisitions or merging with one another. Generally these consolidations are unproductive at best and counterproductive at worst. They seldom promote efficiency or enhance international competitiveness or stimulate technological breakthroughs. They do not result in the creation of *real* values, the building of *new* factories, the development of *new* products or processes, or the employment of *new* workers. The vast majority of these megamergers are a form of paper entrepreneurialism, a means for reshuffling *existing* assets, an exercise in financial razzle-dazzle that benefits the merger midwives of Wall Street but not the American economy" (Adams and Brock 1986, 372).

As the merger frenzy gained momentum, one antitrust barrier after another fell. The first to go were the restraints against vertical mergers. The Reagan administration early on, in 1981, permitted DuPont to gobble up Conoco in the largest takeover to that date. Next to go was the strong rule against horizontal mergers. This was a harder nut for the administration to crack, since horizontals generally involved mergers of competitors and a reduction of competition. The issue was presented in 1984 when LTV, a major domestic steel producer, proposed to acquire Republic Steel, another major domestic steel producer, and the merger was allowed. The administration justified junking the rule by arguing that horizontal mergers of domestic competitors would be allowed whenever the candidate firms claimed that getting bigger was necessary to allow them to "compete" better against foreign producers (Shepherd and Wilcox 1979, 180-1; Geisst, 292-3). To some, the argument that "competition would be strengthened by allowing firms to eliminate their competitors" was ludicrous. Professor Philip Areeda, a leading antitrust law scholar, suggested that it was astonishing that anyone would argue "that the thing that prevents the American automobile industry from competing effectively with Japan is that General Motors is *too small*" (Adams and Brock 1986, 379). Yet both the Antitrust Division and the FTC were in accord on this point, and the door was open for horizontal mergers.

## Junk Bonds and the S&L Disaster

By the end of the 1980s over $250 billion in junk bonds had been issued to finance the merger movement. Many firms had been acquired at high premiums over book value, and many firms had been saddled with incredible amounts of high interest rate debt. All this financial deadweight made it difficult to succeed, unless the merger had produced a degree of market power sufficient to enable them to recoup these unproductive burdens through the collection of monopoly rents from consumers.

By 1987, toward the close of the Reagan era, the stock market had had enough of illogical mergers and acquisitions at unreasonably high premiums, unserviceable junk bonds, a very large number of M&A transactions at very high transactions fees (especially when funded with junk bonds) and useless payments of greenmail out of funds that could better have been used for productive investments. October 19, 1987 saw the market explode in a "Black Monday" crash that sent the Dow down over 500 points in one day (Previts and Merino 1998, 363). The stock market collapse also precipitated the crash of the teetering Savings and Loan industry. The S&Ls had heavily invested in the largely worthless and generally non-performing junk bonds, bought out of savings deposits attracted by high interest rates. Given the poor performance of the junk bonds, especially after the stock market crash eliminated the possibility of refinancing them, the only way to cover the interest payments on existing savings deposits was to pay high enough interest rates to attract new savings deposits. It had become a classic Ponzi scheme.

But the hundreds of billions in losses would not be borne by either the issuers of the bonds or the investors in the S&L's. All the savings and loan losses financed out of mis–invested savings deposits were insured by the Federal Savings & Loan Insurance Corporation (FSLIC), which when faced by the magnitude of the insured losses, itself became insolvent and had to be rescued by taxpayers. In due course, however, the federal government made good on depositor losses. In the end, the cost to the federal government and the American people of Reagan's "regime of corporate control" and the unleashing of the "economic power of American business" as applied to the savings and loan industry, would be roughly $500 billion, more than the total cost of financing the Second World War (Previts and Merino 1998, 378; Mayer 1990, 2). By the time the bailout had to be funded, Reagan was of course out of office, and others would have to suffer the consequences. Few remember Reagan's Depository Institutions Act of 1982, which deregulated the S&L's to allow them to invest in junk bonds and thus finance a substantial portion of the speculative and counterproductive M & A boom.

## Post-Reagan Deregulation and the Move to Monopoly

In banking, Reagan had moved to loosen regulation to allow the banks to duplicate the abuses that led to the imposition of the original controls in the 1930s. During the Clinton administration, this reversion to a pre-New Deal regulatory regime continued as the abuses of the past faded from memory. The Interstate Banking Act of 1994 allowed interstate merger of banks. And there was no objection to the horizontal merger of the Chase Manhattan Bank and the Chemical Bank into the nation's largest bank.

Telecommunications was another area of intense activity. Congress passed the Telecommunications Act of 1996, going a substantial way down the road of deregulating the heavily regulated telephone industry. Utility proponents of deregulation found, not surprisingly, an ideological ally in neoclassical economics. The argument was that deregulation would "create market-driven incentives and new forms of supply" superior to those provided under regulation. Neoclassicals asserted that market power could not continue to exist under deregulation, since it would be "rapidly eroded by new entry." They also assured the credulous that there was no further need to monitor the profit rates being earned by these erstwhile monopolists since, they argued, monopoly cannot exist under deregulation, and "deregulated market forces would put *the most efficient* industry structure in place" (Trebing 2001, 262. Emphasis added.).

The result was that many states adopted various forms of deregulation legislation, often abandoning the standard ratebase and cost accounting reporting requirements, thus making the road back very costly and difficult should the experiment fail. Service and affiliated transactions controls grew lax, and in many areas "greater efficiency" resulted in sharp reductions in service quality and upward price pressure. In rural areas especially, the bankruptcy of the neoclassical prescription has been especially apparent. In Iowa, for example, legislation allowing competitive providers of local telephone services was passed in 1996 (Iowa Code 476.1D) and 1998 and

1999 (Iowa Code 476.101). But as of 2002 the fraction of rural exchanges where significant competition exists is virtually zero. The Iowa Utilities Board (IUB), in fact, appears to have rejected the use of standard measures of monopoly power on the grounds that it is highly unlikely that there will be more than a maximum of two providers of local telephone service in these exchanges in the foreseeable future, *and to insist on competition would mean the rejection of deregulation.* "If the Board were to adopt the HHI [Herfindahl-Hirschman Index; based on number of producers and market shares] as its test for effective competition, the practical effect would be to nullify Iowa Code §476.1D by imposing a standard that is never likely to be met." (IUB 2000, 15-6).[21]

In accounting, as well, the relaxation of regulation allowed the accounting firms to combine business consulting activities with their auditing practices, thus creating obvious conflicts of interest with disastrous results for the nation (the Arthur Anderson/Enron disaster being only one example).

Nationwide, the result of the almost complete abandonment of effective antitrust enforcement by the federal government (with one exception to be dealt with below) has led to a sharp increase in monopoly concentration. As Harry Trebing has put it: "The most distinctive feature of deregulation . . . has been the massive move toward greater concentration at both the national and global levels. Industries that were once considered to be localized monopolies have been transformed into large regional, national, or transnational enterprises. It is less than coincidental that the decline in economic regulation has been matched by a parallel, substantial growth in industry concentration." (Trebing 2001, 263).

One of the areas often cited as a success story for deregulation has been telecommunications. And indeed, compared to fifty years ago, prices are lower today. However, the industry is moving rapidly to re-monopolization.

> In domestic telecommunications, the seven original Regional Bell Holding Companies were reduced to four as Bell Atlantic acquired NYNEX; SBC acquired Ameritech (giving SBC one-third of the national market); and WorldCom acquired MCI. AT&T and WorldCom would now control about 80 percent of the long distance market. Despite efforts to promote competition in local phone markets, the incumbent telephone companies still controlled 97 percent of the market in late 1999. (Trebing 2001, 263, as modified by Trebing 2002 ).

In the electric industry, Trebing also shows that the value of mergers pending or completed has moved from $8.9 billion in 1994 to $233.5 billion in 1999. (Trebing 2001, 264). The result, Trebing tells us, is the emergence of "tight oligopolies," where price discrimination gives preferred rates to preferred customers and slams customers with few options. Trebing's data shows, for example, that for the natural gas industry between 1984 and 1996, wellhead prices fell 21 percent, prices at the city gate (the pipeline delivery point) fell by 17.7 percent, prices to industrial users fell 23.5 percent, but prices to residential customers ***increased*** by 14.4 percent. (Trebing 2001, 265-6).[22] He concludes, "It cannot be assumed that oligopolistic market structures will automatically culminate in the realization of an optimal infrastructure, the realization of all network and coordination economies, or the distribution of these gains to all sectors of the economy" (Trebing 2001, 269).

Deregulation, especially deregulation without the backup of strong antitrust enforcement, is a prescription now, as it has always been, for rapidly expanding abuse of the bulk of American consumers.

## CHICAGO AND ITS ALLIES

Monopoly abuse has always had its defenders and apologists. In the New Economy these are the powerful monopoly interests themselves and their ideological allies in the judiciary, the regulatory commissions, the Antitrust Division, and academe. This section will review the two main theoretical justifications for blocking antitrust enforcement and regulatory action to control monopoly power. The first is the "contestable market" hypothesis put forward by Professor Baumol and his allies. The second is Professor Bork's energetic and paradigm-setting assertion that all that matters is allocative efficiency, and all questions of who benefits and who gets hurt by monopolies are irrelevant.

### The Contestable Market Hypothesis

Recall that in 1974 the federal government launched its antitrust action against AT&T. In the middle of that litigation AT&T employed a group of economists including Professors Bailey, Baumol, Panzer and Willig to assist in developing positions to support the maintenance of AT&T's monopoly. The task was to establish a theoretical basis for the claim that an absolute unregulated monopolist would still be bound to price no higher than the competitive level, since to do otherwise would be to attract instant entry and competitive defeat. (NRRI 1996, 29). The result was the theory of Contestable Markets. It asserted that the price/quantity outcomes of perfect competition would occur even if a single firm had an absolute monopoly, under certain conditions. In such a situation, there would be nothing to gain from antitrust enforcement, and the monopolist could safely be left in place without fear of injury to consumers.

Though the theory was very popular for a while among monopolists and true believers, in the end it became apparent that the assumptions underlying the theory were so empirically unrealistic that the theory applied to virtually nothing. The model rested on the following four critical assumptions (Shepherd 1984, 572):

1) Entry is free and without limit. There are zero sunk costs.
2) The entrant is capable of entering the market instantly at the scale of production of the monopolist, thereby beginning with no cost disadvantage.
3) If the entrant can establish any price advantage at the outset, the entrant wins the entire market of the monopolist.
4) Exit is free.

One need only compare these assumptions with what it would take for an entrant to instantly displace AT&T from its markets, to see that entry would hardly be free; the sunk cost of duplicating AT&T's capital on the ground would be in the tens of billions, if not higher. Entry could not happen overnight, and AT&T and its subsidiaries would have an opportunity to adjust their prices to eliminate any price differential advantage the entrant was relying upon to capture the total market. Furthermore, AT&T is a multi–product firm; just because the entrant has a nominal price advantage in one product, does not mean that it would have an advantage in others. The third assumption is just unrealistic. A firm like AT&T would not simply walk away from its investment because the initial price of the new entrant was marginally lower than its own. There would be a price war, and this would take time. Finally, the risk of losing would be significant for both parties, and the expected value of the loss for the losing party would be overwhelming under Baumol's assumptions, and would substantially exceed the expected value of the normal competitive profits it could anticipate in Baumol's world, were it to prevail. In sum, the theory, by its own terms, does not appear to be applicable to any substantial subset of the normal run of major antitrust cases.

## Borkian Efficiency

In his 900-page *Economics of Regulation and Antitrust*, Kip Viscusi does not quibble on points of principle: "The viewpoint taken in this book is that economic efficiency should be the only objective in antitrust decisions." He bases this viewpoint on Robert Bork's conclusion to the same effect: "Whether one looks at the texts of the antitrust statutes, the legislative intent behind them, or the requirements of proper judicial behavior . . . the case is overwhelming for judicial adherence to the single goal of consumer welfare in the interpretation of the antitrust laws" (Viscusi, et al. 1997, 63-4). It is important to clarify what Bork means by "consumer welfare." "[I]t seems clear the income distribution effects of economic activity should be completely excluded from the determination of the antitrust legality of the activity. It may be sufficient to note that the shift in income distribution does not lessen total wealth, and a decision about it requires a choice between two groups of consumers that should be made by the legislature rather than by the judiciary" (Bork 1978, 111). As Lande (1982, 84) characterizes Bork: "He further asserts that there is 'not a scintilla of support' in the [Sherman] Act's legislative history for 'broad social, political, and ethical mandates' and explicitly rejects distributive issues as a possible area of antitrust concern." (Bork 1966, 7).

There are at least three major problems with Bork's position. The first is that he is wrong about the legislative intent behind the Sherman, FTC, and Clayton Acts. In light of the historical context leading up to the passage of the Acts, it would be strange indeed if Bork were correct and Congress had no interest whatsoever in protecting consumers, farmers, and business people from monopoly abuse, and was only concerned with "allocative efficiency." And in fact, the historic record does not support his assertions on this point. Congressional distaste for the pricing and output consequences of monopoly was rooted in concerns about the distribution of wealth between monopolists, other producers, and consumers, and only secondarily the maintenance of productive efficiency. (Lande1982, 89).

While it is true that the legislative history of the Act does show Senator Sherman praising the trusts for their supposed "efficiency," he himself pointed out in qualification of this praise: "It is sometimes said of these combinations that they reduce prices to the consumer by better methods of production, but all experience shows that *this saving of cost goes to the pockets of the producer.* (Lande, 91. Emphasis in the original). Lande goes on to show that during the debates on the Act: "Senator Sherman termed monopolistic overcharges 'extortion which makes the people poor,' and 'extorted wealth.' Congressman Coke referred to the overcharges as 'robbery.' Representative Heard declared the trusts, 'without rendering the slightest equivalent,' have 'stolen untold millions from the people.' Congressman Wilson complained the beef trust 'robs the farmer on the one hand and the consumer on the other.' Representative Fithian declared that the trusts were 'impoverishing' the people through 'robbery' (Lande, 94-5).

Lande provides a similar analysis of the legislative history of the Federal Trade Commission Act of 1914 and reaches the same conclusions that

Congress, while concerned with not interfering unnecessarily with operating efficiency, was primarily concerned with controlling the coercive and abusive aspects of monopoly power. With respect to the Clayton Act, the results are the same. The remarks of one Senator expressed a desire to protect consumers and to encourage corporate efficiency in the belief that these benefits would be passed on to consumers: "The chief purpose of antitrust legislation is for the protection of the public, to protect it from extortion practiced by the trust, but at the same time not to take away from it any advantages of cheapness or better service which honest, intelligent cooperation may bring." (Lande, 106-126). In light of Lande's analysis, Bork's claim that Congress was concerned only with allocative efficiency, and not at all with the robbery-like aspects of monopoly pricing, seems more like wishful thinking on his part.

The second problem with Bork's analysis is that it assumes that any firm gaining monopoly power will produce the volume necessary to achieve "allocative efficiency," and set price so as clear the market at *that* level of output. Yet it is not clear, as an empirical matter, how one could determine what level of output corresponds to "allocative efficiency." And even if this could be done, why would it be that this Borkian level would correspond to the profit maximizing output and pricing of a monopolist, which the neoclassical monopoly model tells us involves lower output and a higher price than for a competitive firm? Perhaps the answer to this is, as Posner tells us, that only monopolies that extract monopoly rents are objectionable. "The only exclusion of competitors that should be objectionable from an antitrust standpoint is that which results in an increase in the market price above competitive level" (Posner 2001, 200-1). But if so, then how is this consistent with the neoclassical monopoly model, where the unregulated monopolist will be led inexorably to raise prices and restrict output in order to maximize profits? And then wouldn't the "competitive" price and output level be counterfactual and indeterminate? And if, in an enforcement proceeding, the burden of proof on this point is shifted to those injured by the monopolist, will they then not always lose in a Bork-Posner world?

The third problem with the Borkian position is that it focuses on monopolization where the monopolization process results in lower costs of production, as if that situation were standard. Yet it often occurs that Firm 1 acquires Firm 2 (a higher cost producer), and simply shuts down Firm 2's facilities and lays off its workforce. Thus the average cost of production would then be lower than it was when measured across the two firms, but the level of production is much lower as well, and it may well be that to maximize profits the acquiring firm will just raise its prices. Why is this better for consumers, who now pay more and get less?

The response most often heard is that a firm that has some monopoly power and raises its rates above "the competitive level," will be directly confronted with new entry which will force a reduction in prices. But here we have another case of a false universal masquerading as an empirical fact. There is no reason whatsoever to believe *a priori* that in any particular market entry will be cheap and easy. In the small town markets for local telephone service, discussed above, for example, entry is very expensive relative to the size of the market and very risky. Price can be pretty high and service can be pretty bad before entry might be stimulated, and even then, the ability of the incumbent to make short term changes just long enough to defeat the new entrant may still deter entry.

Moreover, if firms are indeed consolidating toward a monopoly in order to take advantage of economies of scale in production, then this is a natural monopoly situation, and regulation is in order. It is extremist and outlandish to suggest that firms should be allowed to coalesce into unregulated monopolies just because the monopoly firm *could possibly* rebuild its production facilities to comprehend the entire market and have a lower average cost relative to the erstwhile competitors producing at fractions of the market. If the monopolist were to build enough capacity to capture the total market through economies of scale, there is every reason to suppose that the price charged and the output level chosen will be the monopoly levels. And even if, *arguendo*, these monopoly levels were to involve higher production and a lower price *than the old competitive levels with no economies of scale*, price will still be above, and production levels will still be below, the hypothetical competitive levels *given* the presence of the economies of scale or potential economies of scale. Thus, in what is probably the most general fact pattern in the heavy and network industries, the situation could be substantially improved through intelligent regulation, while still leaving the monopolist a competitive return. To leave the monopoly intact and unregulated would be to expose consumers to monopoly abuse.[23]

Put another way, when economies of scale permit only one optimum-size producer in a market, it may be desirable for public policy to allow a monopolistic supplier to operate. But the mere fact that a monopolist is allowed to exist does not assure the public of obtaining the benefits of whatever lower costs may be achieved. In fact, the monopolist has an incentive to absorb not only the benefits resulting from the lower cost, but also to raise prices. Consequently, and obviously, the presence of a monopoly, even one based on economies of scale, calls for public regulation. (Phillips 1988, 47).

## CONCLUSION

To summarize, only in the world of fairy tales does the unregulated market produce the best of all possible worlds. Without regulation economic relations tend to be heavily coercive: the fox will eat the hen, the strong will rob the weak, the baron will exploit the serf, the slave owner the slave, the industrialist the worker in the sweatshop, the monopolist the consumer and the competitor. Leaving the market to the mercies of monopolists, manipulators, polluters, robber barons, and financial and accounting con men inevitably results in substantial losses to most participants in the economy and certainly to the average working family. Only the creation and adaptation of intelligent public policy mechanisms for the control of these abuses in and around the marketplace can provide adequate protection for society. The Borkian policy of heads in the sand is a prescription for disaster for all but the predators.

It is also clear that the impact of monopoly power on the distribution of income is a central issue and not, as Bork and Chicago would have us believe, irrelevant. While it is indeed important that the economy operate efficiently in achieving public and private goals within an intelligent system of laws and public policies, productive efficiency will be beside the point if the fruits of that production are diverted by those with monopoly power.

Large concentrations of monopoly power are also inconsistent with democratic decisionmaking. It has been apparent from the end of the civil war onward that political influence is not unrelated to economic power. The more concentrated the economic power the greater the degree of its political influence and the more difficult it is to carry into effect measures to control that power. If democracy is to be preserved, then concentrated economic power has to be dispersed, and has to be dispersed early in the process of its formation before it coalesces into political power.

Protecting society against predatory concentrations of economic and political power has been the role of reformers over the course of the last century and more. Much of what has been achieved has been achieved by the practical intelligence, applied economic craftsmanship, and legal and political savvy of reformers like Commons and La Follette, Brandeis and Wilson, Veblen, Ely, Berle and Means, Bonbright and FDR, and several generations since, all devoted to the improvement of American society and those who participate in it. The battle with the monopolies is fought generation by generation; each new generation has the same battle to win or lose, and its own material wellbeing to achieve and protect.

## NOTES

1 The author would like to thank Professor Kathleen Pulling and Bernerd Lowenthal for their valuable input on a number of points.

[2] Not all great thinkers were enamored of the produce of these new schools of political economy. As Cardinal Newman put it, "Political economy is . . . a science at the same time dangerous and leading to occasions of sin." (Gray 1931, 1).

[3] See also the discussion on this point in David Hamilton (1970, 23-4.)

[4] Aquinas (1225-1274), was largely influenced by Aristotelian thinking and by the great Moslem Aristotelians, Avicenna (980-1037) and Averroes (1126-1198).

[5] With its corollary that any effort to improve outcomes by tinkering with the "natural" operation of the economy will only make things worse and not better.

[6] For example, major killers like typhoid, cholera and dysentery. The typhoid incidence alone in the United States in 1900 was 31 per 100,000, while by 1953 it was less than 0.05 per 100,000 population. See Bureau of the Census (1975, 58).

[7] The life expectancy of all Americans in 1900 was 47.3 years (33.0 years for blacks). By 1995, with reform, this had risen to 71.9. (Sheehan et al. 2000, 10).

[8] See also Friedman (1973, 409ff).

[9] See, for example, Lincoln Steffens (1993).

[10] See, for example, Barney Hope and Michael Sheehan (1985).

[11] These abuses, based as they were in a network industry characterized by high fixed costs and relatively low variable costs, would also be characteristic of many of the major industries and abuses in the "New Economy" of the 1990s onward.

[12] For the whole story see, Henry Demarest Lloyd (1963). For a description of the issue somewhat more sympathetic to the railroads see, Hovenkamp (1991, Chapter 13). The discussion here generally follows Hovenkamp.

[13] The Interstate Commerce Commission was largely abolished by the Staggers Rail and the Motor Carrier Acts of 1980, both part of the deregulatory push at the beginning of the Reagan era.

[14] This brings to mind a hearing several years ago before the Oregon Public Utilities Commission on the topic of the rates being charged by US West . In response to a cross examination question by the author on US West rate levels, a US West vice president told the commission that "*competition* was forcing the company to raise its rates."

[15] Two books which would set the tone of the era were written about the Standard Oil trust. The first was, of course, Henry Demarest Lloyd (1894), *Wealth Against Commonwealth* , while the other was Ida Tarbell (1904), *The History of the Standard Oil Company.*

[16] The purpose of a *quo warranto* proceeding is to determine if a corporation is acting beyond the legal powers granted by its state charter. The *quo warranto* remedy against abusive corporations has become obsolete since state legislatures have generally broadened their corporation statutes to allow corporations to engage in any legal activity.

[17] This discussion relies on Neale and Goyder (1980, 181-2).

[18] This, of course, is the same argument advanced for public enterprise controlled and planned by that very same class of trained managers, with the difference that there is, with some exceptions, oversight and control by the public in the public sector.

[19] For a description of a similar affiliated transaction abuse involving the U S West and Yellow Pages see White and Sheehan (1992).

[20] And it is interesting to note that at the time of the AT&T divestiture, Standard Oil, notwithstanding its own divestiture, was again the second largest company in the country, and second only to AT&T.

[21] Both the HHI (Herfindahl-Hirschman Index) and the older four firm concentration ratio ("CR4") are measures of concentration in an industry based on the number of producers and their shares of the market. For a comparison see Viscusi (1997, 149-52).

[22] For an attack on the neoclassical position approving price discrimination see Sheehan (1991).

[23] For a good brief discussion of economies of scale, declining average costs and natural monopoly see Phillips (1988, 45-8).

# REFERENCES


Adams, Walter, and James W. Brock. 1986. *The Bigness Complex.* New York: PantheonBooks

Arnold, Thurman. 1940. *The Bottlenecks of Business.* New York: Reynal & Hitchcock

Berle, Adolf A., and Gardiner C. Means, 1933. *The Modern Corporation and PrivateProperty.* New York: Macmillan.

Blaug, Mark. 1968. *Economic Theory in Retrospect.* Homewood: Richard D. Irwin

Bolton, Patrick, Joseph F. Brodley and Michael H. Riordan. 2000. Predatory pricing: strategic theory and legal policy. *Georgetown Law Journal* 88:2239-2330.

Bork, Robert. 1966. "Legislative Intent and the Policy of the Sherman Act." *Journal of Law and Economics* 9.

———. 1978. *The Antitrust Paradox.* New York: Basic Books.

Brinkley, Joel, and Steve Lohr. 2001. *U S v. Microsoft*. New York: McGraw-Hill.

Brodie, Abner. 1963. "The Adequacy of Workmen's Compensation as Social InsuranceReview of Developments and Proposals." In *Labor, Management, and Social Policy*. Gerald R. Somers. Madison: the University of Wisconsin Press.

Bureau of the Census. 1975. *Historical Statistics of the United States: Colonial Times to 1970*. Washington, DC: USGPO.

Chamberlin, Edward. 1933. *The Theory of Monopolistic Competition*. Cambridge, MAHarvard University Press.

Chandler, Alfred D. 1977. *The Visible Hand: The Managerial Revolution in AmericanBusiness*. Cambridge, MA: Harvard University Press.

Clark, John Maurice. 1939. *Social Control of Business*, 2nd ed, NY: McGraw-Hill.

Commons, John R. [1923] 1968. *The Legal Foundations of Capitalism*. Madison: University of Wisconsin Press.

Dorfman, Joseph. 1959. *The Economic Mind in American Civilization*. Volume 4. New York: Viking. *and th*

Fine, Sidney. 1956. *Laissez Faire and the General Welfare State: A Conflict In American Thought, 1865-1901*. Ann Arbor: Univ. Michigan Press.

Flynn, John J. Winter 2001. Standard Oil and Microsoft—Intriguing Parallels or Limping Analogies? *The Antitrust Bulletin* 645-733.

Friedman, Lawrence. 1973. *A History of American Law*. New York: Simon & Shuster.

———. 2002. *American Law in the 20th Century*. New Haven: Yale University Press.

Geisst, Charles. 2000. *Monopolies in America*. Oxford: Oxford University Press.

Glaeser, Martin G. 1957. *Public Utilities in American Capitalism*. New York: Macmillan.

Gray, Alexander. 1931. *The Development of Economi c Doctrine*. London: Longmans.

Hamilton, David. 1970, *Evolutionary Economics: A Study of Cha nge in Economic Thought*. Albuquerque: U. New Mexico Press.

Hawley, Ellis W. 1966. *The Ne w Deal and the Problem of Monopoly*. Princeton: Princeton University Press.

Halliday, Stephen. 1999. *The Great Stink of London: Sir Joseph Bazalgette and the Cleansing of the Victorian Capital*. Phoenix Mill: Sutton Publishing Ltd.

Hellman, Richard. 1972. *Government Competition in the Electric Utility Industry*. New York: Praeger.

Hope, Barney and Michael Sheehan. 1985. "Miller and Lux: a study in monopoly power." *The Social Science Journal* 22:31-47.

Hovenkamp, Herbert. 1991. *Enterprise and American Law: 1836-1937*. Cambridge: Harvard University Press.

IUB. (Iowa Utilities Board.) March 1, 2000. "Order Denying Petition to Deregulate." In Re: *U S West Communications, Inc.*, Docket No. INU-99-3.

Lande, Robert. 1982. Wealth transfers as the original and primary concern of antitrust: the efficiency interpretation challenged. *Hastings Law Journal 34:65-151.*

Liebhafsky, H.H. 1976. "Price Theory as Jurisprudence: Law and Economics, Chicago Style." In *The Chicago School of Political Economy*, Warren J. Samuels, ed., East Lansing: Assn. for Evolutionary Economics.

Lilienthal, David E. 1944 *TVA: Democracy on the March*. Chicago: Quadrangle.

Lloyd, Henry Demarest. [1894] 1963. *Wealth Against Commonwealth*. Englewood Cliffs, NJ: Prentice-Hall.

Lovett, William A. 1984. *Banking and Financial Institutions Law*. St. Paul: West Publishing.

Mayer, Martin. 1990. *The Greatest Ever Bank Robbery: The Collapse of the Savings and Loan Industry.* New York: Charles Scribner's Sons.
McCraw, Thomas K. 1971. *TVA and the Power Fight: 1933-1939.* Phila: Lippincott.
Neale, A.D. and D.G. Goyder. 1980. *The Antitrust Laws of the U.S.A.: A Study of Competition Enforced by Law,* 3rd ed. Cambridge: University of Cambridge Press.
NRRI. 1996. *Determining When Competition is "Workable": A Handbook for StateCommissions Making Assessments Required by the Telecommunications Act of 1996.* Columbia, OH: National Regulatory Research Institute.
Peritz, Rudolph J.R., 1996. *Competition Policy in America: 1888-1992: History, Rhetoric,Law.* New York: Oxford University Press.
Phillips. Charles F. 1988. *The Regulation of Public Utilities.* Arlington, Virginia: Public
Utility Reports.
Posner, Richard A. 2001. *Antitrust Law, 2nd Edition.* Chicago: University of Chicago Press.
Previts, Gary John, and Barbara Dubis Merino. 1998. *A History of Accountancy in the United States: The Cultural Significance of Accounting.* Columbus: Ohio State University Press.
Robinson, Joan. [1933] 1969. *The Economics of Imperfect Competition.* London: Macmillan.
Sheehan, Michael. 1991. Why ramsey pricing is wrong: The case of telecommunications regulation. *Journal of Economic Issues* 25:21-32.
———. Robert Lee, and Lisa Nuss. 2000. *Oregon's Prevailing Wage Law.* Portland: Fair Contracting Foundation.
Shepherd, William G. 1984. "Contestability" vs. competition. *The American Economic Review* 74: 572-587.
———. and Clair Wilcox. 1979. *Public Policies Toward Business.* 6th Ed. Homewood: Richard D. Irwin.
Smith, Adam. [1776] 1937. *The Wealth of Nations.* New York: Modern Library.
Steffens, Lincoln. 1993. *Shame of the Cities.* NY: Farrar, Strauss & Giroux.
Sullivan, Lawrence Anthony. 1977. *Handbook of th e Law of Antitrust.* St. Paul: West Publishing.
Tarbell, Ida. 1904. *The History of the Standard Oil Trust.* New York: Harper & Row.
Tool, Marc. 1979 *The Discretionary Economy: A Normative Theory of Political Economy.* Santa Monica: Goodyear.
Trebing, Harry M. 2001. "On the Changing Nature of the Public Utility Concept." *In Economics Broadly Considered: Essays in Honor of Warren J. Samuels.* New York: Routledge.
———. 2002. Telephone conversation of July 8, 2002 updating the information at Trebing —
——.2001, 263, with respect to the Sprint acquisition by Worldcom.
Veblen, Thorstein. 1918. *The Higher Learning in America: A Memorandum on the Conduct of Universities by Business Men.* New York: Hill and Wang.
———. [1904] 1932. *The Theory of Business Enterprise.* New York: Mentor Books.
———. [1921] 1963. *The Engineers and the Price System.* New York: Harcourt Brace.
Viscusi, W. Kip, John M. Vernon, and Joseph E. Harrington Jr. 1997. *Economics of Regulation and Antitrust.* Cambridge, MA: The MIT Press.
White, Evan and Michael F. Sheehan. 1992. Monopoly, the holding company, and assests stripping: the case of yellow pages. *Journal of Economic Issues* 26: 159-82.

12

# TOWARD DEVELOPMENTAL CURRICULUM REFORM: TEACH WHAT? TO WHOM? WHY?

Baldwin Ranson

## INTRODUCTION

In 1989, President Bush convened his Cabinet with all the nation's Governors at a high-profile national education summit. Their agenda was a challenge to American power and prosperity: "the failure of US schools to teach the basic skills needed to keep Americans productive and competitive" *(Time Magazine*, October 9, 1989:60). These leaders reached substantial agreement on how to reform public school curricula—the knowledge, skills, and attitudes taught—to correct that failure. Their agreement took the form of national goals that answer our title questions. Their answer to "*Teach What?*" was to prescribe five academic subjects: English, mathematics, science, history and geography. Their answer to "*To Whom?*" was all American children through high school. Their answer to "*Why?*" was to raise the skills of citizens and workers to compete in the global economy.

This education summit contributed to a new framework for federal policy making. The shift was from piecemeal to "systemic" reform. Federal laws passed since have established similar education goals and sought to align federal programs with state and local efforts to reach them.

Systemic reform is but the latest stage in a seemingly endless cycle of reform. The cycle reflects the difficulty policy makers experience in adjusting public education to two global trends. One is the explosion of scientific and technological (sci/tech) knowledge, which constantly redefines the content of theoretical and practical knowledge and the conditions of economic efficiency. The other is the global aspiration for democracy, which constantly redefines the sense of social equity and the conditions of political participation.

The cycle of reform results from the incompatibility of policies designed to respond to these trends. Democracy is thought to demand curricula for all youths up to the limit of their talents, while the explosion of sci/tech knowledge is thought to demand curricula for the talented few presumed capable of mastering it. Vocational and general curricula devoid of intellectual content are designed for the majority who will start work when they leave high school. Academic curricula devoid of practical applicability are designed for the minority who will pursue higher education.

These alternative curricula give modern forms to ancient dualisms: efficiency versus equity, quality versus quantity, theory versus practice. Policies creating such dualisms are necessarily non-developmental because they are self-defeating. Although both sides are recognized as desirable, gains for one side come at the expense of losses for the other. Every movement toward excellence or quality or theory moves away from equity or quantity or practice.

There is widespread optimism that current systemic reform policies can end this cycle. There are bold assertions that prescribing rigorous *academic* curricula for *all* youths will eliminate the dualisms and advance American education toward all these desirable ends. But despite their bi-partisan popularity and apparent common sense, we judge these policies *not* developmental. They do not eliminate the dualisms; they will prove self-defeating, and the sterile cycle of reform will continue.

The following essay presents grounds for our negative judgment. First we describe the elements of institutional analysis necessary to design developmental policies. Next, we use these elements to generate developmental answers to our title questions. Then we analyze dualistic answers found in five policies proposed prior to the 1989 education summit. We conclude by suggesting how policies in one act that epitomizes federal systemic reform—Goals 2000: The Educate America Act—could be revised to eliminate dualisms and become developmental.

## ELEMENTS OF INSTITUTIONAL ANALYSIS

The cycle of education reforms continues because problems are not being solved. Policies moving in one direction generate opposition that reverses direction and prevents solutions. In contrast, developmental policies establish a direction that is maintained because it progressively solves problems. Designing progressive solutions requires understanding three elements of social analysis. They are the *subject* of inquiry, the *criterion of judgment* guiding choices, and the *principle* guiding data collection. We elaborate John Fagg Foster's understanding of these elements (Tool, 2000).

The *subject* of social inquiry is not individuals but *institutions*, defined as prescribed patterns of correlated behavior. It is through prescribed behavior patterns that individuals in societies carry on life-maintaining functions, such as feeding, sheltering, and educating their populations. It is through prescribing new behavior patterns that policy makers try to improve the performance of life-maintaining functions.

Examples of educational institutions are curricula prescribing knowledge, skills, and attitudes to be taught and methods of teaching; rules for administration and finance; requirements for admission and graduation; etc. Comprehensively, their function is to empower each generation gradually to participate in social life by mastering selected aspects of society's cultural heritage.

As policy makers design institutions to empower each generation, they make choices about which aspects of their heritage to prescribe, for which youths, for which forms of participation—the questions in our title. Their choices are guided by the *criterion* that Foster came to call *developmental continuity.* Joining the words "developmental" and "continuity" focuses attention on the fact that policy makers universally want their societies to thrive and survive. They adjust institutions in order to maintain and improve the performance of institutional functions.

Foster showed that this criterion is universally applied, but with unequal skill. It is difficult to achieve *both* development *and* continuity in each policy. One common mistake is to seek continuity by maintaining existing institutions without development. Conservatives cling to familiar behavior patterns no matter how badly these perform their functions. They adjust new institutions to old ones rather than prescribing more effective behaviors. The opposite mistake is to seek development without continuity. Revolutionaries eliminate existing institutions no matter how badly it dislocates continuous performance of institutional functions. They adjust new institutions to visions of future performance rather than to the maintenance and improvement of existing performance.

These mistakes in pursuit of developmental continuity come from failures to recognize and employ the actual determinants of institutional performance. Performance is a factual matter determined by factors in the environment in which institutions operate. Society's understanding of determining factors is called technology.

We define technology as the stock of knowledge that is applicable to physical phenomena. It is the operational part of the sci/tech knowledge explosion. This stock is developmental in the sense that additions and corrections constantly expand and improve it. Foster showed that technology is valid and applicable across cultures, and that developmental policies improve institutional performance by adjusting to it. The *principle* directing attention to factors determining performance Foster called the *principle of technological determination* (J.F. Foster, 1981).

The principle of technological determination directs policy makers to collect data on how well institutions mobilize determining factors to perform their life-maintaining functions compared to the best performance possible with current technology. If gaps appear between actual and technically possible performance, policy makers prescribe new behaviors to reduce those gaps. Applied to education, the principle of technological determination suggests evaluating the technical competence of various answers to our title questions. Are existing curricula diffusing the knowledge, skills, and attitudes most appropriate for excellent and equitable adult participation? Are alternative curricula prescribed for the most appropriate target audiences? Are the forms of participation for which curricula prepare the most appropriate to promote developmental continuity?

Applying the principle of technological determination is just as prone to error as applying the criterion of developmental continuity. In education, the chief danger is seeking technically competent means to achieve non-developmental ends. It is to adjust educational institutions to other institutions rather than to technically superior alternatives. Let us clarify by explaining a pervasive error of American policy makers.

Our sample of education policies reveals that policy makers want public education to prepare youths for several forms of adult participation, including the use of sci/tech knowledge and the practice of democratic citizenship. But throughout the 20$^{th}$ century, preparation for economic participation predominated. The primary answer to our "*Why Teach?*" question was to close gaps in preparation of workers for employment; in the words of *Time*, "to keep Americans productive and competitive." This answer subordinates educational institutions to occupational institutions, with harmful results.

Preparing youths for economic participation is certainly necessary for developmental continuity. The error is to subordinate public educational institutions to this aim. It leads policy makers to look for factors determining efficient means to turn students into "human capital" ready to occupy a hierarchy of occupations. It leads away from attitudes, skills, and knowledge determining efficient participation in sci/tech and democratic trends.

Societies world-wide distinguish high-skill, high-status, mental occupations from low-skill, low-status, manual occupations. Harnessing youths efficiently to this dual occupational structure justifies sorting them into dual curricula—intellectual for an academically talented minority, practical for the untalented majority.

But sorting students fuels the cycle of self-defeating reforms. Policy initiatives to democratize education through universal access generate opposition because they water down traditional academic curricula. Initiatives to spread scientific knowledge by raising academic standards generate opposition because they restrict access. Compromises calling for all to master academic curricula, or for all to love menial jobs to which vocational curricula lead, fail. "Thinking" curricula with meager applicable content remain a privileged preserve for an academically talented minority, and "doing" curricula devoid of intellectual content remain the dumping ground for an academically challenged majority.

We think the criterion of developmental continuity does not justify subordinating public educational institutions to occupational institutions. We think the principle of technological determination does not justify dualistic curricula to supply workers for mental and manual occupations. We find these answers to our "*Why Teach?*" and "*Teach What?*" questions self-defeating. To alert readers to these errors in our historical sample, we shall introduce mistaken policies with slogans adapted from one of Mao Tse-tung's favorite educational slogans: "politics in command."

Curricula defining educational excellence and equity as mastery by an academic elite of symbol manipulation and memorization skills without immediate practical application, we shall label "academic fallacy in command." Curricula defining educational excellence and equity as mastery by all students of material manipulation skills without immediate intellectual significance, we shall label "vocational fallacy in command." The former explicitly, and the latter implicitly, denies sci/tech competence to the masses—a result incompatible with the aspiration for democracy.

These fallacies are not mutually exclusive. Indeed, they have become more joined as the explosion of sci/tech knowledge raises the symbol-manipulating requirements of the least skilled jobs. But most specific policy proposals put one or the other in command, depending on whether mental or manual employments are most needed in a given economic or political context.

Avoiding these fallacies requires using institutional analysis correctly to eliminate self-defeating dualisms. We demonstrate that use with hypothetical policies to show what developmental curricula could look like. We label our policies "sci/tech inquiry in command."

## SOME HYPOTHETICAL POLICIES

We start by answering our "*Why Teach?*" question. We hypothesize that public education can and should contribute to developmental continuity by empowering all youths to participate in expanding knowledge and democratic life. The larger the percentage of a society's population practicing a scientific style of living and sharing in determining public policy, the better will that society survive and thrive. The more people guiding their lives by evidence, the more quickly and competently will they adjust institutions when evidence warrants.

We observe a gap in empowerment. At present meaningful participation in knowledge and democracy is limited to a small number—those who master academic curricula that lead to higher education. We would close this gap by designing educational institutions that will achieve *universal practice of sci/tech inquiry.*

By scientific inquiry we mean discovering general principles in special-case observations. By technological inquiry we mean discovering special-case applications of scientific principles. Universal practice of sci/tech inquiry will not make everyone a scientist, but it will habituate everyone—starting with the youngest school children—to practice inquiry in their daily lives. John Dewey expressed well how the absence of such practice inhibits developmental continuity. "Without initiation into the scientific spirit one is not in possession of the best tools which humanity has so far devised for effectively directed reflection. [Without initiation one] does not become acquainted with the traits that mark off opinion and assent from authorized conviction" (Dewey, 1916:223).

Our aim for all to use the best tools for reflection sounds similar to the popular aim of "scientific literacy," but is very different. Daily practice of scientific living means a habit of answering questions one asks oneself. Literacy typically means certified ability to use certified taxonomies to answer questions asked by others (Bybee, 1997, throughout but especially p.63; Ranson, 1987). Our universal practice of inquiry is closer to living by what Dewey called the "method of intelligence" (Dewey, 1938:100-12).

"*Teach What?*" We answer "curricula that involve all students at all times in sci/tech inquiry." Such inquiry has procedural but not content requirements. The procedures eliminate dualisms that separate and oppose talent for thinking from talent for doing. They demand thinking and doing in every undertaking. The most theoretical of subjects, e.g., mathematics. is never isolated from practical significance; the most practical of subjects, e.g., driver education, is never isolated from social and intellectual significance. Our ideal is sometimes called an integrated curriculum (Beane, 1997).

The academic fallacy requires science courses to transmit content—primarily taxonomies—by telling and reading (Schmidt et.al., 1997:17). The taxonomies are records of earlier inquiries preserved in symbols. Alfred Korzybski explained the evils of transmitting verbal structures apart from observing the structure of non-verbal phenomena to which symbols refer:

> As we proceed, we must emphasize *order* considering what comes first and what next. This is semantically important, for the usual procedure is entirely different: first, we have our structurally "preconceived" doctrines and languages; next, we observe the structure of the world; and *then* we try to force the observed facts into the linguistic structural patterns. But in the new way, we start with silent observations, and search empirically for structure; next, we invent verbal structures similar to them; and, finally, we see what can be said about the situation, and so test the language. Experience shows that the old habits of labels first, objects next, instead of the structurally natural order of *objects first, labels next,* is semantically pernicious and harmful (Korzybski, 1958:219).

Curricula competent to develop universal habits of inquiry require all students to practice activities of looking for evidence, identifying viewpoints, making connections, considering alternatives, and assessing the importance of whatever content each school's staff, parents, and students determine is of immediate and powerful interest to students (Jackson and Davis, 2000:23; Wheelock, 1998). These activities are taught with the best learning practices: ". . . we have learned [that] human learning . . . is best when it is participatory, proactive, communal, collaborative, and given over to constructing meanings rather than receiving them . . ." (Bruner, 1997:44). Practicing sci/tech inquiry is daily guided by transactions between teachers and learners: ". . . effective teaching is a problem-solving activity that relies heavily on teacher judgment and discretion in developing a situationally effective response" (Elmore et.al., 1988:39).

Summarizing our hypothetical answers to our title questions, we suggest that one necessary answer to "*Why Teach?*" is to reduce the gap in universal empowerment to practice sci/tech inquiry. Our developmental answer to "*Teach What?*" in order to remove that gap is the attitudes, skills, and knowledge used in competent sci/tech inquiry. The most developmental answer to "*Teach Whom*?" is *all* youths—without sorting, competition, or failure.

Although most policy makers share our aim of empowerment for participation in the trends of sci/tech knowledge and democratic living, most policies they have proposed differ greatly from our hypothetical policies. In American history we have discovered only two that approximate our ideal: The Morrill Act of 1862, that created the land grant colleges, and the Servicemens Readjustment Act of 1944, that created the G.I. Bill of Rights. In the last half century, we have not found their equal. Evidence for these assertions follows.

## SOME HISTORICAL POLICIES

### 1948: Vocational Fallacy in Command.

In 1948, President Truman's Commissioner for Education created the National Commission on Life Adjustment Education for Youth. Its charge was described in the pamphlet *Life Adjustment Education for Every Youth* (United States Office of Education, 1948).

The problem addressed had been raised by vocational educators. They assumed that all youths should complete high school as preparation for adult life. But they observed that many—perhaps 60% of the high school age population—dropped out and were prepared neither for mental nor for manual occupations. Recognizing that there were many social and economic causes for dropping out unrelated to schools, the educators nevertheless thought that changes within schools could keep alienated youths in the system. "It has been abundantly demonstrated that almost any apparent block to high-school attendance can be overcome where there is an all-impelling interest in doing so. [Impelling interest of students will come from] the development, try-out, and spread of programs of instruction which will have greater value, meaning, and appeal to more of the youth of high-school age . . . "(iii).

Obviously, these dropouts were not interested in traditional college preparatory, vocational, or general curricula. The Commission did not challenge the content and sorting function performed by those curricula, but did challenge their relevance to this un-served population. The solution proposed was to supplement traditional curricula with "life adjustment" programs that unmotivated students would find more interesting and practical. But what is life adjustment? The Commission vaguely took that expression to mean adjustment to the low-status occupational and social opportunities contemporary society offered such students. "If the plans herein described . . . should help young people better to fill their niches in life, the purposes of this document . . . will have been fulfilled" (iv).

> Life adjustment is impossible unless occupational adjustment occurs. Since they may change jobs many times during their lives, the boys and girls with whom the [reform] is concerned are likely to need resourcefulness and flexibility in order to achieve occupational adjustment. They will hold jobs for which they can make little specific preparation while they are still in school. If by actual work experience a boy can learn the types of jobs he dislikes, he will have made some progress. If, in addition, he can learn to work eight hours a day and can attain competence in some one job which he does like, he is well on his way toward occupational adjustment (97).

Translated into the language of institutional analysis, the National Commission on Life Adjustment Education for Youth sought to contribute to developmental continuity by closing a performance gap. High schools were failing to prepare *all* youths for adult life. To close this gap, its answer to "*Teach What?*" was a life adjustment curriculum. Its answer to "*To Whom?*" was all youths, but especially the alienated. Its answer to "*Why?*" was to prepare youths for adult life, but especially for employment in manual occupations. It explicitly designed this curriculum to improve the practical quality of education, assuming implicitly that it would not diminish intellectual quality.

We agree with the Commission that developmental continuity is served by reducing the number of youths alienated from schools and ill-prepared for adult life. And we endorse its belief that curricula can and must be of impelling interest and appeal before all youths will pursue them to completion. But its proposed curriculum was a faulty means to achieve a faulty occupational objective.

The Commission's life adjustment curriculum incorrectly applied the principle of technological determination by excluding intellectual knowledge, skills, and attitudes—a pattern we are calling the vocational fallacy. It assumed that students' existing interests and future "niches in life" lacked social and intellectual significance, and made no effort to connect them to global trends. It assumed that practical learning is for everyone, but denied that theoretical learning is for everyone. Even if it had proven attractive to alienated students, the Commission's curriculum—adjusted to supposed occupational opportunities—would not have empowered youths meaningfully to increase their participation in adult life or to contribute to social development. Any resulting gain in educational quantity would have been at the expense of educational quality.

Life adjustment policies never gained widespread support or led to legislative enactment. Early in the Commission's career, its title and non-intellectual agenda were ridiculed by critics. In 1954, after sponsoring a number of conferences and publishing two reports, the Commission quietly disappeared, without developmental result. Fifty years later, its problem of adolescents alienated from schools and society remains unsolved and high on the nation's educational agenda.

## 1958: Academic Fallacy in Command.

In the 1950s, the Rockefeller Brothers Fund organized several panels of business and academic experts to assess major problems facing the United States. The panel assessing educational problems published its report in 1958 under the title *The Pursuit of Excellence: Education and the Future of America* (Rockefeller Brothers Fund, 1958).

The report opens with a beautiful statement of the aim of developmental education policies: "widening and deepening the life purposes of our citizens."(v) Educational institutions should promote this aim by helping individuals identify, nurture and wisely use their talents.

But public education has a responsibility to develop talents for more than private purposes. It must view talents as resources to operate social, technical, and economic institutions necessary for a free society. Contemporary society, because of the explosion of sci/tech knowledge, is demanding that the labor force increase its skill and training. Society needs more highly trained talent—specifically scientists, mathematicians, and engineers. But public schools are failing to provide an adequate supply of such talent (6-7). The gap between the supply of and demand for highly trained talent is largely due to high school curricula. Electives presenting a "democracy of subject matters"(26) to students squeeze out important academic subjects, stifling the development of talent, and encouraging talented students to share a "common mediocrity" (33).

The panel attributes public acceptance of academic mediocrity to dualistic thinking, to a "tug of war between equality and excellence in a democracy" (15). Many Americans believe mistakenly that promoting quality is incompatible with promoting quantity, leading them to neglect the gifted. But in fact, democratic society demands encouraging high individual performance. The panel asserts that the dualism is unnecessary: "Fortunately, the demand to educate everyone up to the level of his ability and the demand for excellence in education are not incompatible. We must honor both goals" (22). The panel proposes eliminating the dualism by providing equality of academic opportunity, while recognizing that unequal native capacities and motivations will lead to unequal achievements.

Having satisfied itself that intellectual excellence is compatible with educational equity, and that a "democracy of subject matters" poorly serves talented students, the panel suggests three steps to eliminate mediocre education. First, schools should sort out talented youth. Second, schools should provide guidance to encourage the talented to respond to the nation's manpower needs. Third, the federal government should provide funding to support these policies.

"The general academic capacity of students should be at least tentatively identified by the eighth grade as the result of repeated testings and classroom performance in the elementary grades. An adequate guidance system would insure that each student would then be exposed to the sort of program that will develop to the full the gifts which he possesses" (30). The panel proposes for the academically talented, in addition to the general curriculum prescribed for all, two or three years each of science, mathematics, and a foreign language (27).

Translated into the language of institutional analysis, the Rockefeller Brothers Fund panel on education sought to contribute to developmental continuity by closing a performance gap. High schools were failing to develop all youths' talents to their maximum. To close this gap, its answer to "*Teach What?*" was a challenging academic curriculum. Its answer to "*To Whom?*" was the most academically talented. Its answer to "*Why*?" was to prepare the talented few for the most skilled occupations. It explicitly designed this curriculum to increase intellectual excellence, and explicitly asserted that it would not diminish educational equity.

We agree with the panel's judgment that developmental education policies will widen and deepen citizen participation in society, that the explosion of sci/tech knowledge raises skill and training requirements, and that democracy benefits from universal high performance. But we find its aims and its policies to be self-defeating.

Society clearly needs highly trained scientists, mathematicians, and engineers. And perhaps some necessary but scarce talents restrict the number of people who can master that training. But designing curricula during years of compulsory education to address such specialized needs and abilities is incompatible with curricula promoting universal practice of sci/tech inquiry. It requires sorting youths by talents presumed but not proven to be relevant to the practice of sci/tech inquiry. It encourages high school students to narrow their interests to future employment possibilities rather than widening and deepening their interests through practice of immediately usable attitudes, skills, and knowledge. The result cripples the academically talented by depriving them of practical studies, and excludes the rest by denying them intellectual studies.

The "*Why Teach?*" answer of meeting projected shortages of trained manpower subordinates public educational institutions to occupational institutions. It assigns to schools responsibility for correcting supply-demand imbalances in labor markets rather than for eliminating gaps in intelligent social participation. It requires sorting students into groups bound for high status or low status occupations. Designing public school curricula for future specialists commits the academic fallacy, and creates the very dualism the panel hoped to eliminate. It makes high school science courses gates to later mastery of advanced science, not avenues for engaging all students in practicing science relevant to their daily lives.

But appearing amidst public praise for Soviet science education, and shock at the enemy's successful launch of two satellites, the Rockefeller report contributed to a national sense of crisis and a rapid policy response in the form of The National Defense Education Act of 1958. That legislation closely echoed the report's policy recommendations.

> The Congress hereby finds and declares that the security of the Nation requires the fullest development of the mental resources and technical skills of its young men and women. The present emergency demands that additional and more adequate educational opportunities be made available. The defense of this Nation depends upon the mastery of modern techniques developed from complex scientific principles. It depends as well upon the discovery and development of new principles, new techniques, and new knowledge.
>
> We must increase our efforts to identify and educate more of the talent of our Nation (*US Statutes at Large*, 1959:1581).

The NDEA authorized significant expenditures on science education, but was soon identified with elitist curriculum proposals (Lazerson, 1985, chapter 2). It failed to achieve its basic purpose of making academic science more appealing and of providing the economy with adequate highly trained manpower. A quarter century later, another prestigious panel proposed similar curricula in similar language to solve the same problem.

## 1965: Vocational Fallacy in Command.

In the 1960s, the nation's attention shifted. The Cold War intellectual threat from the Soviet Union paled before a hot war in Viet Nam and urban riots. In this new setting, a new kind of education study led to a different national policy response, even as it continued to adjust educational institutions to occupational institutions.

In 1964, a Research Conference on Education and Cultural Deprivation at the University of Chicago reviewed the state of knowledge in that field and recommended policies to solve related problems. Its work was published the following year under the title, *Compensatory Education for Cultural Deprivation* (Bloom et.al., 1965).

The report's first paragraph identifies the problem to be addressed: youths who are excluded from public education are subsequently excluded from increasing sectors of the occupational system. Manpower requirements for unskilled workers are diminishing, with adverse effects on youths weeded out by their lack of academic talent. Academic curricula exclude the disadvantaged, making education a "status-giving and selective system" rather than "a system that develops each individual to his highest potential" (2).

Children of low-income families are especially prone to exclusion from public education. Perhaps one-third of high school entrants do not graduate, often because of "experiences in homes which do not transmit the cultural patterns necessary for the types of learning characteristic of the schools and the larger society" (4). Those experiences start with biological deprivation—the inability to satisfy basic needs dependably. They continue with cultural deprivation—the absence of intellectually stimulating environments. They lead deprived children to find formal education uncongenial and defeating.

> . . .the culturally deprived child has difficulty in learning for its owns sake and in learning for the approval of an adult. He values things and activities which are concrete and which have immediate and tangible rewards. He has difficulty in seeing the relevance of much of school learning since he is unable to comprehend fully or accept the deferred and symbolic gratification that the middle-class child has come to accept. . . . It is difficult for him to learn to be quiet and to attend to a flow of words . . . from the teacher (21).

The report's recommendations start with meeting physical and developmental needs of children before entering school. After enrollment, it recommends assessing each child's level of development in order to adapt materials and learning approaches to each child's readiness to learn. No child should be made to repeat a grade; all should experience continual success. And the report argues that schools are responsible for more than academic curricula. "We do not regard the school as the agency for the solution of the social ills of a society. However, we do regard the schools as providing a setting in which all can learn under as nearly ideal conditions as possible. Furthermore, the school is responsible not only for the learning of subject matter and intellectual skills, but also for the learning of basic attitudes and values" (31).

At the secondary level, the report recommends identifying at-risk children and providing them with special programs. These programs should emphasize basic language and reading skills, as well as work experiences to facilitate the transition to employment in the manual occupations to which deprived youths might aspire. "The student should be moved to as complex a type of work as he can master and increasingly his work experiences should be related to the types of jobs for which there will be greatest need in industry and the community" (39).

*Compensatory Education for Cultural Deprivation* can be translated into the language of institutional analysis as follows. Academic failure prevents many poor youths from completing their school preparation for manual occupations. A curriculum competent to reduce such failure will teach basic academic and vocational content in ways that are less academically demanding and more palatable for deprived youths. Reducing rates of academic failure will expand educational quantity, and will not harm educational quality.

We concur with the authors' judgment that excluding youths from public education harms the developmental continuity of society. We also concur with their recommendations to meet biological and cultural development needs of all youths. But we find their curricular recommendations understandably but regrettably failing to eliminate self-defeating dualisms from public education.

Their "*Why Teach?*" answer was non-developmental but politically expedient. It accepted the tradition of subordinating educational institutions to economic institutions. It recommended means to raise rudimentary academic success of the deprived to meet occupational demands, but did not explore ways to eliminate academic barriers to universal practice of life-enhancing sci/tech knowledge, or possibilities of schooling as a vehicle for present rather than future social participation.

Their "*Teach What?*" answer was developmental in intent, but yielded too much to curricula devoid of intellectual content. By endorsing the dualism between thinking and doing curricula, it missed an opportunity to make academic curricula more practical and vocational curricula more intelligent.

Their "*To Whom?*" answer was likewise developmental in intent. It sought to reduce the sorting effect of public schools by helping traditionally excluded youths master basic academic and vocational curricula.

These recommendations fit well the mood engendered by President Johnson's agenda to promote civil rights and eliminate poverty. The

Elementary and Secondary Education Act of 1965 quickly turned much of the report into public policy.

> In recognition of the special educational needs of children of low-income families and the impact that concentrations of low-income families have on the ability of local educational agencies to support adequate educational programs, the Congress hereby declares it to be the policy of the United States to provide financial assistance . . . to local educational agencies serving areas with concentrations of children from low-income families to expand and improve their educational programs by various means (including preschool programs) which contribute particularly to meeting the special educational needs of educationally deprived children (*US Statutes at Large, 1966:27*).

The Elementary and Secondary Education Act started distributing federal funds to school districts according to the number of poor children enrolled, without specifying the types of services these children should receive. At five-year intervals, Congress amended, expanded, and reauthorized the Act in a continuing effort to reduce performance gaps between deprived and other youths. Up to 1994, Congress had amended and expanded the Act seven times, but deprived youths continued to be excluded at unacceptable levels. In 1994, the "Goals 2000: The Educate America Act" tackled the problem once again, still using the thinking of 1965.

## 1973: Vocational Fallacy in Command.

The National Commission on the Reform of Secondary Education was established by the Charles F. Kettering Foundation in 1972. Its report published a year later, *The Reform of Secondary Education*, calls for national education goals to respond to rising levels of student dissent, racial discord, and absenteeism, and to falling levels of enrollment, academic performance, and funding. The Commission reports widespread feelings that both compensatory and vocational education are failing the increasingly diverse student population, and develops thirty-two recommendations to cure these ills. It begins by defining education developmentally as learner-centered achievement.

> The ultimate purpose of public secondary schools and school systems in American is to provide educational opportunities to satisfy both the common and the unique needs of the individuals who aggregate to the

> total population. Public secondary schools are responsible for delivering a quality education to all youth. . . .To accomplish this mission, a school must diagnose each learner's needs, concerns, and cognitive and affective styles, and cut its cloth to fit each design (National Commission on the Reform of Secondary Education, 1973:26).

But after recognizing the diversity of students, the Commission suggests that secondary school might be unable to meet the needs of each, and should reduce the compulsory attendance age: "By the age of fourteen, a student who has not developed some motivation toward learning is not likely to profit from compulsory schooling" (41-2). Comprehensive high schools should stop being custodial institutions, and be assigned national education goals that "give the schools a new alignment to the needs of society" (30). And the needs of society are not learner-centered achievement but an adequate supply of trained workers.

> The secondary school must seek to prepare students for a successful life of work through increasing their occupational options. It must ensure that those students who wish to do so acquire job-entry skills before leaving high school (32-3).
>
> A national objective of great importance is the upgrading and expansion of occupational education for all, until all secondary school students who wish to do so can leave high school equipped with marketable skills whether or not they plan to continue their education (52).

The Commission recognizes and resents the inferior status of vocational curricula compared to academic curricula: "Education for leisure still looms larger than education for work" (51). It seeks to diminish this dualism by revitalizing apprenticeship through a massive proliferation of work-study programs capable of qualifying students for *any* occupation in their community. "High school curricula should be expanded so that all adolescents can participate in cooperative work-study programs while pursuing other educational interests. The traditional barriers between vocational and academic 'tracks' must be eliminated to permit students to cross lines in pursuit of their individual educational goals" (54).

In the language of institutional analysis, the National Commission on the Reform of Secondary Education judged that public education must contribute to developmental continuity by providing practical learning for *all* youths. It found a performance gap caused by the unpopularity of vocational curricula. Its answer to "*Why Teach?*" was to reduce that gap. It thought that technically adequate means to that end were expanded vocational curricula made available to all. These curricula were designed explicitly to increase the practical excellence of high schools, with the implicit assumption that they would not diminish intellectual excellence.

We agree with the Commission that practical learning is vital for all youths. But not if it is simply added to impractical academic learning, and not if it is only practical for employment. This Commission's report was completely unresponsive to the educational potentials and demands of sci/tech knowledge and democratic aspirations.

Its "*Why Teach?*" answer aimed more to raise the status of vocational education than to satisfy the common and unique needs of a diverse student body. It came close to limiting the responsibilities of public schools to preparing workers for existing occupations. Its "*Teach What?*" answer, like that of the National Commission on Life Adjustment Education in 1948, contained nothing to engage youths in the intellectual aspects of the sci/tech trend or to prepare youths for full participation in society. Its "*To Whom?*" answer urged vocational mastery for all high school students, but did nothing to eliminate the low status of curricula leading to low status jobs.

The Kettering Foundation report did not lead directly to legislation. But a decade later, its call for national education goals and performance-based instruction was picked up by a more influential report. And two decades later its call for expanded occupational education had become part of systemic federal reform legislation.

## 1983: Academic Fallacy in Command.

The '60s and '70s were decades of social confusion, conflict, and chaos. In education they were decades of experimentation and innovation, often promoted with federal funds. Not surprisingly, the '80s brought a reaction. In 1981, President Reagan's Secretary of Education created the National Commission on Excellence in Education to examine the quality of education in the country. The context was a sense that the nation's preeminence in commerce, industry, science, and technological innovation was being eroded by other nations' advances. Its report published in 1983, *A Nation at Risk: The Imperative for Educational Reform*, sparked a reform effort that continues actively into the 21st century.

The Commission's report asserts that the average graduate is less well educated than in earlier generations and less likely to be ready for either college or work. Echoing the findings of the Rockefeller panel in 1958, it calls for the restoration of excellence in education, coupled with the maintenance of equity. The dualism can be eliminated by changing youths from unmotivated learners into dedicated and hard working learners: "Our goal must be to develop the talents of all to their fullest. Attaining that goal requires that we expect and assist all students to work to the limits of their capabilities. We should expect schools to have genuinely high standards rather than minimum ones, and parents to support and encourage their children to make the most of their talents and abilities" (National Commission on Excellence in Education, 1983:13).

A major cause of mediocre educational performance is electives chosen from a "curricular smorgasbord," permitting students to choose the general track rather than college preparatory or vocational tracks. The Commission disapproves of this democratically-motivated policy. It proposes requiring "Five New Basics" as minimum requirements for high school graduation—four years of English, three years each of math, science, and social studies, and one year of computer science. These courses appear to respond to technological imperatives of modern society: "Whatever the student's educational or work objectives, knowledge of the New Basics is the foundation of success for the after-school years and, therefore, forms the core of the modern curriculum" (24).

Anticipating concerns that such a traditional academic curriculum might be inaccessible to the disadvantaged and uninteresting to the alienated, the Commission asserts "that everyone can learn, . . . that a solid high school education is within the reach of virtually all" (24).

In addition to recommendations regarding content, the Commission suggests standards and expectations that teachers should maintain, the time that should be devoted to the New Basics, and sanctions for students who reduce that time by absenteeism and tardiness. The report ends with a sermon for students: "You forfeit your chance for life at its fullest when you withhold your best effort in learning. . . . When you work to your full capacity, you can hope to attain the knowledge and skills that will enable you to create your future and control your destiny" (35).

In the language of institutional analysis, the National Commission on Excellence in Education sought to contribute to developmental continuity by closing a performance gap. High schools were failing to develop all youths' talents to their maximum. To close this gap, its answer to "*Teach What?*" was a basic academic curriculum. Its answer to "*To Whom?*" was to all students. Its answer to "*Why?*" was to prepare all youths to participate in the economy in either skilled or unskilled occupations. The New Basics curriculum was explicitly designed to harmonize demands for educational excellence and equity.

We agree with the Commission on Excellence in Education that developmental continuity is promoted by education that evokes dedication and hard work from students. And we agree that all can master intellectually challenging subjects. But the purposes for which and the means by which it proposed achieving such behaviors were self-defeating because commanded by the academic fallacy.

The "*Why Teach?*" answer remained to meet a national employment need defined by "leaders" rather than educational needs defined by student interests and requirements for social participation. This answer could be appropriate for trade and professional schools. It is inappropriate for public schools.

The "*Teach What?*" answer repeats the academic fallacy found in *The Pursuit of Excellence* in 1958, prescribing arid academic subjects as competent to prepare youths for employment, sci/tech knowledge, and democratic participation.

The "*Teach Whom?*" answer of 1983 seems different from the 1958 answer, but the difference is superficial. The panel in 1958 aimed its academic courses at the most talented minority, ignoring the low-level academic skills needed by the masses. The Commission in 1984 sought to raise student mastery of low-level as well as high-level skills. In both reports, sorting by academic talent would determine who mastered what curriculum.

These answers to our title questions were not developmental because they perpetuated self-defeating dualisms that deprive the masses of intellectually excellent education, and deprive the scholastically inclined of practically excellent education. But *A Nation at Risk* was widely applauded and generated a flurry of reform activities, among them President Bush's 1989 education summit. The goals developed at that summit remained but fond hopes for the elder Bush, but they became proud achievements for President Clinton. With minor revisions, they became law in Goals 2000: The Educate America Act signed in 1994.

Because this act recycles many of the policy proposals in our historical sample, it provides a useful vehicle for summarizing what we have identified as flaws in those proposals and our suggestions for eliminating those flaws. This act recommends eight concrete goals to improve the performance of public education in the United States. We shall examine each goal to consider its technical competence to raise the skill level of the workforce—the ubiquitous purpose that we reject for public education—and to raise the number of Americans practicing sci/tech inquiry and empowered to participate in democratic life—our suggestion of developmental purposes.

## 1994: Goals 2000. Making Self-defeating Policies Developmental.

The declared purpose of Goals 2000: The Educate America Act is to provide a framework for creating a vision of excellence and equity to guide Federal education programs, and for meeting National Education Goals established by its first title. The framework will promote "coherent, nationwide, systemic education reform" by assisting state and local governments to develop and certify "high-quality, internationally competitive content and student performance standards" and opportunity to learn standards, and to assure equal opportunity for all students to meet "high academic and occupational skill standards, and to succeed in the world of employment and civic participation." (*US Statutes at Large*, 1995:128) We summarize this complex statement in the form of an answer to our question "*Why Teach?*" The Act's purpose is to close a gap in the international competitiveness of the United States by raising academic performance as a step toward raising the skill level of the workforce.

With the Act serving as "a cornerstone of the national strategy to enhance workforce skills," (129) its purpose clearly focuses on preparation for economic participation. But it does not ignore our hypothesized purposes of expanding participation in reliable knowledge and in democratic life. The standards for content, performance, and skills to which it refers will surely include large elements of sci/tech knowledge. And promoting equal opportunity and success in civic participation will surely address aspirations for democracy.

Nor does the Act ignore our concern to eliminate the dualism between excellence and equity. Its definitions of standards to be met show that educational excellence continues to mean measurable mastery of specified academic subjects: "(4) the term 'content standards' means broad descriptions of the knowledge and skills students should acquire in a particular subject area. . . .(9) the term 'performance standards' means concrete examples and explicit definitions of what students have to know and be able to do to demonstrate . . . proficien[cy]"(129). Its definition of the youths supposed to benefit from the reforms shows that educational equity continues to mean providing equal opportunity:

(1) [T]he terms "all students" and "all children" mean students or children from a broad range of backgrounds and circumstances, including disadvantaged students and children, students or children with diverse racial, ethnic, and cultural backgrounds, American Indians, Alaska Natives, Native Hawaiians, students or children with disabilities,

> students or children with limited-English proficiency, school-aged students or children who have dropped out of school, migratory students or children, and academically talented students and children; . . . (*ibid*)

We shall question Congress's success in harmonizing excellence and equity in the eight factors it has chosen as national goals. We shall also question its success in harmonizing economic, scientific, and democratic purposes in its design of educational institutions for "all children to prepare them to participate fully as workers, parents, and citizens; . . .(128)

"(1) *School Readiness*. . .By the year 2000, all children in America will start school ready to learn." (*US Statutes at Large* 1995:130).

The first goal is a direct descendant of proposals published in *Compensatory Education for Cultural Deprivation* in 1965. It targets the same deprived children, and seeks to compensate for the same harmful effects of poverty, while avoiding flaws in the Elementary and Secondary Education Act that actually created barriers to academic achievement. The objective of the school readiness goal is to reduce academic failures of *poor* children by meeting the physical and intellectual needs of *all* children before they enter school, and by assuring that *all* will have access to developmentally appropriate preschool programs and parental support. But as with its predecessor, efforts to reach this goal create conditions for the very academic failures it intends to avoid.

When school readiness is treated as readiness to climb the academic ladder, the rungs of which are academic performance and skill standards, lacking readiness appears as a flaw in children—most frequently in poor children. The unready are labeled as possessing risk factors: "Teachers and parents of kindergarten children rated a child's ability to sit still and pay attention as essential or very important to his/her being ready to start school. . . . Parents were asked about their children's overall activity level and ability to pay attention. . . . Thirteen percent of parents report their children encounter difficulties in paying attention. Difficulty in paying attention varies by children's sex, mother's education, welfare receipt and race/ethnicity" (National Center for Education Statistics [NCES], 2000:41-2).

Preprimary curricula designed to counter risk factors come to center on skills considered necessary for success higher up the ladder, whether or not the skills be developmentally appropriate, useful, or interesting. "In kindergarten, children develop literacy skills such as recognizing letters and understanding the letter-sound relationship at the beginning and ending of words. At kindergarten entry, 31% understood the letter-sound relationship at the beginning of words, and 18% at the end of words, compared with 74 and 54, respectively, by the end of kindergarten" (NCES, 2001:20).

Preschools and kindergartens become gatekeepers, ready to certify that their "graduates" are skilled enough to survive increasingly academic primary school curricula. The children most at risk are drilled in basic skills and never develop more complex skills (*ibid*). If judged unready for first grade, they are held back—flunked—and thereby introduced to failure even before their first contact with formal education. Since grade retention is the best indicator of future dropping out, (Lunenburg, 1999:18) their academic future is jeopardized in the name of overcoming their "flaws." Far from reducing school failure, preschools are turned into "academic boot camps" that create failure.

> To some policymakers an accelerated pace for learning and pressure to master the next-grade's content may seem to imply a tremendous victory for educational excellence. It sounds as if today's kindergartners are learning more. However, the escalation of academic demand is seen to be detrimental by almost all experts in both early childhood education and subject-matter specialists because too often the escalation is focused narrowly on isolated pre-reading and numerary skills without opportunities for more integrated, conceptual learning, and because it fosters teaching methods that are incompatible with how young children learn" (Shepard,1990:159-61).

Contrary to the intent of Congress, the goal of school readiness has reduced rather than increased the quality of preprimary programs available to the most needy. Commanded by the academic fallacy, which defines educational excellence as mastery of isolated academic skills, the first goal promotes developmentally *in*appropriate curricula and early academic failure. The results are neither excellent nor equitable.

The school readiness goal was not reached by 2000 (NCES, 2001:4). It will never be reached by recycling self-defeating policies like those proposed in *Compensatory Education for Cultural Deprivation* in 1965. But there are alternative meanings of readiness that are not self-defeating.

Developmental alternatives could include making preprimary education part of the free public school system. Preschools and kindergartens could become society's first publicly organized and financed providers of learning environments and resources not available in homes. And rather than demanding that youths be ready "to sit still and pay attention," these schools could demand of themselves that they be ready to engage the attention of all youths at whatever age entry be permitted.

Preprimary curricula could have children practice sci/tech inquiry and democratic living, not as preparation for future success but as essential means for coping intelligently with current environments. Children could develop habits of generalizing from special-case observations, recognizing special-case applications of generalizations, and taking responsibility for logical consequences of decisions based on inquiry. Then they would not need special high school courses in citizenship (goal 3) or special policing for anti-social behavior (goal 7) because they would have the habits and inclinations appropriate to desirable behaviors. In their daily lives they would harmonize excellence and equity.

"(2) *School Completion*. . .By the year 2000, the high school graduation rate will increase to at least 90 percent" (*US Statutes at Large*, 1995:130).

The second goal is the same as that addressed in *Life Adjustment Education for All Youths* in 1948. It intends to improve the readiness for employment of alienated adolescents by insisting that they get "a high school degree or its equivalent." But the legislation in 1994 does nothing to make schooling less repellent or more relevant to drop-outs.

When school completion is treated as the final step up the public school academic ladder, adolescents are asked to master academic basics considered necessary for success in entry-level jobs. They are presented with a duty to conform to an uncongenial and personally irrelevant curriculum as a condition of economic participation.

Making high schools gatekeepers to certify job skills generates self-defeating behavior patterns that increase alienation from school. It encourages sorting and segregation, as academically weak, low-income and minority students are disproportionately funneled to low quality schools with rigid discipline and tracking procedures and high drop out rates (Fine, 1991:14,22). Low-achieving students receive demeaning treatment, and are often pushed out of full-time schooling toward the GED [General Education Diploma] as if it were a credential equivalent to a diploma (Fine, 1991:83-8; Lunenburg, 1999:21).

The school completion goal of a 90% graduation rate, eliminating the gap between minority and non-minority drop outs, was not reached by 2000, even using biased statistics that count the GED as completing school and don't count the prison population as failing to complete school (NCES, 2001:43). The second goal will never be reached without learning lessons from *Life Adjustment Education for All Youths*.

A first lesson is that the holding power of schools depends on their ability to provide curricula of "all-impelling interest" to students. High schools, just as preprimary schools, must give youths compelling reasons to "pay attention." They can demand a commitment from students only as they fulfill a reciprocal commitment to serve students' current interests and needs.

A second lesson is that curricula must genuinely empower students to participate in society. Curricula that seek to adjust the poor to low-quality occupations that will never offer enough jobs or adequate pay create neither excellence nor equity for the poor or for society.

A developmental alternative is to treat school retention as a challenge to make schools make themselves relevant to *all* students. We believe that a curriculum of sci/tech inquiry could arouse the enthusiastic interest of alienated students. Eliminating curricula based on the academic and vocational fallacies could raise genuine school completion rates and, in the process, achieve without policing the safe schools sought in goal 7. Students attending schools with enthusiastic interest will shun drugs and violence.

"(3) *Student Achievementt and Citizenship*. . .By the year 2000, all students will leave grades 4, 8, and 12 having demonstrated competency over challenging subject matter including English, mathematics, science, foreign languages, civics and government, economics, arts, history, and geography, and every school in America will ensure that all students learn to use their minds well, so they may be prepared for responsible citizenship, further learning, and productive employment in our Nation's modern economy" (*US Statutes at Large,* 1995:131).

Three objectives are stated for goal 3: improved academic performance; ability to reason; and involvement "in activities that promote and demonstrate good citizenship, good health, community service, and personal responsibility; . . ."(*ibid*) The first is the heart of this Act's systemic education reform. It follows *The Pursuit of Excellence* in 1958 and *A Nation at Risk* in 1983 in listing academic subjects that students should master, and in claiming that academic competency is compatible with equity. It follows *The Reform of Secondary Education* in 1973 in prescribing tests to motivate and certify performance. It does not make clear how competency in using one's mind and in citizenship is to be motivated and certified.

Repeated testing of academic mastery throughout the academic ladder nakedly exposes the academic fallacy. That fallacy blindly assumes that skill at answering questions asked by others is a competent proxy for skill at making productive and informed answers to questions that one asks oneself.

Testing may motivate students and teachers to study approved answers, but it is antithetical to learning to use one's mind to find competent answers to genuine questions—which is the essence of competent inquiry. There is no room for originality or personal relevance in answering test questions (Corbett, 1991).

Testing may serve to document degrees of excellence, but it is antithetical to equity. It is meant to sort students so that some negative sanction can be imposed on poor performance. And those most prone to poor academic performance will always be those least well served by academic curricula—the poor. Flunking them to achieve goal 3 creates conditions that defeat goal 2.

Testing circumscribes curricula by defining which knowledge and skills are relevant to academic success. Relevance to academic success has no necessary relationship to relevance to real life success. In Colorado, a number of elementary schools are using a core reading program produced by McGraw-Hill, the company that produces the statewide Colorado Student Assessment Program. Teachers choose this reading program in part because it includes "test-taking skills such as filling in little circles with a pencil. It's called bubbling"(Hubler, 2001:29A). The costs in student time, public money and narrowed skills resulting from frequent testing have not been calculated.

Congress prescribed frequent testing to demonstrate "competency over challenging subject matter." It suggested *no* means for students to acquire or demonstrate competency in using their minds well or in responsible citizenship. Goal 4 on teacher education, examined below, includes the suggestion that more information about American government will generate responsible citizenship, and goal 7 on safe schools suggests providing more information about drugs. These clauses reveal a faith that academic information communicated verbally by teachers can change the behavior of poor students who are better informed about the legal system and the effects of drugs than their teachers can ever be.

Federal statisticians have come up with one measurable proxy for responsible citizenship. They measure how many students "participate in community service," which appears to mean some sort of volunteer work, even if schools require it. "In 1999, 60% of the students participated in community service when their school required and arranged it, and 54% participated when their schools arranged but did not require service. Fewer students participated when the school required participation without arranging an activity (35%) or neither required nor arranged an activity (29%)," (NCES, 2001:30).

If volunteering be considered the epitome of responsible citizenship, then policy makers' vision of democratic society is shamefully inadequate. It is pitiful that they pay such great attention to achieving academic excellence, but simply mention in passing the enormously more important issues of excellence in citizenship and in thinking.

The Goals 2000 legislation succeeded in expanding the scope and frequency of testing, but raising academic performance and narrowing interracial gaps—the purposes for which expanded testing occurred—were spotty, achieved in some grades in some subjects and not achieved in others

(NCES, 2001:17-8,56). There is no evidence that the subsidiary goals of better citizenship and better thinking were achieved.

A developmental alternative to Congress's third goal would make excellence in citizenship and in thinking primary objectives. Students could display both by active inquiry into and resolution of public policy issues of concern to them. The academic ladder and testing would have to be eliminated, with subject matter being sought out only when relevant to student inquiry and issue resolution.

"(4) *Teacher Education and Professional Development*. . .By the year 2000, the Nation's teaching force will have access to programs for the continued improvement of their professional skills and the opportunity to acquire the knowledge and skills needed to instruct and prepare all American students for the next century" (*US Statutes at Large,* 1995:131).

This goal has been present but not prominent in many earlier policy initiatives, and there is nothing inherently self-defeating in it. But it implies that poor student performance results from widespread poor teacher preparation, and it proposes improving teacher performance by increasing their specialized mastery of academic subjects—imposing the academic fallacy more firmly on public education.

The futility of increasing academic specialization of teachers is revealed in Title VIII of Goals 2000: The Educate America Act. That title, "Minority-Focused Civics Education," prescribes "substantive academic instruction in the principles, institutions and processes of American Government" to teachers of minorities and Native Americans so they can pass on this "knowledge and understanding of the American system of government." (209-10) It is an affront to teachers and minority students to suggest that civics education can increase the excellence or equity of the public education to which they are subjected. "Knowledge and understanding of the American system of government" are irrelevant substitutes for practical curricula that actively involve teachers and minorities in sci/tech inquiry and democratic living.

"(5) *Mathematics and Science*. . . By the year 2000, United States students will be first in the world in mathematics and science achievement" (*US Statutes at Large*, 1995:132).

This goal explicitly recognizes the global importance of the explosion of sci/tech knowledge. But just like *The Pursuit of Excellence* and *A Nation at Risk*, it fails to empower all students to participate in that explosion. Instead, it foolishly challenges the most academic American youths to excel on international tests. It promotes two academic fields, despite the fact that mastery of their technical details has traditionally turned off, and purposely been used to eliminate, the bulk of students. It perpetuates the untested hypothesis that mastery of their technical details is useful for most mental occupations. Just like goal 3, goal 5 is incompatible with excellent and equitable education for all. Of course, this goal was not achieved by the year 2000 (NCES, 2001:25-8).

"(6) *Adult Literacy and Lifelong Learning*. . .By the year 2000, every adult American will be literate and will possess the knowledge and skills necessary to compete in a global economy and exercise the rights and responsibilities of citizenship."(*US Statutes at Large*, 1995:132).

This goal only indirectly impacts public school curricula. One of its prime objectives is that "all workers will have the opportunity to acquire the knowledge and skills, from basic to highly technical, needed to adapt to emerging new technologies, work methods, and markets through public and private educational, vocation, technical, workplace, or other programs; . . . (*ibid*). It is in harmony with vocational programs proposed in *The Reform of Secondary Education* in 1973. Why such job-specific skills should be a responsibility of public schools or how they will make the workforce into more responsible citizens is not explained. In its 2001 study, the NCES did not report changes since 1994 (NCES, 2001:29).

"(7) *Safe, Disciplined and Alcohol- and Drug-Free Schools*. . .By the year 2000, every school in the United States will be free of drugs, violence, and the unauthorized presence of firearms and alcohol and will offer a disciplined environment conducive to learning"(*US Statutes at Large*, 1995:132).

This goal was not made explicit in any of the historical policies we examined, although concern about dropouts has often reflected concerns about delinquency. The only relation between this goal and curricula is authorization to local educational agencies to propose programs that might include "Developing and implementing innovative curricula to prevent violence in schools and training staff how to stop disruptive or violent behavior . . ." (207).

Goal 7 tries to eliminate undesirable behavior by imposing discipline rather than by removing the causes for such behavior. It does not recognize the possibility that the academic fallacy driving all its curricular proposals might itself contribute to disruptive or violent behavior. It does not recognize that the poor are the most likely to run afoul of policing rules because the academic environment is so repellent to them.

If the intent of goal 7 is to have students reject anti-social behavior and practice constructive citizenship, then policing will not work. Schools must become places where students engage in healthy and rewarding activities that they would not want disrupted—an attitude that will be developed only if schools are healthy and rewarding places from kindergarten on.

"(8) *Parental Participation*. . .By the year 2000, every school will promote partnerships that will increase parental involvement and participation in promoting the social, emotional, and academic growth of children" (*US Statutes at Large* 1995:133).

This goal recognizes that learning healthy and productive attitudes, knowledge, and skills in schools must be a continuation of healthy and productive learning at home. It does not recognize that the homes least likely to provide healthy and productive learning are low-income homes, or that it is poverty itself that stifles healthy and productive learning. Instead, it places a responsibility on public schools to promote learning at home despite poverty. The statisticians just report the inequity as they report the failure to achieve goal 8. "[M]ost of the statistically significant increases in family activities, such as reading, telling stories, and singing songs with their child, that occurred between 1993 and 1999 were among white children from two-parent households with family incomes above the poverty threshold and with mothers who speak English at home" (NCES, 2001:89).

## CONCLUSION

Examination of a sample of public school curricular reforms in the United States has revealed a small number of answers to our title questions. The answer to "*Teach What?*" has been various academic and vocational subject matters, skills, and attitudes. The answer to "*To Whom?*" has been either academically talented or deprived youths. The answer to "*Why?*" has always been to prepare youths for employment and citizenship.

These answers have been efforts to achieve developmental continuity while responding to the global explosion of sci/tech knowledge and aspirations for democracy. But they have achieved more continuity than development. There has been continuous subordination of education policy to employment policy, continuous commitment to academic and vocational fallacies, continuous lip service to democratic equity.

These answers create dualisms that render them self-defeating. Sorting students into high- and low-status curricula to prepare them for high- and low-status occupations generates resistance that is little muted by claims to provide equal opportunity for all to achieve high status. Curricula preparing for employment have overshadowed and perverted curricula appropriate to other forms of social participation. These self-defeating traits are already visible in Goals 2000: The Educate America Act.

The principle of technological determination suggests how Goals 2000: The Educate America Act could be revised to eliminate dualisms and make it developmental. That principle directs attention to existing gaps in school performance. Both the quality and the quantity of preparation of youths to use sci/tech inquiry and to participate in democratic society are much below technically possible levels. Closing these two gaps is necessary to eliminate opposition between educational quality and quantity.

The institutional adjustment suggested here to close these gaps and eliminate dualisms is to transmit the best theory and practice of sci/tech inquiry to all youths. The first step proposed to close both gaps is to end the subordination of education policy to employment policy. Public school curricula should be driven by judgments of the knowledge, skills, and attitudes most appropriate for full participation of all youths in the intellectual, political and economic life of American society. The second step proposed is to avoid the academic and vocational fallacies. All curricula should impart knowledge, skills, and attitudes in their full theoretical and practical reality. Maintaining the unity of theory and practice permits taking the third step of eliminating tracking. When all curricula are both theoretical and practical, the need for tracking students according to academic talent disappears, along with its undemocratic consequences.

As written, Goals 2000: The Educate America Act is not developmental. Frustration with its perpetuation of the sterile cycle of reform has prompted some to mount the barricades to oppose its self-defeating policies and policy makers: ". . . we must stand up and say 'No!' . . . Goals 2000 knows no barriers. And so we are forced to create a stink."(Ohanian, 2000:355) But becoming partisans in an interest-group based political system is seldom productive of developmental change. A more instrumental approach is to perfect our analytical skills, the better to expose the self-defeating nature of dualistic policies. The more clearly we analyze failures to understand technological determination and to achieve developmental continuity, the more persuasive will developmental curricular reforms appear.

## REFERENCES


Beane, James A. 1997. *Curriculum Integration.* New York:Teachers College Press.

Bloom, Benjamin S. et.al. 1965. *Compensatory Education for Cultural Deprivation.* New York: Holt, Rinehart and Winston.

Bybee, Rodger W. 1997. *Achieving Scientific Literacy.* Portsmouth, NH: Heinemann.

Corbett, H. Dickson. 1991. *Testing, Reform, and Rebellion.* Norwood, NJ: Ablex Publishing Corporation.

Dewey, John. 1916. *Democracy and Education.* New York: Macmillan.

_______. 1938. *Experience and Education.* New York: Macmillan.

Elmore, Richard F. et.al. 1988. *Steady Work.* Santa Monica, CA: Rand Corp.

Fine, Michelle. 1991. *Framing Dropouts.* Albany: State University of New York Press.

Finnan, Christine et.al. 1995. *Accelerated Schools in Action.* Thousand Oaks, CA: Corwin Press.

Foster, John Fagg. 1981. The effect of technology on institutions. *Journal of Economic Issues* 15(4):907-13.

Hubler, Eric. 2001. DPS "[Denver Public Schools] tests effects of consistency." *The Denver Post,* November 11:29A.

Jackson, Anthony W. and G.A. Davis . 2000. *Turning Points 2000.* New York: Teachers College, Columbia University.

Kogan, Barry S. 1997. *Common Schools, Uncommon Futures.* New York: Teachers College Press.

Korzybski, Alfred. 1958. *Science & Sanity.* Clinton, MA: The Colonial Press.

Lazerson, Marvin, et.al. 1985. *An Education of Value.* Cambridge: Cambridge University Press.

Lunenburg, Fred C. and Beverly J. Irby. 1999. *High Expectations. An Action Plan for Implementing Goals 2000.* Thousand Oaks, CA: Corwin Press.

NCES (National Center for Education Statistics). 2000. *America's Kindergartners.* U S Department of Education.

_______. 2001. The Condition of Education, 2001. http://nces.ed.gov/pubsearch/ pubsinfo.asp?pubid=2001072.

National Commission on Excellence in Education, 1983. *A Nation At Risk.* Washington DC: Government Printing Office.

National Commission on the Reform of Secondary Education, 1973. *The Reform of Secondary Education.* New York: McGraw-Hill.

Ohanian, Susan, 2000. Goals 2000. What's in a name? *Phi Delta Kappan* 81(5):345-55.

Ranson, Baldwin. 1986. Planning education for economic progress: distinguishing occupational demands from technological possibilities. *Journal of Economic Issues* 20(4):1053-65.

_______. 1987. "Questioning the meaning of literacy." *Education Week* 29 April, p.28.

_______. 1988. Rural education and economic development in China, Mexico, Japan, and the United States. *Comparative Education Review* 32(2):213-25.

Rockefeller Brothers Fund. 1958. *The Pursuit of Excellence.* Garden City: Doubleday.

Schmidt, William H. et.al. 1997. *Many Visions, Many Aims. A Cross-national Investigation of Curricular Intentions in School Science.* Dordrecht: Kluwer Academic Publishers, volume 2.

Shepard, Lorrie. A. 2000. *Flunking Grades.* New York: Falmer Press.

Tool, Marc R. 2000. *Value Theory and Economic Progress. The Institutional Economics of J. Fagg Foster.* Boston: Kluwer Academic Publishers.

United States Department of Education. 1990. *National Goals for Education.* Washington DC: Government Printing Office.

United States Office of Education. 1948. *Life Adjustment Education for Every Youth.* Washington DC: Government Printing Office.

*United States Statutes at Large.* Washington DC: Government Printing Office. 1959, volume 72. 1966, volume 79. 1995, volume 108, part 1.

Wheelock, Anne. 1998. *Safe to be Smart.* Columbus, OH: National Middle School Assn.

13

# POLICIES TO PROVIDE NON-INVIDIOUS EMPLOYMENT

Deborah M. Figart

## INTRODUCTION

Labor markets are rife with hierarchical distinctions between different categories of work and different groups of workers. Relative wages signify the relative "worth" or "value" of particular forms of work (and types of workers). Class distinctions are often grounded in employment status. Racial-ethnic and gender discrimination in labor markets maintain inequality. Full-time employees are presumed to be more stable and career-oriented than part-time workers. Paid work itself is treated as a marker of one's social contribution, implicitly and explicitly devaluing unpaid work in homes and communities.

Neoclassical labor economics treats these distinctions as either deserved, short-lived, or both. Unimpeded labor markets are hypothesized to reward those whose productive contributions warrant it, providing the incentives that benefit society as a whole. Irrational and inappropriate behavior is weeded out by competitive forces. Commutative justice, based on the equality of exchange between wages and the marginal revenue product of labor, is taken to be the hallmark of fully functioning labor markets.

Institutional economics takes a different approach. As noted by Thorstein Veblen in *The Theory of the Leisure Class*, economic institutions generate comparisons between people "in respect of their relative worth or value." These "invidious" comparisons or distinctions often express "an aesthetic or moral sense" of relative worth (Veblen 1994 [1899], 34). While Veblen's original focus, appropriate to his time, centered upon invidious distinctions between the leisure classes and the working classes, his work encompassed other forms of hierarchy, including, notably, those based on gender. Although he avowed that his use of the term "invidious" is merely technical, and not meant in a pejorative sense, Veblen was attuned to the tendency of economic institutions to make invidious distinctions that promote ceremonial over instrumental value.

Applied to labor markets, this institutionalist framework challenges the neutrality and efficacy of market mechanisms in determining the relative value of jobs and workers. Employment hierarchies may rigidly reflect and reproduce pre-existing social practices (Figart, Mutari, and Power 2002). This happens because wages, the allocation of jobs, and other conditions of employment carry larger social meanings about the relative worth and value, as well as the appropriate place, of particular groups of people. Some people are deemed deserving of what are perceived to be "good" jobs, while others are not. The distinction between "good" jobs and "bad" jobs frequently promotes ceremonial over instrumental value. For example, this distinction serves to creates the identity of a male breadwinner as a full-time worker of deserving social status, while undervaluing much of women's socially necessary paid and unpaid labor.

An over-reliance on market mechanisms has rendered a gap between, in the words of Marc Tool (2001 [1979]), "what is" and "what ought to be." What is needed is "progressive institutional change" (Bush 1978, 1989). Paul D. Bush argues that change is progressive when it replaces ceremonially based standards of judgment with those that are instrumentally based (1989, 455). Public policy, according to Bush, is one means of advancing progressive institutional change.

With regards to labor market policy, progressive public policy should have as its goal the elimination of merely ceremonial distinctions in favor of policies that seek to develop human potential, capabilities, and well-being (Tool 2001 [1979], 90-93; Figart, Mutari, and Power: ch. 10). Workers should be treated fairly, meaning that recognition of the worth of their contributions should not be distorted by unequal allocations of power and status (Dugger 1989). Workers should not be excluded from full and equal participation in the world of work on the basis of class identity, race-ethnicity, gender, nationality, or sexual preference (Peterson 1994, xi). Finally, the work of society is more than paid work. It also entails the ongoing work of families, or the social reproduction of the future labor force. Life's work, in its many forms, creates value and should be rewarded accordingly.

This chapter is concerned with policies that would stock the labor market with so-called "good" jobs. Though I will discuss multiple aspects of job quality, total compensation (pay plus benefits) is central. Therefore, institutional employment policy would call for jobs in which workers receive remuneration adequate to sustain themselves and their families according to prevailing social norms. Further, good jobs are jobs that enable workers to participate in family, community, and political life.

## WHAT IS A "GOOD" JOB?

In contemporary advanced industrialized economies, one's position in the labor market confers status. In part, this is a remnant of the institutional arrangements of the United States' Keynesian welfare state of the postwar period. Job creation was a major economic goal and being a breadwinner was the basis for certain entitlements. Leisure does not carry the same cachet that it did in Veblen's day, nor is productive employment as disparaged. Yet, not all jobs are considered breadwinner jobs, the jobs of full economic citizens.

The distinction between "good" jobs and "bad" jobs is more than ceremonial. In addition to conferring status, "good" jobs provide access to resources. Resources enable people to achieve well-being that, according to Amartya Sen (1999), is dependent upon both meeting basic needs and having choices about how to live. Tool also views "the expansion and maturation of individual's discretionary capacity and role" as a normative economic goal (2001 [1979], 91). The expansion of "good" jobs enhances social well-being by replacing invidious status distinctions with democratic development of what Tool terms "human resources."

Non-invidious employment policy means creating good jobs within market economies. In order to suggest policies to provide non-invidious employment, it is necessary to come to an understanding about what, exactly, is a good job. There is a long history of discussion and debate about good jobs versus bad jobs in the literature, primarily within economics and sociology. For example, drawing upon the work of institutional scholarship in the 1950s, research on labor market segmentation in the 1970s sought to catalogue the hierarchical rankings of jobs in the economy.

Early accounts of dual labor markets sought to explain poverty and unemployment among disadvantaged workers as resulting from structural barriers rather than the intrinsic worth of individuals. A distinction between a primary sector and a secondary sector received considerable attention (Doeringer and Piore 1971). Yngve Ramstad carefully reviews the history and research in dual labor market theory and submits that it also explains job allocation and wage outcomes. According to Ramstad, "The dual labor market theory . . .is clearly the right sort of theory, that is, *a type of institutional theory*" (1993, 215).[1]

Dual labor market literature is largely inductive, drawing from case studies of specific firms and analyses of the structure of labor markets in the economy of a particular time and place. Such studies reveal the invidious distinctions embedded in existing social practices. These social practices shape an individual's place within the social order. The primary sector, it was advanced, contains good jobs, those with higher pay, steady full-time, year-round work, opportunities for promotion, and higher unionization rates. Jobs in the secondary sector are lower-paid, unstable and dead-end, and less likely to be covered by a collective bargaining agreement. It would be an oversimplification to classify white-collar employment as primary and blue-collar employment as secondary. Unionized precision production and skilled craft occupations in factories, construction sites, and in the transportation sector have higher average pay and benefits than nonunion service sector jobs cleaning offices and hospitals, for example.

A declining share of employment in the manufacturing sector following World War II and the rise in services sparked a debate on eroding job quality stemming from the "deindustrialization" of America. Several authors (notably Bluestone and Harrison 1982) were critical of the growth of a low-paid and labor-intensive service economy. Nevertheless, it is unwise to assume that jobs in the service industry, newly created or jobs in offices that date to the rise of big business at the turn of the last century, were "bad" jobs. Service industries are both a high-wage and a low-wage sector. The financial sector offers high-salaried work. Low-wage services include child care, cleaning, and food service employment. In fact, the distribution of earnings in the service sector is more unequal than in the manufacturing sector. According to a study by economist Joseph Meisenheimer (1998, 28), the best compensated workers in some service industries earn considerably more than the best compensated in other industries; but the lowest paid workers in services also fare worse than lower-paid workers elsewhere.

These observations have led labor economists in the institutional and Marxian traditions to suggest that both the primary and secondary sectors had, in fact, primary and subordinate jobs within them (Gordon, Edwards, and Reich 1982; Reich 1984; Craig, Garnsey, and Rubery 1985; Amott and Matthaei 1996). For example, unionized blue-collar craft jobs (mostly filled by white men) fell into the lower core of the primary sector while white-collar employment of hospital technicians (mostly filled by white women), fell into the upper segment of the secondary sector.

Beyond these broad occupational rankings, institutional scholars have identified the distinctions made between diverse jobs within occupational categories. Pay is but one measure to classify jobs and is likely "the single most important element of job quality in the view of most workers" (Meisenheimer 1998, 24). Recently, scholars have sought to provide a richer analysis of the overall desirability of specific jobs. Jencks, Perman, and Rainwater (1988) thought it was important to integrate nonmonetary characteristics into a newly-proposed index of job rankings.

These authors culled 48 job characteristics from a national telephone survey in the United States, the 1980 Survey of Job Characteristics. Of these, fourteen (earnings plus thirteen nonmonetary variables) had statistically significant effects on the way workers evaluated their jobs. The nonmonetary factors included: hours, vacation time, on-the-job training, risk of job loss, educational requirements, proportion of repetitive work, relative position ("Does your boss have a boss?"). Also important were organizational setting such as union coverage, state/local employee, federal employee, and working conditions such as whether and to what extent workers get dirty, decide their own hours, and are subjected to frequent supervision (see Jencks, Perman, and Rainwater 1988). Using multiple regression analysis, a (weighted) index of job desirability was constructed.

While the index was highly correlated with pay, the thirteen nonmonetary job characteristics, taken together, were twice as important as earnings in determining a job's desirability. Further, accounting for nonmonetary factors increased estimates of labor market inequality. Specifically, all other things equal, monetary and nonmonetary payoffs were higher for men and whites compared to women and people of color. Because overall job desirability varies more than pay, it is crucial to consider multiple factors in defining what it means to have a good job.

The Jencks, Perman, and Rainwater study was a significant advance in assessing how job quality is defined. As a result, researchers acknowledged that people themselves place more value on job aspects such as autonomy, fulfillment, and ability to balance work and family, according to Chris Tilly (1997). More importantly, Tilly adds, "bad jobs can no longer be described as vestigial" (1997, 269). Bad jobs formed the core of the economy in the age of globalization, economic restructuring, post-Fordism, or whatever term one prefers for the economic paradigm of the late twentieth century. Tilly provides a reflective, longitudinal look at seven key dimensions of job quality in the United States. The analysis indicates that overall, jobs have become "unambiguously worse" in the past two or three decades. Indicators that have fallen include real wages, union density, job permanence or security, and upward mobility. The trends toward wage flexibility, employment flexibility, and functional (or internal) flexibility have led to a decline, rather than an increase, in job quality (Mutari and Figart 1997). And finally, workplace advances in "total quality management," "lean production," and other fashionable trends in the management/organizational literature and practice, have led to less worker control.

Tilly's verdict is substantiated by an excellent longitudinal empirical study of changes in job quality. Maury Gittleman and David Howell (1995) perform a cluster analysis of 621 jobs in order to better classify labor market segments, which the authors refer to as contours, and assess change from 1973-1990. Though many of their variables are similar to those in the Jencks, Perman, and Rainwater study, Gittleman and Howell augmented the model by considering more elements of job characteristics. In addition, usage of the Current Population Survey and the *Dictionary of Occupational Titles,* rather than a one-time telephone survey, enabled an extended examination.

First, the authors have clustered jobs into six contours, augmenting the labor market segmentation literature: Independent Primary (private and public sectors); Subordinate Primary (white-collar and blue-collar); and Secondary (blue-collar and "people-centered" service). White men are most likely to work in the independent primary sector (see also Dickens and Lang 1993). White-collar jobs in the subordinate primary sector are typically female-dominated occupations such as nurses, bank tellers, and typists. Their blue-collar counterparts would be truck drivers and production workers in transportation, communications, public utilities, and construction. The secondary sector contains jobs in retail services and other low-paid work as child care workers, household workers, teachers' aides, office clerks, including many jobs that are female-dominated and/or minority-concentrated. Low-wage manufacturing and construction occupations are the blue-collar equivalents of the people-centered service jobs. Within the contours, the distribution of jobs by race and gender is consistent with the early descriptions of dual and segmented labor markets: women and people of color predominate in the secondary and subordinate primary contours.

Second, Gittleman and Howell describe the shifts in the distribution of employment by race and gender between 1973 and 1990. The authors find that black and Hispanic men suffered an especially sharp drop in the quality of their jobs as well as a worsening job mix. White, black, and Hispanic female workers experienced an improvement in their job mix. Unfortunately, at the same time as job mix improved for some groups, job quality within each job contour generally declined. For instance, the share of workers covered by employer's group health insurance fell while the share of involuntary part-time employment expanded.

Since 1995, when the US government released its first systematic data on nonstandard employment, the relationship between job quality and nonstandard jobs has received increased attention. Nonstandard employment typically includes on-call work, day labor, temporary help agency employment, employment with contract companies, independent contracting or other self-employment, and part-time employment. A key study by Kalleberg, Reskin, and Hudson (2000) provides further proof of the link between "bad" jobs and nonstandard employment. In this notable study, these authors conceptualize bad jobs as those with low pay and without access to health insurance and pension benefits. They conclude that the growth of nonstandard jobs is indeed problematic because the quality of these jobs is poor. Gains in supposed flexibility come at a high price (see also Golden 2000).

To summarize, the distinction between good jobs and bad jobs is based on factors besides wages. In addition to a fair compensation package of sizable, family-sustaining earnings and benefits, good jobs are marked by employment security and good working conditions. Unfortunately, the proportion of bad jobs in the United States labor market has been increasing. Since job quality provides a crucial signal of the social value or worth of individuals and groups in contemporary capitalism, the growth of "bad" jobs heightens social inequality. The remainder of this chapter considers the following question: How can we turn this around?

# ELIMINATE INVIDIOUS DISTINCTIONS BETWEEN HIGH-WAGE AND LOW-WAGE WORKERS

The phrase "living wage" is used to express the idea that wages should provide a decent standard of living, given current social norms. The assertion that all labor is worthy of earning a minimal, socially-defined level of subsistence directly challenges the invidious, productivity-based distinctions rationalized by neoclassical labor economics. Current living wage campaigns, like those led by organized labor in the earlier part of the twentieth century, involve discussions of fairness. Living wage activities fall into two categories: (1) efforts to raise state and federal minimum wages; and (2) campaigns to establish a living wage for contractors doing business with local government. These policies tie income to employment in the paid labor market. They do not supplant the need to secure basic income, discussed by Charles Clark in chapter 5 of this volume.

## Raise the Federal Minimum Wage

In the US, the first national minimum wage, established in 1938, was 25 cents per hour. (Most individual states also have their own minimum wage laws; only Arizona and Louisiana lack them.) The federal minimum hourly wage reached $1.00 by 1956, $2.00 by 1974, and $3.10 by 1980. Prior to the 1980s, maintaining the value of the minimum wage had steady support in the US Congress, across party lines. It was raised regularly, especially in periods of high inflation. After years of not keeping pace with price changes during the 1980s, the two most recent stepwise increases in the minimum wage in 1996 and 1997 were to $4.75 and $5.15 per hour, respectively.

From 1938 through the 1960s, the minimum wage hovered at or above 50 percent of the average hourly wage of production and nonsupervisory workers in the private sector. Fifty percent was seen as a target for fairness by policymakers (Figart 2001, 113-115). Since the 1970s, wages in general, and the federal minimum wage in particular, have diminished in buying power. If the real value of the minimum wage in 2000 were equivalent to the real value in 1968, its peak, the wage would be $7.92 per hour. Wages of persons paid by the hour have also lagged behind productivity, profits, and the salaries of upper-level management. A related complication that serves to impoverish workers is the fact that nearly 30 percent of wage and salary workers are not even subject to minimum wage legislation, especially workers in private households and in industries such as finance, insurance, real estate, and state and local government.

The view that the minimum wage labor force is comprised of teenagers and other transient workers is false. A demographic picture of the low-wage labor markets tells a much different story. More than two-thirds are adults over the age of twenty and more than sixty percent are women. Compared with their representation in the US labor force as a whole, minimum wage earners are disproportionately African-American (15 percent) and Hispanic (20 percent). Those earning the minimum wage are committed workers, averaging 30 hours of paid work per week. And 47 percent work full-time year-round. Nearly 40 percent are the sole breadwinners in their families (Figart 2001, 116-117). Unfortunately, some low-wage workers spend substantial portions of their post-school careers in minimum or near-minimum wage jobs (see Carrington and Fallick 2001). Increases in the minimum wage, therefore, do effectively reach those who need it most—poor, generally less educated, disadvantaged working adults in low-income families, especially women with children.

Seeking to reverse the erosion in the value of the federal minimum wage, ten states (as of January 1, 2001) have set their own minimum wages higher than the federal standard (Nelson 2001). The State of Washington, in particular, serves as a model. It became the first state to index the minimum wage to the rate of inflation, by easily passing a state-wide ballot initiative in the November 1998 general election. A minimum of $6.72 on January 1, 2001 was thereafter annually indexed to the Consumer Price Index (CPI-U). Certainly, a strong case should be made for every state to adopt the actions of the State of Washington.

Raising the minimum wage to a living wage and indexing it to inflation is public policy that really should be addressed federally. Currently, however, the existing federal wage floor, low as it is, is under attack from the political right. There are proposals floating through the halls of the US Congress to allow states to opt out of any future minimum wage increases. A study by the Economic Policy Institute (Rasell, Bernstein, and Boushey 2001) contends that no states should opt out; the authors marshal economic evidence of who benefits from increases in the minimum wage. The benefits of a higher minimum wage to low-wage workers, their families, and the macro economy far outweigh the alleged costs of wage hikes. The intangible benefits of a minimum wage, one that provides a true living wage standard, is the elimination of invidious distinctions between deserving and undeserving workers.

## Adopt Municipal Living Wage Ordinances

The declining real value of the federal minimum wage gave rise to a new living wage movement in the 1990s, which continues into the 21st century. The contemporary living wage movement—actually a relatively decentralized collection of local movements—attempts to transcend minimal notions of subsistence institutionalized in the low level of the current wage floor. The most tangible product of a local living wage campaign is a particular type of municipal ordinance placed before legislators and voters.

Living wage ordinances require private sector employers who receive public funds (through contracts, tax breaks, or subsidies) to pay their workforce a living wage. This living wage is defined at a level above the prevailing minimum wage. Advocates justify such market intervention by arguing that public tax dollars should not be used to subsidize employers who pay poverty-level wages. Living wage campaigns are also a response to privatization and contracting out of public services, a trend that has replaced unionized "good" jobs with disposable work forces.

Baltimore passed the first living wage ordinance in December 1994, defining a "living wage" as an hourly wage rate of $6.10 in 1995, increasing to $7.70 by 1999. The movement accelerated geometrically during its first years of growth. The initial ordinance in Baltimore was followed a year later by two ordinances, Santa Clara County, California, and the city of Milwaukee, Wisconsin. The number doubled to four in 1996 and doubled again to eight in 1997. Between December 1994 and December 2001, a total of 69 separate living wage ordinances were approved across the United States. Many ordinances call for wages between $6.50 and $8.00 an hour, with a range of $6.25 to $12.00 an hour. Most require some amount of health benefits or a slightly higher wage without benefits; others mandate vacations or sick leave.

Although the majority of these ordinances were passed in city governments, also adopting ordinances between 1994 and 2001 were fourteen counties, two school boards, two townships, and one university (Wesleyan University). Regionally, the ordinances reach from northeast (Boston) to the west (Portland) and through the central states (Minneapolis, Chicago, Omaha and San Antonio) to the southwest (Los Angeles and Tucson). The southeast is not represented, with the exception of Alexandria, Virginia, a suburb of Washington, DC, and the Richmond, Virginia, School Board. The largest national clearinghouse of community groups, the Association of Community Organizations for Reform Now (ACORN), has been active in nearly all of these living wage campaigns. ACORN has a web site to help activists, allowing us to follow the progress of the movement.[2]

A major drawback of utilizing a municipal ordinance as a strategy is limited coverage and effectiveness. Because they are local and do not cover the entire low-wage labor market, living wage ordinances do not reach as many workers as minimum wage laws. This has not stopped opponents from fighting hard to defeat them. Using their neoclassical economic toolkit, foes claim that if the local wage is raised, then the costs of doing business will rise and the quantity of employment demanded will fall. Competing research by the Economic Policy Institute, University of Massachusetts economist Robert Pollin, and other scholars has found that job loss and other hypothesized negative economic and fiscal consequences have not happened (Weisbrot and Sforza-Roderick 1996; Pollin and Luce 1998; Niedt, Ruiters, Wise and Schoenberger 1999; Kraut, Kinger, and Collins 2000). Living wage movements, therefore, advocate that creating good jobs is a continuing and crucial social goal. It is one that can augment other aspects of the public interest.

## ELIMINATE INVIDIOUS DISTINCTIONS BY WORK HOURS AND EMPLOYMENT STATUS

During the post-World War II period, the forty-hour work week was a social norm in most industrialized countries. This standard work week is one of the many economic institutions that has been unraveling in recent decades. Initiatives to increase flexibility in employment practices and working conditions have included more diversity in work hours. The first wave of flexible work hours included the expansion of part-time jobs and "overtime" as a regular practice (Figart and Mutari 2000). In the US, this trend has resulted in a simultaneous increase in people working short hours and people working long hours (Golden and Figart 2000). The quest for flexibility in the number of employees has also led to the growth of nonstandard employment, particularly temporary and contingent work.

While the part-time jobs that have been created are typically the "bad" jobs of secondary sector employment, overwork inhibits other workers, especially those in professional and managerial jobs, from fully participating in family and community life. Workers are provided with two, limited options: a "mommy track" of part-time or temporary jobs with limited career prospects or a "male model" of more-than-full-time breadwinning. Invidious distinctions based on work hours thus carry gendered messages, reinforcing gender inequality in the labor force (Figart and Mutari 2000).

Improving the compensation, stability, and working conditions of part-time and contingent jobs would reduce the penalties associated with flexibility. Reducing full-time hours—not simply by restraining overtime, but by shortening the standard work week to thirty hours—would create a new social norm, one that could enable breadwinners to be caregivers as well. With long-hour part-time jobs and short-hour full-time jobs, invidious distinctions based upon hours could melt away.

### Create Good Jobs for Part-Time, Contingent, and Temporary Workers

Employment arrangements for "nonstandard work" vary greatly. Given such diversity, the conditions of part-time workers may even be at the top of the hierarchy. Part-time work is steady and regular, if not well compensated. Nevertheless, the nearly one out of five US workers employed part-time suffer low wages and reduced opportunities for career development and lack health insurance coverage and pension benefits. Differential treatment of part-time employees is especially of concern for the growing number of workers whose employment part-time is *involuntary*. A majority of part-timers who are men typically fall into this category, though there are differences across countries (Tilly 1996; O'Reilly and Fagan 1998). During economic contractions, the proportion of involuntary part-time employment expands.

Contingent workers, on the other hand, do not have an implicit or explicit contract for ongoing employment. Nonstandard work is thus also performed by independent contractors, on-call workers, workers in temporary help agencies, and workers provided by contract firms. Data on contingent and alternative employment arrangements has been collected in biennial supplements to the Current Population Survey since February 1995. According to the latest survey by the Bureau of Labor Statistics in February 2001, the proportion of workers in all of these types of employment arrangements amounts to about 13.4 percent of total employment (US BLS 2001; Hipple 2001; Kalleberg et. al 1997). The majority of these workers are employed in service industries, notably private household and education services. Though contingent workers are found in both low- and high-skilled occupations, in general, median weekly earnings and access to benefits are relatively lower than for noncontingent workers. In fact, median weekly earnings were 45 percent lower in 2001. Eligibility for employer-provided health insurance is only about half of comparable noncontingent workers. Pension coverage is even less prevalent.

Reducing the number and proportion of nonstandard jobs is key to fair employment policy. As Jonathan Hiatt (1995) has phrased the issue, "The growing problem of abuse and marginalization of what has become known as the 'contingent work force' is no longer a secret" (739). But we are well beyond the research in the mid-1990s that exposed the extent of the problem. It is time to act. At the very least, part-time and contingent workers should be eligible for benefits in proportion to their hours of work. In 1997, the European Union passed a Directive on Part-Time Work, extending employment benefits and social security provisions to part-timers on a pro rata basis (Mutari and Figart 2000, 235).

Workers in nonstandard employment arrangements need access to many of the policies to eliminate invidious employment discussed in this chapter (for further reading, see Barker and Christensen 1998; Carré et al. 2000). They need pay and benefit equity, a living wage or, if hours are too low, a basic income plus social security coverage and access to health insurance. They need to be covered by labor legislation; currently, only workers employed full-time, permanently, by a single employer at a fixed location, are eligible for union organization under the National Labor Relations (or Wagner) Act of 1935. They need to be covered by other federal employment regulations and policies (discussed below) such as the Equal Pay Act, nondiscrimination or equal employment opportunity provisions of Title VII of the Civil Rights Act, and the Family and Medical Leave Act. Other employment laws where nonstandard workers are overlooked include those governing occupational health and safety, worker layoff notifications and retraining, and age discrimination. In sum, nonstandard workers need to escape the conditions of a secondary labor market, and not be treated like undeserving, second-class citizens. This means turning their bad jobs into good jobs.

### Extend Overtime Penalties to Uncovered Workers

In addition to establishing the first federal minimum wage in the US, the Fair Labor Standards Act of 1938 established the 40-hour work week as the norm. The FLSA did this by mandating that hourly wage employees covered by the Act would receive an overtime premium or penalty of "time and one half" for each hour in the week that they worked beyond 40. Enforcement is under the Wage and Hour Division of the Department of Labor, the same division that oversees the minimum wage.

Unfortunately, the FLSA excludes numerous workers from coverage. Ever since 1938, salaried workers, especially executives, supervisors, administrators, and professional employees, have been exempt. Almost half of these are workers in professional specialty occupations. These workers must meet salary and job duties requirements too. Also exempt from the minimum wage and overtime provisions are certain seasonal employees, temporary or contingent farm workers, and casual employees such as babysitters. Those additionally excluded from receipt of overtime pay include many transportation employees, employees of broadcasting stations, domestic service workers, farm workers, and employees of motion picture theaters. There are partial exemptions as well.

The effect of these exclusions has meant that the overtime regulations of the FLSA have become weaker and less central to the economy, especially with the decline of covered manufacturing jobs. The number of white-collar workers excluded from coverage is especially large. The latest estimates from the Department of Labor show that about 40 million workers, or one-third of all wage and salary employees are exempt from the overtime provisions (US Department of Labor 2001). The proportion of those employees who are exempt has risen both absolutely and relatively. The nature of jobs in the service sector has contributed to this trend.

Exempt jobs (no overtime pay) in retail trade and other service industries, as well as employment in professional specialty occupations, have been growing faster than non-exempt jobs. Currently, over 62 percent of professional specialty workers are exempt. Consider the restaurant industry as an example. The National Restaurant Association reveals that the salary of one-quarter of their assistant managers is below $20,000 (Linder 2000, 250). These employees, by virtue of their job title, are exempt. A former assistant manager at a Pizza Hut relates a telling story of this alleged managerial work: "[T]he glow of being a manager and being in charge fades as you're mopping that floor at two o'clock in the morning" (quoted in Linder 2000, 253). The typical work week was 50 hours, sometimes upward of 60 or 70 hours. For the number of hours worked, the salary of an assistant manager often amounts to less than the federal minimum wage.

Lower-paid white collar employees, employed in what could be termed the subordinate primary sector, deserve to be covered by the wage and hours provisions of the FLSA. A statutory overtime premium of at least 50 percent, if not 100 percent, is required.[3] At the same time, we need statutorily to limit mandatory overtime. Currently, workers do not have the right to refuse to work overtime. Unfortunately, many working parents do not have backup child care arrangements, and mandatory overtime hurts working families.

Beyond these reforms, however, we need to radically restructure our definition of what it means to be a "full-time" worker. This means, first of all, reducing weekly hours to a thirty-hour standard. It also entails challenging assumptions about labor market attachment over the life cycle, enabling employees to sustain careers while taking time for education, family, and/or political and community involvement. Flexible work hours schemes must provide individual workers with real choices and control over their schedules, not unacceptable trade-offs between important aspects of their identities.

## ELIMINATING INVIDIOUS DISTINCTIONS BY GENDER AND RACE-ETHNICITY

Within labor markets, good jobs and bad jobs are often allocated on the basis of the gender and race-ethnicity of the worker. This leads to discrimination against individuals, but also differences in remuneration, status, working conditions, and access to job ladders on the basis of the gender-typing and sometimes the racial-ethnic typing of particular occupations or jobs. The characteristics of good jobs are generally associated with occupations held by white males, while working women and men of color are concentrated in subordinate sectors. There is substantial literature suggesting that this is more than coincidental. Women's jobs were historically constructed under the assumption that they were temporary or secondary earners. Pay could be lower and training and investments in human or physical capital could be minimal, creating a reinforcing cycle of low productivity and wages (Humphries and Rubery 1995, 4). Even when women are highly skilled, compensation is depressed by the undervaluation of caring, working with people, manual dexterity, and other characteristics of women's work.

The good jobs held by white males were created as jobs for primary breadwinners. Employer policies, labor activism and negotiations, and labor market regulations were constructed to reinforce gendered social practices such as the male breadwinner family and married women's domestic labor (Figart,

Mutari, and Power 2002). At the same time, the male breadwinner family, though hegemonic, was never universal. Regional economies historically relied upon the labor force participation of both men and women of color, especially African-American men and women. Minority-concentrated jobs were structured for co-breadwinners, thus diminishing individual salaries and opportunities for advancement. Working conditions based on relations of subservience continued long after slavery. Discrimination external to labor markets (for example, in housing and education) has limited access to good jobs. Further, employers, influenced by social norms, have often placed African-Americans and other people of color at the end of the hiring queue (Cherry 2001, 9). Despite almost four decades of equality policies meant to eliminate invidious distinctions based on gender and race-ethnicity, an unfair allocation of good jobs and bad jobs persists, in part because such policies have been institutionalized in a compromised fashion.

## Remove Loopholes from the Equal Pay Act

Under the Equal Pay Act of 1963, sex discrimination was defined as unequal pay where men and women worked in the same job. The wording and administration of the proposed equal pay policy changed substantially compared with earlier versions of the bill introduced just after World War II (for the history of passage, see Figart, Mutari, and Power 2002, ch. 8). The final Act contained several compromises. First, the language of equal pay for employees performing work of *comparable* quality or quantity was weakened. The Equal Pay Act legislates equal pay for equal work on jobs the performance of which requires equal skill, effort, responsibility, and which are performed under similar working conditions. This stipulation protects women in male-dominated and integrated jobs but not the majority of working women.

The jobs in which most women are employed are not subject to provisions of the Equal Pay Act. Roughly 60 percent of women are employed in female-dominated occupations and numerous others work in segregated job sites, divisions of a company, or specializations. Many of these jobs—serving meals, running cash registers, cleaning buildings, and assisting health care providers—are in expanding sectors of the economy.

Further, the Equal Pay Act is an amendment to the Fair Labor Standards Act rather than a separate, "stand alone" piece of legislation. The original bills called for proactive investigation and fixing of remedies by a separate equal pay division within the Labor Department. Instead, this became the responsibility of the pre-existing Wage and Hour Division, already authorized to enforce the minimum wage and overtime provisions of the FLSA; eventually it was moved to the US Equal Employment Opportunity Commission. These administrators respond to employee complaints; they do not initiate investigations. Enforcement of equal pay ultimately lies with the courts. Litigation, however, depends upon the initiative and resources of employees themselves, often limited unless supported by a local or national union. Therefore, another loophole that needs to be closed is access to information about wages and salaries.

The US Equal Employment Opportunity Commission compiles data summarizing the number of individuals filing charges for the types of discrimination covered in the Equal Pay Act and Title VII of the Civil Rights Act. A perusal of summary statistics from 1992 through 2000 indicates that less than 2 percent of the total charge filings by individuals are alleged violations of the Equal Pay Act (US EEOC 2001). Rather than viewing this as evidence of a lack of gender discrimination, it seems more likely that enforcement of the Act is not reaching the majority of working women.

Statistics on the gender-based wage ratio (female as a fraction of male wages) provide a telling story. Before the Equal Pay Act was passed in 1963, the gender-based wage ratio, based on median annual earnings, was 64 percent in 1955, falling to 61 percent in 1960. Following passage of the Act, the ratio remained about 60 percent until 1980. The most marked improvement occurred in the 1980s, rising to 72 percent in 1990, then inching to 73 percent by 2000 (Figart, Mutari, and Power 2002, Figure 2.5). Policy analysts such as the Institute for Women's Policy Research in Washington, DC, report that over half of the so-called "improvement" in the 1980s was due to an erosion of men's real wages. At the end of the twentieth century, there was still a substantial, relatively stable gap between what men and women earn.

During more than twenty years of debate over federal equal pay legislation, there were never any proposals to mandate equal pay by race. Race as a basis for equal pay was excluded from the Equal Pay Act. In contrast, race discrimination in labor markets was legislatively defined as a lack of access to particular jobs. This was the provenance of separate equality legislation, the employment provisions (Title VII) of the Civil Rights Act of 1964. While the Equal Pay Act focuses on a specific form of wage discrimination, unequal pay for equal work, Title VII prohibits discrimination in hiring, firing, promotion, and the terms and conditions of employment, including remuneration. It covers more forms of discrimination, including race, sex, religion, and national origin. Equal opportunity policies were primarily designed to address discrimination by race, religion, and national origin (Burstein 1985; Harrison 1988; Blankenship 1993). The category of "sex" was added to protected classes at the last minute. Many argue that the amendment mandating equal treatment by sex was partly an attempt by conservatives to sink the legislation, although working women's advocates also supported the measure.

To remedy these loopholes, one important bill that has been under consideration in the US Congress is the Fair Pay Act (FPA). The FPA (S. 684 and H.R. 1362 introduced in the 107th Congress on April 3, 2001) would outlaw discrimination in pay for female-dominated or minority-dominated jobs that are equal in skill, effort, responsibility, and working conditions to comparable male-dominated jobs, even if the actual work is dissimilar. For example, within companies, employers could not pay jobs that are held predominantly by women or people of color less than jobs held predominately by men or whites if those jobs are equivalent in value to the employer. As in the Equal Pay Act, exceptions are permitted for wage differentials based on seniority, merit, or quantity and quality of work. The FPA also addresses the "information gap" by requiring employers to release summary payroll statistics by gender, race, ethnicity, and job category. Workers would then know how their own pay stacks up to other jobs at the same workplace. Finally, the bill would forbid retaliation, protecting workers from being fired for discussing salary with coworkers, and it would allow workers to band together to bring class action lawsuits for discrimination in pay.

Another proposed bill, the Paycheck Fairness Act (S. 77 introduced January 22, 2001 and H.R. 781 introduced February 28, 2001, both in the 107$^{th}$ Congress), would strengthen enforcement of equal employment opportunity. The bill would expand compensatory and punitive damages for equal pay violations, treating gender-based wage discrimination like discrimination based upon race or ethnicity. The Paycheck Fairness Act also calls for research, education, and outreach, calling on the Secretary of Labor to propose voluntary guidelines to show employers how to evaluate jobs with the goal of eliminating invidious disparities.

## Strengthen Affirmative Action

It is not controversial to argue that individual workers should be provided equal employment opportunities (EEO). Policies to counteract invidious distinctions by gender and race-ethnicity have sought to remove pernicious barriers that prevent individuals from having access to opportunity. However, from an institutionalist perspective, it is clear that individuals enter labor markets shaped by history, culture, and past practices. In a now-famous analogy, President Lyndon B. Johnson described two runners in a race, one weighted down with a ball-and-chain. It is not sufficient, he argued, to stop the race, remove the hindrance, and then ask the once-encumbered runner to compete from the rear. True equality of opportunity requires redressing the inequality of starting positions.

The role of public policy in undermining the rigidities that result from historical practices is more controversial, and this is reflected by extensive litigation over the appropriateness and extent of affirmative action (AA) policies. The name refers to the proactive nature of efforts to hire and promote groups who are under represented. Thus, affirmative action requires that employers make distinctions on the basis of gender and race-ethnicity but asserts that such distinctions are not invidious.

The controversial nature of affirmative action has led the courts to narrowly define the scope of appropriate policies. Affirmative action programs are primarily voluntary, not broadly mandated by law for all employers. Since President Johnson signed an executive order covering government contractors, these employers are required to have affirmative action plans in place, with a "good faith effort" made to achieve their goals. The courts may also impose affirmative action plans on particular employers found, as a result of a lawsuit, to have a pattern of discrimination. Outlining goals and timetables to meet those goals is acceptable. Quotas, the most controversial tool for affirmative action, are frequently called "reverse discrimination" (Woody 1999). In general, quotas have not been permitted by the courts.

Some firms have voluntarily adopted affirmative action, to one degree or another. Organizations that advertise that they are EEO/AA employers are seeking to better utilize the human capital of a diverse labor force and, specifically, attempting to facilitate occupational integration by race and gender. But have largely voluntary, piecemeal approaches to EEO enforcement and affirmative action worked?

In an extensive survey of empirical research on the effectiveness of equal opportunities policies, Lee Badgett and Heidi Hartmann (1995) find positive, yet modest, results. Race- and gender-conscious policies have barely altered the race-based and gender-based wage gaps. Affirmative action has mainly improved the employment opportunities for nonwhites in managerial and professional jobs in the 1970s, but its effect has been diminished after lax enforcement by the Reagan Administration. The impact of EEO/AA has been greater in the public sector than in the private sector. AA has slightly reduced the gender gap in wage premiums paid by many companies. Finally, affirmative action programs in the 1970s and 1980s had an impact on race-based employment shares. In federal contractor private firms with affirmative action hiring practices, black employment grew more rapidly than in the general economy (see also Leonard 1990; Rodgers and Spriggs 1996; Cherry 2001, ch. 9).

Hiring is not the only employment practice where affirmative action needs strengthening. The status of workers over the life-cycle is equally critical to their income and employment status. Women and people of color tend to be more concentrated into "bad" jobs with dead-end career ladders. Case studies within the internal labor market literature have sought to bring attention to this issue (see Hartmann 1987; Figart 1989).

Though positive results have been relatively limited, renewing our commitment to affirmative action by compelling it for all employers, regardless of firm size, is an important policy objective. We have seen that success was greater during periods of aggressive enforcement and economic growth. Barbara Bergmann's book, *In Defense of Affirmative Action* (1996), recounts the benefits of diversity in the following:

> Perhaps the most important reason for valuing the introduction of diversity into workplaces is that it helps dismantle two caste systems—one based on race and another based on gender—that have been responsible for a great deal of misery. A caste system dictates that your social status forever be that which you were born into, limits your choices of occupations, regardless of your talent and taste, and visits automatic disrespect on those at the bottom of the caste pecking order. (107-108).

To eliminate the dead-end structure of the internal labor market for secondary jobs, "bridge positions" or "crossover positions" need to be established to allow employees to move both laterally and vertically. Such career development programs involve a commitment to internal upgrading as opposed to outside recruitment. Creative programs bargained by public sector labor unions representing female-dominated white collar jobs (e.g., by the American Federation of State, County and Municipal Employees) can serve as a model for further efforts.

## REDUCE INVIDIOUS DISTINCTIONS BETWEEN PAID AND UNPAID LABOR

The standard so-called "labor-leisure" trade-off in neoclassical labor economics textbooks is not accurate. Institutional analysis would improve upon the neoclassical approach in two ways. First, hours that are not devoted to paid labor are more correctly termed "non-income time." Every nonpaid work hour is not used for leisure. In fact, there has been considerable discussion in academic and policy circles that leisure has been declining (see Schor 1991; ILO 1995; Schor 2000).

Second, sound employment policy acknowledges that the unpaid work of families is valuable to society. A good job provides ample opportunities to help balance work and family responsibilities. As a result, we need to remove the invidious distinctions between work in the labor market that is paid and work in the home that is unpaid. A broad commitment to employment policies that help to balance work and family would not be seen as interfering with free and unfettered markets; as will be shown below, the societal benefits from public policy would far outweigh the costs.

### Count and Value Unpaid Labor

Feminist economists have long argued that systems of production and reproduction do not operate autonomously. Analyses of the economic value of domestic labor highlight the public interest in providing for social reproduction. The labor force needs nourishment and replenishment. Household labor, caring labor, the work of families, and social reproduction have value (Waring 1988; Folbre 1994; Benería 1992; Himmelweit 1995). And things that have value ought to be counted.

National income and product accounts, the primary source of data for determining Gross Domestic Product (GDP) in the US and in other nations, only measures activities for which money is exchanged. Scholar-activists have sought to remedy this omission of unpaid labor from these accounts. By incorporating domestic labor into a nation's official statistics, advocates hope to gain symbolic acknowledgment of caring labor and influence the construction of economic policy. Recognizing unpaid labor is not a new idea in the economics discipline. The subject dates to the work of Charlotte Perkins Gilman and Margaret Reid (Folbre 1991; Aslaksen and Koren 1996).

The United Nations has provided estimates of unpaid household work from time-use studies (UN 1991, 1995). Not surprisingly, the surveys show that women spend longer hours each week than men in unpaid household work; the trends are similar in developed and developing regions of the world. Economists have also provided estimates of unpaid work. The research has covered numerous countries (see, for example, Aslaksen and Koren 1996; Cloud and Garrett 1996; Ironmonger 1996). Canada has been a global leader in the measurement of unpaid work through time use surveys; the latter were incorporated into Canada's general social surveys in 1986 (Mutari 2001).

But merely counting the work of families is not remuneration for that labor. How can we pay for the costs of caring? During the immediate post-World War II era, a male breadwinner or family wage provided for many family needs, though the unpaid labor of women was unrecognized. The male breadwinner family, however, is no longer hegemonic. If we are not going to pay these costs via a male breadwinner wage, then we need to find other methods of paying the costs of caring, preferably ones that promote gender equity.

## Mandate Paid Family and Medical Leave

An Institute for Women's Policy Research report on the cost to Americans of the lack of family and medical leave contains a telling statement about US public policy: "Historically, the most common parental leave policy in the United States was for firms to terminate a woman's paid employment and to let her bear the costs of subsequent unemployment and of finding a new job" (Spalter-Roth and Hartmann 1990, 2). More than six decades after sweeping legislation establishing Social Security and covering matters such as child labor, minimum wages, and maximum hours, contemporary US policy still does not adequately address paid parental leave. The United States Congress did pass the Pregnancy Discrimination Act of 1978, prohibiting employment discrimination on account of pregnancy. Pregnancy is treated just like any other temporary disability. A measure of job security is provided.

We still lack a coordinated, gender-neutral policy providing *paid* parental and family leave. The Family and Medical Leave Act (FMLA), signed into law by President Bill Clinton in 1993, guarantees employees up to 12 weeks of *unpaid* leave in order to care for a newborn child, an adopted or foster child, a seriously ill child, parent, or spouse, or for employees themselves to recover from an illness. An employee's current job, or a comparable position, is protected during the leave. Employers must also continue health benefits for the leave-taking employee. The legislation covers employees working in companies or organizations with at least 50 employees within a 75-mile radius. Eligibility is also restricted to employees who have worked at least 20 work weeks for that employer in the current or preceding calendar year. Though 66.1 percent of the labor force is covered by the FMLA, only 54.9 percent of employees are eligible (US Department of Labor 1996, 62-65). Since the leave is generally unpaid, usage figures are well below this. Workers at the low end of the earnings distribution cannot afford to take the unpaid leave. The gap between those who need leave and those who use leave is particularly high for African-Americans (Gerstel and McGonagle 1999).

The FMLA did spur family leave coverage, but less than 2 percent of family leaves in the private sector are paid (Waldfogel 1999). The United States stands virtually alone—along with Australia and New Zealand—among advanced industrialized countries in not providing paid family leave and other family-friendly policies. In addition to policies that help bolster income for the poor and replace income for those who cannot work, European and Canadian social policy provides paid leave to parents, both mothers and fathers. Over 120 countries provide paid maternity leave. Paid leave ranges from 10 weeks in Switzerland to 72 weeks in Sweden (see Lewis 1993; Ruhm and Teague 1995; Kamerman and Kahn 1997; Kamerman 2000; Wisensale 2001).

Statistical analyses show that the macroeconomic effects of providing family and medical leave are positive, increasing labor force participation and lowering unemployment. Comparative research suggests that the costs to employers are negligible, and managers report increases in employee morale and decreases in employee turnover. The benefits to society are substantial (Wever 1996; Albelda and Manuel 2000). Caring labor becomes valued to our families, our communities, and our economy.

Some path-breaking research has estimated the dollar costs to workers and society of the lack of parental and medical leave (IWPR 1989; Spalter-Roth and Hartmann 1990). This research was utilized to urge passage of the Family and Medical Leave Act of 1993 and to encourage expansion of the federal legislation today. Workers who must take leave without pay, or cut back on their hours, or quit jobs because of childbirth, adoption, or caring for a family member who is ill suffer lost earnings. Companies lose when employees use their sick days to care for children and family members, employee turnover rises, and productivity and morale suffers. Taxpayers fund part of the costs in the form of unemployment benefits to those parents who have lost their jobs when they must be absent from work to care for sick children. Poorer families also turn to public assistance to cover lost wages and to Medicaid if their employer-sponsored health care coverage is lost. In their report, *A Workable Balance*, the US Department of Labor's Commission on Family Leave found that 20 percent of FMLA leave-takers with family income below $20,000 were forced to seek public assistance for income replacement. Almost 10 percent of all who took leave were forced go on public assistance (Holcomb 2001). These aggregate losses amount to billions of dollars.

Ideally, family and medical leave should be guaranteed by and funded by general revenues through federal social welfare policy, as in Europe and Canada. One alternative being explored is providing and funding paid leave though state Temporary Disability Insurance (TDI) programs. Funds are collected for TDI in the same manner as unemployment insurance. Employees and employers both pay a small percent into the state trust fund. Currently, five US states (California, Hawaii, New Jersey, New York, and Rhode Island) and Puerto Rico allow employees to take leave with partial replacement of earnings for some period of weeks. Pregnancy is defined as a temporary disability, and therefore maternity leave is partially funded for a period of time. In addition to providing wage replacement, TDI plans generally cover a larger share of the work force and are more generous in the duration of leave than the FMLA. At the end of the Clinton administration, the US Department of Labor finalized regulations to allow states to offer unemployment insurance trust fund payments to parents who require time off from work to care for newborns or newly adopted children.

As of 2001, at least 26 US states are considering legislation to provide or extend paid family and medical leave. Policy research is demonstrating the efficacy of extending TDI programs to expand leave beyond childbirth or utilizing the Unemployment Insurance (UI) system to fund paid leave (see Hartmann et al. 1995; Boldiston 1998; National Partnership for Women & Families 2000; Albelda and Manuel 2000; Naples and Frank 2001). In her testimony for the Illinois General Assembly, for example, Vicky Lovell (2000) estimated the program cost for that state at $61 million, or $10.71 per worker per year. The average annual per employee cost is calculated to be $10.81 in Massachusetts (Albelda and Manuel 2000). A new study on the fiscal viability of extending TDI in New Jersey to encompass parental leave and leave for ill family members estimates the cost to be in the range of $113 to $134 million per year (Naples and Frank 2001), lower than an earlier IWPR estimate. Academic and policy research estimates that expanding unemployment insurance to cover birth and adoption leave only ranges from $11 to $29 per worker per year (Hartmann et al. 1995; Lovell 2000; IWPR 2000). Adding other kinds of family leave could increase the costs to as much as $100 per worker per year (Forsberg 2001), still a bargain to help sustain working families.

In 1999, the National Partnership for Women & Families, a nonprofit, nonpartisan organization focused on education and advocacy, launched a campaign for paid family leave. Their objective is to make family and medical leave affordable for all working Americans. In *Why Americans Need Family Leave Benefits and How They Can Get Them* (Holcomb 2001), a report available from the National Partnership in paper format and on their web site, the organization seeks to reach workers and policymakers (see also National Partnership 2001). Researchers and activists across the US are currently working to show that the direct costs are relatively low while the socioeconomic benefits are significant.

## Legislate Real Welfare Reform

"Welfare reform" was passed in the form of the Personal Responsibility and Work Opportunity Act of 1996. It replaced the decades-old Aid to Families with Dependent Children (AFDC) with Temporary Assistance for Needy Families (TANF). This law mandated that states enforce work requirements and decrease benefits to recipients who have been enrolled for a 2-year spell; it also placed a 5-year limit on lifetime benefits. The legislation is punitive and forces caregivers into the labor market. Any job will do, regardless of whether it pays enough to support children, regardless of whether it offers health care insurance, vacation or sick leave, or any other aspects of compensation that are available to the American middle class. The moralistic discourse used to defend these provisions defines poor mothers as socially inferior and undeserving of income support because they are neither married nor full labor market participants.

The so-called welfare reform legislation has been extensively critiqued by other scholars and even political "insiders" (see Ellwood 1996). Readers can also consult the chapter in this volume by Janice Peterson. In general, real welfare reform should have two guiding principles: (1) "make work pay" and (2) value unpaid caring labor. Policies to provide a living wage, policies such as shortening the work week to help reconcile paid work and family life, and approaches to securing affordable family and medical leave were discussed above.

The primary objective, from an institutional perspective, is to eliminate invidious comparisons between poor mothers and others. Since economic status carries implications for social status, such comparisons will only disappear if we reduce poverty overall and especially poverty among the working poor. Merely dropping persons from the "welfare rolls" does not alleviate their life conditions. They are still poor. Reports from "leaver studies" show that the number of welfare caseloads have dropped since 1996. These findings shed little light on the effectiveness of welfare reform. About half of leavers, in fact, had on average lower post-exit than pre-exit household incomes (Primus, Rawlings, Larin, and Porter 1999; Bavier 2001; Loprest 2001). In the late 1990s, the health of the overall macro economy was largely responsible for leavers' employment rates and improvement in socioeconomic indicators (Schoeni and Blank 2000; Blank 2001a; for a review see Blank 2001b). In an economic downturn, these so-called gains will be seen for what they really are, temporary.

Numerous social scientists and children's advocates have offered blueprints for reforming welfare, even prior to passage of the 1996 legislation (see Levin-Waldman 1997; Handler and White 1999; Schram 2000). One such proposal titled "Help for Working Parents" was penned by feminist economists Barbara Bergmann and Heidi Hartmann (1995). The same players involved in the policy debates in the mid-1990s are gearing up for the reauthorization of Temporary Assistance for Needy Families in 2002.

## Decouple Heath Insurance from Employment

The United States spends more money as a percent of GDP on health care than other industrialized countries of the world. In the US, 64 percent of persons in 2000 were covered by a health insurance plan tied to their employment, for part or all of the year. Persons over the age of 65 qualify for Medicare. The poorest, who meet the eligibility requirements for Medicaid, are able to utilize health care though that program. This leaves millions of Americans without access to health insurance in general or even access to a family physician. With the exception of South Africa, the United States is the only industrialized economy that lacks national health insurance; it has neither a "single-payer" system nor some other alternative providing universal access. In the Canadian model, for instance, government-sponsored health insurance is provided by each province (See also the Chapter in this volume by Michael Keaney.).

The US Census Bureau tracks the extent of health insurance coverage each year (see US Census Bureau 2001). The statistics reveal the invidiousness of the American system of tying health care insurance to employment. The proportion of coverage rises with income. It rises with the size of the firm in which one is employed. Full-time workers have more coverage than part-timers. Coverage varies by race-ethnicity, age, and gender. Hispanics are far less likely to be covered than white non-Hispanics. The coverage rate for African-Americans and Asians and Pacific Islanders is also lower than the rate for whites. Women are slightly more likely to have coverage than men.

In 2000, 14 percent of the US population were without health insurance coverage *for the entire year*. This amounted to nearly 39 million persons. Approximately 12 percent of children, a slightly smaller fraction than the US average, were not covered. Following on the heels of welfare reform legislation, a number of innovative children's health insurance programs have been implemented in the states, through state-federal partnerships. States' Medicaid disbursements are augmented with federal funds from the State Children's Health Insurance Program (SCHIP), a program that was attached to the Balanced Budget Act of 1997. The allocation over ten years (under a matching formula with the states) is to help states provide health insurance to children from low-income families. The funds have allowed states to increase their Medicaid income eligibility limits or establish separate child health insurance programs. The United States is bridging the coverage gap for America's children but not for their parents. One out of six mothers caring for young or school-aged children lack health insurance.

In access to health care, distinctions between children and parents, between workers and nonworkers, between full-time workers and part-time workers, between large and small firms, and between high-paying jobs and low-paying jobs are invidious; they presuppose that some groups are more deserving than others. The Census Bureau 2000 figures indicate that 93 percent of those households with annual incomes of at least $75,000 have health insurance, but the corresponding figure for households with incomes less than $25,000 is only 77 percent. Overall, 30 percent of poor persons were uninsured in 2000. The near-poor, those working but poor, are a group having among the highest rates of non-coverage; more than half of the working poor, 55 percent, lack health insurance. Finally, full-time employment is not a guarantee. Roughly 15 percent of persons who worked full-time in 2000 were uncovered.

Private markets are not the answer for the provisioning of health care. In microeconomics language, there are numerous market "imperfections." Robert Kuttner points to externalities: "Social-health measures offer positive externalities—general benefits that market logic fails to discern and price accurately" (1997, 110). Higher quality care and more universal care can be provided for less cost (see, for example, Rasell 1996; Kuttner 1997). It requires exploring various aspects of health care, costs, and delivery: reducing the length of private drug company patents, shared government-private ownership of medical discoveries and drugs that were supported with government funds, increasing preventative care and health maintenance, considering tort reform, etc.

The current health care system is not working. It is time to consider bold alternatives. The link between health care and a job makes little sense and exists not by design, but by historical accident (Cadette 2001). Opinion polls of Americans have revealed broad support for universal health insurance (Jacobs 2001). Financing a national health insurance system would require a combination of private-public cost sharing, through payroll and other taxes, premiums, deductibles, and general revenues. There are likely to be economies and efficiencies that would arise from a single-payer system or universal health insurance.

## CONCLUDING COMMENTS

Invidious employment stigmatizes categories of work and workers, creating status-based hierarchies in labor markets. Distinctions between high- and low-wage jobs, long hours and short hours, men and women, whites and people of color, and paid and unpaid labor create value judgments about the relative worth of economic contributions. While neoclassical economists view such hierarchies as necessary to provide incentives, institutional economists do not treat work as a disutility. Instead, the incentive (or habit) to work can be cultivated through the progressive institutional change. Good jobs create good workers; bad jobs generate bad habits.

The social-value principle proposed by Tool in *The Discretionary Economy* (2001 [1979]) offers two relevant criteria for advancing the policy agenda outlined above. First, progressive policies must promote "the continuity of human life" (293). In a market economy, this means providing each member of the community with access to jobs paying a living wage and other benefits, without discrimination by race-ethnicity, gender, or other invidious categories. The continuity of human life also requires policies and institutions that value the sphere of social reproduction, especially unpaid work performed in homes and communities. Family and work are aspects of our lives that cannot be separated from each other. Policies to advance one sphere must necessarily consider the other.

Tool's second criterion is the "noninvidious recreation of community through the instrumental use of knowledge" (293). Each person in a community has "inherent potential and worth" (295). We need a culture that nourishes this potential. In a market economy, it is good jobs (well paid, with benefits, and permitting individuals time for family and community life) that tangibly enable people to fulfill their potential and thus promote social well-being.

## NOTES

1 On the replacement of "good" jobs with "poor" jobs due to the growing service sector in advanced capitalist economies, Ingrid Rima (2000) would concur with institutionalists that "Neither contemporary [neoclassical] labor market models nor [Keynesian] macroeconomic models seem comfortable in addressing this constellation of events" (171). Rima, however, rejects labor market segmentation theory. She offers a post-Keynesian "disaggregated macroeconomic model," arguing that sectoral differences in the jobs that people hold are due to the degree of competition in product markets more so than the sociological or cultural characteristics of workers.

2 The URL is: http://www.livingwagecampaign.org/.

3 In the last few sessions of the US Congress, there has been some consideration of amending the FLSA to allow employees to substitute compensatory (comp) time in lieu of overtime pay. Though there can be no doubt that workers need more time for themselves and their families, the so-called flexibility provided under the proposals benefits employers more than employees (Golden 1998; Walsh 1999).

## REFERENCES

Albelda, Randy and Tiffany Manuel. 2000. *Filling the Work and Family Gap: Paid Parental Leave in Massachusetts.* Boston: Labor Resource Center, University of Massachusetts-Boston.

Amott, Teresa and Julie Matthaei. 1996. *Race, Gender, and Work: A Multi-Cultural History of Women in the United States*, revised edition. Boston: South End Press.

Aslaksen, Iulie and Charlotte Koren. 1996. Unpaid household work and the distribution of extended income: the Norwegian experience. *Feminist Economics* 2 (3): 65-80.

Badgett, M.V. Lee and Heidi I. Hartmann. 1995. "The Effectiveness of Equal Employment Opportunity Policies." In *Economic Perspectives on Affirmative Action.* Margaret C. Simms, ed. Washington, DC: Joint Center for Political and Economic Studies, 55-97.

Barker, Kathleen and Kathleen Christensen, eds. 1998. *Contingent Work: American Employment Relations in Transition.* Ithaca, NY: ILR Press.

Bavier, Richard. 2001. Welfare reform data from the survey of income and program participation. *Monthly Labor Review* 124 (7): 13-24.

Benería, Lourdes. 1992. Accounting for women's work: the progress of two decades. *World Development* 20 (11): 1527-60.

Bergmann, Barbara R. 1996. *In Defense of Affirmative Action.* New York: Basic Books.

———. and Heidi Hartmann. 1995. A welfare reform based on help for working parents. *Feminist Economics* 1 (2): 85-89.

Blank, Rebecca M. 2001a. What causes public assistance caseloads to grow? *Journal of Human Resources* 36 (1): 85-118.

———. 2001b. Declining case loads/increased work: what can we conclude about the effects of welfare reform?" *Economic Policy Review* [Federal Reserve Bank of New York] 7 (2): 25-36.

Blankenship, Kim M. 1993. Bringing gender and race in: US employment discrimination policy. *Gender & Society* 7 (2): 204-26.

Bluestone, Barry and Bennett Harrison. 1982. *The Deindustrialization of America.* New York: Basic Books.

Boldiston, Carolyn. 1998. *Estimating the Cost of Using New York's Temporary Disability Insurance Program to Provide Partial Pay to Covered Workers During Le aves Taken Under the Family and Medical Leave Act.* Latham, NY: Fiscal Policy Institute.

Burstein, Paul. 1985. *Discrimination, Jobs, and Politics: The Struggle for Equal Employment Opportunity in the United States since the New Deal.* Chicago: University of Chicago Press.

Bush, Paul D. 1987. The theory of institutional change. *Journal of Economic Issues* 21 (3): 1075-1116.

———. 1989. The concept of 'progressive' institutional change and its implications for economic policy formation. *Journal of Economic Issues* 23 (2): 455-464.

Cadette, Walter M. 2001. *Financing Health Care: There Is a Better Way.* Policy Note 2001/3. Annandale-on-Hudson, New York: The Jerome Levy Economic Institute of Bard College.

Carré, Françoise, Marianne A. Ferber, Lonnie Golden, and Stephen A. Herzenberg, eds. 2000. *Nonstandard Work: The Nature and Challenge of Changing Employment Arrangements.* Champaign, IL: Industrial Relations Research Association.m

Carrington, William J. and Bruce C. Fallick. 2001. Do some workers have minimum wagecareers? *Monthly Labor Review* 124 (5): 17-27.

Cherry, Robert. 2001. *Who Gets the Good Jobs? Combating Race and Gender Disparities*. New Brunswick, NJ: Rutgers University Press.

Cloud, Kathleen and Nancy Garrett. 1996. A modest proposal for inclusion of women's household human capital production in analysis of structural transformation. *Feminist Economics* 2(3):93-119.

Craig, Christine, Elizabeth Garnsey, and Jill Rubery. 1985. Labour market segmentation and women's employment: a case study from the United Kingdom. *International Labour Review* 124 (3): 267-20.

Dickens, William T. and Kevin Lang. 1993. "Labor Market Segmentation Theory: Reconsidering the Evidence." In *Labor Economics: Problems in Analyzing Labor Markets*, William Darity, Jr., ed. Boston: Kluwer Academic Publishers.

Doeringer, Peter B. and Michael J. Piore. 1971. *Internal Labor Markets and Manpower Analysis*. Lexington, MA: D.C. Heath and Company.

Dugger, William M. 1989. " Radical Institutionalism: Basic Concepts." In *Radical Institutionalism: Contemporary Voices*. William M. Dugger, ed. Westport, CT: Greenwood Press.

Ellwood, David T. 1996. Welfare reform as I knew it.. *The American Prospect* (May-June) 22-29.

Figart, Deborah M. 1989. Collective bargaining and career development for women in the public sector. *Journal of Collective Negotiations in the Public Sector* 18 (4): 303-315.

———. 2001. "Raising the Minimum Wage and Living Wage Campaigns." In *Squaring Up: Policy Strategies to Raise Women's Incomes I n the United States*, Mary C. King, eds. Ann Arbor: University of Michigan Press.

———. and Ellen Mutari. 2000. Work time regimes in Europe: can flexibility and gender equity coexist? *Journal of Economic Issues* 34 (4): 847-871.

——— .———, and Marilyn Power. 2002. *Living Wages, Equal Wages: Gender and Labor Market Policies in the United States*. London: Routledge.

Folbre, Nancy. 1991. The unproductive housewife: her evolution in nineteenth-century economic thought. *Signs: Journal of Women I n Culture and Society* 16 (3): 463-84.

———. 1994. *Who Pays fo r the Kids? Gender and th e Structures of Constraint*. London: Routledge.

Forsberg, Mary E. 2001. *Put in Perspective Family Leave Strikes Needed Balance*. Trenton: Jersey Policy Perspective. Available: http://www.njpp.org/familyleave.html

Gerstel, Naomi and Katherine McGonagle. 1999. Job leave and the limits of the family and medical leave act. *Work and Occupations* 26 (4): 510-534.

Gilman, Charlotte [1898] 1966. *Women and Economics*. New York: Harper and Row.

Gittleman, Maury B. and David R. Howell. 1995. Changes in the structure and quality of jobs in the United States: effects by race and gender, 1973-1990. *Industrial and Labor Relations Review* 48 (3): 420-440.

Golden, Lonnie. 1998. Working-time policy, hours determination, and regulatory reforms in the United States and other industrialized countries." *International Review of Comparative Public Policy* 10: 51-75.

———. 2000. "Better Timing? Work Schedule Flexibility Among US Workers and Policy Directions." In *Working Time: International Trends, Theory and Policy Perspectives*, Lonnie Golden and Deborah M. Figart, eds. London: Routledge, 212-231.

———. and Deborah Figart. 2000. Doing something about long hours." *Challenge* 43 (6): 15-37.

Gordon, David M., Richard Edwards, and Michael Reich. 1982. *Segmented Work, Divided Workers: The Historical Transformation of Labor in the United States*. Cambridge: Cambridge University Press.

Handler, Joel F. and Lucie White, eds. 1999. *Hard Labor: Women and Work in the Post-Welfare Era.* Armonk,NY: M.E. Sharpe.
Harrison, Cynthia. 1988. *On Account of Sex: The Politic s of Women's Issues, 1945-1968.* Berkeley: University of California Press.
Hartmann, Heidi I. 1987. "Internal Labor Markets and Gender: A Case Study." In *Gender in the Workplace,* Clair Brown and Joseph A. Pechman, eds. Washington, DC: The Brookings Institution.
———, Young-Hee Y oon, Roberta Spalter-Roth, and Lois Shaw. 1995. *Using Temporary Disability Insurance to Provide Paid Family Leave: A Comparison with the Family and Medical Leave Act.* Washington, DC: IWPR.
Hiatt, Jonathan P. 1995. Policy issues concerning the contingent work force. *Washington and Lee Law Review* 52: 739-753.
Himmelweit, Susan. 1995. The discovery of 'unpaid work': the social consequences of the expansion of 'work.'" *Feminist Economics* 1 (2): 1-19.
Hipple, Steven. 2001. Contingent work in the late-1990s. *Monthly Labor Review* 124 (3): 3-27.
Holcomb, Betty. 2001. *Why Americans Need Family Leave Benefits and How They Can Get Them.* Washington, DC: National Partnership for Women & Families. Available: http://www.nationalpartnership.org/download/genaud.pdf
Humphries, Jane and Jill Rubery. 1995. "Introduction." In *The Economics of Equal Opportunities,* Jane Humphries and Jill Rubery, eds. Manchester, UK: Equal Opportunities Commission.
International Labour Office. 1995. *Working Time Around the World.* Conditions of Work Digest, Vol. 14. Geneva: ILO.
Institute for Women's Policy Research. 1989. *Unnecessary Losses: The Costs to Workers of the Lack of Family and Medical Leave, Wyoming.* Washington, DC: IWPR.
———. 2000. *Paid Family and Medical Leave: Essential Support for Working Women and Men.* Washington,DC:IWPR Publication#A124. Ironmonger, Duncan. 1996. Counting outputs, capital imputs and caring labor: estimating gross household product. *Feminist Economics* 2 (3): 37-64.
Jacobs, David C. 2001. "Prospects for National Health Insurance in the United States." In *The Future of the Safety Net: Social Insurance and Employee Benefits,* Sheldon Friedman and David C. Jacobs, eds. Urbana-Champaign, IL: Industrial Relations Research Association,.
Jencks, Christopher, Lauri Persan, and Lee Rainwater. 1988. What is a good job? A new measure of labor-market Success. *American Journal of Sociology* 93 (6): 1322-57.
Kalleberg, Arne L. et al. 1997. *Nonstandard Work , Substandard Jobs: Flexible Work Arrangements in the US.* Washington, DC: Economic Policy Institute/Women's Research & Education Institute.
———, Barbara F. Reskin, and Ken Hudson. 2000. Bad jobs in America: standard and nonstandard employment relations and job quality in the United States. *American Sociological Review* 65 (2): 256-278.
Kamerman, Sheila B. 2000. From maternity to parental leave policies: women's health, employment, and child and family well-being. *Journal of the American Medical Women's Association* 55 (2): 96-99.
———. and Alfred J. Kahn, eds. 1997. *Family Change and Family Policies in Great Britain, Canada, New Zealand, and the United States.* Oxford: Clarendon Press.
Kraut, Karen, Scott Kinger, and Chuck Collins. 2000.*Choosing the High Road: Businesses That Pay a Living Wage and Prosper.* Boston: Responsible Wealth/United for a Fair Economy.
Kuttner, Robert. 1997. *Everything fo r Sale: The Virtues and Limits of Markets.* New York: Alfred A. Knopf.
Leonard, Jonathan. 1990. The impact of Affirmative Action and Equal Employment Law on black employment. *Journal of Economic Perspectives* 4 (Fall): 47-63.

Levin-Waldman, Oren M. 1997. *The New Welfare: How Can It Be Improved*?"(Working Paper No. 184). Annandale-on-Hudson, NY: The Jerome Levy Economics Institute of Bard College.

Lewis, Jane, ed. 1993. *Women and Social Policie s in Europe: Work, Famil y and the State*. Aldershot, UK: Edward Elgar.

Linder, Marc. 2000. "*Moments Are the Elements of Profit": Overtime an d the Deregulation of Working Hours Under the Fair Labor Standards Act*. Iowa City, IA: Fonpihuà Press.

Loprest, Pamela. 2001. How are families who left welfare doing over time? A comparison of two cohorts of welfare leavers. *Economic Policy Review* [Federal Reserve Bank of New York 7 (2): 9-19.

Lovell, Vicky. 2000. "Paid Family and Medical Leave: Supporting Working Families in Illinois." Testimony for the Illinois General Assembly, House Committee on Labor and Commerce, Subcommittee on Unemployment Insurance for the New Workforce. September 7.

Meisenheimer, Joseph R. II. 1998. The services industry in the 'Good' versus 'Bad' jobs debate. *Monthly Labor Review* 121 (2): 22-47.

Mutari, Ellen. 2001. "Gender-Based Policy Analysis and National Statistical Programs on Gender: A Comparative Analysis. (Working Paper), Committee on Social Indicators of Women's Status, Institute for Women's Policy Research.

———. and Dborah M. Figart.1997. Markets, flexibility, and family: Evaluating the gendered discourse against pay equity. *Journal of Economic Issues* 31 (3): 687-705.

——— . and———. 2001. "The Social Implications of European Work Time Policies." In *Working Time: International Trends, Theory and Policy Perspectives*, Lonnie Golden and Deborah M. Figart, eds. London: Routledge, 232-250.

Naples, Michele and Meryl Frank. 2001. *The Fiscal Viability of New Jersey Family-Leave Insurance*.(Working Paper). Trenton, NJ and New Haven, CT: The College of New Jersey and Bush Center for Child Development and Social Policy at Yale University.

National Partnership for Women & Families. 2000. *State Family Leave Benefit Initiatives: Making Family Leave More Affordable*.. Washington, DC: National Partnership for Women and Families.

———. 2001. *Family Leave Benefits: A Menu of Policy Models fo r State and Local Policy Leaders*. Washington, DC: National Partnership for Women and Families.

Nelson, Richard R. 2001. State labor legislation enacted in 2000. *Monthly Labor Review* 124 (1): 12-24.

Niedt, Christopher, Greg Ruiters, Dana Wise, and Erica Schoenberger. 1999. *The Effects of the Living Wage in Baltimore*. (Working Paper No. 119). Washington, DC: Economic Policy Institute.

O'Reilly, Jacqueline and Colette Fagan, eds. 1998. *Part-Time Prospects: An International Comparison of Part-Time Work in Europe, North America and the Pacific Rim*. London: Routledge.

Peterson, Janice. 1994. "Introduction." In *The Economic Status of Women Under Capitalism: Institutional Economics and Feminist Theory*, Janice Peterson and Doug Brown, eds. Brookfield, VT: Edward Elgar.

Pollin, Robert and Stephanie Luce. 1998. *The Living Wage: Building A Fair Economy*. New York: The New Press.

Primus, Wendell, Lynette Rawlings, Kathy Larin, and Kathryn Porter. 1999. *The Initial Impact of Welfare Reform on the Incomes of Single-Mother Families*. Washington, DC: Center on Budget and Policy Priorities.

Ramstad, Yngve. 1993. "Institutional Economics and the Dual Labor Market Theory." In *Institutional Economics: Theory, Method, Policy*, Marc R. Tool, ed. Boston/Dordrecht: KluwerAcademicPublishers.

Rasell, Edith. 1996. "Health Care Reform." In *Reclaiming Prosperity: A Blueprint for Progressive Economic Reform*, Todd Schafer and Jeff Faux, eds. Armonk, NY: M.E. Sharpe.

———. Jared Bernstein, and Heather Boushey. 2001. Step up, not out: The case for raising the federal minimum wage for workers in every state. (EPI Issue Brief #149. Washington, DC: Economic Policy Institute.

Reich, Michael. 1984. Segmented labour: time series evidence, hypotheses and evidence. *Cambridge Journal of Economics* 8 (1): 63-81.

Reid, Margaet G. 1934. *Economics of Household Production*.New York: John Wiley.

Rima, Ingrid H. 2000. Sectoral changes in employment: an eclectic perspective in 'good' jobs and 'poor' jobs. *Review of Political Economy* 12 (2): 171-190.

Rodgers, William M. III and William E. Spriggs. 1996. The effect of federal contractor status on race differences in establishment-level employment shares, 1970-1992. *American Economic Review* 86 (2): 290-293.

Ruhm, Christopher J. and Jackqueline L. Teague. 1995. *Parental Leave Policies in Europe and North America.* (NBER Working Paper No. 5065) Cambridge, MA: NBER.

Schoeni, Robert F. and Rebecca M. Blank. 2000. *What Has Welfare Reform Accomplished? Impacts on Welfare Participation, Employment, Income, Poverty, an d Family Structure.* (Working Paper no. 7627). Cambridge, MA: National Bureau of Economic Research.

Schor, Juliet B. 1991. *The Overworked American: The Unexpected Decline of Leisure*. New York: Basic Books.

———. 2000. "Working Hours and Time Pressure: The Controversy about Trends in Time Use." In *Working Time: International Trends, Theory and Policy Perspectives*, Lonnie Golden and Deborah M. Figart, eds. London: Routledge.

Schram, Sanford F. 2000. *After Welfare: The Culture of Postindustrial Social Policy*. New York: New York University Press.

Sen, Amartya. 1999. *Development As Freedom*. New York: Alfred A. Knopf.

Spalter-Roth, Roberta M. and Heidi I. Hartmann. 1990. *Unnecessary Losses: Costs to Americans Of the Lack of Family and Medical Leave*. Washington, DC: Institute for Women's Policy Research.

Tilly, Chris. 1996. *Half a Job: Bad and Good Part-time Jobs in a Changing Labor Market.* Philadelphia: Temple University Press.

———. 1997. Arresting the decline of good jobs in the USA. *Industrial Relations Journal* 28 (4): 269-274.

Tool, Marc R. [1979]. 2001. *The Discretionary Economy: A Normative Theory of Political Economy*. New Brunswick,NJ: Transaction Publisher.

United Nations (UN). 1991. *The World'sWomen 1970-1990: Trends and Statistics*. New York: United Nations.

———. 1995. *Human Development Report*. Geneva: United Nations.

US Bureau of Labor Statistics. 2001,. "Contingent and Alternative Employment Arrangements, February 2001." Washington, DC: US Department of Labor News Release.

US Census Bureau. 2001. "Health Insurance Coverage: 2000." (Current Population Reports P60-215). Washington, DC: US Department of Commerce.

US Department of Labor, Commission on Family Leave. 1996. *A Workable Balance: Report to Congress on Family and Medical Leave Policies*. Washington, DC: US GPO.

US Department of Labor, Employment Standards Administration, Wage and Hour Division. 2001, January. *Minimum Wage and Overtime Hours Under the Fair Labor Standards Act*. Washington, DC: US GPO.

US Equal Employment Opportunity Commission. 2001."Charge Statistics FY 1992 Through FY 2000." Available: http://www.eeoc.gov/stats/charges.html.

Veblen, Thorstein. [1899]1994. *The Theory of the Leisure Class*. New York: Penguin Books.

Waldfogel, Jane. 1999. Family leave coverage in the 1990s. *Monthly Labor Review* 122 (10): 13-21.

Walsh, David J. 1999. The FLSA comp time controversy: Fostering flexibility or diminishing worker Rights?" *Berkeley Journal of Employment and Labor Law* 20 (1): 74-137.

Waring, Marilyn. 1988. *If Women Counted: A New Feminist Economics*. New York: Harper Collins.

Wever, Kirsten S. 1996. *Assessing Temporary Wage Replacement for Family and Medical Leave.* Cambridge, MA: Radcliffe Public Policy Institute.

Weisbrot, Mark and Michelle Sforza-Roderick. 1996. *Baltimore's Living Wage Law: An Analysis off the Fiscal and Economic Costs of Baltimore City Ordinance 442.* Washington, DC: The Preamble Center for Public Policy.

Wisensale, Steven K. 2001. *Family Leave Policy: The Political Economy of Work and Family in America.* Armonk, NY: M.E. Sharpe.

Woody, Betty. 1999. "Affirmative Action. " In *The Elgar Companion to Feminist Economics,* Janice Peterson and Margaret Lewis, eds. Cheltemham, UK: Edward Elgar, 1-9.

# 14

# POLICY IMPLICATIONS OF THE NEW INFORMATION ECONOMY

William H. Melody

*We can perhaps assume that the use of a medium of communication over a long period will to some extent determine the character of knowledge to be communicated and suggest that its persuasive influence will eventually . . . lead to the emergence of a new civilization.*

H.A. Innis, (1950) *Empire and Communication*

## INTRODUCTION

An ever more popular theme in the scientific literature, government policy documents and the popular press, is that technologically advanced economies are in the process of moving beyond industrial capitalism to information-based economies. This transformation is expected to bring profound changes in the form and structure of economic, social, cultural and political systems. European Union (EU) integration and the North American Free Trade Agreement (NAFTA) are just two illustrations of this ongoing restructuring of economies and societies (Melody 1985a).

This transformation is being driven by the development and pervasive application of information and communication technologies and services (ICTS). The electronics, computer, telecommunication, media and information content industries constitute a $US trillion-plus global industry sector. It is the fastest growing sector of the global economy and is expected to remain so for the foreseeable future. Most national governments are counting on these industries to provide the primary stimulus to their future economic growth.

If one were to believe the "blue sky" speculation and industry promotion about the technological and service possibilities in this field, one would quickly conclude the new ICTS will solve all of society's problems. A more realistic assessment of the process of transformation to an information economy may provide a little deeper understanding and help fashion more realistic policies by governments and market decisions by industries. (Melody 1996).

This chapter examines some characteristics of "information" in the new information economy, and the important policy issues and implications they raise. The term "information economy," rather than the currently popular "knowledge economy" is selected deliberately because— as this chapter will demonstrate—it is not at all clear that an expansion of information in the economy will necessarily lead to an expansion of knowledge. This remains to be demonstrated and is likely to depend significantly on the development and application of effective government policies at both national and international levels. This chapter focuses on the common general characteristics of information economies, and does not take up the very important issues arising from the great differences among national economies. Hence the use of the generic term, "new information economy."

## MAJOR FORCES DRIVING ECONOMIC TRANSFORMATION

The primary forces driving the transformation of national, regional and global economies are dramatic changes in technologies, policies, and markets. This has involved the combination of the development and increasingly pervasive applications of ICTS on the one hand, and the worldwide movement to market liberalization and deregulation on the other. The conversion of telecommunication (telecom) networks and all forms of communication and information content to digital standards is creating an electronic network foundation that facilitates exchanges and transactions of all kinds. Electronic commerce and the next generation Internet represent the next step in this process. Together with liberalized markets and reduced barriers to trade, this will ensure the 21st century information economy is primarily an international, or even global economy (Sheehan and Tegart 1998).

In an agricultural economy, land is the most valuable resource attracting investment capital. In an industrial economy, manufacturing plants, machinery and other forms of physical capital are the focal point of investment activity. In the information economy, the expectation is that people will be the central resource attracting investment because information is essentially produced, stored, and applied by humans. Whereas the industrial economy was an era of physical capital with labour employed to facilitate its needs, the information economy is expected to be an era of human capital with investment in the skills, competences, and capabilities of people being the central activity.

This suggests that the information economy can provide for a considerably higher level of human development than the industrial economy, for the conversion of what we know as the "labour force" into information or knowledge workers, and for a significant expansion in investment in education, training, research and development—the major formal knowledge generating and distribution activities. It also suggests the possibility for a more widespread distribution of the wealth generated in the knowledge economy because the human resources attracting this increased investment are also workers and consumers.

Therefore, the most important elements of the new information economy that require examination are:

1) the increased generation and use of information as both an economic resource and a product exchanged in markets;
2) the development and use of advanced high speed telecom networks—the information infrastructure—for electronic commerce and related next generation Internet activities;
3) the increased emphasis on the role of human capital as the principal producer, repository, and disseminator of information;
4) the continuation of major market deregulation at both national and international levels.

## THE INFORMATION/COMMUNICATION FOUNDATION OF ECONOMIC INSTITUTIONS

The functioning of any economy or society depends upon information, and the efficient and effective communication of it among society's members. Information is generally interpreted as a "stock" concept, a store of knowledge and values. Communication is a "flow" concept, reflecting the process of transmission and exchange of information, knowledge and values, which itself creates information influencing knowledge and values. "Information" and "communication" provide different analytical perspectives on essentially the same phenomena. An examination of the information characteristics of any economy must focus on its communication characteristics. New communication networks are often the driving force behind the generation of vast quantities of information.

In the broadest sense, the social, cultural, political and economic institutions in any society are defined in terms of the characteristics of the shared information within and among those institutions. (Innis 1951). In the narrower economic sense, it has been recognized generally that the most important resource affecting the economic efficiency of any economy, industry, production process or household is information and its effective communication. Now that entire industries and major sectors of technologically advanced economies are devoted to information—the search for it, the creation of it, the manufacture, storage, classification, summarization, selection, editing, interpretation, hoarding, purchase, sale, and broadcast of it—the economic characteristics of information are beginning to be recognized as an area in which precious little is known. Yet it is apparent that the characteristics of information define the state of knowledge that underlies all economic and social systems. They affect the nature of economic markets and the structure of industry. They affect the internal structure of organizations ranging from corporations to government agencies, political parties, universities, labour unions, libraries and volunteer groups. They affect the formation of social and cultural networks; the nature of work and leisure; the role and definition of education; the structure, content and effective control of the mass media; and the information environment through which public opinion is formed.

Equally significant is the fact that institutions also generate information for the external environment that is employed by organizations and individuals for decision-making. For any particular institutional structure in society, there will be an associated information and communication structure that will influence how that society functions. Some institutional structures will provide stronger incentives for the creation and diffusion of information than others. Moreover, the type and quality of information is likely to change as a result of changes in institutional structure. If institutional change is desired, it may be necessary to change the information structure as a prerequisite to, or as an essential aspect of, effective institutional change.

The importance of information flows and communication patterns to the establishment and maintenance of particular institutions has been understood since earliest times. Trade routes and communication links were deliberately designed to maintain centers of power and to overcome international comparative disadvantages. Britain still benefits substantially from its historically established communication links with its former colonies, long after the empire's formal demise. Universal telephone service was adopted as a policy objective in the US and other countries to encourage economic and social interaction within the country as a way of promoting national unity. The EU is attempting to foster a new European identity by promoting increased communication and information exchange as a basis for stimulating increased trade among its member countries and completing the single European market (Innis 1950).

## SOME CHARACTERISTICS OF INFORMATION MARKETS

In reality, of course, all societies have been information societies. The most significant change between technologically advanced societies and the oral tradition of the Greek city-state—still practised by some native cultures today—is not in the role of information in society, but in the way that information processes are institutionalized. The dominant form of information creation and exchange has shifted from oral discourse flowing outside the bounds of formal market arrangements to the establishment of information generating, storage and transmission institutions, the commodification of information and its exchange through markets. Perhaps the most significant change is not the volume of information, but the structure, the distribution, the institutions, and the dependence on particular institutions (Melody 1987).

Information is often regarded as something equivalent to a natural resource, a mother-lode of objective, unbiased facts to be sought out by diligent search. For example, this view underlies such concepts as "freedom of the press" in Western democracies. Although the press has been recognized as having biases of its own that influence the direction of its search, the information that is found, and how it is interpreted, there is a classification of information that can be analysed usefully as having the characteristics of a primary resource, an information commons for society.

The stock of knowledge in society at any one time, that is, the skills and education of the populace, the detailed factual information relating to such things as the working of production processes, the interrelationships and interdependencies of different sectors of the economy etc., collectively represent a primary resource of society. The value of this stock of knowledge to society depends upon how pervasively it is spread throughout society, and upon the institutions for maintaining, replenishing and expanding the stock of knowledge, i.e., its education and training system, and research generating new knowledge. Economic and social benefits come in the form of improved decision-making of all kinds throughout the economy.

Once information has been generated, the cost of replicating it is very much lower than the cost of generating it in the initial instance. The consumption of information by one user does not destroy it, as occurs with almost all other resources and products. The information remains to be consumed by others, the only additional costs being those associated with bringing the same information and additional consumers of it together under conditions where it can be consumed, i.e., learned. And once a given level of penetration is reached, a multiplier effect comes into play with many types of information, as the information is spread throughout society by informal communication processes outside the formal processes of learning and training.

Hence, although the costs of adding to the stock of knowledge may be very great there are generally significant economies in distributing that information throughout society, and to other societies if the incentive exists to do so. The implications of this economic characteristic of relatively low cost replication of information can be extremely beneficial under some circumstances such as the spreading of knowledge throughout society, for example, information about AIDS. But it can create special problems and difficulties under other circumstances, for example, for a smaller society attempting to protect its culture from being engulfed by the spread of information and values from a dominant neighbour.

Unfortunately, in the new age of information, much of the new information that is generated has its greatest economic value in scarcity rather than in widespread distribution. For example, information that has become important as a resource input to industrial, commercial and professional activities is specialized information sought to provide "inside" or superior knowledge of the behaviour of consumers, suppliers, competitors, government decision-makers, etc. In essence, in imperfect economic markets, this inside information for private consumption strengthens the negotiation or market power position of the organizations or individuals that have access to it. Such information may or may not be costly to obtain, but its economic value clearly lies in its scarcity, that is, in the monopoly of information. Once such information becomes generally known to all interested parties, its economic value dissipates drastically.

Specialized information services for the private consumption of a restricted clientele are springing up almost daily. They range from special research studies of the details of international markets for transnational corporations to confidential assessments of the negotiating strength of a specific customer, competitor, trade union, or government. They include remote sensing satellite data identifying the detailed swimming patterns of schools of fish, and pinpointing the location of mineral resources and the progress of crop growth in distant countries. They include the DNA of specialized crops and even people in distant lands. In recent years there has been a significant increase in claims of intellectual property rights (IPR) over an ever increasing range of information, and even basic data that may have future economic value.

Many governments have taken steps to attempt to restrain the march of information IPR and markets into the details of people's personal lives and to regulate the conditions of access to certain kinds of data banks, for example, credit, medical, and tax files. The pursuit, sale and use of information in accordance with the incentives of the marketplace clearly cannot be totally unrestricted. But the production characteristics of (1) the relatively high costs of establishing most databases and information services; and (2) the relatively low costs of extending the market for services already created; provide a powerful tendency toward centralization and monopoly on an international basis. Thus, competitive forces in many information markets are likely to be rather weak. This, in turn can be expected to raise important issues of national and international government policy relating to IPR and competition policy. The inherent conflict between maximizing prices in quasi-monopoly information markets and the social efficiency of societal distribution at marginal costs approaching zero will be a central issue in policy debates about information economy policies.

## EXTENDING THE LIMITS OF MARKETS

The rapid rise of information markets is made possible primarily by the interaction of advances in computer and telecom technologies. Advances in the computer industry have pushed back the intensive limit of the potential information market by reducing the costs of generating more and more kinds of data. Advances in telecom have pushed back the extensive geographical limit to encompass national and global markets. However, it is important to identify and explore the economic implications of the new technology facility systems that provide the infrastructure within which information is generated and processed, and over which it travels. Included as well are the hardware and the information services, and the information content that is provided over the facility systems.

What are the implications of markets without geographical limits, and an enormous expansion of information in the so-called information economy? The conventional economic theory of markets would suggest that more information and better communication can only improve the functional efficiency of markets. It should lead to expanded competition and an increased role for the market in allocating resources in society. More considered analysis, in light of the experience of the last quarter century, raises questions about this oversimplified analysis. In particular, it raises the possibility that improved information and communication networks may be fundamentally altering the structure of markets so that, at least in many instances, they function less efficiently and play a less significant role in allocating resources.

With respect to knowledge and understanding, it is not at all clear that the new ICTS have led to an improved condition. Studies of transnational corporations have shown that those corporations with the most sophisticated and complex decision-making systems employing enormous volumes of information make no better decisions than firms making similar decisions with less information. Studies have shown that stock brokers, with access to many more sources of information for their stock purchase and sale decisions, have made no better decisions in the stock market than individuals who have not had access to modern sophisticated information sources. In light of the great expansion of information, most corporations have reduced their planning horizons because their ability to forecast the future has substantially declined, despite all of this additional information. With substantially improved statistical data and descriptive information about the workings of the economy, our understanding of the economic system is not demonstrably better than it was in the 1950s. Are the new information and communication technologies introducing more complexity, instability and uncertainty into our economic and social systems than the increased information will permit us to understand and control?

Moreover, the benefits of these technologies are not likely to be distributed uniformly across markets. Certain segments of society are likely to be made poorer in both absolute and relative terms. These new technologies permit many markets to be extended to the international and global level. But it is the largest national and transnational corporations and government agencies that have the greatest need for, and the ability to take full advantage of, these new opportunities. For them the geographic boundaries of markets are extended globally, and their ability to administer and control global markets effectively from a central point is enhanced. These changes have been a significant factor in stimulating the wave of mergers and takeovers involving the largest transnational corporations in recent years. The diseconomies of size and scope provided by increasing administrative costs and reduced effectiveness of information processing and communication in very large organizations can be reduced substantially by the application of information and communication technologies.

The manner in which these technological developments are being implemented creates possibilities for creating significant barriers to entry for all but the largest firms, thereby accelerating tendencies toward concentration. In fact, in many industries smaller firms are likely to find themselves disadvantaged because of the new technological developments. For example, telecom systems in most countries are being redesigned to meet the technically sophisticated digital data requirements of high-volume, multiple-purpose, global users—integrated services digital networks, supplied over high speed broadband transmission lines. For traditional, simpler communication requirements, such as basic telephone services, the upgraded system will serve quite well, but at substantially increased cost to smaller users. Unless there is public policy intervention, the telecom options available to small, localized, and even regionalized businesses are not likely to reflect their unique needs. Rather, their range of choice among services and prices on the common telecom network is likely to be dictated by the global needs of the largest firms and government agencies. In similar fashion, the terms and conditions for access to many new data banks provide substantial benefit to high volume transnational corporations, but prohibitive cost to small domestic companies, particularly in developing countries. (Mansell and Wehn 1998).

In most major industries the new competition that has developed from the globalization of markets is intensified oligopolistic rivalry among transnational corporations. The firms that can now leap across market boundaries are already dominant firms in their respective product/service and geographical markets. Their entry has a major impact on the structure of the supply side of the market just entered, which stimulates a major strategic response from the established dominant firm(s). This is not dynamic competition responding to the invisible hand of market forces as assumed in economic theory, but rather a type of medieval market jousting, an oligopolistic rivalry for the control of market territory. The rivalry is directed to obtaining a long-run position of market entrenchment and dominance in particular foreign national submarkets. (Schumpeter 1950).

In attempting to achieve these long-term dominant market positions, the transnational corporations are often assisted by governments of their respective host countries. Many governments adopt policies and positions that assist their respective transnational corporations, and even participate in international marketing. Thus the oligopolistic rivalry among transnational corporations involves a strong element of nationalism and direct government involvement on both the demand and supply sides of the market exchange.

Taken collectively, these changes introduce new elements of risk and uncertainty into the economic system. But the greater the geographic coverage of a transnational corporation, the more risk and uncertainty can be diversified, although not for the particular production locations dependent on them. Indeed, major structural imbalances in regional economic development have been documented in several countries.

Historically, the current revolution in telecom technologies can be compared in certain respects with the effect of the introduction of the telegraph upon the structure of markets in the last century. In a detailed study of these developments in the United States, Richard DuBoff (1983) concluded, "the telegraph improved the functioning of markets and enhanced competition, but it simultaneously strengthened forces making for monopolization. Larger scale business operations, secrecy and control, and spatial concentration were all increased as a result of telegraphic communications." DuBoff noted that "increasing market size helped 'empire builders' widen initial advantages which at first may have been modest."

It is apparent that decision-making in our society at all levels—governmental, corporate and individual—is becoming increasingly dependent on highly complex information and communication systems. The information acquires value because the decision-making systems in society are being structured so as to be dependent upon highly specialized information delivered over complex, high-technology telecom networks. As the dependence becomes greater, the economic value of the information becomes greater because the opportunity cost for following any alternative path also becomes greater.

## KNOWLEDGE AND EFFICIENCY, OR INFORMATION OVERLOAD?

For centuries the written record of the most important information in society was safeguarded by monks. Societies, at least as judged in today's terms, were characterized by information scarcity. The demand for information greatly exceeded its supply. Both the spreading of established information to wider sectors of society and the accumulation of new information tended to enhance knowledge and understanding. This might be characterized as the acquisitive phase of information accumulation.

Because demand far outran supply, and the costs of replication were extremely high, books were enormously valuable. This information was guarded carefully. The most valuable books were chained to an immovable object. But the monks did much more than physically guard the information. They controlled access to it by making decisions with respect to who could read what books for how long, thereby imposing an information class system upon society. But perhaps even more significant was the fact that they taught selected people how to read, and they read the books to other selected groups that did not know how to read. Even for those who could read, the monks provided the appropriate contextual interpretation of the information. In sum, they exercised a high degree of monopoly of knowledge because of their unique position as gatekeepers to the information. The monks were information professionals who exercised an extremely important and powerful role in their societies.

Over the last fifty years, we have seen the transition from a condition of information scarcity to one of information surplus. It used to be that professional people, including PhD students and professors in economics, were expected to be able to review personally all of the important information in their field and make their own judgements with respect to relevance and significance. But now that is not possible. As if the explosion in books, journals, newsletters and related print material were not enough, now this is being supplemented by a rapidly growing body of electronic information sources that may ultimately dwarf the information available in print. The sheer volume of supply of information vastly exceeds that which can be individually assessed.

But this information is merely the raw material—some people would say data—for the creation of useful information products and services. If this raw material is to be useful, it must be structured and processed to meet particular objectives. Indeed, without a compass to guide one through this sea of incomprehensible decontextualized information, one can easily drown in a flood of incomprehension. In quantitative terms, too much information may be worse than too little because it is more likely to create confusion and suspend independent thought. One sees evidence of this problem in a variety of ways. The large consulting firms, which advise corporations and governments with respect to major decisions, used to define their role as bringing more information to bear on decisions so they were enriched, that is, "more informed." However, the consultants do not justify their role in these terms any more. Now they are in the information destruction business. They justify their role by advising managers as to the 90 per cent of the available information that can he destroyed or ignored because it is not the key information for the decisions to be taken. Now the consultants point to the relevant information and protect decision-makers from the wave of unhelpful information that threatens to engulf them.

In addition, studies of corporate decisions have been made comparing decisions taken by corporations that employ all the latest information, technology and available databases with decisions taken by other firms that are not making full use of the information technologies and available databases. They have not been able to demonstrate that the resulting decisions are any better. In fact, a significant characteristic of decision-making in the information economy is that as more information has become available to guide decision-makers, the planning horizon for decisions has been shortened because of a growing inability to make good forecasts. The dynamic character of ICTS has created an environment in which the additional information has not been adequate to overcome the increased uncertainty created.

It is clear that data and raw information require context and meaning to be understood. Once again, society needs a professional class to guide it to the relevant information. Today we call this class of consultants, "information professionals." But the functions that are required, although still in their evolutionary phase, are not all that different from those of the old monks. The new "electronic monks" will not be guarding the scarce information, but they will be guiding users to the relevant information. The old monks may have been defending the information storehouse; the new electronic monks will provide the compass to guide users through the ocean of information. But in each case, it is the monk who stands at the gateway to the information that will lead to knowledge and understanding. If most of society is wallowing in a sea of incomprehensible information, will it be any better off than if it wallowed in a sea of ignorance?

The plethora of new database and information services now being developed will expand the opportunities for those with specialized and higher-level professional qualifications and relatively high incomes. In the process—and for the most part quite inadvertently—some traditional public markets and social services will be disadvantaged. The correlation between an improving quality and variety of telecom services and a declining quality and variety of postal services—a clear trend in most developed countries since the 1970s—is not accidental, and carries significant social implications that are not yet fully understood. It is important to emphasize that the impact upon the less educated and the poorer classes of society will not be restricted to the displacement of social and public services. The greater impact may well be in the restructuring of information and communication networks and markets in ways that will deny them access.

It is evident from this analysis that increased ICTS can serve to improve the efficiency and equity of markets or to create market imperfections, inefficiencies and equity distortions. The effects in reality will depend largely on the effectiveness of public policy and market regulation at the international, national and industry levels.

## THE STRUCTURE OF INTERNATIONAL MARKET LIBERALIZATION POLICIES

### Financial Markets

The worldwide deregulation of markets has proceeded at a very uneven pace. The virtually complete deregulation of the financial markets, in combination with new global information and communication financial networks, has provided for such rapid movements of money capital around the world that it has become a cause of instability. The volume of international financial exchanges is now more than twenty times greater than the value of trade in goods and services, which has prompted some analysts to interpret the information economy as "casino capitalism." This is associated with increased volatility in stock markets, currency markets, and economic activity in regions and small nations that are vulnerable to the resource allocation decisions of large foreign governments, transnational corporations and financial traders and speculators. Clearly liberalization of the financial markets has gone too far. Increased regulation of international financial markets is needed to reduce incentives for speculation and market manipulation in order to achieve greater stability and efficiency.

## Product and Services Markets

The liberalization of international product and services markets is proceeding slowly through negotiations at the World Trade Organization (WTO) and related regional organizations on a sector-by-sector and industry-by-industry basis, but major steps in liberalizing markets have been taken over the last 15 years. More industries are subject to global competition, and consumers can buy more products and services in global markets. Deregulation has had, and is having a demonstrable impact on product and services markets and on resource allocation.

However, the structure of liberalization has been very biased in the direction of goods and services that the most powerful countries wish to export. The most significant barriers to trade, through import tariffs, taxes and domestic subsidies, are established in the agriculture and textile sectors of North American and European countries. These are the sectors in which developing countries have a demonstrable international comparative advantage. If they are to be able to use the ICTS to gain access to world markets and overcome their poverty and underdevelopment, they must be allowed access to liberalized global agriculture and textile markets. The WTO must pursue a more balanced policy of market liberalization in the interest of all countries.

## Labour Markets

The liberalization of international labour markets has yet to get off the ground, due primarily to the fear in the rich countries of being invaded by the army of surplus unemployed from developing countries. Economic immigration to the rich countries is restricted to that needed to fill specific skilled and unskilled labour shortages. The impeccable logic of the efficiency of markets and the improved productivity from resource allocation on a global scale, which is immediately accepted for money capital, accepted in principle for physical capital in product and services markets, somehow doesn't apply to human capital, which remains highly regulated, with even tighter restrictions being adopted by many rich countries today. Neither this inefficiency in the allocation of human capital, nor its accompanying hypocrisy in the rich countries, is sustainable. In the "so-called" global information economy, the policies of liberalization must be extended to the labour market. A global information economy can only function efficiently if there is a global market for human capital. Global markets must function in the best interests of the people of the globe, not just those in rich countries.

Clearly there is considerable evidence of market failures in some labour markets, as there is in some capital and product markets. An immediate deregulation of the world's labour markets might create even more instability than deregulation of the capital markets. The challenge is to consider steps to the efficient deregulation of all resource markets in a coordinated and balanced approach. This suggests a very clear policy agenda to improve the allocation efficiency of all resources in a global information economy that includes the continuous gradual liberalization of global labour markets.

## Intellectual Property Rights: Information Ownership

In the global information economy, information becomes a valuable resource for many applications, and a valuable product for others. More and more information is being recognized as "economically valuable" by increasing claims of intellectual property rights (IPR). Considerable information that used to be publicly available is no longer so, and monopolies of information are being established in the wealthiest countries and corporations. Laboratories and libraries in developing countries (and in some areas even in the US) can no longer afford to subscribe to scientific journals and reports. The application of monopoly pricing to specialized information monopolies protected by expanding interpretations of IPR, based on historic traditions of patents and copyright in the industrial economy, is artificially restricting access to information and distorting information markets.

Under the existing application of IPR in the information economy, information markets will continue to function inefficiently and lead to increases in the gap between rich and poor, both within countries and between countries. Outdated IPR legal protections make most information markets both highly inefficient and inequitable. They provide a major artificial barrier to trade. The establishment of liberalized IPR laws and regulations for the information economy that promote economic efficiency and equity must be a high priority for national governments and international agencies, including the WTO.

## PRODUCTIVITY IN THE NEW INFORMATION ECONOMY

### Access to the Information Infrastructure

The foundation for the information economy and advanced information and communication services will be a transformed and upgraded telecom network that will provide the information infrastructure over which the new electronic services will be supplied. Broadband telecom network connections will be needed in the workplace, home, schools and all other centers of activity, just as the telephone is needed now. The new information infrastructure will be the most important public utility of the twenty-first century economy. Almost all countries are in the process of developing and/or implementing policies relating to the establishment of new national broadband information infrastructures. These developments require a considered reassessment of public policy relating to the supply of public utility services in the new economy, comparable to that developed for telephone, electricity, gas and transport for the industrial economy. What is the best institutional structure for ensuring an efficient universal provision of information infrastructure services under conditions that are accessible by all those who desire it is a fundamental policy now being debated in many countries (Melody 2002).

Those without access to basic information infrastructure services will be denied access to information and the ability to act on the content conveyed, whether it relates to economic, social, cultural or political activity. There is already concern about a "digital divide" in access within the US and other wealthy countries, and also between the rich and poor countries. Recognizing that the majority of the world's population has never had access to a telephone, it is apparent that the problem of information infrastructure access will deny them access to the information economy until there is a major global policy commitment to extend the advanced telecom network dramatically.

## INFORMATION/COMMUNICATION TECHNOLOGIES AND SERVICES (ICTS): PRODUCTIVITY IMPROVEMENTS

Although the information/communication sector of the economy is extremely important in providing a foundation for a modern economy, the major transformations that will bring about an information economy lie elsewhere. For the most part, the new information/communication technologies and services are intermediate goods. Their primary benefit lies not in their intrinsic value, but in their applications for other purposes. The productivity potential for an information economy lies in the potential for applying these technologies and services to change the way business is done, e.g. electronic commerce, the way organisations and industries are structured, and the way people choose to conduct their lives.

Banking and finance has been a leading applications sector. The industry has been restructured on a global basis. Banks have reorganised the way they function. We can readily recognise that we do our banking and finance very differently today than ten or even five years ago. Other industry sectors, including transport and tourism, manufacturing and services are at earlier stages in their respective transformation processes. Despite official government pronouncements by most countries announcing national commitments to Information Society policy goals, public sector applications lag noticeably behind private sector applications. It is particularly ironic because it is in the sectors of education, health and government administration where the potential benefits of information/communication technologies and services are arguably the greatest. The extent of productivity improvements for the economy will depend significantly upon innovative service applications in the public sector (Melody 1997).

### Defining the Public Interest in Public Information

Liberalization reforms of the telecom and other infrastructure segments of the economy have provided much needed new opportunities for private initiative for the development of the information economies. But governments have yet to mark out the domain of the public interest in the new market environment. An important question that has not yet been addressed is, what will be the universal information needs of the general public in the information economy and information society? If society is going through a transformation to a condition where information takes on increasing importance, then presumably there will be a definable set of public information needs essential to the maintenance of participatory democracy.[15] This information will be necessary for individuals to function effectively as workers, managers, consumers, and knowledgeable, responsible citizens. The public information commons that will be essential to enable information economies to be inclusive rather than exclusive has yet to be defined or even seriously examined (Melody 1990).

## COMPETITION AND REGULATORY POLICIES FOR CONCENTRATED OLIGOPOLIES

It is apparent that the dominant industry characteristic in the information economy will be highly concentrated oligopolies, especially in the information and communication industries. Information, communication infrastructure, and network communication services markets all have powerful economic tendencies to concentrated oligopoly market structures—what Trebing has called "tight oligopoly." (Trebing 1994, 1997). This raises a dilemma for governments with respect to the application of traditional competition laws and/or direct regulation.

The existing body of economic knowledge tells us that oligopoly yields market failure in the form of inefficiency, instability, and indeterminacy. Too little output is produced and too much capacity is established for that output so that excess capacity will serve as an artificial barrier to entry. The rivalry tends to focus on non-price factors, often heavy marketing which provides an additional artificial barrier to entry. Prices are generally set well above costs, and significant price discrimination is typical, except when external factors or a rise in uncertainty stimulates a price war. Concentrated oligopolies often engage in explicit or implicit self-regulation to preserve market share and oligopoly profits. Some oligopolies engage in significant R&D and technological development, which can lead to crashing the barriers to entry of another industry, inter-industry rivalry and "waves of creative destruction." But the transition to the new paradigm is likely to be highly inefficient and path dependent, leading to new industry arrangements which are far from efficient, and very often simply restructured oligopoly.

The traditional analysis is helpful to a degree, and utility regulation attempts to address some of the inefficiency characteristics of concentrated oligopoly. However, economic analysis of market failures and imperfect markets in recent years has developed additional insights into some of the distinct characteristics of network industry markets. Developments in the economics of networks have clarified the characteristics of both production and consumption network externalities (Economides 1996, Shapiro and Varian 1999). This becomes extremely significant in the information infrastructure and information industries as capacity networks are unbundled from service networks and an increasing number of players participate interdependently in competitive/cooperative relations to develop capacity and supply services.

Opportunities for strategic opportunistic behaviour, i.e., imposing network costs on others while realizing revenue from the contributions of others, will tend to promote inefficiency and instability. There are significant economies of scale and scope in networks, but we have learned most of these can be achieved without being internalized to the firm. For most information services on the information infrastructure, there are increasing returns in market expansion. Markets with these distinctive characteristics need rules if operator initiative is to be directed toward efficiency and universal service development. Regulation can influence where the oligopoly market rivalry is focused in the information infrastructure sector. Revised competition laws focused particularly on concentrated oligopoly, rather than simply on monopoly power, can help make information and network services markets workable. (Trebing 1994, 1997).

## ECONOMIC GROWTH AND HUMAN CAPITAL INVESTMENT

It is by now clear that the ICTS revolution will not provide a wave of economic expansion in capital-intensive physical assets, comparable to the past waves of investment initiated by the railway, electricity, natural gas and the automobile. Each of these past innovations required enormous investments in physical infrastructure that carried with them massive employment of relatively unskilled and semi-skilled labour. In contrast, the information revolution is being driven primarily by skilled labour, representing a much smaller portion of the labour force. For the first time in the history of capitalism, the primary driving economic force is not physical capital, but human capital – the investment in skilled labour (Freeman and Soete 1994).

This is evident in the R&D that is yielding continuous innovations, even in the ICTS equipment manufacturing industries, which are increasingly dominated by software development. Just as computer software grew from almost nothing in the mid-1960's to become larger than the computer hardware industry 20 years later, so a similar process has now begun in the telecom sector, most dramatically illustrated by the explosion of Internet services. The driving force is the information content and the communication capabilities, not the physical facility systems.

This is also true in the applications of information/communication technologies and services throughout the economy, and even in the delivery of new services to the home. Experimental trials around the world over the last decade have demonstrated that investments in state of the art technologies and services are not enough. There must be far more investment both in understanding consumer needs and in enhancing the consumer skill base before there will be widespread acceptance of these services. Thus there is increasing evidence that the pace at which the new technologies and services are driving the process of transformation to an information economy depends primarily on the pace of productive investment in human capital, i.e., the skill base of labour, management, consumers and policy makers (Mansell and Steinmueller 2000; Becker 1993; Schultz 1972).

In some respects this is a very positive state of affairs for it implies some very promising tendencies. First, it could significantly reduce the oscillations in the business cycle, which, in the past have been aggravated by the rise and fall of enormous investment in location-specific fixed physical capital. Investment in human capital can avoid these fluctuations. Further, in times of deficient aggregate demand in an information economy, it will be investment in human capital that should be the priority need to stimulate renewed economic growth. A second important characteristic of investment in human capital is that it closes the gaps between the traditional distinct economic activities of investment, employment, service provision and benefit to the population. In the industrial economy, investment frequently does not provide satisfactory employment, and a significant portion of the economy cannot take advantage of the goods and services on offer. If the priority infrastructure investment is in human capital, then the needs of people as workers, as consumers and as citizens, can be met with the same investment. It is both a resource input and a service output at the same time (Freeman and Louca 2001; Machlup 1980).

## CONCLUSION

An information economy is so different from an industrial economy, and the understanding of economists and policymakers about its characteristics so limited at this stage, that we do not have nearly enough knowledge and understanding to manage an information or knowledge-based economy. To paraphrase Kenneth Boulding (1966), "the knowledge of economics does not include the economics of knowledge." It is one of those areas that economists have long recognized, but rarely pursued. Only now that information and knowledge are becoming central to the next phase of capitalist economic development is the subject beginning to get some concentrated attention.

Thus at present we have only very poor indicators to help tell the difference between productive and unproductive investments in information and human capital. Like any other from of investment, bad investments will simply waste resources. For example, by the best indicators available, the US invests more per person on education than any other country, but gets far less benefit from this investment than many other countries. At present we have only crude measures for identifying precisely where productive investments in information and human capital development might be made, or even identifying very clearly where good investments have been made. The best indicators available identify short run skill shortages, which are often misleading for the purpose of building the long run productive capacity in human capital that will best serve a country's population and interests. In fact, we don't know how to conceptualize adequately or measure the productivity of specific investments in human capital. This is one reason for the IT productivity paradox that economists have been debating for the past quarter century.

At the micro level we don't know much more about the characteristics of information as resource inputs into production processes or service outputs from them. Information is not a commodity in the conventional sense, and we are just beginning to develop the conceptual economic and legal foundations for different forms of intellectual property in information.(Noll 1993).

Yet, sustained growth in future information economies will require investments in human capital as a high priority policy tool of governments — for macro economic management of the economy, for enhancing the micro economic performance of specific economic sectors, for building competitive advantage in regional and global markets, and for enhancing individual income and well being. If successful, the so-called "economic man" of industrial capitalism, the servant of accumulating physical capital, can be transformed back into a multi-dimensional human being whose human development is served by investment in the accumulation of human capital.

This chapter has identified some distinctive characteristics and priority policy implications of the new information economy, and signalled the directions in which policies must change if the new information economy is to function more efficiently and equitably than the old industrial economy. The analysis has demonstrated that it cannot be assumed the new economy will be better than the old. Although it offers great potential, it also offers greater possibilities for systemic market failures. More than the old economy, the new one will require the guidance of wise public policies if the potential benefits are to be achieved. That will require a better understanding of the new information economy than economists or policymakers have so far acquired.

## REFERENCES


Antonelli, C. ed. 1991. *The Economics of Information Networks*. Amsterdam: Elsevier.

Becker, Gary S. 1993. *Human Capital: A Theoretical and Empirical Analysis, with Special Reference to Education* (3rd edition). Chicago: The University of Chicago Press.

Boulding, K.E. 1966. The economics of knowledge and the knowledge of economics.*American Economic Review* 56, May.

DuBoff, R. 1983. The telegraph and the structure of markets in the United States, 1845-1890. *Research in Economic History* 8: 253-77.

Economides, N. and D. Encaoua,. 1996. Special Issue on network economics: business conduct and market structure. *International Journal of Industrial Organization* 14.

Freeman, C. and F. Louca,. 2001. *As Time Goes By: From the Industrial Revolutions to the Information Revolution*. Oxford: Oxford University Press.

Freeman, C. and L Soete. 1994. *Work for All or Mass Unemployment*. London & New York: Pinter Publishers. Innis, H. A. 1950. *Empire and Communication*. Toronto: University of Toronto Press.

Innis, H. A. 1950. *Empire and Communication*. Toronto: University of Toronto Press.

———.1951. *The Bias of Communication*. Toronto: University of Toronto Press.

Lundvall, Bengt-Ake and Bjorn Johnson. 1994. The learning economy. *Journal of Industry Studies* 1: 2, Dec.

Machlup, Fritz. 1980-84. *Knowledge: Its Creation, Distribution and Economic Significance* (3 Volumes). Princeton, NJ: Princeton University Press.

Mansell, R. and W.E. Steinmueller. 2000. *Mobilizing the Information Society: Strategies for Growth and Opportunity*. Oxford: Oxford University Press.

Mansell, R. and U. When. eds. 1998. *Knowledge Societies: Information Tehnology for Sustainable Develment*. Oxford: Oxford University Press. (Published for the United Nations Commission on Science and Technology for Development).

Melody, W. H. 1985a. The information society: implications for economic institutions and market theory. *Journal of Economic Issues* 19 (June): 523-39.

———. ed. 1985b. The information society: unveiling some contradictions. *Media, Culture and Society* 7:3.

———. 1987. Information: an emerging dimension of institutional analysis. *Journal of Economic Issues* 21 ( 3): 1313-39.

———.1990. "Communication Policy in the Global Information Economy: Whither the Public Interest?" In *Public Communication: The New Imperatives. Future Directions for Media Research*. M. Ferguson, ed. London: Sage 16-39.

———.1996. Toward a framework for designing Information society policies. *Telecommunications Policy* 20(4): 243-59.

———. ed. 1997. *Telecom Reform: Principles, Policies and Regulatory Practices*. Lyngby: Technical University of Denmark..

———. 1999. Human capital in information economies. *New Media and Society* (1): 39-49.

———. 2002. "Designing Regulation for 21st Century Markets." In *The Institutionalist Approach to Public Utility Regulation*. E. Miller, and W. Samuels, eds. East Lansing, MI: Michigan State University Press.

Noll, R. G. 1993. "The Economics of Information: A User's Guide." In *Institute for Information Studies in The Knowledge Economy: The Nature of Information in the 21st Century*. Queenstown, MD:Aspen Institute.

Reich, Robert. 1992. *The Work of Nations*. New York: Vintage Books.

Schultz, Theodore W. 1972. "Human Capital: Policy Issues and Research Opportunities." In *Human Resources*, Fiftieth Anniversary Colloquium, Vol. VI, *NBER*.

Schumpeter, J.A. 1950. *Capitalism, Socialism and Democracy*. 3rd edition. New York: Harper.

Shapiro, C. and H.R.Varian. 1999. *Information Rules: A Strategic Guide to the Network Economy*. Boston: Harvard Business School Press.

Sheehan, P. and G. Tegart, eds. 1998. *Working for the Future: Technology and Employment in the Global Knowledge Economy*. Melbourne: Victoria University Press.

Soete, Luc, 1997. *Building the European Information Society for Us All*. Brussels: European Commission Directorate-General for Employment, Industrial Relations and Social Affairs.

Trebing, H.M. 1994. The networks as infrastructure—the reestablishment of market power. *Journal of Economic Issues* 28(2) June.

———.1997. "Emerging Market Structures and Options for Regulatory Reform in Public Utility Industries." In *Telecom Reform: Principles, Policies and Regulatory Practices*, W.H Melody, ed. Lyngby: Technical University of Denmark.

# 15

# AN INSTITUTIONALIST PERSPECTIVE ON ENVIRONMENTAL GOAL SETTING

Kurt Stephenson

## INTRODUCTION

At the most basic level, environmental policy can be thought of as addressing two fundamental questions: 1) how to establish environmental goals and 2) how to achieve those goals. Environmental goal setting addresses questions of what ambient physical, chemical and biological conditions should exist in our nation's air and water resources. Once the desired ambient conditions have been identified, the policy means to achieve those conditions—such as emission technology and performance standards, emission taxes and subsidies, transferable emission allowances, educational programs, or moral "suasion"—must then be established.[1]

Within the economics profession, the original institutional economics (OIE) offers a unique perspective to the study of environmental economics and policy. The distinction between OIE and other schools of economic thought is perhaps clearest over the issue of how environmental goals should be established. Drawing strength and support from the intellectual heritage of John R. Commons and John Dewey, the OIE perspective on environmental goal setting is distinguished from other schools of thought with respect to the role and efficacy of democratic processes in environmental policymaking and the role of analysis in decision-making. This approach stands in sharp contrast to neoclassical, Austrian, and in some instances, ecological economic perspectives to environmental goal setting. The objective of this chapter is to describe more fully an OIE perspective on environmental goal setting and distinguish it from others perspectives within the economics profession. The chapter will conclude by outlining some implications an OIE perspective holds for developing an applied, policy-oriented research program related to environmental goals setting.

## PERSPECTIVES ON ENVIRONMENTAL GOAL SETTING

The environmental goal setting process involves establishing social environmental goals and developing ambient environmental standards. Social environmental goal setting requires identification of the level and type of end uses (environmental quality) desired from a shared (common-pool) environmental resource. With respect to atmospheric resources, air quality goals might include the level of protection for human health, aesthetic objectives related to visibility, and the protection of terrestrial or aquatic vegetation and wildlife (e.g. from acidified rain). For water resources, water quality goals might include varying degrees of protection of human health, types and extent of recreational uses, commercial uses (commercial fisheries), and species protection.[2]

Environmental goals articulate social aspirations for a particular resource, but are not measurable policy criteria. Ambient environmental *standards* are criteria by which achievement of environmental goals are measured for policy purposes. Ambient standards provide quantifiable measures that determine whether the broad, social objectives are being achieved. Ambient standards, in essence, establish the critical linkage between articulation of societal values related to environmental quality and the legal system that would ensure achievement of those goals. These ambient standards may be expressed as physical, chemical, or biological measures of the ambient environment. The Clean Air Act, for instance, requires the Environmental Protection Agency (EPA) to establish chemical standards in the form of maximum allowable ambient concentrations for six pollutants. The criteria used to establish achievement of a water quality goal could include the level of chemical standards (e.g. ambient phosphorus concentrations), physical standards (temperature), or biological standards, (e.g. bacteria counts or a biological index ) (National Research Council 2001).

Environmental goals and standards must be established with the recognition that airsheds and watersheds serve other nonenvironmental objectives (Kneese, Ayres and D'Arge). Airsheds and watersheds receive waste discharges from a wide range of human induced activities—sediment and chemical runoff from crop production, air emissions from personal and public transportation, effluent from human waste, etc.. Yet, the disposal of human created wastes can also diminish the quantity and quality of environmental services and amenities wanted or needed by the people. This reality sometimes requires difficult choices to be made concerning competing social, economic, and environmental ends. It is increasingly being realized that there is no achievable air quality standard capable of eliminating all human health risks. The recent Supreme Court decision concerning the EPA's new ambient air quality standards for particulates and ozone highlighted the difficulty of choosing between health risks and foregone economic opportunities (Coglianse 2000). Similarly, water quality objectives must be established by considering and balancing multiple and often competing uses of the riparian environment. For example, great interest is being expressed in reestablishing robust wild salmon populations throughout the Pacific Northwest. Yet, people also desire economic opportunities and other natural amenities in the region. Some biologists argue that wild salmon restoration will be difficult or impossible in many watersheds given the numerous stressors associated with population growth and associated economic activities (Lackey 2000; Moscrip and Montgomery 1997). Furthermore, intentionally introduced nonnative species of game fish (bass, walleye, striped bass) are flourishing in the modified riparian environment at the expense of native salmon species, further compounding restoration efforts (Lackey 2000). This last example also illustrates that choices concerning environmental goals not only require deciding between competing environmental and economic goals (salmon or inexpensive hydropower) but between different environmental goals (salmon or smallmouth bass fishery?)

Given these realities, how should environmental goals and standards be selected? At the most general level, this question can be answered in three ways: analytical computation (conducted by either economists or biologists), private negotiation (markets), or political negotiation (democratic processes). Within economics, adherents to each of these perspectives can be clearly distinguished. OIE, however, is the only school of thought that provides clear and unambiguous support and justification for the democratic alternative.

## An Institutionalist Perspective

Institutionalist economists have long recognized that formal rules and informal customs establish the foundations for a functioning, successful economy. John R. Commons devoted a significant amount of his professional energies toward identifying and explaining these foundations, which he referred to as working rules (Commons 1924, 1934). These working rules recognize the inescapable interdependencies between people and define rights and responsibilities of market participants to deal with these interdependencies (Commons 1924). Property rights, a critical element of these working rules, define scope of control over resources and productive assets. Market prices emerge within the confines of a specific set of working rules. All observed prices are in effect contingent prices—contingent on the particular set of working rules existing at a place and time. Many institutionalists following the Commons tradition have elaborated and expanded on these fundamental insights (Samuels 1992, Schmid 1989, and Bromley 1989).

Given the importance of these working rules to economic performance, it is not surprising that economists writing in the OIE tradition are particularly interested in the origin and evolution of these working rules. The working rules of the economy are derived, to a large extent, from deliberative social action. While informal customs and habits are an integral element of these working rules (Hodgson 1998a), working rules for much of the formal economy are a product of cumulative, discretionary, judicial, legislative, and administrative rule-making processes (Rutherford 1983).[3]

The working rules of the economy are critical in settling fundamental conflicts between competing interests. Interdependencies, particularly those related to use of the environment, are ubiquitous and many of these interdependencies reflect incompatible economic uses (Samuels 1971). When these incompatible uses become acute, government or some social collective modifies or addresses these working rules to determine whose interests or what uses will take precedence (Samuels 1971; Schmid 1989). At the most fundamental level, environmental goals setting is about clarifying rights and responsibilities among competing interests with respect to the environment.[4]

Consider discharge of chemical compounds into a waterbody. Working rules (in this case property rights) would identify the rights and responsibilities for two fundamentally distinct users of the resource: those using it for waste disposal and those who use it for nonwaste disposal, e.g. recreation, aesthetics, production input (Shabman and Stephenson 1996a). The emitter of compounds may cause diminished commercial or recreational opportunities downstream. The compounds may also represent health risks to certain segments of the downstream population. How should these incompatible uses be resolved? One option might be to assign rights to the downstream users of the water. In such a case, the waste emitters would be prevented or held liable for the damages imposed on others. At the other extreme, rights to use the waterbody could be granted exclusively to waste emitters. Downstream users could not legally prevent emitters from discharging into a waterbody. If no explicit social decision is made regarding use of a waterbody, the defacto rights structure rests with the emitter. Failure to explicitly assign rights, however, could still be considered an implicit social sanction to the emitters (Schmid 1989). Still a third option would be to identify some socially acceptable level of risk and damage to downstream users and grant emitters the authority to discharge up to, but not exceed, this level.

Because some uses of a waterbody are incompatible, choices have to be made concerning who can harm whom. If the emitter receives the rights, then downstream users may be harmed. If downstream users receive the rights, the emitter faces higher costs and perhaps lost business opportunities. Ronald Coase is perhaps best known for stressing the dual nature of harm, but with respect to this dimension of Coasian reasoning, an OIE perspective is in absolute agreement.

The dual nature of any property rights structure highlights the choices that must be made—where the rights and responsibilities lie and who can harm whom and to what degree—but offers no insight in what right structure should be selected. From an OIE perspective, there is no analytical method to resolve this choice over which set of working rules is correct or right. The rules selected ultimately rest on how the community weighs the values behind these competing uses. Federal water quality policy as embodied by the Clean Water Act reflects that a combination of rights structures exist simultaneously. Certain categories of waste emitters face requirements to install and operate technologies that minimize the water quality impacts. Other types of waste emitters are granted defacto rights to emit waste. Certain agricultural producers, a subset of what are called nonpoint sources dischargers, may discharge waste into waters of the United States with relative impunity (Stephenson, Shabman, and Geyer 1999). In this case, rights to use a waterbody rest to a large extent with the waste emitters. Federal water quality law provides downstream users very limited rights to prevent or limit certain types of farm operations from using a waterbody for waste disposal. Additional evidence and social support of this rights structure for nonpoint sources can be found in voluntary cost-share arrangements. Federal and state cost share programs pay agricultural producers to voluntarily implement effluent control practices to reduce their damages to downstream users. The historical presumption is that someone else (typically government agencies) must offer cash assistance to induce farm operators to reduce or control effluent discharges.

Regardless of what one individually thinks about this rights structure, it currently enjoys the collective sanction. When the Clean Water Act was drafted in the early 1970s, a collective decision was made to exclude many agricultural emitters, but not industrial or municipal emitters, from mandatory waste control requirements. In the collective choice process, agricultural producers are exempted from mandatory controls because of perceptions of fairness (ability to pay), potential sources of conflict between related right structures (particularly between effluent control and land use control), the relative contribution of such sources to water quality impairments, and deeply held beliefs about the preservation of agrarian lifestyles. Obviously, these values may come in direct conflict with other social values related to water quality objectives and the existing rights structure (set of working rules) will change over time.[5]

Thus, the OIE perspective stresses that the choice of what working rules are selected is ultimately based on collective decision processes. Furthermore, a social valuing process based on democratic processes and feedback ensures that these working rules continue to change and evolve to reflect underlying social values. This adjustment, refinement, and creation of the working rules of the economy provides the social sideboards on market activity and helps ensure that market activity produces outcomes consistent with underlying ethical and social values (Commons 1924).

## An Austrian Perspective

The emphasis and interest concerning the importance of the working rules for economic performance in general, and environmental policy in particular, are now well recognized by many economists writing outside the OIE tradition. For example, economists writing in the Austrian tradition, self-labeled "free market environmentalists" (FME), readily acknowledge the fundamental role of government in establishing and enforcing property right systems (Anderson and Leal 1991). While acknowledging this role, the FME economists argue that such property rights, once assigned, should be made private and transferable to the maximum extent possible.

In the context of air and water resources, the FME economists argue that private entities should be assigned the rights to the atmosphere or watershed (Smith 1995). Neighborhood associations, for example, could be initially assigned the rights to the atmosphere above their jurisdictions or the water within their boundaries. But for the FME economist, these rights should then be transferable. Waste emitters should be allowed to negotiate with the neighborhood associations to legally dispose of their waste within their jurisdiction (Smith 1995). Any unauthorized waste being discharged on the property would be subject to enforcement action. Through these market transactions, the neighborhood associations and emitters would decide for themselves appropriate environmental goals for their location.

From an Austrian perspective, transferring rights between emitters and the various types of nonemiting users is no different conceptually than transferring rights to goods traditionally traded in markets. Markets are a way to resolve conflict and competition over resources. At some level recreational use and waste disposal are mutually exclusive uses—emitting waste into a waterbody reduces recreational uses. Yet, use of my neighbor's sports car is equally exclusive. If my neighbor has rights to it, I do not. If my neighbor is driving it, I cannot. In the case of the sports car, the existing personal property working rules govern the use and transfer of rights to use a car. Potential competing uses of the sports car are settled through market exchange. I obtain the right to use that vehicle through a market transaction. For the FME perspective, the only difference between the sports car and establishing a water quality goal through markets, is that the rights to the water resource are not well established and nontransferable. Establishing those rights make the car and water quality conceptually equivalent.

Furthermore, the FME economist would argue that market exchange would result in outcomes that more accurately reflect people's environmental values and preferences. According to Fred Smith (1995, 72) "only under a system where resources are privately held will people have the ability to accurately express their environmental values." Markets facilitate a discovery process for parties on both ends of the transaction (Kirzner 1997). For the recreational user or other nonemitter, new environmental conditions and economic opportunities require individuals to constantly reevaluate and discover preferences and opportunities. Facing the difficult choice of deciding how to allocate a limited budget would also more accurately reveal people's preferences for environmental protection. For the waste emitter, the requirement to pay for the use of the environment would also create incentives to search for and create new ways to prevent pollution.

A variety of technical and practical objections can be raised against a market transaction approach to environmental goal setting. At a practical level transferable atmospheric or water quality rights may be infeasible to implement because of the high costs of establishing and transferring rights between the multitudes of possible interests (Park 1996). The Austrian may reply that such obstacles are not insurmountable and transaction costs can be reduced by either technological innovation or better design of the right system (Smith 1995; Shabman and Stephenson 2000). The OIE economist may be skeptical of the ability to overcome these technical implementation barriers, but the OIE critique of the FME position reaches a much more fundamental level. In short, the institutionalists argue that environmental goals and sports cars cannot be made fundamentally equivalent because they are fundamentally different.

The difference between environmental goals and automobiles rests ultimately in a distinction between social values and individual preferences. In reference to environmental policy, philosopher Mark Sagoff makes perhaps the most clear and eloquent distinction between the two (Sagoff 1988, 1994, 1996, 2000). When people make a choice about what type of automobile to buy, they must decide what is good for them. Yet, people do not view all decisions in such narrow, self-interested terms. People view many public policy decisions through a different set of lens. When deliberating, debating, and deciding many public policy questions, people frame discussions in terms of ethical or moral commitments or obligations. By definition, these commitments and obligations are made without reference to the self (Bromley 2000). At its core, democratic deliberation and decision-making focuses attention primarily on what citizens aspire to achieve as a community, not what individuals want personally (Sagoff 1996). Acting as citizens rather than consumers, people voluntarily decide to impose restrictions and costs on themselves in order to achieve the principles and values of the community.

In short, people simultaneously view themselves as both citizens and consumers and assume different perspectives depending on the type of decision being made (Shabman and Stephenson 1996b). The distinction between moral commitments and individual preferences is not just an academic distinction. The distinction is simply an acknowledgement and recognition that people frame and understand choices differently depending on the specific decision context. Institutionalists recognize that a given community may deem it inappropriate to exchange child labor, sex, etc. through private exchange. Citizens of the United States no longer allow children to work in factories or mines because of moral and ethical reasons and not because of barriers to negotiating a transaction. The fact that a mine owner may be willing to pay a good wage to a child and obtain consent from the parents to employ the child was eventually considered irrelevant. The decision to limit employment of children was made from a perspective of what a good community ought to do—the "right" thing to do—and not whether it satisfied the preferences of the transacting parties. Similarly, citizens may also agree that a good society should establish minimum acceptable levels of risk in the workplace. Once established, these community standards are not then placed for sale to the highest bidder.

The experience in the United States suggests that these distinctions apply to environmental goal setting. The nation's air and water quality laws reflect a moral judgment that environmental protection should establish aggressive air and water quality standards that protect both people and the ecological system. The broad aim of the Clean Water Act is to "restore and maintain the chemical, physical, and biological integrity of the Nation's waters." (101(a), 33 U.S.C. 1251 (a). Similarly, the Clean Air Act instructs the EPA to establish national ambient air quality standards that protect human health. These broad goals were not established or subject to revision based on what someone would pay for them but reflect a moral obligation to protect and safeguard the health of the populace and the ecosystem. These statements are an expression of what a good society should strive for. We protect nature not necessarily for what services the environment personally provides us but because protecting ecosystem is an important end in and of itself (Dworkin 1994).

This moral commitment that people express for the environment does not then imply that the OIE perspective would argue for a pristine environment – environmental quality that existed prior to anthropocentric-induced damage. OIE is built on the philosophic foundations of pragmatism. Pragmatism acknowledges that pursuit of environmental goals must be made with an acknowledgement and understanding of the biological constraints, physical limits and economic costs of the achieving these goals. The establishment of ends-in-view with reference to the available means is one of the most fundamental contributions of pragmatist philosophers like John Dewey to OIE thought.

Given the impact on the natural environment is unavoidable, the pragmatist approach would recognize the impossibility of eliminating all human and ecological harm from waste discharges. Society may express a deep commitment to improving the riparian ecosystem functioning, but such a commitment must be expressed within the confines of social, biological, physical, and economic realities. While a pragmatist may express a deep commitment to minimizing the impacts on the riparian environment, a pragmatist would also recognize that the concrete stormwater channels that used to be the Los Angeles River will never again approximate the riparian conditions that existed in 1800 or achieve the water quality conditions of a stream running out of the Sierra Nevada Mountains. From an OIE perspective, water quality goals should be different for the Los Angeles River and a stream in Yosemite National Park. Because pristine or uniform environmental goals cannot be realistically achieved does not mean that the moral commitment to air and water quality protection is compromised. Rather, the OIE perspective recognizes that the means of achieving environmental quality must be part of the ongoing ethical and moral discussions over establishment of environmental goals and standards (Sagoff 1988).

The distinction between private preferences and social values justifies the use of collective choice processes to debate and decide appropriate levels of environmental quality. From an OIE perspective, individual preference satisfaction through market exchange is simply inconsistent with people's expressions of ethical and moral commitments to environmental quality. Yet, the distinction between private preferences and moral commitments also implies a *limit* to which collective choice making processes should be applied in environmental policy. While collective choice processes may be favored as a means to address environmental goals, the OIE perspective recognizes the efficacy of relying on private incentives and decision-making as means to achieve socially determined ends. In short, institutional economists express support for allowing significant individual discretion on how to achieve environmental goals (Hayden 1995; Samuels 1992).

To clarify the point, OIE economists would not rule out, *a priori*, the use of market mechanisms as a means to achieve socially determined ends in environmental policy. Market arrangements could be established between waste emitters *after* environmental goals have been determined. Such market-like systems are sometimes referred to as cap-and-trade. An effluent or emission load cap is the maximum emission load that can be discharged without violating a given environmental standard. Thus, the waste load cap limits waste discharges within the confines of socially determined goals. Once the environmental goal and effluent cap have been established, the fixed and limited number of discharge allowances is distributed among the waste emitters. Allowance holders may transfer these allowances to existing waste emitters and new emitters must buy allowances from the existing stock of allowances before being allowed to legally discharge. OIE support for such markets for discharge rights stem from the fact that such rights structures are created *within* socially prescribed bounds. Markets for discharge allowances are a set of working rules that ensure market outcomes are consistent with social values.

Despite a strong social planning legacy (Rutherford 2001), an OIE perspective would not rule out the use of limited market exchange to achieve environmental goals. Given the pragmatist foundations, the performance of discharge allowance markets would be evaluated against other policies to achieve environmental goals. At least some OIE practitioners recognize and appreciate the potential and power of markets to stimulate innovation, motivate private interests, and organize economic activity for many of the same reasons Austrians advocate the use of markets (Samuels 1992; Hodgson 1998b).

## Role of Government

Scholars with the OIE perspective recognize the fundamental role of government in establishing environmental goals, but this conclusion is hardly unique within environmental economics. With the exception of the Austrians, most environmental economists would agree that government has a more active and positive role to play. Neoclassical environmental economists, for example, justify government's role in establishing environmental goals based on the existence of externalities or transaction costs. Neoclassicists are quite confident in expressing the limitations of markets to provide adequate levels of environmental quality. While neoclassical economists are often accused of uncritical support for markets, mainstream environmental economists express an almost total *lack* of professional attention to, and advocacy of, market processes in setting environmental goals.

Given widespread acknowledgement for the need of government intervention to establish environmental goals, the question then becomes "how will government decide which environmental goal to pursue?" Conceptually, at least two approaches to collective choice making can be identified. These two approaches can be described as (a) rational analysis and (b) democratic deliberation. While this may represent a stylized polarization of approaches, it does nonetheless describe some strong differences in the conceptual underpinnings of the different schools of thought. Among mainstream economists, there is a strong tendency to subscribe to the rational analytic approach. While there are elements of a rational analytic perspective in OIE, it is argued here, that OIE is the school of thought most firmly committed to deliberative democratic processes as a way of establishing environmental goals.

## Rational Analysis and Neoclassical Economics

A rational analytic approach creates an analytical framework that aims to *answer* the question of "which environmental goal" should be pursued? The rational analytic approach relies on analysts to follow a formal decision logic. Such a logic begins with identifiable, preferably quantitative, decision criteria. Formal rules and procedures then are evaluated, weighed (valued), and chosen from among competing alternatives based on these decision criteria (March 1982). These procedures would provide the basis for an "objective" analysis and identify the "best" or "optimal" answer to the above question (Shabman 1985).

Within mainstream (neoclassical) economics, the rational analytic perspective is exemplified by formal benefit-cost analysis. With respect to environmental goal setting, benefit-cost analysis purports to weigh the values of the different competing environmental services in terms of willingness to pay. These various monetized values people place on different environmental end states are weighted against the cost of achieving those end states. The environmental goal that maximizes the difference between monetized benefits and costs is considered "optimal." In writing about establishment of national ambient air quality standards, Heather Ross (2001, 14) writes "there is only one way to make this determination properly, and that is by weighing costs and benefits."

Benefits and costs, derived from neoclassical welfare theoretic concepts, are, at the conceptual level, an individual's values (preferences) for different environmental goals or end points quantified in a common denominator of dollars. Benefit-cost analysis rests on the argument that the choices individuals make in market exchange provide the data that analysts can use to translate people's preferences into money terms. The premises of this revealed choice framework are that individuals know their preferences for goods and services (states of the world) before being confronted with a choice, that people are willing to pay to satisfy those preferences, and whatever an individual chooses is in the interests of that individual (Shabman and Stephenson 1996b).

The benefit-cost analyst exhibits similar reverence for individual preferences as the Austrians. From the perspective of the benefit-cost analyst, the objective of public policy should be the satisfaction of individual preferences. Rather than creating a market for people to express these preferences, the neoclassical economist proposes to measure the private preferences that cannot be adequately expressed in a market context. Like the Austrians, the neoclassical benefit-cost analyst makes no distinction between moral and ethical commitments and preference satisfaction. According to Michael Hanemann (1995, 105) "modern theory of social choice considers it immaterial whether preferences reflect selfish interest or moral judgment." As described above, the OIE economist would consider the two quite distinct in matters of public policy.

The commitment to quantify individual preferences for different states of the environment raises the challenge of monetizing values not expressed as market transactions. Mainstream environmental economists devote considerable intellectual resources to developing, refining, and promoting so-called nonmarket valuation techniques (e.g. contingent valuation, hedonic price, and travel cost methods) to meet this challenge (Cropper and Oates 1992). In the air quality arena, nonmarket valuation techniques have been used to monetize reduced human health risks and increased visibility from more stringent air quality standards. In the water quality literature, nonmarket valuation studies have monetized individual preferences for recreational opportunities, endangered species, habitat, and aesthetics. Indeed, mainstream environmental economists view the development and application of these nonmarket valuation techniques as the chief contribution economics can make to environmental goal setting (Cropper 2000).

The commitment to measure individual preferences is supported, in part, by a profound ambivalence toward the political processes (Shabman 1985). Advocates of benefit-cost analysis often express concerns that the political process cannot be trusted to reflect all the individual preferences people hold for the environment. The explicit justification for nonmarket valuation research is often the claim that monetization is necessary in order for environmental values to be accounted for in public decision processes. The implication of this argument is that decision participants will somehow overlook or place a zero value on the environment unless the benefits of ecosystem services are quantified in the same units as costs (Loomis et al. 2000).

Proponents of systematic benefit-cost analysis often express concerns that rent seeking in political processes distort the representation of preferences. Benefit-cost analysis, according to advocates, could help insulate the choice of environmental goals from purely political forces and give voice to the disenfranchised. Stokey and Zeckhuser (1978) reflect the underlying belief that benefit-cost analysis can more comprehensively and completely reflect individual preferences than the political process when they write:

> One of the great virtues of the benefit-cost approach is that the interests of individuals who are poorly organized or less closely involved are counted. (This contrasts with most political decision making procedures.) Even when pushed by powerful interest groups, projects whose benefits do not outweigh their costs will be shown to be undesirable. The benefits and costs accruing to all—to the highway builders, the environmentalists, the "little" people," the users and providers of services, the taxpaying public—will be counted on a dollar-for-dollar basis. Benefit-cost analysis is a methodology with which we pursue efficiency and which has the effect of limiting the vagaries of the political process (151).

Thus, as a general approach to environmental goal setting, comprehensive benefit-cost analysis purports to offer a practical substitute, rather than a complement, to political choice processes (Shabman 1995). Preferences for environmental quality need to be measured and political choice processes do not allow for complete and unbiased expression of these environmental preferences. The entire premise of systematic benefit-cost analysis is to decide what is efficient or optimal. If a public decision process decides otherwise, the decision is often considered either inefficient or deficient.

Many benefit-cost advocates are careful to point out that such analysis should not be the sole factor in deciding among environmental goals. Rather, these economists argue that benefit-cost analysis should be performed and used as *input* into the policy process (Oates 1999; Arrow et al. 1996). One may then ask the benefit-cost analyst, "why should comprehensive monetization of different states of the environment even be offered as an input?" If the rational analyst took an instrumentalist perspective, the analyst would first ask what economic analysis would help participants in a public choice process evaluate tradeoffs and make choices among competing ends. Yet, this is not the question that the neoclassical economist asks. Rather, the rational analyst structures intellectual efforts and resources as if their responsibility is to answer the question of what environmental goal to pursue. For the benefit-cost advocate, the choice of an environmental goal is framed by the dictates of welfare economics rather than the needs of the public choice process.[6]

The criticisms of benefit-cost analysis in public policy are voluminous. Within OIE, critics have long pointed out that neoclassical welfare theory is theoretically incapable, regardless of the policy pronouncements of the applied benefit-cost practitioner, of making efficiency judgments (potential pareto optimal allocation) concerning choices between alternative institutional arrangements, e.g., the working rules of the economy (Bromley 1989, Mishan 1980, Swaney 1987). Expressed differently, benefit-cost analysis cannot decide between competing social values when values are subject to change and social judgment (Samuels 1992). The intention here is not to repeat these criticisms in reference to environmental goal setting. If OIE support for deliberative democratic processes as a way to establish environmental goals were based on criticisms of benefit-cost analysis alone, the OIE alternative would be weak. This, however, is not the case. The OIE perspective offers clear, positive support for democratic alternatives over a rational analytic one as a way to establish environmental goals and standards.

## Democatic Deliberation and Institutional Economics

The institutionalists believe that deliberative democratic processes are more than a decision-making forum (Shabman 1985). Often democratic processes are portrayed as mere exercise in coalition building and vote trading among well-defined interests. While these activities may be part of the process, the OIE theorist also understands that democratic processes are an effective means of social inquiry. Deliberative democratic processes allow for the expression, discovery, transformation, and creation of social beliefs and policy preferences; the accommodation of diverse and diffuse knowledge and interests; and the creation of social cohesion and purpose.

From an OIE perspective, democratic deliberation is a process of social learning and transformation that cannot be replicated by the rational analytic model. Giandomenico Majone (1989) reflects an OIE perspective by stating:

"In a free debate, persuasion is a two-way interchange, a method of mutual learning through discourse. Real debate not only lets the participants promote their own views and interests but also encourages them to adjust their views of reality and even to change their views of the process" ( 8).

Democracy is thus viewed as a deliberative process that is capable of creating and transforming policy preferences. The process of social deliberation and debate forces participants to entertain a wide range of perspectives and critically evaluate and defend their position. As a social learning process, these positions and beliefs will evolve and change. OIE has a long intellectual history of subjecting existing preferences and beliefs to inquiry and critique (Veblen 1899). Consequently, the OIE perspective rejects the neoclassical notion that public policy should take preferences as they are. The power and legitimacy of democratic decision-making derives in part from an ability to change preferences or create shared beliefs where none existed before.

The reliance and support for democratic decision-making is also based on the acknowledgement that knowledge and interests are diffuse and fragmented. John Dewey in particular stressed the idea that no man or limited set of men is wise enough or good enough to rule others without their consent (Dewey 1939). Deliberative democratic processes provides an opportunity for people to bring their perspectives and insights to the policy decisions.[7] Charles Lindblom (1979; 1990) in particular stresses the advantages of incorporating informal knowledge from citizens and nontechnical decision participants in public decision processes.

Yet, democratic processes are more than a way simply to make decisions. The process of participation itself provides a valuable social function (Dewey 1954). Hank Jenkins-Smith (1990) summarized this perspective: "Individuals gain immeasurably from the process of participation, feeling their way from vague predisposition to reasoned viewpoint through debate and thereby gaining the type of human fulfillment that can only be derived from taking part in governing the public forces and institutions that so thoroughly affect our lives. In this view, democratic processes are fundamentally educational." (78)

Thus it matters to citizens how decisions are made. Imagine a process to decide water quality standards for a regional stream system. A decision could be made by relying on analysts to measure individual preferences. The analysts would identify the water quality standard that maximized net benefits based on these measurements. In contrast, a deliberative democratic process could be created that would grant interested citizens the authority to investigate, debate, and ultimately decide what is the most appropriate water quality standard for the stream system. Imagine further that both decision-making frameworks would produce the exact same result—the exact same water quality standard. The water quality standards are the same but the outcomes of these two decision processes cannot be considered equivalent. One approach makes a decision; the second makes a decision but raises the community's overall knowledge of the stream system and builds a sense of citizenship.

Given the open-ended and transforming nature of deliberative democratic processes, those with the OIE perspective make no claim that there exists a unique or optimum outcome (Samuels 1992; Bromley 2001). They argue that environmental goals should be a product of a democratic process, but they do not offer a specific procedure or analytical framework for producing "answers" to the question of which environmental goal or standard is to be sought. Institutionalist scholars offer no particular insight into whether a region should strive to restore a salmon fishery or introduce a bass fishery in its place. OIE scholars do not claim to offer a method or calculation that would determine whether an ambient ozone concentration should be 10 parts per million or 8 parts per million. John R. Commons once remarked to a group of his students that he had no system, only a process (Ramstad 2001). That comment, related to his notions of reasonable value, could just as easily apply to environmental policy as to labor policy.

## Rational Analysis and Ecological Economics

It should be noted that neoclassical economists are not the only economists that advocate a "rational" analytic approach to environmental goal setting. Another rational analytic perspective would require biological and ecological analysts, rather than benefit-cost analysts, to identify environmental goals. While benefit cost and biological approaches use different criteria to establish environmental goals, both rely on analysts (experts), rather than social deliberation and debate, to guide environmental goal setting.

Elements of what is becoming known as ecological economics frequently support such a biological analytic approach. Ecological economists may call for "carrying capacity" analysis to establish environmental goals and standards. Carrying capacity analysts seek to identify, through quantification, "sustainable" levels of development. "Sustainable" is defined with respect to a variety of ecological "limits" identified by analysts (Ekins and Simon 2001; Daly 1996). Carrying capacity analysts assert that hard, quantifiable standards can be identified to determine "critical" ecosystem functioning and the ambient standards necessary to support those critical ecosystems. For example, sustainable levels of ambient sulfur dioxide concentrations would be established that do not have "detrimental effect on human health" or do not "threaten critical ecosystems" (Ekins and Simon 2001, 6).

Carrying capacity analysis differs from benefit-cost analysis in that the analysis is conducted in physical units rather than in monetary terms. Furthermore, benefit-cost analysts purport to identify the optimum environmental goal while carrying capacity analysts seek to identify the minimum benchmark for an acceptable ("sustainable") environmental goal. Yet the two approaches share the common theme of establishing environmental goals based on objectives identified by a rational analytic procedure—benefit-cost analysts maximize net benefits and carrying capacity analysts strive not to violate analyst-identified ecological limits. Environmental goals are defined with respect to the analyst's notions, not those resulting from public deliberation, of what are proper environmental goals. In both biological and benefit-cost analysis, it is the analysts and their corresponding analytical computations that provide the criteria necessary to establish environmental goals and standards.

It should be recognized, however, that some economists writing in the OIE tradition sometimes express sympathetic support for the carrying capacity approach. Dietz and van der Staaten (1992, 42), for example, state that "there is only one way to prevent overexploitation of the ecological utilization of space: specified standards being sustainable from an ecological point of view. This implies that standards are directly derived from the functioning of ecocycles." While such a position may reflect a general belief that economic growth should occur within the confines of ecological boundaries, those with an OIE perspective ultimately cannot identify what those boundaries are in the absence of a social valuation process. Ecosystems do not have a point of view. People do. In this sense, the OIE perspective is unapologetically anthropocentric. From an ecosystem perspective, the Los Angeles River might be decidedly dysfunctional, but this observation tells us nothing about whether this physical reality is acceptable or what water quality standards should be established in a highly modified urban setting. The admission that standards should be sustainable from an ecological point of view cannot answer the question of whether a productive bass fishery should be established in a Pacific Northwest stream that once supported wild salmon. What are considered sustainable environmental goals cannot be defined without reference to the values people express for the environment.

A deliberative, open process capable of tapping diverse interests and multiple sources of knowledge also is a process that diffuses the exercise of power. Rationalistic approaches to establishing environmental goals would place more control over decisions, such as what environmental standard to use, into the hands of unelected bureaucrats or self-appointed experts. Klein and Miller (1996, 273) once remarked, "institutionalists would not advocate the appointment of value czars." As a matter of consistency, this general sentiment applies to the benefit-cost analysts who claim the ability to measure the preferences people hold for the environment or biologists (and ecological economists) who would claim to know what those values should be.

## POLICY CONTRIBUTIONS

OIE economists express strong support for "scientifically informed and democratically guided debate" as a means to establishing environmental goals (Hodgson 1997, 62). The reliance on democratic deliberation means that institutional economists do not presume to judge what the correct, sustainable, optimal, or efficient water quality goal or standard should be (Bromley 2001, 43). At the same time, the existence of strongly held social values by the public related to environmental protection severely limits OIE support for the Austrian-oriented market driven approach to establishing environmental goals. Given the rejection of a rationalistic or market approach in favor of deliberative democratic process, how can those with an OIE perspective contribute to and facilitate environmental goal setting policy?

While the OIE literature offers a coherent conceptual alternative to the environmental goal setting process, applied OIE research related to environmental goal setting is minimal. The existing OIE literature provides little in the way of practical examples and illustrations of how the OIE perspective is applied in specific goal setting under the air and water quality programs. The lack of applied OIE research is unfortunate because the OIE perspective has much to add to environmental policy-making.

The OIE conceptual approach does offer at least two general conclusions for how policy economists can contribute and facilitate the goal setting process. First, the OIE perspective suggests a particular avenue of research and study of environmental goal setting processes. Given the importance of working rules to the economy, institutional economists have a strong imperative to investigate the *decision processes* of environmental goal setting. In short, institutionalists should be interested in the study of the rules for making rules (Shaffer 1989). Second, the OIE perspective leads to some general conclusions about how economists should actively contribute to environmental policy (how to participate within a given process). While the pragmatic foundations of OIE do not support an analytical method to answer the question of which environmental goals to pursue, it does not follow that economists have nothing to contribute analytically to the environmental goal setting process.

## Deliberative Democratic Processes

To argue that democratic deliberation and processes should be fundamental to the establishment of environmental objectives represents a broad conceptual and philosophical position. It does not contribute to the debate about *what* deliberative, democratic process should be used in environmental goal setting. Democracy is not a monolithic concept (Tilman 1987). There are a number of ways a process can be organized to decide and establish environmental goals.

Currently, Congress delegates responsibility for establishing environmental standards under very broad statutory goals to the Environmental Protection Agency (EPA). The federal EPA may then delegate some standard setting authority to state environmental agencies. In the current form, the environmental standard setting process is largely built around an administrative rule-making process directed by agency bureaucrats. Over the past decade, there has been growing pressure to introduce more deliberative debate and negotiation in this administrative process (Cannon 2001). Some commentators propose incremental reforms that would introduce more public input and consultation into an administrative process (Coglianse 2001). More systemic calls for reform—often under the general label of negotiated rule-making and collaborative decision-making—call for more systemic restructuring that allows the affected parties more authority to decide for themselves what environmental standards are to be established (Freeman 1997; Harter 1997).

As an intellectual tradition, the OIE impulse would be to favor more inclusive, deliberative processes to establish working rules (Tool 1985). For instance, Commons advocated changes in the way workplace rules should be established. He recognized that establishment of such rules required an exercise of collective power, but he advocated a process that would channel the energy of interest groups into an inquiry and search for reasonable solutions (Ramstad 2001; Chasse 1997; Rutherford 1983). Commons, for example, advocated the formation of commissions populated with representatives of the affected parties to determine workplace rules. He felt that the ensuing bargaining process among the parties would best facilitate the development of rules that would most likely be accepted and followed willingly (Commons 1934; Ramstad 2001). Commons' proposals gave explicit recognition of the efficacy of deliberative, pluralistic processes in establishing the working rules of the workplace (Chasse 1997).

Despite the growing interest in reforms to infuse the administrative rule-making process with more characteristics of an open, deliberative negotiation, relatively little systematic research has been conducted concerning how and whether such specific reforms would improve the environmental rule-making process (Beierle and Konisky 2000). Given their intellectual history and tradition, OIE economists have a professional interest in the study of the processes for establishing environmental goals and standards. Research questions confronting public policy are: how can participation be made meaningful and effective? What outcomes can various reforms be expected to achieve? How can different environmental standard setting processes be evaluated?

A research agenda for OIE scholars should strive to identify criteria that would be valuable in evaluating the efficacy of a particular environmental standard-setting process. Evaluative criteria might include the level of participation and involvement by affected parties, the degree to which technical and scientific information can be integrated into the process (thus utilized by the decision participants), the ability to produce agreement on standards among different interest groups, and the ability to produce robust and enduring outcomes. Institutionalists have a particular interest in how power and influence may manifest itself in particular rule-making structures.

A future research program should provide for the evaluation of different standard-setting processes and the criteria of judgment incorporated. How do proposed changes measure up against these criteria? Are the criteria themselves products of warranted inquiry and subject to instrumental validation? An OIE research agenda concerning the environmental standard setting process should also identify the conditions that facilitate the achievement of these recommended outcomes. For instance, researchers may investigate how technical expertise can be better integrated into public decision processes and/or what conditions or structures of rule-making tend to reduce conflict between competing interests.

The OIE empirical research tradition could provide a valuable contribution to the study of the "rules for making rules." Mainstream economists seek to identify general laws governing individual behavior (conventional microeconomics) or to investigate behavior in stylized, simplified settings (game theory). These general laws are applied and then used to provide insights into behavior in specific situations. While such an approach provides its own set of insights, the OIE-oriented study of rule-making behavior seeks to understand the reasons why people do what they do within specific institutional contexts. Working to identify behavior and relationships within specific decision contexts forces OIE economists to pay close attention to not only the role financial incentives play in rule-making but also how participant behavior is conditioned by formal rules, informal customs, and belief systems.

The methodological approach of institutional economics is also well positioned to establish tentative relationships between the rule-making structures, behavior, and outcomes that are evolving and interconnected (Dugger 1979; Wilber and Harrison 1978). The contribution provided by the institutionalist approach is that these connections and relationships are established to a significant degree through comprehension of the decision process as it is understood and viewed from the participants themselves. Such an approach has inescapable conclusions for the way research is conducted. The OIE economist conducting research on the process of environmental goal setting cannot do so from the confines of an office or lab. An OIE approach requires detailed understanding of the process that can only come from a more participant observer approach to research. The OIE approach must move beyond generalities and statements of principles into understanding the way decisions are made "on the ground."

The importance of such a research approach can be illustrated by comparing differences in environmental standard setting between the air and water programs. While establishing air and water quality standards might raise the same conceptual challenges, the actual standard setting process differs considerably between the two programs. These differences can only be understood by first realizing that the statutory structure, regulatory rules, and regulatory "culture" of the water program differs in substantive ways from the federal air program. These differences are then layered onto the different physical properties of air and water pollution (the adverse impacts of effluent discharge tends to be much more localized than air emissions). Understanding the rule-making behavior in the existing system will require research that is sensitive to how a specific institutional context creates barriers and opportunities to the environmental goal setting process and what types of reforms are better adapted to one program versus another.

## Analytical Contributions

Regardless of the specific rule-making process, what can the OIE economist contribute to the process of establishing environmental goals and standards? It is argued here that an OIE perspective does not provide the policy economist with any special or unique analytical tools. Rather, what the OIE perspective provides is a unique perspective on how economists participate in the public decision-making process (Shabman and Stephenson 2000). From an OIE perspective, deliberative democratic processes stand at the center of collective choice processes. Technical economic analysis is not structured as if it were intended to make the decision confronting the public choice process, but rather to facilitate and complement the process. The OIE perspective instructs the policy economist to be more attentive to what decision participants need, rather than what the discipline says they need. As Daniel Bromley (2001) states:

> The better strategy, when economists come to debates over public policy, is to abandon the contrived need to offer truth rules. Rather, the better strategy is to let the citizenry and policy makers speak for themselves, and let us use those voices—without the imposition of economistic judgments—as our best evidence of the reasons for their behavior. We may usefully point out important economic concepts that might well help to clarify issues—and narrow the range of feasible options. But this input must be in the nature of assistance, not in the nature of denouncing chosen policies as Pareto inferior (41).

This perspective implies that economists should be prepared to contribute analysis and expertise to the policy process in ways that are amenable, desirable, or credible to other decision participants.

With this said, the specific analysis, logic, and methods that may be most valuable to decision participants may be quite orthodox. Concepts familiar to all economists—opportunity costs, marginal analysis, and the importance of incentives—may be some of the most valuable contributions an economist can make to the policy debate (Shabman 1984, 1985 1995; Rhodes 1985; Bromley 2001). Analysis may clarify specific economic consequences of policy alternatives under consideration (Sagoff 1988). For instance, economic analyses might investigate the range of possible costs or economic impacts of different environmental standards. The costs of achieving different levels of environmental qualities provide evidence about the potential sacrifices a community must make for reduced health risks or improved environmental amenities. Such analysis may highlight how the cost burden of a particular environmental standard is distributed among the population and suggest mechanisms for sharing costs in ways that are considered more equitable. Regional fiscal impact modeling may provide governments with insights into how land use changes necessary to achieve different water quality standards may influence government revenues and costs. In quantifying costs, clarifying the incidence of costs, or identifying regional economic impact, the economist with an OIE perspective may draw from the same quantitative tool kit as the mainstream economist.

While the technical tools may be similar, the professional orientation and attitude toward what should be done with those tools is what distinguishes the rational analytic perspective from an OIE perspective. The essence of establishing environmental goals and standards is the balancing of the social and economic consequences of different standards against the commitments to improved environmental quality. If policy economists view deliberative democratic processes as the forum for deciding this balance, economic analysis should aim to facilitate and acknowledge this balancing without claiming any authority or special insight to *do* the balancing (Shabman 1985).

Such a perspective means that the policy economist must be flexible in contributing analysis to the policy debate. It is conceivable that decision participants might view nonmarket valuation studies that monetize environmental services as an instrumental element of the decision process. The institutionalists may be skeptical of such a calculation and feel compelled to point out the underlying assumptions and implications of such analyses, but institutionalists should not rule out its use in the policy process *a priori*. The relevant test is the potential contribution analysis has to make to the process of public deliberation, debate and judgment (Shabman 1995; Shabman and Stephenson 2000).

With this perspective, recent research provides some insights into what types of economic analyses decision participants find particularly credible and useful in the environmental decision processes (Stephenson 2000; Stephenson and Shabman 2001). Cost analysis is a particular type of economic analysis that is conducted in almost every environmental policy decision. Quantifying the costs of different degrees of stringency in an environmental standard is valuable to the policy process because it illuminates the choice confronting decision participants in clear, familiar and understandable terms. Participants easily understand control costs and foregone economic activities in dollar terms.

The same may not be true for systematic monetization of the environmental end states (Shabman 1993). Estimates of the changes in environmental conditions may be best understood and debated as changes in physical units—fish populations, acres of high quality aquatic habitat, or the probability of certain health risks rather than stated in dollar terms. Consider the challenge of returning wild salmon to some watershed in the Pacific Northwest. Decision participants consider a number of policy alternatives that have different restoration costs and levels of success. For instance, decision participants might best understand the choice confronting them in terms of the restoration costs of returning X number of salmon. In such a case, decision participants are quite capable and willing to weigh tradeoffs and compare alternatives without standardizing outcomes in dollar terms (Stephenson 2000; Stephenson and Shabman 2001). In fact, monetizing the environmental service may actually obscure choices, inhibit problem solving, and create unnecessary conflict if decision participants are better able to understand environmental changes in natural units. Furthermore, if decision participants view it as their *responsibility* to debate and decide whether the economic consequences (costs) justify the environmental improvement, decision participants may view systematic monetizing of benefits as usurping their authority to choose.

## SUMMARY

The intellectual foundations laid out by institutional economists such as John R. Commons and the pragmatic philosophy of John Dewey provide a justification and broad outline for a unique perspective within the economics profession on environmental goal setting. The OIE perspective relies on democratic processes to establish ambient air and water quality goals and standards. The remaining challenge for contemporary OIE economists is to embark on a research program to provide conceptual detail and the empirical content to the OIE perspective.

## NOTES

[1] The conceptual distinction between goal setting and methods to achieve goals does not deny the interplay between ends and means. Obviously, neither ends nor means are constant or independent. Changes in pollution control knowledge and technology, for example, will influence the efficacy of achieving different environmental objectives. The process of deciding environmental goals may necessarily involve discussion of how the goal is to be achieved (Cannon 2001). The organization of this paper does not deny the interplay between ends and means, but isolating the discussion of goals (ends) provides a conceptual framework for illustrating a distinct OIE perspective on environmental policy.

[2] In order to keep the scope of the paper focused, discussion of environmental goal setting is confined to air and water quality examples. The goal setting process may be necessary for any "common-pool" or open access resource. Natural resource management systems may establish aggregate goals and standards for the consumptive use of wildlife species. For example, commercial fisheries management regimes might establish total allowable catch limits. Water quantity management programs might establish minimum stream flow conditions.

[3] The Austrians, however, would place more emphasis on the "spontaneous" or informal origin of a property right system than do those working in the OIE tradition.

[4] Given that these interdependencies and conflicts are everywhere prevalent, the externality concept has limited usefulness. Since interdependencies are ubiquitous, so too are externalities. Consequently the existence of an externality cannot in and of itself justify collective action or amendment of the working rules.

[5] It is increasingly recognized that these sources are now the primary barrier to achieving water quality standards in many watersheds. A significant part of the debate concerning major proposed revisions to the water quality regulations (so-called TMDL or total maximum daily load) is a debate over whether the current rights structure should be revised to better facilitate achievement of water quality goals and standards. For the OIE, these conflicts between competing moral commitments can only be resolved through democratic processes.

[6] This observation is the product of numerous conversations with Leonard Shabman about the role of benefit-cost analysis in public policy.

[7] The OIE perspective towards the function of democratic process in collective choice making parallels the Austrian perspective of the function of market process in private decision-making. Austrian economists stress how market processes for private goods are able to utilize and create knowledge widely distributed through the economy. For the Austrians, this function of markets cannot be replicated by rational calculations. Using similar reasoning but applied to a different decision making context, those with an OIE perspective believe that deliberative democratic processes are best able to utilize and create knowledge for collective problem solving. Democracy, as it has been said many times before, facilitates a competition of ideas.

# REFERENCES


Anderson,Terry L. and Donald R. Leal. *Free Market Environmentalism.* Boulder Colorado: Westview Press.

Arrow, Kenneth J., Maureen L. Cropper, George C. Eads, Robert W. Hahn, Lester B. Lav, Roger G. Noll, Paul R. Portney, Milton Russell, Richard Schmalensee, V. Kerry Smith, and Robert N. Stavins. 1996. Is there a role for benefit-cost analysis in environmental, health, and safety regulation? *Science* 272 (April): 221-222.

Beierle, Thomas C. and David M. Konisky. 2000. Values, conflict, and trust in participatory environmental planning. *Journal of Policy Analysis and Management* 19 (Fall) 4: 587-602.

Bromley, Daniel W. 2001 "Economics and Public Policy: the Essential Logic of Pragmatism." Paper presented at the Lund School of Economics and Management, Lund University, Sweden, September.

———. 2000. "The Two Realms of Reason: Calculation and Sentiment." Paper presented at the 7th Ulvön Conference on Environmental Economics, Ulvön Sweden, June 18-21.

———. 1989. *Economic Interests and Institutions: The Conceptual Foundations of Public Policy.* Oxford: Blackwell.

Commons, John R. 1924. *The Legal Foundations of Capitalism.* New York: Macmillan.

———. 1934. *Institutional Economics: Its Place in Political Econ my.* New York: Macmillian.

Cannon, Jon. 2001. "Bargaining, Politics, and Law in Environmental Regulation." In *Environmental Contracts: Comparative Approaches t o Regulatory Innovation in the United States and Europe.,* E. W. Orts and K. Deketelaere, eds. London: Kluwer.

Chasse, J. Dennis. 1997. John R. Commons and the special interest issue: not really out of date. *Journal of Economic Issues* 31:4 (December): 933-949.

Coglianese, Cary. 2000. The constitution and the costs of c lean air: Is the Clean Air Act unconstitutional? *Environment* 42:9 (November): 32-37.

———. 2001."Is Consensus an Appropriate Basis for Regulatory Policy?" In *Environmental Contracts.* Eric W. Orts and Kurt Deketelaere, eds. London: Kluwer Law International.

Cropper, Maureen L. 2000. Has economic research answered the needs of environmental policy? *Journal of Environmental Economics and Management* 39 (May): 328-350.

———. and Wallace E. Oates. 1992. Environmental economics: A survey. *Journal of Economic Literature* 30 (June): 675 – 740.

Daly, Herman E. 1996. *Beyond Growth.* Boston: Beacon Press.

Dietz, Frank J. and Jan van der Straten. 1992. Rethinking environmental economics: missing links between economic theory and environmental policy. *Journal of Economic Issues* 26 ( March) 1: 27 – 51.

Dewey, John. 1939. "The Democratic Form." In *Intelligence in the Modern World: John Dewey's Philosophy.* Joseph Ratner, ed. New York: Modern Library.

———. 1954. *The Public and Its Problems.* Denver: Swallow.

Dugger, William M. 1979. Methodological differences between institutional and neoclassical economics. *Journal of Economic Issues* 13 (December) 4: 899-909.

Dworkin, R. 1994. *Life's Dominion.* New York: Vintage.

Ekins, Paul and Sandrine Simon. 2001. Estimating sustainability gaps: methods and preliminary applications for the UK and the Netherlands. *Ecological Economics* 37:1 (April): 5-22.

Freeman, Jody. 1997.Collaborative governance in the administrative state. *UCLA Law Review.* 45 (October): 1 – 9.

Harter, Philip J. 1997. Fear of commitment: an affliction of adolescents. *Duke Law Journal* 46 (April): 1389 - 1423

Hanemann. W. Michael. 1995. "Contingent Valuation and Economics. " In *Environmental Valuation: New Perspectives.* K.G. Willis and J.T. Corkindale, eds. Wallingford: CAB International.

Hayden, F. Gregory. 1995. Instrumentalist policy-making: policy criteria in a transactional context. *Journal of Economic Issues* 29 (June 1995) 2: 361 - 84.

Hodgson, Geoffrey M. 1997. "Economics, Environmental Policy and the Transcendence of Utilitarianism." In *Valuing Nature? Economics ,Ethics, and the Environment.* John Foster, ed. London: Routledge.

———. 1998a. The approach of institutional economics. *Journal of Economic Literature* 36 (March)1: 166-192.

———. 1998b. Socialism against markets? A critique of two recent proposals. *Economy and Society* 27 (November): 407 - 433.

Jenkins-Smith, Hank. 1990. *Democratic Politics an d Policy Analysis.* Fort Worth: Harcourt Brace.

Kneese, Allen V., Robert U. Ayres, and Ralph C. D'Arge. 1970. *Economics and the Environment.* Washington DC: Resources for the Future.

Kirzner, Israel M. 1997. *How Markets Work: Disequilibrium, Entrepreneurship andDiscovery* .London: Institute of Economic Affairs.

Klein, Philip A. and Edythe S. Miller. 1996. Concepts of value, efficiency, and democracy in institutional economics. *Journal of Economic Issues* 30:1 (March): 267-277.

Lackey, Robert T. 2000. "Restoring Wild Salmon to the Pacific Northwest: Chasing an Illusion? " In *What We Don't Know About Pacific Northwest Fish Runs– An Inquiry into Decision-Making.* Patricia Koss and Mike Katz, eds. Portland: Portland State University.

Lindblom, Charles E. 1990. *Inquiry and Change.* New Haven: Yale University Press.

———. and David K. Cohen. 1979. *Usable Knowledge.* New Haven: Yale University Press.

Loomis, John B., et al. 2000. Measuring the total economic value of restoring ecosystem services in an impaired river basin: results from a contingent valuation survey." *Ecological Economics* 33 (April): 103-117.

Majone, Giandomenico. 1989. *Evidence, Argument and Persuasion in the Policy Process.* New Haven: Yale University Press.

March, James. 1982. Theories of choice and making decisions. *Society* 20 (November-December): 29-39.

Moscrip, A. L. and D. R. Montgomery. 1997. Urbanization, flood frequency, and salmon abundance in Puget lowland streams. *Journal of the American Water Resources Association* 33 (6): 1289-1297.

Mishan, E. J. 1980. How valid are economic evaluations of allocative changes?" *Journal of Economic Issues* 14 (1980) 1: 143 – 161

National Research Council. 2001. *Assessing the TMDL Approach to Water Quality Management.* Washington DC: National Academy Press.

Oates, Wallace E. 1999. "An Economic Perspective on Environmental and Resource Management: An Introduction.". In *The RFF Reader in Environmental and Resource Management*. W. Oates, ed. Washington DC: Resources for the Future.

Park, William. 1996. Environmental regulatory reform: discussion. *Journal of Agricultural and Applied Economics* 28 (July) 1: 126 - 29.

Ramstad, Yngve. 2001. John R. Commons's reasonable value and the problem of just price. *Journal of Economic Issues* 35 (June) 2: 253-277.

Rhoads, Steven E. 1985. *The Economist's View o f th e World: Government, Markets, and Public Policy.* Cambridge: Cambridge University Press.

Ross, Heather L. 2001. Clean air - is the sky the limit? *Resources* 143 (Fall) 13-16.

Rutherford, Malcolm. 2001. Institutional economics: then and now. *Journal of Economic Perspective* 15 (Summer) 3: 173-194.

———. 1983. J. R. Commons's Institutional Economics. *Journal of Economic Issues* 17 (September) 3: 265 – 288.

Sagoff, Mark. 1988. *The Economy of the Earth: Philosophy, Law, and the Environment.* Cambridge: Cambridge University Press.

———. 1994. Should preferences count? *Land Economics* 70 (May) 2: 127 - 44.

———. 1996. On the value of endangered and other species. *Environmental Management* 20 (Number 6): 897-911.

———. 2000. At the monument to General Meade, or on the difference between beliefs and benefits. *Arizona Law Revie w* 42 (Summer): 433-462.

Samuels, Warren J. 1992. *Essays on the Economic Role of Government, Volume 1.* New York: New York University Press.

———. 1971. Interrelations between legal and economic processes. *Journal of Law and Economics* 14 (October): 435 – 50.

Shaffer, James Duncan. 1989. "On the Fundamentals of the Economic Role of Government – The Rules Governing Economic Activity." In *Fundamentals of the Economic Role of Government.* Warren J. Samuels ed. New York: Greenwood Press.

Schmid, A. Allan. 1989. "Economy and State: An Institutionalist Theory of Process and Learning." In *Fundamentals of the Economic Role of Government.* Warren J. Samuels, ed. New York: Greenwood Press.

Shabman, Leonard. 1984. Water resources management: policy economics for an era of transitions. *Southern Journal of Agricultural Economics* 16 (July) 1: 53 - 65.

———. 1985. Natural resource economics: methodological orientations and policy effectiveness. *A merican Journal of Agricultural Economics* 67 (December) 5: 1030-34.

———. 1993. "Bargaining, Markets, and Watershed Restoration: Some Elements of a New National Water Policy. " In *Water Resources Administration in the United States: Policy, Practice and Emerging Issues.* Martin Reuss, ed. East Lansing: Michigan State University Press.

———. 1995. "Bargaining and Water Disputes: A Perspective on the Coming Debate." In *Water Quantity/Quality Management and Conflict, Resolution: Institutional Processes, and Economic Analysis.* Ariel Dinar and Edna Tusak Loehman eds. Westport: Praeger.

———. and Kurt Stephenson.1996a. Environmental policy reform: a taxonomy of economists' perspectives. *Journal of Agricultural an d Applied Economics* 28 (July): 117 - 125.
———. and Kurt Stephenson. 1996b. Searching for the correct benefit estimate: empirical evidence for an alternative perspective. *Land Economics* 72 (November): 433 - 49.
——— and Kurt Stephenson. 2000. Environmental valuation and its economic critics. *Journal of Water Resources Planning and Management* 126 (November/December) 6: 382 – 88.
Smith, Fred L. 1995. Markets and the environment: a critical reappraisal. *Contemporary Economic Policy* 13 (January) 1: 62-73.
Stephenson, Kurt, Leonard Shabman and L. Leon Geyer. 1999. Toward an effective-based effluent allowance trading system: identifying the statutory and regulatory barriers to implementation. *The Environmental Lawyer* 5 (June) 3: 775-815.
———. and Leonard Shabman. 2001. Nonmarket valuation in hydropower relicensing: an application of a pattern modeling approach. *Journal of Economic Issues* 35:2 (June): 497-504.
———. 2000. Taking nature into account: observations about the changing role of analysis and negotiation in hydropower relicensing. *William and Mary Environmental Law and Policy Review* 25 (Winter) 2: 473 - 498.
Stokey, Edith and Richard Zeckhuser. 1978. *A Primer for Policy Analysis*, New York: W.W. Norton.
Swaney, James A. 1987. Elements of a neoinstitutional environmental economics. *Journal of Economic Issues* 21 (December) 4: 1739-1779.
Tilman, Rick. 1987. The neoinstrumentalist theory of democracy. *Journal of Economic Issues* 21 (1987) 3: 1379 – 1401.
Tool, Marc R. 1985. *The Discretionary Economy: A Normative Theory of Political Economy.* Boulder: Westview Press.
Veblen, Thorstein. [1899] 1956. *The Theory of the Leisure Class* . Middlesex UK: Penguin Books.
Wilber, Charles K. and Robert S. Harrison. 1978. The methodological basis of institutional economics: pattern model, storytelling, and holism. *J. of Econ.. Issues.* 12 (Mar): 61- 89.

# 16

# POLICY CONCERNS REGARDING ECOLOGICALLY SOUND DISPOSAL OF INDUSTRIAL WASTE MATERIALS

F. Gregory Hayden

## INTRODUCTION

Early in the Twentieth Century, Thorstein B. Veblen argued that private business enterprise "has taken over the [natural] resources by a process of legalized seizure, and has used them up as rapidly as may be . . . ." (Veblen 1919, 98). One of the most important natural resources seized and used up has been the living systems destroyed by industrial waste disposal. Improper waste disposal, in addition to resulting in disease problems for humans and other species, results in a loss of living systems upon which people and industry depend. Some of the services nature provides include purification of water and air; regulation of atmospheric chemistry; storage, detoxification, and recycling of human waste; natural pest and disease control; regulation of the chemical composition of oceans; maintenance of soil fertility; and nutrient storage and recycling. The attempt to replace these critical ecosystem services as they have been overwhelmed and destroyed by waste disposal has led to excessive resource costs and a burden in trying to maintain a standard of living.

The purpose of this chapter is to discuss policy concerns regarding ecologically sound land disposal of industrial waste materials. The disposal of hazardous, toxic, and radioactive waste has been and will continue to be a serious and growing problem associated with industrial society.[1] Land disposal is the most common method of disposing of wastes, but land disposal is not a permanent solution because even "secure" landfills fail in time. The consideration of industrial waste disposal brings to mind media coverage of colossal waste disposal failures such as the pollution of Love Canal by Hooker Chemical and Plastic Corporation with DDT and PCB emissions; the incineration of chlorinated wastes by the Solvay corporation to produce new chlorinated compounds including dioxins and furons more toxic than the original waste; the global transfer and burial of mercury wastes in Spain by the Bayer corporation; the contamination of groundwater on a global scale with aldicarb by the Rhone-Pauler corporation; the dumping of millions of gallons per day of carcinogenic and teratogenic chemical waste into the Atlantic Ocean by the Ciba Corporation; the illegal storing and disposing of large quantities of hazardous chemicals by Bordon Chemicals and Plastics that contaminated the groundwater in poor and minority communities; the dumping of millions of pounds of carcinogenic PCBs into the Hudson River in New York by General Electric corporation, and so forth. This entire chapter could be filled with a continuous list of such examples. Why are there so many such cases?

One reason is that people in general and economists in particular have not wanted to recognize and deal with the ugly and noxious side of high output and mass consumption economies.[2] Although production has never occurred without the involvement of the ecological system, that fact is rarely recognized in production theory and analysis, and the consideration of waste disposal is even more rare.

The main reason for the dismal waste disposal record is the fact that most of the institutional and technological decision making regarding industrial production, pollution emissions, and waste disposal has been dominated by powerful corporations.[3] Corporate "power, dominance and dependence are ubiquitous in industrial clusters and networks as they are in the socio-economy in general" (Elsner 2000, 431). Thus, the power of corporations to make such decisions will be an overarching concern in the discussion below. Economists seldom include the ecological system in their paradigms, and when they do, their approach is inconsistent with societal norms. Furthermore, their paradigms mainly serve corporate efforts to increase pollution, avoid remediation, and provide for unsafe disposal.

The institutionalist approach to problem solving guides the endeavor of this chapter because, as John Groenewegen emphasized, there is a "necessity to have a good understanding of the social beliefs, the rules, and habits of the actors involved in order to grasp who determines 'efficiency' in what terms" (2000, 18). Thus, the first task is to review an institutionalist approach to social beliefs and norms because beliefs and norms justify institutional activities.

## GENERAL APPROACH OF INSTITUTIONAL ECONOMICS REGARDING EFFICIENCY CRITERIA

The general institutionalist approach for analysis is outlined in Figure 1, which demonstrates a world view synthesized from knowledge from the social sciences. Figure 1 emphasizes that in order to gain a sufficient understanding of a problem area, the relevant values, social beliefs, institutions, technology, ecological system, and attitudes need to be defined and integrated in a complex open system analysis (see Hayden 1989). A hazardous waste facility conceived to fit a specific context needs to be embedded. The American Chemical Society stated in 1984 that "to manage

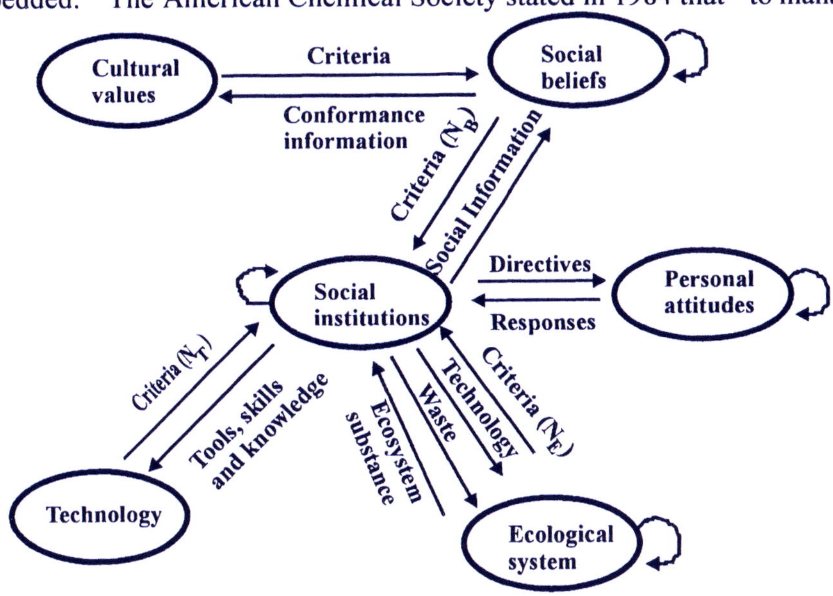


*Figure 1.* **Institutionalist Integrated System**

hazardous waste successfully, the situation must be viewed as a whole. This is the most critical need of all. Solutions to the hazardous waste problem require a multi-disciplinary effort that takes into account the technological, social, political, and economic factors of the issues. Concentrating solely on waste-disposal technologies is akin to treating the symptoms of an illness without considering the cause. The technological issues of hazardous wastes affect all of society" (Salcedo, Cross, Jr., Chrismon 1989, 61).

The normative criteria illustrated in Figure 1 are most important for understanding and analyzing the institutions and technologies of production and waste disposal, the latter also being a production process. The three normative sets of criteria are social belief criteria ($N_B$), technological criteria ($N_T$), and ecological system criteria ($N_E$). All three are criteria for the judgment of social institutions. Social beliefs are expressed in legal statutes, contracts, agency rules, regulations, operating procedures, and legislation. An example of such legislation is the Resource Conservation and Recovery Act (RCRA). "The RCRA was passed by Congress in 1976 to deal with the problem of hazardous waste disposal. EPA (US Environmental Protection Agency) was required to establish performance criteria for treatment, disposal, and storage facilities and to create a manifest system for tracking waste from their manufacture to their disposal" (Lester and Bowman 1989, 734).

$N_T$ and $N_E$ are not defined in an anthropocentric sense. Technology does not think about and decide upon normative criteria. Technology is the combination of tools, skills, and knowledge that is combined by social institutions such as corporations ( Hayden 1998). The technological norms are the criteria conveyed to society as a result of the combination selected by particular societal units. Once selected and adopted, technology becomes woven into the social fabric "in such a fashion as to build its own necessity" (Hamilton 2001, 746). Likewise, no assumption is being made that an ecological system designs beliefs from mental reflection. Instead, $N_E$ represents the normative criteria consistent with the maintenance of a particular kind of ecological system as institutions apply technology to the ecosystem in order to take resources and dispose of waste. To change institutionalized waste disposal systems, policymakers need to change the set of criteria, $N_E$, used to judge the systems.

It is through institutional structures and patterns that the various normative criteria are expressed. Likewise, institutions are the battleground for the clash among various criteria. For example, there is a traditional social belief ($N_B$) to protect workers' health, yet a new technology may be implemented that requires a new technological norm ($N_T$) for a certain level of cancer among the workers. Environmental analysis submitted by corporations as part of a licensing process for a particular technological design for waste disposal is to include projections for the expected level of cancer. The policy process will decide which set of criteria are to be applied to evaluate the institutional and technological structure. Or, as a different example, persons may decide they would like to alter the current ecosystem by implementing new criteria ($N_E$) for less waste to be delivered from corporations to groundwater. This would initiate a conflict between new criteria and current technological criteria ($N_T$).

The normative criteria are necessary for a society to establish efficiency (Hayden 1998). $N_B$, $N_E$, and $N_T$ have sets of subcriteria which are delivered to institutions with authority such as courts. The designated subcriteria become the standards to be applied by the institutional authority to determine efficiency. Efficiency means the ability to produce or achieve a desired effect. For society, the desired effects are determined by the normative criteria which are utilized to evaluate and judge efficiency.[4] For example, courts deliver authoritative codes and regulations to corporations in order to establish the obligations of corporations with regard to requirements to protect the ecosystem. In turn, the corporation given authoritative power delivers requirements to processing units such as a factory. The requirements, for example, deal with supervising, auditing, monitoring, producing, storing, loading, transporting, and disposing of hazardous waste. For efficiency, the requirements must be enforced and consistent with normative criteria.

Economists in the neoclassicalist tradition disagree with the social science approach to norms and efficiency, thus, their ideas are utilized to undermine democratic deliberations. First, neoclassicalists believe democracy is about autonomous self-directed individuals bargaining in the market place, while the institutionalist view is that the rules for markets and bargaining are a small part of the whole social or economic structure and that both markets and bargaining are to be judged by normative social criteria. Furthermore, to avoid anarchical activities like the midnight dumping of toxic waste, persons cannot be autonomous or self-directed. Persons spend their lives in institutional relationships. "These relationships overlap, intersect, interact in a complex interplay of discourse and action" (Anderson & Englehardt 2001, 6).

Second, the neoclassical tradition refuses to recognize system norms and instead concentrates on rules; rules justified in terms of pecuniary enhancement without reference to social morality. For neoclassicalists, the rules are to guide procedures without concern for social or ecological outcomes or consequences. Of course, without norms, it is not possible to make judgments about what rules ought to exist and about whether the consequences from the rules are consistent with the normative components. Market rules are emphasized in the neoclassical paradigm so as not to have to judge market consequences by society's moral and ethical standards that have been established to judge the legitimacy of markets. As John Dewey explained, conclusions are not possible when analysis is separated from either the relevant context or consequences (Dewey 1938). To separate the analysis of rules from their real-world context and from the impact of those rules on nature leads to the degradation of nature and limits knowing.

Third, neoclassical economists provide a narrow definition of efficiency by defining it procedurally[5] and in purely pecuniary terms. Their criterion of efficiency is expressed in the phrase "marginal benefits equal marginal costs" (MB=MC)[6] and they refer to concerns about other desired effects as not being efficiency concerns. Such a conception of efficiency does not address such concerns as the desirability of the resulting distribution of hazardous waste, distribution of income, or the social and ecological consequences of economic activity. This pecuniary criterion begs the question of the nature of the institutional structure and of the ecological system. Nevertheless, the myriad desired social and ecological effects must be judged if economic activity is to serve the community at large and not just the powerful few.

## CORPORATE POWER: POLICY DOMINATION, PREVARICATION, AND ARROGANCE

The corporation is a dominant and aggressive institution in modern society, and we have yet to discover how to counter its growing power and guide its operations for the general welfare. The founders of the United States did not forsee the problems of corporate power because at that time, the dominant social institutions were religion and family, the latter being where most commercial ownership and decision making resided. A major concern at the time was the separation of church and state, but a crucial concern today is the capture and domination of government by integrated corporations. Today the dominant institutions are corporations and government. As with many other social problems—from campaign finance to low wages—the accelerated pace of environmental degradation and the improper disposal of hazardous, toxic, and radioactive waste are mainly the result of the corporate domination of other social institutions.[7]

As participant-observer of waste disposal decision processes, the author advises all legislative bodies and governmental agencies that the first order of business is twofold with regard to deciding upon how and with whom to design waste disposal processes. The first is to know the problem and the second is to define the alternative power structure involvement that corresponds to alternative waste disposal policies.

With regard to the first, the kind and extent of the waste problem needs to be determined by the governmental bodies before informed political decisions are possible. That is not the approach usually taken. Usually corporations lobby for a solution that requires a particular approach to the problem to be accomplished by corporate domination or, in many cases, lobbying for particular corporations to undertake the task. Then, upon being contracted for the task, the corporations define the problem consistent with the waste disposal technology they want to build or consistent with the kind of ecosystem damage they feel is beneficial to their associated corporate structure. The integrated systems approach suggested above will not be followed by the corporations. When legislative bodies forsake the right and duty to define the problem, the likelihood of an outcome consistent with serving the general welfare and preventing an ecological disaster are remote. Instrumental institutionalists have always emphasized the importance of problem definition and emphasized that the problem being considered should guide the analysis.[8]

With regard to the second, it is imperative that the power structure with which corporations are associated be articulated and understood before getting into bed with them in order to prevent a giant with a bad reputation from rolling over and crushing the public later. Usually the corporate power structure is more powerful than the government agency in a relationship. In most cases, a corporation is given a contract to take the lead, and, consequently, all the crucial decisions are made before the public is aware of the process. By the time the public becomes aware of what is happening and decides against the project because of the corporation's reputation or because of the inappropriate disposal technology, the government is already contractually committed and brings pressure on citizens to encourage their compliance (see Minnesota example below).

The corporations are usually so powerful in these cases that when the public begins to pressure for change, the corporations just turn to more attorneys and public relations companies, and begin a campaign of lies and deceit ( Greer and Bruno, 1996). They arrogantly move forward. Their lies are not necessarily told in order to fool anyone, but, rather, because in public processes they are expected to give an answer. Any answer serves the purpose because the excessive power of corporations in these situations means any answer will suffice. To boldly prevaricate demonstrates power. Mark Twain wrote: "When in doubt; tell the truth." These corporations are not in doubt, they are quite sure of their power. Once, as a commissioner, the author pointed out to the officer from a large global energy company that what had been stated about a proposed waste facility licensing process was inconsistent with reality—"it was a fantasy." Did the officer bother to defend his plan? No. His response, in a public meeting with media coverage, was: "I agree its kind of hard to separate reality from fantasy in this project" (*Lincoln Journal Star* May 16, 1996). His answer received bold print coverage in the newspaper, as he should have expected it would. What did he care? He received a big laugh from the officials representing other corporations, and, furthermore, it served the purpose of informing the agencies and advocacy groups from the various states involved that they could not depend on reliable data or candid answers. Arrogance, ignorance, and the absence of ethical standards make for heady behavior when supported on a platform of excessive power.

Political scientists have found that affiliated corporations can capture and dominate governmental agencies and commissions by being bound together in a "subgovernment." The concept of a subgovernment "is based on the observation that relatively small groups of actors dominate certain sectors of the political system" (Duffy 1997, 4). There are usually three different groups involved. They are (1) government bureaucrats in executive positions, (2) a governmental committee, such as the members of a congressional committee or commission, and (3) a special interest group (usually a corporate network). Hazardous waste disposal is especially well suited for subgovernment activity because such arrangements thrive on quiet agreements among the parties and also because citizens generally would rather not think about or deal with such waste. Most studies emphasize subgovernments operating at the national level, although they also operate at the state and local levels, especially with commissions dealing with concerns such as water, waste disposal, energy generation, and irrigation. Jeffrey M. Berry (1989, 240-1) characterizes the basic elements of the subgovernment as:

- A small group of actors playing a dominant role in developing policy in a particular field;
- Policy making as consensual, with quiet bargaining to produce agreements among the affected parties;
- Partisan politics exerting little impact on the relatively autonomous and stable arrangements (Bolduc 2001, 35).

Daniel McCool has explained that "as a descriptive device the subgovernment concept has been consistent with what can be observed in policymaking" (1998, 555). The author's own policymaking experience confirms McCool's observation. The subgovernment network is based on organization, with the inter- and trans-organizational relationships serving the social and economic decision making process. (An articulation of such a waste disposal network can be found in Hayden and Bolduc 2000.) The subgovernment makes no pretense of being a form of democracy. The network responds to whatever the management of various organizations can gain in their transactions with each other. According to Thomas Birkland, the striking features of the subgovernment network are the mutually reinforcing nature of the relationships among the parties and the fact that the government regulators do not tend to impose their ideas (2001, 96). This is an example of what Paul D. Bush has called "ceremonial encapsulation" ( Bush 1983, 1987, 1991). This is a situation in which the problem-solving process of the community has been "encapsulated" by powerful vested interests in order to control the type and use of technology to serve their own ends at the community's expense. This is clearly the case in the matter of waste disposal.

If democratic deliberations are to be allowed to guide the institutional and technological design of a hazardous waste disposal facility to successful fruitition, it is imperative that the task not be handed off to any group dominated by a powerful corporate network. The power structure studies need to be completed before making legislative decisions and before signing contracts. The most effective means the author has found for defining a corporate power structure is to find how the corporations are bound together through the use of overlapping "power blocs" (Hayden, Wood, Kaya 2002). A power bloc is the set formed by the interlocks of the boards of directors of four corporations, as follows: Peter Kiewit & Sons'<=>Berkshire Hathaway<=>CalEnergy Co.<=>Illinois Power. This is an example of four corporations with energy interests who are producers of hazardous, toxic, and radioactive waste. The directed lines between the corporations represent the exchange of one or more directors between corporations. The combination of the four corporations is one power bloc.

A study of the corporate power structure of a multi-state compact for the disposal of low-level radioactive waste found that among the 72 corporations that were most involved in the network, the dominant corporations are involved in a large number of different conjoint power blocs. As examples, among some of the large well-known global corporations, Berkshire Hathaway is a member of 421 different power blocs among the 72 corporations; Peter Kiewit & Sons is a member of 489 different power blocs; Entergy is involved in 319; CalEnergy participates in 570; and Illinois Power is a member of 555 different overlapping blocs (Hayden, Wood, Kaya 2002). When the number of different power blocs shared by pairs of corporations was analyzed, data consistent with the number of power blocs was found regarding their integration. As examples, Berkshire Hathaway shares 86 different power blocs with CalEnergy; CalEnergy shares 112 with Peter Kiewit, and Peter Kiewit shares 88 with Berkshire Hathaway (Hayden, Wood, Kaya 2002). This radioactive waste disposal compact is not only the victim of corporate capture, it is the most dense and extensive network found in the surveyed literature. The capacity for influence by citizens of the five states making up the multi-state compact is very limited against such a system of global giants. Not surprisingly, the engineers and scientists of the corporations with contracts to design, build, and operate the radioactive waste disposal facility for the compact, designed the scientific methodology, techniques, and database to be utilized by the state government agency designated to make the decision about the license application of the same corporations. (This is another real-world manifestation of Bush's theory of ceremonial encapsulation.) In their arrogance, the corporate engineers and scientists wrote journal articles to explain how they completed and implemented the methodology for the state agency to use to evaluate and judge the corporations' own license application (Paton, et al. 1989; Cawley, et al. 1990; Bisese, et al. 1991). The methodology is a sham and is inconsistent with federal and state law; yet, it was utilized by the state agency.

## CORPORATE POWER: UTILIZATION OF THE COASE THEOREM

Neoclassical economists have developed a theoretical concept that giant corporations now use to rationalize business practices that, in fact, create more pollution, reduce cleanup and remediation of waste sites, and make more insecure and less effective waste facilities. It also is used to promote public policies that result in greater resource costs, deterioration in public health, and the destruction of vital ecosystems, all of which must be borne by the community at large. The concept is known as the Coase theorem (Coase 1960). The Coase theorem is couched in terms of the MB=MC criterion of "efficiency." A standard economics textbook portrayal of the theorem is presented in Figure 2.It shows the relationship that presumably exists between the polluter and the pollutee (the individual or group of individuals who suffer the adverse effects of pollution generated by the polluter). Dollar values are measured on the vertical axis and the level of pollution is measured on the horizontal axis. The downward-sloping line, EA, is the marginal benefits (MB) curve, and the upward-sloping line, OM, is the marginal cost (MC) curve.

The MB curve measures the benefits to the producer, who generates pollution in the production process. It is downward sloping because each additional unit of output (which entails additional units of pollution) adds less to total benefits than previous units of output (pollution). At point A,

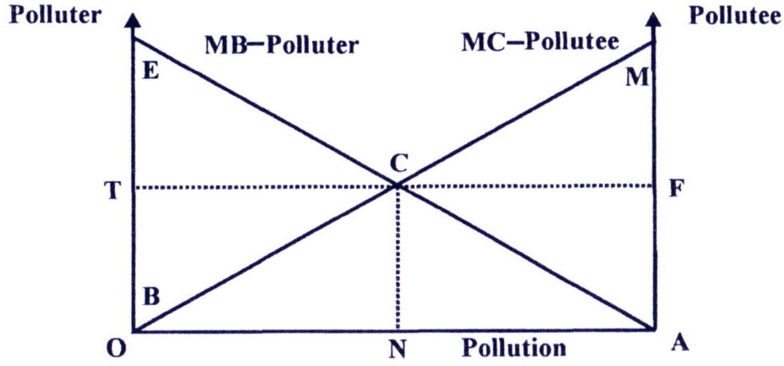


*Figure 2.* **Coase Theorem Bribe**

MB is equal to zero, because benefits are maximized at that point. When benefits are maximized, the producer has no pecuniary incentive to increase production (pollution) beyond that point. Thus, point A represents the maximum level of production and pollution in the absence of any constraints placed on pollution.

The MC curve measures the additional cost to the community of reducing additional units of pollution. It is upward sloping because of the theoretical presumption that it costs more in terms of the sacrifice of scarce resources to eliminate or remediate damages from each additional unit of pollution.[10] According to this analysis, the "optimal" or "efficient" level of pollution, point N, is determined when MB=MC is at point C.

In other words, the Coase Theorem states that greater "efficiency" is achieved if, for example, a corporate polluter is given the right to come into an area and produce waste that causes cancer and destroys the monetary value of homes in the neighborhood. Under the Coase scheme, the pollutee is required to bribe the polluter to reduce the amount of pollution or increase the level of cleanup and remediation. This is like the Mafia coming into an area and requiring protection payments from businesses with the threat that the businesses will be damaged and their owners beaten if they do not pay. The less they pay, the more the damage; the more they can pay, the greater the protection.

Referring again to Figure 2, the "Mafia geometry" of the Coase theorem can be portrayed as follows: If the pollutee can afford to pay the bribe of AF, the corporate polluter will cut back on the level of carcinogenic emissions by AN because at point C, the marginal benefit to the polluter (MB) is equal to the marginal cost of the pollutee (MC). If the pollutee can afford only to pay a lesser amount, the pollutee will be the recipient of more cancer and the polluter will be willing to provide more carcinogenic emissions, consistent with the lower bribe paid.

Although basic foundational assumptions and real-world facts are in conflict with the Mafia approach, it is still promoted by neoclassicalists as an ideal of efficiency. Recall that efficiency means "to achieve a desired effect" and that to judge whether desired effects have been achieved, criteria based upon social norms must be utilized. Neither the destruction of traditional property rights nor bargained cancer levels is consistent with social criteria. The desired effect, as defined by society's moral and ethical standards, is inconsistent with the Coase approach which is an attempt to avoid such standards. First, the Coase approach is an attempt to establish the argument that "efficiency" should be determined by a procedure rather than by judging outcomes. If the bribe procedure is followed, then according to neoclassicalists, the optimal efficiency is achieved. The proof is based on the tautology that because property rights are changed to require persons to pay a bribe in order to protect their health and environment, then it is efficient because that procedure is followed. Neither the use of tautologies nor the attempt to ignore consequences is acceptable. Second, the Coase approach is an attempt by neoclassicalists to set aside the myriad social criteria that society wants applied, and to dictatorially state that only their narrow bribe procedure, which is inconsistent with societal criteria, should be utilized.

Occasionally, there is recognition that the Coase approach is inconsistent with social morality and, therefore, is neither moral nor legal. David Zilberman correctly states that "society may decide that some behavior will simply not be tolerated" (2001, 12). The Comprehensive Environmental Response, and Liability Act and the Resource Conservation and Recovery Act clarify that polluters are required to provide full remediation with regard to damage from hazardous waste emissions and disposal. Bribes from pollutees for less remediation are not required or allowed.

Although Zilberman's statement is correct, it is not sufficiently inclusive. First, when society does decide to allow or require processes such as particular property structures, or market–like bargaining as in the case of trading pollution credits, those processes are part of society. Therefore, normative criteria and rules to allow for payoffs to guide and determine efficiency are established by society. Second, the Coase approach leads to confusion because of what is termed a "category mistake." A category mistake is the treatment of facts or concepts as if they really belong to one logical type or category, when they belong to another. An illustration of this mistake is as follows: "To say that the square root of four is white . . . makes no sense because it is impossible meaningfully to predicate color of a number . . . . An economist who asks how much citizens would pay for opinions that they advocate through political association commits a category mistake. The economist asks of objective beliefs a question that is appropriate only to subjective wants. . . . One cannot establish the validity of these beliefs by pricing them, nor can that mechanism measure their importance to society as a whole" (Anderson, Mandelker, Tarlock 1984, 35).

Of course, as is usually explained, there is a whole range of other reasons from within the Coase paradigm that make Coase and its Mafia geometry irrelevant, such as huge transaction costs, uncertainty, lack of knowledge and information, rent seeking, unique elasticities, lack of prices on pollution, inability to form the pollutees into an association, and the inability of species and ecosystem processes to bargain and bribe. In addition, "imposing rigid private property or central authority on a multispecies resource use system that has evolved over centuries may not only adversely affect the very human groups who have been responsible for successfully husbanding resources but may adversely affect the ecological function of the resource systems" (Becker and Ostrom 1995, 125).

Coase advocates claim to be attempting to use the market to solve the pollution/waste disposal problem. This, however, is inconsistent with the market approach, which requires that consumers pay a price sufficient to cover all costs. The market approach is consistent with the "polluter pays" rule, which requires the producer to pay for all costs of pollution prevention, remediation, and waste disposal. The "pollutee pays" rule shifts the costs away from the consumer of the product onto the pollutees.

Whether critiqued from within or outside, the Coase theorem fails. So what is its purpose? Can we just ignore it when developing ecological policy? No, because the corporate opposition uses it. Although scientifically irrelevant, it has propaganda value for corporations because its ideological base comes from the ideology of market capitalism. Just as the neoclassical paradigm provided cigarette companies with arguments that it is efficient to encourage smoking because cigarettes kill people, the Coase apparatus allows corporations to claim that the science of economics demonstrates that pollution levels should be higher, remediation requirements less strict, and waste disposal more risky. Of course, research centers stand ready to provide arguments in support of the propaganda.

The corporate push to change Superfund legislation is an example. The argument is explained and supported by David Rubenson and Jerry Aroesty of Rand Corporation. They explain that: "Superfund—originally passed in 1980—still exemplifies a form of federal responsiveness to grass–roots concern about hazardous waste sites. It is associated with the concepts of 'the polluter pays,' direct government intervention with numerous outlays, and strict and several retroactive liability. If the program was intended to assure attention to the prompt mitigation of visible threats to health and quality of life, then it has been successful largely through emergency removals and as a mechanism for affected communities—sometimes even those with limited political influence—to voice concerns and draw attention to nearby hazardous waste sites" (1994, 5). After that kind of acknowledgement of the success of Superfund, we might have expected the authors to call for an extension of Superfund concepts to other areas. Instead, their paper is devoted to hypothetical and rhetorical statements about the need for change. They complain that Superfund was influenced "less by fundamental policy concerns than by mistrust. . . ." (2). However, fundamental policy should be influenced by mistrust, given the power and record of the cooperative oligopolies that have been involved. The authors complain that because of the history of corporate policy (Love Canal) and EPA malfeasance, the various pieces of legislation regarding hazardous waste "are unusually prescriptive, detailed and complex" (2), even "defining the thickness of landfill liner" (2). Well, yes, given the reality of subgovernments surrounding federal and state regulatory agencies, that has been necessary. General legislation is not sufficient; specific and detailed requirements are necessary to assure enforcement.

Next, Rubenson and Aroesty raise Coase kinds of arguments, saying we could better adapt industrial processes "to better balance economic and environmental costs and benefits" (4). Their "balance" is an argument for more pollution, less remediation, less secure disposal, and lower monetary costs for the corporations. Balance is not the issue; fulfilling societal norms about the ecosystem and human health is the issue.

They question whether "Superfund phobia" is "still a desirable way to influence behavior" (4) because "the message about the potential hazards and uncertain liability of generating new waste has been delivered" (4). The message has been delivered, and it should continue to be delivered because it can so quickly be unlearned to increase profits. The authors believe that: "An alternative to Superfund phobia is to alert generators. . ." (4). The generators are already very alert to their waste emissions. The authors suggest we replace "polluter pays" with the neoclassical tools of "taxes and fees" which "would facilitate more effective and innovative policy approaches" (4). Yes, there would quickly be new policies for innovations in technology to create more waste and more unsafe disposal facilities. Moreover, given the monopoly power of the corporations, they will be able to shift taxes and fees. In addition, as explained below (Figure 4), to change the technological design of capital does not relieve society of the stock of old waste. New "innovations" will make the stock grow faster or slower. It will grow slower if the polluter pays policy is maintained.

The polluter pays principle is now being introduced into Eastern Europe because one of the perils of privatization has been an increased problem with hazardous and radioactive waste as industry has been privatized. "In the wake of the collapse of the command economies in Eastern Europe. . .many observers anticipated that the privatization of state-owned enterprises and the transition to a market based economy would in and of itself lead to a significant reduction of the amount of pollutants generated within the former Soviet bloc. . . ." (Darst 2001, 131). Experience has been quite different. Consequently, "independent waste management organizations modeled on those in use throughout the European Union supported by 'polluter pays' financing schemes are emerging in the 10 EU candidate countries of Central and Eastern Europe (CEEC), a study commissioned in 1998 by the Environment Directorate General of the European Commission has determined" (*The International Radioactive Exchange* October 15, 2001). The polluter pays principle should continue to be strengthened, enforced, and implemented more widely because if the social beliefs and comcomitant legal standards retreat, pollutees will suffer the toxicity of corporate power.

## CORPORATE POWER: DISTRIBUTION OF WASTE

Hazardous, toxic, and radioactive waste is not distributed equally, efficiently, fairly, randomly, or rationally across the social, temporal, spacial, income, or socioeconomic milieu. The distribution has been determined mainly by corporate decision makers without much influence from democratic institutions. Thus, the location of such waste and its consequences have been distributed to fall most heavily on the least powerful.[11] Toxic waste facilities "are often located in communities that have high percentages of poor, elderly, young, and minority residents. A high concentration of uncontrolled toxic waste sites is found in Black and Hispanic urban communities. . .and large commercial hazardous waste landfills and disposal facilities are more likely to be found in rural communities in the southern Blackbelt" (Bullard 1990, 103). As the affluent became more aware of the consequences of hazardous waste and aware of the reputations of corporations that refused to adequately care for waste, the affluent became more organized in preventing waste disposal in their communities. The actions by the affluent to protect themselves have resulted in corporations more intensely targeting waste facilities to powerless poor, minority, and rural communities. Some argue that institutional racism has been the major influence on siting policy. The correlation, however, seems to be different. The siting of waste disposal facilities has been concentrated in African-American, Hispanic, Native American, and rural communities in the United States because they have the least power. Remember that when the noted neoclassical economist, Lawrence Summers, argued for dumping cancer causing waste from the industrial world onto people in Africa, it was not a racial argument. He argued for it because they are poor (*The Economist* 1992).[12] The real point is that the poor, in Africa or elsewhere, simply do not have the political power to fight against the dumping of hazardous waste in their proximity.

In the case of siting waste disposal facilities, "where the primary conflict opposes the interests of a corporation to those of local residents affected by its operations, citizens rarely believe for long that the state is neutral and impartial. They find themselves having to struggle with the state, which they perceive as representing interests other than their own" (Young 1983, 178). This has led to the situation where the willingness on the part of communities to accept a waste facility is at an all-time low because public distrust of government and corporate officials charged with finding solutions is at an all time high. Numerous studies have found this to be the case. Richard Krannich and Stan Albrecht's study on nuclear waste disposal is an example. They concluded that the legacy of distrust is clearly evident in the findings and that the mistrust influences people's perceptions about health and safety of nuclear disposal projects. "Such concerns are exacerbated by the history of previous failures on the part of governmental agencies to deal with radioactive problems and the public's substantial distrust of those assigned responsibility for such activities" (Krannich and Albrecht 1995, 450).[13] In most cases of waste disposal, those assigned responsibility are private corporations with horrible records. The contribution of dangerous materials and lack of trust means that groups in affluent communities can organize the political muscle to stop a siting, thus, the facility is placed where such muscle cannot be organized because of lack of funds for political campaigns, lawsuits, lobbying, and hiring experts. Both new technology and new institutional structures are necessary in order to make dangerous waste centers safe and acceptable, and to provide distribution on a more rational and equitable basis than by raw political muscle.

The popular philosophical conceptions about justice and distribution have not been helpful to assist in guiding the reform of waste site distribution. "Nearly all theories of justice in contemporary philosophical and political discourse, including utilitarian theories, contract theories like Rawls and Nozick, and even critics of liberal theory like Neilsen, are distributively oriented theories" (Young 1983, 176). Although distributively oriented, they are of little assistance in the distribution of waste disposal for a number of reasons. First, most are based on some kind of utility maximization concept, but utility does not exist in the real world. Second, utilitarian theories, although rhetorically adopted by authoritarion collectives like the Nazi powers of World War II, are neither internally consistent nor operational.

Third, the non-utilitarian ideas are "me first" ideas, although Rawls' ideas are tempered in that respect. Rawls explains that his theory of justice is meant to facilitate obtaining an overlapping consensus on what basic rights and liberties are necessary to advance one's own views (English 1991, 8). Fourth, they are based on an idea of bargaining among atomistic individuals, while the real-world effort of attempting to deal with the location of waste disposal facilities needs to be based on how to reach a reasonable consensus among overlapping institutional organizations. Finally, the philosophies mentioned emphasize given procedures rather than emphasizing outcomes and how to change procedures to achieve outcomes. A number of scholars have commented on the last issue. Mary English stated: "To realize justice in its fullest sense—as encompassing outcomes as well as procedures and societal as well as individual considerations—it seems that a shared conception of the good *is* necessary" (1991, 9). In addition to ignoring concerns about reaching agreement on what consequences are good, philosophies driven by "the distributional orientation precludes considering questions of the justice of decision making structures" (Young 1983, 176).

The ideas of philosophers like Rawls, Nozick, and Neilson have influenced bureaucracies in corporations and government agencies. Corporate and government bureaucrats working together often follow the principle that justice is reached if their procedures are followed about how to site, how to determine probabilities, what relationships to consider, and so forth. In the siting case she studied, Iris Young found that: "The issue of justice raised by community residents in the siting case, however, calls into question just those institutional structures that justify some decision making procedures. They claim that communities should have the right to participate in such siting decisions, either in having the power to approve, disapprove, or be party to approval" (Young 1983, 177). Gregory McAvoy observed pressures used by the State of Minnesota in its attempt to site a waste facility according to its own predetermined policies. The state used its power to pressure for policies that did not have widespread support among citizen groups. "The disparity in resources between citizens and the state and the fact that the agency seeking to find a site was also providing information as to its safety made the education effort suspect in the minds of some citizens. In addition, the state tried to induce consent by promising financial compensation and by using moral suasion to convince citizens that opposing the facility was inimical to the general welfare" (McAvoy 1994, 727). Although this kind of state pressure is consistent with Rawls' idea of imposing a comprehensive doctrine, it caused the people in Minnesota to be more suspicious. In addition, "the state's efforts to induce support for its programs challenge conventional pluralist understandings of policymaking, which emphasize the impact that citizens have on policymakers, rather than the effect that public officials have on citizens" (McAvoy 1994, 727).

As John Dewey and Marc R. Tool have emphasized, instrumentalist philosophy is the guidance needed in a democratic society where both the design of decision-making institutions and technologies and their expected consequences need to be determined by democratic processes. According to Tool, the core significance of government agencies "is not so much their power to direct and constrain—their powers of mandamus and injunction—although that is real and significant, rather it is their instrumental and facilitative capacity to provide the *community* with a common vehicle for public-policy formation and implementation" (Tool 1979, 201).If government agencies provide such instrumental capacity, potentially affected communities will accept safe disposal facilities and reject unsafe ones. If the principle of self-determination by the community is taken seriously as a fundamental principle of justice, the decisions to reject an unsafe facility is rational. As Young explained, if a proposed "facility is harmless enough to render its rejection by a community irrational, then it should be possible to find a community that will agree to site it. If on the other hand, it really is the case that no community, if given the choice, would agree to have a plant like that proposed . . . then it should follow that such a plant is not a good solution to the problem of hazardous waste" (Young 1983, 182).

## SECOND LAW OF THERMODYNAMICS, ENTROPY, AND POLLUTION

Although the main concern here is about waste disposal rather than waste production, some understanding of the latter is necessary in order to help form expectations and principles about the former. To do so, the importance of thermodynamics, entropy, and joint products will be recognized. Agricultural economists are the only economists who have generally been concerned with joint products. This is odd since all production processes create multi-products, some of which may be designated goods and some as bads. Some bads require waste disposal systems to protect persons, other species, beauty, and ecological system processes.

Production is, in part, the transformation of energy and matter; therefore, entropy is a component of the material base of the production-ecosystem nexus. In physics, there are two different kinds of entropy: Thermodynamic entropy and configurational (sometimes called logical) entropy.

Thermodynamic entropy follows from the second law of thermodynamics. The second law states that, in a closed system, when there are changes of energy from one form to another, some useful energy is converted to a useless form and, therefore, the energy available to do useful work decreases. It is not possible to complete any real physical process with as much useful energy as there was at the beginning—some is always wasted in a closed system. Thermodynamic entropy is defined as the quantitative measure of the amount of thermal energy not available to do work. Available energy can never increase, so its opposite, entropy, can never decrease. "If the system is isolated and closed so that it does not exchange matter or energy with any other system, its entropy increases, with every physical action or transformation that occurs inside the system. Entropy can never decrease in an isolated system . . . ." [Ayres, Robert U. 1998, 190].

Configurational entropy is a measure of disorder or randomness in a closed system. Again it is a negative concept, in this case the opposite of organization or order. A piece of ice in which the water molecules are held in an ordered solid state has a lower entropy (more order) than the highly dispersed and rapidly moving molecules in water vapor. The mining of a resource from a site with high grade ore in conjunction with its final disposal into the environment in the form of mine wastes, generates an increase in configurational entropy—from the ordered molecules of the concentrated ore to the disaggregated slagheap and dissipated heat. "Both the mining of a resource from a site with high grade ore as well as its final disposal into the environment, e.g. in the form of mine wastes generates a continuous increase of our planet's entropy" (Faber and Wagenhals 1988, 230). The greater the disorder of a sample of matter, the higher its entropy. Thus, there is an interdependence between entropy and the concentration of a resource, on the one hand, and between entropy and potential environmental pollution due to mine wastes and dredged materials on the other" (230). Entropy in this sense is the formal measure of the total extent of disorder in a closed system.

But, alas, all production systems in the real world are open systems—neither isolated nor closed. Therefore, predetermined entropy calculations are not available for real-world production relationships. What is important is to recognize that all production systems must produce the joint products of wasted energy and disordered material. "In a real world system, there is a finite rate of energy exchange with the environment. If it is slow relative to the time frame of interest, we treat the system as isolated" [Christie 1994, 34]. Thus, entropy theory informs us that, in addition to the social dimensions explained above, entropy is another dimension that should be considered and measured for the particular process being evaluated.

Advice often heard from advocates for a cleaner environment is that technology should be selected and production organized so that waste does not exist. For example, a leading textbook in environmental science recommends opposition to disposal facilities in order to encourage government officials and waste producers to undertake changes to prevent pollution (Miller 1998, 590-91). That is not possible without repealing the second law of thermodynamics. It may be that we should try as much as possible to select technology so that one unit's waste is another unit's input, as is the rule in ecological systems. However, it is impossible to produce without waste output and it is impossible to design a waste disposal process that does not produce additional waste.

Being concerned about entropy is certainly not conclusive in designing technological systems. Dioxin (TCDD), which is a waste product of the chemical industry, can accumulate in body fat and promote cancer by activating DNA. The dioxin is neatly captured in the fat, the cancer is growth, and the molecules are orderly, yet, we do not want it. Furthermore, there are other physical laws, such as the rate of penetration of radioactive isotopes through various kinds of materials, and there are biological laws, such as the law of tolerance between chemical factors and species in an ecosystem, that need to be considered.

Some have attempted to give entropy a mystical and/or deterministic quality, and in the process they have made the word hopelessly ambiguous.[14] Recently Matthew Forstater wrote that, due to entropy, "the inputs utilized in production in the current period . . . must be replaced in the output of the current period for the system to be able to operate again in the following period" (2001, 2). In addition to being inconsistent with the history of the utilization of coal, the statement is very inconsistent with what physicists have written about entropy.

Thermodynamic entropy seems to have been adopted by many economists to find a new deterministic iron law to prove that economics is even more dismal than earlier economists had conveyed. First, as explained above, there are different definitions of entropy in physics. Second, those different definitions of entropy for different concepts have been neither correlated with each other nor found to have common measures. Third, additional definitions have developed as the concept was introduced into biology to explain the evolution of organizations. Fourth, the result of attempting to mix entropy and biology has mainly been confusion. "The confusion can be eradicated if we . . . admit that Earth's biological system is open to organizing input from outside" (Klyce 2001, 9). (We could add, as is the economic system.) Peter Medawar explained the confusion as follows: "The audacious attempt to reveal the formal equivalence of the ideas of biological organization and thermodynamic order . . . must be judged to have failed (1984, 226). If biologists cannot construct an iron law from entropy, it is doubtful that social scientists might. We can, however, borrow concepts from physics and biology, as relevant, for the analysis of particular production and waste systems. Such borrowing is not done to try to find determinative concepts, but, rather, to utilize concepts that help to discover viable policy regarding disposal of waste produced from multiple output production centers.

## MULTIPLE OUTPUTS

As instrumental institutionalists have emphasized for a century, the social process known as a production center, i.e., a factory, has numerous social, economic, and ecological consequences or outputs, such as the confirmation of some and disruption of other social beliefs. Factory consequences include distribution of income, disease, mangled limbs, pension benefits, products for sale, health care, thermodynamic entropy, hazardous toxins, alienation, and so forth. Factory studies have been extensive, and they have shown that there is no factory with a single output. Some of the consequences of production centers are found to be "goods" and some are found to be "bads." In some cases, societal evaluation institutions have found all the resulting outputs to be sufficiently bad to ban future production and sales. This includes an array of bads for which there was ample market demand, like DDT and dangerous baby carriers. What is a good output and what is a bad output depends on the moral standards and philosophy being applied and the adequacy of the measurement and policy.

Economists have traditionally adopted production function concepts divorced from joint products, ecological resources, and waste emissions. Production sets have been represented as functioning without resources from the ecosystem, without waste as an output, and, in addition, without a context of the exhaustibility of resources and expansion of waste flows and stocks. The Cobb-Douglas production function, which reigned for decades as the primary representation of production by neoclassicalists, had only a single output represented and only two inputs; capital and labor. There was no waste output (or other joint outputs). On the input side, there were no ecological resources, entrepreneurial ability, energy, financial capital, technology, and so forth. "The neoclassical tendency to omit [natural] resources as factors of production has one critical weakness. It is the simple physical fact that energy is *used up* in the economic production process, but cannot itself be created or 'produced' by human activity" (Ayres, Robert U. 1998, 204). The more energy and other ecological resources used because of inefficient or wasteful production processes, the less resources are available for other uses, one being waste disposal. As environmental issues became a concern in economics, waste emissions were treated as simply another factor input (Cropper and Oats 1992, 679). That obviously was not helpful, since a waste emission is an output, not a factor input.

Waste emissions, as economists began to emphasize, are an inevitable part of the production process. Robert Ayres and A.V. Kneese stated in 1969 that "there has been a tendency in the economics literature to view externalities as exceptional cases. . . .We believe one class of externalities—those associated with the disposal of residuals resulting from the consumption and production process—must be viewed differently. They are a normal, indeed, inevitable part of these processes" [1969, 282]. In 1975, Nicholas Georgescu-Roegen wrote that "given the entropic nature of the economic process, waste is an output as unavoidable as the input of natural resources" [1975, 357].

More recently, Stefan Baumgärtner has emphasized that to consider unwanted pollutants as special cases of joint production misleads policymakers into believing that waste can be eliminated by regulation or taxation. He wrote: "Single production will turn out to be a mere idealization, not existent in the real world; and environmental pollution as a consequence of the process of production appears as an inherent effect, rather than an exceptional external effect, of production" [2000, 69]. Baumgärtner, is developing a new joint-production economics based on the transformation of energy and matter. Figure 3 demonstrates one of his conclusions (Baumgärtner 2000, 25). Even when limiting production to a consideration of physical inputs and outputs, there are a number of both, to include ecological inputs and waste outputs. The brown coal fired power plant has four different kinds of waste emission outputs complementing the output of

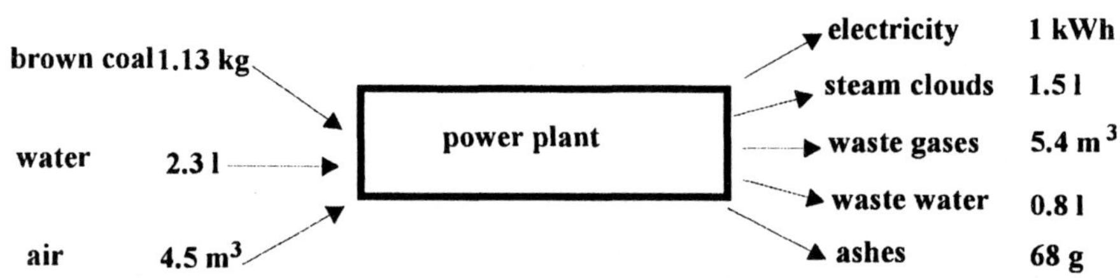


*Figure 3.* **Some of the Inputs and Outputs of a Brown Coal Fired Power Plant**

electricity. Both the extraction and use of energy to produce electricity and the disposal of waste cause environmental damage.[15]

A widely-held view is that a decrease in emissions from an industry due to a decrease in capital or the adoption of new capital containing technological innovations leads to a decrease in waste for disposal. For example, the introduction of new end-of-pipe technology in the North Rhine-

Westfalia region of Germany led to a 52–percent decrease in cadmium emissions from electricity production from 1955 to 1988 as electricity production increased (de Bruyn 2000, 216). Such an example is certainly a testimonial about how to have a major impact on emissions by improving technology. It, however, is not a blueprint for how to reduce the stock of hazardous waste. The graph on the left in Figure 4 (adapted from

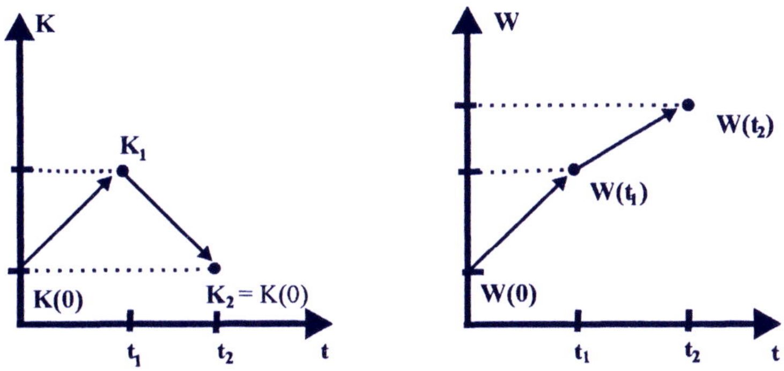


*Figure 4.* **Relationship Between Capital and Waste**

Baumgärtner 2000, 252) is an illustration of an initial capital stock K(0) at time period t=0. In the graph on the right, the corresponding stock of hazardous waste is illustrated. As the capital stock increased in the production center to $K_1$ in time period $t_1$, the stock of waste increased to $W(t_1)$. Next, assume that the capital stock fell in time period $t_2$ to its original level due to depreciation or a new investment policy so that $K_2=K(0)$. The growth rate of K is negative, thereby decreasing the rate of waste emissions. However, between $t_1$ and $t_2$, the stock of waste continues to increase. Any emission level will increase the stock of waste. Although the stock of capital has fallen, the disposal problem has worsened. The same would be the case due to technological improvements.

This reality speaks to the argument that the high rates of pollution emissions due to dirty industries moving to third-world countries should not be a concern because after the countries become rich they can change policies to less dirty technology in order to enhance environmental quality. The radical supporter of economic growth from dirty industries postulates a positive long-run relationship between economic growth and environmental quality (de Bruyn, 2000, 2), while the strong antagonist argues that no improvement can be made without getting off the growth path (3). In simple terms, Figure 4 suggests both are wrong. Even the antagonist argument assumes that if capital is held stable for no growth, the waste stock will fall. It will, instead, continue to grow. Thus, when countries are cursed with dirty industries, they can expect the large stock of waste to grow in the future.[16]

## DISPOSAL AS SERVICE PRODUCTION CENTERS

The stock of waste indicated in Figure 4 creates centers of production for disposal services. Such disposal services may be a pipe that dumps the waste into a river, a pumping system that injects it into a water aquifer, or an elaborate disposal plant that treats or stores the waste. University engineering libraries are full of books, reports, and computer programs with detailed plans for and about impacts from various kinds of disposal services—ranging from aerobic degradation by bacteria to injection into water aquifers for filtration. Two characteristics that stand out from that literature are that waste disposal processes always produce waste and that the stock of waste does not remain stable and immobile. Whatever the disposal processes, there are mobile chemical leachates, gases, radioactive leakages, ash, heat, oxides, and so forth produced by those processes. The scientific literature contains models of the plumes and risk contours of the new joint products created by the hazardous disposal sites and waste treatment centers. Whatever the disposal method, the stock of waste produced does not remain stable. The particular stock may depreciate, such as by a natural loss of radioactivity. Or, nature's assimilation capacity for dangerous pollutants may lead to a natural deterioration of the amount of waste stock. Its lack of stability may be exhibited by the stock remaining the same but spreading through a medium like air, water, and soil. Or, it may become mobile through the movement of humans and animals to which it has adhered. In addition, it may be chemically or physically transformed into other substances, some that may be more harmful, some that may be less so. Or, technology may be applied to change waste into an inert substance. Some of these kinds of changes are flows from the stock, however, mobility should not be confused with a flow. A change in location of a stock does not constitute a flow.

Baumgärtner states: "The assumption that there is no natural deterioration of waste amounts to saying that joint outputs that enter the natural environment as emissions remain there *in one form or the other* . . . (2000, 250). That is correct, but not relevant. Some forms are harmful and some are not. The stock of feedlot manure from animals and sewage from humans can be composted and changed chemically and physically into another form to be absorbed by plants to produce food and forests. Changing the form of waste stocks is a major concern in a world where, as Baumgärtner demonstrated, the flow of pollution emissions is strictly positive in an economy with a positive stock of capital (2000, 251). The form and amount of some emissions can be changed to be less harmful, into a form that is actually a positive resource, or one which deteriorates. Such changes require policies for institutional and technological changes involved in waste disposal.

What Clarence E. Ayres taught us about technology and its evolution is important for understanding why it is crucial for policymakers to become involved early in the process of technological design and implementation. If technology that is inappropriate for waste disposal is implemented, substantive evolution toward appropriate technology should not be expected. First, one of Ayres's important contributions was that technology is not tools (i.e., machines, computers, and so forth). It is the *combination* of tools, skills, and knowledge. This is too little understood by those in the corporations who are in charge of establishing the technology. They are mainly engineers who do not realize that the selection of particular tools stipulates requirements for a whole set of skills and knowledge. In addition, the engineers stipulate the kind of institutional structure that provides the tools, skills, and knowledge and how they are to be combined, as explained above (see Figure 1). Thus, the corporations are engineering social institutions as well as tool selection. The institutional and technological engineering can be costly in pecuniary terms, if it is undertaken in a manner consistent with social and ecological needs. If, on the other hand, the corporation adopts institutional and technological engineering in such a way as to shift the social and ecological costs of pollution onto the community at large, it can substantially increase its profits. This is known as "cost shifting." Thus, one reason for the corporate resistance to correct technology after it has been adopted is that it will lose the profits attained through cost shifting. Moreover, as Ayres emphasized, once institutional and technological practices are put in place, they become rigid and resistant to change.

Second, Ayres's explanation of technological evolution clarifies that new technology is a new combination of previous technology (Ayres, C.E. 1962). Thus, the technological path is usually an extension of a current technological base, especially given the institutional stasis. Thus, if the wrong kind of technology is established, we can expect that any new disposal process will be an extension of the old. For example, when corporations were allowed to drill holes to inject waste into subsoil and water acquirfers, it should not have been a surprise that their new technology would be to drill deeper and use higher pressure injection techniques, thereby making for a dangerous waste plume too deep and diffused for recovery or mediation. Again, this means it is important for public policymakers to become involved early to guide corporate activity.

The work of Georgescu-Rogen that was considered his weakest can also provide guidance for technology policy regarding waste. He has been adversely criticized (rightly so) for formulating a fourth law of thermodynamics which stated that matter becomes progressively unavailable through dispersion and dissipation and that dispersed matter is irretrievable even if available energy is plentiful. He said this will proceed to the point where all matter is unavailable. This, however, is not consistent with physics or the world around us. (Why do economists have a need to formulate deterministic iron laws?). Gold and uranium that is diffused in seawater can be recovered. Carbon sequestration is the use of plant photosynthesis to take carbon dioxide from the atmosphere and store carbon in the soil in order to mitigate the greenhouse effect. Phytoremediation is the process of using living plants to remove heavy metals and other pollutants from soil and water.

What can be learned from Georgescu-Rogen is that waste disposal technology should not be designed so as to create unnecessary levels of diffusion and dissipation of resources. This would make remediation of waste sites and retrieval of resources very expensive. This idea is related to configurational entropy which is a measure of disorder or randomness. His concern is relevant for policy even if his physical law failed to be immutable. He did not need a "fourth law." An example of disorder and randomness that leads to excessive costs is the low-level radioactive waste disposal system that has been utilized by nuclear energy generators, hospitals, industry, and research centers. Traditionally, large amounts of such radioactive waste is shipped by the train load to waste facilities with an intent to store it for millions of years. This waste is composed of materials exposed to radioactivity such as wood scaffolding, old concrete, materials from hospitals, clothing, ore from uranium mining, and so forth. In the first instance, much more radioactive material was created than necessary—more random exposure. It was not necessary to allow so much material to be become radioactive. Thus, waste facilities far larger than what was necessary became a necessary burden. Moreover, the method used mingles all the different materials that have been exposed to different isotopes—some isotopes with a dangerous half-life of three months, others with a dangerous half-life of millions of years. This disorder and random mixing makes it impossible to retrieve the material with a three-months half-life after it is no longer dangerous and move it to the city dump, which is less expensive to maintain. Another example is that only a small fraction of the municipal and industrial waste streams are hazardous; yet, they are responsible for groundwater contamination from landfills. Had they not been randomly mixed with the nonhazardous waste, protection and remediation would be much less expensive. These examples demonstrate Georgescu-Rogen's concern because different elements become increasingly mixed together and more difficult to separate from each other. A different set of institutional operations and technologies would make remediation and retrieval easier.

## CONCLUDING REMARKS

Throughout this chapter, the need for a different set of institutions and technologies has been part of the approximately twenty-five policy conclusions articulated. Policy conclusions have been reached about principles explaining why institutional and technological changes are necessary and principles explaining how to proceed to make the changes. A major question throughout has been about why citizens have not been able to expect reasonable instrumental policy solutions to be implemented. The main reason is institutional failure. As explained, one such failure has been the ideology within the popular economic and philosophical paradigms. However, the major institutional failure is due to the domination of policymaking, design, implementalism, and operation of waste disposal processes by large powerful corporations responsible for much of the production, disposal, and remediation of hazardous, toxic, and radioactive waste.

The United States has the best set of environmental protection laws, procedures, and criteria one might hope to find as a legal code designed to alleviate problems associated with waste disposal. This legal apparatus is associated with the world's greatest accumulation of highly educated scientists and engineers available to conduct studies and construct facilities. Moreover, the economic resources devoted to the problems of waste disposal are staggering—whether considering facility construction, remediation of leaking facilities, disease, or loss of living systems. We fail to improve the situation because most studies, decisions, facility design, remediation, storage, and disposal of waste is guided by corporations. The corporation is an institution that dominates waste production and disposal processes both inside and outside of government. As a consequence, the exemplary environmental laws and the highly advanced science of waste disposal are not adequately utilized to serve the interests of the community at large. The growing problem of hazardous waste is not the result of the lack of knowledge or inadequate law; it results from the failure to reform institutions so that democratic processes, rather than the vested interests and power of giant corporations, direct the development of social policy.

## NOTES

1 Land disposal includes open dumps, surface impoundments, sanitary landfills, "secure" chemical landfills, and underground injection wells. Sanitary landfills are engineered for non-hazardous wastes, however, many of the waste streams delivered to them contain hazardous materials that are responsible for groundwater contamination. For an excellent

nontechnical description and explanation of the toxicology, contamination level, location, human health concerns, and regulation of waste disposal, see R. Allan Freeze (2000).

2 Within the past year, the author has received two new books about the environment, and neither contained anything about the waste problem created from production processes. One book was about the economics of natural resources and the other was about the economics of the environment. Yet, neither made mention of waste disposal. This example demonstrates that science is a social construction. The social beings who function in our society—people in general—seldom consider the creation and disposal of hazardous waste in either their paradigmatic view or their myth making, and economists generally have constructed their paradigms consistent with the myths of their society.

3 During the year, 2001, *The Wall Street Journal* published numerous excellent news articles that explain the ability of different groups composed of major global corporations to successfully promote policy, complete the passage of legislation, and obtain executive orders for the benefit of the corporations. The same corporations are responsible for both the production and disposal of most industrial waste.

4. For an example of the use of codified criteria to evaluate the efficiency of the financial assurance plan contained in a license application for a radioactive waste facility, see F. Gregory Hayden and Scott Fullwiler (2001).

5 The problem with this kind of rigid approach to procedure is addressed later in the section on "Corporate Power: Distribution of Waste."

6 The notion of the MB=MC criterion will be put in a broader social context in the discussion later of the so–called "Coase theorem." With the MB=MC criterion, presumably, the rational economic actor will undertake an activity up to a point where the addition to total benefits from the activity is just equal to the addition to total costs. The standard neoclassical Principles of Economics textbook claims that when MB=MC, net benefits (total benefits minus total costs) are maximized.

7 An article by James A. Swaney and Paulette I. Olson provides an extensive description of ecological damage by corporate interests in various countries (1992, 9-21).

8 For an introudctory discussion of instrumental institutionalism, see the first chapter of this book written by Marc R. Tool and Paul D. Bush.

9 When the value of the marginal curve is equal to zero, the value of the related total function is maximized.

10 This is based on the neoclassical economists' belief in the law of diminishing marginal returns of variable resources used in the production of goods and services.

11 Determining the real distribution of hazardous waste impacts has not been attempted in literature surveyed. Instead, facility and site location have been used as a substitute for the final destination of waste impacts. However, the social pattern of risk and impacts may be much different than indicated by facility location. Scoping techniques could be utilized to determine all the populations reached through underground waste plumes, migration leachate, diseases carried by animals, movement of radioactivity through the soil, gases from disposal sites carried by the wind, contaminated water supplies, and so

forth. Moreover, toxicity and waste characteristics could be utilized to determine differences in the danger of waste exposure for different groups.

12 When he was the chief economist at the World Bank, Lawrence Summers wrote a policy memorandum in which he utilized the neoclassical paradigm to argue for dumping hazardous waste in the habitat of the African poor. He argued that such dumping would be more efficient in the MB=MC sense because the present discounted value of life is far lower than it is in industrial nations. Because the MC of the waste, measured in terms of loss of life, would be much lower, more waste should be generated and dumped. This is a demonstration of the conflict between social morality and the implications of neoclassical logic. Once his memorandum was leaked to the public, Summers protested that it was not written to be taken seriously as a policy document. Such a rationalization does not, however, change the fact that his argument is a precise rendering of the neoclassical logic on the point. In an editorial note, *The Economist* pointed out that it would be difficult for economists to argue against Summer's ideas from a neoclassical point of view (*The Economist* 1992).

13 Studies from the US Environmental Protection Agency have documented a history of unsafe hazardous waste, reporting that between 80 to 90 percent of all hazardous wastes are disposed of in an unsafe manner (Salcedo, Cross, Jr., Chrismon 1989, 51), and Berry Johnson and Christopher De Rosa report the number of uncontrolled waste sites at 40,000 (1997, 1). Protesting citizens are aware of that history, thus, their adverse "reaction to proposed hazardous waste sites is an understandable response to past indiscriminate management of hazardous wastes" (Salcedo, Cross, Jr., Chrismon 1989, 51).

14 Ambiguity usually leads us to quit using a word. One such example is the word "holistic." It had a specific meaning in the scientific world. However, it was adopted by numerous groups, was used extensively, and was given so many different meanings without distinct borders, that the scientific community started using substitutes. We are at about the same position with conceptual words like "entropy" and "chaos," and "thermodynamic" is in danger of gaining the same reputation. To use the word "entropy" with various ill-defined meanings within the same discipline means we are at the point that it should be abandoned or, at least, its original meaning recaptured. As Clarence E. Ayes said to his students: "Words are tools, therefore, like a scissors, they should cut—they should cut away most of the world. Otherwise they are useless." Literature professors write about topics such as the entropic chaos of complexity, economists about topics such as chaos in the distribution of income due to ignorance of entropic trends. Neither use of the term has anything to do with the meaning of entropy and neither cuts. A term like "terrible" would probably better convey the meaning intended in both cases. When any concept is extended to explain too much, as has been the case with entropy, it often explains nothing.

15 There is no reason to expect the production functions of the different joint products to be the same. The level and direction of the marginal product as well as the level and direction of the absolute product can be different for the output that is for sale than for the waste output that is for disposal.

16 A casual survey of reports about third–world macroeconomies indicates that such countries actually ratchet down spending for environmental protection as their economies become more dependent on business cycles. During the upside of the cycle, industries hold environmental protection expenditures at a low level due to the excessive competition

in the global economy. During downturns in the cycle, environmental protection is reduced to a minimum, from which it seldom recovers in the next upturn.

# REFERENCES


Anderson, Frederick R., Daniel R. Mandelkerer, and A. Dan Tarlock. 1984. *Environmental Protection: Law and Policy* . Boston: Little, Brown and Company.

Anderson, James A. and Elaine E. Englehardt. 2001. *The Organizational Self and Ethical Conduct.* Fort Worth: Harcourt College Publishers.

Ayres, Clarence E. 1962. *The Theory of Economic Progress.* New York: Schocken.

Ayres, Robert U. and Allen V. Kneese. 1969. Production, consumption, and externalities. *American Economic Review* 59:282–297.

Ayres, Robert U. 1998. Eco-thermodynamics: economics and the second law. *Ecological Economics* 26:189-209.

Baumgärtner, Stefan. 2000. *Ambivalent Joint Production and the Natural Environment: An Economic and Thermodynamic Analysis.* Heidelberg: Physica-Verlag.

Becker, C. Dustin and Eleanor Ostrom. 1995. Human ecology and resource sustainability: the importance of institutional diversity. *Annual Review of Ecological Systems* 26: 113–33.

Berry Jeffrey M. 1989. "Subgovernments, Issue Networks, and Political Conflict." In Richard A. Harris and Sidney M. Milkis, eds. *Remaking American Politics*, 239-260. Boulder: Westview Press.

Birkland, Thomas A. 2001. *An Introduction to the Policy Process: Theories, Concepts, and Models of Public Policymaking.* New York: M. E. Sharpe.

Bisese, Patrick L., Charles N. Cawley, Mark A. Hunter, and Michael A. Sabbe. 1991. Readiness review for site characterization: a systems approach. *Nuclear Plant Journal* 9:80–88.

Bolduc, Steven R. 2001. *The Problem of Complex Technology in Public Policy Design: A History and Policy Evaluation of Low-Level Radioactive Waste Policy in the United States.* Ph.D. Diss., University of Nebraska–Lincoln.

Bullard, Robert D. 1990. Ecological inequities and the New South: black communities under siege. *The Journal of Ethic Studies* 17:101–115.

Bush, Paul Dale. 1983. An exploration of the structural characteristics of a Veblen–Foster defined institutional domain. *Journal of Economic Issues* 17:35–65.

_________. 1991. Reflections on the twenty–fifth anniversary of AFEE: philosophical and methodological issues in institutional economics. *Journal of Economic Issues* 25:321–46.

_________. 1987. The theory of institutional change. *Journal of Economic Issues* 21:1075–1116.

Cawley, Charles N., Mike A. Sabbe, Patrick L. Bisese, John H. DeOld, and Jay D. Ringenberg. 1990. An approach to the licensing of a mixed waste unit. *Transactions of the American Nuclear Society* 61:179–187.

Christie, John R. 1994. "A Survey of Thermodynamical Ideas." In Peter Burley and John Foster, eds. *Economics and Thermodynamics: New Perspectives on Economic Analysis*, 23–37. Boston: Kluwer Academic Publishers.

Coase, Ronald H. 1960. The problem of social cost, *The Journal of Law and Economics* 3: 1–44.

Cropper, Maureen L and Wallace E Oates. 1992. Environmental economics: a survey. *Journal of Economic Literature* 30:675–740.

Darst, Robert G. 2001. *Smokestack Diplomacy: Cooperation and Conflict in East–West Environmental Politics.* Cambridge, MA: The MIT Press.

de Bruyn, Sander M. 2000. *Economic Growth and the Environment: An Empirical Analysis.* Boston: Kluwer Academic Publishers.

Dewey, John. 1938. *Logic: The Theory of Inquiry.* New York: Henry Holt and Company.

Duffy, Robert J. 1997. *Nuclear Politics in America: A History and Theory of Government Regulation.* Lawrence: University of Kansas Press.

Elsner, Wolfram and John Groenwegen, eds. 2000. *Industrial Policies After 2000.* Boston and Dordrecht: Kluwer Academic Publishers.

Elsner, Wolfram. 2000. "An Industrial Policy Agenda 2000 and Beyond–Experience, Theory and Policy." In Elsner and Groenwegen, 411–486.

English, Mary. 1991. Siting, justice, and conceptions of the good. *Public Affairs Quarterly* 5:1–17.

Faber, Malte and Gerhard Wagenhals. 1988. "Towards a Long–Term Balance Between Economics and Environmental Protection." In Willem Salomons and Ulrich Förstner, eds. *Environmental Management of Solid Waste Dredged Material and Mine Tailings.* New York: Springer–Verlag.

Forstater, Mathew F. 2001. "Notes on Environmental Economics and Classical Political Economy." Center for Full Employment and Price Stability. University of Missouri–Kansas City. Online Available from http://iml.umkc.edu/econ/AFEE/ Environmental _Economics_and_CPE.html; Internet; accessed on 25 June.

Freeze, R. Allan. 2000. *The Environmental Pendulum: A Quest for the Truth About Toxic Chemicals, Human Health, and Environmental Protection.* Berkeley: University of California Press.

Georgescu-Roegen, Nicholes. 1975. "Energy and economic myths." *Southern Economic Journal* 41:347–381.

Greer, Jed and Kenny Bruno. *Greenwash: The Reality Behind Corporate Environmentalism.* New York: The Apex Press, 1996.

Groenwegen, John. 2000. "Introduction: Industrial Policy; Issues, Theories, and Instruments." In Elsner and Groenwegen, 1–21.

Hamilton, David. 2001. Comment provoked by Mason's 'Duesenberry's contribution to consumer theory.' *Journal of Economic Issues* 35:745–747.

Hayden, F. Gregory. 1998. "Normative Analysis of Instituted Processes." In Sasan Fayazmanesh and Marc R. Tool, eds. *Institutional Theory and Applications: Essays in Honor of Paul Dale Bush, Volume 2.* Cheltenham, UK: Edward Elgar.

_______. 1989. *Survey of Methodologies for the Valuing Externalities and Public Goods.* Conducted under subcontract to the Cadmus Group with funding by the US EPA, Office of Environmental Planning, Contact 68-01-7363.

———.and Scott T. Fullwiler. 2001. Analysis of the financial assurance plan in the license application for a low-level radioactive waste disposal facility. *Journal of Economic Issues* 35:373–383.

———. and Steven R. Bolduc. 2000."Contracts and Costs in a Corporate/ Government System Dynamics Network: A United States Case." In Elsner and Groenwegen, 35-284.

———. Kellee Wood, and Asuman Kaya. 2002. The use of power blocs of integrated corporate directorships to articlulate a power structure: case study and research recommendations. *Journal of Economic Issues* 36: 671-706.

Johnson, Barry L. and Christopher T. DeRosa. 2001. "The toxicological hazard of superfund hazardous waste sites." *Reviews of Environmental Health* 12 (December 1997): 235–251. Online Available from http://www.atsdr.cdc.gov/toxhazsf:html; Internet; accessed 1 August.

Klyce, Brig. 2001. "The Second Law of Thermodynamics and What's New." *Cosmic Ancestry*. Online. Available from www.panspermia.org/secon/2w.htm; accessed on 28 June.

Krannich, Richard S. and Stan L. Albrecht. 1995. Opportunity/Threat responses to nuclear waste disposal facilities. *Rural Sociology* 60:435–453.

Lester, James P. and Ann O'M. Bowman. 1989. Implementing environmental policy in a federal system: A test of the Sabtier-Mazmanian model. *Polity* 21:731–753.

*Lincoln Journal Star*. May 16, 1996.

McAvoy, Gregory E. 1994. State autonomy & democratic accountability: the politics of hazardous waste policy. *Polity* 27:699-728.

McCool, Daniel. 1998. The subsystem family of concepts: a critique and a proposal. *Political Research Quarterly* 51:551–570.

Medawar, Peter. 1984, *Plato's Republic.* Oxford: Oxford University Press.

Miller, Jr., G. Tyler. 1998. *Living in the Environment: Principles, Connections, and Solutions.* 10th Edition. Boston: Wadsworth Publishing Company.

Paton, Richard F., Charles N. Cawley, and Jay D. Ringenberg. 1989. "Using a Regutatory Matrix to Identify Requirements and Evaluate Project Compliance." Low-Level Waste Proceedings of the Symposium on Waste Management. Published by Arizona Board of Regents. Tucson, AZ.

Rubenson, David and Jerry Aroesty. 1994. "Hazardous Waste Policy: Unfinished Business." RAND Issue Papers. Online. Available from http://www.rand.org/publication/IP/IPI/ip141.html; Internet; accessed on 5 August. 1999.

Salcedo, Rodolfo N., Frank L. Cross, Jr., and Randolph L. Chrismon. 1989. *Environmental Impacts of Hazardous Waste: Treatment, Storage, and Disposal Facilities.* Lancaster, PA: Technomic Publishing Company, Inc.

Swaney, James A. and Paulette I. Olson. 1992. The economics of biodiversity: Lives and lifestyles. *Journal of Economic Issues* 26:1–26.

*The Economist*, February 8, 1992.

*The International Radioactive Exchange*. October 15, 2001.

Tool, Marc R. 1979. *The Discretionary Economy: A Normative Theory of Political Economy.* Santa Monica, CA: Goodyear Publishing Company, Inc.

Veblen, Thorstein. 1919. *The Vested Interests and the State of the Industrial Arts*. New York: B. W. Huebsch.

Young, Iris M. 1983. "Justice and Hazardous Waste" In Michael Bradie, Thomas W. Attig, and Nicholas Rescher, eds. *The Applied Turn in Contemporary Philosophy*. Bowling Green, OH: Bowling Green Studies in Applied Philosophy.

Zilberman, David. 2001. "Externalities and the Selection of Policy Tools: Other Considerations." Department of Agricultural and Resource Economics, University of California–Berkeley. Online. Available from http://are.berkeley.edu/~zilber /EEP101 /Lecture-Summary-PDF/ Lec06-coase-theorm.pdf; Internet; accessed on 16 July.

# 17

# GLOBALIZATION: AN INSTITUTIONALIST PERSPECTIVE

Gladys Parker Foster

## INTRODUCTION

Globalization has taken on at least two different meanings in the current literature. It is defined here as a process of institutional change in the modes of intercourse among nations and regions of the world, prompted by technologies that increase the volume of exchange of knowledge, culture, and commerce. This positive position reflects that of Thomas Friedman (1999), who sees globalization as the integration of capital, technology, and information across national boundaries. On the other hand, there are many who look at globalization as the takeover and augmentation of world commerce by increasingly powerful and rich multinational corporations (MNCs), driven by narrow and self-serving corporate goals and values without regard to human welfare. To them, globalization appears to be out of control and the MNCs without accountability.

Clearly, the world is beset by problems that seem not to go away and often even to get worse as globalization advances. The United Nations Development Programme (UNDP) reports that eighty countries have per capita incomes lower than a decade ago, and sixty countries have grown steadily poorer since 1980 (Gates 2001, 6). Another UN estimate is that one-fifth of the world's population consumes eighty-six percent of the world's services and goods, while the bottom fifth consumes less than three percent (Lindblom 2001, 162). In the United States, CEO compensation during the 1990s went from 85 times what blue collar workers make to 475 times (Frank 2000, 7). Underdeveloped nations' external debt exceeds $2.5 trillion, Fidel Castro reports, and an outrageous mechanism of subjugation and exploitation goes with it (Castro 2000, 282).

When one takes a hard look at the world economic situation, certain realities become apparent. One is that globalization is here to stay. Neither technology nor political power can be expected to undo it. The question becomes, then, not whether it is good or bad but how to deal with the associated problems. From an institutionalist perspective, the question would be what kinds of institutional changes are appropriate.

A second reality is that, while many if not most of the problems we see appear to be the old familiar ones, there has nonetheless been a change, and that is a change in economic philosophy. For more than twenty years nations everywhere have been much friendlier to market values than previously, and along with that goes an unwillingness to go against the *laissez-faire* philosophy of non-interference with the market. George Soros calls this trend "market fundamentalism" (Soros 1998; 2000). George DeMartino refers to it as global neo-liberalism (DeMartino 2000, 11-16).

Jeff Gates, however, believes it is not necessary that a neo-liberal philosophy be applied to a globalized world:

> The problem with globalization is *not* the corporate entity, as some insist. Nor is globalization a problem *per se.* The malady lies in the combination of: (a) the narrow bandwidth of values to which the corporate entity mechanistically attunes its operations (i.e., financial values), and (b) the current state of corporate ownership—abstract, remote and concentrated. The result is a globalizing economy that is experienced by most as disconnected, speeded-up and dumbed-down. The solution lies in evoking a policy mix insistent that business methods mature so that ownership patterns quickly become more personalized, localized and human-sized. In a private property system, that is the only sensible way globalized private enterprise can attune its operations to the legitimate concerns of those influenced by its operations.
>
> Globalization has the potential to be a positive force. However, under neoliberal-informed rule-making, globalization instead has emerged as a capital markets-led, government-backed process that radically redistributes wealth . . . (Gates 2001, 5).

Jonathan Mitchie, in the introduction to a book he co-edits on global instability, takes a similar view:

> Economic liberalisation is simply the form that such globalisation is currently taking, given the global neo-liberal regime. Thus, many of the problems which appear to stem from globalisation are due to the neo-liberal regime of deregulation and *laissez-faire* within which these

> developments are occurring (Mitchie 1999, 3). . . .It is necessary to expose the current complacent orthodoxy in mainstream economics, and challenge the fatalistic belief that the new globalised economy rules out any change of course. . . . [T]he fact that the economy is becoming inceasingly internationalised does not dictate the form that this process is taking. The free-market, *laissez-faire* agenda is one being pursued by those who benefit from such a deregulated winner-take-all environment. It is not the only choice. And for the majority of the world's population, it is an inappropriate one (Mitchie 1999, 6).

Nobel laureate Amartya Sen also expresses positive thoughts about globalization, along with a hope that proper attention be paid to the deprived:

> Indeed, we cannot reverse the economic predicament of the poor across the world by withholding from them the great advantages of contemporary technology, the well-established efficiency of international trade and exchange, and the social as well as economic merits of living in an open society. Rather, the main issue is how to make good use of the remarkable benefits of economic intercourse and technological progress in a way that pays adequate attention to the interests of the deprived and the underdog. That is, I would argue, the constructive question that emerges from the so-called anti-globalization movements. . . . [M]any of the anti-globalization protesters, who seek a better deal for the underdogs of the world economy, are not—contrary to their own rhetoric and to the views attributed to them by others—really "anti-globalization." It is also why there is no real contradiction in the fact that the so-called anti-globalization protests have become among the most globalized events in the contemporary world (Sen 2002, A4, A5).

In this essay, we see the increased interconnectedness of globalization as exciting and enriching, providing greater opportunity and holding forth the promise of facilitating problem-solving. The thesis of this essay, then, is that it is not globalization *per se* but the application of a neo-liberal philosophy that is responsible for the dismal economic scene and that institutional adjustments can and should be the avenue both for addressing the problems and for developing the potential promise of globalization.

## INSTITUTIONS AND ECONOMIC THEORY

If ever an economic philosophy were uniquely equipped to analyze globalization and institutional change, it is institutional economic philosophy. It differs sharply from the traditional neoclassical economic paradigm that prevails today both in academia and, predominantly, in government policies.

Traditional theory assumes the institutional structure to be given, and at this point in history this means the market structure. It does not question the adequacy of the market but in fact uses it as the criterion of judgment with which to assess economic policies. Thus economists of this persuasion are likely to recommend policies of privatization, *laissez-faire*, deregulation, and the like, in order that business firms rather than the polity may be the decision-makers in determining economic policy.

Institutional economic theory rests on a fundamentally different philosophy. Its analytical focus is on institutions, which it defines as prescribed patterns of correlated human behavior (Foster [1972] 1981, 939-40; Foster [1948] 1981, 320; see also Tool 1979, 73). Accordingly, it regards economics as a study of economic institutions, that is to say, institutions having to do with the provision of the means of life. Therefore, instead of being given, the existing institutional structure is subject to analysis and thus to possible recommendations for change. Note that, whatever their structure, institutions are inescapably present. An economy cannot function without them. But it will be obvious that the particular pattern of institutions differs in different cultures and also changes within a society with the passage of time.

In all societies, however, institutions embody two contrasting value systems and patterns of behavior, an idea conceived and developed by Thorstein Veblen, the founding father of institutional economics. The first of these value systems, generally referred to as the instrumental or technological "ought," posits ideas as instruments of problem-solving with the goal of enhancing human welfare. The second, the ceremonial "ought," seeks to preserve power, status, and hierarchical invidious differentiation. Veblen was wont to refer to the first of these two behavioral patterns as the industrial and the second as the business or pecuniary. Employments having to do with workmanship or production would fall under the first category and those having to do with ownership or acquisition under the second (Veblen [1899] 1933, 155; see also Veblen 1904, 314). An apt illustration of the distinction between the two kinds of behavior was offered by Paul D. Bush in quoting the response of the CEO of United States Steel to a Congressional Committee: "United States Steel is not in the business of producing steel, it is in the business of producing profits" (Bush 2000).

Institutional theory goes on to explain that problems arise in society when, as technology advances, the existing institutional structure is rendered inadequate to carry on the economic process efficiently. In other words, behavior is not being correlated as effectively as existing knowledge would permit (Tool 1979, 78). The phenomenon called globalization provides an example. The explosion of technological and scientific advances has made possible the proliferation of processes and gadgets that connect societies everywhere as never before through trade, travel, electronic communication, and so on. Multinational corporations (MNCs) find that the world is their stage as they seek out and control markets in pursuit of their own ends, without accountability inasmuch as existing institutions lack means of oversight and control. Thus MNCs have the capability of manipulating one country against another in an effort to secure favorable tax concessions, relaxed labor and environmental standards, trade advantages, and so on, as they pursue their goal of enlarging their power and maximizing pecuniary gain.

Institutional economic theory, unlike mainstream economic doctrine, makes possible analysis of such matters in its theory of change. J. Fagg Foster has put forth a theory of institutional adjustment, a theory that he formulated with the idea that it would be applicable to any society at any time, at any place, at whatever stage of development.

Foster begins with a principle termed "technological determination," which is simply

> that social problems can be solved only by adjusting the institutional structures involved in the problem so as to bring them into instrumentally efficient correlation with the technological aspects of the problems. What is meant by 'instrumentally efficient correlation' is that the instrumental functions of the institutions in question be carried on at a level of efficiency tolerable to the members of the institution in view of the possibilities indicated by those same technological factors. . . . [T]he technological aspects of human know-how are characteristically more dynamic in the developmental sense than are the institutional aspects. The inclusive reason for this is that the ceremonial functions of institutions directly stimulate active support of an institutional structure, even though its instrumental functions are recognizably below what could be accomplished within the existing technological know-how. And so it is that most frequently the comparatively developmental character of technology results in social problems.
>
> Not only is technology determinate of institutional problems in the sense that it creates such problems, but also it is determinate of the

solutions in the sense that it constitutes the basic data which must be taken as given in social problems [Foster [1948] 1981, 932-33].

A second principle of institutional adjustment, called "recognized interdependence," means that "the immediate pattern of any institutional adjustment is specified by the pattern of interdependencies recognized by the members of the institution." In other words, "the new pattern of behavior must be specified in conceptual form before it can emerge into the new pattern of behavior." The third principle, called "minimal dislocation," means that any institutional modification "must be capable of being incorporated into the remainder of the institutional structure" (Foster [1948] 1981, 929-33; Foster [1972] 1981, 939-42; Foster 1948, 364-82; see also Tool 2000, 92-95].[1]

It is necessary now to look at the criterion of judgment used in making these institutional adjustments. As suggested earlier, the criterion of judgment, that is, the locus of value, is found in the instrumental/technological way of behaving. Marc R. Tool, building on the work of Veblen, John Dewey (1938), Clarence Ayres (1944), and Foster, explains the necessity of the application of a criterion of judgment as follows.

> [A]ll economic systems, whatever the stage of their development, confront problems in three major areas of the economic process: determining the level, the character, and the distribution of real income. We need only add . . . the equally elemental recognition that these decision areas continuously involve two sorts of . . . judgment. First, all such decisions, by whomever made, become structural directives to pattern and organize economic functions in particular ways. Policy directives to increase taxes, create a budget surplus, cut interest rates, revamp 'success indicators,' or introduce a guaranteed annual minimum income, are examples. Second, all such decisions require a response to the query, 'Which direction is forward?' That is, a choice of or among institutional structures is always involved, and a criterion of choice defining what ought to be must be employed in choosing among alternatives (Tool 1979, 81).

To this end he advances what he terms a non-ideological principle of social value:

> We now affirm that that direction is forward which provides for *the continuity of human life and the noninvidious re-creation of community through the instrumental use of knowledge.* We consider the foregoing to

> be a criterion of judgment, a social-value principle, which is general in its relevance to the social process, to the functional components of that process (economy, polity) and to choices among institutional forms which organize that process (Tool 1979, 292-93; italics in the original).

As might be expected, this social value principle is not necessarily applied unconditionally by decision-makers in the community. In fact, Veblen, Ayres, and Foster have all attested to the common reluctance to alter the existing institutional structure and the common desire to retain as much as possible of the ceremonial ways of behaving.

As a consequence, Bush argues, the two value systems, the instrumental and the ceremonial, while inherently incompatible, "are intertwined within the institutional structure through a complex set of relationships" (Bush 1987, 1079). He explains that ". . . ceremonially warranted patterns of behavior can contain instrumental behavior and . . . instrumentally warranted patterns of behavior can contain behavior that has ceremonial characteristics" (Bush 1987, 1082). To demonstrate the most commonly occurring of these patterns he developed a concept, "ceremonial encapsulation," which analyzes the complexity of these relationships and is extremely useful in elucidating their applicability in modern society.

The logic of ceremonial valuation, Bush says, may be used to rationalize any combination of behaviors, not only ceremonial but also instrumental ways of behaving. All that is required is a plausible argument to validate any particular correlation of behavior. A vivid example is found in the canoe-building practices of the Trobriand islanders described by Bronsilaw Malinowski. Two kinds of behavior are involved in canoe-building, one ceremonial and the other instrumental. For the first, the magician must make an offer to the woodsprite that presumably inhabits the tree and utter an incantation to get him to leave the tree. For the second, the canoe builder chops down the tree and builds the canoe. In this activity, "ceremonial considerations are dominant, and a ceremonially warranted standard of judgment correlates the behaviors of the magician and the craftsman. The instrumental behavior of the craftsman is 'encapsulated' within a ceremonially warranted pattern of behavior" (Bush 1987, 1083-84; see also Bush 1994, 651; and Bush 1997).

Now, what is to be said about the role of the market in the globalization phenomenon? In a comprehensive and insightful study of what he terms the market system, Charles E. Lindblom helps to show how that system relates to the question of globalization (Lindblom 2001). Noting that information has become the basic resource in modern society, he asks how these highly mobile new resources of information or knowledge are to be organized or coordinated. There being not much advocacy for either the nation-state or a new world state to assume the role, he says this is all the more reason to understand the market system. Calling it the big globalizer, he says the market is the major institutional instrument for undercutting the autonomy of individual nation-states and for quickening the restless movement of labor and capital over the face of the earth (Lindblom 2001, 13). "Indeed, in our time the market system has become a global coordinator of cooperative performance of at least a billion people. No other method of social cooperation matches the market system in scope and detail. . . .No government has ever organized so many people in such an articulated and detailed assignment of performances. . . .Moreover, there exists a global market system but no world state" (Lindblom 2001, 40-41). As a consequence, he asserts, corporations, banks, and international political elites make momentous decisions with little democratic control (Lindblom 2001, 242).

Ironically, the corporation, he observes, may indeed be the quintessence of the market system, but it is also internally a non-market or even an anti-market institution. It is a way of achieving coordination of some activities through managerial command rather than through market interactions. To that extent it is a rival to, rather than an instrument of, market system coordination (Lindblom 2001, 75).

The corporation also acts in many ways to curb democracy. Market elites "undertake in public discourse, in the schools and churches and in the mass media an assault on the mind designed to create a conformity of thought endorsing the market system. . . .Democracy is curbed by an assault on the minds of the masses that persuades them to live within the rules of the market system rather than become 'masters of the situation'" (Lindblom 2001, 232, 234).

Giving the corporation the rights and powers of a legal person, he asserts, also is an assault on democracy. In the international order, the corporation has become increasingly visible as a challenge to democracy (Lindblom 2001, 239-40). MNCs can bring more power to bear on the states than the states can bring to bear on them. Beyond that, market elites from corporations and banks have joined with state elites to establish institutions that are assigned certain powers of central direction of the international economy, the International Monetary Fund (IMF), and the European Central Bank, among others. These international institutions are far removed from the voters in the member nation-states but are easily accessible to corporations (Lindblom 2001, 239-41).

The bedrock case for the market system rests on the merits of mutual adjustment as a fundamental social coordinating process. The general claim here, he continues, is only a claim that, among other institutions and social processes, some form of market system for some sphere of human interaction is of great value. But it is essential that it be supplemented by other forms of social coordination such as the state, the family, the corporation, and the interactions of civil society, for example, political parties, clubs, museums, and the like (Lindblom 2001, 275-77). .

One can see echoes here of some of the protests at the World Trade Organization (WTO) meetings in Seattle in 1999 and at subsequent international forums, the most notable being the Group of Eight meetings in Genoa in 2001, where the protesters were reported to number as many as 100,000. Most observers have found it easy to denigrate the protesters as unfocused, uninformed, even anarchic and Luddite. This misses the point. Although the issues were varied, the level of information was spotty, and indeed the protests seemed unfocused, the agonizing about the condition of the globalized world can hardly be said to be misplaced. An argument could be made, also, that two common strands did emerge: 1) objection to rich-country domination of decision-making in multilateral institutions, and 2) objection to bad results for the poorest people (Walker and Hofheinz 2000). And Mike Prokosch gives the protesters credit for mobilizing people in an extraordinary array of ways—defending workers' rights, saving the earth, reclaiming democracy, and narrowing the gap between rich and poor. It will always be a plural movement, he says, which is not a bad model for global cooperation (Prokosch 2000, 10). The point, then, is that policy makers should acknowledge the validity of much of what the protesters have been saying and try to address problems accompanying globalization.

Decision-making by corporate financial managers, at least in the US, has resulted in the ceremonial encapsulation of technological improvements by all too many firms, with harm to consumers, to employees, and sometimes even to shareholders.

Where democracy prevails, however, although it is obvious that citizens do not always take advantage of their opportunities, options are available. They can opt to use regulation, for example, to curb the power of economic elites to ceremonially encapsulate technology. It is democracy alone that allows the correction of errors, through education, open discourse, and political action. And, as Foster was fond of saying, it is not even essential that the electorate understand the exact nature of the problem, because "if the shoe pinches" voters can "throw the rascals out." Thus, as institutionalists argue, if the propensity of the common man is to preserve the comfortable and familiar, and therefore to resist needed institutional adjustment, recourse is available through the self-correcting nature of a democratic system.

## FOREIGN TRADE AND INVESTMENT

International trade must be discussed at some length here for a number of reasons. It has exhibited dramatic growth as a proportion of GDP all over the world and, as a consequence, it has increasing relevance to the issue of globalization. Moreover, exchange, which goes back as far as recorded history, occurs in societies of all ideological persuasions and within various kinds of institutions. Communist countries, for example, have used price as an institution helpful in distribution. And the family, generally regarded as an institution patterned essentially along feudalistic lines, buys goods and services in the marketplace. Additionally, trade is important in the present context because it is one of the focal points of protest against globalization. The publicity from the protests has helped to reveal the fact that trade is not well understood by protesters, workers, and the general public.

The principle of comparative advantage, as formulated by David Ricardo, has been the dominant model for trade in economic theory for 180 years (Ricardo [1821] 1973, 81-83]. This principle demonstrates, as is well known, that trading can benefit both trading partners by providing more output with the same level of inputs, even if one trader can produce both items traded more cheaply than the other trader. As Jagdish Bhagwati observes, it is strongly counterintuitive to believe that both countries could gain from trade in such a circumstance (Bhagwati 2000, 90). Why should one produce an item that can be produced at lower cost elsewhere? And how can a high-wage country export goods to a low-wage country?

Ricardo's principle of comparative advantage provides an answer to these questions. The mathematical logic of the principle is sound. In addition, the principle satisfies the institutionalist theory of value as enunciated by Foster [see Foster [1948] 1981, 932): Producing greater output with the same level of inputs is instrumentally efficient.[2]

As might be expected, however, when efforts are made to apply the principle of comparative advantage in the real world, substantial complexities and points of disagreement arise, and these disagreements have generated a considerable body of literature. Some of this literature is used to inform the following analysis.[3]

What is perhaps the most important difficulty encountered in applying the comparative advantage principle arises from the fact that generally costs, that is, prices, of items traded in the real world are expressed in money terms rather than in real terms. This becomes a problem because price is an institution and, as seen above, institutions exhibit both instrumental and ceremonial attributes. In institutionalist terms, market prices reflect not only instrumentally warranted valuations, but also ceremonially warranted valuations. The price of a BMW, for example, is warranted, in part, by the instrumental efficiency of a finely engineered automobile, but it is also warranted, in part, by the ceremonial status the car confers on its owner. As a consequence, price may not reflect real costs.

Space considerations do not permit a discussion of price theory here except for the following observation. Prices of goods produced by MNCs are likely to be oligopolistically determined; that is, sufficient market power is likely to exist to permit prices to be set above real costs. Thus, instrumentally warranted valuations may be encapsulated in ceremonially warranted valuations, with a consequent distortion of gains actually realized from trade. Bhagwati considers this question. He refers to oligopolistic pricing as an externality destructive of the free trade position and contends that it is better to fix the market failure than to forgo free trade (Bhagwati 2000, 91-93). Indeed, this would be a "first-best" solution. Unfortunately, however, in the present political climate, "fixing" prices is an alternative seemingly not now and not likely soon to be "on the agenda." The "second-best" solution of pursuing freer trade nonetheless remains a worthwhile goal inasmuch as it has the advantage of securing the lowest possible price to the consumer, providing some gain, even if the real costs of production are not accurately reflected in relative prices. But oligopolistic pricing clearly is a significant economic problem, one that deserves continuous attention and oversight, along with correction where possible. Anti-trust enforcement, public-utility regulation, "jawboning," and use of the media are among the policy options that should always be ready to be utilized.

Another major difficulty encountered in efforts to realize a comparative advantage from international trade was foreseen by Joan Robinson. In addressing a "real-time effect," she looks at the possibility of a country choosing to specialize in the "wrong" product: . . . "[T]he imposition of free trade on Portugal killed off a promising textile industry and left her with a slow-growing export market for wine, while for England, exports of cotton cloth led to accumulation, mechanization and the whole spiraling growth of the industrial revolution" (Robinson 1978, 103).

This raises the question of a dynamic rather than a static approach to the theory of comparative advantage. This strategy has been used by James M. Cypher and James L. Dietz in looking at the evolution of the international trade price, that is, changes in the terms of trade (Cypher and Dietz 1998, 305-14; also see Prasch 1995, 428, and Cypher's chapter in this volume). As Cypher and Dietz point out, the comparative advantage analysis is static, that is, it is like a snapshot. Thus, they suggest that it is instructive to track the terms of trade to see what happens over time. If prices change a new "snapshot" must be taken, as the gains from trade that existed earlier will change and may even disappear. As a result a new product mix may become preferable.

This study provides a corroboration of the argument of Raul Prebisch to the effect that developing nations face a disadvantage because of their reliance on exports of primary products, which are likely to suffer falling prices relative to the prices of the manufactured products that are the major exports of developed nations (Prebisch 1950). Cypher and Dietz show that over time the nation producing a primary product actually may come to realize a loss from continuing to specialize and to trade, at the same time that the other trading partner continues to realize a benefit. This is a valuable insight. And putting actual numbers on the size of the gain or loss allows a judgment to be made as to whether there is a net gain, that is, whether the gain realized by the advantaged partner is greater than the loss realized by the disadvantaged partner. Furthermore, such an analysis permits the judgment that even if there is a net total gain, this exchange may not be optimal as long as the less developed partner is the one that is disadvantaged by the exchange. The study demonstrates, then, that developing countries are justified in feeling aggrieved over the level of prices of the goods they export relative to those they import. Fidel Castro reports that "the purchasing power of such commodities as sugar, cocoa, coffee and others is 20 percent of what it used to be in 1960; consequently, they do not even cover the production costs" (Castro 2000, 284).

The Cypher-Dietz study can lead to insights relative to global policy options. One desirable option would be for developed trading nations to offer compensation in the form of foreign aid rather than to forgo the gains to be realized from trade. Another conceivable option would be for the developing nations to organize, as OPEC nations have done with respect to oil, to restrict the level of output of, say, coffee or bananas. Similarly, nations could engage in import substitution, as has often been recommended, either singly or in concert, the result of which could be a decrease in the prices of manufactured products because of reduced demand. Institutionalists would favor market intervention by governments, say, for example, the Group of Eight, which show some responsiveness to their constituencies, instead of action by MNC cartels.

The comment of Joan Robinson is a reminder of the perils faced by countries in making choices regarding specialization. As originally formulated, the concept of comparative advantage was generally thought of as applicable to fixed "natural" resources, assumed to be "given" in the sense that they were endowments of nature. Institutionalists would argue, incidentally, that even "natural" resources are not given because they are a function of the state of the industrial arts. In any case, the concept is now thought of as applicable to any kind of product or service. A consortium of countries in the European Union, for example, has succeeded in gaining a market for Airbus. Do we, Charles E. Wilber asks rhetorically, want a steel industry or an electronics industry (Wilber 1998, 469)?

Not sufficiently recognized is the fact that opportunity cost, which underlies the question of comparative advantage as well as other questions relating to cost, is determined by the institutional structure as well as the technology it encapsulates. If instrumentally warranted knowledge is brought to bear on the use of resources technologically determined to be available to the community, but not previously accessible to it because of the ceremonial encapsulation of the technology, then the "scarcity conditions" previously taken for granted are fundamentally altered. Lester Thurow makes the point that in this high-tech era man-made brainpower industries are the only source of comparative advantage. In any event, complexity is added when industries that depend on research and development and human skills dominate the system. The global economy is a dynamic one, always in transition, he continues; there is often no chance for those not in the industry to enter it quickly enough (Thurow 1996, 68-72).

On this point, one might wonder if sometimes the seemingly frantic search for a likely product for export, as in niches of the telecommunications industry, for example, might in fact be counterproductive. Can the necessary adjustments be made rapidly enough and smoothly enough to bring forth the expected gain? Losses from the disruption may more than offset the expected gains. Prasch observes that time, while it is not incorporated in the principle of comparative advantage, can be a very potent reality in the real world (Prasch 1995, 428).

The principles of institutional adjustment developed by Foster can be useful in analyzing such a situation. As technological change impinges on the existing institutional structure, a judgment may be made that greater efficiency could be realized from changes in that structure, in this case perhaps from a decision to concentrate on a different product of research. This course of action may be indicated by the application of the first principle of institutional adjustment, that of technological determination. That is, the attempted adjustments would make instrumentally better use of the technological factors. But such a change will not be successful unless the second and third principles as well can be implemented. The second, the principle of recognized interdependence, refers to the pattern of interdependencies recognized by the members of the institution. That is, the new pattern of behavior must be specified in conceptual form, and those involved must recognize their actual relationships as specified in the new pattern. Otherwise, the new pattern simply does not eventuate into action; no one can perform a new activity without deliberately directing his efforts in the novel activity. In other words, the proposed changes must be brought as problematic factors into the comprehension of the persons involved. The third principle, that of minimal dislocation, discloses the limits of adjustment in terms of rate and in terms of degree and area (Foster [1948] 1981, 932-34; see also Foster 1981, 907-13; Foster [1943] 1981, 923-28].

As mentioned above, however, the application of the three principles is complicated by the existence of another theoretical phenomenon explained by Foster and further developed by Bush, the fact that institutions exhibit both instrumental and ceremonial patterns of behavior:

> On the one hand, every institution serves to bring the activities of individuals to bear in a contributory way on the instrumental function, which is the collaborative activity of the group. For example, through such institutions as contract, the market, the wage system, and so forth, the activities of a large number of persons may be correlated so as to result in the erection of a building, or in the provision of foodstuffs, or in the performance of a ballet. . . .
>
> On the other hand, every institution serves a completely different kind of function: It serves to differentiate between persons and groups in invidious terms. The boss may be identified in terms of his instrumental function, but he also may be identified in terms of prestige, honor, deferential attitude, or power. . . .
>
> It is important to keep in mind the distinction between the instrumental and the ceremonial functions of institutions. Otherwise we shall be unable to see very clearly the part technology plays in social problems (Foster 1981, 908).

Returning to the literature on comparative advantage, Dell Champlin and Paulette Olson argue that trade today is more likely than not to be determined institutionally. The most important factors underlying foreign direct investment are the legal environment, the industrial relations climate, and favorable government policies (Champlin and Olson 1999, 447-48).

One area in which choices are made, and indeed very controversial and consequential ones, has to do with standards of production regarding environmental impact and worker safety and working conditions. The best solutions are not necessarily immediately apparent. Prasch suggests the desirability of seeking worldwide agreement on choices that are appropriate (Prasch 1999, 416). In this vein Lance Compa argues that it might be feasible to honor choices if they are benign, that is, made for health and safety standards or because of cultural or language factors, but not to honor choices resting on comparative advantage generated by violating workers' rights and suppressing wages (Compa 1998, 61). The question involves what is often referred to as free trade versus "fair trade" or "managed trade."

George DeMartino addresses this issue in an even-handed, thorough, and thoughtful way. Historically, he says, free trade meant the absence of government restrictions, including tariffs, quotas, licenses and other policy instruments that target trade flows (DeMartino 2000, 195). Fair trade critics of free trade do not, he continues, reject the concept of comparative advantage *per se* nor the logic of the free trade argument predicated upon it. But they demand that countries adopt ethically defensible labor and environmental practices as a precondition for trade, and they argue that differences across nations in policy regimes may obstruct the mutual benefits usually associated with free trade. For example, low labor and environmental standards may give a nation comparative advantage (DeMartino 2000, 195-98).

Such arguments are reasonable and have a strong appeal. But consider the following: Negotiators from developing countries frequently oppose certain standards, notably those regarding working conditions and the environment, arguing that trade is more important than such problems at certain stages of development and noting that the US and other advanced industrial countries ignored such standards in an earlier stage of their own development (Adams 2001, 4-6; see also Prasch 1999). Arthur MacEwan contends that the history of the US and other advanced capitalist countries teaches us that virtually all such countries found economic success in protectionism, not free trade, Britain being the only exception (MacEwan 1991, 6-7). It is also pointed out that in recent years some countries that are advancing the most rapidly are practicing managed trade (Collins and Miller 2000, 43). On the other hand, Paul Krugman offers Thailand as an example of one of those export-led success stories that are the best advertisement for the WTO and its free-trade agenda. Pre-globalization society in Thailand was nasty, brutish, and short—for example, in 1975 only one rural Thai in six had access to safe drinking water, while today it is four out of five. Most of the complaints about trade that developing countries make, he goes on, involve their desire for more, not less, trade, and they fear those who want to impose environmental and labor standards that they believe they cannot afford (Krugman 2000; see also Sachs 2002, A18).

A major question, however, remains. That is, to what extent is it *possible* to make trade the vehicle for securing high labor and environmental standards. The fact is that poor countries simply would have to stop trading rather than to try to lift such standards higher than their GDP can support. Wages and environmental standards are low because the countries are poor, and such countries desperately need their export industries (see Krugman 2001). In such instances there may be alternatives to stopping trade.

Bhagwati maintains that the freeing of trade should be accompanied by institutional changes. For example, the WTO could require payment of some compensation or allow for some retaliatory tariffs. He notes that Carla Hills used such measures in the EU hormone-fed beef disputes. In addition, the US could agree to finance protective devices that fishermen in poor countries are being asked to use. Bhagwati points out that UN embargo procedures are available and also suggests working with organizations such as the International Labor Organization (ILO), UNICEF, the UN Environmental Protection Agency, the International Committee on Human Rights, and the like. Another possibility would be the use of labeling, such as "Dolphin-safe Tuna," or "Free Range Chicken." The use of Trade Adjustment Assistance is also available. In addition, the media can be used to point out abuses (Bhagwati 2000, 98-102, 153, 160, 175, and 206).

One could argue with the permitted measures. The point is that such matters often can be adjudicated successfully in the WTO and elsewhere if *democracy, representation, and transparency prevail.* This, indeed, may be the most important argument made by the protesters regarding globalization. This is where the often invoked "level-playing-field" idea makes sense: All nations should have the opportunity to participate in negotiations relevant to them. Such requirements could be expected to ameliorate substantially the grievances cited by protesters. The difficulty, of course, is that not all nations are democratic. An immediate solution to this problem is not apparent. However, the US should promote democracy at every opportunity, a principle that has often been violated in the past.

As for the question of insisting on higher standards, while it is often appropriate to strive for higher standards and the harmonization of standards, countries arguably should have some right to determine their own priorities. Bhagwati enlarges upon this idea, arguing that there is no reason that two traders have to accept the same standards. If clean water and clean air are both prized, for example, Mexico may choose clean water first and clear air second, while the US does the reverse. It is illegitimate to force one's standards on others on grounds of unfair trade. He also notes that, while the so-called "race to the bottom" is a theoretical possibility, much empirical research shows little relevance since MNCs typically, although not always, seem to use the more environmentally friendly technology even when not required, and little evidence exists that governments actually lower standards in order to attract investment. Rather, the "race to the bottom" occurs more on the fiscal dimension when nations (or states within) offer cheaper land, tax breaks, and so on (Bhagwati 2000, 82-84, 91, 98-99, 153, 160).

Similarly, Gary Burtless contends that there need *not* be "a level playing field" in the sense that laws affecting trade should be identical, just as they are not identical in different states in the US. Suppose that one trading partner wants less pollution, while another wants higher output from the industries that pollute. Both can get what they want. There are caveats, of course. If pollution crosses national boundaries a different approach will be necessary. As noted above, standards should be determined democratically in so far as possible. Of course, not every group or nation will get what it wants. This does not mean there should be no rules. There is need for legal infrastructure, for example, regarding rights, contracts, and so forth, so producers will have the confidence to trade. The Uruguay Round of the General Agreement on Tariffs and Trade (GATT), the last round, which created the WTO, reflected such considerations. Members committed themselves to tariff reductions but also agreed to an international tribunal that will impose sanctions if one country reneges, as well as to other measures.

Burtless also refutes the notion of a "race to the bottom" presumed to result from different standards and rules. A generous public health care system can affect trade patterns: Industries with high medical costs will be less competitive, while industries with low costs will be more competitive, with industry as a whole not affected. The situation is similar, he continues, with respect to worker and environmental standards. In some cases productivity will be increased and thus costs will fall, in which case competitiveness will not be affected. In other cases such costs may reduce workers' take-home pay. But if the regulations deliver social benefits greater than social costs, then they are sensible, and this will be true in both open and closed economies. Then too, regulations may *attract* capital instead of discouraging it. The tourist industry prefers a cleaner environment. Nor does capital necessarily flee when governments increase taxes to finance infrastructure, education, and other amenities that increase productivity. In sum, free trade and mobile capital do not preclude a society from adopting activist social welfare policies; the public goods provided are valued by firms and people (Burtless et al 1998, 94-97, 114-27; see also Lavin 2002, A18; also Sachs 2001, A18).

What should be said, then, about freer trade, meaning lower tariffs and quotas, versus fair trade or managed trade? The most reasonable answer is that both must be goals and they need not be incompatible. Lance Compa contends that whether trade is free or conditional, it requires rules (Compa 1998, 64). Paul Hawken, Amory Lovins, and L. Hunter Lovins express it well: "Market competition, like any sport, works only if there is a rulebook adhered to by all the players and enforced by honest umpires" (Hawken et al 1999, 282).

Little mention has been made of one of the most serious objections to the operation of comparative advantage, the harm it can do to displaced workers, or, indeed, to failed industries. Even if the overall result of freer trade is beneficial to the community as a whole, and many liberals as well as conservatives think that it is (see, for example, Reich 2000, 56; Thurow 1996, 71, 74; Klein 2001; Gordon 1958), the problem is that the benefits often are very unevenly distributed. The loss of jobs resulting from imports is obvious and serious to those affected, while the advantages spread around to the rest of the population from lower prices of imports and from increased sales of exports are scarcely noticeable. Furthermore, there may be a question of losing an entire industry, even a major one, as David Moberg argues may happen in the US in the case of steel. "Over the past four years, 32 percent of the nation's steel producers—that's 29 companies, including the third and fourth largest—have gone into bankruptcy. Thirteen have stopped operating altogether. Several others teeter on the edge of bankruptcy or closure. . . . Few steel companies are earning enough to cover operating expenses; virtually none are covering their financing costs." There are several reasons for this: the resurgence of Asian economies producing a sudden surge of steel exports, high fixed costs, over capacity, the necessity of paying health benefits for 600,000 retired workers and spouses, an overvalued dollar, and other obstacles. If the US wants to retain a serious manufacturing base, with skilled, well-paying jobs, "then preserving the steel industry is crucial" (Moberg 2002, 23-25; but see also Sachs 2001, A18).

When a country faces such problems it is of the utmost importance to have in place fiscal and monetary policies of full employment. When jobs are readily available, protectionist policies are much less likely to be advocated. As John Maynard Keynes argued, trying to solve the problem of unemployment by the search for markets, with wars often the result, is no longer necessary (Keynes 1936, 381-83). In addition, job adjustment assistance, education and training, a good health care system, dealing with problems of racism and sexism, regulation of campaign finance, a progressive tax structure, and other progressive policies should be implemented.

One more problem should be mentioned, the liberalization of capital and financial markets. The international financial institutions, says Nobel laureate Joseph C. Stiglitz, have pushed the ideology of market fundamentalism, to the detriment of developing nations that have allowed the IMF and other international financial institutions to manage globalization for them. Hot money pours into a country, fueling speculative real estate booms; then investor sentiment changes and the money is pulled out. Prudent behavior requires countries to set aside reserves equal to the amount of short-term lending, with the result that if a firm is borrowing $110 million from a US bank, it may be paying interest of 20 percent, while the government sets aside a corresponding amount, on which it in effect receives 4 percent. The opportunity cost is high; the money could have been much better spent on building rural roads or constructing schools or health clinics. Some of the East Asian success stories such as Korea and Taiwan, by contrast, have managed globalization on their own, creating their own enterprises, with governments taking an active hand in managing the economy with high regulation of the financial markets (Stiglitz 2002, 16-19; see also Faux 2002, A23).

A major failure of understanding is the belief that when the principle of comparative advantage is found inoperative or ineffective it should be replaced with a policy of absolute advantage. But in addition to the theoretical argument against this, there is the fact of actual trade patterns in the world. If comparative advantage is to be abandoned, it must be done on grounds other than the supposed superiority of absolute advantage. Those who think that low-wage countries have an advantage should note that the US has the most difficulty competing with countries such as Canada, the countries of the European Union, and Japan—the highest wage countries in the world, says Eamonn Fingleton. In fact, nations whose wages at last count were higher than in the US include Switzerland, Germany, Denmark, Sweden, and Austria, all of whom enjoy booming exports to the US And Japan, where wages are the world's highest, and who continues to run a substantial trade surplus with the US (Fingleton 2000, 20). Also significant is the fact that exporting industries in any country pay wages about five to fifteen percent above the national average (Burtless et al 1998, 46).

The fact is that in the basket of commodities that enter into international trade some will have a comparative advantage and some will have a disadvantage in trade with a low-wage country, and the same will be true in trade with a high-wage country. For example, in trade with Mexico the US would be likely to have an advantage in small appliances and a disadvantage in embroidered garments. In 1999, the US exported $112 billion of products to Mexico, a low-wage country, and imported $126 billion. In the same year the US exported $129 billion of goods and services to Canada, a high-wage country, and imported $229 billion. The US had a so-called unfavorable balance with both countries, one high-wage and one low-wage.

Facts such as these are explainable because the foreign-exchange mechanism does work to reflect prices, as does the average-unit-cost mechanism (that is, it is cost per unit of product, not cost per hour of labor, that is of account), and more than tolerably well when one considers the enormous and growing volume of trade. The volume of worldwide exports has increased from 8 percent of GDP in 1950 to 26.4 percent today (Melloan 1999, A27).

What the theory of comparative advantage says and what it does not say seems to be widely misconstrued. It speaks only to the increased outputs realizable when two products traded have different cost ratios. It has nothing to do with the level of employment; other theories speak to that. Nor does it require full employment to be relevant.[4] It does not affect discrimination or exploitation or opportunities for education and training. It does not adjust unfair pay scales. Such problems would still exist if trade were reduced or abandoned altogether. The principle is simply one of the theoretical constructs that can be useful in determining effective trade policy.

## INTERNATIONAL ORGANIZATIONS

Not all problems in a globalized world can be attributed to the application of a neo-liberal ideology. There are problems directly caused by globalization, problems that occur because of the absence of necessary international infrastructure and the inability of the nation-state and other existing institutions to cope, for example, with problems arising from the global reach of MNCs. Thus attention must be given both to developing new institutions and to modifying existing institutions

Clearly now is a time for institutional innovation. The United Nations was not designed to oversee the behavior of MNCs or to adjudicate monetary and financial disputes. Could it be redesigned to provide infrastructure for a global economy? The answer to this is not clear. In any case, the UN framework should be used where possible to create agencies that could take on additional tasks, some relating to trade, for example, as it does in matters such as air traffic, weather, and other areas. But perhaps the more obvious route at this time would be for some changes to be made in existing institutions, notably the WTO, the IMF, and the World Bank.

International financier George Soros is working on an extremely attractive plan which he refers to as an "Open Society Alliance," a political alliance complementing NATO, with two objectives: 1) to help the evolution of open societies within countries, and 2) to foster development of international law and international standards of behavior. What makes a society open is that its citizens are free to decide how society should be organized. Preconditions for membership include a democratic constitution, the rule of law, freedom of speech and press, and an independent judiciary. The Alliance would provide membership to any country that subscribes to its objectives. It would use both sticks and carrots, especially the latter. Soros suggests the Alliance should work on strengthening the IMF to provide liquidity and offer rewards and on converting the World Bank to a World Development Agency. He sees the WTO as an important institution that provides the ground rules for free trade and should work on its labor and environmental standards, compensating developing countries for introducing standards. He does not want to elaborate on the Alliance, suggesting that the details should be worked out by the participants. In any event, such an alliance could be the international organization that has been lacking in providing supervision of MNCs and international financial markets and so on (Soros 2000, 280-360). The US, says Soros, could regain its position as leader of the free world by forming an alliance of like-minded states devoted to developing the principles of open society internationally and internally within individual countries (Soros 2000, 335).

Soros suggests that the IMF should be made to function pretty much as a world central bank, particularly to act as a lender of last resort, and for this it should be given resources and responsibility. In a recent interview he suggested it should be enabled to issue Special Drawing Rights (SDRs) on short notice to countries in urgent need (Bank 2002, B1). Also the IMF should penalize irresponsible lenders instead of insisting only on government belt-tightening (see Soros 1998, 121, 134, 181, 183; Soros 2000, 251, 280; Soros 2001; also Sawyer 1999, 19-20). What the IMF should *not* do is fairly clear: it should not insist on debt repayment and the reduction of social programs such as education, health care, and the like. In terms of the present analysis, it should renounce monetarist and neoclassical policies in favor of an institutionalist agenda of progressive social change predicated on Tool's social value principle as the criterion of judgment.

The World Bank, for its part, should focus on helping the very poor more than the less poor, and it should do this through more grants and more positive incentives to enable countries to comply with better labor and environmental standards (Soros 2000, xix, xx, 346, 350). Again, such policies would lessen the need for restrictions on trade. The International Financial Institution Advisory Committee issued a report in March of 2000 advising that both the IMF and the World Bank should cancel loans owed by the poorest countries and should provide more grants rather than loans. Even the Secretary of the Treasury, Paul O'Neill, has advocated this change in policy. The IMF should refocus its lending on emergencies, short term, while the World Bank should do long-term development aid. Finally, the US should increase foreign aid (Meltzer and Sachs 2000).

It is worth noting that some of the strategies designed by John Maynard Keynes sixty years ago continue to find support in this area. James Galbraith, noting that the system of floating exchange rates and unregulated international capital markets could easily fail, recommends planning for a transition in the global financial system toward an effective multilateral regulatory and stabilization system. He suggests it is time to examine a return to a Bretton Woods framework of fixed but adjustable exchange rates among the major currencies, backed by a multilateral reserve (Galbraith 2001, 4). Another initiative, frequently recommended, is that nations should attempt to gain some control over runaway financial transactions and to lessen global inequality by adopting a proposal made by James Tobin to tax foreign exchange transactions. Tobin contends that over $1.5 trillion a year could be yielded by a 0.5 percent tax (Arestis and Sawyer 1999, 151). A natural complement to the Tobin tax would be a "Keynes tax" on the sale of any financial asset held less than, say, one or two years, as well as a capital gains tax, especially on cross-border trade (Crotty and Epstein 1999, 430-31).

## OTHER AVENUES FOR CHANGE

One of the most promising and exciting venues for redirecting the world order is the Internet. This could help to push power down to the people. One thing that makes it promising is that those now in power, the market elites and government elites that Lindblom refers to, have not found ways to inhibit or control it. Although access to the Internet unfortunately is not sufficiently available in developing nations (see Castro 2000, 251), the good news is that it connects 689 million people and 172 million Internet hosts (*US News and World Report* 2002, 69), and it is growing rapidly. By using e-mail and the Internet, <strangebedfellows.com,> individuals have organized and energized the resistance to mindless globalization. In Seattle, Internet users organized effectively to demand human rights and labor standards from nations dependent on the rich market of the US (Safire 1999). This was a decentralized, non-ideological resistance to the IMF and the WTO.

Not sufficiently covered by the media are nongovernmental organizations (NGOs). They constitute, according to Benjamin R. Barber, "another internationalism, forming a crystal around which a global polity can grow." For example:

- Jody Williams creates a worldwide civic movement that enacts a treaty for a ban on land mines.
- A Bangladeshi visionary, Mohammed Yunus, develops an idea for microfinancing, which makes loans to women in third world societies.
- Citizen groups use "Good Housekeeping seal" methods to underwrite safe fisheries and support rug manufacturing without child labor.
- Peter Armstrong's <oneworld.org> and Globalvision's <mediachannel.org> are diverting the new telecommunications from pure commerce to the public interests of global society.
- Hundreds of NGOs gather in new international organizations such as CIVICUS, the World Forum on Democracy, and Transparency International, and begin to develop civic networking across nations, courtesy of the World Economic Forum at Davos, Switzerland.

- More than a dozen democracies—including not only the center-left regimes led by Bill Clinton, Lionel Jospin, Gerhard Schroder, and Tony Blair, but also South Africa, Argentina, Brazil, and Chile—met in Berlin in June of 2000 to discuss how they might redress international injustices.
- A few weeks later, nearly one hundred nations met in Warsaw to seek an even broader consensus for a democratic concert of nations.

Although there are many forces arrayed against such initiatives, Barber suggests that a global public opinion is in the making, a significant starting place for countervailing power (Barber 2000, 16-19; see also Barry 2000).

An additional example of international cooperation is the International Performance Measurement and Verification Protocol, formed in 1997 by top financial firms and the US Department of Energy, creating a market where loans to finance energy and water savings can be originated as quickly as they can be sold into the new secondary market. Since its founding the protocol has been adopted in more than twenty countries, including Brazil, China, India, Russia, and Ukraine (Hawken et al 1999, 268).

Freedom and democracy are mentioned again and again, usually more or less in the background, in discussions on development. Amartya Sen, however, stresses that freedom and democracy are a central force for development. Economists in particular tend to identify economic inequality with income inequality, says Sen, while he, on the other hand, is concerned with inequality with respect to education, health care, unemployment, social exclusion, literacy, nutrition, and mortality. Markets must be supplemented by the creation of basic social opportunities for social equity and justice, and this is especially important in developing countries. Sen sees freedom as a causally effective factor in generating rapid change. Women, in particular, need more freedom because of their role in population control. The organizing principle of development is the overarching concern with the process of enhancing individual freedoms and the social commitment to that end (Sen 1999, 108, 143-44, 225, 297-98).

An organization such as the "Open Society Alliance," mentioned above, could implement ideas such as these offered by Greider: 1) set up a worldwide unitary taxation system for MNCs; 2) regulate and tax financial capital, beginning with a tax on foreign exchange; 3) put ceilings on interest rates; 3) regulate or close down offshore banking centers; 4) prohibit governments at all levels from granting tax favors in exchange for investment; 5) reform the terms of trade; 6) end tax subsidies to MNCs that block labor rights for foreign workers; and 7) write off bad debts in poor countries (Greider 1997, 96, 317-26). Greider senses that a new ideology is struggling to be born. There are new compatible strands of thought arising from the feminist movement, labor unions, and religious organizations. These could synthesize a new global vision he calls "global humanism" (Greider 1997, 468-69; see also DeMartino 2000, 24-26).

Michael Hardt and Antonio Negri also see a fundamentally new global system emerging:

> Anti-globalization is not an adequate characterization of the protesters. . . The protesters are indeed united against the present form of capitalistic globalization, but the vast majority of them are not against globalizing currents and forces as such; they are not isolationist, separatist or even nationalist.
>
> The protests themselves have become global movements, and one of their clearest objectives is the democratization of globalizing processes. This should not be called an anti-globalizing movement. It is pre-globalization, or rather it is an alternative globalization movement—one that seeks to eliminate inequalities between rich and poor and between the powerful and the powerless, and to expand the possibilities of self-determination.
>
> A different and better future is possible. . . .We are beginning to see a multitude emerge that is not defined by any single identity, but can discover commonality in its multiplicity (Hardt and Negri 2001, A23).

## CONCLUDING COMMENTS

Technology—the technology of information and communication and the technology of transporting goods and people—has created the revolution we refer to as globalization. Ideas are being exchanged and used as instruments of progress.[5] The spread of technology has had positive social value. But to the degree that the technology has been ceremonially encapsulated by those who seek narrow pecuniary gain at the expense of the spread of benefits to the general population, the impact has been negative. Millions remain outside the reach of technology, alienated and impoverished. Additionally, change has been so rapid that institutions have been unable to keep up, leaving many international activities without needed oversight.

Within a nation-state, the institutional arrangements designate who is responsible and accountable—the monarch or other authoritarian figure or, in a democracy, the elected representatives of the people. In the world as a whole, however, there is no electorate organized to choose representatives. As a result, we are all connected, but there is no responsible agency in charge. Lindblom poses what he rightly terms a frightening question: How can democratic control over international institutions be achieved for an "electorate of several billion people of diverse aspirations and understandings?" (Lindblom 2001, 242; see also Faux, A22).

As Thomas Friedman points out, the technology of globalization is changing the nature of human relationships: "The global marketplace today is an Electronic Herd of often anonymous stock, bond, currency and multinational investors, connected by screens and networks." The Electronic Herd is merciless, although not infallible (Friedman 1999, 94). What is his solution? There must be a balance between the "Lexus" and the "olive tree," Friedman tells us, that is, we must continue to embrace the magic and promise of technology while preserving the safety nets, the culture, the community, the traditions, the man tending his olive tree.

A most exciting phenomenon in this globalized world is the promise of the Internet. Largely through it, says Jeremy Brecher, the protester movement has exhibited a powerful worldwide outreach linking people at the grassroots around the world, which has been termed "globalization from below" (Brecher 2001, 1). Brecher reports an appropriate response on the part of global activists since the attacks. They defined the attacks as criminal acts, not acts of war, and they defined the appropriate response as mobilizing international law, not military violence. They are a part of a swelling "global justice" movement, calling for justice not vengeance. Even those most critical of US imperialism and even "hard hat" labor unions have joined the rest of the US in condemning the attacks and urging justice. The movement blames neither trade nor the US for the world's ills. "Rather, . . . it calls for worldwide cooperation to protect human and labor rights, the environment, and people's livelihoods. . . .There is no longer such a thing as national security—security must be global to be secure. . . .The fundamental conflict in the world today remains globalization from above vs. globalization from below" (Brecher 2001, 1-3).

## NOTES

[1] Foster in his later years was contemplating an additional principle of institutional adjustment, or, alternatively, a reformulation or extension of the second principle, to the effect that not only must the participants in an institutional adjustment understand, they must also have the energy and the physical capacity to participate. It has to do with the characteristics of human effort.

[2] Foster supported in conversation and in his lectures the principle of comparative advantage and the goal of free trade.

[3] Additional articles by institutional economists relating to the subjects of trade and globalization may be helpful to the reader (Atkinson 1999, 335-41; Atkinson 1998, 419-26;

Ernst and Ozawa 2002, forthcoming; Ho 1998, 375-83; Larudee and Koechlin. 1999, 419-26; Went 2000, 655-77).

[4] Consider, for example, the following illustration of comparative advantage: Suppose that a secretary is more productive than her boss in both secretarial and managerial tasks. The secretary, however, has a comparative advantage in secretarial work while the boss has a comparative advantage in managerial work. Such a division of labor, then, will increase productivity. (A recommended policy implication might be a rectification of pay differentials.) This kind of situation can and no doubt often does prevail at any level of employment. A similar situation can exist in textile production versus steel production within the same country, as well as in almost any kind of work imaginable. The principle of comparative advantage can be relevant and useful for analysis at any level of employment.

[5] Louis Menand, in his recent Pulitzer-prize winning book about the development of the pragmatic philosophy in America—which is the philosophy that underlies institutionalist thought—says that ideas and beliefs are "instruments for coping. An idea has no greater metaphysical status than, say, a fork" (Menand 2001, 361).

# REFERENCES


Adams, Bob. 2001. World trade: not easy being green. *The National Voter.* 50: 3-7.

Arestis, Philip and Malcolm Sawyer, 1999. "What Role for the Tobin Tax in World Economic Governance?" In *Global Instability: The Political Economy of World Economic Governance.* Jonathan Mitchie and John Grieve Smith. eds. London: Routledge.

Atkinson, Glen. 1999. Developing global institutions: lessons to be learned from regional integration experience. *Journal of Economic Issues* 33: 335-41

———. 1998. The political economy of liberalization and regulation: trade policy for the new era. *Journal of Economic Issues* 32: 419-26.

Ayres, C. E. 1944. *The Theory of Economic Progress.* Chapel Hill: University of North Carolina Press.

Bank, David. 2002. The man who would mend the world. *Wall Street Journal,* (March 14). B1.

Barber, Benjamin R. 2000. Globalizing democracy. *The American Prospect* 11: 16-19.

Barry, Colleen. 2000. World leaders address prosperity gap. *Denver Rocky Mountain News,* (June 4).

Bhagwati, Jagdish. 2000. *The Wind of the Hundred Days: How Washington Mismanaged Globalization.* Cambridge: The MIT Press.

Brecher, Jeremy. 2001. <sysop@zmag.org> Now more than ever: a global movement for global justice. *ZNet Commentary* (September 28). 1-3.

Burtless, Gary, Robert Z. Lawrence, Robert E., Litan, and Robert J. Shapiro. 1998. *Globaphobia: Confronting Fears about Open Trade.* Washington, DC: Brookings Institution Press.

Bush, Paul D. 1999. "Ceremonial Encapsulation." In Philip Anthony O'Hara, ed. *The Encyclopedia of Political Economy, Vol. I.* London: Routledge, 80-82.

———. 2000. Foster memorial lecture. University of Denver. (April 21).

———. 1987. The theory of institutional change. *Journal of Economic Issues* 21:1075-1116.

Castro, Fidel. 2000. *Capitalism in Crisis: Globalization and World Politics Today.* Melbourne: Ocean Press.

Champlin, Dell and Paulette Olson. 1999. The impact of globalization on US labor markets: redefining the debate. *Journal of Economic Issues* 33: 443-51

Collins, Jessica and John Miller. 2000. Know-nothings and know-it-alls: What's wrong with the hype about globalization? *Dollars and Sense*. 231: 41-43.

Compa, Lance. 1998. A fast track for labor. *The American Prospect* 9: 60-64.

Crotty, James and Gerald Epstein. 1999. A defense of capital controls in light of the Asian financial crisis. *Journal of Economic Issues* 33: 427-33.

Cypher, James M. and James L. Dietz. 1998. Static and dynamic comparative advantage: a multi-period analysis with declining terms of trade. *Journal of Economic Issues* 32: 305-14.

DeMartino, George. 2000. *Global Economy, Global Justice: Theoretical Objections and Policy Alternatives to Neoliberalism.* London: Routledge.

Dewey, John. 1938. *Logic: The Theory of Inquiry.* New York: Holt, Rinehart & Winston.

Ernst, Dieter and Terutomo Ozawa. 2002. National sovereign economy, global market economy, and transnational corporate economy. *Journal of Economic Issues* 36:547-55.

Faux, Jeff. 2002. A deal built on sand. *The American Prospect*; Special Supplement (Winter). A22-A24.

Fingleton, Eamonn. 2000. Unsustainable. *The American Prospect* 11: (August 14) 18-21.

Foster, J. Fagg. 1981. The effect of technology on institutions. *Journal of Economic Issues* 15: 908.

———. [1972] 1981. The fundamental principles of economics. *Journal of Economic Issues* 15: 937-42.

———. 1948. Lectures. "Value and Its Determinants." (Department of Economics, University of Denver). Taped and Transcribed.

———. [1948] 1981. Syllabus for "Problems of Modern Society." *Journal of Economic Issues* 15: 932-34.

———. [1943] 1981. The theory of institutional adjustment. *Journal of Economic Issues* 15: 923-28.

Frank, Thomas. 2000. *One Market Under God: Extreme Capitalism, Market Populism, and the End of Economic Democracy.* New York: Doubleday.

Friedman, Thomas. 1999. *The Lexus and the Olive Tree.* New York: Farrar, Straus and Giroux.

Galbraith, James K. 2001. <pae_news@btinternet.com> The war economy. *Post-Autistic Economics Newsletter.* 9: (October 19) 4.

Gates, Jeff. 2001. <pae_news@btinternet.com> The global economy. *Post-Autistic Economics Newsletter* 9: (October 19). 5.

Gordon, Wendell. 1958. *International Trade: Goods, People, and Ideas.* New York: Alfred A. Knopf.

Greider, William. 1997. *One World, Ready or Not: The Manic Logic of Global Capitalism.* New York: Simon and Schuster.

Hardt, Michael and Antonio.Negri. 2001. What the protesters in Genoa want. *The New York Times, Op-Ed.* (July 20) A23.

Hawken, Paul, Amory Lovins, and L. Hunter Lovins. 1999. *Natural Capitalism: Creating the Next Industrial Revolution.* Boston: Little, Brown and Company.

Ho, P. Sai-wing. 1998. Multilateral trade negotiations and the changing prospects for their world development: assessing from a southern perspective. *Journal of Economic Issues.* 32: 375-83.

Keynes, John Maynard. 1936. *The General Theory of Employment, Interest and Money.* New York: Harcourt, Brace.

Klein, Philip A. 2001. Institutionalist perspective on globalization. Paper presented at meetings of the Association for Institutional Thought. Reno, Nevada. (April 19).

Krugman, Paul. 2000. Poor countries don't want to be "saved." *Denver Rocky Mountain News,* (February 21).

———. 2001. Trade protests are misguided. *Rocky Mountain News,* (April 24).

Larudee, Mehrene and Tim Koechlin, 1999. Wages, productivity, and foreign direct investment. *Journal of Economic Issues*. 33: 419-26.
Lavin, Douglas. 2002. Globalization goes upscale. *Wall Street Journal*, (February 1). A18.
Lindblom, Charles E. 2001. *The Market System*. New Haven: Yale University Press.
MacEwan, Arthur. 1991. The gospel of free trade: the new evangelists. *Dollars and Sense* 171: 6-9, 20.
Melloan, George. 1999. Welcome to the Seattle World's Fair, circa 1999. *Wall Street Journal*, (November 30). A27.
Meltzer, Allan and Jeffrey D. Sachs. 2000. A blueprint for IMF reform. *Wall Street Journal*, (March 8).
Menand, Louis. 2001. *The Metaphysical Club: A Story of Ideas in America*. New York: Farrar, Straus and Giroux.
Mitchie, Jonathan. 1999. "Introduction." In *Global Instability: The Political Economy of World Economic Governance*. Jonathan Mitchie and John Grieve Smith. eds. London: Routledge.
Moberg, David. 2002. A parade to oblivion. *The American Prospect* 13: 23-25.
Prasch, Robert E. 1999. Developing the principle of a managed trade system. *Journal of Economic Issues* 33: 411-17.
———. 1995. Reassessing comparative advantage: The impact of capital flows on the argument for laissez-faire. *Journal of Economic Issues* 29: 427-33.
Prebisch, Raul. 1950. *The Economic Development of Latin America and Its Principal Problems*. New York: United Nations.
Prokosch, Mike. 2000. Realizing Seattle's potential. *The Progressive Populist* 10. (December 15).
Reich, Robert. 2000. A new China deal. *The American Prospect* 11: (April 24) 56.
Ricardo, David. [1821] 1973. *The Principles of Political Economy and Taxation*. New York: Everyman's Library.
Robinson, Joan. 1978. *Aspects of Development and Underdevelopment*. Cambridge: Cambridge University Press.
Sachs, Jeffrey D. 2001. Democrats should back free trade. *Wall Street Journal*, (December 4). A18.
Safire, William. 1999. Clinton saved US.dignity with message in Seattle. *Denver Rocky Mountain News*, (December 7).
Sawyer, Malcolm. 1999. Minsky's analysis, the European single currency, and the global financial system. Working Paper No. 266. The Jerome Levy Economics Institute of Bard College Summary. 8: 19-20.
Sen, Amartya. 1999. *Development as Freedom*. New York: Alfred A. Knopf.
_______. 2002. How to judge globalism. *The American Prospect*; Special Supplement. A2-A6 (Winter).
Soros, George. 1998. *The Crisis of Global Capitalism: Open Society Endangered*. New York: Public Affairs.
_______. 2001 Interview. National Public Radio. (November 3).
_______. 2000. *Open Society: Reforming Global Capitalism*. New York: Public Affairs.
Stiglitz, Joseph S. 2002. Globalism's discontents. *The American Prospect*; Special Supplement. (Winter). A16-A21.
Thurow, Lester. 1996. *The Future of Capitalism*. New York: William Morrow and Company.
Tool, Marc A. 1979. *The Discretionary Economy: A Normative Theory of Political Economy*. Monica: Goodyear Publishing Company.
______. 2000. *Value Theory and Economic Progress: The Institutional Economics of J. Fagg Foster*. Boston: Kluwer Academic Publishers.
*US News and World Report* 2002. 132: 69.

Veblen, Thorstein. 1904. *The Theory of Business Enterprise*. New York: Charles Scribner's Sons.
———. [1899] 1934. *The Theory of the Leisure Class*. New York: Modern Library.
Walker, Marcus and Paul Hofheinz. 2000. Prague's subdued protests score points. *Wall Street Journal* (September 25).
Went, Robert. 2000. Game, set, and match for Mr. Ricardo? The surprising comeback of protectionism in the era of globalizing free trade. *Journal of Economic Issues* 34: 655-77.
Wilber, Charles K. 1998. Globalization and democracy. *Journal of Economic Issues* 32: 465-71.

# 18

# GLOBAL INDUSTRIAL POLICIES

Wolfram Elsner

## INTRODUCTION

The characteristics of the "new" economy are to be seen not so much in the hypermanias of the high-tech stock markets that have turned out, with their recent depressions, to be rather conventional. They have to be seen as knowledge-based, clustered, and networked economies. They manifest considerable intensification of direct interdependencies among economic agents, where the outcome of A directly depends also on the behavior of B, and vice versa. This has always been true of modern economies, as institutionalists and socio-economists have routinely contended. But it has become so intense, obvious, and ubiquitous that it can by no means be ignored any longer in either standard theory or policy formation.

The direct interactions in which agents are involved, by virtue of their increased interrelatedness, cannot sufficiently be guided by a more or less spontaneous, but inherently power-based, mechanism called "the market," which presumably operates with arms-length, short-run, spot-contract relations based on prices. Markets and prices no longer carry the information or facilitate future expectations required to guide individual behavior and to coordinate agents in the more complex situations that involve direct interdependencies.

Why have information and coordination problems risen in prominence in the "new" economy, in contrast to the older manufacturing-based economy?

First, microelectronic/digital and net-based technologies, which have come to dominate the technological basis of the economy, have considerable informational and organizational impact. With the nearly unlimited opportunities to produce, process, store, diffuse, and communicate data, information selection and its effective use have become a major problem in making effective economic choices. Electronic information is available at near zero marginal costs, adding yet another aspect to the well-known "collective-good" character of information. This is all the more significant since information is mostly used invidiously; that is, it involves the opportunistic use of asymmetric information. With its ubiquitous "external" effects, the production of new information and related systemic innovations carry a considerable amount of uncertainty for individual agents. When coordinated through markets and prices only, this uncertainty leads to a considerable amount of potential informational and innovative lock-in among individual agents. Net-based technologies and ubiquitous technological complementarities make "externalities" of individual decisions predominant. Net externalities render basic, systemic, and net-based innovations as complex decision-problems that call for more complex forms of coordination, specifically among small and medium-sized agents.

Second, manufacturing and services, though ever more fragmented, have become ever more interdependent. Manufacturing oriented service has become a directly interdependent relation that involves all the problems of information externalities mentioned. Thus, service requires a collective learning relationship with manufacturing agents. This requires more complex forms of coordination than those that markets and prices can provide.

Third, globalization is a politically organized phenomenon with one-sided, regulated "deregulations"—concessions and exemptions for capital interests, following the "neo-liberal" market ideology. However, a largely global deregulated economy has proven to be not really workable and, indeed, not feasible, even for the most advanced and powerful corporate agents. It has increased fragmentation and direct interdependencies on a global scale, and with this has come increased uncertainty at a level that cannot be managed by individual agents through markets and the price system.

Hence, this situation is characterized by "externalities," "collective-good" and related coordination problems. The lack of institutional embeddedness, through which the conventional states provide minimum structure and stability, permits the corporate economy worldwide to strive to pursue its own private interests through practices designed to reduce complexity and uncertainty. These practices, basically, consist of localization/regionalization and local clustering. That is, corporate agents try to develop new spatial forms of coordination among suppliers, assemblers, customers, public, and intermediate agents based on proximity, local embeddedness and long-run, close, dense, and continued interaction.

There are additional coordination problems associated with these three problems of the "new" economy. Markets and prices are less effective institutional arrangements than ever. Indeed, they may never have been sufficiently effective even under conventional manufacturing circumstances. Corporate agents have developed substitutes for "markets." They are increasingly supported by the state which has protected them through standard-setting, permissive collusion policies, and high "intellectual property rights" barriers. Individual strategies to catch up with these problems range from monopolistic behavior to collusion, "cartelling" and other restrictive practices.

Progressive institutional change would include networking on an equal and open source basis, seeking sustainable coordination. It would require the unlocking, acceleration, and stabilization of related innovative processes through the support of public industrial policies (IP).

Some evolutionary theories, specifically evolutionary game theory, have demonstrated that progressive coordinated solutions can be made feasible through collective learning in institutions of coordination and cooperation in a self-governing system among private agents. However, the underlying societal "dilemma-structures" (externalities, collective goods) persist, rendering emergent self-governing private processes to be highly time-consuming and fragile, if, indeed, they are not locked-in and inoperative.

Clearly, there is a necessary role for public industrial policy (IP) to play in the "new" economy! This role must focus on informational and collective learning aspects of the system of interdependent agents. Hence, it must focus upon their continuous interactions and their learning of coordination, i.e., institution-building and institutional change. It needs to unlock, accelerate, and stabilize the processes of learning and institution-building. Industrial policy must be developed as an interactive relation between the public agent and the interactive system of private agents. In this sense, it can be said to be doubly-interactive. It needs to assist private agents in solving collective industrial problems such as basic, systemic, and net-based innovations, the improvement of industrial structures, and the collective production of common location factors, e.g., specific "soft" infrastructures of common interest.

Industrial policy may act through direct coordination or through the change of incentive structures of the public agent (where incentives need not be pecuniary in the first instance). It should also shape the institutional structure by changing the arena and conditions of private interactions, e.g. through changing expectations and changing current behavior. In this way, IP focuses upon processes and futurity. Its role is to help strengthen conditions for the emergence of progressive institutional arrangements, for example, network structures that support effective learning and instrumental problem solving. In this paper we develop an institutionalist conception of industrial policy.

First, we will describe the institutionalist understanding of IP and of international global relations. Second, we will consider the implications of the "new" economy for shaping an interactive learning and institutions-focused IP approach. Third, we will examine the current global economic regime, developing some basic prerequisites for implementing the principles of a collective-learning and institutions-building IP approach at the global level. We will also attempt to identify measures needed to establish such an IP regime. Finally, we will take a close look at the building blocks of such a global IP regime. We will examine the regional/local systems where the dominant learning-to-learn takes place and where the cultural equipment to participate in global processes is generated. It will be shown that local/regional industrial policies can be highly interactive, problem-solving, and institutionally-oriented to fulfill their roles as the cornerstones of an effective global IP regime.

## THE INSTITUTIONALIST APPROACH TO GLOBAL ECONOMIC POLICIES

### Instrumentalism

The institutionalist conception of economics is that of a science which supports real problem solving. It is a policy-oriented approach to inquiry. Impairments of the socio-economic provisioning process are analyzed through inquiry into the determining factual means-consequences relations. It offers an "instrumental" analysis of the conditions of problem solving. The ceremonial aspects of the behavioral structure are expected to be problem-perpetuating, generating impairments to the production and distribution of real income. Problems are evaluated through the elaboration of instrumentally warranted criteria of judgment to facilitate social provisioning and problem solving.

These judgmental criteria include "the continuity of the human life process" (see Tool [1979] 2001, 292; 1994, 406), which enables recurrent interaction, collective learning, and the adjustment and/or emergence of institutions as the instruments of coordination to facilitate collective problem solving. The idea of continuity also implies that institutional arrangements contribute to the expectation that members of the community have a common future of continued interactions. This expectation, in turn, influences their present behavior, specifically their inclination to learn the institutions of coordination and cooperation. Institutionalist instrumental value theory also includes the notion of the "recreation of community," which envisions institutional changes that arise out of innovative collective action. Finally, it sets forth the idea of non-invidious, non-ceremonial change. This means that the incentive structure of the socio-economy should not be changed in such a way as to stimulate more status and power-oriented behavior which undermines the inclination and ability of members of the community to enter into collective learning processes.

## Policy

Public policies, generated through the specific collective action of the state (political and administrative) on the local, national, and international levels constitute an indispensable element of promoting instrumental problem solving. This can be accomplished through individual problem-solving behavior in a world of direct interdependencies only if such behavior is embedded in an appropriate framework of incentives and of expectations of a common future of continued interaction. Institutionalist policy making, accordingly, is concerned with arrangements that organize processes instrumentally (Hayden 1994). It consciously rejects the dominance of power and status over collective problem solving. It also forestalls the ceremonial encapsulation of the community's fund of knowledge by self-interested elites (Bush 1987; 1994).

Institutionalists reject the notion of the "spontaneous generation" of the institutional system. Complex modern economies cannot sufficiently organize themselves through private actions. These provisioning systems require an adequate framework to render sufficiently stable processes for resolving problems. Evolutionary processes among the private agents do not automatically provide adequate stability and problem solving; they need to be embedded in a structure of incentives and expectations created through planned collective action, i.e., public policy.

The institutionalist conception of policy formation is also "relativistic" (Hayden 1994) in the sense that it does not posit a universal "best solution," or "best institutional structure," or "best evolutionary process." The viability of institutional arrangements depends on time, space, the ecosystem, and the specific knowledge fund of the society. These contextual factors differ over time, from nation to nation, and often among local/regional communities, as well.

## International Economic Relations and Policies

The institutionalist "international" perspective is not so much physically or spatially oriented as it is oriented with respect to cultural-institutional distance. International relations are viewed as intercultural exchanges among socio-economic entities (Adams 1994). These, in turn, have developed under regional time-space conditions, as specifically regional path-dependent historical courses. As exchange relations extended beyond their regional-cultural borders and became inter-social exchange, inter-cultural institutions emerged along side the existing intra-cultural and intra-regional settings (Palan 2000, 13). Intercultural overarching institutions have emerged, blurring cultural boundaries. Nevertheless, the region remains the main locus of cultural emergence, cultural reproduction, and cultural change, because it is the arena of relatively more frequent interactions and more intense collective learning. In this way, the regional culture creates and recreates the abilities and competencies of agents to enter and participate in inter-cultural exchange.

Against this background, international policies are focused on institutional arrangements that coordinate an international economy in which regional socio-economic entities incorporate inter-cultural interactions, solve common problems, and create certain international "collective goods" (Adams 1994). Institutionalist international economic policies proceed from a consideration of international direct interdependencies among regional socio-economic entities. It contemplates shaping those international institutions into entities capable of instrumental problem solving (Lower 1994). Thus, such policies are not only concerned with physical infrastructure (e.g., traffic, telecom) but also with institutional, organizational, legal, administrative, and political infrastructure.

The problems created by the foreign financial portfolios and direct investments of "stateless" transnational corporations have led institutionalists to develop proposals for inter-regionally coordinated industrial policies as well as international organizations that can bring about effective social control to achieve social and economic stabilization. Transnational corporations have successfully dominated trade, production, technology and prices in international, regional, and local markets. Aided and abetted by the widespread acceptance of the myths of "free market" ideology, transnational corporations have been able to pressure national, regional, and local governments to subvert their own public interest by making endless investment concessions to the transnational corporations.

## COORDINATION PROBLEMS IN THE "NEW" ECONOMY

The "new" economy is increasingly characterized by digital, microelectronic and net-based technologies. These have considerable impact. Information— in contrast to a conventional manufactured good— displays the features of a "collective good" (Hutter 2001). This is emphasized by the fact that it is available under the new technological conditions at near to zero marginal costs. Therefore, there are pervasive tendencies in the "markets" to produce information at "suboptimal" levels and of complete lock-ins of information and innovation production under conditions of individualistic decision-making (Miller 2001). Prevalent net-based technologies and "systemic" innovations, with their complex technological complementarities, involve technological or net-externalities that are ubiquitous in individual decisions with respect to the production or purchase of these technologies. They make lock-ins a ubiquitous, latent feature of production and use of related goods. Basic, systemic and net-oriented innovations can no longer be generated in the same way that they were in conventional manufacturing regimes. Furthermore, manufacturing and services have become more interdependent (Antonelli 1998). Innovation in manufacturing has become an interdependent and interactive process between manufacturing and knowledge-intensive services. This involves the "externalities" of information as mentioned above (for example, Ruys 2000). Therefore, a manufacturing-oriented service can be provided only as communication in a common learning process.

Finally, globalization is a political and bureaucratic phenomenon, organized, on the one hand, by highly selective processes of deregulation, liberalization, and empowerment of capital and corporate interests and, on the other hand, by national regulation, bureaucratization, authoritarian control of social interests. The advocates of the transnational corporate economy have always welcomed this one-sided liberation. However, the "under-socialized" global economy imposes *too little* "structure" on the decision making of the individual corporate agents.

The corporate economy, insufficiently coordinated by the "market," in fact, cannot deal with the increased level of uncertainty that comes with the "neo-liberal" model of deregulated globalization (Armstrong 2001, 533, 541). It establishes its own private, substitute arrangements to reduce uncertainty and complexity to manageable levels. Regionalization and regional clustering in new industrial districts with suppliers, services, project partners, customers, societal and public agents have become the dominant form of spatial organization of the most advanced, most fragmented, most highly technological and most globalized parts of the corporate economy (Feser 1998; Maillat & Grosjean 1999; Elsner 2000a). In spite of the rhetoric of globalization, the corporate economy is looking for spatial and cultural proximity; that is, some form of local embeddedness, structure, certainty, and collectivity. Only these conditions, however, permit the organization of complex, systemic innovations because they allow for the emergence of repeated interactions, common collective learning, the stabilization of future expectations, cultural proximity, and common tacit knowledge and even the enhancement of social capital albeit in reduced and distorted forms. (Grabher (ed.) 1993; Saxenian 1994).

Common to all these features of the "new" economy is the fact that there are fundamental and new coordination problems in an economy that is increasingly characterized by direct interdependencies, "externalities," "collective goods," and severe information and expectations problems. In order to establish substitution solutions to compensate for the failures of globally disembedded markets, the corporate economy deploys standard setting, cooperation and networking as new forms of coordination (Piore 2001), together with more conventional and more restrictive forms such as the use of market power and monopolistic practices, collusion, "cartelling" and lobbying for high "intellectual property rights." The corporate agents in the "new" economy try to surmount the arms-length and one-shot spot-contracting market relations to establish stable mid-term relations that are largely resistant against price changes and involve collective learning processes and networking.

These private solutions, however, are insufficient substitutes. As mixtures of progressive and regressive practices, they indicate the need for more comprehensive social forms of organization and management (Baker 1996; Pratt 1997; Lamberton 2001). This means that industrial policy must include process-oriented interventions, such as subsidies and non-pecuniary incentives, direct coordination, and framework measures, such as the change of expectations of the private agents concerning the recurrence, permanence, and time horizon of their interactions. Hence, the whole informational and institutional setting is at stake in developing a modern IP approach (Hart 1992; Elsner & Huffschmid 1994; Jessop 1994; Lane 1995, 167 ff.; Amable & Petit 1996; Belussi 1999; Jones 1999; Rycroft & Kash 1999, 211-223; Yu 2000; Elsner 2001a).

Among the conditions of more progressive and instrumental institutional forms of coordination are socially and politically embedded network structures that provide for a more effective collective learning. Scholars have elaborated whole sets of conditions for a favorable network of responsive and responsible governance. Included are the equal rights of the members, control of power, the avoidance of hub-and-spoke structures, open access and entry, a diversity among agents, multiple centers of discretion, diversity of structures, redundant and parallel processes, and cultural embeddedness. Taken together, they ensure a continuous abundance of new ideas and innovations (see e.g. Powell & Smith-Doerr 1994; de Bruijn & ten Heuvelhof 1995; Maggioni 1997; Elsner 2000a).

# GLOBAL GOVERNANCE AND POLICIES

## The Current Globalization Mechanism: An Exclusively Regulated Regime

In contrast to prevailing ideology and rhetoric, current globalization is not a natural, spontaneous, evolutionary, or market-selected process. But it is highly political, regulated, bureaucratic, and authoritarian. It is carefully organized by the most powerful national governments and by the international economic organizations they have created as their policy instruments. Its mechanism is neither "neo" (new) nor, in any reasonable understanding, "liberal." Its character is determined by its one-sided societal structure in its provision of a global physical economic infrastructure (Kingston 2000; Perraton 2001). During the past two decades, the leading governments have given high priority to, and strategically pursued, the globalization as an exclusive arena for private commercial, financial, and corporate interests. Transnational corporations have increasingly been forced by capital turnover requirements, increased profit rate demands of the speculative financial markets, and by the new shareholder culture to dominate their home markets (see, e.g., Lower 1994). An essential ingredient of deregulated globalization has been a shift in the character of the corporation from production and investment to the exercise of power, employment downsizing, and the redistribution of income to shareholders (Lazonick & O'Sullivan 2000; Jones 2000; Williams 2000; Barnet & Cavanagh 2001a). To put the matter in Veblenian terms, globalization has accelerated a shift from the "industrial employments" to the "pecuniary employments" in transnational corporations (Veblen [1904] 1975).

"Neo-liberal" globalization, therefore, has been rightly characterized as a "program of deliberate destruction of collectivity," (Bourdieu 1998, 110) and as an "undermining-the-public-interest-policy worldwide" (Wallach 2001), It has served the vested interests of powerful transnational corporations rather than the public interests of the nations and regions affected( McMichael 2000).

Leading governments have deliberately kept the traditional social state functions below this global level of organization and have tried to keep the remainder of society apart from the deregulated global arena. Individuals, social organizations and political organizations, popular initiatives and movements are denied participation in the global arena. They are carefully kept within national and regional boundaries and subordinated to increasingly new paternalistic, neo-feudalistic kinds of politics, specifically vis-a-vis the labor force and the social security systems (Standing 2001). For a general discussion of social exclusion in the processes of international integration, see, e.g., Schoukens and Carmichael (2001). In the wake of nationally and regionally restricted social interests, facing excessive economic competition, and an increasingly fierce structural "war" among economic locations, it is no wonder that a society can be easily rendered a playground for nationalist, regionalist, religious, and fundamentalist ideologies that strive to gain control of the power of the state. Such movements turn out to be both a complement to, and a cornerstone for, this kind of globalization; and they wind up undermining it as well. (Heilbroner 1993; Rodrik 1997; Kingston 2000).

## A Power, Wealth and Income Redistribution Mechanism

The globalization regime has completely changed the power, assets, income distributions, and the premises of interactions among the societal groups on the regional, national, and global levels. The traditional institutional arrangements and the attendant distribution of costs and benefits have been drastically modified. Thus, the global economic system has changed its character and dynamics, becoming a predominantly redistributive and socially polarizing mechanism (Chossudovsky 1997; Amin 1999; Williams 2000). The redistribution of power, opportunities, wealth, and income has become the dimension of the economic system that displays the greatest dynamics. The *World Development Report 2000/2001* of the World Bank and UNICEF provide broad statistical evidence of the fact that today there is the *most unequal* international income distribution since statistics have been reconstructed, i.e. , since the year 1800. Among the 100 financially most powerful organizations of the world there is a increasing number of private corporations and a decreasing number of nation states. A tiny group of individuals controls more income and wealth than the majority of the world's population (Kingston 2000). This is not surprising since the "neo-liberal" ideologies of the most powerful governments have led them to establish what they term to be an "efficient" market mechanism as the dominating instrument of global integration. Largely disembedded "neo-liberal" markets, however, turn out to be a highly power-based systems with an increasingly unequal distribution of power (Kingston 2000). Thus, the global economy, its integration process, and its dynamics are increasingly determined by an uncontrolled system of unequally distributed power.

The United Nations Organization is the one system of international political governance that offers a developmental and equalizing approach to global problems through its elaborate mechanisms of peaceful and participatory conflict resolution. But its authority in international affairs has been deliberately eroded. It has been financially undermined and politically depreciated. With respect to today's essential global decisions, it plays only a secondary role as it is accepted at best as a helping hand.

## Hierarchical Unification; Reduced Problem-Solving Capacity

Against this background, the literature has demonstrated that the nations, regions and economic locations worldwide, far from yielding any kind of balanced development, have been reorganized into a system of what is called hierarchical unification (Unger & van Waarden (eds.) 1995; Ruigrok & van Tulder 1995; Keyman 1997; Barnet & Cavanagh 2001b). They do not participate on an equal basis but are integrated into a hierarchical system of center-periphery subordination and dependency. This means that national and local cultures, that have developed unique characteristics through countless regional interactions in response to regional conditions, are under increasing pressure to adapt to and emulate the behavior of the wealthy, powerful, and "successful" centers of the global economy (Unger and van Waarden (eds.) 1995).

In consequence, the global system increasingly loses its cultural diversity (Keyman 1997; Kingston 2000; Mander 2001; Barnet and Cavanagh, 2001b. With this decline comes a reduced problem-solving capacity since, more than ever, "power is detached from responsibility and those who make decisions are separated from those who are affected by them" (Retallack 2001, 202). As they lose their cultural traditions and regionally adapted institutional problem-solving procedures, nations and regions of the world are losing their traditional national sovereignty and capacity for social control, which are necessary for self-sufficiency. New technologies, in addition, impose an acceleration of global innovation processes so that they tend to outpace the ability of local institutions to adapt to new exigencies (McClintock 1996).

The global system has run into an "institutional disequilibrium" that reduces its ability to provide the global public goods, the demand for which has increased because of the growing global direct interdependencies (Padoan 2001). The increased production of global public "bads," and the decreased ability of problem solving have been widely discussed, for example in the area of natural environmental problems (Giampietro and Mayumi 1998; Conca 2000; Görg and Brand 2000; and Retallack 2001). A global system with a reduced cultural and institutional diversity will—as is true for all complex systems—lose its capacity to solve problems and to absorb shocks of any kind. It loses its resilience.

### Counter-Productive & Excessive Competition Among Nations

Finally, the national and local cultures, the regions, the cities, and economic locations have been forced through globalization into a deregulated, power-dominated, and "homogenized" system, involving increased competition called "free trade" in the "world market." It imposes fierce competition on the majority of locations in their struggle to attract highly mobile and globally footloose investment capital, that nevertheless makes itself scarce, to their regions. This devastates local communities and subverts their national, regional, and local public interests (Lower 1994; Chossudovsky 1997; Wallach 2001; Morris 2001). A subsequent *race to the bottom* among regional economies as they compete for the "scarce" global capital is an inevitable consequence and has been widely described and discussed (Wilson 1996; Martin 1997; Sinn 1997; Lindlar and Trabold 1998; Nayeri 1998; Conca 2000).

Competition among a vast majority of powerless, immobile, and "inelastic" local entities vis-à-vis powerful and highly "elastic" investors, has reached an intensity that has proven to be counterproductive in nearly every respect. Such a regime does not leave enough room for the majority of national/local cultures to develop their own locally-adapted solutions to their problems. Competition forces them—either by the "market" forces of private power exertion or by the "visible hand" of the powerful governments and their international organizations—to behave in ways that run contrary to their public interests (Braunstein and Epstein 1999; Lovering 1999; Amin 1999; McMichael 2000; and Elsner 2001b). Local democratic participation, the community's capacity to collectively learn to innovate and call upon their historically developed institutions of coordination and cooperation, are undermined. Thus, the very source of their capabilities to enter international exchange is dried up. No wonder that this globalization regime also leads to repercussions in forms of an increasingly aggressive nationalism, regionalism, and religious fanaticism.

## BUILDING A LESS INVIDIOUS PROBLEM-SOLVING GLOBAL ECONOMY

All in all, we are facing a global system that creates more problems than it solves, while the global and local capacities to solve problems have been reduced. The whole global system, therefore, must be reorganized to increase its problem-solving capacity, its resilience and its ability to reestablish and strengthen structural policies accordingly.

Two basic conditions for an institutional structure that provides instrumentally more effective outcomes follow from the above:

First, the resilience of the global system and the support of inter-regional collective learning, coordination, and institutions-building processes must be restored. An institutional reform should allow for the spatial-cultural entities to interact on an equal (non-invidious) basis. This means that the national, regional, and local economies with respect to their historical, cultural, and geographical settings must be taken seriously. This is necessary to reestablish cultural diversity at the global level. This requires a rejection of all kinds of cultural universalism and essentialism that justify social, political and economic dominance (Elsner 2000c).

Second, enabling cultural diversity worldwide requires a reduction of the current level of "homogenized" excessive competition among the spatial-cultural entities in order to restore their capacities to decide and act according to their local problems and to their historically developed institutions. This involves some globally effective framework measures to be taken so that national and local abilities to act in a democratic and participatory way can be restored.

## Protect Cultural Diversity and Develop Equality-Based Interaction

The global system has to be analyzed as an interactive inter-regional system of national and local cultural-spatial entities. Global physical infrastructures, real-time electronic communication, legal, political and administrative homogenization, increased unification and integration into hierarchical structures and the increased global production of collective "bads" such as poverty, inequality, refugee migration and environmental deterioration, all have increased the direct interdependencies among them. To permit instrumentally-warranted coordinated behavior vis-à-vis the global "collective goods," the global system of cultural-spatial entities has to be reorganized on an equitable, power-free basis where every culture has an equal voice and its freedom of action to care for its own local problems. Nations and local cultures have to be acknowledged with respect to their specificity and differences. Cultural diversity has always existed and has to be secured for the future. As in biological systems, it has proved to be a crucial to complex socio-economic systems in securing their learning, innovation, and general economic effectiveness (see, e.g., Delorme and Dopfer (eds.) 1994). The notion of cultural diversity can be carefully applied in an evolutionary framework to global cultural interactions (Elsner 2000b).

Biological systems are organized to provide for permanently high levels of diversification in order to maintain sustainability. While it is important to avoid crude biological and evolutionary analogies, it seems clear that protecting cultural diversity and equal rights of the diverse cultural entities seems to be the only way to prevent the global system from a continued shift into a power-based hierarchical unification and cultural imperialism. To protect cultural diversity worldwide implies deliberate restrictions against cultural exports from the mighty to the less mighty, and the conservation and further development of the specific cultural identities of the latter. Rather than externally imposing a hierarchical integration of cultures, effective learning and innovation can be supported, as the natural system demonstrates.

The conception of self-guided development also includes self-guided time-requirements and rejects the idea of a continuous acceleration of socio-economic processes. The processes of common learning of coordination and of trust- and institutions-building are time-consuming and cannot be accelerated by external pressures from the "world-markets." These pressures, rather than accelerating processes, would cause social costs through reduced collective learning. As has been stated: "all encompassing. . .marketization might foster *adaptation* in the short run, the consequent loss of organizational diversity will impede *adaptability* in the long run" (Grabher & Stark 1997, 533). In contrast, protected diversity allows for a learned, voluntary, trust-based global integration at a speed specific to the needs of the individual economy. Protected diversity of national/local cultures has become a widely discussed and advocated issue in international relations and policy analyses (see, for example, Sugden 1996; Keyman 1997; Grabher & Stark 1997; Giampietro & Mayumi 1998).

De Martino (2000, 128 ff.) has argued that, in a world of inequality, cultural and moral universalism will yield cultural imperialism. However, since cultures can only be mutually defined and constituted, and the borders between them are socially constructed, cultural relativism would not yield a sustainable basis for inter-cultural interaction as relativism would put the ever-present insider-outsider relation in question. The view to be rejected, he argues, is not so much universalism but essentialism, which presumes that cultural rules could reflect timeless and universal values. Further, both essentialism and relativism should be rejected in favor of a moderate universalism as a non-imperialist, internationalist ethic tolerant of cross-cultural differences that allow for diverse communities to identify. The intent behind an anti-essentialist universalism is "harmonization of global capabilities."

To suggest a global institutional reform of the world-market regime, to suggest a system of diversity and a set of framework policy measures, however minimal, will no doubt involve some kind of "universalism." De Martino, however, considers his moderate universalism, or "ethical internationalism," to serve as a guideline for policy intervention and a well-endowed global policy regime to foster a more equal development. However, caution is warranted. In a power-based, unequal, and redistributive global regime, any arrangement that allows for an interventionist policy inevitably will bear, and might easily be converted into, a vehicle to exert imperialist intervention. In order to undermine the regime of cultural and economic imperialism, it is necessary to avoid any arrangement that allows for any kind of interventionism into any community in which moderate universal/internationalist value criteria prevail.

Cultural diversity and normative/moral non-invidious relativism must be given the highest priority if the global system is to prevent the dominance of the mighty over the non-mighty in the technological, economic, social, cultural, normative aspects of national, regional, and local communities. In sum, the *global protection of cultural diversity must be the highest value of a global institutional reform.*

International and regional industrial policies have been drafted elsewhere for the European Union (EU) to implement a structural policy strategy for protected diversity (Elsner 2000c, 87). It advocates a change in the understanding of "regional development support" in order: (a) to include the support of a relatively "isolated" regional development, (b) to cover possible extra costs of regions that do not implement the usual imported or imitated "modernizations," and (c) to explore their own specific and path-dependent historical course of development. This implies that the diversity of local agents—profit and non-profit, public, societal, and commercial—have to be involved on an equal basis to formulate a regional development strategy. The EU, for instance, with its well developed regional and network policies, should redefine its regional and structural policies to include the promotion of such development strategies as a European pilot program. Roger Sugden formultated it as a general rule: "Strategies must take account of particular histories. . . .it is not even sufficient simply to be rooted in local histories, multinational webs can only be borne out, and be grown from, such histories" (Sugden 1996, 28). Or, as Mander has recently put it: "The answer. . .is. . .to bring real power back to the local communities, while supporting communities. . .who attempt to stand in the way of the juggernaut" (Mander 2001, 57).

## Contesting Excessive "Competition"

As has been explained, the fierce kind of "competition" that takes place on a unified, homogenized basis among communities has proved to be counterproductive to global and local problem solving. Fierce "homogenized" competition can even be analyzed as a form of structural "war" among economic locations that resembles the culture of military warfare (Elsner 2000b). It is a power-based struggle for resources; it is a system of mutual conquest of home markets; a system for the redistribution economic opportunities from the powerless to the powerful.

The need to reduce the level and kind of competition in favor of some kind of learning interaction among diverse entities has been widely discussed in recent years (De Martino 2000, 152 ff., 184 ff.). It requires a certain set of internationally implemented social, cultural, and environmental minimum standards to prevent the race to the bottom by lowering prices for local environmental assets and local labor. International codes of conduct for local economic development and promotion, the consumption of labor and local environment by investors, and a more binding form of spatial planning would have to be included. These are the very areas where the leading group of powers has always deliberately exercised its discretion in order to prevent any progress toward agreements of this kind at the international level.

Such a code could include minimum prices for labor, space, land, and natural assets. It could also include restrictions on interregional cultural export, where the import of foreign models goes beyond the path-dependent funnel of future opportunities of a region. This would reduce the considerable social costs from destruction of local institutions, webs and capabilities. Discussions of the global standards of conduct have led to the development of a wide range of operative standards, index regulation proposals, and charters (see, e.g., McClintock 1996; De Martino 2000, 219-236; Standing 2001).

It is obvious that defensive minimum standards and code strategies designed to reduce excessive competition must deal with the current domination of production, labor, environment, social and cultural processes by disembedded, speculative agents. When financial speculation becomes a dominant feature of the economy, it might rightly be termed a "casino economy." The drastic reform proposals for the global financial system and the capital markets include the widely discussed Tobin tax and measures to re-connect the volatile pecuniary flows to real processes and to domestic or local public control. Needed as well is control over short-term capital flows, a comprehensive reform program for the IMF, World Bank and other power-based international economic institutions and their transformation into a set of developmental agencies. Also on the reform agenda is the taxation of transnational corporations to nurture a global development fund, and new governance of the foreign direct investment (Lower 1994; Palley 1999; Harris 1999; Braunstein & Epstein 1999; Barnet & Cavanagh 2001a). The global financial system, therefore, has to be changed to be geographically rooted and to "cater. . .to the interests of local and regional economies" (Barnet, Cavanagh 2001a, 69).

**"Localization" and Global Interaction on an Equal Basis**

We do not intend to advocate a comprehensive program of desirable minimum standards or far-reaching sets of industrial and financial policy measures. This is intended, rather, to be an instrumental approach, incorporating the criterion of changing the institutional framework to reduce excessive competition. The purpose is to recreate opportunities, capabilities, and competencies on the national, regional, and local levels, making it possible for these communities to deal with their own problems. This means re-connecting agents, community, place, and nature on a procedural, interactive, sequential, and learning basis (Norberg-Hodge 2001). Therefore, the intention here is not to repeat the usual advocacy of the creation of new international organizations, or even of internationally-coordinated industrial policy. Reducing excessive competition means enabling the regional-cultural communities, however vaguely defined, to act with a higher level of competence in dealing with their regional real production problems.

This seems to be the only way to build future global governance on the basis of the knowledge and competencies of regional socio-economic cultures. This would ential a guarantee of representation and voice for all regions. It would also involve the building of a new global institutional framework for inter-cultural interaction and exchange on an equal basis, allowing for a global "dialogical climate" (De Martino 2000, 237; Standing 2001, 180). It is a defensive approach that will "assist in working out institutional arrangements that will allow societies to continue to engage in international trade and production without substantial damage to the social fabric" (McClintock 1996, 242). What must be avoided is the pervasive cultural imperialism that leads to the complete breakdown of global exchange and the oppressive nationalism, regionalism, racism, and religious fanaticism that would follow in its wake.

The "re-localization" of resources, rights, and competencies brings responsibility, capability, and agency back to where the problems are and where the people are "immediately aware and directly affected" by them (Retallack 2001, 202). Localization is not a relapse into an historical constellation that has already passed into a romantic ideal; it is the re-connection of action to real world problems; it is the only sensible way to engage in instrumental problem solving. Contrary to the usual globalization rhetoric, instrumental problem solving seems to be effective on a small scale

(Morris 2001, 122 ff.; Hines and Lang 2001). It allows for an "economics as if community matters" (Morris 2001, 124).

## LOCAL INDUSTRIAL POLICIES

Regional-cultural entities are not generally well-prepared competently to act with respect to their own problems and equally to interact on the inter-regional and global level. They have to undertake to enable themselves, with their regional individual, organizational, societal, and public agents to gain the collective and public action competencies required. The corresponding IP approach for the regional communities displays features parallel to those explained for the global level, i.e., it must be oriented to interactions, common learning processes, institutions-building, and institutionalized coordination. This is why we have called it an interactive IP approach. It focuses on the institutional arrangements for interactive processes (Elsner 2001a).

It is a policy approach that can be integrated into the broader institutionalist conception of a negotiated, transparent, participatory, and instrumentally-oriented economy. Therefore, it is less "defensive" than the global approach and more proactive. It is operational since it is located where most of the problems, and the people affected by them are located (Mizrahi 1998; Belussi 1999; Weiler et al. 2000; Norberg-Hodge 2001; Elsner 2001a). The interactive IP approach provides for the resolution of typical economic problems, such as income growth, jobs creation, the improvement of the industrial structure, and the creation of common factors of production (i.e., locational factors including all kinds of infrastructures). All are characterized by direct interdependencies and thus are collective-good or coordination problems that cannot sufficiently be solved by the market mechanism (Elsner 2001a). It is necessary, therefore, for the public agent to interfere with the private process to shape and reform the conditions of the private interaction in order to accelerate and stabilize the learning-to-coordinate and learning-to-cooperate process. Formal analysis and practical experience indicate that this can be done by two sets of instruments: first, changing incentive structures (Klein 1990) to include a wide range of non-pecuniary incentives, e.g., informational measures; second, shaping future expectations of the private agents that directly determine their current behaviors (Redding 1996; Axelrod 1997). Here, the public agent may persuade private agents that they have a common future where they will, with high probability, meet and interact with each other. They may also lend support for parallel corporate measures to develop new markets (see, e.g., the case studies in Elsner 2001a, and in de Bruijn and ten Heuvelhof 1995).

This implies a new interaction between the system of private agents and the public agent which is designed to be focused on the process of private institutions-building rather than being directly interventionist. Therefore, the approach also allows for a "lean" policy. One reason is that private agents appear to respond to small, non-pecuniary changes of conditions of interaction such as informational incentives or the deliberate shaping and changing of future expectations (Elsner 2001a).

The public agent is required, with the consent of the governed, to define the "public interest" with respect to the kinds of behavior private agents must consistently adhere to over time. We have called this new private-public interaction as *meritorics* and described the role it plays in the more comprehensive institutionalist conception of the negotiated economy (Elsner 2001a, 70). A new, strong, self-conscious and proactive role of the public agent is obviously required here, regardless of the fact that his action and financial funding may be "lean."

We have also described this approach as a *meso* approach, since theory, formal analysis, and practical experience lead to the conclusion that the essential supporting factors for publicly initiated, accelerated and stabilized processes of private collective learning of institutionalized coordination are to be found in meso-economic platforms where the probability to meet the same agent again in the future is definitely positive (Elsner 2001a, 74). This has to do with well-known factors such as proximity, density, group size, and mobility. Thus regions, industries, sectors, industrial clusters, and networks, professional or social *groups* of any kind become the focal points of processes of effective institutions-building and, therefore, the focus of institutionally oriented interactive IP. Economic policies, in general, should be redefined as institutional policies, that is as structural (industrial and regional) policies.

This approach is consistent with a strand of the modern cluster and networks literature. The analysis of supporting conditions for the good governance of co-operations and networks has resulted in many more specific policy suggestions concerning the internal structure and process of those platforms, e.g., the openness and the life cycles of networks, their behavior over time to keep the focus continuously on learning, problem solving, and innovation (see e.g. Elsner 2000a, 2001a). The approach confines the public shaping of the conditions of private interaction, coordination, and institutions-building to well-defined problems with "collective-good" dimensions. Thus, it does not deny that private agents may be competitors in some "markets," nor does its conception of institutions of coordination and cooperation imply illusions of an omnipresent harmony of interests. The prisoners' dilemma, specifically, illustrates the coexistence of competitive and cooperative dimensions and the lasting tension between them. The present approach makes sure that this basic tension is ubiquitous and will tend to last in the background, even under conditions of well developed cooperation and networking. This is why coordination is such a complex and non-trivial achievement. Increasing the overall efficiency of problem solving would seem to justify a further elaboration and application of this interactive IP paradigm.

## CONCLUSION

The approach to global industrial policy presented here starts from an analysis of direct interdependencies in what we have termed the "new" economy. It is concerned with current global regimes that foster social disembeddedness, social exclusion, institutional uniformity, power concentrations, and inequality within and among nation states. It deals with the increased complexity and predominance of the coordination problem among agents of all kinds. However, its primary concern is not the formulation of interventionist policies as such. It is focused, rather, on the institutional environment and its reform. It seeks to nurture directly interactive processes among agents meeting on an equal basis. This requires a careful consideration of their learning processes and their capacity to bring about institutional changes by which they are collectively enabled to cooperate in solving problems with "externalities" and "collective-good" dimensions.

The public agent, in turn, has to be qualified and able to define problem-solutions as publicly "merited" goods. Accordingly, the IP agent also has to set up a whole institutional-instrumental nexus that is able to unlock learning and innovation processes, to accelerate and to stabilize them. Critical here is the shaping of (mainly non-pecuniary) reward structures. The IP agent must nurture the expectations of private agents that there will be a strong common future and offer public mediation of private disagreements in order to secure that common future.

The view developed here is that industrial policy must be designed to help unlock and sustain processes of interactive, inter-cultural institutions-building for global instrumental problem solving. Local agency competencies seem to be the most essential precondition for an effective global economic system. In the final analysis, the global framework that has been proposed here is designed to undermine global patterns of power that give rise to imperialism and violence in inter-cultural relations. Thus, industrial policy must have the capability to deal with real problems and to be responsive to those affected by them. Reconnecting at the local level responsibility, affectedness, and qualified agency appears to be the vital precondition for developing an instrumental institutionalist global industrial policy regime.

## REFERENCES

Adams, John. 1994. "International Economic Relations." In *The Elgar Companion to Institutional and Evolutionary Economics.* G.M. Hodgson., W. J. Samuels, M.R. Tool, eds. Aldershot UK, & Brookfield US: Edward Elgar.

Amable, Bruno and Pascal Petit. 1996. New scale and scope for industrial policies in the 1990s. *International Review of Applied Economics* 10. 1:23-41.

Amin, Samir, 1999. "Capitalism, Imperialism, Globalization." In *The Political Economy of Imperialism: Critical Appraisals.* R.M.Chilcote, ed. Boston, Dordrect & London: KluwerAcademic Publishers.

Antonelli, Cristiano. 1998. Localized technological change, new information technology and the knowledge-based economy: the European evidence. *Journal of Evolutionary Economics* 8:177-198.

Armstrong, Peter. 2001. Science, enterprise and profit: ideology in the knowledge-driven economy. *Economy and Society* 30.4:524-552.

Axelrod, Robert. 1997. *The Complexity of Cooperation. Agent-Based Models of Competition and Collaboration.* Princeton, N.J.: Princeton University Press.

Baker, Peter. 1996. Spatial outcomes of capital restructuring: 'New industrial spaces' as a symptom of crisis, not solution. *Review of Political Economy* 8: 263-278.

Barnet, Richard and John Cavanagh. 2001a. "Electronic Money and the Casino Economy." In *The Case Against the Global Economy. And for a Turn Towards Localization.* E. Goldsmith and J. Mander, eds. London: Earthscan.

———. and———. 2001b. "Homogenization of Global Culture." In *The Case Against the Global Economy. And for a Turn Towards Localization..* E. Goldsmith and J. Mander, eds. London: Earthscan.

Belussi, Fiorenza. 1999. Policies for the development of knowledge-intensive local production systems. *Cambridge Journal of Economics* 23:729-747.

Bourdieu, Pierre. 1998. *Contre-feux.* German edition: *Gegenfeuer. Wortmeldungen im Dienste des Widersrtand gegen die neoliberale Invasion.* Konstanz: Universitätsverlag.

Braunstein, Elissa and Gerald Epstein. 1999. "Creating International Credit Rules and the Multilateral Agreement on Investment. What are the alternatives?" In *Global Instability. The Political Economy of World Economic Governance.* J. Michie and J.G.Smith, eds. London & New York: Routledge.

Bush, Paul D. 1987. The theory of institutional change. *Journal of Economic Issues* 21:1075-1116.

———. 1994. "Theory of Social Change." In *The Elgar Companion to Institutional and Evolutionary Economics.* G.M. Hodgson, W.J. Samuels and M.R.Tool, eds. Aldershot UK & Brookfield US: Edward Elgar, 2:291-296.

Chossudovsky, Michel. 1997. *The Globalisation of Poverty. Impacts of IMF and World Bank Reforms.* Penang (Malaysia): Third World Network.

Conca, Ken. 2000. The WTO and the undermining of global environmental governance. *Review of International Political Economy* 7.3:484-494.

de Bruijn, Johan A. and Ernst F. ten Heuvelhof. 1995. "Policy Networks and Governance." In *Institutional Design.* David L. Weimer. ed. Boston, Dordrecht & London: Kluwer Academic Publishers.

Delorme, Robert, and Kurt Dopfer. eds.1994. *The Political Economy of Diversity; Evolutionary Perspectives on Economic Order and Disorder.* Aldershot, UK & Brookfield, US: Edward Elgar.

De Martino, George. 2000. *Global Economy, Global Justice. Theoretical Objections and Policy Alternatives to Neoliberalism.* London, & New York: Routledge.

Elsner, Wolfram . 2000a. "An Industrial Policy Agenda 2000 and Beyond - Experience, Theory and Policy." In *Industrial Policies After 2000.* W. Elsner and J. Groenewegen, eds. Boston, Dordrecht, & London: Kluwer Academic Publishers.

———. 2000b. "Diversität und Kooperation sozio-ökonomischer Kulturen. Globale Krise oder Erhalt kultureller Identitäten". In B. P. Priddat (Hg.*), Kapitalismus, Krisen, Kultur,* Marburg: Metropolis, S.

———. 2000c. "Globalisierung - Standorte-,Krieg' oder Kooperation der Regionen." In *Ökonomie eines friedlichen Europa.* E. Altvater and B. Mahnkopf, eds. Muenster: Germany: Agenda 75-89.

———. 2001a. Interactive economic policy: toward a cooperative policy approach for a negotiated economy. *Journal of Economic Issues* 35.1:61-83.

———. 2001b. Krieg der Standorte oder Kooperation der Regionen. Leitbilder der Globalisierung. (War Among the Economic Locations or Cooperation of the Regions. Alternative Visions of Globalization). *Blätter für deutsche und internationale Politik.* 46.1:105-113.

——— and Huffschmid, Joerg. 1994. "Industrial Policy." In *The Elgar Companion to Institutional and Evolutionary Economics.* G.M. Hodgson, W.J. Samuels, and M. R.Tool., eds. Aldershot UK & Brookfield US: Edward Elgar 1:343-351.

Feser, E. J. 1998. "Old and New Theories of Industry Clusters." In *Clusters and RegionalSpecialisation.* M. Steiner, ed. London : Pion.

Giampietro, Mario, and Kozo Mayumi. 1998. Another view of development, ecological degradation, and north-south trade. *Review of Social Economy* 56:20-36.

Görg, Christoph and Ulrich Brand. 2000. Global environmental politics and competition between nation-states: on the regulation of biological diversity. *Review of International Political Economy* 7 (3):371-398.

Grabher, Gernot, ed.1993. *The Embedded Firm. On the Socioeconomics of Industrial Networks.* London & New York: Routledge.

———. and David Stark. 1997. Organizing diversity: evolutionary theory, network analysis and postsocialism. *Regional Studies* 31(5):533-544.

Harris, Laurence. 1999. "Will the Real IMF Please Stand Up. What Does the Fund Do, What Should It Do?" In *Global Instability. The Political Economy of World Economic Governance.* J. Michie and J.G. Smith, eds. London, & New York: Routledge.

Hart, Jeffrey. 1992. The effects of state-societal arrangements on international competitiveness: steel, motor vehicles and semiconductors in the United States, Japan and Western Europe. *British Journal of Political Science* 22:255-300. Repr. 1995 in: *Industrial Policy* W.Grant, ed. Aldershot UK, Brookfield US: Edward Elgar. 1995. 59-104.

Hayden, F. Gregory. 1994. "Institutional Theory of Economic Policy." In *The Elgar Companion to Institutional and Evolutionary Economics.* G.M. Hodgson, W. J. Samuels. and M. R.Tool, eds. Aldershot UK, Brookfield US: Edward Elgar. 1:392-397.

Heilbroner, Robert L. 1993. *21st Century Capitalism.* New York: W.W. Norton.

Hines, Colin and Tim Lang,. 2001. "The New Protectionism of 'Localization'." In *The Case Against the Global Economy. And for a Turn Towards Localization.* E. Goldsmith and J. Mander, eds. London: Earthscan.

Hutter, Michael. 2001. Efficiency, viability and the new rules of the internet. *European Journal of Law and Economics* 11:5-22.

Jessop, Bob, 1994. "Changing Forms and Functions of the State in an Era of Globalisation and Regionalisation." In R. Delorme and K.Dopfer, eds. *The Political Economy of Diversity: Evolutionary Perspectives on Economic Order and Disorder.* Aldershot UK & Brookfield US: Edwad Elgar.

Jones, Evan. 1999. "Industrial Policy." In *Encyclopedia of Political Economy.* P. A. O'Hara, ed. London & New York: Routledge, 1:503-505.

Jones, Marc T. 2000. The competitive advantage of the transnational corporation as an institutional form. *International Journal of Social Economics* 27: 943-958.

Keyman, E. Fuat, 1997. "Globalization, State, Identity/Difference. Toward a Critical Social Theory of International Relations." New Jersey: Humanities Press.

Kingston, William. 2000. A specter is haunting the world; the specter of global capitalism. *Journal of Evolutionary Economics* 10:83-108.

Klein, Daniel B. 1990. The microfoundations of rules vs. discretion. *Constitutional Political Economy* 1:1-19.

Lamberton, Donald McL. 2001. "The Knowledge Based Economy: Better Living or Bigger Profits?" In *Innovation, Economic Progress and the Qualitiy of Life.* G. Sweeney, ed. Cheltenham UK, Northampton (Mass.) US: Edward Elgar.

Lane, Christel. 1995. *Industry and Society in Europe. Stability and Change in Britain, Germany and France.* Aldershot UK & Brookfield US: Edward Elgar.

Lazonick, William and , Mary O'Sullivan. 2000. Maximizing shareholder value: a new ideology for corporate governance. *Economy and Society* 29.1:13-35.

Lindlar, Ludger, and Hearld Trabold. 1998. Globalisation, unemployment and social inequality: A farewell to welfare? *Konjunkturpolitik* 44,:1-30.

Lovering, John, 1999. Theory led by policy? The inadequacies of the new regionalism in economic geography illustrated from the case of Wales. Paper presented at the Economic Geography Research Group Seminar, London, July 3, 1998, published in *International Journal of Urban and Regional Research* 1999.

Lower, Milton. 1994. "International Economic Policy.". In *The Elgar Companion to Institutional and Evolutionary Economics.* G. M. Hodgson, W. J. Samuels and M.R. Tool, eds. Aldershot UK, & Brookfield US: Edward Elgar. 1:419-423.

Maggioni, Mario A. 1997. "Firms, Uncertainty and Innovation Policy." In *Economics of Structural and Technological Change.* G. Antonelli, and N. De Liso,eds. London & New York: Routledge.

Maillat, Denis and Nicolas Grosjean. 1999. "Globalisation and Territorial Production Systems". In *Innovation, Networks and Localities.* M. M. Fischer. et. al. eds. Berlin et al.: Springer.

Mander, Jerry. 2001. "Technologies of Globalization." In *The Case Against the Global Economy. And for a Turn Towards Localization.* E. Goldsmith, and J. Mander, eds. London: Earthscan.

Martin, Andrew. 1997. What does globalization have to do with the erosion of welfare states? Sorting out the issues, Centre for Social Policy Research, Univ. Bremen, ZeS-Arbeitspapier 1/1997.

McClintock, Brent. 1996. "International Trade and the Governance of Global Markets." In *Political Economy for the 21st Century* C. J. Whalen, ed, Armonk (NY) & London: M. E. Sharpe.

McMichael, Philip. 2000. Sleepless since Seattle: what is the WTO about*? Review of International Political Economy* 7.3:466-474.

Miller, Edythe S. 2001. The Impact of technological change on market power and market failure in telecommunications. *Journal of Economic Issues* 35:2:385-393.

Mizrahi, S. 1998. "Regional Cooperation and Innovative Industries: Game-theoretical Aspects and Policy Implications." In *Clusters and Regional Specialization. On Geography, Technology and Networks.* M. Steiner, ed London: Pion.

Morris, David. 2001. "Free Trade: The Great Destroyer." In *The Case Against the Global Economy. And for a Turn Towards Localization.*. E. Goldsmith and J. Mander, eds. London: Earthscan.

Nayeri, Kamran. 1998. The world economic and social situation on the eve of the 21st Century. *Review of Political Economy* 10:233-244.

Norberg-Hodge, Helena. 2001. "Shifting Direction: From Global Dependence to Local Interdependence." In *The Case Against the Global Economy. And for a Turn Towards Localization.*. E. Goldsmith and J.Mander, eds. London: Earthscan.

Oltra, Vanessa and Eric Schenk. 1998. "Evolution of Cooperation with Local Interactions and Imitation." In *The Economics of Networks*, P. Cohendet, et. al., eds. Berlin, Heidelberg & New York: Springer .

Padoan, Pier Carlo. 2001. "Globalization, Regionalism and the Nation State: Top down and Bottom up." In *Globalization, Institutions and Social Cohesion.* M. Franzini, and F. R. Pizutti, eds. Berlin, Heidelberg & New York: Springer.

Palan, Ronen. 2000. "New Trends in Global Political Economy." In *Global Political Economy. Contemporary Theories.* R. Palan, ed. London & New York: Routledge 1-18.

Palley, Thomas I. 1999. "International Finance and Global Deflation. There is an Alternative." In *Global Instability. The Political Economy of World Economic Governance.* J. Michie and J. G. Smith, eds. London & New York: Routledge.

Perraton, Jonathan. 2001. The global economy; myths and realities. *Cambridge Journal of Economics* 25:669-684.

Piore, Michael J. 2001. The emergent role of social intermediaries in the new economy. *Annals of Public and Cooperative Economics* 72.3:339-350.

Powell, Walter W. and Smith-Doerr, Laurel. 1994. "Networks and Economic Life." In *The Handbook of Economic Sociology.* N. J. Smelser and R. Swedberg, eds, Princeton & New York: Princeton University Press and Russell Sage Foundation.

Pratt, Andy. 1997. "The Emerging Shape and Form of Innovation Networks and Institutions." In *Innovation, Networks and Learning Regions*? J. M.Simmie, ed. London, & Bristol (Penn.) : Jessica Kingsley Publ.

Redding, Stephen. 1996. The low-skill, low-quality trap: strategic complementarities between human capital and R&D. *The Economic Journal* 106:458-470.

Retallack, Simon. 2001. "The Environmental Cost of Economic Globalization." In *The Case Against the Global Economy. And for a Turn Towards Localization.* E. Goldsmith and J. Mander, eds. London: Earthscan.

Rodrik, Dani, 1997. *Has Globalization Gone Too Far?* Washington: Institute for International Economy.

Ruigrok, Winfried and Rob van Tulder, 1995. *The Logic of International Restructuring.* London, & New York: Routledge.

Ruys, Pieter H. M. 2000. "Service-Specific Governance Regimes." Paper presented at the Annual Conference of the International Society for New Institutional Economics. Tuebingen, Germany.

Rycroft, Robert W. and Don E, Kash,. 1999. *The Complexity Challenge. Technological Innovation for the 21st Century.* London, & New York: Pinter.

Saxenian, Annalee. 1994. *Regional Advantage. Culture and Competition in Silicon Valley and Route 128.* Cambridge (Mass.) & London: Harvard University Press.

Schoukens, Paul and Laurence Carmichael, 2001. "Social Exclusion in Europe: Testing the Limits of European Integration." In *Social Exclusion and European Policy.* D. G. Mayes J. Berghman and R. Salais. Cheltenham, eds. UK & Northampton US: Edward Elgar.

Sinn, Hans-Werner. 1997. The selection principle and market failure in systems competition. *Journal of Public Economics* 66: 247-274.

Standing, Guy. 2001. "Global Flexibility: Economic Integration, Social Disintegration?" In *Globalization, Institutions and Social Cohesion.* M. Franzini, M. and F. R. Pizzuti, eds. Berlin, Heidelberg, & New York: Springer .

Sugden, Roger, 1996. "Multinational Economies and the Law of Uneven Development." Occasional Papers in Industrial Strategy, No. 37, Research Center for Industrial Strategy. The University of Birmingham.

Tool, Marc R. [1979] 2001. *The Discretionary Economy: A Normative Theory of Political Economy.* Santa Monica (CA): Goodyear Publ. Co.

———. 1994. "Instrumental Value Theory." In *The Elgar Companion to Institutional and Evolutionary Economics.* G. M. Hodgson, W. J. Samuels and M. R. Tool, eds. Aldershot UK & Brookfield US: Edward Elgar. 1:406-412.

Veblen, Thorstein B. [1904] 1975. *The Theory of Business Enterprise.* Clifton, NJ: Augustus M. Kelley.

Unger, Brigitte, and Frans van Waarden (ed.s). 1995. *Convergence or Diversity? Internationalization and Economic Policy Response.* Aldershot, UK & Brookfield, US:Avebury.

Wallach, Lori, 2001. "The World Trade Organization's Five-Year Record: Seattle In Context." In *The Case Against the Global Economy. And for a Turn Towards Localization.* E. Goldsmith and J. Mander, eds. London:

Weiler, Stephan, Eric Scorsone, and Madeleine Pullman. 2000. Information linkages in local economic development. *Growth and Change* 367-384.

Williams, Karel. 2000. From shareholder value to present-day capitalism. *Economy and Society* 29:1:1-12.

Wilson, J. D. 1996. "Capital Mobility and Environmental Standards: Is there a TheoreticalBasis for a Race to the Bottom?" In J. Bhagwati, R.E. Hudec, eds. *Fair Trade And Harmonisation: Prerequisites for Free Trade?*, Cambridge (MA):World Bank. 2000. *World Development Report: 2000-2001.* New York: Oxford University.

Yu, Tony F. L. 2000. A new perspective on the role of the government in development.Coordination under uncertainty. *International Journal of Social Economics* 27: 994-1012.

# 19

# RECENT TENDENCIES IN DEVELOPMENT ECONOMICS: BRINGING INSTITUTIONS BACK IN?

James M. Cypher

*No area of economics has experienced as many abrupt changes in its leading paradigm since World War II as has economic development. The twists and turns in development economics have had profound implications for development policy (Adelman 2001, 103).*

*. . . .the development debate . . . has cycled. First institutions and culture explained everything, then were irrelevant, then were explicable themselves and efficiency enhancing, then they [were] partially inexplicable and possibly even dysfunctional, and finally now there is a recognition that institutions, rather than being efficiency promoting and filling in the gaps resulting from market failures, are possibly even impediments to efficiency as they seek to preserve existing inequalities and power relationships (Stiglitz 2000, 8-9).*

## INTRODUCTION[1]

This chapter critically analyzes some major recent analytical tendencies in development economics. In particular, the focus will be on key points of contention within the field of study as expressed through the writings of a number of prominent contributors. Most particularly, this chapter will concentrate on the role of institutions and institutional innovation in the context of development. After numerous complex twists and turns, development economics—as currently practiced by many, but not all—has returned to its "big picture" roots as expressed in the research of the "pioneers of development." The pioneers—among them Paul Rosenstein-Rodan, Gunner Myrdal, Ragnar Nurkse, Albert Hisrchman, and W. A. Lewis—gained prominence in the early postwar years with their broad, generalized, and often Keynesian approach to development issues (Cypher and Dietz 1997, Ch 5).

## THE 1970s, 1980s, 1990S: FOLLOWING THE TWISTS AND TURNS

By the late 1970s, however, a new dynamic dominated the field: Building on the work of P.T. Bauer, Hla Myint and Ian Little, writers such as Deepack Lal and Anne Krueger (currently First Deputy Managing Director of the International Monetary Fund—the number two position) commenced a neoliberal counter-revolution which resonated in the developmental institutions such as the International Monetary Fund (IMF) and the World Bank (Cypher and Dietz 1997, Ch. 7). Their critique of the "statist" predilections of the "pioneers" and their belief that states in general in developing nations were largely "predatory," entities incapable of countering "rent seeking" clients—in fact willingly facilitating such rent-seeking, while engaging in or fostering "directly unproductive activities" (DUP)—led them to advocate a wholesale reduction in the quantitative and qualitative purview of the state. By the mid-1980s the scathing attacks of the neoliberals had crystallized into John Williamson's "Washington Consensus" which signified a confluence of opinion among the IMF, the World Bank, The Agency for International Development (AID), the Interamerican Development Bank (IDB), influential conservative think-tanks (such as the Cato Institute and the Heritage Foundation) and the US Treasury and State Departments regarding the proper course for all developing nations to pursue: an open capital account, liberalization of foreign trade, elimination of all restrictions regarding Direct Foreign Investment, free-fluctuating foreign exchange rates (or currency boards or dollarization), privatization of parastate firms, imposition of "flexible" labor market rules, shredding or elimination of the social safety net (softened somewhat in the 1990s as crises have erupted), abandonment of both full-employment fiscal and monetary policy, along with industrial policies, etc. (Cypher 1998; Williamson 1998).

By the mid-1990s, however, the neoliberal approach had created its own critics, some launching their attacks from the highest reaches of the World Bank—such as Joseph Stiglitz—Chief Economist of the World Bank—and Ravi Kanbur (Wade 2001). Undeterred by the mounting criticism of neoliberalism, the IMF and the World Bank reemphasized their neoclassical premises: Throughout the 1980s and well into the 90s, the IMF/WB had focused on "structural adjustment" policies to bring borrowing nations into compliance with the precepts of the Washington Consensus. Structural adjustment lending, commonly entailing "cross conditionality" between the IMF (which lent largely within a one-three year time frame) and the World

Bank (which often extended "concessional" below market loans for intermediate periods) focused not on short-term balance of payments problems, or long term infrastructure programs, but rather on *strategies* such as a new trade or currency regime, or a new set of parameters for fiscal budgeting. As evidence mounted in the 1990s that these new and highly interventionary policy initiatives were not serving to overcome fundamental problems of development, attention shifted toward the perceived need for *institutional change.* Thus, we find the beginnings of *second stage structural adjustment programs* beginning in the mid-90s, pushing the IMF/WB and other elements of the Washington Consensus into what is essentially "nation (re)building." The distinction between first stage structural adjustment programs (SAPs) and those of the second stage is, at the margin, somewhat vague: The original SAPs were a decidedly quantum leap upward in interventionary scale, with the IMF/WB dramatically shifting their role to engage in policy matters heretofore thought to be purely the purview of sovereign nations. While risking over generalization, it could be argued that the first stage SAPs were essentially focused on "getting the fundamentals right"—such as the rate of inflation, the magnitude of the trade deficit, the growth rate of GDP, the policy on tariffs, the exchange rate, the size of the government's annual budgetary deficit, openness regarding Direct Foreign Investment, and so on. The goal was twofold: (1) "get prices right"—eliminate subsidies and tariffs and other "distortions" to the free market ideal—and (2) "get policies right"—eliminating "populist" full-employment policies and countercyclical policies along with industrial policies—such as the support for credit allocation from state-owned development banks.

In contrast, second stage SAPs seek to penetrate to the core of developing societies, setting the basis for a new "path" of development (Cypher 1997): "New" institutional economists (NIE), such as Douglas North (1998), have emphasized the importance of "path dependence"—history matters. Present outcomes are the result of past decisions, past events, inculcated cultural practices, and institutions built, nurtured and evolved from decades or centuries past, according to the theory of "path dependence". Widespread acceptance of the theory of "path dependence" at the IMF/WB has led to an attempt to persuade developing nations to "get a new history" through a radical restructuring of institutions in developing nations. Institutions must be "market friendly"—meaning, essentially, that institutions are needed only to the degree that they contribute to the creation of a neoclassical model of a competitive market economy. "Getting a new history" demands the euthanasia of institutional structures which are seen to inhibit the functioning of "free" markets. On a practical, or applied, level what this may mean has been left vague—in fact, even the meaning of the term "institution" is treated vaguely in recent, representative, compendiums published by the World Bank and the International Economic Association (Meier and Stiglitz 2001; Haymi and Aoki 1998). Nevertheless, it is now argued by many mainstream development economists that the missing factor, what Irma Adelman terms *the* "X-factor," is an institutional foundation/structure conducive to the achievement of economic development (Adelman 2001).

The present orientation within the field of development economics arises from many, complex factors—among them should be mentioned at least three pivotal events: First, the meltdown of the Mexican economy in 1994/95 entailed the failure of the most concerted combined effort by the IMF/WB—of loans extended, advice proffered (and followed), guided by the steering mechanism of "surveillance" conducted by the IMF. Mexico's nearly non-stop tutelage by the IMF/WB began in earnest in 1982 with the outbreak of the debt crisis and culminated in the six-year presidential term of Carlos Salinas (1988-1994). Mexico had long been portrayed as a model of economic reform by the US government, the Fund and the World Bank as it entered the vortex of forces which drove the nation to the worst economic collapse since the Great Depression in late 1994. Never had the IMF/WB had a more dutiful pupil than Carlos Salinas—whose all-powerful political party, the PRI, ensured that the policies pursued by the IMF/WB were faithfully executed.

Second, the Asian Crisis of 1997 shattered the IMF/WB myth that openness to foreign trade, and an export-led development strategy were the keys to ascendance from underdevelopment. In the aftermath of the Asian rupture the IMF/WB sought valiantly to portray the East Asian nations as victims of their own, unique brand of "crony capitalism." But to trained observers this stance was, at best, unconvincing, as had been the IMF/WB's assertion that the success of the Asian "tigers" was attributable to their compliance with the neoclassical model of competitive free market capitalism (Evans 1998; Akyuz, Chang and Kozul-Wright 1998; Wade and Veneroso, 1998; Chang 2000).

Third, the Russian debt default/crisis of 1998 finally dissuaded many at the IMF/WB of their embrace of "shock treatment" as a means to "transition" former Soviet states to neoclassical competitive free market capitalism.

There is no one common thread running through these three events, and all were at first depicted as arising from superficial causes: Mexico's case was attributed to an over-valued exchange rate, not to more determinate structural causes (Cypher 1996). Asia's was attributed to "crony capitalism" but it was, in fact, primarily a result of both an indiscriminate opening of the capital account (at the behest of the IMF/WB) and a Minsky-like explosion of debt creation—an *endogenous* financial reality of contemporary capitalism. Meanwhile, in Russia, the favorite scapegoat was "gangster capitalism;" but this crisis actually arose as a result of IMF/WB engineered "asset stripping" programs which they funded and supported under the heading of "privatization."

Thus, while there was no common thread—following Irma Adelman's hypothesis that development economics has long followed a tendency to seek one single cause (constraint "X") as the determining factor to be overcome in remedying underdevelopment—some orthodox development economists began to place primary emphasis on the need to create/transform/alter *institutions* (Adelman 2001, 104). Their sense of immediacy—in terms of support for a new central thrust in development economics—did not merely appear as a result of the major failures in development policy traceable to the Mexican, Asian and Russian crises of the 1990s. Aggregate data, too, revealed some alarming tendencies which cause all but the most dogmatic to reflect on their enthusiasm for the Washington Consensus: A annual United Nations Development Program publication, *The Human Development Report* had revealed in 1996 that after decades of development policymaking the global share of income accruing to the bottom 20 percent of the world's population had fallen from 2.3 percent in the mid-1960s to only 1.4 percent in the mid-1990s, while during the same time period the share of the top 20 percent had risen spectacularly from 70 percent of global income to 85 percent (Yusuf and Stiglitz 2001, 249). Table I, below, records the dramatic failure of the neoliberal era to deliver on its promises of a growth explosion ("unleashing capitalism") as a result of high IMF 'conditionality' and aggressive SAPs imposed across a broad swath of developing nations in the 1980-1998 period:

*Table I*: Median Unweighted and Weighted Growth in GDP Per Capita
(percent per year—inflation adjusted real growth)

| Unweighted | Developed Nations | Developing Nations |
|---|---|---|
| 1960-1979 | 3.4 | 2.5 |
| 1980-1998 | 1.8 | 0.0 |
| Weighted | ___ | 0.8 |

Sources: William Easterly, "The Lost Decades: Explaining Developing Countries' Stagnation," 1980-98, typescript, World Bank, January 2000. Branko Milanovic, "True World Income Distribution 1988 and 1993."Policy Research Paper 2244, Development Research Group, World Bank, November 1999.

The "weighted" inclusion calibrates the median rate of growth in countries' per capita GDP growth with regard to population size. Thus, this method shows a higher median growth rate for developing nations (0.8 vs 0.0) due to the relatively strong performance of China and India—nations with populations above one billion. China's per capita growth, at 6.3 percent in the 1988-99 period, and India's, at 4.9 percent, are remarkable exceptions to the two "lost decades" under neoliberal policymaking (World Bank 2000, 274). What is most remarkable, however, is the fact that neither China nor India are examples of successful applications of neoliberal/neoclassical policymaking. China has continued to utilize a unique combination of central planning and the market, while India has been pressed since 1991 to adopt the Washington Consensus, but has failed to do so. All in all, objective observers—faced with the data in Table I—are forced to question the efficacy of the simple nostrums of neoclassical development theory, and this has opened the way to the new focus on institutions.

## INSTITUTIONS, WHICH INSTITUTIONS? THE IDEOLOGICAL AND EMPIRICAL DEBATE

While it seems true that there has never been so much emphasis on institutions as one finds today (save in the late 1940s and early 1950s when the "pioneers" of development offered their many, and varied, theoretical formulations of underdevelopment) the underlying methodological homogeneity of the pioneers is not to be found among current practitioners of orthodox development economics. Thus a debate presently rages over how institutions should be altered; which—if any—institutions are functional in terms of fostering development; and how—if at all—the current record of development in many key nations should be understood within the context of their institutional composition. What can be said, without great fear of contradiction, is that the preeminent development institutions are uncertain as to how they should respond to the proposition which they now espouse: institutions matter. There is unanimity, however, in terms of acceptance of the idea that troubled, poor nations cannot exit from their development dilemmas simply through the adoption of accepted practices and conventional norms regarding the application of macroeconomic policy to problems of trade, tariffs, taxation, state budgeting, central bank stabilization, and so on. "Getting prices right;" are necessary but very far from sufficient conditions. Nations must go much further than ever before; they must participate in engineering an institutional transformation. Joseph Stiglitz, then a special advisor to the World Bank, underscored this point:

> Besides ensuring that the state at the national level performs its own functions well, the state also has a role to play in helping to alter other institutions in a country. Once it is recognized that the institutional arrangements in a society might not be efficiency enhancing, but rather power and wealth preserving, then a new rationale for collective action arises: not just to correct market failures, but to alter non-market institutional arrangements that impede efficiency and increase inequality. These institutional arrangements are sometimes, but not always, creatures of political processes . . . . (Stiglitz 2000, 8)

States, according to Stiglitz, have a vast role to play in "provid[ing] the institutional infrastructure required for a market economy" (Stiglitz 2000, 8).

But how, and to what end? Addressing this question is no simple matter. In attempting to do so, it will become clear that by far the most detailed and creative work on this matter of the role of institutions in development has been undertaken by an enterprising and creative group of heterodox economists, sociologists and political scientists, none of whom consciously employs the language and method of the "original" institutional economics (OIE), but all of whom operate within the broad scope and purview of institutional economics. While it is somewhat simplistic to do so, one can view the dispute over the role of institutions in development as threefold, as both Peter Evans and Stiglitz have emphasized (Evans 1998, 67; Hellman, Murdock and Stiglitz 1998, 255-256): 1. The Market-Friendly Perspective; 2. The Market Enhancing View; 3. The Developmental State Approach. The market-friendly perspective fits comfortably within the conservative confines of the neoliberal/neoclassical paradigm, while the market enhancing view insists that current development dilemmas have their roots in a failure of collective action. Forward movement in the field of development will demand acceptance that the state and the market are coequal, complimentary institutions. Finally, the developmental state approach breaks with the market-focused view, while simultaneously rejecting the idea of the state as a demiurge. The market, here, is an embedded institution—embedded in a broad range of social forces and institutions. While being but one broad institution, the "state" is viewed as the preeminent coordinator and creator of the development process. In the following sections of this chapter a deeper analysis of the role of the state as the preeminent institution, and the dispute surrounding the role of the state, is offered.

## THE MARKET FRIENDLY PERSPECTIVE

The neoliberal/neoclassical position of orthodox development economics regarding the state—and the many institutions which might be linked to or derived from state policy—is that the government's role should be limited to ensuring both property rights and competition. At the same time, it is presumed that a greater role for the state cannot be allowed because, *a priori,* all further state "intervention" will introduce "distortion" from the perfectly-functioning competitive model, thereby introducing "inefficiencies". This perspective is derived from the famous Arrow-Debreau model of competitive general equilibrium which introduces numerous assumptions regarding the behavior of individuals and markets—assumptions which are broadly inappropriate for a developing nation which has not yet reached the capitalist mode of production and that exists in a twilight of social and economic forces which could be described as neo-feudal/neo-capitalist. Kenneth Arrow and Gerard Debreau were silent on the role of institutions in their competitive equilibrium model, but it can be safely inferred that they assumed a splendid set of institutions—all needed to make their flawless model of competitive equilibrium determinate. In any case, their silence on the matter has been shared by staunch neoclassicals. Any careful analysis of the broad range of institutions needed to make possible such a competitive equilibrium, however, would quickly demonstrate the improbability of *any* developing nation meeting the minimal requirements assumed. For example, a monetized economy would necessitate a very complex, institutionally embedded, modern financial system including functioning deposit banks, investment banks, a efficient method of raising long term capital, a short-term capital market, a broad-based market for corporate stock shares and, unless foreign trade is ruled out by assumption, a complex set of efficient institutions sufficient to meet the challenge of the foreign exchange markets along with the financing needed to fund current account and capital account transactions, as well as a central bank with a competent, merit-based technocratic professional cadre operating with sufficient autonomy from the central government. Here we have introduced but one complex of institutions—the financial system. As any practitioner of development policy will likely affirm, the *absence of many* of the institutions needed to finance a perfectly competitive market society is the *pervasive reality* throughout most of the developing regions. But, of course, this is only the beginning of a long list of institutions needed to meet the conditions of the fictitious economy devised by Arrow and Debreau.

Undeterred, neoclassicals have seized upon the "Solow model" of growth to affirm that development is merely a process of adding more, and better capital, and more and better labor to a "production function" which will then provide the means for "growth convergence" with the formerly poor developing nation actually catching-up to the developed nations in terms of per capita output—institutions are assumed to be functional, as in the case of the Arrow-Debreau model (Cypher and Dietz 1997, 125-127).

Much of the work of the "pioneers" of development built upon market failures—externalities, dualism, increasing returns, vicious and virtuous circles, etc. For some of the pioneers underdeveloped nations were in general equilibrium—a low level trap. In most of the work of the "pioneers", ubiquitous market failures could be resolved only through creative public policy. (Careful students of Colonial policy might find that many such "market failures" were the results of conscious institutional policy making by the then dominant powers—a matter that received too little attention from the "pioneers".) Critics of the work of the "pioneers" such as Myint, Bauer, Little and Krueger were adamant in their stress of "government failures" which they saw as inevitably arising from nearly all state "interventions." Most widely cited in this regard was Krueger's writing on "rent seeking" and "directly unproductive activities" (DUP)—which conjures an image of an inevitable predatory state apparatus emerging, should a developing nation fail to follow the strictures of the Arrow-Debreau/Solow construct (Krueger 1974, 1993).

In the early 1990s the World Bank returned to the theme of the role of state-nurtured institutions within the development process with their publication of *The East Asian Miracle: Economic Growth and Public Policy* (World Bank 1993). In this study the Bank was forced to take a step back from its embrace of the "rent seeking" hypothesis and acknowledge that industrial policy had played a role in the success of the Asian tigers. However, the Bank took great pains to argue that the distinguishing characteristic of East Asia's "interventions" was their "market-friendly" nature. Thus, it was argued, East Asia's success was essentially premised on "getting the basics right," including controlling inflation, adopting competitive exchange rates, and maintaining macroeconomic stability, while the main thrust of the report sought to assert that the underlying success was due to heavy and sustained infrastructure outlays, and above all a strong commitment to education. Most important was the Bank's acknowledgement that the Asian tigers had created new institutions through their industrial policies which allowed for a highly functional relationship to develop between private sector firms and government bureaus thereby driving investment forward at tremendous pace. This was a great concession to those who had long maintained that the rapidly developing Asian nations were not merely passively following a market-induced export-led model of development. Still, however, the Bank sought (unsuccessfully) to underplay the centrality of industrial policy, awkwardly insisting that in any case the

Asian experience could not be duplicated in the future, and that the real lessons to be learned were that Asia's limited interventions all derived from a consistent inner-logic—they were "market friendly," and quite limited in scope.

In recent years, as the emphasis on institutions among leading orthodox development economists has increased, Douglas North's work has been widely, and approvingly, cited. At the International Economics Association conference, North presided—offering a "summary evaluation" (North 1998). The World Bank's 1999 conference on "the Future of Development Economics" included the participation of 36 luminaries in the field, among them five Nobel Prize Laureates—most prominent of which was North. North has been typified by Geoffrery Hodgson as a proponent of "orthodox neoclassical theory, particularly in the adoption of standard, mechanical versions of maximizing rationality" (Hodgson 1994, 399). North's work, nonetheless, was repeatedly and positively cited by participants of the two conferences. And, there can be little doubt that North, whose experience with developing nations seems to be non-existent—as is the case for far too many of the major orthodox development economists—perceives development to be driven by the maximizing goals of individuals working successfully through the market, insofar as they are generally unimpeded by the "distortions" of government. North begrudgingly confirmed the *possibility* of effective and limited state interventions in institution building, but he was quick to evoke the work of Krueger (1974; 1993)—yes, market failures *could* be remedied by interventions, but then such interventions might well result in government failures, potentially larger than the market failures that prompted the intervention (North 1998, 553-554).

But, to take a case in point, a review of what is known regarding a pet project of the "market friendly" school—privatization—directly disconfirms the tenets of Krueger, North and many others. Joseph Stiglitz was able to examine a broad cross section of research examining the efficacy of "first stage" privatizations. His conclusion are suggestive of the probable results of currently ongoing "market friendly" second stage structural adjustment programs which, like the privatizations, seek structural change of a nation's institutions:

> I can easily point to a model for [institutional] change that does not work: that [is the] underlying strategies of the [IMF/WB] in promoting privatization. A [IMF or WB] mission would go to the country, explain the virtues of privatization and in particular how privatization would increase efficiency and stem the corruption that was bleeding the country

> Of course, in reality privatization allows corrupt government officials to steal not just a fraction of today's rents (profits), but a fraction of (the present discounted value) of all future rents . . . .
>
> There are some state enterprises, however, that have been as or more productive than corresponding private firms. Advocates of privatization treated such success cases as an aberration, and presumed it would be easier to privatize than reform, that is to figure out what made the successful state enterprises productive, and apply those lessons more broadly (Stiglitz 2000, 16).

Unlike other fields of economic analysis, the role of the World Bank in setting the research agenda and providing a central focus to research through its annual publication of the Bank's *World Development Report* (WDR) is unparalleled. Robert Wade describes the creation of the WDR in the following terms:

> The *World Development Report* published annually is the Bank's flagship publication. Each number takes a theme and presents the Bank's conclusion on it . . . . The WDR is a political document in the sense that as the Bank's flagship, its message must reflect the ideological preferences of key constituencies and not offend them too much; but the message must also be backed by empirical evidence and made to look "technical."
>
> The core budget ranges from $3.5 to $5 million, handsomely supplemented from trust funds and foundations. Each WDR has a print run of at least 50,000 in English, some have gone over 100,000, and smaller numbers are translated into seven languages. (Wade 2001, 1435-1436).

Given this, it is of central interest to note that the WDR for 2002 is entitled *Building Institutions for Markets.* The report focuses on three areas: Firms, Government and Society. Aside from an insistence that more "openness" to foreign trade will both enhance economic growth and build strong pro-market institutions—a point largely refuted by Dani Rodrik's important study *Making Openness Work*—the Bank's study is a loosely assembled pastiche of anecdotes and vague discourses on the need to build institutions which have been previously defined in North's terms (Rodrik 1999).

Uppermost in the matters addressed in the WDR for 2002 is that "policymakers building institutions first need to assess what is inhibiting market development" (World Bank 2002, 10). This unify theme—pursuing institutional change only to the degree that such change leads toward further development of competitive markets—is taken as an article of faith by the Bank, offered uncritically and with only offhand and often inappropriate justification through a very selective citation of research. Drawing directly on the work of North, institutions are defined merely as rules, norms of behavior, conventions and codes of conduct. Further following North, the main constraint to economic development is construed as high transaction costs which arise from unclearly defined property rights and low levels of competition. In the Bank's view, the task of development is one of building incentive compatible, "effective" institutions. The matter can be addressed most directly, argues the Bank, through containment and restriction of the role of the state to an essential "Night-Watchman State" keeping the rules of the competitive market and ensuring property rights (World Bank 2002, 3-8). Alert readers will note the Bank's predilection for highly inappropriate metaphors which are intended to bolster the "market friendly" approach of the text: For example, the improvements of the 12th Century Genoese traders and those of the 11th Century Maghribi traders are utilized to, apparently, shed light on appropriate policies that 21st Century nations should adopt. Obviously, given a near static level of technological change, nations could *only* improve their efficiency by dropping transaction costs—which could come through improved trading practices. But, this begs the question: Are poor nations underdeveloped because they have not sought out every opportunity to cut transaction costs in trade (or elsewhere)? Clearly, transaction costs in a less developed nation can be quite high, and lowering some of these costs could well be a priority. But the transaction cost approach, so beloved by the New Institutionalists, actually (if implicitly) assumes away the development dilemma. Development, at least in the view of the "original" institutional economics (OIE) occurs when the society undertakes continual improvements in the *process of production* through the adoption of improved technological processes or enhanced forms of organization. One-off improvements could come from dropping transaction costs, but then what? For a society to successfully engage in development an ongoing, endogenous process of productivity enhancing change must occur. Rationalizing trade practices cannot cause development, nor did the Genoese traders ever rise above the status of clever traders—a temporary status eroded by the shift of trade patterns to the Atlantic and away from the Mediterranean after 1500.

The strongest and most consistent argument advance by the WDR of 2002 is that development hinges on the willingness to "open" less developed nations to trade. Here the Bank does not look back to the history of Latin

America in the 19th Century. Yet, throughout much of the 19th Century Latin America was as "open" as any region in the world. The price of manufactures fell and Latin America imported them. The price of raw materials rose, and Latin America became increasingly specialized in the export of a wide range of primary products and agricultural goods. The end result of this "openness" and "specialization" was that Latin America fell victim to global overproduction in the commodities markets, which was speeded by the widespread innovations in synthetics that served as substitutes for many primary products. Failing to build its productive base and enhance its productivity levels through investment, Latin America fell behind—the gap between the per capita income of Latin America and the advance industrial nations widen in the closing decades of the 19th Century (Bulmer-Thomas, 1994, 46-154). "Openness" as advocated by the Bank will not induce development, because a market-led economy, such as those built in Latin America, will not ensure a "export-investment nexus." That is, a society must have some linkage between the *sphere of trade* and the *sphere of production.* As the research of Alice Amsden shows (to be discussed below) successful nations have, in fact, selectively opened to foreign trade, while utilizing adept forms of state intervention to create and nurture a "export-investment nexus." As well trained neoclassicals, the Bank's many economists have no grasp of the fundamental role that technological dynamism must play in the development process. Their theorizing remains locked in the pre-industrial *sphere of trade (or circulation).* The Bank foresees broad effects occurring merely by opening a nation to trade: Nations will learn about new technologies and perhaps acquire new organizational/managerial structures. Even, we are told, "policymakers can import whole aspects of the institutional system: laws, regulations and enforcement systems" (World Bank 2002, 18). And, of course, there was a time when developing nations did just that—this time period was known as Colonialism. A brief study of this historical period will show that with few, highly unusual exceptions, Colonialism forced upon the developing regions inappropriate and unassimilated institutions that had been regarded as implicitly "superior" to those that had evolved in the Colonies (Cypher and Dietz 1997, Ch 3).

Anxious to provide Medieval historical examples, the Bank can selectively forget Colonialism and the long history of Latin America's experiment with "openness." History as a method of verification of hypotheses is used in a highly selective manner by the Bank. The Bank does caution readers of the WDR of 2002 that the elixir of openness could be thwarted by government regulations, particularly those that imposed constraints on the free operation of factor markets—such as labor laws and labor unions. As an antidote, the Bank cites with approval the more aggressive practices of some Indian employers who have recently become "adept at circumventing labor market regulations and resisting union pressure" through the use of, for example, lockouts of their employees (World Bank 2002, 137). The Bank does acknowledge that the opening of a nation to trade may cause temporary dislocations. Begging the question, the Bank then proceeds to state that in the first instance adjustment to trade's dislocation effects can best be addressed by further liberalization of the labor markets (World Bank 2002, 143). In essence, then, should a rapid opening to trade undermine key sectors of a developing nations economy, thereby creating significant unemployment the first and best and most "market friendly" remedy would be to eviscerate whatever labor laws exist in a developing nation and let the wage level fall, perhaps to subsistence or below.

While the Bank cites much research to support its views on the necessary direction of institutional change, and while most of the cited research has been sponsored by the Bank, Dain Rodrik's widely-cited study of the issues posed by the Bank regarding the centrality of trade openness to the development process received no acknowledgement. Yet Rodrik has completed several econometric studies which clearly defy the Bank's approach. One of his major findings is that there is *no* evidence that exporters yield positive externalities for other firms. Thus, concludes Rodrik "there is no economic argument for government policies that favor export activity" (Rodrik 1999, 37). Further, "openness will likely exert pressures that widen income and wealth disparities" and "will leave countries vulnerable to external shocks. . ." (Rodrik 1999, 13-14). Summing up his broad empirical studies he finds: "The evidence is clear: although countries that grow fast tend to experience rising export-GDP ratios, the reverse is not true in general" (Rodrik 1999, 33). Merely opening, as urged by the Bank, along with tighter definitions of property rights and a freer reign for the market, will not speed development. More probably, it will retard development. At minimum, then, institutional change designed to promote development must be substantially different from that advocated by the "market friendly" approach.

## THE MARKET ENHANCING APPROACH

As Chief Economist of the World Bank, Joseph Stiglitz had ample opportunity to reflect on the "market friendly" view, and at the 1999 World Bank conference he further enraged his critics by articulating his contempt for the prevailing IMF/WB acceptance of the neoclassical model of development.[2] Calling for a wholesale reorientation of World Bank research to be focused on institutions and institutional change—a theme widely echoed by many conference participants—rejecting the "fundamentals" approach and advocating what he termed "modern economic theory," Stiglitz blasted neoclassicals, and proponents of the Public Choice theory of the state (such as Krueger):

> Neoclassical theory contends that the particular set of institutions in an economy does not matter . . . . History does not matter. Not even the distribution of wealth matters if one is interested solely in efficiency . . . . And in leaving out institutions, history and distributional considerations, neoclassical economics leaves out the heart of development economics. Modern economic theory argues that the fundamentals are not the only deep determinates of economic outcomes.
>
> Neoclassical theorists could not, of course, turn a blind eye to the fact that the kind of [Solow model-based] convergence predicted by theory was not occurring, and thus they had to look to some "outside" intervention. *Government failures provide an easy way out* . . . . Many versions of such theories are inherently unsatisfactory. . . .the "government-induced distortion" theory of underdevelopment does not do well in explaining key aspects of the development process (Hoff and Stiglitz 2000, 390-391).

While the "market friendly" view claims that laissez faire competitive markets are inherently efficient, the "market enhancing" approach is built upon the premise of the existence within developing nations of pervasive market failures that must be addressed through creative and evolutionary institution building. Rather than a minimalist government, the "market enhancing" view of these advocates of institutionalism in the field of development economics suggests a government actively involved in facilitating the efficient functioning of markets. As an advocate of this perspective, Stiglitz and his associates propose creative bank regulations, promotion of joint state-private research consortiums, market promotion, government-business coordination councils, and standard settings (Hellman, Murdock and Stiglitz 1998). But they also insist that *control* of economic activity remains with the private sector, while an activist state must be employed to foster development as a *complement* to the private sector—a view that many "original" institutional economists (OIE) have long held, apparently unknown to these self-described proponents of "*modern* economic theory."

Peter Evans argues that the "market enhancing" approach has emphasized the "profit-investment nexus" devising policies that ensure that highly profitable conditions result in economic growth through recurring cycles of profitability—investment—higher profit—greater investment. This virtuous circle cannot be assumed in developing nations, where the cycle is often profitability and speculation in real estate, or profitability and capital flight. To achieve the virtuous nexus, Evans argues (based on East Asian experience) that "a combination of subsidies and selective protection against external competition is the first step" (Evans 1998, 67). Here it can be seen that the "market enhancing" approach challenges the underlying dogma of the IMF/WB Washington Consensus model; that is, that openness, i.e. free trade based in static comparative advantage, is *the* key to development and convergence.

In terms of versatility and creativity Dani Rodrik's research offers the best, and by far the clearest, exposition of the "market enhancing" approach. Rodrik's contribution to the contemporary literature of development has been massive, and cannot be adequately summarized here. While Stiglitz's work demonstrates his deep grasp of economic theory and his creative insights which have pushed a body of theory to new and higher levels, Rodrik is a very convincing econometrician who willingly challenges many of the dogmatically-held but empirically unsupported views of orthodox IMF/WB economic analysis. Here a survey of Rodrik's work will be restricted to his contribution to the International Economic Association conference of 1998 and to a World Bank conference paper written in 2000, entitled "Development Strategies for the Next Century" (Rodrik 2000).

The prevailing view of the causes of economic stagnation and decline in developing nations, in the orthodox perspective, is that these nations failed to allow free market forces to operate, while constructing a regime utilizing a combination of state intervention—known generally as Import Substitution Industrialization policies (ISI)—and markets. According to the IMF/WB, nations that employed ISI, but were open to foreign trade, or used ISI in a more "market friendly" way, did better than other nations. Rodrik rejects these claims as a misspecification of the issue, showing that even within a sample of the E. Asian economies one can use an analysis centering on institutions to show why some of these economies achieved growth levels much higher than others. Thus, the issue is not state intervention vs. market, but rather strong institutions vs. fragmented institutions. Societies with strong institutions have higher levels of education per capita and less ethnolinguistic political and social fragmentation. Additional indicators of *institutional quality* are measured by Rodrik as a function of four variables: (1) The quality of the bureaucracy, with nations scored higher on the basis of expertise, autonomy from the private sector, efficiency of government service and superior modes of recruitment. (2) The rule of law, defined in terms of strong courts and orderly succession of political power. (3) Risk of appropriation. (4) Repudiation of contracts by government, or postponement of payment of obligations. In an econometric test of eight Asian nations, Rodrik is able to show very high correlations between his key "institutional" variables and the growth of productivity (Rodrik 1998, 91). Thus, even among high-performing Asian nations, those nations which exhibit the strongest institutional structures perform better. The inference, then, is that—rather than the degree of openness, or the willingness to pursue 'market friendly" policies—a key variable assumed by the Washington Consensus to be the underlying cause of economic backwardness, the state, can in fact be a determinate factor in achieving high growth.

For Rodrik the evidence clearly points to the efficacy of ISI policies—a position of apostasy—in the 1940-1970 period. When nations driven by strong ISI policies began to experience trouble in the late 1970s this was not due to excessive state intervention, but rather to factors such as the oil price spikes, monetarist policies that rapidly drove global real interest rates to unexpected heights and a general global slowdown which constrained the exports of the developing nations. At that juncture some developing nations did much better than others—those that had strong institutions, particularly in E. Asia, weathered the downdrafts of the early 1980s and continued strongly to expand. Latin American nations, in contrast, experienced turbulence because they had deeper social divisions and weaker institutions which were incapable of adequate conflict management. Nations with strong institutions are able to manage macroeconomic shocks better, they are able to respond quicker with new strategies and policies. Those with weaker institutional structures will more likely enter into a period of protracted dispute, possibly escalating. Nations with a highly unequal distribution of income and wealth provide another indicator of a society that will likely encounter a "coordination problem"—a protracted period of dispute and disarray in response to a macroeconomic shock. In Rodrik's view, based upon an extensive body of research, the issue of growth after 1980 has little to do with a nation's openness to trade, the range of ISI policies, or the strategies and scope of government interventions (Rodrik 2000, 11). "The countries that got into trouble were those that could not manage openness, not those that were insufficiently open" (Rodrik 2000, 12). Meanwhile, under pressure from the IMB/WB to reform (fragment) their safety net—particularly through the privatization of their Social Security programs and/or health programs—throughout much of Latin America a sense of economic insecurity has grown, and with it a deepening resistance to and a "backlash" against IMF/WB structural adjustment programs has been nurtured.

Still, Rodrik notes that the IMF/WB has failed to grasp the real lessons of the "lost decades" of the 80s and 90s: The IMF/WB now seek "institutional reform" as the resolution of their own failed, ideologically driven, policies. "Hence, as it comes to be operationalized, the new view of development results in a racheting up of [IMF/WB] *conditionality* and a narrowing of the space within which policy can be conducted" (Rodrik 2000, 28). What then, according to the "new view", must be done? Rodrik points to the advocacy of "extreme convergence" whereby developing nations will be pressured to adopt US-style policies, and institutions—real and imagined. Thus, the "market friendly" dogma would encourage a range of neoliberal policies that have scant possibility of being enacted even in the pro-market US, such as full privatization of Social Security, elimination of protective labor legislation, etc. Rodrik argues that the crux issue here is that many developing nations *do* need extensive institutional reform, but that however reasonable might be some of the reforms advocated by the IMF/WB such reasonable new standards:

> Are the wedge with which a broader set of policy and institutional preferences—in favor of open capital accounts, deregulated labor markets, arms-length finance, American style corporate governance and hostility to industrial policies—are imparted on the recipient countries. [This] agenda focuses too much on institutional reforms needed to make the world safe for capital flows, and therefore necessarily diverts political capital and attention from institutional reforms in other areas. (Rodrik 2000, 30)

In the final analysis, then, the empirical research demonstrates the efficacy of the "market enhancing" approach, yet the dilemmas of the developing nations become even more acute as the IMF/WB (ignoring this research) seeks "institutionally centered" second stage structural adjustment programs designed to prioritize the globalization agenda of transnational corporate capital.

## THE DEVELOPMENTAL STATE

Well beyond the theoretical and epistemological parameters of the IMF/WB lies a body of well-documented research demonstrating the need for a set of institutions which are not merely "market enhancing." From the perspective of Developmental State theory the need for a set of institutions which guarantees functional collective action is not merely a coequal to the need for well-functioning markets in the pursuit of economic development. Using a framework which Thorstein B. Veblen ([1915] 1964; [1934] 1964) would have found highly relevant and in line with his research into the development of Germany and Japan, advocates of the developmental state argue that the state must be both a locus for a broad array of institutions *and* a means to directly spark and redirect the accumulation process. The relation between state and capital is not one of equality—the state has to have the means to discipline capital, and the capability of functioning entrepreneurially as a 'first mover' inaugurating new industries and sectors. Regarding a developing nation's policies toward openness, the state cannot accept static comparative advantage—it must be able to *recreate* comparative advantages as a nation climbs through stages of technological development. Here technology is viewed as an "institution" in that nations must pursue a technological policy—one that eventually leads them to technological autonomy. At its core, a developmental state must have the capacity for leadership vis-à-vis its relationship with capital—a juxtaposition which only can arise when the state has a highly trained, 'exceptional' bureaucracy at its command, and the means to guarantee compliance from capital in return for state-supported assistance, or preference, which has been proffered to foster national development.

Peter Evans' research in this area is perhaps the most detailed. His term *embedded autonomy* attempts to evoke an institutional structure wherein the state is *embedded* in social relations with the private sector—relations are "close" through joint management schemes, perhaps, or through meetings, panels, commissions, etc., which allow for a deep understanding by the relevant state bureaus of the needs and capabilities of the private sector. While a relationship of trust and mutual communication is essential, so equally, is *autonomy*—state bureaus, in their (1) promotion, (2) oversight and (3) regulation capacity cannot become *captured* by the private sector. For advocates of the development state theory it is the muscular, independent, entrepreneurial state to be found in particularly in Japan, Korea and Taiwan which opens the door to the possibility of rapid and sustained economic development. Yet, the state cannot demand mere "followership" from the private sector. The state needs to foster conditions whereby a "highly capable, coherent business community" is created and sustained (Evans 1998, 69).

The creation of a functioning bureaucracy leading and guiding the accumulation process does not necessitate the eradication of all mediocrity, mendacity and clientelism but rather is conditioned upon the insulation of key economic bureaus—this is the lesson of Asia's success, and it is transferable.

Another major proponent of the Developmental State is Alice Amsden. Her recent book, *The Rise of the Rest,* makes a resounding case for manufacturing as the core activity giving rise to development (Amsden 2001). But, the successful incorporation of the manufacturing sector is viewed, above all, as arising from new institutions put into motion through astute government development policies which hinge on the creation of a new control mechanism between government and the private sector—*the principle of reciprocity*.

Reciprocity is the link between government support and industrial performance. Development banks, in particular, used reciprocity to break the hold of family-based managerial cadres in top firms, insisting that support (tariffs, duty-free intermediate inputs, etc.) will occur only if qualified professionals are in control of firms. Nations "sneak ahead" if they rely on developmental banking (which imposes control mechanism to overcome governmental failure), local content management (forcing producers to sequentially rely on greater local content), selective exclusion (keeping some domestic markets closed to foreign firms/trade) and national firm formation (creating strong national firms with growing knowledge-based production capabilities). In this context sneaking ahead involves avoidance of the doctrines of the IMF and the World Bank regarding Direct Foreign Investment—DFI lags rather than leads waves of expansion of domestic investment. The foundational basis of capital formation and technological deepening comes in the first instance from public sector investment, and not from DFI.

Amsden's work is perhaps the most detailed effort yet to focus on the role of manufacturing in the process of development: Her study centers on "the rest"—those developing nations that did not *fall behind* the advanced nations in the last half-century. Included here are China, India, Indonesia, South Korea, Malaysia, Taiwan, Thailand, Argentina, Brazil, Chile, Mexico and Turkey. These nations produced 4.9 percent of world manufacturing in 1965, and 17.4 percent of it in 1995 (Amsden 2001, 2). They stood in stark contrast to other "developing" nations because: "countries without robust manufacturing experience tended to fall further behind, and the developing world became divided between those that were excluded from modern world industry and those that were redefining its terms" (Amsden 2001, 1-2).

Rejecting "new" institutional economists (OIE) emphasis on "transaction costs" as a core cause of underdevelopment, Amsden argues that the basic problem of development is "too few knowledge-based assets" not too little infrastructure or education. Knowledge, argues Amsden, is conceptual, firm-specific and proprietary, and most intensely created, utilized and supported through the growth of a manufacturing sector—"the heart of modern economic growth." (Amsden 2001, 3). The technological capabilities most instrumental in fostering the acquisition and development of this crucial component of the development process are: (1) *production capabilities,* (2) *project execution capabilities,* and (3) *innovation capabilities*.

Moving from a predominantly agricultural, backward, nation suffering from a shortage of skills to membership in "the rest" required nations to adopt an Industrial Policy centering on the principle of *reciprocity*—the state created a new institutional structure designed to minimize both market failure and government failure. Amsden shows that, predominantly, this was achieved through the shrewd utilization of "development banks" such as Mexico's Nacional Financiera and Brazil's BNDES, or through other means, such as entry restrictions on foreign capital, tariff protection, subsidized credit, duty exemptions for machinery imports, and so on. As important as they have proven to have been, the development banks were only part of a much larger and much criticized system known as Import Substitution Industrialization (ISI). ISI when it worked—which was very often, in spite of the constant criticism which orthodox economists have levied against it—demanded in exchange for some favorable treatment in specific industrial sectors that these sectors would achieve specific *performance standards* such as the achievement of an efficient scale of production or the employment of non-familial professionals in top positions in key firms. While acknowledging that corruption was commonly present to some degree, Amsden insists that when ISI meant a *dense* network of rules and reciprocity requirements the stimulus provided through ISI was in fact complimented by rapid sectoral growth, often bringing positive externalities and virtuous circles into play, as well.

"The rest" rose in conjunction with "getting the control mechanism right" rather than by getting the prices "right." Over a century of sluggish development was reversed and unprecedented manufacturing ensued. Growth rates of manufacturing output per capita grew faster for decades *outside* the North Atlantic than inside it (Amsden 2001, 11-12).

Different nations met the challenge of constructing their ISI policies in many varying ways. Amsden makes a convenient distinction between those "integrationists" who failed to create "national*ist* innovation systems to champion 'national leaders' with their own proprietary knowledge-based skills" (Amsden 2001, 14). Those who failed to achieve this threshold Amsden refers to as the "integrationists" and their fate has been to fall into a subordinate position vis-à-vis foreign capital, with Mexico after 1980 proving to be the best example. Meanwhile, the "independents," such as Korea and Taiwan have forged strong manufacturing capabilities due to the ability of nationally-owned firms to achieve first mover advantages and economies of scale. Building manufacturing ability involves the creation of a cadre of experienced, qualified engineers and mangers and this occurs only through a complex process of *institutional evolution:* ". . .manufacturing experience is not simply a stock of knowledge. It is a stock of knowledge that passes through *a specific historical and institutional filter"* (Amsden 2001, 15-16). National leaders in manufacturing arise more commonly in nations that had a relatively solid background in manufacturing prior to WW II *and* were able to break-free of the hold of foreign firms over the manufacturing sector.

As central as manufacturing is to the development process, Amsden nonetheless emphasized the need for a relatively high level of income equality—a characteristic which distinguished most Asian economies from other regions, particularly Latin America. In nations with highly unequal distributions of land a power bloc forms to thwart industrialization because landowners achieve Ricardian rents from land. Through their receipt of such rents the rate of return to agriculture remains high which then slows or forestalls the shift to manufacturing because of the relatively lower rate of return. Consequently, if income inequality is associated with a highly unequal land tenure system a nation's "core competency" will remain in agriculture—this sector will exhibit "absorptive capacities" which curb a necessary process of institutional evolution as the inheritors of landed estates cling to their landholding pattern of life. Amsden's findings demonstrate that nations which are experiencing relatively greater degrees of income equality are also those able to concentrate their efforts on national leader firms and the acquisition of production skills (Amsden 2001, 191).

If nations can sidestep the trap of agricultural dominance and proceed to build national leader firms, such firms will proceed to create cutting-edge skills along with proprietary control over such skills. A major stumbling block for those who have pursued manufacturing as the avenue to development occurs when nations grapple with the complexities of acquiring technological proficiency. This can occur when a nation manages through state intervention to both increase the level of technical education and education in general and provide through targeted subsidized credit the means for national firms to acquire modern production equipment. A new elite of managers and engineers who exhibit production know-how, are able to execute production projects *if* they are able to work with an educated, skill-based, labor force. Solving the dilemma of development demands the "visible hand" of the state, which would accord well with Karl Polayni's perspective regarding the process of institutional transformation. Amsden observes:

> The developmental state was predicated on performing four functions: developmental banking; local-content management; "selective exclusion" (opening some markets to foreign transactions and keeping other closed); and national firm formation. As a consequence of these functions, "the rest" finally made the requisite three pronged investment

> to enter basic industry—in large scale plants, in hierarchical managements—cum technological skills, and in distribution and marketing networks. Two principles guided developmentalism: to make manufacturing profitable enough to attract private enterprise through the allocation of . . . (subsidies) and to induce such enterprises to be results-oriented and to redistribute their monopoly profits to the population at large. (Amsden 2001, 125)

Of all of the instruments that the state can utilize, the most efficient is that of development banking in Amsden's view, because of these banks abilities to encourage and to achieve key policy goals such as export expansion, local-content targets in production and price stability. Above all, developmental banks, and the state in general, must impose adequate "performance standards" as a counterpart to the assistance provided—the most important of which would be large expenditures on research and development (Amsden 2001, 206) Contrary to the "market friendly" approach of the World Bank, Amsden shows that for developing nations virtually every case of successfully rising manufacturing exports has been due to ISI policies.[3] Successful nations have been *selectively strategically seclusive* rather than merely "open" as the World Bank recommends.

Another requisite element, in direct opposition to the views of the World Bank, is the distancing a nation must achieve from would-be foreign transnational corporations. As bearers of Foreign Direct Investment (FDI), transnationals (TNCs) are commonly viewed in the development literature as constituent elements of any positive program for development. However, Amsden shows that a partial correlation analysis demonstrates that FDI is *negatively correlated* with a nation's ability to produce research and development, patents, scientific publications and scientists and engineers engaged in research and development. Furthermore, the *sooner* a nation accepts the entry of TNCs the less likely a nation will develop the national independence needed to create strong national leaders (Amsden 2001, 208-212) Nations which encourage or do not consciously discourage TNCs from acquiring local firms through majority ownership mergers are also nations with low research and development levels. Thus, screening out TNCs from all but limited sectors of a nations economy seems to be the best policy for national success.

Far from the "market friendly" dictates of the World Bank that firms develop within the context of the private sector, Amsden's research demonstrates that state-owned firms frequently became national leaders crowding-in other private firms due to their positive externality impacts—as many of the "pioneers" of development had argued in the 1940s and 1950s.

Other positive externalities include aggregate increases in research and development (through research institutes) which could be appropriated by national firms and the incubation of entrepreneurial capabilities which could be spun off into the wider economy.

It is an axiom of the "market friendly" approach, propounded by the World Bank and other multilateral "development institutions," that developmentalism, or ISI, founders of necessity due to distortions of market forces which generally lead to "government failures" much more profound than the market failures that ISI sought to remediate. But, based on her extensive study of numerous concrete cases—rather than the abstract methodology so favored by the multilateral institutions—Amsden affirms that:

> 'government failures' can no longer be taken for granted if governments do use institutional mechanisms to raise productivity and jump start industrial growth. Government failures may be inevitable in the absence of systematic machinery to prevent them, but not necessarily in the presence of such machinery. . . .The reciprocal control mechanism of 'the rest' was hardly perfect. But it illustrates the possibilities of minimizing government failures even in economies plagued by 'moral hazard' and corruption but enjoying manufacturing experience.
>
> There has not thus far been widespread recognition of the systematic machinery that countries in 'the rest' put in place, implemented and monitored to avoid government failure and to pursue developmental goals. Yet 'getting the control mechanism right' whether or not prevailing prices were 'right' was central to the postwar process of catching up. (Amsden 2001, 290)

## CONCLUSIONS

Bringing institutions back in to development theory has proven to be complex and divisive. Building on the work of the "pioneers" of development, particularly in terms of their emphasis on the role institutions play in either retarding or assisting development, is not a straightforward proposition, given the current state of the field of development economics. Unlike most academic fields of research in economics, development economics itself is both nurtured and burdened by globe-straddling "development" institutions with billions of dollars to spend, and thousands of economists to deploy. Who and what dominates their research agenda, and to what ends, must be taken into account in evaluating the nature of the new trend toward the assertion that institutions, and therefore history, matter.

The development institutions, particularly the IMF/WB, are now well-along in their attempt to impose second-stage structural adjustment policies which hinge upon institutional transformations of the "market friendly" nature. This thrust stands at odds with a mass of recent research, only some of which has been discussed in this chapter, which makes the case, irrefutably, that while institutional transformations can and should be supported they need be, at minimum, of the "market enhancing" type. And, most preferably they should be in the direction of building and sustaining "developmental states."

Alice Amsden, in particular, has presented a carefully reasoned challenge to orthodoxy based not on irrelevant vignettes or flights of theoretical abstraction but on a mass of carefully compiled case studies of an important subset of developing nations—those that have actually demonstrated their ability to engage in sustained development. As Amsden demonstrates, manufacturing is the core activity of these nations. Their success has been based not on lowering transactions costs, nor will the lowering of such costs, as argued by the "New Institutionalists" create conditions sufficient for sustained economic growth. Rather, nations have to develop their own proprietary skills, which are firm-specific and found in the acquisition and creation of knowledge-based assets (production, project execution and innovation capabilities). To reach this threshold, nations must adopt dynamic Import Substitution Industrialization policies that embed reciprocal relationships between opportunities extended to national firms and fulfillment of the requirements and objectives of the developmental state. The visible hand of a control mechanism is a necessary constituent in the struggle to achieve national production competitiveness.

## NOTES

1. I am grateful to Ha-Joon Chang for his detailed comments on an earlier draft of this chapter.

2. In addition to the works cited in this section by Stiglitz, a useful edited compendium of his writings is *The Rebel Within: Joseph Stiglitz and the World Bank* (Chang 2001).

3. This has also been the case for the now developed nations—an important point eloquently argued in *Kicking Away the Ladder: Development Strategy in Historical Perspective* (Chang 2002).

# REFERENCES


Adelman, Irma. 2001. "Fallacies in Development Theory and Their Implications for Policy." In *Frontiers of Development Economics.* Gerald Meier, and Joseph Stiglitz, eds. Washington: The World Bank and Oxford University Press.

Akyuz, Yilman, Chang, Ha-Joon, and Kozul-Wright, Richard. 1998. New perspectives on East Asian development. *Journal of Development Studies* 34 (6): 4-36.

Amsden, Alice. 2001. *The Rise of the Rest.* Oxford: Oxford University Press.

Bulmer-Thomas, Victor. 1994. *The Economic History of Latin America Since Independence.* Cambridge: Cambridge University Press.

Chang, Ha-Joon. 2000. The hazard of moral hazard: untangling the Asian crisis;". W*orld Development.* 28: (4): 775-788.

———. (ed.). 2001. *The Rebel Within: Joseph Stiglitz and the World Bank.* London: Anthem Press.

———. 2002. *Kicking Away the Ladder: Development Strategy in Historical Perspective.* London: Anthem Press.

Cypher, James. 1996. Mexico: financial fragility or structural crisis. *Journal of Economic Issues* 30 (2): 451-462.

———. 1997. Los vicisitudes de los países en vías de ajuste estructural. *Deslinde;* no. 20, 28-47.

———. 1998. The slow death of the Washington Consensus on Latin America. *Latin American Perspectives* 25 (6): 47-51.

———, and Dietz, James. 1997. *The Process of Economic Development.* London: Routledge.

Evans, Peter. 1998. Transferable lessons? Re-examining the institutional prerequisites of East Asian economic policies. *Journal of Development Studies* 34 (6): 66-86.

Hayami, Yujiro, and Masahiko Aoki,. 1998. *The Institutional Foundations of East Asian Economic Development.* London: Macmillan.

Hellman, Thomas, Murdock, Kevin and Stiglitz, Joseph. 1998. "Financial Restraint and the Market Enhancing View." In *The Institutional Foundations of East Asia Economic Development.* Yurjiro Hayami and Masahiko Aoki, eds. London: Macmillan.

Hodgson, Geoffrey. 1994. "Institutionalism, 'Old' and 'New'." In *Institutional and Evolutionary Economics.* Geoffrey Hodgson, Warren Samuels, and Marc Tool, eds. Cheltenham, UK: Edward Elgar.

Hoff, Karla and Stiglitz, Joseph. 2000. "Modern Economic Theory and Development". In *Frontiers of Development Economics.* Gerald Meier, and Joseph Stiglitz, eds. Washington: The World Bank and Oxford University Press.

Krueger, Anne. 1974. The political economy of the rent-seeking society. *American Economic Review* 64 (3): 291-303.

———. 1993. *Political Economy of Policy Reform in Developing Countries.* Cambridge: MIT Press.

Meier, Gerald and Joseph Stiglitz, (eds.). 2001. *Frontiers of Development Economics.* Washington: The World Bank and Oxford University Press.

North, Douglas. 1998. "The Institutional Foundations of East Asian Development: A Summary Evaluation." In *The Institutional Foundations of East Asia Economic Development.* Yujiro Hayami, and Masahiko Aoki, eds. London: Macmillan.

Rodrik, Dani. 1998. "TFPG Controversies, Institutions and Economic Performance in East Asia." In *The Institutional Foundations of East Asia Economic Development.* Yujiro Hayami, and Masahiko Aoki, eds. London: Macmillan.

———. 1999. *The New Global Economy and Developing Countries: Making Openness Work* Washington, D.C.: Overseas Development Council and Johns Hopkins Press.

———. 2000. Development Strategies for the Next Century. 41. http://orion.forumone.com/ABCDE/ files.fcqi/145_Rodrik_ Japan.pdf

Stiglitz, Joseph. 2000. Development Thinking at the Millennium. 1-28. http://orion.forumone.com/ABCDE/files.fcgi/211_stiglitz.pdf

Veblen, Thorstein B. [1915] 1964. *Imperial Germany and the Industrial Revolution.* New York: Agustus M. Kelley.

______. [1934] 1964. "The Opportunity of Japan." In *Essays in Our Changing Order.* Leon Ardzooni, ed. New York: Augustus M. Kelley.

Wade, Robert. 2001. Making the World Development Report 2000: attacking poverty. *World Development* 29 (8): 1435-1441.

———. and Frank Veneroso. 1998. The Asian Crisis: The High-Debt model versus the Wall Street-Treasury-IMF complex. *New Left Review;* no. 228, 3-23.

Williamson, John. 1998. "Latin American Reform: A View From Washington." In *Economic Reform in Latin America.* Harry Costin and Hector Vanolli, eds. Orlando: Dryden.

World Bank. 1993. *The East Asian Miracle: Economic Growth and Public Policy.* Washington: The World Bank.

———. 2000. *World Development Report.* Washington: The World Bank.

———. 2002. *World Development Report.* Washington: The World Bank.

Yusuf, Shahid and Joseph Stiglitz. 2001. "Development Issues: Settled and Open." In *Frontiers of Development Economics.* Gerald Meier, Joseph Stiglitz .eds. Washington: The World Bank and Oxford University Press.

# ABOUT THE AUTHORS

**Paul D. Bush** is Professor Emeritus of Economics, California State University, Fresno. His research and writing have focused on the philosophical foundations of institutionalist methodology and the theory of institutional change. He is a Past President of the Association for Institutional Thought (AFIT) and the Association for Evolutionary Economics (AFEE). He is also a founding member of the European Association for Evolutionary Political Economy (EAEPE) and has been awarded an Honorary Life Membership by EAEPE. His publications include: "The Theory of Institutional Change," *Journal of Economic Issues* (1987); and "The Methodology of Institutional Economics," in Tool, ed. *Institutional Economics* (1993).

**Charles M. A. Clark** is Professor of Economics, Tobin College of Business, and Senior Fellow, Vincentian Center for Church and Society at St. John's University, New York. He has authored or edited eight books, the most recent of which is *The Basic Income Guarantee: Ensuring Progress and Prosperity in the 21st Century* (2002). The most recent of his over 70 professional publications are: "Wealth and Poverty: On the Social Creation of Scarcity," *Journal of Economic Issues*, (2002), and a three part essay on economic equity in Network's *Connections* magazine (2002).

**James M. Cypher is** Professor of Economics at CSU Fresno. He has written widely on economic development. He is the author of State *and Capital in Mexico: Development Policy since 1940*, (Westview 1990) and co-author (with James Dietz) of *The Process of Economic Development* (Routledge 1997). His work focuses on the state-led aspects of industrialization in developing nations. He has contributed chapters to eight books and published over 50 articles in scholarly journals. He has taught and/or done research at the American University in Washington DC, and at universities in Mexico and Chile.

**Wolfram Elsner** is Professor of Economics and Director of the Institute for Institutional and Socio-Economics, University of Bremen, Germany. He is a specialist in the fields of industrial and regional economics. He also is Head of the Planning Division of the Ministry of Economic Affairs of the State of Bremen and Director of the Bremen Economic Research Institute. He is co-editor of *Industrial Policies after 2000*, (Kluwer, 2000). He has published in the *Journal of Economic Issues* and in the *International Review of Applied Economics*. He was AFEE's Clarence Ayres Visiting Scholar in 1995, and is a member of the EAEPE Council, 2002-2003.

**Deborah M. Figart** is Professor of Economics at Richard Stockton College in Pomona, New Jersey. Her interdisciplinary research on discrimination, minimum wages, emotional labor, working time, and public policy has been published in book volumes and social science journals, including the *Journal of Economic Issues, Social Politics, Work and Occupations, Industrial Relations, Feminist Economics*, and *Review of Social Economy*. She serves on the elected Boards of AFEE and the Association for Social Economics. Her most recent book, co-authored with Ellen Mutari and Marilyn Power, is *Living Wages, Equal Wages: Gender and Labor Market Policies in the United States*, (Routledge 2002).

**Peter Fisher** is a professor in the Graduate Program in Urban and Regional Planning at the University of Iowa, where he has taught since 1977. His research and teaching interests are centered on state and local government finance, economic development policy, and poverty and income inequality. He has served as a consultant on tax issues, welfare reform, and economic development policy for state government agencies, labor unions, and non-profit organizations. He is co-author, with Alan Peters, of *Industrial Incentives: Competition among American States and Cities* (Upjohn Institute for Employment Research, 1998), and of a forthcoming book on enterprise zones.

**Gladys Parker Foster** was Adjunct Professor of Economics at the University of Colorado at Denver. She studied with C. E. Ayres and J. Fagg Foster, leaders in the development of "neoinstitutional" economics. From the late 1940s until his death in 1985, she worked closely with Foster (her husband) studying the substance and implications of neoinstitutional economics. After his death, she completed her PhD in economics at the University of Colorado. Her research and writing address the endogeneity of money and Keynes's *General Theory*, the economics of women, and global economic problems. Her articles have appeared in the *JEI* and elsewhere. She has served on the Board of Directors of AFEE and AFIT.

**F. Gregory Hayden** is Professor of Economics at the University of Nebraska-Lincoln. His fields are public policymaking and environmental economics. Recent co-authored journal articles include "The Use of Power Blocs of Integrated Corporate Directorships to Articulate a Power Structure" and "Analysis of the Financial Assurance Plan in the License Application for a Low-Level Radioactive Waste Disposal Facility" in the *JEI.* He served as a Special Assistant to the Governor of Nebraska; as Commissioner on the Central Interstate Low-Level Radioactive Waste Compact Commission; and as a member of the Ecosystem Valuation Forum, US Environmental Protection Agency. He is a recipient of the AFEE Veblen-Commons Award.

**Michael Keaney** is a lecturer in economics, finance and international political economy at Mercuria Business School, Vantaa, Finland. His research interests include the political economy of health care provision. He is currently working on various projects concerning state-business linkages and rivalries in the global political economy. As well as having published articles in various journals, including the *Journal of Economic Issues, Review of Social Economy,* and *Critical Sociology*, he is the editor of *Economist with a Public Purpose: Essays in Honour of John Kenneth Galbraith* (Routledge, 2001). He is also an editor of the *Review of Radical Political Economics* and *Capitalism Nature Socialism.*

**Philip A. Klein** is Professor Emeritus of Economics at Pennsylvania State University. He has taught at a number of universities in the US and abroad. He was on the staff of the National Bureau of Economic Research and is a Senior Research Scholar at the Economic Cycle Research Institute. He has had Fulbright Fellowships in France, Yugoslavia, and Italy. His fields of expertise are business cycles, economic theory, and institutional economics. He is the author of *Beyond Dissent: Essays in Institutional Economics* (1994), co-author of *Forecasting Financial and Economic Cycles* (1994), and of many journal articles. He is a recipient of the AFEE Veblen-Commons Award.

**William H. Melody** is Professor, Center for Information and Communication Technologies, Technical University of Denmark; Visiting Professor at London School of Economics, and at LINK Center, University of Witswatersrand, South Africa. He is Managing Director of Learning Initiatives on Reforms for Network Economies, www.lirne.net. He is author of "Designing Utility Regulation for 21$^{st}$ Century Markets" in Miller & Samuels: *The Institutionalist Approach to Public Utility Regulation,* Michigan State Press (2002)*; The Triumph and Tragedy of Human Capital: Foundation Resource for the Global Knowledge Economy,* Delft University Press (2002); and editor of *Telecom Reform: Principles, Policies and Regulatory Practices DTU Press* (1997).

**Edythe S. Miller** is former Chairwoman and Commissioner of the Colorado Public Utilities Commission. Her fields of specialization are economic philosophy and regulatory and public utility economics. Recent publications include *The Institutionalist Approach to Public Utility Regulation* (co-edited with Warren J. Samuels), Michigan State University Press (2002), and

"Economics in a Public Interest," *Journal of Economic Issues* (June 2002). She is a recipient of the Association for Evolutionary Economics Veblen-Commons Award (2002) and the Transportation and Public Utilities Group of the American Economics Association Distinguished Member Award (1993). She is currently an Adjunct Professor of Economics at the University of Denver, University College.

**Janice L. Peterson** is a Senior Analyst at the United States General Accounting Office, where she works on retirement income policy issues. Her areas of specialization are public sector and labor economics. She has written extensively on institutional and feminist economics. She is co-editor of The *Elgar Companion of Feminist Economics* (1999) and co-editor of *The Economic Status of Women Under Capitalism* (1994). Her work on the economic status of women and welfare policy has been included in a number of edited volumes. Her articles have been published in the *Journal of Economic Issues, Journal of Social Economy*, and *the Social Science Journal.*

**Baldwin Ranson** was Professor of Economics at Western State College of Colorado and the American University in Bulgaria. Since retiring, he has accepted many volunteer teaching assignments in Russia and Central Asia. He has made an extensive comparative study of the educational systems of the US, Mexico, Japan, Korea, China, Bulgaria, and Russia. He has published several articles on institutional economics and comparative educational systems, including "The Institutionalist Theory of Capital Formation," *JEI* (1987); and "Education for Modernization: Meritocratic Myths in China, Mexico, the US and Japan," *JEI* (1988). He edited "The Papers of J. Fagg Foster," *JEI* (1981). He served two terms as President of AFIT.

**Michael F. Sheehan** is a partner in Fisher, Sheehan & Colton, a firm of economists and practicing attorneys in Oregon. He specializes in regulatory and forensic economics and public finance on the economics side, and regulation and public policy on the law side. He is co-author of *Oregon's Prevailing Wage Law* (2000) and a number of articles, studies and prepared testimony on issues ranging from the economics of high level nuclear waste disposal in Utah to predatory practices of dominant telephone carriers in Iowa. He has taught economics at several universities, is a past President of AFIT, and has served on the Editorial Board of the *JEI.*

**Kurt Stephenson** is an Associate Professor in the Department of Agricultural and Applied Economics at Virginia Tech. His research interests include market-based environmental policies, water resource policy, and the role of economics in public policy. Current sponsors of his research include the

National Science Foundation, Environmental Protection Agency, Natural Resources Conservation Service, and the Rappahannock River Basin Commission. His co-authored paper, "Environmental Valuation and Its Economic Critics," was published in the *Journal of Water Resources Planning and Management* and was selected as the best theory-oriented paper in 2000 by the American Society of Civil Engineers, Environmental & Water Resources Institute Planning and Management Council.

**Marc R. Tool**, is Professor Emeritus of Economics, CSU, Sacramento. He served as editor of the *Journal of Economic Issues* 1982-1991. His primary research focus is on social value theory in economic analysis. Among the five volumes he has authored are *The Discretionary Economy* 3rd ed. (2001) and *Value Theory and Economic Progress, The Institutional Economics of J. Fagg Foster* (2000). He has served as an editor and co-editor of eight volumes on institutional and evolutionary economics. He is Past President of AFEE and of AFIT and a Founding and Life Member of the European Association for Evolutionary Political Economy (EAEPE). He was the recipient of the AFEE Veblen-Commons Award in 1988.

**Harry M. Trebing** is Professor Emeritus of Economics, Michigan State University. He is Founder and Director of the Institute of Public Utilities, MSU (1966-1992), with responsibility for annual conferences, and educational programs for state and federal regulators. He served as the Chief Economist for the Postal Rate Commission and for the Federal Communications Commission. He is a Past President of AFEE and a recipient of the Veblen-Commons Award. He is a Past Chair of the Transportation and Public Utilities Group of the AEA and a recipient of the Distinguished Member Award. He has received distinguished service awards from National Association of Regulatory Utility Commissioners, National Association of State Utility Consumer Advocates, and four major universities. He is the author of numerous publications in economics.

**L. Randall Wray** is Professor of Economics and Senior Research Associate with the Center for Full Employment and Price Stability at the University of Missouri-Kansas City. He is also a Senior Scholar at the Jerome Levy Economics Institute of Bard College. He is the author of *Understanding Modern Money: The Key to Full Employment and Price Stability* (Elgar, 1998) and *Money and Credit in Capitalist Economies* (Elgar 1990). He is also the author of numerous scholarly articles in edited books and academic journals, including the *Journal of Economic Issues, Cambidge Journal of Economics, Review of Political Economy,* and *Journal of Post Keynesian Economics.* He is a past President of AFIT.

# Index


**A**

Abortion, in social agenda of social conservatives, 332
Abuse, fostered by concentrations of poor families, 124
Academic curriculum, sorting of students into, 349–378
Access to information, 425
ACORN. *See* Association of Community Organizations for Reform
Actual budget, structural budget, cyclical budget, distinguished, 65
ADC. *See* Aid to Dependent Children
AFDC. *See* Aid to Families with Dependent Children
Affirmative action, 394–396
*Affluent Society*, 262
African Americans, 392
  in minimum wage force, 386
  urban communities, toxic waste sites in, 475
Agency for International Development, 550
AID. *See* Agency for International Development
Aid to Blind, 163
Aid to Dependent Children, 163
Aid to Families with Dependent Children, 164, 166, 400
Aldicarb, dumping of, 462
American Broadcasting Company, 269
American Enterprise Institute, 189
Ameritech, 268, 338
Antimiscegination laws, 31
Antitrust enforcement, crippling of, 333–337
AOL-Time Warner merger, 269
Arthur Anderson, 287–314
Asian economic crisis, 146
Association of Community Organizations for Reform, 387
Atomic Energy Commission, subordination of scientists' authority, 28
Atomic scientists, subordinated authority of, 28
AT&T, 266, 291, 333, 338

**B**

Babylonia, origins of money of account in, 98
Bank of England, 87
Banking, 85–114
  alternative approach to, 94–102
  Bank of England, 87
  barter economy, 97–100
  Community Reinvestment Act, 110
  credit controls, 109
  Currency School-Banking School, 85–94
  favored groups, lending to, 110
  Federal Open Market Committee, 93
  Federal Reserve, 9, 87
  financial services, provision of, 109
  Glass-Steagall Act, 110
  Great Depression, 89
  International Monetary Fund, 102
  money, origins of, 97
  post-war period, 90–94
  pre-war period, 85–90
  private property, development of, 97
  Real Bills Doctrine, 89
  Real Business Cycle Theory, 94
  reserve ratios, 108
  taxes-drive-money approach, 98
  treasury bill rate, 90
  World Bank, 102
Barley, as basis of monetary unit, 97
Barter economy, 97–100
Basic income, 133–156
  American basic income system, hypothetical, 149–151
  arguments for, against, 152–154
  capital mobility, 146–147
  conservatives views of, 152–153
  costs of, 150
  defined, 133–137
  distributional impact, 151–152
  economic crises, 146
  economic institutions of twentieth century, 143
  equity, defined, 134
  federal government revenues, 151
  funding for, 150
  globalization, 143
  Great Society programs, 140
  household income, by quintile, 1999, 152
  income distribution effects, 151
  Keynes-Beveridge model, 143, 144
  labor market flexibility, 147
  liberals, views of, 154

macroeconomic policies, 144
microeconomic policies, 144
negative income tax, 153
"new economy," challenges of, 142–147
payments in 1999, 150
poverty
business cycle peaks, 1959–99, 141
economic growth
1959–2000, 141
relationship between, 140–142
rates of, actual, predicted, 142
productivity gains, 144
social justice, 137–139
technological impact, 145–146
trade liberalization, 146
trickle-down economics, 140
welfare state approach, 148
work, role of, 148
Bayer corporation, 461–462
Bell Atlantic, 291, 338
Bell holding companies, 266
Biopiracy, by pharmaceutical companies, 190
Block grant funding, 166
Bordon Chemicals and Plastics, 462
British National Health Service, 209
British Telecom, 291
Brown coal fired power plants, 482
*Building Institutions for Markets,* 559
Burlington Northern Railroad, Santa Fe Railroad, merger of, 324
Bush, Paul D., biographical sketch, 577

C

Cable television, telephone companies, mergers of, 324
Capital Consultants, 317
Capital mobility, basic income and, 146–147
Carbon sequestration, 486
Cartesian dualism, neoclassical school of economics, basis in, 254
Cash welfare entitlement, elimination of, 166
Cato Institute, 550
CBS, 269
Centralization of economic power, 251–286. *See also* Deregulation; Globalization; Monopolies
antitrust, 264–275
authoritative groups, identification of, 261
Clayton Act, 272
communication, standard industrial code classification, 268
competitive local exchange carriers, 268
consolidation of corporations, 267–270
deregulation, 264–275
economic consequences of, 277–279
electricity, deregulation of, 265–266
Energy Policy Act, 265
Federal Communications Commission, 265
Federal Energy Regulatory Commission, 264
Federal Trade Commission, 267
federal transportation, deregulation of, 264
firms, control of market, 262
globalization, 275–279
government response, 271–275
International Monetary Fund, 275
merger movement, 270–271
natural gas industry, deregulation of, 264
neoclassical school of economics
basis in Cartesian dualism, 254
definition of economics, 254
economic policy shaped by, 256
methodology, 254–255
power, concepts of, institutionalism approach, 258–260
power structures, in societies, 261
privileged groups, identification of, 261
regulation, assault on, 264–265
social beings, humans as, 260–262
technology, institutions, distinction between, 258
telecommunications, deregulation of, 266–267
trade, capital mobility and, 276–278
World Bank, 275
World Trade Organization, 275
Ceremonial encapsulation, 27–28
of technology, 28
Ceremonial institutions, defined, 23
Chase Manhattan Bank, 337
Chemical Bank, 337
Children, industrial exploitation of, 321
China, per capita growth, 554
Cholera, efforts to eradicate, 195, 321
Church, as authoritative group, 261
Ciba Corporation, 462
CIVICUS, 514
Civil Rights Act, Title VII, 389
Clark, Charles M. A., biographical sketch, 577
Clayton Act, 272, 330
Clean Water Act, 321
CLECs. *See* Competitive local exchange carriers
Clinton health care plan, 186, 191, 193, 199, 206
CMS Energy, 298
Coal fired power plant, 482
Coal mines, children working in, 321

Coase theorem, 470–475
Collective bargaining, 11
Collectivism, 54–57
Comcast, 287–314
Commission on Excellence in Education, 367
Committee for Economic Development, Research and Policy Committee, 65
Communcation economy, 411–432
  access, to information infrastructure, 425
  economic institution foundations, 413–414
  economic transformation, forces driving, 412–413
  European Union, 411
  financial markets, 422–423
  human capital investment, economic growth and, 428–429
  information markets, characteristics of, 415–417
  information monopolies, 424
  information ownership, 424–425
  intellectual property rights, 424–425
  international market liberalization policies, 422–425
  labor markets, 423–424
  North American Free Trade Agreement, 411
  oligopolies, competition, regulatory policies, 427–428
  overload of information, 420–422
  product markets, 423
  productivity, 425, 426–427
  public interest in, 426–427
  services markets, 423
  specialized information services, 416
Community Reinvestment Act, 110
*Compensatory Education for Cultural Deprivation,* 361, 362, 369–370
Competition among nations, globalization and, 534
Competitive local exchange carriers, 268
Conservative think-tanks, perspective on economic development in developing nations, 550
Consolidation of corporations, economic power centralization with, 267–270
Conspicuous consumption, as demonstration of ability to pay, 14
Contestable market hypothesis, 339–340
Contingent workers, 388–390
Control, economic theory, relationship between, 6–7
Copper, origin of usage as money, 97
Credit controls, 109
Crime, fostered by concentrations of poor families, 124
Cultural diversity, global industrial policies and, 535–537
Cumulative causation, concept of, 17–19
Currency School-Banking School, 85–94
Curriculum, 349–378
  academic curriculum, 349–378
  Commission on Excellence in Education, 367
  dual curricula, 353
  Elementary and Secondary Education Act, 363
  global trends, 349
  Goals 2000: The Educate America Act, 367–376
  low-income families, children of, 361
  National Commission on Excellence in Education, 365
  National Commission on Life Adjustment Education for Youth, 356–358
  National Commission on Reform of Secondary Education, 363
  National Defense Education Act, 360
  national education summit, 349
  parental participation, 376
  Research Conference on Education and Cultural Deprivation, 361
  Rockefeller Brothers Fund, 358
  School Readiness, 369
  sorting of students, 353
  technological determination, principle of, 352
  vocational curriculum, sorting of students into, 349–378
Cyclical budget, actual budget, structural budget, distinguished, 65
Cypher, James M., biographical sketch, 577

**D**

Darwin, challenge to neoclassical school of economics, 318–320
DDT, dumping of, 461
*In Defense of Affirmative Action,* 395
Defined-contribution plans, health care, usage of, 200
Democracy, institutional change and, 34–36
Democratic sovereignty, public policy and, 30–32
Demonstration effect, patterns of behavior, 27
Depository Institutions Act, 337
Deregulation, 264–275, 287–314. *See also* Globalization
  of cable industry, 291
  Clayton Act, 272

communication, standard industrial code classification, 268
competitive local exchange carriers, 268, 291
consequence, 300–303
consolidation of corporations, 267–270
economic consequences of, 277–279
electricity, 295
aftermath of, 297–300
deregulation of, 265–266
response to deregulation, 296–297
Energy Policy Act, 265, 295, 310
Federal Communications Commission, 265, 290
Federal Energy Regulatory Commission, 264, 295
Federal Trade Commission, 267
federal transportation, deregulation of, 264
globalization, 275–279
government response, 271–275
Hepburn Act of 1906, commodities clause of, 306
Herfendahl-Hirschman Index, 309
International Monetary Fund, 290
Interstate Commerce Commission, creation of, 304
laissez faire doctrine, 303
long distance interexchange carriers, 291
merger, 270–271
acquisition guidelines, establishment of, 308–309
natural gas industry, deregulation of, 264
origins of, 289–290
public utility industries, 264–314
Public Utility Regulatory Policy Act, 295
reform, 305–310
savings and loans, 336–337
Securities and Exchange Commission, 295
telecommunications, 266–267
response to, 290–292
trade, capital mobility and, 276–278
Wisconsin Advanced Plan, 309
World Bank, 275, 290
World Trade Organization, 275
*Descent of Man,* 319
Developing countries, 549–576
Agency for International Development, 550
Development State theory, 566–572
Interamerican Development Bank, 550
International Economic Association, 552
International Monetary Fund, 550
market enhancement, 562–566
market friendly approach, 556–562
Solow model of growth, 556
World Bank, 550
*World Development Report,* 556
Development State theory, 566–572
*Dictionary of Occupational Titles,* 383
Dioxins, dumping of, 461
Discrimination, in employment, 392–394
Disease prevention initiatives, underevaluation of, 195
Dislocation, minimal, principle of, 26
Disney Corporation, 269
Disposal of industrial waste. *See* Industrial waste
Distribution of income, 133–156
American basic income system, hypothetical, 149–151
arguments for, against, 152–154
capital mobility, 146–147
conservatives views of, 152–153
costs of, 150
defined, 133–137
distributional impact, 151–152
economic crises, 146
economic institutions of twentieth century, 143
equity, defined, 134
federal government revenues, 151
funding for, 150
globalization, 143
Great Society programs, 140
household income, by quintile, 1999, 152
increasing unequality of, 120
Keynes-Beveridge model, 143, 144
labor market flexibility, 147
liberals, views of, 154
macroeconomic policies, 144
microeconomic policies, 144
negative income tax, 153
"new economy," challenges of, 142–147
payments, 1999, 150
poverty
business cycle peaks, 1959–99, 141
economic growth
from 1959 to 2000, 141
relationship between, 140–142
rates of, actual, predicted, 142
productivity gains, 144
social justice, 137–139
technological impact, 145–146
trade liberalization, 146
trickle-down economics, 140
welfare state approach, 148
work, role of, 148
Division of labor, divisive effects of, 194
Doctors
patients, as partners, 209
proletarianization of, 206

Domestic abuse, psychological damage from, 197
Drug discounts, Medicare, 193
Dual curricula, 353
Duke Energy, 298
Dwelling, progressive tax, Social Security, 247
Dynegy, 298

**E**

Economic incentives, taxes as, 121–124
*Economics of Regulation and Antitrust,* 340
Education, curriculum, 349–378
  academic curriculum, 349–378
  Commission on Excellence in Education, 367
  dual curricula, 353
  Elementary and Secondary Education Act, 363
  global trends, 349
  Goals 2000: The Educate America Act, 367–376
  low-income families, children of, 361
  National Commission on Excellence in Education, 365
  National Commission on Life Adjustment Education for Youth, 356–358
  National Commission on Reform of Secondary Education, 363
  National Defense Education Act, 360
  national education summit, 349
  parental participation, 376
  Research Conference on Education and Cultural Deprivation, 361
  Rockefeller Brothers Fund, 358
  School Readiness, 369
  sorting of students, 353
  technological determination, principle of, 352
Electricity, deregulation of, 265–266
Elementary and Secondary Education Act, 363
Eli Lilly, 189
Elsner, Wolfram, biographical sketch, 577
Employment, 379–410
  affirmative action, 394–396
  African-Americans, 392
    in minimum wage force, 386
  Aid to Families with Dependent Children, 400
  Association of Community Organizations for Reform, 387
  Baltimore, first living wage ordinance, 387
  Civil Rights Act, Title VII, 389
  contingent workers, 388–390
  discrimination, 392–394
  equal employment opportunities, 394
  Equal Employment Opportunity Commission, 393
  Equal Pay Act, 389, 392
    loopholes in, 392–394
  ethnicity, 391–396
  Fair Labor Standards Act, 390
  Family and Medical Leave Act, 389, 398
  family leave, paid, 397–400
  gender, 391–396
  gender equity, 396–397
  "good" job, defined, 380–384
  health care, percent of GDP spent on, 401
  health insurance, 401–402
    U.S. population without, 401
  high-wage, low-wage workers, distinctions made between, 385–387
  Institute for Women's Policy Research, 397
  manufacturing, declining share of employment in, 382
  medical leave, paid, 397–400
  Medicare, 401
  minimum wage, raising, 385–386
  municipal living wage ordinances, 386–387
  National Partnership for Women and Families, 399–400
  overtime penalties, 390–391
  paid, unpaid labor, distinctions made between, 396–402
  part-time workers, 388–390
  Personal Responsibility and Work Reconciliation Opportunity Act, 400
  Pregnancy Discrimination Act, 398
  race and, 391–396
  State Children's Health Insurance Program, 402
  Survey of Job Characteristics, 382
  Temporary Assistance to Needy Families, 400
  Temporary Disability Insurance, 399
  temporary workers, 388–390
  unpaid labor, 396–397
  welfare
    caseloads, 168–169
    reform of, 400–401
  work hours, employment status and, 388–391
Employment Act of 1946, 50–51, 54, 56, 57
Encapsulation, ceremonial, 27–28
Energy Policy Act, 265
Enhancement of human life, as role of economics, 73, 80
Enron, 287–314

Environmental policy, 433–460, 461–492
  African-American urban communities, toxic waste sites in, 475
  aldicarb, 462
  Austria, 438–442
  Bayer corporation, 461–462
  Bordon Chemicals and Plastics, 462
  brown coal fired power plant, 482
  capital and, relationship between, 483
  carbon sequestration, 486
  Ciba Corporation, 462
  Clean Air Act, 434–457
  Coase theorem, 470–475
  corporate power, policy domination by, 466–470
  DDT, 461
  dioxins, 461
  disposal services, 484–486
  Environmental Protection Agency, 434–457, 464
  furons, 461
  General Electric corporation, 462
  government, role of, 442–443
  greenhouse effect, 486
  groundwater, contaminated, in minority communities, 462
  Hispanic urban communities, toxic waste sites in, 475
  Hooker Chemical and Plastic Corporation, 461
  institutionalist integrated system, 463
  Love Canal, 461
  mercury wastes, 461–462
  neoclassical school of economics, 443–446
  PCBs, 461, 462
  pollution, 478–481
  production of, 478–481
  radioactive waste, 475
  radioactive waste disposal system, 486
  Resource Conservation and Recovery Act, 464
  Rhone-Pauler corporation, 462
  Solvay corporation, 461
Environmental Protection Agency, 464
EPA. *See* Environmental Protection Agency
Equal employment opportunities, 394
Equal Employment Opportunity Commission, 393
Equal Pay Act, 389, 392
  loopholes in, 392–394
*Equality and Efficiency: The Big Trade-Off,* 137
Equity, defined, 134
Ethnicity, employment discrimination, 391–396
European Union, 411
*Expropriation of Health,* 196

**F**

Factories, children working in, 321
Fair Labor Standards Act, 321, 390
Family and Medical Leave Act, 389, 398
Family break-up, taxation and, 117
Family leave, paid, 397–400
Fannie Mae, 110
Farmers, as favord group, lending to, 110
Favored groups, lending to, 110
FCC. *See* Federal Communications Commission
Federal Communications Commission, 265, 331
Federal Energy Regulatory Commission, 264
Federal Open Market Committee, 93
Federal Power Commission, 331
Federal receipts, 72
  GDP, unemployment, compared, 74
  percent of GDP, 79
Federal Reserve, 9, 87
Federal Reserve Act of 1913, 89
Federal Reserve Board, 331
Federal Savings & Loan Insurance Corporation, 336
Federal spending, percent of GDP, 53, 78
Federal Trade Commission, 267, 341
Federal transportation, deregulation of, 264
Federal Water Pollution Control Act, 321
Figart, Deborah M., biographical sketch, 578
Financial services, provision of, 109
Firms, control of market, 262–286
Fiscal impact, fiscal policy, distingished, 67
Fiscal policy, 47–84
  collectivism, 54–57
  Committee for Economic Development, Research and Policy Committee, 65
  Employment Act of 1946, 50–51, 54, 56, 57
  federal spending, percent of GDP, 53, 78
  fiscal impact, distingished, 67
  fiscal stance, distinguished, 64, 70–73
  Great Depression, 48, 49
  Great Society programs, federal spending, 78
  Humphrey Hawkins Act of 1978, 55
  inflation, productivity, unit labor costs, compared, 77
  Keynesian theory, 49–51
  normative, legitimacy of, 54–60
  OPEC, 58
  Phillips Curve, 48, 55, 57–60, 63
    1960–69, 61

1960–99, 62
political scientist, approach to government, 52
potential GDP, concept of, 69
productivity, in United States, deterioration of, 75
public sector, 76–79
rational expectations hypothesis, 60
role of economics, 73, 80
role of government, 52–54
Say's laws, 50
September 11th, 2001, effect of, 57
structural budget, actual budget, cyclical budget, distinguished, 65
theory, policy, linkage, in economic analysis, 49–53
unemployment
GDP, federal receipts, expenditures, compared, 74
inflation, parity of, 60–79
usefulness, 73–76
Fiscal stance, fiscal policy, distinguished, 64, 70–73
Fisher, Peter, biographical sketch, 578
FMLA. *See* Family and Medical Leave Act
FOMC. *See* Federal Open Market Committee
Food and Drug Administration, lobbying by insurers, 199
Foster, Gladys Parker, biographical sketch, 578
*Foundations of Economic Analysis,* 4
Founders of institutionalist policy, 3–4
Freddi Mac, lending to, 110
Freedom of speech, 32–34
FSLIC. *See* Federal Savings & Loan Insurance Corporation
FTC. *See* Federal Trade Commission
Furons, dumping of, 461

**G**

Gas industry, deregulation of, 264
Gatreaux Program, Chicago, 125
Gay rights, in social agenda of social conservatives, 332
GDP, federal receipts, unemployment, compared, 74
Gender, employment discrimination and, 391–396
Gender equity in employment, 396–397
General Electric corporation, 462
General Telephone and Electronics, 291
*General Theory,* publication of, 2
German political philosophy, conception of state, 304
Glass-Steagall Act, 110, 330
GlaxoSmithKline, 189
Global Crossing, 288, 300–303
Global industrial policies, 523–548
competition, 537–539
coordination problems, 528–530
cultural diversity, 535–537
equality-based interaction, 535–537
global governance, 531–534
globalization mechanism, 531–532
hierarchical unification, 533
income redistribution, 532–533
instrumentalism, 526–527
international economic relations, 527–528
local industrial policies, 540–542
localization, 539–540
policy, 527
problem-solving global economy, 534–540
Global One, 287–314, 291
Globalization, 143, 275–279, 493–521
CIVICUS, 514
Group of Eight meetings, Genoa, 501
International Committee on Human Rights, 508
International Labor Organization, 508
International Monetary Fund, 512, 513
international organizations, 512–514
International Performance Measurement and Verification Protocol, 515
Internet, access to, in developing nations, 514
"Open Society Alliance," 512, 515
Special Drawing Rights, to countries, 513
Transparency International, 514
United Nations, 512
Development Program, 493
embargo procedures, 508
World Bank, 512, 513
World Development Agency, 512
World Economic Forum, 514
World Forum on Democracy, 514
World Trade Organization, 512
Seattle protests, 501
Goals 2000: The Educate America Act, 367–376
Gold, origin of usage as money, 97
"Good" job, defined, 380–384
Government
economy, relationship of, laissez-faire conception, 2
relationship to economy, laissez-faire conception, 2
Government receipts, as percent of GDP, 79
Granger Movement, 322, 324
Great Depression, 48, 49, 89, 221
Great Society programs, 140

federal spending on, 78
*Great Transformation,* 143
Greece, original coinage issued in, 100
Greenhouse effect, 486
Groundwater, contaminated, in minority communities, 462
Group of Eight meetings, Genoa, 501

**H**

Hayden, F. Gregory, biographical sketch, 578
Hazardous waste. *See* Industrial waste
Health care, 183–219. *See also* Health insurance
American Enterprise Institute, 189
biopiracy, by pharmaceutical companies, 190
British National Health Service, 209
Clinton health care plan, 186, 191, 193, 199, 206
community development, public health and, 203–206
defined-contribution plans, usage of, 200
division of labor, divisive effects of, 194
doctors
patients, as partners, 209
proletarianization of, 206
Food and Drug Administration, lobbying by insurers, 199
high risk patients, doctors turning away, 207
Hippocrates, 207
HMOs, 199, 207
management controls exercised by, 199
managed care organizations, 199, 207
Medicaid, creation of, 194
medical malpractice litigation, 209
medical-industrial complex, 196
medicalization of health care, 196
Medicare
creation of, 194
prescription drug discounts, 193
rising costs of, 198
objectification of psychological conditions, 197
Osler, William, 211
patient empowerment, 208
patient-doctor relationship, trust in, 211
patient-provider relationship, reconstruction of, 206–209
percent of GDP spent on, 401
preferred provider organizations, 199
prescription medicine, to over-the-counter medicine, 199–200
privatization of human suffering, material purpose served by, 197
real income, 202–203
researchers, rewarding of, at expense of clinician, 210
Soviet Union, collapse of, 184
specialization, in health care, 194
television commercials, as public relations campaign, 191
vested interests, distinctions serving, 186
World Bank, 195
Health insurance
employment and, 401–402
U.S. population without, 401
Health maintenance organizations, management controls exercised by, 199
Herfendahl-Hirschman Index, 338
Heritage Foundation, 550
High risk patients, doctors turning away, 207
High-wage workers, low-wage workers, distinctions made between, 385–387
Hippocrates, 207
Hispanic urban communities, toxic waste sites in, 475
Hispanic-Americans, in minimum wage force, 386
Historical origins, use of money, 97–100
Homeowners, as favord group, lending to, 110
Hooker Chemical and Plastic Corporation, 461
House of Morgan, 329
Household income, by quintile, 1999, 152
Housing regulations, use of, 125
Human behavior, economic theory and, 9–10
Human life, enhancement of, as role of economics, 73, 80
Humphrey Hawkins Act of 1978, 55

**I**

IBM, 332
*ICC v. Cincinnati RR,* 324
"Illegitimacy bonus," 168
ILO. *See* International Labor Organization
Income inequality, before, after income taxes, 120
Industrial accidents, 321
Industrial waste, 461–492
African-American urban communities, toxic waste sites in, 475
aldicarb, 462
Bayer corporation, 461–462
Bordon Chemicals and Plastics, 462
brown coal fired power plant, 482
capital and, relationship between, 483

carbon sequestration, 486
Ciba Corporation, 462
Coase theorem, 470–475
corporate power, policy domination by, 466–470
DDT, 461
dioxins, 461
disposal services, 484–486
Environmental Protection Agency, 464
furons, 461
General Electric corporation, 462
greenhouse effect, 486
groundwater, contaminated, in minority communities, 462
Hispanic urban communities, toxic waste sites in, 475
Hooker Chemical and Plastic Corporation, 461
institutionalist integrated system, 463
Love Canal, 461
mercury wastes, 461–462
PCBs, 461, 462
production of, 478–481
radioactive waste, 475, 486
Resource Conservation and Recovery Act, 464
Rhone-Pauler corporation, 462
Solvay corporation, 461
Inflation
productivity, unit labor costs, compared, 77
unemployment, parity of, 60–79
Information economy, 411–432
access, to information infrastructure, 425
economic institution foundations, 413–414
economic transformation, forces driving, 412–413
European Union, 411
financial markets, 422–423
human capital investment, economic growth and, 428–429
information markets, characteristics of, 415–417
information monopolies, 424
information ownership, 424–425
intellectual property rights, 424–425
international market liberalization policies, 422–425
labor markets, 423–424
North American Free Trade Agreement, 411
oligopolies, competition, regulatory policies, 427–428
overload of information, 420–422
product markets, 423
productivity, 425, 426–427
public interest in, 426–427
services markets, 423
specialized information services, 416
Information markets, characteristics of, 415–417
Information monopolies, 424
Information ownership, 424–425
Institute for Women's Policy Research, 397
Institutional change theory, of neoinstitutionalism, 1–46
Institutionalism
ceremonial encapsulation, 27–28
ceremonial institutions, defined, 23
conspicuous consumption, 14
control, economic theory, relationship between, 6–7
cumulative causation, 17–19
defined, 4
democracy, institutional change and, 34–36
democratic sovereignty, public policy and, 30–32
demonstration effect, patterns of behavior, 27
derivation of term, 4
development of, 3–12
economic theory, institutions as focus, 7
foundational concepts, 1–46
founders of, 3–4
freedom of speech, 32–34
human behavior, economic theory and, 9–10
laissez-faire relationship of government, economy, 2
majority rule, 34
minimal dislocation, principle of, 26
neoclassical school of economics, compared, 1–46
neoinstitutionalism, 12–29
elements of, 12
institutional change theory, 11–12
methodology of, 12
original institutionalism, neoinstitutionalism, distinguished, 10–11
political foundations, economic policy, 29–36
process, economic theory and, 8
recognized interdependence, principle of, 25
rejection of neoclassical school of economics, 9
social status, consumption and, 14
task of economists, 2
technological institutions, defined, 23

technology, ceremonial encapsulation of, 28
unification of economic science, 4–5
Veblenian theory, 13–17
Institutions, as focus of economic theory, 1–46
Intellectual property rights, 416, 424–425
Interamerican Development Bank, 550
Interdependence, recognized, principle of, 25
International Committee on Human Rights, 508
International Economic Association, 552
International Harvester, monopoly power, 323
International Labor Organization, 508
International Monetary Fund, 102, 275, 512, 513, 550
International Performance Measurement and Verification Protocol, 515
Internet, access to, in developing nations, 514
Interstate Banking Act, 337
Iron, origin of usage as money, 97

**J**
Jefferson, Thomas, on full development of human personality, 212
Junk bonds, 336–337

**K**
Keaney, Michael, biographical sketch, 579
Keynesian theory, 49–51
Klein, Philip A., biographical sketch, 579

**L**
Labor costs, productivity, inflation, compared, 77
Laissez faire doctrine, public utility industries, deregulation, 303
Laissez-faire doctrine, in relationship of government, economy, 2
Latin American economic crisis, 146
Libertarian perspective, 31
Living wage ordinances, 386–387
Loan agreements, development of money in, 97
Local government receipts, as percent of GDP, 79
Love Canal, 461
Low-wage workers, high-wage workers, distinctions made between, 385–387
Lydia, original coinage issued in, 100

**M**
Macro-economic management, 47–84
collectivism, 54–57
Committee for Economic Development, Research and Policy Committee, 65
Employment Act of 1946, 50–51, 54, 56, 57
federal spending, percent of GDP, 53, 78
fiscal impact, distinguished, 67
fiscal stance, distinguished, 64, 70–73
Great Depression, 48, 49
Great Society programs, federal spending, 78
Humphrey Hawkins Act of 1978, 55
inflation, productivity, unit labor costs, compared, 77
Keynesian theory, 49–51
normative, legitimacy of, 54–60
OPEC, 58
Phillips Curve, 48, 55, 57–60, 63
1960–69, 61
1960–99, 62
political scientist, approach to government, 52
potential GDP, concept of, 69
productivity, in United States, deterioration of, 75
public sector, 76–79
rational expectations hypothesis, 60
role of economics, 73, 80
Majority rule, 34
*Making Openness Work,* 559
Malnutrition, taxation and, 117
Managed care, 199, 207
Manufacturing, declining share of employment in, 382
MAPP. *See* Mid-Continent Power Pool
Marriage promotion policies, opposition to, 172
Medicaid, creation of, 194
Medical leave, paid, 397–400
Medical malpractice litigation, increase in, 209
Medical-industrial complex, 183–219
Medicalization of health care, 196
Medicare, 401
creation of, 194
prescription drug discounts, 193
rising costs of, 198
Megawatt hours, futures markets for trading, 296
Melody, William H., biographical sketch, 579
Mercury wastes, dumping of, 461–462
Merger movement, centralization of economic power with, 270–285

Merril-Lynch, 317
Metals, origin of usage as money, 97
Metropolitan fragmentation, local taxation and, 124–128
Metropolitan planning organizations, 126
Mexican economic crisis, 146
Microsoft trial, 329
Mid-Continent Power Pool, 298
Miller, Edythe S., biographical sketch, 579
Mines, children working in, 321
Minimal dislocation, principle of, 26
Minimum wage, raising, 385–386
Mirant, 298
Monetary policy, 85–114
  alternative approach to, 94–102
  Bank of England, 87
  barter economy, 97–100
  Community Reinvestment Act, 110
  credit controls, 109
  Currency School-Banking School, 85–94
  favored groups, lending to, 110
  Federal Open Market Committee, 93
  Federal Reserve, 9, 87
  financial services, provision of, 109
  Glass-Steagall Act, 110
  Great Depression, 89
  historical origins, use of money, 97–100
  International Monetary Fund, 102
  loans, development of, 97
  money, origins of, 97
  post-war period, 90–94
  pre-war period, 85–90
  private property, development of, 97
  Real Bills Doctrine, 89
  Real Business Cycle Theory, 94
  reserve ratios, 108
  taxes-drive-money approach, 98
  treasury bill rate, 90
  World Bank, 102
Money, origins of, 97–100
Monopolies, 315–348. *See also* Globalization
  antitrust enforcement, crippling of, 333–337
  "Black Monday" crash, 336
  Bork, Robert, 340–343
  Burlington Northern Railroad, Santa Fe Railroad, merger of, 324
  Capital Consultants, 317
  Clayton Act, 330
  Clean Water Act, 321
  contestable market hypothesis, 339–340
  Darwin, challenge to neoclassical school of economics, 318–320
  Depository Institutions Act, 337
  Fair Labor Standards Act, 321
  Federal Communications Commission, 331
  Federal Power Commission, 331
  Federal Reserve Act of 1913, 89
  Federal Reserve Board, 331
  Federal Trade Commission Act, 341
  Federal Water Pollution Control Act, 321
  Glass-Steagall Act, 330
  Granger Movement, 322, 324
  Herfendahl-Hirschman Index, 338
  House of Morgan, 329
  IBM, case against, 332
  *ICC v. Cincinnati RR*, 324
  industrial accidents, 321
  on information, 424, 427–428
  Interstate Banking Act, 337
  mergers of cable televisions and telephone companies, 324
  Microsoft trial, 329
  *Munn v. Illinois*, 324
  New Deal, 328–331, 333
  new economy, Sherman Antitrust Act, 326
  *Northern Securities Case*, 326
  Occupational Health and Safety Act, 322
  price discrimination, 323
  Public Utility Holding Company Act, 330
  railroads, 323
  *Railway v. Illinois*, 324
  Rockefeller's Standard Oil Trust, 325
  Rural Electrification Administration Authority, 331
  Safe Drinking Water Act, 321
  savings and loans, deregulation of, 336–337
  Securities Act of 1933, 322
  Securities and Exchange Act, 322, 330
  Securities and Exchange Commission, 331
  Sherman Antitrust Act, 325
  Standard Oil, 326
  Standard Oil Trust, 323, 326
  *Swift & Co v. United States*, 326
  Tennessee Valley Authority, 331
  *United States v. Darby*, 321
  *United States v. E.C. Knight Co.*, 326
  Vanderbilt, Cornelius, 323
  workers' compensation, 162, 163, 321
Mother's Pensions, 162–163
Multinational corporations, 493–521. *See also* Globalization
Municipal living wage ordinances, 386–387
*Munn v. Illinois*, 324

**N**

NAFTA. *See* North American Free Trade Agreement

*Nation at Risk: The Imperative for Educational Reform,* 365
National Commission on Excellence in Education, 365
National Commission on Life Adjustment Education for Youth, 356–358
National Commission on Reform of Secondary Education, 363
National Defense Education Act, 360
National education summit, 349
National Partnership for Women and Families, 399–400
Natural gas industry
  deregulation of, 264
  residential customer, price rise to, 339
Negative income tax, 153
Neoclassical school of economics
  basis in Cartesian dualism, 254
  Darwin, challenge to, 318–320
  definition of economics, 254
  economic policy shaped by, 256
  government analysis, 115–117
  institutionalism, compared, 1–46
  methodology, 254–255
  during recent administrations, 1–46
  rejection of, 1–46
Neoinstitutionalism, 12–29
  elements of, 12
  institutional change theory, 11–12
  methodology of, 12
  original institutionalism, distinguished, 10–11
New Deal, 11, 328–331, 333
New economy. *See also* Centralization of economic power; Deregulation; Public utilities
  challenges of, 142–147
Normative, legitimacy of, 54–60
Normative fiscal policy, legitimacy of, 54–60
North American Free Trade Agreement, 411
*Northern Securities Case,* 326
NYNEX, 268, 338

**O**

Occupational Health and Safety Act, 322
Old Age Assistance, 163
Old Age Insurance, 163, 164
Oligopolies, competition, regulatory policies, 427–428
OPEC, 58
Open Society Alliance, 512, 515
Original institutionalism, neoinstitutionalism, distinguished, 10–11
OSHA. *See* Occupational Health and Safety Act
Overtime employment, 390–391

**P**

PacTel, 268
Palace, origination of money within, 98
Parental participation, in education, 376
Part-time workers, 388–390
Patient empowerment, 208
Patient-doctor relationship, trust in, 211
Patient-provider relationship in healthcare, reconstruction of, 206–209
PCBs, dumping of, 461, 462
Penal system, origination of money from, 98
Personal Responsibility and Work Reconciliation Opportunity Act, 170, 400
Peterson, Janice L., biographical sketch, 580
Pfizer, 189
Pharmaceutical companies, biopiracy by, 190
Phillips Curve, 48, 55, 57–60, 63
  1960–69, 61
  1960–99, 62
Police power of taxation, 121
Policy, theory, linkage, in economic analysis, 49–53
Polio, eradication of, 195
Political foundations, of economic policy, 29–36
Political scientists, approach to government, 52
Pollution, environmental. *See* Industrial waste
Potential GDP, concept of, 69
Poverty
  business cycle peaks, from 1959–99, 141
  economic growth
    1959–2000, 141
    relationship between, 140–142
  rates of, actual, predicted, 142
  taxation and, 117, 124–125
Power, concepts of, institutionalism approach, 258–260
Power structures, in societies, 261
Prayer in schools, social agenda of social conservatives, 332
Preferred provider organizations, 199
Pregnancy Discrimination Act, 398
Prescription drug discounts, 193
Prescription medicine, to over-the-counter medicine, 199–200
Price discrimination, 323
Private property, development of, 97

Privatization of human suffering, material purpose served by, 197
Privatization of Social Security, 239–243
Privileged groups, identification of, 261
Productivity
 deterioration of, in United States, 75
 inflation, unit labor costs, compared, 77
Progressive tax, 115–132
 assault on, 117–120
 distribution of income, increasing unequality of, 120
 economic incentives, taxes as, 121–124
 educational deficits, 117
 family break-up, 117
 Gatreaux Program, Chicago, 125
 income inequality, before, after income taxes, 120
 malnutrition, 117
 metropolitan fragmentation, local taxation and, 124–128
 metropolitan planning organizations, 126
 neoclassical school of economics, government analysis, 115–117
 police power of taxation, 121
 poor job prospects, 117
 poverty, 117, 124–125
 regressive taxation, 119
 rental housing regulations, use of, 125
 social Darwinism, impact on poor, 119
 subdivision regulations, 125
 substance abuse, 117
 zoning, 125
Proletarianization of doctors, 206
PRWORA. *See* Personal Responsibility and Work Reconciliation Opportunity Reconciliation Act
Psychological conditions, objectification of, 197
Public confidence in Social Security, 239
Public health. *See also* Health care
 community development and, 203–206
 underevaluation of, 195
Public power, 11
Public relations campaign, television commercials as, 191
Public utilities, 264–314. *See also* Globalization
 cable industry, 291
 Clayton Act, 272
 communication, standard industrial code classification, 268
 competitive local exchange carriers, 268, 291
 consolidation of corporations, 267–270
 economic consequences of, 277–279
 electricity, 295
  deregulation, 265–266, 296–297
   aftermath of, 297–300
 Energy Policy Act, 265, 295, 310
 Federal Communications Commission, 265, 290
 Federal Energy Regulatory Commission, 264, 295
 Federal Trade Commission, 267
 federal transportation, deregulation of, 264
 globalization, 275–279
 government response, 271–275
 Hepburn Act of 1906, commodities clause of, 306
 Herfendahl-Hirschman Index, 309
 International Monetary Fund, 290
 Interstate Commerce Commission, creation of, 304
 laissez faire doctrine, 303
 long distance interexchange carriers, 291
 merger, 270–271
  acquisition guidelines, establishment of, 308–309
 natural gas industry, deregulation of, 264
 Public Utility Regulatory Policy Act, 295
 reform, 305–310
 Securities and Exchange Commission, 295
 telecommunications, deregulation of, 266–267
  response to, 290–292
 trade, capital mobility and, 276–278
 Wisconsin Advanced Plan, 309
 World Bank, 275, 290
 World Trade Organization, 275
Public Utility Holding Company Act, 330
*Pursuit of Excellence: Education and Future of America,* 358

**Q**

*Quest for Certainty,* 20
Qwest, 287, 300–303

**R**

Race
 employment discrimination and, 391–396
 in social agenda of social conservatives, 332
Racial segregation, political fragmentation and, 126
Racism, distinctions inherent in, 31
Radioactive waste
 disposal system for, 486
 dumping of, 475
*Railway v. Illinois,* 324
Ranson, Baldwin, biographical sketch, 580

Rational expectations hypothesis, 60
RCRA. *See* Resource Conservation and Recovery Act
Real Bills Doctrine, 89
Real Business Cycle Theory, 94
Recognized interdependence, principle of, 25
*Reform of Secondary Education,* 363
Regressive taxation, 119
Rejection of neoclassical school of economics, 1–46
Relationship of government, economy, laissez-faire conception, 2
Reliant Resources, 298
Rental housing regulations, use of, 125
Research Conference on Education and Cultural Deprivation, 361
Researchers, medical, rewarding of, at expense of clinician, 210
Reserve ratios, 108
Resource Conservation and Recovery Act, 464
Rhone-Pauler corporation, 462
Rockefeller, 325–327
Rockefeller Brothers Fund, 358
Role of economics, 73, 80
Royalty, as authoritative group, 261
Rural Electrification Administration Authority, 331
Russia, debt default of, 552

S

Safe Drinking Water Act, 321
Sallie Mae, 110
Santa Fe Railroad, Burlington Northern Railroad, merger of, 324
Savings and loans, deregulation of, 336–337
Say's laws, 50
SBC, 338
SCHIP. *See* State Children's Health Insurance Program
School curriculum. *See* Curriculum
School Readiness, 369
Schools, prayer in, social agenda of social conservatives, 332
Scientific knowledge
  efforts to suppress, 28
  explosion of, 349
SEC. *See* Securities and Exchange Commission
Securities Act of 1933, 322
Securities and Exchange Act, 322, 330
Securities and Exchange Commission, 331
September 11th, 2001, effect of, 57
Sheehan, Michael F., biographical sketch, 580
Sherman Antitrust Act, 325, 326
Shortfall, Social Security, 219–250
Silver, origin of usage as money, 97
Smallpox, eradication of, 195
Social beings, humans as, 260–262
*Social Control of Business,* 316
Social Darwinism, impact on poor, 119
Social insurance, 161
Social justice, 137–139
Social Security, 11, 164, 219–250
  commission to "modernize," 239–243
  financial shortfall, 219–250
  Great Depression, 221
  long-term prospects, 225–231
  privatization of, 239–243
  public confidence in, 239
  reform, 231–243, 243–248
  Social Security Trust, funds, 219–250
  tax on dwelling, progressive, 247
  transformation to advance-funding model, 221–231
  trust funds, 219–250
Social status, consumption and, 14
Solow model of growth, in developing countries, 556
Solvay corporation, 461
Sorting of students, 353
Southern Pacific, Union Pacific, merger of, 324
Southwest Bell, 268
Sovereignty, democratic, public policy and, 30–32
Special Drawing Rights, to countries, 513
Specialization in health care, 194
Specialized information services, 416
Speech, freedom of, 32–34
Sprint, 291
Standard Oil, 326
Standard Oil Trust, 323, 325, 326
State Children's Health Insurance Program, 402
State government receipts, as percent of GDP, 79
Steel plant closings, 16
Stephenson, Kurt, biographical sketch, 580
Structural budget, actual budget, cyclical budget, distinguished, 65
Students
  as favored group, lending to, 110
  school curriculum. *See* Curriculum
Subdivision regulations, taxation and, 125
Substance abuse, taxation and, 117
Survey of Job Characteristics, 382
*Swift & Co v. United States,* 326

**T**
TANF. *See* Temporary Assistance to Needy Families
Task of economists, 2
Taxation, progressive, 115–132
  assault on, 117–120
  distribution of income, increasing unequality of, 120
  economic incentives, taxes as, 121–124
  educational deficits, 117
  family break-up, 117
  Gatreaux Program, Chicago, 125
  income inequality, before, after income taxes, 120
  malnutrition, 117
  metropolitan fragmentation, local taxation and, 124–128
  metropolitan planning organizations, 126
  neoclassical school of economics, government analysis, 115–117
  police power of taxation, 121
  poor job prospects, 117
  poverty, 117, 124–125
  regressive taxation, 119
  rental housing regulations, use of, 125
  social Darwinism, impact on poor, 119
  subdivision regulations, 125
  substance abuse, 117
  zoning, 125
Technological determination, principle of, 352
Technological impact of basic income, 145–146
Technological institutions, defined, 23
Technological knowledge, explosion of, 349
Technology
  ceremonial encapsulation of, 28
  institutions, distinction between, 258
Telecommunications, deregulation of, 266–267
Television commercials, as public relations campaign, 191
Teligent, 293
Temple, origination of money within, 98
Temporary Assistance to Needy Families, 165–177, 400
Temporary Disability Insurance, 399
Temporary workers, 388–390
Tennessee Valley Authority, 11, 331
Theory, policy, linkage, in economic analysis, 49–53
*Theory of Business Enterprise,* 15
*Theory of Economic Progress,* 23
*Theory of Leisure Class,* 15, 262, 379
Time Warner, AOL, merger, 269
Tool, Marc R., biographical sketch, 581
Trade, capital mobility and, 276–278
Trade liberalization, 146
"Traditional values," return to, 332
Transparency International, 514
Treasury bill rate, 90
Trebing, Harry M., biographical sketch, 581
Trickle-down economics, 140
Trust, in patient-doctor relationship, 211
Typhoid, efforts to eradicate, 195, 321

**U**
UNDP. *See* United Nations Development Program
Unemployment
  GDP, federal receipts, compared, 74
  inflation, parity of, 60–79
  taxation and, 117
UNICEF, 508
Unification of economic science, 4–5
Union Pacific, Southern Pacific, merger of, 324
Unionism, 11
Unit labor costs, productivity, inflation, compared, 77
United Nations, 512
  Development Program, 493
  embargo procedures, 508
  Environment Protection Agency, 508
United States Steel, 16
*United States v. Darby,* 321
*United States v. E.C. Knight Co.,* 326
Universal health care, 183–219
  American Enterprise Institute, 189
  biopiracy, by pharmaceutical companies, 190
  British National Health Service, 209
  Clinton health care plan, 186, 191, 193, 199, 206
  community development, public health and, 203–206
  defined-contribution plans, usage of, 200
  division of labor, divisive effects of, 194
  doctors
    patients, as partners, 209
    proletarianization of, 206
  Food and Drug Administration, lobbying by insurers, 199
  high risk patients, doctors turning away, 207
  Hippocrates, 207
  HMOs, 199, 207
    management controls exercised by, 199
  managed care organizations, 199, 207
  medical malpractice litigation, 209
  medical-industrial complex, 196

medicalization of health care, 196
Medicare
creation of, 194
prescription drug discounts, 193
rising costs of, 198
objectification of psychological conditions, 197
Osler, William, 211
patient empowerment, 208
patient-doctor relationship, trust in, 211
patient-provider relationship, reconstruction of, 206–209
preferred provider organizations, 199
prescription medicine, to over-the-counter medicine, 199–200
privatization of human suffering, material purpose served by, 197
real income, 202–203
researchers, rewarding of, at expense of clinician, 210
Soviet Union, collapse of, 184
specialization, in health care, 194
television commercials, as public relations campaign, 191
vested interests, distinctions serving, 186
World Bank, 195
Unpaid labor, paid labor, distinctions made between, 396–402

**V**

Vanderbilt, Cornelius, 323
Verizon, 268
Veterans, as favored group, lending to, 110
Viacom, 269
Vietnam War, distrust of government with, 331
Vocational curriculum, sorting of students into, 349–378

**W**

War, psychological damage from, 197
Waste disposal services, 484–486
Watergate, distrust of government with, 331
Welfare reform, 157–182, 400–401
Aid to Blind, 163
Aid to Dependent Children, 163
Aid to Families with Dependent Children, 164, 166
block grant funding, 166
cash welfare entitlement, elimination of, 166
economic recession, impact of, 175–176
employment, welfare caseloads and, 168–169
family formation, 170
"illegitimacy bonus," 168
marriage promotion policies, opposition to, 172
Mother's Pensions, 162–163
Old Age Insurance, 163, 164
Personal Responsibility and Work Reconciliation Opportunity Reconciliation Act, 170
poverty, 169–170
public assistance programs, 161
social insurance, 161
social provisioning, 158–159
Social Security Act, 164
Survivor's Insurance, 164
Temporary Assistance to Needy Families, 165–177, 170–172
Unemployment Insurance, 163
"welfare mothers," 164
welfare state, 159–161
welfare-to-work strategies, effectiveness of, 174
Work Opportunity Reconciliation Act, 165
Workmen's Compensation, 162, 163
Welfare state, basic income, contrasted, 148
Welfare-to-work strategies, effectiveness of, 174
Wergeld, practice of, evolution of money from, 98
Wheat, as basis of monetary unit, 97
Williams, long-distance carrier, 287–314
Work, role of, basic income and, 148
Work hours, employment status and, 388–391
Work Opportunity Reconciliation Act, 165
Workers' Compensation, 162, 163, 321
World Bank, 102, 195, 275, 512, 513, 550
World Com, 287–314
World Development Agency, 512
*World Development Report,* 556
World Economic Forum, 514
World Forum on Democracy, 514
World Partners, 291
World Trade Organization, 275, 512
Seattle protests, 501
WorldCom, 338
Wray, L. Randall, biographical sketch, 581
WTO. *See* World Trade Organization

**X**

Xcel Energy, 298

**Z**

Zoning, taxation and, 125